ON THE INFORMATION HIGHWAY

THE FUTURE OF WORK IN CANADA

J. William Pfeiffer, Ph.D., J.D.

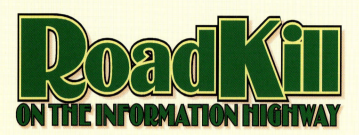

Copyright © 1999 by Pfeiffer & Company

Design and graphics: John Robertson
Senior editor: Marian Prokop
Editor: Angela Barker
Permissions editor: Kimeiko Hotta-Dover
Cover cartoon: Uku Casements

Pfeiffer & Company 57 Oriole Gardens
Toronto, Ontario,
Canada M4V 1V9
Tel.: 416-964-9486
Fax: 416-964-6738
drp@idirect.com

Canadian Cataloguing in Publications Data

Pfeiffer, J. William
RoadKill on the Information Highway:
The Future of Work in Canada

1. Economics   2. Geopolitics   3. Business

ISBN: 1-894334-99-X $39.95

Printed in Canada

Printing 1 2 3 4 5 6 7 8 9 10

Requiem to the Great Depression

— June ,1935

With unemployment at 27%, thousands of men, fed up with their life in BC relief camps, boarded CPR freight trains bound for Ottawa.

Riots broke out when they were stopped at Regina.

This workers' action led to the "Red Scare," a groundless belief that 1919-Russian-type Bolshevism would topple the country.

This experience is a vibrant testimony to the power of the forces that compel Haves and Have-Nots against each other in troubled times.

Dedication

To **Copernicus,** the mind and spirit that told the world, after 14 centuries of Ptolemaic belief, that the earth was *not* the stationary centre of the universe. And to the stout hearts and nimble minds of those who allowed themselves to hear his message.

To **my fellow Canadians,** I apologize if any of my observations are offensive to you. I know that this book will challenge many of your long-standing beliefs, but my heart is well-intentioned and my caring for and appreciation of our society is very profound.

To **our sacred cows,** may they rest in peace.

My task, which I am trying to achieve, is to make you hear, to make you feel... it is above all, to make you see, and that is everything. **— Joseph Conrad**

Table of Contents

I DON'T CARE IF IT IS YOUR LUNCH HOUR - GET OUT THERE AND FIND OUT IF CANADIANS ARE SATISFIED WITH THEIR JOBS...

Canada's Credit Rating

Debt monitors say they want to see deep and sustained cuts in the country's $583 billion AFD.

A rating upgrade would reduce Ottawa's borrowing costs as well as those of the provinces, whose credit always ranks below that of the federal government.

The only way the sovereign credit rating is going to be improved is if they make big strides in debt reduction.
— *Salomon Smith Barney,*
major New York brokerage firm

Canada's 1972 hockey victory over Russia:
"The Shot Heard 'Round the World"

*T*rying to understand our world from the media is like trying to tell time by looking at the second hand of a watch — the information is virtually meaningless without the context of the other hands.

This book is the owner's handbook for Canadians who want to understand the way our country really works. What are our unique strengths and weaknesses as we enter the new millennium?

Acknowledgments

This book represents more than 2 years of research and includes data gathered from more than 3,000 newspaper clippings from such diverse sources as the *Victoria Times-Colonist* on the West Coast to the *Kugluktuk Miner* on the North Coast and to the *St. John's Telegraph* on the East Coast. *The Globe and Mail* and the *Ottawa Citizen* were particularly instrumental. It also represents more than 2,000 Internet sources and over 150 books. During the course of this research I have grown to rely on StatsCan and a variety of the advocacy groups acknowledged by their inclusion in Appendix D. CBC, particularly the "old" 2-hour version of *Politics,* with Don Newman and Nancy Wilson, was a daily inspiration and often an excuse to take a break from the task of writing.

We have endeavoured to recognize the sources where they were unique and have given great attention to trying to keep our sources straight. If we have omitted recognizing a unique source, it is a result of the immensity of the project, and something that we will correct in subsequent printings if it is brought to our attention. We ended up with more than 300 acknowledgements through text and image references and citations; a truly complex undertaking.

Such an enormous undertaking cannot be a solo journey and I wish to express my particular thanks to senior editor, Marian Prokop; editor, Angela Barker; graphic artist, John Robertson; researcher, Kay Ray; and to my right hand, Kimeiko Hotta, who handled the very complex permission issues.

Special Acknowledgment

To Deborah, whose unqualified support made the book possible.

Preface

The particular undercurrents of writing a book usually mean that, during the creative process, new information and insights alter the shape and form to some substantive degree. Although I have been involved in "creating" more than 50 books in the last 30 years, the amount of reshaping that happened while writing this book was far more extensive than I had experienced previously.

> *Anyone whose world seems relatively stable, and who thinks life is business as usual, isn't paying attention.*
> — *Angus Reid, Shakedown*

My self-defined task, when I conceived this book, was fairly straightforward — to explain, in non-academic terms, what was happening to the evolving nature of work in Canada. What seemed like a clear-cut undertaking became increasingly complex as it became apparent that, while redefining work is a global phenomenon, the texture of those changes in Canada are uniquely inter-woven into the very distinctive fabric of our history, culture and geography.

Much of the complexity that has evolved in the creation of this book can be explained in terms of **General Systems Theory**. Grossly simplified, this concept says that the world is much like a spider's web — altering one strand impacts most other strands and changes the very nature of the whole. In other words, if we fail to see the connections between disparate and sometimes seemingly unrelated aspects of our world, we are doomed to get less than our good nature and abundant resources warrant.

Dependence is a psychological mind-set that is necessary for children to be able to survive when they lack the resources to be self-reliant; dependence that survives the age of autonomy is, for the most part, highly dysfunctional, in that it thwarts the development of independence.

In contrast, **counter-dependence** is a psychological mind-set most prevalent in adolescents; in the most basic sense it means "doing the opposite of what is expected or requested by an authority figure." Frequently, counter-dependence is accompanied by an awareness that the acted-out behaviour is not in the best interest of the actor; but, even with that knowledge, it is considered "better" than acquiescing to "wishes" of the authority figure. Such behaviour thwarts the development of the independent behaviour that leads to maturity.

Like all developed countries, Canada's predilections are tempered by both global realities and the unique interpretations that we give to those events. Many of our "realities" are strongly influenced by our love-hate relationship with the colossus economy of the US — in much the same way that Belgium and Luxemburg respond to France, and Austria, Denmark and The Netherlands respond to Germany.

To understand the Canadian psyche and the impact of our reluctance to accept the evolutionary realities of the nature of work in the global information age, we must systematically examine both our often inappropriate over-dependence on the UK and its traditions and our counter-dependence towards the US. Substantial roots of our ineffectiveness in the transition to the new age are imbedded in these complex issues.

Another important foundation of contemporary Canada is rooted in our monopolistic heritage of being founded on the antiquated mercantile economics of The Hudson's Bay and Northwest companies. This has produced what I call **wardism**, that is, an over-reliance on governments to care for our every need.

It is against these and many similar, but lesser quirks of our national psyche that I have attempted to render a picture of where we are at this moment in history and what we need to do to break out of these mind-numbing, creativity-dampening, self-made constraints to adapting to the new world.

I really think it is time we begin making ourselves relevant to the rest of the world — because if we do not, it will pass us by.

The monster nations, such as the US, India, Japan and China, are like supertankers; once they make a turn, they set the course for everyone else.

We must become the sleek, light yacht, out there in front of the great ships of state, racing ahead, probing the wind, testing the currents, and setting the course. And we can only succeed if we demonstrate the will to do it. In other words, we have to start, as a country, to pull together, instead of allowing ourselves to be pulled apart.[1]

This book has also evolved to be a celebration of the many things that we do exceptionally well. For most of us, Canada is truly the best place in the world to live; yet for far too many others, life could be vastly improved by changing some antiquated assumptions and fostering increased self-reliance.

The title and cover graphic should give the clear message that this book is intended to be iconoclastic. However, the scope is not limited to criticism – a restricted approach that is too often the fodder of popular "gloom and doom" books. **This book ultimately is about prescriptions and treatments** — what needs to be done to ameliorate the pain and provide for a better transition to the information age. This is a time when Canadians should be told what they NEED to know, not what they want to hear.

Although I explain the dangers we are facing — and we are facing some exceedingly extreme dangers as we go through this transition period — I devote most of the book to creating an awareness of opportunities. This is a time of incredible opportunity — if we can get our minds in the right place.

We are not in a transformational period, as many noted writers, such as Professor Richard G. Lipsey would suggest. What is happening will not be "followed by a period of sustained secular boom within a more stable economic structure, beginning around the start of the next millennium and lasting for a period measured in decades."[2]

We are in a period of endless transitions — with no anticipated time to stop and rest from the struggle of change. Modern change theory is based on Kurt Lewin's 1940's action research model that defined change as a process of unfreezing, movement and refreezing. The refreezing period just will not be happening anymore. Things are moving much too fast for that luxury.

While some economists tout sustained economic growth as a cure-all, I see it as a smokescreen that keeps us from focussing on unsustainable population growth and the disastrous chasm that is developing between the Haves and Have-Nots of society.

As a former academic, I have had to wage a constant personal battle to remember that *the audience for this book is the average Canadian,* not other academics. I accept that I will be criticized for over-simplifying some very sophisticated topics, but my purpose is not to impress academics but to assist in bringing the big picture into a shared perspective.

This book is printed in an innovative, and hopefully useful, new format. In the wired world, an electronic magazine is called an e-zine — a magazine in an electronic format. This book is a b-zine, a book in a magazine format. It also has a companion web site to help keep the data current. The book is designed to be read in any order, after the brief introduction.

I end the book with some action plans of things I think we should be doing to bring about major changes in our country. These are contained in Chapter 14, which summarizes the conclusions and recommendations found in the text of the book.

At all times I tried to remember that 1 out of every 6 people was not born in this country — the most pluralistic and diverse culture in the world. Even readers who are Canadian by birth may find that they have been taught a very biased perspective of history.

Then too, a great many of us may have forgotten our school lessons. One of my favourite expressions is a mild corruption of Santana's famous quote, "Those of us who fail to remember our history are doomed to repeat grade 11."[3]

J.Wm.P.
Toronto, November, 1998

Vancouver's Lions Gate Bridge — built with Guinness beer money in 1938.
A tribute to free enterprise — private financing of public works.
Contrast to "A Tale of Two Bridges," page 117.

*We know things are bad.
Worse than bad, they're crazy.*

*I'm not going to leave you alone,
you've got to get mad!*

**I'm as mad as hell, and
I'm not going to take it anymore!**

— *Network,* 1976 movie classic

Economic IQ

Economic ignorance — the absence of knowledge about how the global economy works — is excessively common in Canada and is at the heart of the complacency with which we accept staggering amounts of misinformation and nonsense from our politicians. We are the victims of naive and myopic media coverage, poor education and our own apathy.

Literal Roadkill on roads and highways is the result of the ignorance of the wild and semi-wild animals about cars and trucks. Figurative *RoadKill on the Information Highway* is the result of ignorance about how the global economy works at the end of the 20th century. The next side bar is a way of gauging the amount of ignorance that abounds in the country today. **Economic ignorance causes RoadKill on the Information Highway.**

Economic Ignorance

Among the more striking information from the 1998 Liberal Party's poll was that:
- **80%** of Canadians were surprised that the deficit was gone.
- **60%** did not know the difference between deficit and debt.
- **40%** did not know how many millions are in one billion.

This illustrates an extreme lack of sophistication in basic Economic IQ. Just to make sure we are speaking the same language:
- **Deficit** is the amount that annual spending exceeds annual income.
- **Debt** is the accumulation of deficits created in previous years.
- **One Billion** is 1,000 millions. (See page 11 to understand what $1 billion buys.)

Sections of this book explore these areas in detail and describe how we are already doing enough social spending by world standards. However, the effectiveness of these programs is crippled by rampant false assumptions, institutionalized self-interests and the pathetic mismanagement of the allocated resources.

The end of the federal deficit creates what is grossly mislabeled as a "surplus." Of the Canadians who were polled, 44% want this "fiscal dividend" to be spent on increased social programs, 33% on debt reduction and 23% on tax reduction.

Prime Minister Chrétien's *1997 Red Book* solution was to allocate half to increased spending and the remaining half between tax reduction and debt relief. The 1998 Liberal convention voted for an allocation of 40% to debt reduction, 30% to increased social spending and 30% to tax relief. Fiscal conservatives want 50% for debt reduction and 50% for tax relief. The global uncertainty in world financial markets at the end of 1998 is forcing the federal liberals to reexamine their election priorities and may result in a more conservative approach with a great emphasis on tax and debt reduction.

As you read — and hopefully understand — this book, you will dramatically increase your Economic IQ and be better qualified to know where this money **should** go and how to influence the behaviour of our governments.

What Does the Country Earn? Owe?

The Gross Domestic Product (GDP) of a country is the combined value of all the goods and services produced. The personal equivalent is your total annual income. Canada's GDP is about $800 billion.

The Acknowledged Federal Debt (AFD) of Canada is, in terms of an amount frequently dispensed by the media, $583 billion — or about $20,000 for *each* of Canada's 30 million people. The ratio between the AFD and the GDP is 63.5% — an increase of 60% in the last 10 years and one of the highest of the economically developed nations. (See page 112.) When we add in provincial *acknowledged* debt, the ratio is an astounding 119% of GDP .

While the enormity of our financial obligation is mind-boggling, it is just one segment of the sordid story, reflecting only the *acknowledged* portion of the debts. The Canada Pension Plan (CPP) and its Quebec counterpart (QPP) have unacknowledged debt — for which no provision for repayment has been made — in excess of $1.2 trillion, greater than the acknowledged debts of all levels of government. Federal and provincial crown corporations owe hundreds of billions of dollars in debts, too, that are guaranteed by our governments. **Add all of these debts and obligations together, and we see that our true national debt is well in excess of $2 trillion.**

Who's Paying the Bill?

Another way to conceptualize deficits and debts is that they are really just indefinitely deferred taxes. In a nutshell, in the last 50 years, our elders have been on a spending binge that amounts to the biggest inter-generational heist in history. The bill for this profligate lifestyle is being left to our future generations. By the time you have finished this book, you will see that the concern about what to do with the so-called "surplus" is gallows humour at the most obscene level imaginable.

Fixing Our Financial Mess

▶ We *must* increase our economic IQ so that we can understand the issues.

▶ We *must* eliminate wasteful spending and demand accountability of our politicians.

▶ We *must* demand that our education system create workers who can compete in the information age.

▶ We *must* learn to consume and pollute less, and make sacrifices to pay for a half century of grossly irresponsible behaviour.

▶ We *must* slaughter a lot of our sacred cows.

Paradigms and Paradigm Shifts

It was the best of times,
it was the worst of times,
it was the age of wisdom,
it was the age of foolishness,
it was the epoch of belief,
it was the epoch of incredulity,
it was the season of Light,
it was the season of Darkness,
it was the spring of hope,
it was the winter of despair,
we had everything before us,
we had nothing before us.

These are the famous opening words of Charles Dickens' *A Tale of Two Cities,* which is set in London and Paris in 1775, at the beginning of the Industrial Revolution. Today, more than 200 years later, these profound words are hauntingly true for Canadians as we find ourselves at the beginning of the Information Revolution.

Sadly, for some of us, **today is the worst of times,** and we have nothing before us!

But for some of us, **today is the best of times,** and we have everything before us!

In Dickens' England, at the end of the 18th century, life expectancy was less than 40 years, the literacy rate was less than 10% and it took a year to get a message to Australia and back. There was no humane social safety net.

Today, at the end of the 20th century, life expectancy in Canada is almost 80 years; the literacy rate, according to StatsCan, is much improved but, **by international standards it is pathetic**. Given the amount of money spent on education — 30% of Canadians cannot read simple English, 36% cannot perform simple arithmetic and over 42% of adults have limited literacy skills; however, we can get a message to Australia and back at the speed of light. There is concern that we may be developing some gaping holes in our social safety net.

One camp of economic and social writers — Drs. Stanley Aronowitz and William DiFazio in *The Jobless Future,* and James Rifkin in *The End of Work,* represent the Gloom and Doom School. Another camp of writers — most notably Toronto's Nuala Beck in *Excelerate,* and Don Tapscott's digital-focused books represent the Boundless Optimism School.

Who is right? Both are right — to a degree. For some of us, the future holds unparalleled opportunity, while for others the future is bleak, stark and exceptionally grim. What both groups have in common is a pervasive angst — 47% of Canadians who have jobs now fear they could lose them in the next year or so.[4] We are hell-bent on a path that will dissolve the middle class and turn us into a world and a nation of Haves and Have-Nots. The great restructuring of the new millennium is happening all around us and, as we begin to understand the new rules of the information age, everything seems to be changing at once. Historically and objectively, this change process is really nothing new; people have always experienced such upheaval because of continuous geopolitical and economic change. **It is when change happens to us or those that we care about the most, that it becomes very real.**

It is human nature to fear the unknown, especially when we do not understand the context of the change. This book is the road map that we need to help us see where we are going.

What Do You See in the Drawing?

The classic drawing below dates from 1888, and is presented in most basic psychology courses. Do you "see" a young woman with a feather in her hair, or a haggish old woman?

This illusion is very interesting, because you can see one or the other **but not the two simultaneously**; that is very apropos in terms of the business world we look at today. It is possible to see the old hag as you read the unemployment figures or articles about what is happening to the poor as the social safety net tatters. However, it is also possible to see the young woman, as employment goes up and industry and government layoffs lessen. Heightened awareness of both the bad news and the good news is the major purpose of this book. The world is changing at an unprecedented pace; the key to understanding how we can best cope with change is to understand the new rules of the information age.

Some people approach change with fear and dread. If we are afraid of change, we are going to see and experience the old woman.

But if we can look at change as opportunity, this is an incredibly exciting time. We will see the young woman rather than the old hag.

WHAT DO YOU SEE?

A beautiful young woman or an old hag?

"If you always do what you have always done, you'll always get what you always got."

Is that true today?
The answer is yes, if the rules have remained the same; and no, if the rules are different.

Most of us are conditioned to believe that if we do something in the way that we have done it in the past, it is a reasonable expectation that we are going to get the same results, and that just simply is not true when the paradigm is changing.

A Mental Role Play

Imagine that you were going to an interview for a job that you really wanted. As you are getting ready to go out the door, you find a spot on your clothes and change. Traffic's a little heavier than usual, too. These are things that happen to all of us all the time.

Fortunately, when you get to the building where you are going, there is a parking spot right in front. You pull up next to the car in front of the empty spot, reverse gears, get ready to parallel park **and somebody comes into the parking spot nose first behind you!** You really want this job, and you are running late.

What is the feeling that goes through you?

Whatever your mood, imagine that you get out of the car and go to talk to the person driving the car. *Think about the potential interaction.*

Now, imagine that you find the other driver is your mother's best friend, a woman who walks with a cane. Do you experience some change?

Let's take another scenario. This time the other vehicle is a van, and on the side of the van it says **Hell's Angels Road Service**, and there is a big burly dude driving the truck. Experience another change?

It is possible to change your frame of reference yet again. This time the other driver is a well-dressed 40-ish businessman. Imagine the interaction you may have with that person. People will have a variety of exchanges, from saying fairly loud things to some fairly soft things. In Canada, we are traditionally more likely to say polite and courteous things, but there are times when we all are stressed!

Next, *remember whatever you "said" to that person.* Just then, the person in the spot in front of you honks and says he or she is leaving, so you move up one spot and go on to your interview.

You get to your interview, wait a few minutes, and guess who is sitting behind the desk? Yes, it is the businessman who took your parking spot!

The point of this exercise is to get you to think about how quickly paradigms shift in our everyday life. Part of the message today is the speed with which you make those changes. What we are talking about is a moving target: you think you understand the situation, but what you probably do not understand is that the situation has already changed. By the time most organizations have defined the problem and agreed on a course of action, they are solving a problem that no longer exists.

Science and Paradigm Shifts

Thomas Kuhn's *The Structure of Scientific Revolutions* appeared in 1962, revolutionizing the way we think about change. The version of scientific reality that preceded Kuhn, often referred to as modernism, saw science as an accumulation of all that had been learned over history, with each new law adding its weight to others to form scientific truth. Kuhn saw that accumulated scientific beliefs profoundly altered major new discoveries in a way that all science was altered. He discerned science as having an accepted world view, or "paradigm," of its environment. This scientific paradigm explains everything that science holds as its "reality." Most scientists accepted any activity consistent with the existing paradigm and tended to exclude inconsistent thought.

Eventually, anomalies arise that the paradigm cannot resolve. Then someone steps outside of the existing paradigm and proposes a new principle or law. When the scientific community accepts the proposed change, the science experiences a "paradigm shift," and the new science proceeds within the new paradigm.

Kuhn's concept of paradigms and paradigm shifts is very useful in understanding the changes that take place in all aspects of life — scientific, social, political and economic. Whether in the sciences, or in other aspects of our lives, paradigm shifts seem to have common characteristics:

• Paradigm shifts are a reality in every aspect of life; things change and we must adjust to that new reality.

• Constant shifts in major paradigms tend to make our lives very difficult to understand.

• You cannot abandon a paradigm until you have a new one to put in its place, because it is our paradigms that allow us to function.

• It usually takes a relatively long time to effect a paradigm shift — typically 20 to 40 years — or about the span of a generation.

In the 2nd century, the Ptolemaic paradigm of the universe was developed. (See Ptolemy sidebar, page 5) and for 14 centuries people believed that the untrue was true.

As we look at some institutions today, we can see paradigms that are very much like Ptolemy's paradigm — out of date when the world has changed.

40 years in the Desert

Many of us can recall the *Old Testament* story about Moses leading the Jews out of Egypt. We are told about this band wandering in the desert for 40 years. The younger members were ready to settle in the promised land, but the older generation wanted to return to Egypt, to the land that they knew. It has been speculated that the transition could not have happened until the older generation died out.

When taking into account the story of the wandering band of Jews, it appears that there has not been much change in that aspect of human nature in the last 2,000 years. (See Kuhn's observation, above.)

Educated, intelligent, successful adults rarely change their most fundamental premises.

— Max Planck, German Nobel Laureate

I believe that Planck's observation is categorically true. We tend to stick by most things that have made us successful in the past. It's a kind of "hell-or-high-water" approach to life. We know something works, so we will keep doing it.

The most important thing we learn when we perceive things differently is in paradigm shifting, or the "Aha!" experience, when we finally see the whole picture from a different perspective. The more bound we are by initial perception, the more potent the "Aha!" experience!

The paradigm shift you experienced in each of the parking spot situations puts the reality into a totally different perspective. We can see a reality that is replaced by a limited view — a reality that is critical for us to understand in our daily lives.

Another interesting example of a recent paradigm shift is the environmentally friendly movement of society towards recycling. Twenty years ago all of our bottles and glassware, and most of our newspapers went into the trash. Today, most communities have recycling programs, and for most of us, it has become a psychologically painful experience to throw a can in the trash. We look around for nearby recycling bin, and frequently we find one.

These tumultuous times are perceived as dangerous by many people. Danger in turn generates a fear response that is characterized by the high-adrenaline fight-or-flight feeling. Because the human emotional system cannot maintain a fear response for an extended period, the fear eventually becomes anxiety and/or angst.

Kurt Lewin's classical model of social change defined the process as "unfreezing," movement and "re-freezing." Accelerated change means that for most of us, our lives are in a constant state of unfreezing and movement *without* the opportunity to relax that comes with the re-freezing time.

BC's Lighthouses

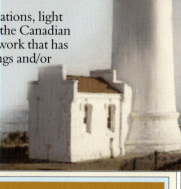

In a typical display of political temerity, the Canadian government has abandoned its plans to automate the remaining 27 staffed lighthouses in BC.

At each of these light stations, light keepers are employed by the Canadian Coast Guard to perform work that has been eliminated by closings and/or automation at the other lighthouses in the province.

There are no data to support the contention that safety has been compromised in anyway.

Paradigm Shifts and Future Trends

Six important paradigm shifts identified by Morris Shechtman that are affecting the business world today are:

- Caring for people is not synonymous with taking care of people.
- A person's ability to change is not a function of capacity, but of choice.
- We need to change our attitudes towards change.
- We must redefine what constitutes acceptable work, moving from adequacy to peak performance.
- Who we are personally is inextricably connected to who we are professionally; the goal is to lead blended, not balanced lives.
- We must create value-driven personal and work lives.[6]

A Paradigm Shift:
1987-96 Global Transfers of Major Conventional Weapons

155

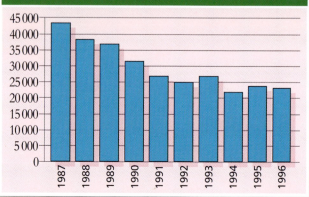

© 1997 UFS, Inc.

> IT'S NOT SO BAD LIVING IN THE PAST - IT'S JUST SUCH A LONG COMMUTE IN THE MORNING...

The Commonwealth:
An Obsolete Paradigm

Canadians are ready for radical change in some arenas and, as all political parties fight to hold the centre-right position, we have seen only moderate resistance to the sweeping changes being implemented by provincial premiers — Ralph Klein (Progressive Conservative) in Alberta, Roy Romanow (New Democratic) in Saskatchewan, Mike Harris (Progressive Conservative) in Ontario, John Savage (Liberal) in Nova Scotia, and, at a Federal level, finance minister Paul Martin (Liberal).

Another arena ripe for change is that of the Commonwealth. Every Commonwealth meeting brings together 54 heads of government from the countries that made up the British Empire in those heady days when every country not only knew its place but also knew that beyond question Britain was the top country. In those days there were no heads-of-government meetings because only the British government mattered. As colonialism waned, significant ties remained among the countries of the former Empire: preferential tariffs, wide-reaching scholarship programs, sporting and cultural exchanges and generous foreign aid policies. It has been argued that Britain's relationship with many of its former colonies remained exploitative, but for the developing countries that made up most of the Commonwealth membership, there was no better club in the world to belong to in order to receive aid and to market goods in the UK.

The question is, when is enough enough? The Commonwealth Games are neat, but so what? What has the Commonwealth done for us — or for anyone else, for that matter — lately?

The interminable crises that seem to rotate constantly among the Commonwealth's African members have sapped the energy of the industrialized member countries, but they are not the only problems. The endless bickering and threats (with occasionally disastrous flare-ups) between India and Pakistan, the frequently insulting verbal attacks by the quixotic Malaysian President, and the civil war in Sri Lanka seem to have no solutions. Britain, more preoccupied than ever with its European relationships, has run out of patience with the Commonwealth. And its sports competitions and cultural exchanges are not enough to justify keeping the organization alive.

Changing from the
Ptolemaic to the Copernican Paradigm

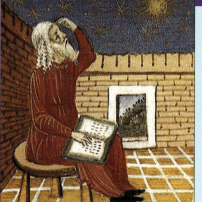

Ptolemy, the most famous astronomer and geographer of the ancient world, theorized that the earth was the stationary centre of the universe.

The Ptolemaic paradigm was associated with so much important truth, and the whole presented such a coherent scheme for the explanation of the heavenly movements, that it was not seriously questioned until Copernicus published his discoveries in 1543: The sun was actually the centre of our solar system. Thus, for 1400 years, people had believed the untrue to be true.

The intellectual slumber of the Middle Ages was destined to be awakened by the revolutionary doctrines of Copernicus. It may be noted that the time at which he discovered the scheme of the solar system coincided with a remarkable epoch in the world's history. The great astronomer had just reached manhood at the time when Columbus discovered the New World.

However, Copernicus delayed publishing his discoveries until he was a very old man. He had a well-founded apprehension of the storm of opposition that they would arouse.

He finally yielded to the entreaties of his friends, and his book was sent to press. But before it made its appearance to the world, Copernicus was dying. A copy of the book was brought to him on May 23, 1543. We are told that he was able to see it and touch it, but nothing more; and he died a few hours afterward.

Too Hot to Touch: Decriminalizing Drugs

While examples on the lack of courage by politicians abound, one of the better examples is certainly the unwillingness to respond to the changing attitudes about decriminalizing drug laws. There is no question that the famous 1996 *National Review* cover story, "The War on Drugs Is Lost," captures the sentiment of a remarkably broad segment of social/political activists, from the hard-right Fraser Institute and the Libertarian Party to the hard-left NDP. We had a Royal Commission on the subject in the 1970's, and its recommendations to decriminalize have been supported by most law enforcement agencies. *The Globe And Mail* and the *Ottawa Citizen* have called for reconsideration — but nothing happens because of a lack of will. (See more about the cost of inaction on page 88.)

TheWill toChange:

The Big Picture

The beaver has long been a symbol of Canada, and is more revealing than most people know. Well-known for its unwillingness to change and its inability to adapt, the beaver is like the old marquis in Charles Dickens' *A Tale of Two Cities* who, representing the aristocracy at the time of the French Revolution, said, "I will die perpetuating the system that I was born to."

Commitment to the common good is missing in Canada today, as almost all of us are focused on issues of self-interest. This is not just a political foible, but true for surplus maritime bureaucrats, depleted Ontario teachers, and BC salmon fishers. There is no populist will to change because there is no common vision for the future of work.

While the unemployed in the Atlantic provinces stand guard over their work temples — empty processing plants and idled coal mines — workers from Saskatchewan are demonstrating mobility.

> *Change is opportunity!*
> — *Jack Walsh*
> *CEO, General Electric*

The Will to Change is really about our basic personal perception of change. Do we see change as opportunity, like GE president Jack Walsh, or are we willing to die rather than alter our attitudes, like the old marquis?

This book is about telling the truth, something that is difficult to swallow for those who prefer to perpetuate false hopes through lies. This reality is something that Kim Campbell and the Progressive Conservatives learned after she admitted in her 1993 electioneering that unemployment and debt could not be resolved in a single term in office.

Former British Prime Minister Margaret Thatcher's privatization and tough fiscal policies laid the foundation for the UK's strength today. The current Prime Minister, Tony Blair, did 2 years' worth of changes in his 1st 100 days in office. The new Canadian government, in contrast, took the summer off after getting elected in the spring of 1997.

Canada's Symbol: The Beaver

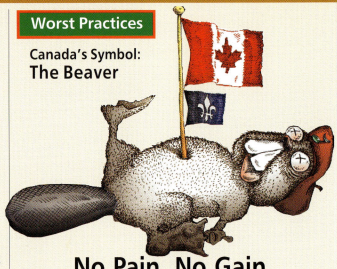

No Pain, No Gain

Personal orientation to "pain" is similar to how we react to change. There are those that like to pull the band-aid off as quickly as possible and get it over with; others prefer the slow removal that protracts the time of pain but reduces the intensity. Similarly, there are those who prefer to jump into cold water, while others would rather enter the water slowly and avoid the sudden shock of the jump. Change is very analogous in that, even when we accept that we must change, some of us prefer the fast method and others prefer to proceed slowly. The implementation of The Common Sense Revolution in Ontario by Premier Mike Harris — with his "let's-jump-and-get-it-over-with" philosophy — has challenged those who prefer the slow-and-steady approach. These people, coupled with Luddite-types (see page 58) who oppose any change, with the intention of avoiding pain altogether, constitute a significant resistance to the Common Sense Revolution. Does the Harris government have the political courage to do the right thing in the face of mounting public dissent and significant drops in popularity? Leadership and courage are rare commodities in political life. Let's hope that, for the sake of the people, the province and the nation, Mike Harris proves to be the exception to the rule.

> *We trained hard, but it seemed that every time we were beginning to form up into teams, we would be reorganized.*
> *I was to learn later in life that we tend to meet any new situation by reorganizing; and a wonderful method it can be for creating the illusion of progress while producing confusion, inefficiency, and demoralization.*
> — *Petronius Arbiter,*
> *Roman centurion, 210 BCE*

I HAVE A NEW PERSONAL CRUSADE.

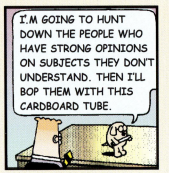

I'M GOING TO HUNT DOWN THE PEOPLE WHO HAVE STRONG OPINIONS ON SUBJECTS THEY DON'T UNDERSTAND. THEN I'LL BOP THEM WITH THIS CARDBOARD TUBE.

THAT WOULD INCLUDE EVERYONE ON EARTH EXCEPT YOU AND ME.

LEAN OVER HERE.

Five Lessons from Canadian Geese

There is an interdependence in the way geese function which is useful to understand for team functioning.

Consider the following:

FACT: As each bird flaps its wings, it creates an "up lift" for the bird following. By flying in a "V" formation, the whole flock adds 71% greater flying range than if each bird flew alone.

LESSON 1: If we have as much sense as geese, we'll know that people who share a common direction and sense of community can get where they are going quicker and easier because they are traveling on one another's thrust.

FACT: Whenever a goose falls out of formation, it suddenly feels the drag and resistance of trying to fly alone. It quickly gets back into the formation to take advantage of the "lifting power" of the goose immediately in front.

LESSON 2: If we have as much sense as geese, we will stay in formation with those who are headed in the direction we want to go.

FACT: When the lead goose gets tired, it rotates back into the formation and another goose flies at the point position.

LESSON 3: If we have as much sense as geese, we will take turns doing the hard tasks and will share leadership roles. We'll also take the opportunity to rest and nurture ourselves so that we come back strong and renewed.

FACT: The geese in formation honk from behind to encourage those up front to keep up their speed.

LESSON 4: If we have as much sense as geese, we will make sure that our "honking" from behind is encouraging, and not something less helpful.

FACT: When a goose gets sick or wounded or shot down, two geese drop out of formation to follow her down to help and protect her. They stay with her until she is either able to fly again or dies. Then they launch out on their own with another formation or catch up with their flock.

LESSON 5: If we have as much sense as geese, we will stand by one another.[8]

Nowhere to Go But Forward

The explorer Cortez, faced with a mutinous crew who wanted to return to Spain rather than follow him in the dangerous conquest of Central America and Mexico, is reported to have ordered his lieutenants to burn his ships during the night. While the story is apocryphal, it has an important moral: **Sometimes we can only move ahead when the option to stay put or return home has been removed.**

During the agrarian revolution, small farmers tried to hold onto their rural lifestyle long after mechanization had destroyed the viability of such enterprises. In the same way, the Atlantic fishers do not seem to be able to let go of their dead industry. A Cortez mentality would torch the empty fish processing plants to send a clear message that the fishers must move on to new and different lives.

A Quick Tire Change

How fast could you change a tire on an automobile? Most physically capable people could do the job in 10 to 15 minutes. With practice you might cut your time to as little as 3 minutes.

If the task is redefined as the need to simultaneously change all 4 tires in less than 10 seconds, as it is in Formula One car racing, then you need to create a new paradigm. The *concept* of changing your paradigm is easy to understand, actually making the change is extremely difficult. For many of us like an old cigarette commercial used to say, we "would rather fight than switch."

Since people do not give up paradigms easily, there usually needs to be compelling external force to make us change the way we perceive the world. Typically, low to moderate amounts of pressure to change only drive us more deeply into the old behaviour. It is painful to watch the BC salmon fishers replay the same futile song-and-dance that their Atlantic cousins have been doing unsuccessfully for the last 20 years.

The Burning Oil Rig

In the circumstance of a fire conventional wisdom and safety training mandated that workers on a North Sea oil rig stay on the platform, awaiting rescue, rather than potentially perishing in the icy water. Ironically, when a terrible fire did occur, only those who dived off the rig ended up surviving.

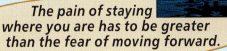

The pain of staying where you are has to be greater than the fear of moving forward.

Best in Class

Best Practices   Worst Practices

Another key concept in the contextual part of this book is called "best-in-the class" or "best practices." Conversely the same principle can be used to learn lessons from the "worst-in-class."

It used take about 6 years to design an auto; that was just the industry standard cycle time. Toyota revolutionized the automobile industry by cutting it to 3 years and then to 2 years. When Ford, at least by legend, was first waking up to the need to dramatically reduce design time, they developed a new way of working that has been labelled the start of North American best-in-class applications.

The story, whether it is true or apocryphal, has in fact been told hundreds if not thousands of times. Ford engineers were sitting around the table talking about the locking system on the car. Engineer A, says, "I think this new system will work," and engineer B says, "If we just adapt the old system, we will get this." Talk goes around the table, and finally some engineer says, "Let's quit looking at what we are doing and look outside. Which automobile company in the world has the finest locking system? Let's borrow freely from that concept." The best locking system was, in fact, Jaguar; Ford subsequently bought Jaguar for its engineering expertise. The same principle applied when Ford looked at suspension systems — they looked at Volvo and Mercedes Benz. Think best-in-class!

We will examine some examples of best practices when we begin comparing what we do in Canada to some other countries. "Who is doing it better?" There is also a corollary in, "Who is doing it worse?" When things are not working, we do not have to repeat mistakes that other people have made.

As examples, Alberta and Korea are delivering more effective education than the average province or Canada. New Zealand is an excellent case study in massive privatization, and the UK's privatization experience is loaded with lessons on pitfalls that can be avoided in privatization. Denmark has set the pace for a post-cold

Ford Taurus

war "small" nation by creating a 5,000-person combat-ready brigade to meet its UN commitments. Hong Kong can teach us much about how a different tax system can stimulate economic growth. Chile has led the world in moving to fully funded private pensions — a model that has been successfully adopted by Peru, Argentina and Colombia.

Sometimes best practices come from what would seem to be unlikely sources. Bangladesh, one of the world's poorest countries, for example, has developed a highly successful model of micro-funding for small businesses. Called the Lending Circle, the model funds very modest loans — sometimes as little as $500 — to entrepreneurs or would-be entrepreneurs. (See page 34.)

Portugal, once the poor cousin of the European Union, has demonstrated the rigour, discipline and great financial restraint that has qualified it for first-round inclusion in the Euro—the common EU currency — while France, an economic powerhouse in relative terms, almost failed to meet the stringent requirements established by the Maastricht Treaty.

The key question that we must ask ourselves, and demand that politicians at all levels ask, is "Who in the world is doing it the best and how could we make it work even better in Canada?" In business, the general approach is to look first within the company, then within the industry and finally outside the industry. A bank wishing to establish an information-age training program for new supervisors may find rich ideas in the practices of the Body Shop, McDonald's, or even Ben and Jerry's legendary US ice cream company.

In school reform, for example, a board or the provincial minister could look to schools that are performing better (i.e., yielding significantly better test results), or it could look to Alberta's system that is clearly out-performing all other provinces (at a lower cost). There are lessons to be learned from Germany, The Netherlands and Japan. There are also some massive failures such as US and UK failures with inner-city schools; these examples bear further examination so as not to repeat the same mistakes they have made.

Best Practices

Boeing's "Cheaper-Better-Faster"

Taking a page from the play book of successful auto makers, aircraft giant Boeing Co. is adopting more efficient practices, which will reduce its aircraft development time from 60 months to 12 months, and lower the cost of development from $8.4 billion to $1.4 billion.

Changes include requiring plants to develop a more generic approach, rather than "product-specific" tools, so they can quickly shift gears along with airline demand for different models. The plan, known as the "cheaper-better-faster" project, also requires that the company shift towards more single-sourced, pre-engineered supplies.

Boeing's twin-engine 777 was launched in 1990, but did not have its first delivery until 1995. As a company official says, "Unless things drastically change we will never develop an all-new airplane."

New Zealand
A Blueprint for
Economic Reform

In the 1950's, New Zealand was among the 5 wealthiest countries in the world. By the late 1970's, it had fallen close to 20th. It had one of the poorest performing economies of the Western world; had not dealt well with the oil crisis; had high import barriers and high levels of farm subsidies; a national debt approaching Third World proportions; a top tax rate of 66%, and a welfare system that the country could no longer afford. From 1975 to 1983, the economy barely grew; the only thing that grew was unemployment — from 0% to 5%.

In 1984, a period of reform started, which has been described by the OECD as the most comprehensive undertaken by any Western country in recent decades.

What Happened?

Financial Sector: The foreign exchange crisis led to a decision to massively devalue the currency, free float the exchange rate, and then deregulate the financial sector. New banks were allowed to operate.

Agriculture: Farm production and processing account for nearly 12% of New Zealand's GDP. Two-thirds of total farm output is exported, earning 60% of total export revenue. Agriculture, however, is too big to be carried by the rest of the economy. Assistance to farmers peaked in 1984, contributing to 30% of total agricultural output. That was unsustainable and, a year later, almost all subsidies were withdrawn — and *all* agricultural subsidies were gone within 2 years. Now assistance is limited to spending on research, inspection, quarantine, and pest control. Farmers are fully exposed to market forces, and the agricultural sector is now the least assisted in the OECD.

Trade: Tariffs were reduced to 1/3 of what they had been, and the country opened up its market to international competition. Now, more than 90% of all imports enter free of any quota, duty, or other restriction. In the meantime, the country's manufacturing base has flourished. While exports of all goods increased 5% in 1994, manufactured goods increased by 7%.

Market Reforms: The public sector used to run everything — some estimates suggest as much as 60% of the economy. In 1984, the government decided the state should not be involved in any activities that could be more efficiently run by the private sector. The 1st step was corporatization through the State Owned Enterprises Act of 1986, which involved getting enterprises run on a commercial basis and requiring them to make a profit. The 2nd step was privatization, or removing the government as an owner.

Public Sector Reform: The public sector decreased in size from 88,000 in 1984, to 36,000 just 10 years later: a reduction of 59%. New Zealand made managers fully accountable — permanent heads became CEOs on contracts to provide certain outputs. Central controls on finance and personnel were freed up, and managers were allowed to set pay and conditions and use capital to the best advantage. Departments could buy and sell their own assets without any further appropriation or authority.

Real-World Accounting System: The country also introduced accrual accounting, and became the only Western government to produce its national accounts in this way, giving a clear idea of the unfunded liabilities of the government. Three key aspects of the government reforms were very successful:
- Transparency in the activities and processes of the government;
- Liberation of managers from central input controls; and
- New financial management and accounting systems.

The Fiscal Responsibility Act of 1994 required all government financial reporting to be in accordance with generally accepted accounting practices, and the government had to publish a comprehensive set of accounts annually and before any election.

Results of 10 Years of Reform: In 1994, New Zealand was ranked 9th overall among the OECD in the World Competitiveness Report. It ranked 1st in the world for government policy designed to develop a competitive business environment.

For 2 years running, the government has balanced its budget. In 1984, the *deficit* was 9% of GDP. In 1996, the *surplus* was more than 4% of GDP (NZ$2.6 billion), rising to 7.5% by the end of 1997. Public debt as a share of GDP was nearly 52% in 1992, and is projected to be down to 18% by 1998. Net foreign currency debt was totally paid off by June 30, 1997.

Government spending as a percentage of GDP — 41% in 1991 — is targeted to be below 30%. Despite this reduction in spending as a percentage of GDP, spending on education overall has been steadily increasing. It was the top expenditure priority in the budget just recently announced; at more than 5% of GDP, it is higher than that in the UK, Australia, the US and Canada.

When accrual accounting was introduced, New Zealanders discovered the government's net worth in 1992-1993 was negative $7.7 billion. By 1996, the government's net worth was positive.

By 1996, unemployment had dropped from a 1992 high of 10.9% to 6.6%. Excellent employment gains continued through 1997.[9]

Auckland's yacht harbour

Zero Basing

The anecdote in the sidebar, great Caesar's Ghost (this page) captures the spirit of how we incorporate our existing standards and paradigms into innovations without stopping to ask why. Most of us carry on relationships based on a mind-set that things "must" be done a certain way. Zero basing is the process that simply asks, "Let us imagine we were starting all over; how would we do it differently?" I am going to ask that question about some of the things in which our government is involved. If we zero base, we will repeatedly ask, "Why in the world are we doing that in that particular way?" Think Best-in-Class and Zero Basing.

There is an old story about cooking a turkey that is extremely relevant to the point at hand. A young couple was busy preparing for its 1st Thanksgiving dinner together. In the process of preparing the turkey, the husband sliced the tail off. The wife, in the best possible spirit, asked, "Why did you do that?" He answered, "Because you always cut the tail off the turkey." She kept quiet and, as luck would have it, his mother was coming to dinner. When she showed up, they asked her the same question. She looked at them with great disbelief and said, "Because you always cut the tail off!" When the grandmother arrived, they asked her also, and she replied, "Well, when I first got married we had only a very small roasting pan. The only way to fit the turkey in was to cut the tail off. That's why I cut the tail off, but I don't know why anyone else does."

PEI and the Other Mini-Provinces

There are lots of things we do that are "turkey tails" in life. Prince Edward Island is an anachronism in size and population (5,200 sq km and 130,000 people). It is less than 1/6 the size of Vancouver Island. Ile d'Anticosti, located in southeastern Quebec, is more than 1½ times larger in area than PEI. It would take almost 5 PEIs to fill Lake Winnipeg, and about 6 to fill Great Bear Lake.

It is common sense to amalgamate the 4 Atlantic Provinces into a single province; it would still be the smallest province in area and larger than only Saskatchewan in population.

If we stuck to turkey tails of the past, women would not be able to vote, Japanese-Canadians would be interned and expelled, racism would abound and Indian children would still be going to residential schools to get "Europeanized."

Constitutionally, the Imperialist Paradigm currently gives Canada a Queen, a Governor General and Lieutenants Governor, Judges by Appointment, and a worthless Senate that is even less meaningful than the British House of Lords that it imitates. Given the robust nature of change in the UK, it is likely that the House of Lords will be discarded long before Canada makes the logical move to a proportionally-based elected senate that could have a more substantive role than political patronage.

> *I can't understand why people are afraid of new ideas; I'm afraid of the old ones.*[5]

Great Caesar's Ghost!
The real reason why things never change

The US and Canadian standard railroad gauge — the distance between the rails — is 4 feet, 8.5 inches. Why that exceedingly odd number? Because that is the way they built them in England, and the North American railroads were built by English expatriates. Why did the English people build them like that? Because the 1st rail lines were built by the same people who built the pre-railroad tramways, and that is the gauge they used.

Why? Because the people who built the tramways used the same jigs and tools for building wagons, which used that wheel spacing. OK! Why, then, did the wagons use that odd spacing? Well, if they tried to use any other spacing, the wagons would break on some of the old long-distance roads, because that was the spacing of the old wheel ruts. So, who built the old rutted roads? The 1st long-distance roads in Europe were built by Imperial Rome for the benefit of its legions and have been used ever since. The initial ruts, which everyone else had to match for fear of destroying their wagons, were first made by Roman war chariots, which, because they were made for or by Imperial Rome, were all alike in the matter of wheel spacing.

So, the Canadian standard railroad gauge of 4 feet, 8.5 inches derives from the original specifications for an Imperial Roman army war chariot. Specs and bureaucracies live forever.[10]

Perseveration Pathology

If zero basing is asking, "What could we do differently?" then perseveration must be its opposite. Psychologists use the term "perseveration" to describe the repetitive use of the same word or idea in response to a stimulus, even when the stimulus changes. It is considered a sign of psychiatric illness. An associated phenomenon known as "perseveration of memory" occurs when we insist on "remembering" the details of an event even after we have been informed that the event did not happen or did not happen in the way that we remember. Many Canadians are afflicted by perseveration of memory. They repeat the familiar myths of our history even as they must know that they no longer explain much about us.

The  Word

How Much Is a Billion Dollars?

To understand and discuss macro-economic issues, it is essential to appreciate the value of a billion dollars. How much work is needed to earn a billion dollars? What can you buy for a billion dollars? Most of us get lost in the millions. We know that there are about 30 million people in Canada, and 10 times that number in the US. China has a billion people; and the world population is somewhere between 5 and 6 billion.

Rule of Thumb
$1 million will buy 1,000 computers for our schools

Rules of Thumb

How can we understand the significance of a billion dollars? What meaning does it have to the average person? StatsCan's "average" income data can give us some clues. The 2 most common ways of expressing "averages" are mean and median. The mean income is determined by adding all of the incomes together and dividing by the 15 million individual tax returns filed each year. Using this method, the average Canadian male earns about $30,000 a year; the average Canadian female earns about $26,000 a year . The other principal way that average is determined, by Revenue Canada, is by the median — or the middle point — where half of the personal income tax returns are above and half are below. Using this method, the national median income is about $19,000. The significant difference between the mean income and the median income indicates the gap between the haves and the have-nots in our society. Given that we are trying to understand the meaning of a billion dollars, we can make a reasonable generalization and say that **the average Canadian earns $20,000-$25,000 a year.**

Vancouver's prestigious Fraser Institute has designated June 27 (1998) as Tax Freedom Day, or the day when we start working for ourselves rather than our governments. That means that virtually half of the income we earn goes to various governmental bodies through direct and indirect taxation. **The average individual has about $10,000-$12,500 a year in disposable income.**

If we divide the median annual disposable income into a billion dollars, the result shows that *it takes 105,820 individuals, working for a year, to create a billion dollars in spendable income.* Put another way, it takes 105,820 individuals working for a year to create a billion dollars in tax revenues.

If we use mean income numbers of $28,000, the same mathematical

Rule of Thumb
$1 billion is the lifetime disposable income of 2,500 Canadian workers

process works out to *only* 71,429 individuals, working for a year to create a billion dollars in spendable income.

Since our purpose is to create a quick method of grasping the meaning of a billion dollars, it is probably reasonable to use the total of 80,000 to 90,000 "average" individuals, working for a year, to generate a billion dollars in taxes and a billion dollars in disposable income. Clearly there are some rounding errors, but since we are developing a rule of thumb, let us go with some number between 71,429 and 105,820.

You are going to work approximately 40 years during your life — at the median and mean average salaries. In today's dollars, you would gross between $756,000 and $1,040,000. Since we know that the government will take half of that in various taxes, this means your lifetime net disposable income is between $378,000 and $520,000. That means that it takes the lifetime work of between 1,923 and 2,646 people to make a billion dollars in disposable income, adding a few people who cannot work because of physical and mental handicaps; a billion dollars is the lifetime disposable income of at least 2,500 workers.

Another way to understand how much a billion dollars is would be to realize what it will buy. The Confederation Bridge, connecting PEI to the mainland, cost a billion dollars. The privately constructed Highway 407 that runs for 36 kilometres north of Toronto — Canada's 1st totally electronic tollway — cost about a billion dollars.

PEI's Confederation Bridge
What $1 billion buys!

We now have some way to better understand the announcement that the 6 cities that were amalgamated into the Greater Toronto Area have a combined *unfunded* debt — mostly pensions — of a billion dollars.

On a provincial level, Quebec and Ontario have acknowledged and unacknowledged debts of about $150 billion *each*; combined, this represents the disposable income guaranteed during a year by somewhere between 21 and 32 million workers! (Remember Canada only has 15 million workers.) This staggering number does not include the unfunded debts of the federal government, the other provinces or crown corporations.

How Much Is a Trillion?

A trillion is a lot more people than there are in the world or the number of years that Earth has existed.

Canada's GDP will not reach $ 1 trillion until at least 2005; Canada's debts today exceed $2 trillion.

A trillion is a thousand times a thousand times a thousand times a thousand.

Rule of Thumb
$1 trillion is $1 million a day for 2,808 years

Victoria's crest as Queen-Empress of India

LOCATION	AREA (Square Miles)	POPULATION
Great Britain, **EUROPE** Cyprus, Gibraltar, Malta	157,500	43,210,00
AFRICA Basotoland, Bechuanaland, British East Africa, British Somaliland, Cape Colony, Egypt, Gambia, Gold Coast, Natal, Nigeria, Northern Rhodesia, Nyasaland, Sierra Leone, Southern Rhodesia, Swaziland, Transvaal, Uganda, Walvis Bay	2,150,000	37,900,000
AMERICA Antigua, Bahamas, Barbados, Barbuda, Bermuda, British Guiana, British Honduras, Canada, Grand Cayman, Grenada, Jamaica, Montserrat, Nevis, Newfoundland, St. Christopher, St. Lucia, St. Vincent, Tobago, Trinidad, Virgin Islands and other small islands of the Caribbean and West Indies	3,094,000	6,898,000
ASIA Aden, Brunei, Ceylon, Hong Kong, India, Labuan Island, Malay Federated States, North Borneo, Papua, Sarawak, Singapore	1,700,000	296,500,000
AUSTRALIA New South Wales, New Zealand, Northern Territory, Queensland, South Australia, Tasmania, Victoria, Western Australia	3,100,000	4,000,000
ATLANTIC OCEAN Ascension, Falkland Islands, Gough Island, St. Helena, South Georgia, South Sandwich, Tristan da Cunha and other small islands	8,670	6,200
INDIAN OCEAN Amirante Islands, Andaman Islands, Chagos Islands, Christmas Island, Cocos (Keeling) Islands, Kuria Muria Islands, Laccadive Islands, Maldive Islands, Mauritius, Nicobar Islands, Seychelles Islands, Socotra, Zanzibar and other small islands	1,200	400,000
PACIFIC OCEAN Antipodes Island, Bounty Islands, Campbell Island, Chatham Island, Ellice Islands, Fiji Islands, Gilbert Islands, Kermadec Islands, Lord Howe Island, Norfolk Island, Pitcairn, Southern Solomons and other island groups	7,500	150,000
Gross area of land mass: 57,510,000.[11] **GRAND TOTAL**	10,200,00	387,400,000

The British Isles are correctly known as the "United Kingdom of Great Britain and Ireland," but everyday terms favoured "Great Britain," "Britain, " or to the dismay of the Scots, Welsh and Irish, simply "England."

There were many different forms of imperial rule and it was not always clear whether a territory was in or out of the Empire. For example, Transvaal in 1897 was only debatably a member as an autonomous republic whose foreign affairs were under British control; Egypt was under British military occupation, but not yet formally annexed; and Cyprus was under Turkish sovereignty, although administered by Britain.

Figures for area and population are approximate.

Areas in red represent the British Empire's domain.

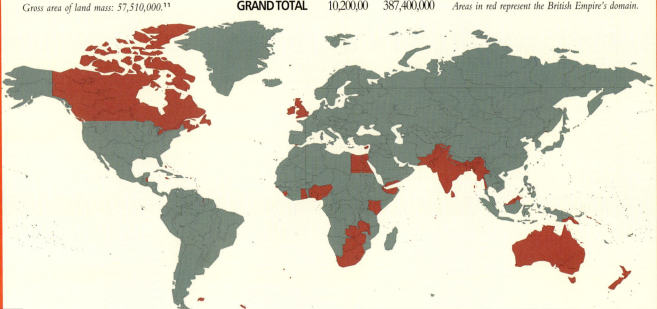

Our Home and Native Land!

Myths and Realities

It may be true that you can't go back, but a clear view of the past can help you keep an eye on the future.[12]

Recreating the Canadian Identity

Since WWII, Canada has dramatically changed its mythical history — the common understanding of a past that holds us together and makes us feel that we are part of a common enterprise. Many of those profound changes have not yet touched the hearts and minds of the average "traditional" Canadian. Daniel Francis' book, *National Dreams*, does an insightful job of reminding that things are not what they used to be.

The RCMP has come a long way from its Yukon gold rush roots to joining Mickey Mouse as a Disney icon of pop culture. The tremendous sacrifices of our military also have come a long way from Vimy Ridge and Dieppe (see page 183) to the sordid debacle of Somalia and blatant sexual harassment charges. The glory of the CPR's last spike has become obsolete in a world of indifference towards the railways. Our treatment of aboriginals, though more humane than that of our Australian and US cousins, is mired in the reality of 300 years of failed social policy, crowned by myriad blatant abuses of the residential schools system.

For the 1 in 6 Canadians who were born elsewhere, the reality of today tends to be much stronger than the ghosts of our past. For most of the rest of us, if we even bother to care, the myths of the past may be more potent than they deserve to be.

Perhaps one of our most costly myths is that there is such a thing as Canadian Culture that needs to be defended from outside influences — especially the US. The facts are:
• 95% of our feature films are foreign,
• 70% of the Canadian book market is of imported books,
• 84% of retail sound recordings feature foreign content.

Canadians traditionally tell pollsters (and almost anyone else who will listen) about their unique multicultural policies, their universal health care system and their role as the world's peacekeepers.

We end up back at the core premise of this book: **The major handicap of the nation is ignorance.** It is difficult to protect a culture when we are limited to approaching issues in an historical vacuum.

Consider the following from an Angus Reid poll of 18-24-year-olds:
• Almost half could not name the 1st prime minister.
• A majority thought that Neil Armstrong was the first Canadian in space. [Marc Garneau]
• About a third thought that Norman Rockwell was a Canadian artist.

Canadian schools are struggling with how to teach about a national identity in a country that is politically fragmented, regionally divided, pluralistic and increasingly multi-ethnic. Citizenship education has resurfaced as a public issue as we examine the question, "What is Canada and what does it mean to be a Canadian?"

Frank McKenna, former Premier of New Brunswick, wrote in "Commentary" in *The Globe and Mail*:

"In my travels from one end of Canada to the other, I have been struck by 2 things: the unequivocal greatness of our country, oddly juxtaposed with the often passionless esteem in which we hold it." He concluded, "We are at a pivotal point in our history. Our discipline and forbearance have put us in a position to redirect our energies towards renewing our national vision. Our Canadian canvas is now ready for bold and sweeping brush strokes that will give all Canadians renewed hope and optimism."[13]

This book is about finding that national vision by both appreciating the things that we do well and understanding the mistakes that we are making that erode our optimism. There are dozens of charts and graphs in the book that show how Canada is doing compared to other countries. Sometimes the news is good, and sometimes there is a lesson that we need to learn if we are to create a national vision that stretches from aboriginal to new immigrant and from St. John's to Victoria.

In some ways, the persistent myths about the country are no more real than Potemkin's Villages. (See sidebar, page 16.) When you have finished the tour of Canada that this book offers, you may be ready to become an active participant in creating a new and dynamic vision for this great (albeit flawed) country.

Fathers of Confederation, Charlottetown, 1864

Other countries have too much history; Canada has too much geography. — *Mackenzie King*

EARLIEST TIMES

- 30,000-10,000 BCE - Aboriginals immigrated from Asia.

- The earliest known settlements in Canada date from 12,000 to 17,000 years ago at the Bluefish Caves in the Yukon.

Cabot lays claim

- Excavations at L'Anse aux Meadows confirm that Vikings settled in Newfoundland in about the year 1000.

- In 1497, Giovanni Caboto (John Cabot) landed in Bonavista, Newfoundland (we think) and claimed the land for England's King Henry VII.

- Jacques Cartier explored Canada's interior in 1535. Canada is thought to come from the Iroquoian word for village, Kanata, that Cartier mistakenly applied to the entire region. Cartier's discoveries gave France a claim to Canada and led to French settlements.

17th CENTURY

- In 1605, Samuel de Champlain established the colony of Port Royal in what is now Nova Scotia, and later founded a settlement at Quebec in 1608, trading fur with the Algonquins and Hurons.

- Montreal, founded in 1642, became the centre of the fur trade, but the companies did not encourage settlement because of wars against the Iroquois. By 1660, there were only about 3,000 settlers.

- In 1663, King Louis XIV made New France a crown colony. The Iroquois signed a peace treaty in 1667.

- The "Company of Adventurers of England Trading into Hudson's Bay" was chartered in 1670 by Charles II, and acquired a monopoly of all trade in the area.

18th CENTURY

- New France stretched from Hudson Bay to the Gulf of Mexico and from Newfoundland to the Great Lakes. The heartland was the 20,000 colonists settled along the St. Lawrence. In 1755, there was the expulsion of the Acadians, and a year later, the Seven Years' War in Europe pitted Britain against France.

- In 1759, France was driven out of Canada when Wolfe defeated the French led by Montcalm. Both generals died in this battle on the Plains of Abraham outside Quebec City. By 1763, the treaty ending the Seven Years' War also gave the British sovereignty in New France.

General Wolfe's death on the Plains of Abraham

- That same year, the British issued a Royal Proclamation forbidding Roman Catholics from holding political office. This was overturned in 1774.

- In 1784, the arrival of 30,000 Loyalists into Nova Scotia led to the creation of the colony of New Brunswick.

- An influx of 10,000 Loyalists into Quebec in 1791 led to the division of the colony into Upper and Lower Canada.

19th CENTURY

- Ongoing antagonisms between the British and the Americans culminated in the war of 1812. By 1814, the Treaty of Ghent was signed. Four years later, Britain and the United States agreed to accept the 49th parallel as the international boundary.

- Immigrants from the United States and Europe were lured by free or cheap land, and the economic base of the colonies grew. Tensions between Upper and Lower Canada led to a series of unsuccessful rebellions. In the aftermath, Governor General Lord Durham recommended the union of the Canadas as the 1st step in the assimilation of French Canadians.

- In 1858, Ottawa was chosen as the capital.

- Montreal and Toronto became leading commercial centres, and the Maritime ports prospered. Improved roads and transportation systems, including the completion of the Grand Trunk Railway in 1861, led to further expansion.

- In 1867, the British government passed the British North America Act; Nova Scotia, New Brunswick, Ontario and Quebec became the Dominion of Canada.

- In 1873, the North West Mounted Police was formed.

- Under Prime Minister John A. Macdonald, western expansion grew. In 1870, Manitoba entered the Confederation. When British Columbia joined a year later, Ottawa promised to build a transcontinental railway from sea to sea. The last spike in the Canadian Pacific Railway was driven at Craigellachie, BC in 1885.

Hammer Down — the last spike in the CPR

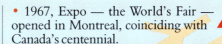

20th CENTURY

• Alberta and Saskatchewan were created in 1905. By 1911, Canada's population was 7,206,643.

• At the onset of World War I, Canadian troops faced devastating losses at Passchendaele. In 1917, Prime Minister Robert Borden introduced conscription and unleashed one of the most bitter political battles in Canadian history.

• In 1919, Winnipeg faced a 6-week General Strike, as workers attempted to achieve better wages, collective bargaining, and improved working conditions.

• By 1921, more than 15% of the workforce was unemployed, and Prairie farmers faced devastating losses when world wheat markets collapsed. The election of 1921 marked the 1st time Canadians could vote for 1 of 3 parties at the federal level: the Liberals, the Conservatives or the Progressives.

• In 1931, Canada achieved sovereign status through the Statute of Westminster.

• In 1940, Unemployment Insurance was proposed, and the Liberals won the federal election.

• Following the Japanese attack on Pearl Harbour in 1941, Japanese-Canadians were interned and their property was confiscated.

• At the same time, immigration had changed the Canadian demographic structure. Canadians of British ancestry now made up 50% of the population, 30% were of French descent and 20% were of other ethnic backgrounds.

• The postwar baby boom and the influx of European immigrants resulted in a 40% population increase between 1945 and 1958.

• By 1945, unemployment insurance and family allowance legislation had been passed.

• Liberal leader Louis St. Laurent was elected in 1948. One of his 1st accomplishments was the entry of Newfoundland into Confederation in 1949. In 1951, his government increased old age pensions and introduced a hospital insurance plan.

• In 1957, the Conservatives under Diefenbaker won a minority government. Diefenbaker introduced the Bill of Rights in 1961 and granted native peoples the right to vote in federal elections.

• Lester B. Pearson's Liberals came to power in 1963. He broadened social welfare by introducing Medicare, the Canada Pension Plan and the Canada Assistance Plan.

• 1965, the Maple Leaf flag is adopted.

• 1967, Expo — the World's Fair — opened in Montreal, coinciding with Canada's centennial.

• Federalist Pierre Trudeau led the Liberals to a majority government in 1968. The Official Languages Act of 1969 adopted French and English as official languages and required federal institutions to provide services in both languages.

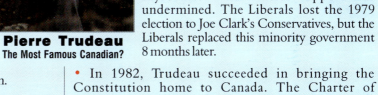

Pierre Trudeau
The Most Famous Canadian?

• In the October Crisis of 1970, Trudeau used the War Measures Act to apply emergency measures of arrest, detention and martial law.

• In 1976, Rene Levesque's Parti Quebecois defeated the provincial Liberals in Quebec, thus fuelling uncertainty over the future of Canada and Quebec. Federally, inflation skyrocketed and Liberal support was undermined. The Liberals lost the 1979 election to Joe Clark's Conservatives, but the Liberals replaced this minority government 8 months later.

• In 1982, Trudeau succeeded in bringing the Constitution home to Canada. The Charter of Rights and Freedoms entrenched bilingualism in the federal jurisdiction and provided for universal language education.

• Trudeau retired in 1984, and John Turner became the Liberal leader. After 16 years of Liberal government, however, the nation elected Mulroney's Conservatives.

• The Conservatives sought to strengthen ties with the US and took steps to attract foreign investment. One of Mulroney's goals was to amend the Constitution Act of 1982 and obtain the support of Quebec. This agreement became known as the Meech Lake Accord.

• In 1987, the Mulroney government negotiated the Canada-US Free Trade Agreement. The Conservatives won a 2nd majority government, and the FTA was approved in December. It took effect on January 1, 1989.

• As the deadline for Meech Lake drew near, Manitoba and Newfoundland withdrew their support and the deal collapsed.

• In 1991, the Conservatives introduced the GST.

• In October 1992, a referendum was held to ratify the Charlottetown Accord (another attempt to bring Quebec into the Constitution), but the deal was rejected.

• In 1993, Mulroney was replaced by Kim Campbell, the country's 1st female prime minister.

• In October 1993, the Liberals came to power under Jean Chrétien with an opposition made up of members of the separatist Bloc Quebecois. The Liberals were re-elected in 1997, and the Western-based Reform Party became the official opposition.

Potemkin's Villages

In 1787, Prince Grigori Aleksandrovich Potemkin, the power behind Catherine the Great, arranged a ceremonial tour for Catherine through south Russia. He gave exact imperatives to the provincial governors along the route, pressuring them to create a display that would impress the empress and her entourage:

...inhabitants dressed in their best
...all houses to be whitewashed
...pigs removed from the highways
...no dead dogs and cats to be seen in any street
...no drunkard to be seen standing outside inn-doors
or be heard using improper language.

Beggars and cripples were moved out of sight. A massive cleanup campaign was launched. New construction was initiated — most of it had not progressed very far when the tour occurred. After Catherine had passed, the new building was terminated and the seamy reality returned. [14]

The Report Card at the End of 1998: Good News and Bad News

The title of Pierre Berton's compelling book, *1967: The Last Good Year,* is very revealing. The 1st revelation is that the centennial year was a "good" year rather than a "great" year, and 2nd was that not much of real quality has happened since.

Balancing the federal budget in 1997 was, of course, good news, but the vast majority of the balancing was circumstantial. The interest rate on the massive federal debt was at a 30-year low and tax collection, thanks to bracket creep, excess EI collections and the stimulation from the roaring US economy, was at a record high. There were some modest reductions in expenditures, but any real savings came on the back of reduced transfers to the provinces. The reality is that despite all the rhetoric, the federal Liberals have continued to do business as usual.

We have not seen the political will at the federal level that we have seen at the provincial level. Premier Klein successfully cleaned house in Alberta, and Premier Harris is attempting a similar regime in Ontario. Saskatchewan, Manitoba and New Brunswick have successfully balanced their budgets. New Brunswick is pressing to market its IT capacity and bilingualism. Nova Scotia has abolished its separate school boards, but in BC, the NDP's anti-business orientation, dependency on natural resources and weakened Asian trading partners, have left it primed for a severe recession as 1999 arrives.

The economic boom of 1998 brought the lowest unemployment rate since the 1990 boom, while the stock exchanges were struggling with problems amplified by Japan's 8-year reluctance to face economic reality, the Asian flu and the implosion of the Russian economy. The loonie plunged to record lows, reflecting the country's dismal decline in productivity. Trade union hostility to the changing global market and the modest success of the economy stimulated costly strikes. Schools are failing to educate our children for the information age, and the gap between the Haves and Have-Nots is widening, with an epidemic of poor children who will be stigmatized for life.

All provinces are not created equal: The economy continues to be dominated by Ontario and, to a lesser degree, by Quebec. This book explores many of the regional differences as we have the opportunity to compare which provinces are doing which things best. The chart of provincial GDP on this page reflects the relative size of the economies of the different provinces and territories.

The next page of the book highlights some of the recent good news about the country; there is genuine reason to rejoice on many fronts. Canada, despite its obvious problems, is much better off than most of the rest of the world. Our cities are safer than most, and no nation is hostile enough towards us to be threatening any conflict. Our poor are middle class by world standards. We remain relatively prosperous but we are no longer purposeful. The people are strong, but the spirit is weak, producing a malaise that, unchecked, can promote our retreating into sectionalism and ethnicity.

Life is comparatively easy but we could make it much, much better if we could find that common vision and work together to make it happen.

Provincial GDP Shares [15]

The dispersion of wealth varies widely across the country, and has remained relatively constant over the past 20 years. As the chart below shows, Ontario and Quebec remain the economic giants with 2/3 of the country's economy.

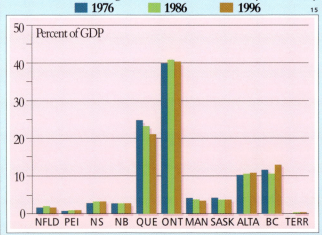

Legend: ■ 1976 ■ 1986 ■ 1996   15

Percent of GDP (y-axis: 0, 10, 20, 30, 40, 50)

x-axis: NFLD, PEI, NS, NB, QUE, ONT, MAN, SASK, ALTA, BC, TERR

IF THE PART OF 'RICK' IN CASABLANCA HAD BEEN PLAYED BY A CANADIAN...

PLAY IT AGAIN SAM! THAT IS — IF IT'S NOT TOO MUCH TROUBLE. I UNDERSTAND IF YOU'RE TOO BUSY. SAY! — WHY DON'T I JUST WHISTLE IT INSTEAD?

UN's Human Development Report 1998

Human development index: The HDI measures a country's achievements in terms of life expectancy, educational attainment and adjusted real income.

1. **Canada**	165. Gambia
2. France	166. Mozambique
3. Norway	167. Guinea
4. USA	168. Eritrea
5. Iceland	169. Ethiopia
6. Finland	170. Burundi
7. Netherlands	171. Mali
8. Japan	172. Burkina Faso
9. New Zealand	173. Niger
10. Sweden	174. Sierra Leone

More Good News from the UN

Canada was ranked 1st in a report from the United Nations as the best country in the world in which to live. By factoring in life expectancy, education and income into a human development index, Canada placed 1st of 174 countries in the UN's 1998 Human Development Report.

Canada does poorly, however, on politically correct indicators like percentage of parliamentary seats occupied by women (13%, compared to Norway, Finland and Denmark with world-leading 38%, 39% and 34% respectively), and the number of female managers and administrators in the labour force.

Our life expectancy is not the best, but it is good, with Canadians living 79.1 years on average. Americans, in contrast, only live 76.4 years.

Canadians seem to agree with the index, since a Decima poll of 1,000 adults found that more than 90% view Canada as the world's best place to live.

The political left, however, seems reluctant to make too much of the figures. They say national averages hide the plight of aboriginals, whose life expectancy is 5 years lower than the national average. Canada also ranks only 9th when the index is adjusted for gender disparity. Canadian women can expect to live longer (80 years) than men, and more women than men graduate from secondary school and enrol in university, but they earn only 72% as much as their male counterparts.

Feelin' Good

Ten reasons why Canadians should feel good about the country in 1998:

1. Growth Goliath. The IMF predicts that Canada will lead the way among Western nations with 3.5% GDP growth in 1998.

2. The Sovereignist Implosion. Quebec's economic ills seem to have reversed the separatist momemtum — the Fall 1998 election will be a moment of truth.

3. The Disappearing Deficit. Thanks to a buoyant economy, Ottawa ran a surplus in 1997-98, the 1st in 23 years.

4. Inflation Deflated. The taming of inflation — ran at a mere 1.8% for 1997 — means low interest rates are here to stay.

5. The Choice of Billions. For the 5th straight year, Canada rates as the world's best country to live in, according to a United Nations survey.

6. Spend Spend Spend. Shopkeepers are smiling as buyers finally begin to splurge, and consumer confidence rises to its highest level since 1989.

7. Live Long and Prosper. Canada ranks 4th among nations in life expectancy. By the year 2000, Canadians will be living an average of 80 years for the 1st time.

8. Export Explosion. Exports have risen from about $190 billion in 1993 to over $300 billion in 1997.

9. Safe at Home. Canada's crime rate has been falling steadily for the past 5 years and was down 2% in 1996.

10. Urban Bliss. Canadian cities continue to be among the most livable in the world.[16]

The Toronto Stampede

The 1993 Grey Cup game between the Bombers and Stampeders at Toronto's SkyDome marked the 1st time in 30 years that Calgary had played in the championship match in Toronto. In 1963, 5 Calgarian cowboys rode their horses through the lobby of the famous Royal York Hotel in a good-natured Stampede-style celebration. Three decades later, the sons and a daughter of those cowboys thought it was an event worth repeating. After shipping the horses to Toronto, they filled up on beer and rode their horses down Front Street to the Hotel. There, they were met at the door by the concierge and the RCMP, who were armed — with carrots and apples!

Pause for a moment to think about that. The potential confrontation was defused with good humour by distracting the horses. If that had happened in Chicago or Detroit, the cowpokes would have been met with tear gas. There is something magnificent in the spirit on both sides of this prank.

The media are too pervasive to let anything stay hidden very long. In this respect, truth and honesty are virtues.

Key Points in
Canada-US Relations

> *Canadians have been educated to be anti-American. Our schoolbooks have taught us that Americans are headstrong and unstable (to say nothing of Expanionist), a result of their excessive indulgence in democracy.* [12]

- 1776: The American Revolution. Canada allied with Britain on the losing side. The differences and aspirations of two separate societies can be traced back to here.

- The War of 1812: Canada was the site for what was basically a dispute between Britain and the US. Canadian forces turned back American forces 5 times. US forces burned what is now Toronto, and the British burned Washington for revenge. These attacks cemented the Canadian will to not be American.

- 1817: The Rush-Bagot Treaty declared that the border between Canada and the US should never again be armed. To this day, it remains the world's longest undefended border (9,000 km).

- 1897: The Yukon Gold Rush. 50,000 Americans came to take part in the prospecting.

- 1911: Prime Minister Wilfrid Laurier lost the national election because of his platform proposing free trade with the US. The opposition won on the platform, "No truck or trade with the Yankees."

- 1918: The US refused to join The League of Nations because Canada was allowed to join independent from Great Britain.

- Late 1930's: William Lyon Mackenzie King, the Canadian PM, tired of British interference, wanted to take advantage of the power and growth south of the border. President Theodore Roosevelt encouraged relations with Canada.

- 1936: Roosevelt visited Quebec. It was the 1st time a US President visited Canada.

- 1940: Roosevelt pledged to support Canada in the event of an attack from overseas. Prime Minister Mackenzie King went to Ogdensburg to sign a defence agreement with the US that tied Canada's defence future to the United States.

- Post-war 1940's: Mackenzie King, wary of the US, abandoned talks about free trade. *Time* magazine published economics article calling Canada the 49th state. King wrote in his diary that he was afraid of US absorption.

- 1950's: C. D. Howe, Canada's US-born "minister of everything," was Prime Minister Louis St. Laurent's right-hand man. The 40's and 50's saw huge foreign investment in Canada. By 1957, Americans controlled 70% of the capital of the petroleum and natural gas industry and 90% of the auto industry.

- 1957-1963: PM John Diefenbaker fought the tide of industry and challenged extensive US investment in Canada. His nemesis was John F. Kennedy.

- 1960's: John F. Kennedy visited Canada. He became angry at Canada for trading with Cuba because of the conflict over the Cuban Missile crisis.

- 1963-1968: PM Lester B. Pearson is accused by Diefenbaker of being a US puppet. Pearson styled himself as a friend of the US.

- 1968-1984: Pierre Trudeau questions Canada's relations with the US. Trudeau went to Washington in 1971 and complained about US tariffs on Canadian exports. In 1972, Nixon returned the visit and faced anti-US demonstrations in Ottawa. Trudeau later announced that Canada must diversify its relationships with other countries to avoid excessive influence by the US. Trudeau established Petrocan and the National Energy Board because by 1972 the energy industry was 99% foreign owned. The National Energy Board lasts only 4 years due to undermining American influence.

- 1984-1993: Under PM Brian Mulroney, the tide turned again with a return to pro-American policies.

- 1987: The Free Trade Agreement is signed.

- 1989: January 1: The Canada-US Free Trade Agreement is implemented.

- 1992: December: NAFTA is signed.

Why Canada Is Not As Productive As the US

US manufacturing labour-productivity advantage over Canada is more than 40%, a dramatic increase over the 23% from the last decade; real US per capita income grew at double the Canadian rate in the 1990-1995 period; Canada is losing its relative share of foreign investment while the US has been increasing its share.

Reasons:

- Canada has been slower to make the transition to a knowledge-based economy.
- OECD has identified Canada as having an innovation gap.
- Labour laws and policies in Canada tend to impose a higher regulatory cost on employers and reduce the flexibility and dynamism of the labour markets.
- Minimum wages tend to be higher and hours of work and overtime regulations tend to be more restrictive.
- Advance notice and severance rules tend to be more stringent.
- Labour laws are more conducive to the formation and retention of unions.
- The high cost of the social safety net and the benefits packages are financed with payroll taxes, which raise the cost of labour, driving jobs out of the country and/or encouraging further substitution of capital for labour.

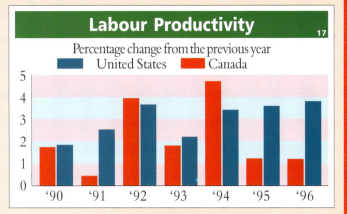

Labour Productivity [17]

Percentage change from the previous year
United States **Canada**

(Bar chart showing percentage change from previous year for United States (blue) and Canada (red) from '90 to '96, vertical axis 0 to 5)

> *The US-Canadian border is not as arbitrary as it appears; for the most part, the watersheds flow away from it.*

On the Border

On a map, you can see border towns and hamlets scattered like paired beads strung along opposite sides of the 9,000-km Canadian-US border. More than 80% of Canadians live within 500 km of the US border; more than 50% live in cities and towns along the southern parts of Ontario and Quebec, close to the Great Lakes and the St. Lawrence River. The people who live in these border communities have different governments but much in common; a person ignorant of the meaning of a national border could easily conclude that these communities are more or less indistinguishable. However, as the poll data in the chart below shows, Canadian and Americans have vastly different attitudes and concerns.

The 1997 Most Important Issues Were... [18]

Canadians:		Americans:	
46%	Jobs	International Affairs	24%
42	Unity	Education	20
24	The Economy	Crime/Violence	20
23	The Deficit	The Economy	15
20	Crime/Violence	Federal Deficit	15
16	Health Care	Drugs	15
		Health Care	14
		Jobs	9

More Americans than Canadians say they go to church, pray and read the Bible, and twice as many say religion influences their political thinking (41% vs. 19%).

Canada's first woman in space, Dr. Roberta Bondar, had to hitch a ride on a NASA spaceship

Defending the Maginot Line of Canadian Culture

While major Canadian authors and journalists comment at length about whether there is, or ever was, such a thing as Canadian Culture, the federal government has put a lot of emphasis on defending it. Heritage Minister Sheila Copps bounces around like a high school cheerleader protecting this illusive, and most likely, imaginary spirit.

"Our identity comes from not having one. As the myth of unity continues to dissolve, and an increasing number of writers, borrowing from the language of cultural theory, have begun referring to Canada as a post-modern, or post-national, country. In a post-national world it is essential not to have the high degree of nationalistic commitment that goes with a unified sense of identity." [12]

Prior to 1967, the purpose of the CBC was simply to offer a national broadcast service. After the Centennial, an act of parliament declared that the CBC must contribute to the development of national unity and provide for a continuing expression of a Canadian identity.

"It's a deal breaker," said a senior MAI negotiator. "Culture is not on the table. If there is no exemption, there will be no deal." (See page 173.) Trying to defend Canadian Culture from the dominant US culture is as futile as the French building a wall to defend against German militarism.

The Original Maginot Line

In the 1930's, France, greatly concerned by the raising German threat, began construction of the Maginot Line stretching 750 kilometres from the Swiss to the Belgian borders. *It was the most elaborate fortification in history.* Every few miles along the defence line were heavily reinforced concrete fortresses, interconnected by a continuous series of underground tunnels at 7 different levels down to a depth of about 50 metres.

The tunnels contained an electric railroad that connected all points along the line of defence, hospitals, troop quarters, command posts — everything necessary to maintain a complete army. Elevators enabled the occupants to go from one level to another.

When Hitler's forces attacked France in 1940, his motorized and armoured divisions simply circled through Belgium and the Netherlands in order to avoid the Maginot Line — what we would call an "end run" in football today.

Thirty-five days after the German attack had begun, the strong point of the Maginot Line, Verdun, was captured.

Common-Law Relations Reflect A Change in Family Values:

The Canadian family is rapidly becoming an unmarried one. Common-law and single-parent families now make up more than 25% of the almost 8 million Canadian families, up from 20% just 10 years ago. Between 1991 and 1996, the number of common-law families jumped 28%, single parent families rose by 19% while married couples increased by less than 2%.

Common-law living is not a new phenomenon, but its popularity has increased substantially in the last 15 years. The prevalence of common-law relationships reflects the changing attitudes of Canadians towards marriage: it appears the common-law union is not only a prelude to marriage, but also an alternative to marriage and remarriage.

For more than a decade, common-law unions have been far more prevalent in Quebec than any other province, accounting for more than 4 of every 10 common-law unions in Canada in 1995, or about 442,000. That was more than 3 times the provincial number in 1981.

Within Quebec, common-law relationships accounted for 21% of all families in 1995, compared with only 11% in 1986 and 7% in 1981. No other region had such a striking trend in both the number and proportional increase in common-law living.

In 1995, for the rest of Canada, the proportion of common-law families was about 9%. It is increasingly popular for common-law couples to have children.

There has also been a decrease in immigration to Quebec, which controls its own separate immigration policy and takes fewer than half as many immigrants per capita as the country as a whole in a clearly discriminatory bid to keep from diluting its "unique" culture.

Family Snapshot
[19]

Percentage of different types of families in Canada

Family Type	1986	1996
Married Couple Families	80.02	73.7
Common Law Couple Families	10.4	12.1
Female Single Parent Families	7.2	11.7
Male Single Parent Families	2.2	2.5

Speed of Life

[20]

Ranking of overall pace of life by country based on 3 criteria: number of minutes it takes a pedestrian to walk 18 metres downtown, number of minutes it takes a postal clerk to complete a stamp-purchase transaction and the accuracy of public clocks.

From fast-paced to slow

1. Switzerland	10. Hong Kong
2. Ireland	11. France
3. Germany	12. Poland
4. Japan	13. Costa Rica
5. Italy	14. Taiwan
6. England	15. Singapore
7. Sweden	16. United States
8. Austria	**17. Canada**
9. Netherlands	

Our National Identity

A Canadian is someone who drinks Brazilian coffee from an English teacup and munches a French pastry while sitting on Danish furniture having just come home from an Italian movie in a German car. He picks up his Japanese pen and writes his MP to complain about the American takeover of the Canadian publishing business.[21]

In the 1950's, 75% of all Canadians were of either British or French background and the country had 2 dominant linguistic forces and 2 cultural traditions with 300 years of local colour added, but that has changed with the recent immigration patterns. (See page 42.) French does not even make the list of the top 14 languages spoken in the homes in Toronto in 1998, and England has dropped to 10th and France to 17th place as a source of immigrants.

Hockey, traditionally Canada's national game, is a contradiction of stereotypes; it requires a special talent to match the image of violently aggressive hockey players with the image of the polite, deferent Canadian. The country is no longer held together by radio or TV coverage of *Hockey Night in Canada*, and the Stanley Cup has been usurped by US teams playing in much larger markets. The possibility of seeing the Leafs and Canadiens playing in the finals has vanished and the dominance of Canadian players has been eclipsed by a torrent of talented European players. Canada is a country without an independence day. Our history reveals no single moment at which the country gained its autonomy.

We cannot find our beginning. There is no Declaration of Independence, no Magna Carta, no Bastille Day. Canada began as a collection of separate colonies belonging to Great Britain, then evolved into an independent nation.

In *Nationalism Without Walls*, Richard Gwyn refers to Canada as the world's first post-modern state, "multi-ethnic, politically decentralized, economically integrated into the global market place." He continues, "Our community is at risk now of being disinvented — of being deconstructed. The Forces arrayed against us include the global economy, neo-conservatism, immigration, multiculturalism and our own indifference." (See pages 42-43.)

Has the country fallen so far behind the times in an era of nationalism that it is in fact ahead of its time in the post-national world? It seems that whether or not we know it and whether or not we want it, Canada is awash in the decentralized, global-market focused reality of the new world order. The only question seems to be whether we go with the flow or fight the transition. Given our history of not facing up to reality, its likely that Toronto and Vancouver will be city states before the Quebec question is answered. Which brings us to the key question addressed in the following sidebar, "What do we do when the horse we are riding dies?"

When the Horse You Are Riding Dies...

Common and practical advice from knowledgeable horse trainers (as well as small children and the intellectually challenged) has a core imperative: "If the horse you're riding dies, get off."

In many facets of the Canadian economy, primarily those sectors that tend to be most insulated from economic realities, such as education, health care, politics, the military and the civil service in general — there is a tendency to choose other less pragmatic alternatives when the horse dies; common alternatives among these institutions include the equivalent of:

1. Buy a new and stronger whip.
2. Try a new bit or bridle.
3. Switch riders.
4. Move the horse to a new location.
5. Ride the horse for longer periods of time.
6. Remind everyone that the horse has always been ridden this way.
7. Appoint a committee to study the horse.
8. Arrange to visit other places where they ride dead horses more efficiently.
9. Increase the standards for riding dead horses.
10. Create a test for measuring the rider's ability.
11. Compare the riding to how it was done in the past.
12. Complain about the nature of horses these days.
13. Invent new styles of riding.
14. Blame the horse's parents, as the problem is often in breeding.
15. If all else fails, tighten the cinch.[22]

Inuit

From Greenland across northern Canada to eastern Siberia is home to about 110,000 Inuit. Distinguished by their more Asian features, the Inuit (singular "Inuk") do not seem to be related to Indians and probably came from the Far East more than 2,000 years ago.

They lived much the same for centuries, but their traditional life has faded as more Inuit have become integrated into the economic and political structures of the countries in which they live. By the middle of this century, for example, most Inuit were Christian.

Petroleum discoveries opened up the Arctic, bringing jobs with the oil companies and on the pipelines. Meanwhile, Inuit knowledge and traditions have made their way into western society, with people who spend time in the cold adopting the hooded coat called the "parka."

Traditionally, the Inuit were people of few possessions: their dogs, home, tools, sled, weapons, kayak, and pieces of folk art. Operating on a "no money" economy, even their homes could be taken over if deserted. Food was shared by all, and land was considered to belong to everybody. Men and women had a symbiotic relationship, with the men hunting and building, and the women preparing the food and making the clothing.

Explorer Roald Amundsen, who completed the Northwest Passage in 1906, observed the influence of civilization on the Inuit and said that, "the Eskimo, living absolutely isolated from civilization of any kind, are undoubtedly the happiest, healthiest, most honourable and most contented among them."

But, as author Daniel Francis points out, "these 2 images – the Inuit as self-reliant hunter (or master craftsman) and the Inuit as tragic victim of progress – seem to be diametrically opposed, but one does not necessarily contradict the other."

The New Inuit Homeland

On April 1, 1999, the Inuit of the Nunavut area of Canada's Arctic ("Our Land" in Inuktitut) will officially take over self-government. The native land claim is the largest in the world. Nunavut covers almost 1/3 of Canada – almost all above the treeline – with a population of 24,000, of whom 85% are Inuit.

The government and representatives for the Inuit signed the Nunavut Act on July 9, 1993. Since then, the new government has been developing and will include Inuit and non-Inuit responsibilities.

Former MP Jack Anawak, an Inuk, was appointed interim commissioner and is directing the spending of more than $150 million to build the new government. Nunavut will have a legislature with 22 MLAs representing 11 ridings.

The Nunavut Final Agreement set rights and benefits to promote Inuit self-sufficiency in a manner consistent with their social and cultural needs and aspirations.

Quebec Inuit Vote Against Separation

The Inuit of northern Quebec voted 95% against the province's separation from Canada. The Inuit rejected Quebec sovereignty, with only 4% voting in favour of separation (and 1% of ballots spoiled). Cree Indians in the province also voted overwhelming against separation, joining the Native claim to 2/3 of northern Quebec, and posing a serious problem to an independent Quebec.

Davis Inlet: Another Sad Tale

A once-heralded $85 million agreement signed by the federal government and the Innu of Davis Inlet has created new and different problems and unforeseen complications.

The money for the 560-member community was thought to be the end of the troubles that began in 1967 when the governments, the local store manager and the priest moved the Innu from their traditional grounds as a way of gathering up a scattered group into one village. The move was a disaster, cutting them off from their hunting, trapping them on the island, and sending the whole community into a well-documented spiral of alcohol and social collapse. Now, the Innu are moving 15 km, back to the mainland.

The actual trouble began with the hiring of a project manager. The Innu felt he wanted to do things his way including putting everything on hold while he went over the whole project and insisting on a scrupulous process of public tenders – a source of continuing discussions between federal officials and the band.

Already behind schedule, the Innu are treading carefully and discovering they do not know very much about business. Greedy people within their own community are pursuing pieces of the action, and the slow start and tensions have resulted in an increase in alcohol abuse and gasoline sniffing.

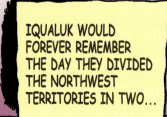

IQUALUK WOULD FOREVER REMEMBER THE DAY THEY DIVIDED THE NORTHWEST TERRITORIES IN TWO...

An Imperial Legacy

The discrimination experienced by aboriginals in Canada's criminal justice system is linked to the experiences of colonialism, according to a recent Royal Commission. Canada's sorry legacy regarding the treatment of aboriginals began when fur traders gave way to waves of immigrant settlers seeking land. Where once the Indians had been most helpful and useful, now they were an obstacle to European visions of progress, justifying colonial policies focussed on getting Indians out of the way.

Canadian Indian policy over most of the last 125 years has been consistently assimilative in its objectives. After Indians were no longer useful for economic or military purposes, the government established a system of reserves designed to "protect and civilize" native people in order that they might eventually assimilate.

It was primarily through the Indian Act and its implementors — the federal Department of Indian Affairs (DIA), created in 1880 — that white man developed the power to guide and shape the conduct of the Natives. They even defined who was and was not "an Indian," reflecting European patriarchy over the matriarchy practised by many First Nations.

Canadian Indian administration from that point consisted of increasing control by government authorities over natives, including attempts to suppress "pagan rituals" such as the Potlatch, efforts to quell traditional native structures of self-government and to implement elected "band councils," and requiring children to attend government-sponsored residential schools. Other examples include initiating a "pass" system whereby Indians could not leave the reserve without permission of the Indian Agent, making it illegal to hire a lawyer to pursue any form of aboriginal rights or land claim, and giving paramountcy to the Indian Act and other federal and provincial laws.

Two significant events heralded a turning point for aboriginals. In a 1973 court case, 6 of 7 Supreme Court judges agreed there *had been* such a thing as "Indian title," but were divided 3-3 on the question of whether that title still existed or had been extinguished. In another case, the Musqueum band asserted that their right to fish was an "existing" Aboriginal right, recognized and affirmed by the Constitution Act. The Supreme Court ruled in their favour.

Status vs. Non-Status Indians

Before 1985, native women who married non-natives, and their children, lost their status — including their right to funding for programs such as medical and dental services, tax exemptions, and money for post-secondary education. Indian men, on the other hand, not only kept their status, but passed it on to their non-native wives as well as their children.

Bill C-31, which was introduced in 1985 to address some of the discrimination, reinstated Indian women, although they were still not given the right to pass full status to their children the same way the men could.

The changes gave as many as 100,000 people who had lost Indian status the right to return to reserves and regain other benefits. The main beneficiaries were native women who had lost status by marrying non-natives, and children from such unions. But the changes caused concern among Indian bands that did not want new members forced on them. The oil-rich Sawridge band of Slave Lake, Alberta, sued, arguing it has the constitutional right to determine its membership. On the other hand, a woman launched her own court case, arguing that the government is ignoring a blatant violation of the Canadian Charter of Rights and Freedoms — discrimination against women.

Under the legislation, Canadian country-music star Shania Twain — who has no proven aboriginal blood — can claim Indian status because she was adopted by her Ojibwa stepfather. On the other hand, Ovide Mercredi, the former national chief of the AFN, says his children have no claim to being Indian because his mother was reinstated with partial rights.

Some reserves can decide their own membership, make exceptions and add non-status people to the band lists, but the rules set by the DIA for its 608 reserves say that where there is no status, there is no membership.

Meanwhile, in Quebec, a growing number of Inuit are complaining that some southerners are marrying their people to take advantage of the benefits provided to the Quebec Inuit by the 1975 James Bay and Northern Quebec Agreement. The historic accord, signed by the region's Inuit and Cree with the federal and Quebec governments, granted the Inuit extensive rights and $90 million in compensation for the construction of the James Bay hydroelectric megaproject.

INDIAN 69%

METIS 26%

INUIT 5%

Anthropomorphic Theater

I'D LIKE TO APOLOGIZE FOR HOW MY ANCESTORS TREATED YOUR ANCESTORS. THERE...THAT SHOULD SQUARE THINGS.

The History of the Assembly of First Nations

- One of the 1st attempts at forming a national presence for First Nations came soon after WWI. The League of Indians in Canada was formed, but failed to attract widespread support.
- After WWII, the North American Indian Brotherhood was established, but it also lacked nation-wide support, broke into regional factions, and disbanded by the 1950's.
- In 1961, the National Indian Council was formed to represent 3 of the 4 major Aboriginal groups: Treaty and Status people, the Non-status people, and the Metis people (the Inuit were excluded).
- Disunity led to the split of the Council in 1968, and the Status and Treaty aboriginal groups formed the National Indian Brotherhood (NIB), while the Non-status and the Metis groups remained united and formed the Native Council of Canada.
- The NIB drew criticism for not being truly representative of all the Status First Nations, and made the transition to becoming the Assembly of First Nations (AFN) in 1982. From being an "organization of representatives from regions" the AFN became an "Organization of First Nations Government Leaders."
- Dr. David Ahenakew was elected the 1st National Chief to the AFN. Ahenakew, along with the leaders of the other 3 aboriginal groups in Canada, attended the First Ministers Conferences (FMC) on Aboriginal rights in Ottawa in 1983, 1984, and 1985, marking the 1st time that Aboriginal Leaders were represented in Constitutional talks that directly affected them.
- The FMCs were a series of Constitutionally guaranteed meetings between the Prime Minister, the Premiers, and the Aboriginal Leaders in order to identify, define and discuss aboriginal and treaty rights.
- The first FMC conference was marked by lack of solidarity among the 4 aboriginal groups. Also prevalent was the position of some provincial governments, who made it clear that they were unwilling to accept any concept of "inherent" aboriginal rights, and that they would only agree to discuss "contingent" aboriginal rights.
- Over the next 2 years, the agenda at these conferences was narrowed to consider the single issue of aboriginal self-government, which led to an impasse between the provinces and the aboriginal groups, again preventing any constitutional consensus defining aboriginal self-government.
- At the 4th and last FMC in 1987, federal and provincial governments unanimously refused to recognize that aboriginal people already had an inherent right to self-government.
- Since this time, the AFN has been actively involved in several areas where Aboriginal concerns are of great importance, including the Meech Lake Accord, the Charlottetown Accord, the Free Trade Agreement with the US, and other legislative business (e.g., Bill C-31).
- Now, the AFN are pushing the federal government for a response to the recent Royal Commission report (see page 27) and its 440 sweeping recommendations.

Potlatch

The word potlatch is Chinook jargon meaning "to give." The potlatch was a ceremonial distribution of gifts and property that was observed by First Nations people of the Pacific coast, from Oregon to Alaska. The ceremonies were a form of barter that had social and ceremonial values as important as or more important than their economic function. Potlatches were a way of honouring the dead and, if successful, could raise the social status of the host. This important ceremony was banned by the federal government between 1884 and 1951, officially because of the "Native treatment of property." The last major potlatch was the Daniel Cranmer potlatch held in 1921, and with it died some of the most powerful work incentives for the younger generations of the Indian communities. The ban against the potlatch was finally lifted in 1951; however, by that time, many tribal identities had been destroyed.

The Indian Act

Canadian Indians are governed by a separate law, the Indian Act of 1876. Provisions in the Act gave the federal government control of Indian affairs including land holdings, land transfers, taxation, local government, education, wills and estates, as well as band membership. The Act only applies to Status Indians, not Metis (of Native and European, primarily French, ancestry) or Non-status Indians (those of Native ancestry who lost status through intermarriage with whites).

The Indian Act, imposed on Natives without any kind of consultation, effectively made Canadian Indians wards of the federal government.

As the reserve system was set up, Natives were forced into dependence on the Indian Act because traditional government, lifestyles, languages and ceremonies were all outlawed. Furthermore, Indian agents were assigned to reserves to enforce various provisions of the Act. The agents were largely responsible for establishing band councils as local governments.

Moreover, the Indian Act restricted the freedom of movement by Canadian Indians. Until the 1950's, Indians were required to obtain special permits if they wished to leave their reserve, and could be arrested if they left without permission from the Indian agent.

In 1927, an amendment was made to the Indian Act making it illegal for Canadian Indians to raise money for Indian political organizations or to pursue legal claims against the government. The amendment was in place until 1951. Canadian Indians were prohibited from voting in federal elections until 1960.

In 1968, public criticism was levelled at the Liberal government of Pierre Trudeau for the paternalistic administration of the Indian Act, so the federal government began looking at ways to dismantle it.

A Special Problem: BC Land Claims

BC is unique in Canada, with dozens of Indian bands whose traditional territories were never ceded or surrendered to non-natives at the time of colonization. Their rights have created widespread uncertainty about resource development and native self-government.

Undefined territorial rights have been the focus of roadblocks and political division for several years, but at least 48 bands representing 2/3 of BC's Indians are now in negotiations for specified areas of Crown land and a degree of self-government, plus cash. The costs of settling all the treaties will reach the billions, most of the cash from Ottawa plus an "equal" value in provincial Crown land transferred to Indian bands.

The Nisga'a Treaty

This mid-1998 potential prototype for BC land settlements, if approved, is going to cost almost $500 million; most of the money will come from Ottawa.

Gitxsan and Wet'suwet'en

The Gitxsan and Wet'suwet'en bands of Northern BC— 2 bands representing 8,000 people — claim their rights include ownership and jurisdiction over their entire 57,000 sq km hereditary territory. It is the longest-running land-claims case in the Commonwealth.

They initially received an almost complete rejection in a 1991 ruling that said native land rights were extinguished before the province entered Confederation and that all native claims were relatively weak in law.

The BC Court of Appeal partly reversed the ruling in 1993 by saying that native rights do exist. But the court did not define precisely what those rights meant in terms of land ownership or self-government.

The Supreme Court of Canada, however, went on to make an historic ruling in their favour, giving aboriginal title a fundamental right in land. The Fraser Institute said the ruling, "practically gives control of 95% of the BC land mass to about 5% of the population."

Australia's Similar Problem

Canada is not alone in dealing with Native land claims. In Australia, the right-wing government, and the powerful National Farmers Federation, insist that the government extinguish all native claims — about 40% of Australia — by pastoral leases held by sheep and cattle ranchers.

In a controversial judgment, the court threw out the notion that Australia was empty land when it was claimed in 1788 for Britain. That ruling re-established the possibility of native title claims over large areas of vacant Crown land, but left unresolved whether native title could also exist on land covered by pastoral leases.

Native Self-Government

Do Indians have an inherent right to self-government, or are they just the 1st Immigrants — Siberian Canadians, as it were — who have to fit into the institutions of society?

Indian leaders quite rightly want to emancipate their people from subservience to the Indian Affairs Department. Yet emancipation cannot occur until Indian politicians begin to tax their own people. The purpose is not so much to save money as to make Indian politicians accountable.

Politics on reserves often consist of a contest among kin-based factions to get their hands on a band government that controls all the land, resource rights, housing, jobs and welfare payments on the reserve.

A bad example is Alberta's Stoney Plain Reserve, for which a judge ordered an investigation, suggesting the reserve may be run like "a dictatorship of a banana republic."

Most band governments are totally dependent on transfer payments from the Department of Indian Affairs. None of their sources of money puts Indian politicians under the discipline of having to tax their own people; the money comes to the band from outside without voters having to reach into their own pockets.

While the battle cry of the American Revolution was "no taxation without representation," it is equally true that there is "no representation without taxation."

Residential Schools

Native Canadians have launched lawsuits against the federal government in connection with abuse at aboriginal residential schools.

The government-run system, which consisted of only 2 schools at the time of Confederation but ballooned up to 80 by 1931, was based on a philosophy of eradicating the language, traditions and values in aboriginal societies. As many as 125,000 Indian, Inuit and Metis children were taken away from their parents and put in institutions — mostly run by religious orders — where officials tried to prepare them to fit into the non-aboriginal world.

The government's racist policies, magnified by mismanagement, underfunding, mistreatment, neglect and horrific emotional, physical and sexual abuse, created generations of victims.

While criminal investigations have been launched in BC, Alberta, Saskatchewan and the Yukon, victims have not found much satisfaction in the conviction of their abusers. Nor do they think multimillion-dollar settlements are the solution. Ottawa would prefer to settle claims on a case-by-case basis, but natives would prefer financial assistance to begin what they call a "healing process" within their communities.

The Royal Commission on Aboriginal Peoples

The Royal Commission on Aboriginal Peoples (RCAP), 5 years in creation at a cost of $60 million, encompasses the results of public inquiries, more than 350 research studies, published reports and round table discussions. Released in November, 1996, it set a record for the most expensive federal probe in Canadian history: it contains 4,000 pages and 440 recommendations.

The report describes the need for a re-balance of political authority, economic resources, and restoration of health and effectiveness to individuals, families, communities and nations. The commission proposed a 20-year plan for aboriginal peoples in the country that would cost Ottawa $2 billion per year, although the government has sent out several signals to indicate that that was not going to happen. We already spend $12 billion a year on Aboriginal Affairs, 50% federal and 50% provincial.

Four key concepts form the strategy in the report:
- Recognizing unique Aboriginal societal and cultural values;
- The inherent right to self-government;
- The nature of Aboriginal nationhood and the need for adequate land; and
- Self-reliant Aboriginal economies.

The RCAP has provided Canadians with a blueprint for a new relationship between the aboriginal and non-aboriginal peoples: a partnership between equals.

To give substance and meaning to this partnership, the commission made specific proposals concerning aboriginal self-government, treaty rights and a new process of negotiating aboriginal land rights. It suggested ways to provide aboriginal peoples with land and resources to build healthy and self-sufficient economies.

Aboriginal people have been deeply frustrated by the inaction of the federal government in the wake of the publication of the report.

> **Royal commissions are Canada's favourite substitute for action. They are created by disingenuous politicians who hope that the pressure on them to take action will be deflected and then dissipated over the often several-year period that such Commissions take to complete their work.**

In response to the call by the RCAP for significant changes in the government's relationship with Aboriginal people, the federal government unveiled "Gathering Strength: Canada's Aboriginal Action Plan." The framework has the objectives of renewing partnerships between governments and Aboriginal groups, strengthening Aboriginal governance, developing a more stable fiscal relationship, and supporting strong communities, people and economies.

Jane Stewart, Minister of Indian Affairs and Northern Development, and Ralph Goodale, Federal Interlocutor for Metis and Non-status Indians, presented the Plan as a "Statement of Reconciliation." (See page 27.) It formally acknowledges the detrimental effects of the historical treatment of Aboriginal people in Canada,

ASSEMBLY OF FIRST NATIONS   TRADITIONAL HEADWARE   OTTAWA

particularly the victims of sexual and physical abuse in the Residential School system, and says the government is deeply sorry.

What it *fails* to do is accept responsibility for past actions, which is seen as some protection for the government against possible legal liability in the dozens of civil suits brought by the victims.

First Nations Chief, Phil Fontaine, accepts belated apology from Federal Minister Jane Stewart

Cynics suggest that the government is basically plea bargaining out of a desire motivated less to right old wrongs than to limit potential claims for damages.

Settling Land Claims by 2000

The time has come for Canadians to face up to the historic mistreatment of aboriginal peoples. The government target for settling all land claims disputes is the year 2000. There are currently 175 specific and 30 comprehensive land claims still to be settled. The government will negotiate with provinces and natives to establish an aboriginal justice system. A 5-step, fast-track process will deal with land claims of $500,000 or less.

A proclamation from the British crown in 1763 promised royal protection for the indigenous peoples, successive Canadian governors and governments have abdicated and abandoned their constitutional responsibility to natives for more than 200 years. **Despite a budget larger than that needed to sustain some Third World countries and a bureaucracy that takes up a 12-page listing in the federal telephone directory,** the Department of Indian Affairs and Northern Development has been unable to help either the country or its charges.

ROADKILL ON THE INFORMATION HIGHWAY

Statement of Reconciliation:
Learning from the Past

As Aboriginal and non-Aboriginal Canadians seek to move forward together in a process of renewal, it is essential that we deal with the legacies of the past affecting the Aboriginal peoples of Canada, including the First Nations, Inuit and Métis. Our purpose is not to rewrite history but, rather, to learn from our past and to find ways to deal with the negative impacts that certain historical decisions continue to have in our society today.

The ancestors of First Nations, Inuit and Métis peoples lived on this continent long before explorers from other continents first came to North America. For thousands of years before this country was founded, they enjoyed their own forms of government. Diverse, vibrant Aboriginal nations had ways of life rooted in fundamental values concerning their relationships to the Creator, the environment, and each other, in the role of Elders as the living memory of their ancestors, and in their responsibilities as custodians of the lands, waters and resources of their homelands.

The assistance and spiritual values of the Aboriginal peoples who welcomed the newcomers to this continent too often have been forgotten. The contributions made by all Aboriginal peoples to Canada's development, and the contributions that they continue to make to our society today, have not been properly acknowledged. The Government of Canada today, on behalf of all Canadians, acknowledges those contributions.

Sadly, our history with respect to the treatment of Aboriginal people is not something in which we can take pride. Attitudes of racial and cultural superiority led to a suppression of Aboriginal culture and values. As a country, we are burdened by past actions that resulted in weakening the identity of Aboriginal peoples, suppressing their languages and cultures, and outlawing spiritual practices. We must recognize the impact of these actions on the once self-sustaining nations that were disaggregated, disrupted, limited or even destroyed by the dispossession of traditional territory, by the relocation of Aboriginal people, and by some provisions of the Indian Act. We must acknowledge that the result of these actions was the erosion of the political, economic and social systems of Aboriginal people and nations.

Against the backdrop of these historical legacies, it is a remarkable tribute to the strength and endurance of Aboriginal people that they have maintained their historic diversity and identity. The Government of Canada today formally expresses to all Aboriginal people in Canada our profound regret for past actions of the federal government which have contributed to these difficult pages in the history of our relationship together.

One aspect of our relationship with Aboriginal people over this period that requires particular attention is the Residential School system. This system separated many children from their families and communities and prevented them from speaking their own languages and from learning about their heritage and cultures. In the worst cases, it left legacies of personal pain and distress that continue to reverberate in Aboriginal communities to this day. Tragically, some children were the victims of physical and sexual abuse.

The Government of Canada acknowledges the role it played in the development and administration of these schools. Particularly to those individuals who experienced the tragedy of sexual and physical abuse at residential schools, and who have carried this burden believing that in some way they must be responsible, we wish to emphasize that what you experienced was not your fault and should never have happened. To those of you who suffered this tragedy at residential schools, we are deeply sorry.

In dealing with the legacies of the Residential School system, the Government of Canada proposes to work with First Nations, Inuit and Métis people, the Churches and other interested parties to resolve the long-standing issues that must be addressed. We need to work together on a healing strategy to assist individuals and communities in dealing with the consequences of this sad era of our history.

No attempt at reconciliation with Aboriginal people can be complete without reference to the sad events culminating in the death of Métis leader Louis Riel. These events cannot be undone; however, we can and will continue to look for ways of affirming the contributions of Métis people in Canada and of reflecting Louis Riel's proper place in Canada's history.

Reconciliation is an ongoing process. In renewing our partnership, we must ensure that the mistakes which marked our past relationship are not repeated. The Government of Canada recognizes that policies that sought to assimilate Aboriginal people, women and men, were not the way to build a strong country. We must instead continue to find ways in which Aboriginal people can participate fully in the economic, political, cultural and social life of Canada in a manner which preserves and enhances the collective identities of Aboriginal communities, and allows them to evolve and flourish in the future. Working together to achieve our shared goals will benefit all Canadians, Aboriginal and non-Aboriginal alike.

On behalf of the Government of Canada

Jane Stewart

The Honourable Jane Stewart, P.C., M.P.
Minister of Indian Affairs and Northern Development

Ralph Goodale

The Honourable Ralph Goodale, P.C., M.P.
Federal Interlocutor for Métis and Non-status Indians

Ticking Time Bomb of Native Population

The volatile combination of numbers published by StatsCan's 1996 census confirms that a swell in the population of natives entering their child-bearing and job-seeking years is coinciding with a rocketing unemployment rate and a collapsing family structure. The prime working-age population of Canada's 800,000 natives will grow by 41% by 2006 and be 62% larger than now by the year 2016. At the same time, Canada's total aboriginal population is expected to grow by more than 50%, double the national rate.

Overall, the average age among Canada's natives is 25.5, while the general population's average is 35.4. The census also showed that the fertility rate among natives is about 70% higher than that of the total population.

They are experiencing a baby boom that will swell their combined population by 300,000- 400,000 in less than 20 years. This means an estimated 30% of Saskatchewan's population will be aboriginal by 2035, and as much as 50% within 50 years.

The frightening aspect is that the social and economic conditions of many natives are already likened to those of the Third World — adult unemployment of 90% in some communities, a suicide rate among young males that is 4 times the rate of the general Canadian population, lower life expectancy, higher infant mortality, and disproportionately higher rates of incarceration, drug abuse and alcoholism. About 33% of native children under 15 live with a single parent, double the Canadian average of 16.4%.

This is a ticking time bomb that could cost the country billions of dollars in increased government assistance if native youth cannot find jobs. The jobless rate among aboriginals already is 25%, almost triple the national average.

Of the total number of aboriginals, 375,000 are marginally integrated Metis. If, for the moment, we set aside the Metis as a separate "problem" and focus only on the members of the First Nations in 600+ bands, we are looking at about 1.5% of the Canadian population that are experiencing virtually every problem known to the Third World's under-developed countries with no reason for optimism. **More bureaucracy is not the solution.**

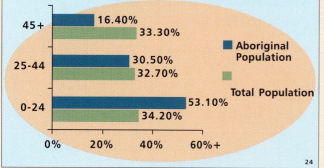

	Aboriginal Population	Total Population
45+	16.40%	33.30%
25-44	30.50%	32.70%
0-24	53.10%	34.20%

0%   20%   40%   60%+

24

The Metis

The French-speaking Metis are people of mixed Native and European — primarily French, Scottish and Irish — ancestry, who consider themselves a distinct nation. In the history of Canada, the Metis have struggled for more than 250 years for public and government recognition of their status as a unique group. For decades, the Metis have suffered the stigma of being seen as First Nations people without receiving any of the advantages of their status or treaty Indian counterparts. To date, social and economic programs funded by the federal and provincial governments have not been available to the Metis, and the Metis have not been eligible to reside on Indian reserves, without marrying a member of the band.

The earliest Metis originated from the intermarriages between the 1st Hudson's Bay Company employees and Indian women. Initially, intermarriage was forbidden by the company, but, under pressure from the officers, the company eventually yielded. Many of the children of these unions were sent to Eastern Canada or to Europe to be educated, with the expectation that they would return to the North to be employees in the fur trade. Because their unique heritage allowed them access to both cultures, they were considered valuable employees of the trade.

The earliest free traders were often Metis, who acquired furs from the trappers and traded them at Red River or in St. Paul, Minnesota. The Red River cart used by buffalo hunters was the trademark of the Metis transportation and, by the mid-1800's, trains of 200 to 300 carts, mainly owned by Metis, were ferrying half of the furs and hides from St. Paul to Red River. These trains not only hauled furs and hides, but also dried buffalo meat, moccasins and other garments sewn from skins; in return, they brought back groceries, tobacco, liquor, dry goods, and ammunition, as well as farm implements and luxury goods.

In an attempt to exclude non-Metis settlers from the Red River settlements, the North West Company fuelled the idea that a territory and separate nation had already begun to develop amongst the Metis. The company warned the Metis that the influx of settlers into the territory would mean an end to their lifestyle and individuality. In 1816, the Metis, fearing this to be true, appointed Cuthbert Grant as "Captain General of all half-breeds" in the country. Under Grant's leadership, the French and English "half-breeds" began to assert their claim to an Aboriginal title and demanded land and compensation from white settlers.

Cuthbert Grant was born in 1793 at Fort Termblante, near the present-day site of Yorktown, Saskatchewan, the son of a North West Trading Company partner and a Cree woman. As was common, at the age of 8 he was sent to Scotland for an education and returned to the Red River settlement at 19 to work as a clerk, eventually being placed in charge of his own post in Qu'Appelle River. Under Grant's leadership, the Metis became more organized.

In 1816, Governor Semple of Red River cut off the pemmican supply routes of the North West Company and Grant planned to reopen them by force. In the skirmish that followed, Semple and 21 of his men were killed, while Grant lost just 1 man. This became known as the "Battle of 7 Oaks."

In the early 1800's, decades of intense rivalry between the NorthWest Company and the Hudson's Bay Company resulted in over-trapping. These events had an adverse effect on the fur trade, and both financially-troubled companies merged in 1821 as the Hudson's Bay Company. This created dramatic changes in the lives of the mixed-blood people who worked for them, including Grant who, with the merger, found his role was no longer required by the new company.

Grant then established the Metis community of Grantown (St. Francis Xavier) near Winnipeg. Under Grant, the Metis became recognized as a "Nation," and he was personally responsible for negotiating treaties with the Dakota, enabling the peaceful settlement of Manitoba.

Today there is a vibrant Metis culture. Michif — which combines French, English and Ojibwa — is the Metis language, and is taught and spoken in Metis schools. There has been a revitalizion of Metis culture with the emergence of Metis heroes and Metis nationalism: Revered leaders include Gabriel Dumont, Louis Riel, and les bois-Brules. These were the leaders of significant confrontations in The Pemmican War, The Red River Rebellion, and the victory at Duck Lake and at Batoche in The Riel Rebellion.

The Alberta Metis Betterment Act of 1938 is a reflection of provincial government attempts to improve the lives and conditions of Metis settlements.

Metis political leaders and political organizations since the 1970's have participated in numerous regional and national aboriginal government conferences to ensure that their concerns would not be overlooked. In the Constitution Act of 1982, the Metis achieved recognition as members of Canada's aboriginal people and their aboriginal rights are now constitutionally guaranteed and protected.

Louis Riel: Hanged for treason

Native Education

Saskatchewan Indian Federated College is a First Nations-controlled university college with campuses in Regina, Saskatoon and Prince Albert. Affiliated with the University of Regina since 1976, SIFC offers undergraduate and graduate university courses in an environment of First Nations cultural affirmation. With more than 1,500 students on and off-campus, SIFC has been an innovator in the development and delivery of academic programs geared to meeting the unique needs of indigenous peoples. Degrees and Certificates are offered in 10 different academic areas.

The philosophy of the hunter is that you take only what you need, and you share the rest.
— Leonard George, *Tsleilwaututh Chief*

Pemmican,
dried meat and tallow sausage,
was the most significant food staple used by westerners.

Riel's Rebellion

Louis Riel was born in Manitoba in 1844 of French, Irish and Native descent. In 1869, the Metis revolted under his leadership. Disaffection began when the Hudson's Bay Company sold the territory of Rupert's Land to the Dominion government. Under Riel, the Metis — fearing for their land rights — captured Fort Garry; however, with the approach of the British forces, Riel escaped from Canada.

Riel lived in exile in the US for a number of years and, in 1884, returned to lead a rebellion in Saskatchewan. At first, he attempted to use constitutional means to present the Metis case, but Prime Minister John A. Macdonald took no action.

Riel believed that his people were being ignored and, in 1885, he organized an armed uprising. His followers raided stores, seized provisions and took several citizens prisoner. A provisional government was set up and Riel called on Major Crozier to surrender the Royal Northwest Mounted Police forts at Carlton and Battleford. Crozier declined and sent out a team to Duck Lake to secure provisions, but they were intercepted and stopped — a force of 99 RCMP and Prince Albert volunteers were defeated by the rebels. Riel extended his rebellion, inciting the Indians to rise up against Hudson's Bay and the government.

In May, government forces took Riel's headquarters and captured the rebel leader. By July, the rest of Riel's followers were captured, and Riel was brought to trial on charges of treason; he was hanged in Regina on November 16, 1885.

Quebec

The Unique Society

The Reality of our French Roots

The British-French conflict in Canada has been going on since before Napoleonic times. Queen Anne's War ended with France losing significant territory, including all of Newfoundland and Nova Scotia. The French settlers (Acadians) were sent back to France or to the French lands in Louisiana.

France abandoned its North American settlers in 1759. Given a choice, instead of taking back Canada, the French chose to trade it for Guadeloupe and Martinique, sugar-producing Caribbean islands.

In old English schoolbooks, the habitant of Quebec always lacked ambition, feared change and was content with the status quo. "He was opposed to change," said a well-used textbook from the 1930's, "and he asked only to be allowed to live as his parents and grandparents had lived and not to be bothered with the improvements and innovations of the energetic, aggressive English." English-speaking Canadians have been more than willing to accept and embellish this version of a rustic, deferential peasant society. Images of the traditional habitant proliferate in our culture. Regardless of image, between 1850 and 1900, half a million Quebeckers left for the US.

The Quebec problem really has not changed since the Battle on the Plains of Abraham, yet politicians and reporters keep trying to make it a fresh issue. Angus Reid says that, "many Quebeckers are yearning for some kind of certainty. Certainty is easier to find among your own people than it is in the outside world. It's also easier to find in the past than in the uncertain present."

Nevertheless, PQ-style nationalism flourishes 250 years later. What does seem indisputable is that most Quebecois have viewed the Conquest as a turning point in their history, the moment when the unique French society that was evolving on the shores of the St. Lawrence was abruptly overwhelmed by a foreign power. Ever since, the Quebecois have been preoccupied with the survival of the French language and culture. For some, this has meant nurturing the desire to create their own country and thereby to undo the events of 1759-1760: to reconquer Quebec for the Quebecois.

Still, the situation continues to baffle and inspire observers around the world. To Americans, it is astounding. "To me it is treason," says a former US envoy. "If the governor of Illinois were saying the things [former Quebec Premier Rene] Levesque said, we would hang him. And then we would try him later, I suppose."

Wee Doe Grant unto the said Governor and Company and theire successors the sole Trade and Commerce of all those Seas Streightes Bayes Rivers Lakes Creekes and Soundes that lie within the entrance of Hudsons Streightes and make create and constitute (them) the true and absolute Lordes and Proprietors of the same Territory

Catalonia: Spain's Quebec

To some people in Spain, Canada-Quebec relations are seen as a role model. The Catalonia region of Spain was conquered nearly 300 years ago, but diehard Catalan nationalists find it hard to forget. A region with its own culture and language — spoken by almost 6 million of Spain's 40 million people — the Catalans want something similar to Quebec's controversial Bill 101.

Like Quebec, the region of Catalonia has an appetite for increasing its power at the expense of the central government. Now, it wants to fly the Catalan flag in the UN and become a full member of the EU.

The Joke:

Former Quebec Premier Jacques Parizeau visits St. Peter at the gates of heaven and asks, "Will the Quebec question ever be solved?" St. Peter says, "Let me check with God." God answers, "Yes, but not in my lifetime."

even pay $17 per kilogram of parmesan cheese protected by a 300% monopoly tariff.

The huge monopoly known as the Liquor Control Board of Ontario is the world's biggest booze retailer, raking in $2 billion a year in net sales after taxes and a profit of $730 million. It is a prime candidate for privatization, but the provincial government has acquiesced in a series of changes that seem designed more to strengthen public support and sympathy for the LCBO as a government-run monopoly than to whip up sentiment for a sale. The 598-store retail chain, facing a fight against privatization by the 4,500-member Ontario Liquor Board Employees Union, is urging customers to claim Air Miles loyalty points when they buy their liquor. It appears the LCBO does not mind if Air Miles help it steal some beer sales from its private-sector twin in Ontario's regulated alcohol duopoly, Brewers Retail Inc.

Ontario electricity consumers can celebrate the provincial government's White Paper on the future of the electricity industry. The proposed policy will finally destroy Ontario Hydro's monopoly. Access to the grid that distributes electricity will be thrown open to all producers, and consumers will be able to buy their electricity from any willing seller at an agreed price, just as they do now with long-distance telephony and natural gas.

This is good news all around, since competition will force down prices and cause a flowering of innovation. Steel plants and pulp mills will turn their waste heat into electricity, benefitting themselves, the environment and consumers. The ecology-minded will sign up for wind-generated power. Cheap hydroelectricity from areas like Quebec and Manitoba will move in. Brokers will spring up, offering consumers packages of gas, electricity, telephony and other services tailored to their needs.

In a competitive market there will be no compelling reason for public ownership of some of the companies. On the contrary, privatization caps the taxpayers' liability for Hydro debt and eliminates the conflict of interest of government as both regulator and industry player. However, the industry will probably not generate enough tax and other revenues to service the debt already acquired, plus existing unfunded liabilities for nuclear decommissioning and spent fuel disposal. More work needs to be done to know for certain if Ontario is wisely, if belatedly, pursuing a path laid out by Alberta, the US Federal Energy Regulatory Commission, numerous American states, and many other industrialized countries, such as Britain, Australia and New Zealand. Canadians in less competition-minded provinces should be asking why they are being denied these choices.

Monopolies:
The Company That Became a Country

Monopoly is the nemesis of efficiency, innovation, discipline and consumer clout. It can only be subdued in 1 of 2 ways: It can be abolished by opening it to vigorous competition, or it can be regulated by effective government. Obliteration of monopolies is always the superior policy, because it gives consumers the room and the tools to look after their own interests, which they inevitably do more competently than would happen with bureaucrats functioning on their behalf.

Canada has a history of monopolies, beginning with the Hudson's Bay Company, which makes us different than any other country, including the US. When the CP railroad was built more than a century ago so that British Columbia would join Canada rather than the US, it was a monopoly also. There was a time when the telephone system was seen as a "natural monopoly," which was probably a logical paradigm for the time, but that time has come and gone and we have all benefitted from the competition.

Today, the national dairy monopoly arbitrarily raises the price of its products, electricity prices are set by absolute monopolies, and alcohol prices are manipulated by monopolies in most provinces. The average Canadian will

> **All countries (provinces and cities) get the governments that they deserve.**

Grain

US conglomerates are positioning themselves for entry into Canada's grain industry as deregulation moves in and trade restrictions are lifted. The grain industry in Canada has traditionally been dominated by farmer ownership, cooperatives and taxpayer subsidies. As the industry moves towards deregulation, it faces the problem of concentrated ownership, leaving Canada's major grain handlers to fight off hostile takeover bids. Canada produces 6% of the world's wheat and accounts for more than 20% of the global export market.

The Canadian Wheat Board has had a monopoly on sales of wheat and barley for more than half a century and currently markets $6 billion worth of grain on behalf of 130,000 farmers. The CWB is currently under attack from Canada's trading partners and farmers who want to market their own grain.

The Board operates as an umbrella sales machine for the industry. It was originally set up to protect farmers in the 1920's by helping them manage risks. However, since then farming has changed dramatically. For example, in the 1940's, the average farm was about 200 hectares. Today the average farm is 600 to 2,000 hectares, with gross revenues in the millions.

To survive in today's environment requires a scale of operations that a protected and subsidized market never demanded. Giant agri-industries dominate almost every commodity on the planet, and grain is facing the same future. These conglomerates are positioning themselves for a takeover in the Prairie grain industry, as the government-sanctioned Board begins to lose power.

Canadian farmers, private grain companies and US farm lobbies have all criticized the Board's monopolistic powers, and it is likely that in 5 or 10 years, as the Canadian industry becomes less regulated, the Board will be shut down.

In the meantime, the image of the Winnipeg-based monopoly as a powerful but benevolent force was shattered in a Manitoba courtroom. A farmer filed a class-action suit against the Board, arguing that it failed in its central task of marketing grain. The Board replied, however, that its mission is not to achieve the best price for farmers, but merely to conduct the "orderly marketing of grain." The court agreed, ruling that the Board owes "no duty of care to farmers."

Yet, the fortunes of every grain farmer are absolutely and completely dependent on the Wheat Board's decision-making. Wheat and other export grains are expropriated without a pre-determined level of compensation. Farmers are paid a pooled price reflecting whatever the Board manages to generate, minus the shipping, handling and storage fees it pays out to its favoured partners.

Consequently, farmers have no way of knowing whether the Wheat Board is doing its job. And they have no other recourse, such as an ombudsman, against incompetent or fraudulent actions by the Board. Unlike nearly any other participant in a modern market economy, farmers have no access to competing service-providers.

According to one analyst, farmers stand to gain from the increased efficiency and the reduced costs. However, consolidation has never traditionally been kind to farmers or consumers.

In 1996, a federal commission came up with a compromise allowing farmers themselves to sell 25% of their wheat crop. Ottawa has been approaching reforms cautiously, but did sanction a plebiscite on whether barley sales should remain under the Board's mandate. Although farmers voted yes, a large minority (37%) voted no. This signals future change. [25]

There must be a big shakeout to make Canada's huge grain industry more efficient, but it will concentrate ownership in fewer hands — including US agrigiants.

Postage Stamp Pricing

"Postage Stamp" pricing is the term for the flat-rate pricing that companies such as Calgary-based Nova Corp., until recently, employed on its gas pipeline system. Using this method, producers charge the same rate to ship their gas to various export points regardless of where their wells are located, with all costs "rolled in" to that rate.

Ending Long-Distance Monopoly

Ever since Montreal-based Teleglobe Inc., was privatized in 1987, its monopoly on overseas long-distance networks from Canada was supposed to end. Already into its 12th year of protected transition — granted to give the company time to prepare for competition — Teleglobe is appealing to cabinet to reverse a decision by the CRTC, which removed restrictions on the routing of overseas phone calls through a 3rd country outside North America and cleared Teleglobe's overseas lines for competitive use.

The decision opened the door to a practice called "switched hubbing," which allows domestic network operators (AT&T, Sprint, Fonorola, Bell) to route overseas calls more cheaply to certain countries. A call from Canada is carried via Teleglobe to the nearest country (or hub), then routed by the cheapest alternative provider (if one exists) to a final destination, resulting in potential savings for the Canadian carrier and its customers. Ending the monopoly could allow Canada to become a discount hub.

Despite the fact that Teleglobe's monopoly will formally come to an end by 1999 — when, through international trade agreements, long-distance companies will be able to route calls through any other cable or system — the company insists the CRTC decision will cause it "irreparable harm."

In reality, the only harm competition will cause is to take a bite out of Teleglobe's long-protected $1 billion market and lighten the pockets of its shareholders.

Wardship:

Destroying Self-Reliance

The easiest way to understand the prosperous Hong Kong economy is to realize that it is nothing like Canada's. Land is scarce, taxes scarcer still. There is a perennial shortage not of jobs, but of labour.

Managing the dollar and running Hong Kong's transparent system of business law are about the biggest functions the government performs. The role of Hong Kong's government is simply to sustain life. They will give shelter and medical care if there is a need. If people want to have more than the bare minimum, they have to earn it.

Low taxes and few services are what most Hong Kong people want. **The free market costs less than being helped through the government.** Almost all older people have bought and sold stocks and properties.

The government makes only about 40% of its money by collecting taxes. There's a flat personal income tax of 15% and a tax of 16.5% on corporations. There is no government property tax. Instead, there is government property, whose prices and related transaction fees — "stamp duties" — make up most of government revenues.

Manufacturing of goods has shrunk since 1980 to a mere 16% of Hong Kong's $1 billion GDP. Finance, property, shipping, export-processing and hotel services account for the rest. Contrast Hong Kong with Canada, which is slowly being weaned off social programs.

On average, Canadians received $26.60 in transfer payments – all income not generated by employment, including public and private pensions – for every $100 of employment income in 1995, down slightly from the all-time high of $26.92 in 1993, but still 31% higher than it was in 1990.

If pensions are excluded, the proportion of income from government social programs was $19.77 in 1995, down from 1994 levels, but still above the $15.60 in 1990.

Don't depend on the government or on big corporations for your paycheque, depend on yourself!

Welfare Failure

A 2-year, $12.5 million program funded by the federal and Nova Scotian governments to get people off welfare has had almost no long-term effect, according to an audit by Coopers and Lybrand Consulting.

The program, designed to help 1,609 people such as youth, single mothers, the disabled and laid-off fishermen get into the workforce, ended in October of 1996. Less than a year later, the participants were back on welfare with no change in attitude.

The report concluded that the program had no impact on individuals' beliefs about the likelihood of maintaining steady employment, or being on social assistance in the longer term, and that many were "lacking the motivation to work: they simply had a poor attitude towards work."

The effects of the program soon disappeared, so that by 10 months following its conclusion, the estimated impact on income support was negligible.

Wisconsin Welfare

The State of Wisconsin recently issued its final welfare cheque, requiring most former welfare recipients to work 40 hours a week at community service jobs or train under a program called Wisconsin Works, or W-2. With the exception of the severely disabled and mothers of babies younger than 12 weeks, people now have a life-long limit of just 60 months to receive cash grants from the state for community service work and job training.

Everyone has unlimited access to day-care subsidies, transportation assistance and employment counselling, and job training is linked closely to the job market. And even though the amount of cash support has dropped, overall funding is up, with the state spending on average 43% more per participant than it did under the old system. In 1997, the state spent $451 million on its welfare program, but this year it expects to spend $645.4 million on W-2.

Although the program has its critics, most of them admit that the work has improved the self-esteem of the participants, made them better parents, and given them a chance to feel pride in providing for their families. In just over a decade, welfare rolls have shrunk from 70,000 to fewer than 14,000 receiving cash grants — a decrease of 80%.[26]

Foreign Aid: Exporting Dependency

Bangladesh was once one of the best at attracting foreign aid; billions made their way into the small country, and the government bloated up to twice its size. The days of foreign donations came crashing to an end, however, when the Third World lost its strategic importance.

Aid declined almost everywhere, and observers predicted disaster. Instead, private investment poured into Bangladesh, exports soared, and its economy grew at its best rate in years.

Foreign aid has taken a back seat to global trade and investment. In 6 years, the amount of official investment going into developing countries has multiplied 6 times. One reason for this change is that developing countries now realize that with reforms they can attract far more money from private sources than they ever could from aid donors.

On the other side, former donors are cutting back for their own fiscal health. Japan, the world's biggest aid donor, plans to cut its development-assistance budget by 10% over the next 3 years; the US has already made big cuts; and Europe's big donors continue to cut back to meet targets required for an EU currency.

Donors are realizing that their aid has little long-term effect if the nations they are meant to help remain poor. While economic growth is not a panacea for poverty, it is the most important factor in improving the quality of life.

Consider Costa Rica, which saw its aid budget of $76 per person reduced by 2/3 at the end of the Cold War. Its economy has soared, with a growth rate of 5.1%, and with the government's winning big investment agreements.

Conversely, Pakistan's aid budget grew by 30% while its own economy ground to a halt. The national treasury neared bankruptcy, and 3 governments were dismissed due to corruption.

There is no relation between more aid and less poverty. A World Bank study found that whenever a country has poor economic policies, foreign aid has no impact on growth or poverty reduction, except to drive out private investment. Recipient countries have to be willing to change: in Zambia and Tanzania — recipients of large amounts of aid from Canada — aid has had little impact because they are not trying to reform.

Countries already on their way up have also benefited. Argentina has financed its debt in private markets, and 57 developing countries have sold bonds on international markets — up from 16 in 1992.

Tax reform has also become important for Third World countries. In India, the government used to collect only 9.6% of earnings, while new reforms could raise $11 billion a year more — 4 times the amount it gets in foreign aid.

The global economy has played a big part in these changes, with trade growing so much that Third World exports are now worth more than 15 times their foreign aid.

It seems that private money is doing what government money could never do. People in developing countries are willing to pay for a large share of development — and there are plenty of them willing to do what the state cannot deliver.

Haiti

Haiti is a country veering towards the edge of famine, with more than 350,000 rural farmers facing starvation due to drought. The principal reason for this crisis is that Haitians are now in such a state of dependence that they cannot grow their own food and sustain themselves.

In addition to famine and drought, the country is experiencing on-going political unrest. Teachers, who had not been paid for 14 months, walked off their jobs. This act, in turn, inspired student demonstrations that culminated in 2 days of rioting, which then evolved into a massive general strike.

Currently 70% of Haiti's budget is made up of foreign aid, and while the gap between the Haves and Have-Nots grows, the IMF and World Bank austerity measures have been criticized for driving the country deeper into unrest. Although there are more Land Cruisers and BMW's than ever in prosperous Petionville, it is said that in Port-au-Prince, people are eating dogs.

Only 2 1/2 years after democratic rule was restored to Haiti by 22,000 US troops, just 5% of the electorate showed up to vote in April 1997 for the 1st round of senate elections.

Meanwhile, Haiti's 5,200-member police force is in no condition to protect the country against the violence already straining the fabric of civil society, much less the surge of criminality that would fill the vacuum left by the now-departed UN peacekeepers, including the 750-man Canadian contingent.

Now, Canada's famed RCMP has been forced to stretch its budget and staff to cover peacekeeping assignments in Haiti. The RCMP currently has 62 officers in Haiti trying to keep the peace and reconstruct civilian police agencies.

Haiti undoubtedly needs the help, but what we already know about the spread of gangsterism in the Caribbean makes clear that the problem does not stop at Haiti's borders.

Best Practices Microcredit

Building on the idea that the poor benefit more from an investment in their self-reliance than in charity or safety nets, micro-enterprise finance is working to put loans at the top of the global development agenda.

The first microcredit lending organization — called Grameen, or the People's Bank — was created in 1976 by a University of Bangladesh economics professor to grant credit to some of the poorest people in the world, especially landless Bangladeshi women, so they could become self-employed.

The idea was soon exported around the world and is already estimated to have benefitted more than 8 million people worldwide. Following a summit held in Washington in 1997, microcredit supporters called for $20 billion to be invested in lending programs by the year 2005, with half the money coming from private enterprise.

> *Empowered individuals, less reliant on the state, will come together and help build strong communities as never before.*
> — *John Ralston Saul, Voltaire's Bastards*

Best Practices:

Avoiding the Wardship Trap in Africa[27]

When we usually think of Africa, we see images of utter despair, poverty, corruption, pestilence, and a whole continent sinking into hopelessness. It is easy to see only the Africa that is broken, but now there are emerging stories of optimism and hope.

What Africans want now from the West is no longer just to be a benefactor, but a partner. They are forcing the shift in aid from handouts to the development of sustainable economies and are realizing that progress comes 1st to those who adopt the principles and practices of capitalist democracy.

> *If you teach someone to fish, instead of giving him fish, then he has a sustainable future.*
> — *Issaias Afewerki, President of Eritrea*

• The newly-independent state of **Eritrea** has adopted the philosophy of self-reliance, avoiding foreign money no matter the source. Since winning independence from Ethiopia in 1992, the nation of more than 3 million carries little debt, has restricted foreign grants to health and education, and has told several private agencies that it no longer needs their help. Aid, they believe, subsidizes but corrupts government, and blocks innovative solutions to problems so that people do not seek out their own resources. Now, the national attitude is "show me, don't tell me."

Eritrea even opted for its own technicians and labourers instead of a multibillion-dollar World Bank loan when it needed a new railway. In 2 years, 42 km have been completed, and 2 steam engines have been restored. For the highway, men and women break rock by hand, illustrating the self-sacrificing character of the Eritreans.

Young people in national service — every male is required to spend 12 months working on rehabilitation projects — are helping to replace tin huts with concrete buildings.

Unlike most of Africa, there is no tribalism or sectarian division, and egalitarianism is ingrained. There is no begging, no corruption and virtually no crime.

• Following 16 years of guerilla warfare that devastated the country, **Mozambique** is slowly recovering. After a peace accord was signed in 1992, the government contracted with the UN to develop a plan that would resettle 95,000 soldiers and 5 million refugees in their home villages. By 1994, $20 million was pulled together by the government and donor countries to pay the unemployed "guys with guns" a minimum salary for 2 years to help them rebuild their farms.

The government has also brought in demining vehicles to get rid of the mines that keep farmers off the lush lands.

(See page 190.) As they begin to prosper, they are hopeful that this will bring more roads and trucks to take their food to market, and return more stores, clinics and schools to the communities.

The government dumped its socialist economic beliefs, adopted market-based capitalism, and accepted IMF plans. Locally, authorities are copying a low-tech alternative to high-maintenance roads, and avoiding paying foreign companies to do the job.

Entrepreneurs are returning to the war-torn beach strip of Xia Xia, setting up restaurants and trailer parks to attract the tourists who once filled its long line of ritzy hotels.

• The once gold-rich West African nation of **Mali** found itself the 4th poorest country in the world, destroyed by wars, colonialism, crashing commodity prices, and bad governments. In 1991, however, a military coup ousted its dictator, oversaw 2 rounds of free and fair elections and installed a civilian president.

Now, district chiefs are no longer appointed from the capital, but elected locally, devolving power to the communities. The Malian Company for the Development of Textiles (CMDT), the state-owned, money-losing monopoly on the country's cotton production, is also decentralizing. The Mali Producers' Union negotiates with CMDT to set prices for the farmer, and the village association receives block earnings. With the pooled profits, villages purchase water pumps, fences, clinics and schools, and pay the teachers. Women pool profits from farming and loan the money out to one another at 9% interest, giving some their 1st independent source of cash.

• Within 2 years of a Marxist coup in 1981, **Ghana's** leader and former military man Jerry Rawlings embraced Adam Smith capitalism, swallowing one of Africa's harshest doses of free-market medicine. Rawlings enlisted the help of Sam Jonah, who became the only black African chief executive of a multinational company (the Ashanti Goldfields) and taught Ghana how to manage its natural resources effectively.

Ghana is also aiming at making itself a middle-income country by 2020, by spinning off responsibility for local governance to district assemblies, and shifting jobs to trained technocrats.

In 1995, Ghana became only the 2nd sub-Saharan nation to have full connectivity to the Internet. Women are getting involved in far-sighted enterprise, too: the country's only maker of sanitary napkins has launched a campaign to teach Ghana's often-infected women to use its hygienic products, while a women's movement — once funded by foreign donors — now gets 95% of its funds from income-generating programs.

Royalists

The Parliamentary System

The monarchy, which has been described as "the moral core of Canadian nationhood," is increasingly irrelevant to most peoples' sense of the country, but it is the pillar on which our system of parliamentary democracy rests. [28] Polls say that 47% of Canadians are for abolition of the monarchy and 44% are for its preservation. But the Parliamentary system is increasingly irrelevant to the issues at hand in a global marketplace.

For example, Question Period, as anyone who has watched it understands, is 9/10 spectacle, 1/10 substance. It is the parliamentary equivalent of gladiatorial combat, with the media sitting in the bleachers egging on the combatants.[28] Each morning, the parties scan the papers and the previous night's news to determine which line of attack in Question Period will maximize their chance of getting media exposure.

Another detrimental tradition in the parliamentary system requires that the minister be appointed from the front benches of the party currently forming the government. Finance Minister Paul Martin, for example, is not qualified for his job — few ministers are. Martin has no formal education in economics and/or finance; his financial wisdom comes from the perspective of a philosophy major trained as a lawyer.

The Senate, modeled on the British House of Lords, is a worthless institution unbecoming a democratic nation in the 21st century. The same can be said for the Governor General and the Lieutenant Governor appointed in each of the provinces.

Last but not least, the 1997 appointment of a woman to the position of Gentleman Usher of the Black Rod demonstrates what happens when you overlay 14th century ritual with contemporary political correctness.

Republicans

The death of Diana, Princess of Wales, sparked much debate over the future of the monarchy in Canada. Some, such as Industry Minister John Manley, say it is time to review the role of the monarchy and look toward the time of either the death or the end of the reign of Queen Elizabeth as an opportunity to change the status quo.

Others argue about the relevancy of a monarchical system in a real democracy. Not only does the "glorious heritage" and symbolism of the monarchy seem particularly irrelevant to Canadians of non-British origin, but it reminds us of an old tradition of top-down governance.

In the current parliamentary system, the sovereign through her agent, the Governor General, still has important constitutional authority as a guardian of last resort. As we look to the future, we should be taking steps to replace the Queen with a President.

In Australia, meanwhile, a constitutional convention held in 1998 considered whether or not the country should become a republic and, if so, which republican model might be put to the electorate to consider. For example, while one faction believes the president should be elected by the general population, delegates of the "Australian Republican Movement" favour a president appointed by a 2/3 majority of Parliament. A referendum will be held on the convention's proposals by the end of 2000.

Several recent opinion polls have shown a narrow majority of Australians — between 51% and 56% — want the country to become a republic. Among decided republicans, more than 2/3 usually state a preference for an elected president over one appointed by Parliament. But when asked under what conditions they would prefer no change, 69% said they preferred Australia's constitutional monarchy to a president appointed by a council.

Australian Prime Minister John Howard conceded that many people had come to the conclusion that having a foreign head of state was "an anachronism" and "no longer appropriate for an Australian nation about to enter the 21st century."

Australia seems ready to become a republic, and it is likely that New Zealand will follow. That would leave Canada alone among the large countries of the Commonwealth, making our politicians look out of touch again with modern Canada.

The disappearance of the nation carries with it the death of politics.[84]

Busbies...
...18th century bearskin hats of the British Royal Guardsmen, cost the lives of 200 Canadian bears a year for replacements.

Too Many People
World Population

Little is known about the size of the human population in early times, but it is estimated that at the close of the last Ice Age (about 9000 BCE), it can only have been a few million. The agricultural revolution led to a great increase, and the population grew to 200 million by the beginning of the common era. For more than 1,500 years, populations grew very slowly as death rates remained high and violent outbreaks of disease affected the more developed parts of the world. Around 1600, the population was about 500 million, only 2.5 times the number 16 centuries earlier.

It took us until 1865 to get 1 billion people on the planet. The main reason for the boom was a decline in the death rate, caused by improvements in hygiene and food supply and, indirectly, the process of industrialization. Then, by 1930, the population doubled to 2 billion — in less than 100 years! The population doubled again by 1985, to 4 billion. Now, there are roughly 5.5 billion people, and estimates say that by 2040, the population could double again. This kind of population growth is staggering. **In the next 50 years, we are going to see living conditions deteriorate dramatically.**

Governments throughout history have wanted their populations to grow to expand the tax base and to increase the ruler's power and wealth. As a result, marriages, larger families and immigration were encouraged. It was also believed that urban growth was advantageous because population would lead to economies of scale and specialization in manufacturing.

Proponents of unlimited growth argue that excessive population will never become a problem for a nation with sufficient scientific knowledge and equitable social institutions. However the current population explosion is having enormous negative economic consequences because most of those people being born are in the Third World where the impact of growth reduces wealth and power since the extremely poor do not contribute to the tax base.

The Third World Population Boom

Asia, Africa and Latin America, which had 1.7 billion inhabitants in 1950, had 3 billion by 1975, a growth of 75%. By 1992, the population of these less-developed regions had risen to some 4.3 billion, representing growth of 41% in a 17-year period. These regions account for more than 80% of the world population today.

In Africa, Asia and Latin America, however, the decades since World War II have been characterized by a continuous increase in population that has been barely containable by programs to curb growth. Such programs have been gradually adopted out of fear that food, energy, and other resources would soon be depleted. For example, despite huge strides in reducing poverty, **nearly 20% of the people in the world live on an income of less than $1.50 a day.**

Life expectancies — the average number of years that a newborn can expect to live, had been increasing everywhere prior to the AIDS epidemic. In the late 1980's, many industrialized countries had life expectancies of more than 75 years, and in Iceland, the country with the highest, the figure was 78. Although in Bangladesh, the expectation is still only 51, life expectancies have been rising faster than 1 year of age per year of time in some poor nations.

With a birth rate of 2.1, children would simply replace their parents. This idea is often referred to as zero population growth, or ZPG.

However, population growth is retarded in less-developed regions where, with their generally poor nutrition and medical care, infant mortality rates remain high. For example, in 1985-1990, the infant mortality rate was more than 150 per 1,000 live births in Africa, 100 per 1,000 in Asia, and 50 per 1,000 in Latin America. **By way of comparison, Canada's infant mortality rate is less than 7 per 1,000.**

Between 1999 and the 2010, the developing world is expected to add more than 700 million men and women to its labour force. In the next 30 years, the labour forces of Mexico, Central America and the Caribbean are expected to grow by 52 million, or 3.5 times the current number of Canadian workers. Worldwide, more than a billion jobs will have to be created over the the next 10 years just to maintain the unsatisfactory status quo.

Meanwhile, new technologies are bringing us into an era of near workerless production at the very moment when population is surging to unprecedented levels.

If the history of the world were a 7-day week, mankind would not appear until the last second of the 7th day!

The clash between rising population pressures and falling job opportunities will shape the geopolitics of the emerging high-tech global economy well into the next century.
— *Jeremy Rifkin, The End of Work*

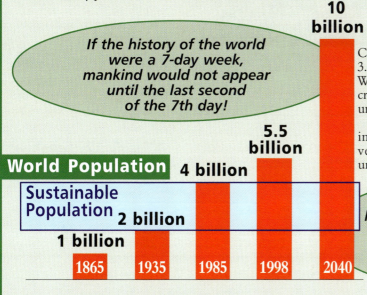

World Population

Sustainable Population

1 billion	2 billion	4 billion	5.5 billion	10 billion
1865	1935	1985	1998	2040

COUNTERPOINT

On a more positive note, poor countries have been able to curb population growth by listening to women and giving them better health care. The world's population grew by *only* 81 million people a year from 1990 to 1995, compared to 87 million annually in the previous 5 years. In fact, global population is growing more slowly than the UN predicted just 3 years ago.

Now, the agency says, it is up to rich countries to do their part. **A global target of $24 billion in annual spending on birth control and reproductive health by the year 2000 is necessary to improve family planning worldwide.**

Meanwhile, RU-486, the revolutionary abortion drug that was developed in France in 1988, is not available to women outside of France, Britain, Sweden, Canada and the US. RU-486 has enormous potential in the developing world where more than 200,000 botched abortions occur each year, but it is being held back by threats from groups with extreme views on family planning.

Despite setbacks such as these, frightening predictions that the world's population will double before the middle of the next century may not come true. For example, Russia is losing about 1 million of its 150 million people every year, as the death rate outstrips the birth rate. Europe, Northern America, Oceania, and the Soviet Union had annual growth rates of only 1.0% from 1950 to 1975. By 1990, Europe and Northern America contained only about 18% of the world's population.

Population growth will probably be most rapid in the Middle East, sub-Saharan Africa and North Africa, with tripling of the population by 2050 and a quadrupling by 2100 likely. In North America, a younger age distribution, a larger inflow of immigrants, and a slightly higher fertility than Europe, is likely to result in a 25% increase. China's population will grow by 37% — despite its attempted single-child family planning policy — while the Indian subcontinent will see a doubling of population and overtake China as the world's most populous country.

In terms of current population density worldwide, the results are surprising: the Netherlands has 375 people per square kilometre, Japan 330, the UK 37, the US 27, Canada and Australia, about 2.9. We seem to have lots of room for more people except that much of our land is largely unusable.

Still, the increase in population will be huge and the population older than 60 is expected to double. On the other hand, the younger population is growing in the less developed countries, where the share of people above 65 will fall to barely 5% — and to 3% in Africa. In more developed regions, the share of older people, which had already soared to 12% by 1990, will rise to 13.5% in 2000. This increasing proportion of older people will exert growing pressure on the systems of medical insurance and pensions that most of the Western nations have established.

Less-developed regions will continue to have a relatively large proportion of dependent children.

Demographic Transition

Demographic transition is the term for a population theory that grew from the diminished rate of population growth in most Western countries this century, when birth rates have generally fallen faster than death rates, and the rates of natural increase are now quite low. According to this idea, every country develops from an initial stage of little or no population growth, with high birth and death rates, to a final stage of similarly negligible growth, but with low birth and death rates. In between is a period of rapid population growth, during which the death rate declines but the birth rate remains high. The fall in the death rate and the subsequent decline in the birth rate are attributed to industrialization, urbanization, mass education, and modernization.

In the modern world, economic and social conditions affect population change mainly through their influence on fertility — all societies control actual reproduction in some manner, particularly through restrictions on marriage. Other factors include social customs that limit fertility through abortion laws, the widespread use of contraceptive techniques, education (especially of women), the age of a woman, the number of children she already has, and the degree of opportunity she has to work outside the home.

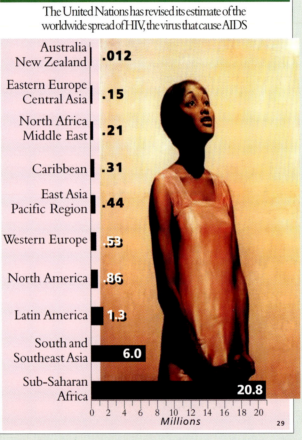

A New, Grimmer Portrait of AIDS

The United Nations has revised its estimate of the worldwide spread of HIV, the virus that cause AIDS

Region	Millions
Australia New Zealand	.012
Eastern Europe Central Asia	.15
North Africa Middle East	.21
Caribbean	.31
East Asia Pacific Region	.44
Western Europe	.53
North America	.86
Latin America	1.3
South and Southeast Asia	6.0
Sub-Saharan Africa	20.8

Millions 29

If you think in terms of a year, plant a seed;
If in terms of 10 years, plant trees;
And if in terms of 100 years,
teach the people. — *Confucian proverb*

Malthusian Theory on Over-Population

In 1798, Thomas Robert Malthus, a British professor and cleric formulated an essay, *The Principle of Population,* that became the basis for contemporary science of demography. For the next 25 years, he extended his theories on what he believed to be the obscenities of unchecked population growth. He hypothesized that, under unchanging conditions, population is inclined to double geometrically (1, 2, 4, 8, 16, 32, 64) each 25 years while food production could only double arithmetically (1, 2, 3, 4, 5, 6, 7). His conclusion was that food production could not keep up with population growth, therefore population growth needed to be impeded.

Malthus rationalized welfare as immoral because it increased population and promoted starvation. His apocalyptic revelation had such widespread advocacy among economic conservatives that Britain declared much of its social welfare programing hopeless.

Although ridiculed by many observers, Malthus' theories were vindicated by the Irish Famine (1845-1849). Severe blight destroyed the potato crop and resulted in more than a million deaths and in 2 million people fleeing to the US and Canada. His theory was further exonerated between 1850 and 1880, when China endured a wave of successive famines resulting in the death of an estimated 50-70 million people.

His pessimistic theories concluded that there needed to be restraints imposed on human reproduction, and while there was validity in his basic premise, his moralistic perspective detracts from his work. To Malthus, moral restraint was essential to reduce the birth rate, and he proposed an "abstinence from marriage, either for a time or permanently… with a strictly moral conduct prohibiting sex in the interval."

Today, those who fear excessive population growth have been called neo-Malthusian. (However, neo-Malthusians are rarely moralistic and have not joined in condemning "vice;" they view contraception as an enlightened means of limiting population.) Core Malthusian ideas have particularly been applied to the poor countries of Asia, Africa, and Latin America, where population growth is great, and famine a real possibility.

The Voluntary Human Extinction Movement (VHEMT), a neo-Malthusian organization, asserts that humans have urges that lead to reproduction, but that the biological urge is to have sex, not to breed. They further assert that culturally induced urges can be so strong that they seem to be biological, but that there is no evolutionary drive to propagate the human species. **Social and religious conformity is probably the controlling cause of most wanted pregnancies.**

Renowned environmental advocate Michael Tobias reinvigorated Malthus' theories in his 1994 book, *World War III.* His warnings of runaway overpopulation and its impact on global ecosystems have earned him many admirers. One of Tobias' mentors, ecologist Paul Ehrlich, predicted in the 1968 best-seller, *The Population Bomb,* that in the 1970's and 1980's, hundreds of millions of people would starve to death. Tobias asserts that Ehrlich and Malthus before him, as concerned and articulate as they were, grossly underestimated the impact of human overpopulation on the quality of our lives and the quality of life for all other kindred forms on this planet.

When Dennis and Donella Meadows wrote *Limits to Growth* in 1997, they were a bit more strident in their cautionary tale, and plotted 5 or 6 of the primary behavioural tendencies of human consumers with regard to waste, energy use and affluents being ejected into the troposphere.

Although the issues have been raised repeatedly, the impact on individual behaviour and national policy have been minimal.

Quinacrine Sterlization

Quinacrine (pronounced KWIN-a-krin) sterilization is a non-surgical permanent birth control for women, which potentially offers millions the best hope for protection against unwanted pregnancies. It could also make an important contribution to the family planning needs of many Third World and developing countries.

The QS method, developed in response to a worldwide demand for sterilization, involves the intrauterine insertion of pellets of quinacrine with a modified IUD. Quinacrine causes fibrosis and scarring when applied to some mucosal membranes, such as the pleural cavity lining and the lining of Fallopian tubes when applied directly. It was this property and the well-established safety of this drug that made it attractive for use in non-surgical female sterilization.

More than 100,000 QS procedures have been performed in more than 20 countries without a single death or a single life-threatening injury. In the hands of a skilled provider, the failure rate is 1%-2% at one year of use. QS can be performed by trained paramedics in the most basic clinic settings for under $1.40.

Culturally-Induced Child Bearing

Because people who plan to create more of themselves are subconsciously aware that this is a mistake, they cannot give their true motivations. We have to translate their rationalizations:
- **I want to carry on the family name.**
  = Trying to please Dad. Cult-of-the-bloodline dupe.
- **I want my kids (who don't exist yet) to have all the things I did not have.**
  = Unfulfilled childhood desires and fantasies.
- **I would like to try for a boy/girl this time.**
  = Ego extension. Gender identity insecurity.
  = Disappointment with existing progeny.
- **I just love children.**
  = Out of touch with inner child, and with existing children.
- **I want someone to visit me when I am old.**
  = Insecurity. Fear of aging. Exploitative personality.
- **I want to give my parents grandchildren.**
  = Still seeking parental approval.
- **I have superior human genes!**
  = Oxymoron! [30]

Canadian Population

Canada's population — about 0.5% of the world's — has doubled in 45 years from just over 14 million in 1951, to 28.8 million in 1996. Overall, Canada's rate of growth slowed between 1991 and 1996, compared to the previous 5-year period. International migration and natural increase added more than 1.5 million people over the past 5 years.

Out of every 100 Canadians, an average of 45 have ancestors from the UK or Ireland, 29 from France, 5 from Germany, 3 from Italy, 2 from the Ukraine and Netherlands and China, between 1 and 2 will be First Nations or Inuit, and 12 from other countries.

For the 1st time since Confederation, Quebec's share of the population has fallen below 25%. Quebec started as 1 of 2 founding nations of Canada, with 43% of the total population, and now finds itself with a shrinking share. It "fears that this trend will lead to a loss of power and political influence," says demographer David Foot. "The supporters of sovereignty are drawn almost exclusively from old-stock French Canadians and, because of their low fertility, there haven't been enough of them to win a majority for their cause."

Compared to the rest of the industrialized world, Canada is still a front-runner in population growth, with a 1.34% annual increase, even though our birth rate hit a record low, with 378,000 births or a rate of only 12.8 babies for every 1,000 people in 1995. In 1996, the average adult woman could be expected to have 1.65 children in her lifetime.

The average annual increases for the rest of the developed countries vary from 0.1% for Italy to 1.0% for the US. The overall number of people on earth rose at an annual growth rate of 1.5%. Our annual population growth is more than 4.5 times the annual increase of the EU — but due to immigration, not domestic procreation.

A feature of rapid population growth is massive urbanization. Consequently, the latest census showed 17.8 million Canadians — or almost 80% — live in 25 metropolitan areas. In addition, 36% of the population live in the 4 most populous metropolitan areas of Toronto, Montreal, Vancouver and Ottawa-Hull.

In 1900, the average person in Canada lived to 50 years of age. Between 1900 and 2000, life expectancy will make an incredible rise from 50 to 80 years.

While the increase is striking for both genders, the growing difference between genders shows that women outlive men by more than 7 years now. Much of this difference can be explained by how few women die in childbirth today. In addition, men used to go off to war and die, worked in more hazardous occupations and lived a rougher life. But it is interesting in Canada that, up until the age of 50, the male and female population is the same. It is after 75 that it is dramatically skewed.

Voluntary Sterilization 31

	Canada	Developed	Developing
Women, under 50	31%	8%	20%
Men	13%	5%	5%

Demographics Highly Overrated

According to a study done by the Royal Bank of Canada, demographics is vastly overrated as an explanation of economic forces; far more important are traditional influences such as changes in interest rates, employment, income and government policies, which "all tend to swamp the role of demographics." To rely on demographics alone is to assume that everything else will remain static, and that we live in a world with few boundaries.

The Canadian and US populations have "virtually identical age structures," but spending on consumer goods and residential construction has been much stronger in the US than Canada in recent years. "Clearly, factors other than demographics explain such a divergence in the performance of the two economies."

Fertility Rate

The *fertility rate* is the average number of children born to each woman while the *birth rate* is the total number of births divided by the size of the population. Canada's fertility rate, which is 1.7 babies per woman, produces one of the highest birth rates among industrialized countries, but well below the 2.1 needed to replace the population.

Fifty-one countries now make the list of nations whose fertility rates are 2.1 or lower. In 1975, the list had only 19 countries. The replacement rate is 2.1 to measure 2 new people to take the place of mother and father plus a margin for childhood deaths. Low fertility rates exist predominantly in the world's wealthiest industrialized countries.

Long-range forecasts point to the world's average birth rate falling to 2.6% during the 1st decade of the next century, contrasted with the developed countries rate of 1.6%. By 2020, the potential birth rate in developed countries could drop below 1.3%.

Meanwhile, population prospects are moderately encouraging. It appears that East Asia nations will join Japan, Europe and North America in bringing their populations under control. Recent experience suggests that the population "explosion" in Africa, Latin America, and South Asia could also be contained with successful programs of socioeconomic development and population control, including late marriage, contraception and abortion.

The Birth Dearth

As the economy moved from an agricultural to an industrial and now to an information age, children have become an economic hardship instead of a necessity. In an agricultural economy, with its great need for cheap, unskilled labour, a large number of healthy children is an advantage. With enhanced government safety nets, proliferating pensions and early retirement packages, each child represents tremendous long-term costs with little or no economic return.

Canadian population grew by 1.34% — the highest of all G-7 industrialized nation.

Understanding Cohort Groups

In their best-selling book (over 300,000 copies), *Boom Bust & Echo: How to Profit from the Coming Demographic Shift,* University of Toronto professor David Foot and journalist Daniel Stoffman contend **that about 2/3 of everything can be explained by demography.** Demography is estimating population size and structure, measuring and analyzing the components of population change (births, deaths, and migration) and those aspects of population structure (composition by age and gender) that help explain its evolution.

> *Everyone is involved in planning for the future — we all need to understand the basics of demography.*

If you were fortunate enough to have been born in some periods, and you have been successful, demographics probably had as much to do with your success as you did. On the other hand, if you were unfortunate enough to be born in other periods, your lack of success may have less to do with you than with the stiff competition you faced.

When it comes to predicting behaviour, the most useful demographic variable is the age composition of the population. For example, in Canada, the combination of a low fertility rate with increasing life expectancy means that the average age of Canadians is increasing. An older society requires fewer goods, which hurts those in the business of manufacturing and selling goods. But an aging society requires many more services, and that means new business opportunities for others.

Understanding Your Cohort

Most of us think of ourselves as individuals and underestimate how much we have in common with fellow members of our cohort. Understanding the size of these cohorts and their predominate characteristics are the keys to understanding how demographics impact you personally.

Pre-World War I: Born before 1915 The most senior of seniors comprise a segment of the population that is currently growing rapidly because they were born when a high birth rate — characteristic of the agrarian economy — was accompanied by a vibrant Canadian economy. Because Canadian women, on average, live 6 years longer than men, this group is predominantly female.

World War I: Born 1915 to 1919 During World War I, many Canadian men went off to battle and, as a result, many Canadian women stopped having babies. That is why the relatively small group of people born during this period have enjoyed a lifelong advantage of having little peer-group competition.

The Roaring Twenties: Born 1920 to 1929 When the soldiers returned from the war in Europe, they quickly made up for lost time — the 1st baby boom. Despite the disadvantage of being part of this large cohort, they have enjoyed a solid prosperity. One intervening factor was that many of them fought in World War II, reducing job competition for those who remained in Canada.

The Depression Babies: Born 1930 to 1939 In such a hard economic period, most Canadians could not afford to have many children, and so the fertility rate declined dramatically. The few children who were born during this decade became truly fortunate. They never had too many worries about finding good jobs, and they were promoted in an accelerated way.

World War II: Born 1940 to 1946 The WWII cohort group was much larger than the WWI cohort because a larger percentage of the 1st group went overseas, and many more lost their lives. There was actually an increase in births during World War II because the economy got a bigger boom than in the previous war.

The Baby Boom: Born 1947 to 1966 Canada's 10 million babies were the loudest per capita boom in the industrialized world. The most likely explanation for this explosion was that the future seemed full of promise, encouraging people to have larger families. One-third of Canadians today are boomers. Front-end boomers earned 30% more than their fathers by age 30; back-enders earned 10% less. The millions of front-end baby-boomers drove up real estate prices and claimed the best jobs; the Generation-Xers entered the labour market just in time for a brutal recession.

The Baby Bust - The Nexus Generation: Born 1967 to 1979 This generation is most noticeable in Ontario and Western Canada. The baby busters have had a pretty good life until now and have had the luxury of being able to pay attention to social issues. An important aspect is that employers usually prefer younger people for entry-level positions, and busters tend to have the better computer skills that today's job market demands. However, this cohort does not have a promising future because of the economic upheaval facing today's workforce.

The Nintendo Generation: Born 1980 to 1995 The outlook for the Nintendo kids is very checkered. They are part of a large cohort and that always means lots of competition. Like the baby boom, the Nintendo cohort has a front end and a back end. The latter group will experience the now familiar disadvantages of arriving at the rear of a large cohort. If they are properly educated, they may arrive ready to work in the post-transition economy. As of 1996, there were 6.9 million members of this generation.

The Transition Future: Born 1996 to 2014 This will definitely be a smaller group and therefore have more opportunities. Immigration policy will be the key ingredient in the ultimate size of this group — an issue addressed in detail starting on the following page.[32]

Immigration

> *Before WWI, people had the right to move from country to country, but false "bad news" about economics, population and prejudice limited that freedom.*

Marketing economist Julian Simon made a case for the economic and moral grounds for expanded immigration in countries such as Canada. "The migration of people from poor to rich countries is as close to an everybody-wins government policy as can be," wrote Simon. (See Counterpoint, page 45.)

Up to and following WWII, however, Canada's immigration bureaucracy operated as an agency excluding non-white, non-Europeans on racist grounds. Explicitly racist language was not removed from Canadian laws until the 1960's.

Before then, Canada's immigration law was racist in wording and intent. The original 1885 Chinese Immigration Act imposed a "head tax" on Chinese immigrants. The 1923 revision effectively terminated immigration from China, and immigration from India and Ceylon was also curtailed. Immigrants from the rest of Asia, South and Central America, Africa, and Blacks from the US — by exclusion provisions that were developed around the turn of the century — were turned away.

Canada's annual immigration over the 20th century has been volatile, ranging from a high of 400,870 in 1913 to a low of 7,576 in 1942. A rising tide of immigration — from just over 50,000 in 1901 to 8 times that figure 12 years later — swelled the population to 7.2 million by 1911. Roughly 1/3 of the immigrants came from Europe — Ukrainians, Russian Jews, Poles, Germans, Italians, Dutch and Scandinavians. In BC there were increasing populations of Chinese, Japanese and East Indians.

Canada has been the world's most accepting country for immigrants, receiving more in relation to our population than any other country, including the US, Australia and New Zealand. Canada also has the world's most accommodating refugee-determination policies.

In 1998, Canada accepted between 200,000 to 225,000 immigrants — almost the same as 1997. Refugees were estimated to number 24,000 to 32,300, up from 1997. In 1997, Canada accepted about 125,000 skilled workers and business-class immigrants, compared to 60,700 family-class arrivals. **Quebec, with 23.5% of Canada's population, will continue to accept only about 12% to 13% of the immigrants.** Quebec has selection powers, so it could easily increase levels — deeply cynical observations observe that open immigration to Quebec would dissolve the separatist problem in 50 years.

Certain aspects of immigration policy and practice adversely impact the job market. Canada currently allows immigration (including a relatively insufficient number of refugees) at a rate equivalent to .92% of the population. This number strains the economy, while the US and Australia admit .46% and .40%, respectively. Although immigration is an integral part of the healthy

"Visible" Minorities

It was not long ago that "visible minorities" in Canada were "invisible." That is because, as recently as 1971, 97% of Canadians were of European ancestry.

Canada's visible minority population has been rising steadily and now stands at 11.2%. The trend will continue as immigration levels remain comparatively high, and most of the immigrants come from Asia, Africa and the West Indies.

The US has been a different story, where affirmative action programs have been driven by 400 years of bad relations between blacks and whites. The Canadian circumstance is quite different because more than 70% of visible-minority Canadians were born outside of Canada, and they do not share the same past.

Cosmopolitan Toronto 33

Toronto is unlike any other city in Canada (or the world) and it is not just size. More than half of Canada's 3.2 million visible minorities live in Ontario; **40% of the visible minorities, 35% of the city's population, live in Toronto, the most cosmopolitan city in the world.**

Who speaks what?

The language spoken most often at home in Toronto in 1996:

1.	English	3,077,405	8.	Tagalog	33,670
2.	Chinese	243,845	9.	Vietnamese	29,910
3.	Italian	96,010	10.	Greek	27,435
4.	Portuguese	68,420	11.	Arabic	22,815
5.	Polish	52,525	12.	Farsi	21,565
6.	Punjabi	51,285	13.	Korean	19,055
7.	Tamil	46,005	14.	Urdu	17,360

diversity we enjoy, strong consideration should be given to reducing the number of immigrants to a level similar to our US and Australian counterparts.

In the face of predicted future immigration pressures from Latin America and Africa, Canada needs to maintain a sensible immigration program that balances our own needs with humanitarian goals. One consideration is that an immigrant population requires large back-up services. For example, in Toronto, where 42% of all new arrivals to Canada settle, 1 in 5 children in area schools speaks another language at home while learning English in school — nearly 2.5 times the national average.

Lastly, while there is a system for rating potential immigrants based on labour market skills, this test is a determinant in less than 30% of cases; the majority are permitted on a "compassionate" basis to join families already here. It would be economically wise to increase dramatically the percentage of "qualified" immigrants.

Demographer David Foot says that, "there should be no illusions about the ability of immigration to make a grey Canada less grey: an immigration policy based on the family ... can never rejuvenate a society."

The Changing Face of Canada

England and France — the "founding" nations of Canada — are no longer sources of significant numbers of immigrants; both have fallen dramatically as source countries: England to 10th and France to 17th.

Immigration Source Countries to Canada[34]

January to December, 1997	
Source Country	**Immigrants**
Hong Kong	22,057
India	19,536
China	18,479
Taiwan	13,278
Pakistan	11,200
Philippines	10,842
Iran	7,475
Sri Lanka	5,060
US	5,028
England	4,018

Immigration Overhaul

A major overhaul of Canada's immigration and refugee-determination systems has been recommended by an independent panel in a report commissioned by Immigration Minister Lucienne Robillard. The report attempts to answer public concern that the system is too cumbersome, backed by insufficient follow-up, and "suffering from a thousand cuts."

Far from saying that Canada is accepting too many foreigners, the report contends that Canada should be competing with other industrialized countries for the "best human capital." Ontario, for example, recently launched a new investor fund, open to foreigners with a net worth of at least $500,000, who are willing to invest $350,000 over 5 years in exchange for a Canadian visa.

Among the report's 172 suggestions is the creation of 2 separate acts — 1 for immigration and citizenship, and 1 for refugees. One of its more controversial proposals is to replace the quasi-judicial Immigration and Refugee Board with an independent Protection Agency, which is designed to be faster, more efficient and far-reaching. Based on the Dutch system, the Agency would provide refugees with access to legal services, documentation centres and housing — and allow case assessment within 15 weeks.

Another recommendation was that skilled workers, investors and entrepreneurs undergo a test to prove they are proficient in either English or French. Currently, 4 out of 5 immigrants have a 1st language other than English or French. Critics charge that history has proven that half of those who did not have English or French learned 1 of the languages within 3 years.

Mandatory English or French is not being welcomed by some who argue that such a proposal violates Canadian tradition and law, and would severely curb the influx of affluent investors. The language barriers would also be unfair to immigrants who are already here and seek to bring their spouses and families into Canada but will have to pay for expensive language training. The authors argue, however, that the requirement reduces the amount of discretion currently in the hands of the immigration and visa officers, while it also urges potential immigrants to prepare themselves better.

Family unification became an even thornier issue when Robillard recently suggested that Canada should reconsider its policy of automatically granting citizenship to everyone born here. Her comments followed a landmark Ontario court decision in which it was decided that a Toronto woman could not be deported to her native Grenada because the rights of her Canadian-born children were ignored. Right now, everyone born on Canadian soil is entitled to Canadian citizenship, no matter who their parents are. In the UK, children born to non-residents do not get citizenship automatically but have to apply before age 18 and demonstrate a "close and continuing link" with Britain, while Australia requires that at least 1 parent be an Australian citizen or permanent resident for a child to qualify. The US extends citizenship to everyone born on its territory.

Another suggestion was that Canada drop the points system for economic immigrants and replace it with criteria that include a minimum level of education, work experience and an ability to earn an income. Currently, the weights assigned to each category or the points awarded are highly subjective. In 1994, of the 230,000 immigrants entering the country, just 14% were selected using the points system.

Under the current system, applicants must obtain at least 70 points. (Entrepreneurs and investors need only 25, as they are not rated on occupation-related factors.) Points are earned for education, job training, experience, occupation, arranged employment, intended destination, age, knowledge of English or French, and personal suitability. A bonus is awarded to those having assisting relatives in Canada, and the self-employed.

Other reforms recommend annual quotas for some immigrant programs instead of overall "target levels," that quotas should not apply to the reunion of spouses or dependent children, that sponsorship be restructured to include "close friends" and same-sex or common-law spouses (but not grandparents), that economic immigrants with the means to support themselves should not be turned away because of their occupations (as happens now), and that the political appointees of the Board be replaced and decision-making authority on refugees go to a group of independent civil servants.

The report said that, "bona fide protection seekers should be encouraged to come forward as soon as possible, and the protection process should be designed to make it in their best interests to do so." The Protection Act would take a more "proactive" role in seeking out genuine refugees abroad.

"Let's look for people who can best adjust and who can best adapt to Canada, who will prosper themselves and help Canada grow," said one panellist. The Minister recently conducted a nationwide consultation and could have new legislation in place by the end of 1998.

A New Immigrant Class

The US has a class of immigrant called the "exceptional alien," which is something Canada should do. After all, Canada values foreigners with sustained and recognized talent in scholarship, the arts, sports, and other endeavors prized by Canadians.

A Sustainable World:
Green Guidelines

Each year about 90 million people join the human race. This is equal to adding 3 Canadas or another Mexico annually. We are reproducing so quickly that we are outpacing the Earth's ability to house and feed us! Forty million acres of tropical rainforest — twice the size of Austria — are being destroyed or grossly degraded every year, 27,000 species become extinct yearly, and nearly 2 billion people lack adequate water.

Information is contradictory regarding the effect of population growth on the environment, which may explain the lax attitude in North America to environmental regulation and protection of basic life support systems like water, air and soil. But we ignore the potential consequences at our peril, according to Thomas Homer-Dixon of the University of Toronto. **The "profligate consumption of non-renewable resources" is contributing to "bloody civil strife and political instability," he warns.** Unless underlying causes are addressed, many countries face a surge of violence.

Modern technologies and improved efficiencies can help to stretch resources. Consumption levels also exert considerable impact. Population pressures work in conjunction with these factors to determine, to a large extent, our total impact on resources.

One example is energy consumption. While the average person in Bangladesh consumes energy equal to 3 barrels of oil yearly, each person in the US consumes an average of 55. When the consumption figures are adjusted for population size, the US still increases its energy consumption 6 or 7 times faster than the more rapidly growing Bangladeshi population.

Industrialized nations, with less than 25% of the world's population, burn about 70% of all fossil fuels. The US alone consumes about 25% of the world's commercial energy, and the former Soviet Union about 20%. In per capita consumption, **Canada burns more fuel than any other nation, followed by Norway and the US.**

Future effects of population growth on natural resources will vary because growth occurs unevenly across the globe. Since 1961, food production has matched population growth in all developing regions except sub-Saharan Africa. In the early 1980's, the UN Food and Agriculture Organization predicted that more than half of all developing nations may be unable to feed their people by the year 2000 using current farm technology.

A UNICEF report on malnutrition issued in December, 1997, indicted that **the lack of proper food is already killing more than 6 million children every year.** That is almost 20,000 deaths every day, or more than 1 child every half second.

Although efforts to deal with the malnutrition issues are well-intentioned, they are focussed primarily on the symptoms rather than *the problem* — **the world just has too many mouths to feed.** The paramount response is to vigorously promote birth control in the developing world. Parents in the developed world should contribute by having only 1 child and adopting the 2nd if they want another.

As a direct result of population growth, especially in developing nations, the average amount of farmland per person is projected to decline. Three factors will determine whether food production can equal population growth:

• **New Farmlands.** Currently, the amount of new land put into production each year equals the amount taken out for various reasons, such as erosion, salt deposits and waterlogging.

• **New Water Sources.** Agricultural demand for water has doubled between 1970 and 2000. Already, more than 70% of water withdrawals from rivers, underground reservoirs and other sources go to crop irrigation.

• **Agrochemical Use.** Pesticides and fertilizers are boosting crop yields. However, in many areas, agrochemicals are too expensive, while in other areas they are overused.

In China, the world's largest dam — the Three Gorges project — will flood a vast area of farmland, and will force 1.3 million people to relocate.

In addition, when both agricultural and non-agricultural needs are taken into account, human population growth may be responsible for as much as 80% of the loss of forest cover worldwide. For example, Haiti, once 100% forested, is now down to 4%.

Population pressure contributes to deforestation not only because of increased demand for farmland and living space, but also because of demand for fuel from wood, on which half of the world's people depend for heating and cooking. By 1990, 100 million Third World residents lacked sufficient wood to meet minimum daily energy requirements, and close to 1.3 billion were consuming wood faster than forest growth could replenish it.

Population and development pressures have also been mounting in coastal areas worldwide for the past 30 years, triggering widespread resource degradation. Throughout much of the world, coastal zones are overdeveloped, overcrowded and overexploited. Already nearly 2/3 of the world's population live along coasts or within 150 km of

The sustainable population of the earth is between 2 and 4 billion — only 2 billion if we consume at the North American level.

one. Within 3 decades, 75% will reside in coastal areas — nearly a *billion* more people than the current global population.

In Canada, a significant majority lives in areas adjacent to marine coast or the Great Lakes. Similarly, nearly 780 million of China's 1.2 billion people, almost 67%, live in coastal provinces or municipalities. Along much of China's coastline, population densities average more than 600 people per square km — in Shanghai, they exceed 2,000.

Coastal development, along with overfishing and pollution are destroying the world's oceans. Overfishing has already depleted commercial fish populations to the point of causing the collapse of fisheries around the world, and scientists say we must act now to prevent further degradation of the marine environment.

Fresh water is predominantly used to grow feed for cattle. As a result, aquifers, rivers, and water levels where ranching occurs are shrinking. Globally, the cattle industry is having a disastrous impact on tropical rain forest areas, which are being cleared to provide open grazing ground for cattle. When that happens, a key ingredient in the planetary recycling system of oxygen and carbon dioxide is lost.

Piecemeal solutions dominate the bureaucracies in charge of overseeing the world's natural resources, and common resources continue to deteriorate. If human society does not succeed in checking population growth, the future will bring widespread social and economic dislocations as resource bases collapse. Unemployment and poverty will increase, and migrations from poorer to richer nations will bring Third World stresses to the developed world.[35]

> The enemies
> of sustainable development
> are **consumption** and **poverty.**
> If we do not deal with population issues,
> we are just prolonging the agony.

We must look beyond our national borders to the impact each of us has on the entire planet. Political boundaries are totally obsolete when thinking about the environment, except that organizational boundaries are necessary to maximize the efficiency of any endeavour.

The answer is to consume less. Families with 3 cars could get by with 2. Those with 2 may be able to get by with 1 — or none at all. These are personal sacrifices and, if your neighbours are not doing it, you are going to be reluctant to do it yourself.

Buildings in the OECD countries use 25% less energy now than they did before 1973, while the energy efficiency of industry has improved by 33%. Worldwide, cars get 25% more km per gallon than they did in 1973. In all, increased efficiency since 1973 has saved the industrialized nations $250 billion in energy costs. Even more savings could be realized through concerted efforts to conserve energy and improve efficiency. Three relatively simple, cost-effective measures could be introduced immediately:
- making compact fluorescent lamps generally available;
- tightening building codes to require better insulation;
- requiring lean-burn engines, thereby saving billions of dollars in energy costs.

> *In terms of energy consumption, when North American parents stop at 2, it is about the same as an average East Indian couple stopping at 60, or an Ethiopian couple stopping at 1,000. "Having babies" is not so much the problem; having adults is what is causing the problems.*

In Canada, consumers have been encouraged through low-interest loans to buy energy-efficient appliances. There are free energy-audits of homes, advice on insulation, promotions for compact fluorescent bulbs, and a push to solar water heating.

Known oil reserves should meet current levels of consumption for 41 years, thanks to better energy efficiency and conservation measures, along with new oil fields brought into production. Natural gas reserves should meet current demand for 60 more years, while coal reserves should last another 200 years.

Canada is also joining other countries in beginning to shut down its nuclear reactors. In the US, 2 more were recently switched off bringing the total decommissionings to 70. All of Sweden's reactors will be phased out by 2010.

We still have a long way to go. **Today, we are among the worst polluters in the world. Ontario ranks 3rd behind Texas and Tennessee in North America.**[35] We have increased our greenhouse emissions by more than 9%, flouting our commitment at the 1992 Rio Summit to stabilize emissions by the year 2000. The provinces were in an uproar over Canada's 1997 promise at Kyoto to reduce gasses to 6% below the 1990 levels by the year 2010 — a demonstration of the supremacy of economic concerns over the environment. The government appears unembarrassed over its failure to fulfill our past promises, and reluctant to commit itself in the UN's efforts to negotiate new targets.

◀ COUNTERPOINT ▶

The Doomslayer

Marketing economist Julian Simon has been called the world's leading "Doomslayer" by *Wired* magazine because of his body of work countering theories of global overpopulation and imminent economic and social disaster.

Simon, a firm believer in the human imagination and human spirit, wrote a piece in 1980 for *Science* magazine, attacking Paul Ehrlich's theories published in his books, *The Population Bomb* and *The End of Affluence*. The article, "Resources, Population, Environment: An Oversupply of False Bad News," was followed a year later by his 1st book, *The Ultimate Resource* — which focussed on human beings, not the number of trees in the forests, oil in the ground or water in the oceans, as the source of expanding wealth.

His 1996 book, *The Ultimate Resource 2*, challenges the alarmist position with charts, graphs and illustrations, providing evidence of the power of human action.

And, although American companies produce more chemical waste than Canada, Canadians dump more into the water. Canada pumped 33 million kilograms of chemical waste into the Great Lakes water compared with 29 million kilograms in the US.

If we do not do something now, by the time we add a few hundred million more consumers, we are going to have to counter a deteriorated environment with a loss of democratic principles. The government will have to initiate regulations that will make a lot of people unhappy. In other words, we can all "voluntarily" do our bit now, or we will not have a choice later.

Basic freedoms will have to be reduced because there will not be enough clean air and water. An exploding population will gradually trigger responses by politicians who, in fear of catastrophe, will initiate reform and make laws that might be tyrannical. This has already happened in Indonesia, where the population of 200 million is predicted to nearly double despite 30 years of effort at control. And in the mean time, lax laws are doing the best they can to encourage destruction on a global scale.

The GATT, for example, is a disaster for the environment because powerful nations are encouraged to plunder forests that should be protected. We are going to need that lumber, so the governments lessen the stringency of their regulations. We are already seeing increased plunder in the Amazon despite 25 years of global consciousness-raising. Environmental causes have fallen on hard times, and it has taken place at the very moment that eco-optimism seems to be rising. As we approach the end of the millennium, we are essentially divided into the pessimists and the optimists.

The Role of Trees

Forest Fires

Trees have an important part to play in reducing Canada's greenhouse gas emissions. The impact from forest fires, however, is far more than the annual human harvest — about 700,000 hectares per year, mostly for pulp, paper and lumber.

Canada lost about 2 million hectares annually to fires through most of the 1980's. But in 1990 alone, due to the pattern of recent droughts, forest fires consumed more than 4 million hectares (an area equal to Nova Scotia and P.E.I. combined).

The 1998 losses will break that record.

It Starts with Science

"The predictions of dire consequences in our reports and other media are rooted in the work of the Intergovernmental Panel on Climate Change. This scientific body pulled together the work of 2,500 scientists around the world who are studying the issue. Their work tells us that if we allow the concentrations of greenhouse gases in the atmosphere to double, then we can expect rapid and unprecedented changes to our climate, with severe consequences for the environment, human health and economic systems." [36]

The ominous sign of the ecological apocalypse is that 20% of the world's population consumes 80% of the resources.

If you are truly concerned about consuming less, you are going to have to be a role model.

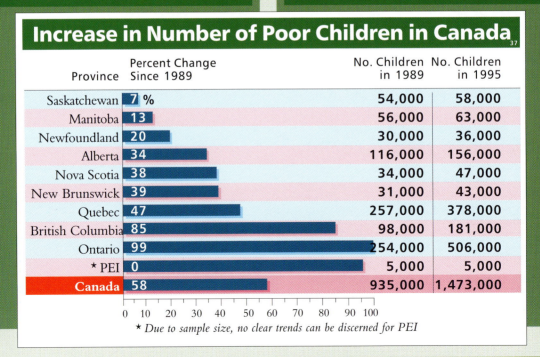

Increase in Number of Poor Children in Canada [37]

Province	Percent Change Since 1989	No. Children in 1989	No. Children in 1995
Saskatchewan	7 %	54,000	58,000
Manitoba	13	56,000	63,000
Newfoundland	20	30,000	36,000
Alberta	34	116,000	156,000
Nova Scotia	38	34,000	47,000
New Brunswick	39	31,000	43,000
Quebec	47	257,000	378,000
British Columbia	85	98,000	181,000
Ontario	99	254,000	506,000
★ PEI	0	5,000	5,000
Canada	58	935,000	1,473,000

0 10 20 30 40 50 60 70 80 90 100

★ *Due to sample size, no clear trends can be discerned for PEI*

World Water Shortage

As the world's population increases, the amount of water available per person decreases. Already some 2 billion people in 80 countries must live with water constraints.

Only 2.5% of all the planet's water is fresh and 2/3 of that is locked up in glaciers and ice caps. The annual renewable fresh-water supply on Earth — rain and snow — is a minuscule 0.000008% of all the water on Earth. And more than half of that disappears through evaporation or transpiration through plants.

For most of the world, the current pattern of water resource utilization is not sustainable. By the year 2025, as much as 2/3 of the world in the lower income categories could be facing moderate to severe water stress, and 35% of the same population could be facing severe stress, as compared to about 9% in 1995. Such shortages will lead to escalating distress over energy, environment, health, food, security, and climatic changes. It could even provoke armed conflicts.

The Arab region, which has the lowest fresh water resources in the world, needs the equivalent of a 2nd Nile River to take care of its needs. The area covers 10.8% of the earth's surface and supports 4.5% of the world's population, but has only 0.4% of the total renewable water resources. Experts say 89% of the water is used for agriculture, 6% in homes and 5% in industry.

Today, much of the Gulf region's thirst is satisfied by desalinization plants and recycled water. Saudi Arabia, the United Arab Emirates and Kuwait rely on desalinated water for more than 70% of their needs. The Arabian Gulf underground water is depleted annually by 80 million cubic metres. The desalinization plants, which make up the deficit, produced 400 million gallons daily in 1997.[181]

Rapid economic development and the numbers of people that prosperity has brought have raised demands for water.

IT, more scientific research, national water policies, and revamped traditional irrigation systems have all been recommended.

Other plans include privatization of water services and projects, boosting water conservation, increasing water resources information, increasing the storage of ground water resources, and monitoring the quality and quantity of ground water.

Water For Sale?

In Canada in general, and Quebec in particular, some people have dreams of "liquid gold" — building a pipeline across the floor of the Atlantic or using oil tankers for water shipments. Quebec is home to 33% of Canada's renewable fresh water. (Canada, the US, China and Russia all have about 9%, while Brazil leads with 18%.)

Companies in Ontario and Newfoundland have also jumped on the bandwagon — a business applied to export about 52 billion litres of water a year from Gisborne Lake, and another wanted to export 600 million litres a year from Lake Superior to Asia. Some argue, however, that water is too valuable to be just another capitalist commodity and are pushing for nationalization of the water trade.

Trading water as a raw resource would make it considered a tradeable good, opening the door to US and Mexican companies to come here and export our water, which also has prompted the idea of a tax on water captured for bottling.

Stabilizing Emissions

"Why do environmental groups keep calling for deep and rapid cuts in greenhouse gas emissions?" write Canadian environmental activists Dr. David Suzuki and Amanda McConnell in their book, *Sacred Balance*. "Why don't they accept the gradual stabilization proposals of some industry groups and governments? After all, stabilization seems like a moderate compromise... And the word itself suggests that if we hold emissions at the levels that existed in 1990, then we will stop the pressure that is changing the climate. The big trouble is, this isn't true. Stabilizing emissions does not mean stabilizing our climate.

"In fact, it condemns us to a new and warmer climate with irreversible ecological damage." [36]

Canadian Life Expectancy at Birth [23]

Year	Both Genders	Males	Females	Difference (Years)
1900 *	50.00	50.00	50.00	0.00
1920-22	59.37	58.84	60.60	1.76
1930-32	61.00	60.00	62.06	2.06
1940-42	64.58	63.04	66.31	3.27
1950-52	68.51	66.40	70.90	4.50
1960-62	71.14	68.44	74.26	5.82
1970-72	72.74	69.40	76.45	7.05
1980-82	75.39	71.88	79.06	7.18
1990-92	77.80	74.61	80.97	6.36
1993	77.95	74.86	81.02	7.16

*Estimated

It seems very convoluted to argue that water is less renewable than oil or gas.

Immigration to Canada since Confederation

39

Number of Immigrants	Year		Year	Number of Immigrants
10,666	1867		1932	20,591
12,765	1868		1933	14,382
18,630	1869		1934	12,476
24,706	1870		1935	11,277
27,773	1871		1936	11,643
36,758	1872		1937	15,101
50,050	1873		1938	17,244
39,373	1874		1939	16,994
27,382	1875		1940	11,324
25,633	1876		1941	9,329
27,082			1942	7,576
29,807			1943	8,504
40,492	1879		1944	12,801
38,505	1880		1945	22,722
47,991	1881		1946	71,719
112,458	1882		1947	64,127
133,624	1883		1948	125,414
103,824	1884		1949	95,217
79,169	1885		1950	73,912
69,152	1886		1951	194,391
84,526	1887		1952	164,498
88,766	1888		1953	168,868
91,600	1889		1954	154,227
75,067	1890		1955	109,946
82,165	1891		1956	164,857
30,966	1892		1957	282,164
29,633	1893		1958	124,851
20,892	1894		1959	106,928
18,790	1895		1960	104,111
16,835	1896		1961	71,689
21,716	1897		1962	74,586
31,900	1898		1963	93,151
44,543	1899		1964	112,606
41,681	1900		1965	146,758
55,747	1901		1966	194,743
89,102	1902		1967	222,876
138,660	1903		1968	183,794
131,252	1904		1969	161,531
141,465	1905		1970	147,713
211,653	1906		1971	121,900
272,409	1907		1972	122,006
143,326	1908		1973	184,200
173,694	1909		1974	218,465
286,839	1910		1975	187,881
331,288	1911		1976	149,429
375,756	1912		1977	114,914
400,870	1913		1978	86,313
150,484	1914		1979	112,096
36,665	1915		1980	143,117
55,914	1916		1981	128,618
72,910	1917		1982	121,147
41,845	1918		1983	89,157
107,698	1919		1984	88,239
138,824	1920		1985	84,302
91,728	1921		1986	99,219
64,224	1922		1987	152,098
133,729	1923		1988	161,929
124,164	1924		1989	192,001
84,907	1925		1990	213,334
135,982	1926		1991	232,020
158,886	1927		1992	253,345
166,783	1928		1993	255,953
164,993	1929		1994	223,912
104,806	1930		1995	212,238
27,530	1931		1996	*250,000
			1997	*250,000

*conservative estimates

Alexander Graham Bell - 1876

World War II

ITS IN YOUR HANDS
HELP FINISH THE JOB
BUY VICTORY BONDS

Yukon Gold Rush - 1897

The Automobile Drives the 20th Century

1969

NAFTA - 1992

Dr. Banting in WWI uniform, Discovery of Insulin - 1920

48

The History of Work:
Gender-Specific Jobs

The intense restructuring of the 1990's, the transition to the information age, is happening. While there is great pain for many, there is nothing really new about this because the economy has always been changing: the String Revolution, the Agrarian Revolution, the Industrial Revolution and now the Knowledge Revolution. In this section, we will focus primarily on the String Revolution and the Industrial Revolution.

The only ones who welcome a change are wet babies; for the rest of us, it is a damn uncomfortable feeling.

The String Revolution[40]

About 40,000 years ago, someone discovered that, by twisting filaments of fibres together, he or she could make string. It opened the door to new ways to save labour and improve the odds of survival. String can be used to tie, catch, hold and carry. From these notions come snares, fishlines, tethers, leashes, carrying nets, handles, and packages, not to mention a way of binding objects together to form more complex tools. It was the innovation that allowed humans to begin to tame their world.

Toward the end of this period, humans abandoned the nomadic way of life. Previously, families had always been on the move, as sources of ready food came and went with the seasons. As the great ice sheets and herds of tundra animals retreated northward, some clans stopped following the animals and began to settle in villages and obtain their food locally.

Due to the warming post-glacial climate, people began to find it possible to live off wild grain and the animals it supported. Settling down and being able to grow as much of something as one wanted not only changed the patterns of childbearing but also changed the types of tasks to be parcelled out.

From Hungary through the eastern Balkans to Greece, there was a profusion of elegant pottery. The idea of baking a container molded of clay in order to make it hard and waterproof had developed around 6000 BCE.

The men did some of the crop tending but also spent much of their time pasturing the flocks. The use of huge draft animals in fields permanently removed the food-producing portion of the economy from the women's domain because such activity was no longer compatible with child raising. Mines, too, were no place to have little children under foot, nor was the smithy. Therefore, metal-working became men's work as well.

Trade and exploration, increased movement of people and new ideas began to alter society dramatically. At the same time, more efficient food production supported ever larger populations, until the villages had become cities. Around

The rarity of warfare had to do with both the sparseness of the population and the lack of great difference between Haves and Have-Nots.

4000 BCE, truly urban civilization sprang up in Mesopotamia, including writing, laws, contracts, tax records, and much else that literacy enables.

It took almost a millennium for the principal changes to reach southeastern Europe, but by 2500 BCE, the sedentary vase painters and weavers were gone.

When people first figured out how to make pottery, they painted it with exquisite designs, but when the potter's wheel was invented and it became possible to mass-produce the pots, the designs rapidly degenerated into a quick swish of the brush.

Matters changed radically in the Bronze Age due to parallel events in China and Europe involving the advent of a new and more versatile textile fibre. About the time metalworking began, animal fibres became available: wool in the west and domestic silk in the east.

The realization that domestic animals could be exploited while alive for wool, milk, and muscle power, not just for meat when killed, revolutionized human society. As the reliance on grain increased, another related task grew up that fit well with child rearing: grinding the grain for use, once it came in from the fields.

Athenian women lost their social equality during the transition from the Bronze Age to the Iron Age. By the dawn of the Classical Age, the married women of Athens, like their Mesopotamian sisters, were held in harem-like seclusion and scarcely allowed out of the house. Their duties were to take care of the food and the servants (if any), to spin and weave the wool, to bear and care for the children, and to obey their husbands.

With women thus sequestered, the commercial aspects of textiles were taken up chiefly by men. Whereas the women in their homes did every step from preparing the raw wool to weaving and sewing the cloth, the men typically managed the sale and trade of the finished products.

When a settlement was overwhelmed and looted, the men who survived the fighting were slaughtered, while the women and children were hauled away to become captive labourers. Such a life was more like serfdom than slavery. Women greatly outnumbered the men, and the majority of them laboured in the textile industry. To get enough women to spin and weave all the wool, the palace warriors continually had to go out raiding for captive female labour. Much of the populace, then, consisted of captive women manufacturing textiles.

The king was responsible for clothing his retainers as well as his servants and slaves, a common practice in the ancient Near East and in medieval Europe. Thus the cloth made by the captive women did not merely dress people but also functioned at the heart of the economy, both domestic and external. [40]

Industrial Revolution

People have always manufactured weapons, tools, clothing, and other goods. For many centuries, these things were made mostly by hand, manufactured in the home or by individual craftspeople. Most people also produced their own food. About 200 years ago, this system began to change as people began to produce manufactured goods in factories. They did not have time to tend their farms, and so they began to buy their food.

England was the birthplace of this Industrial Revolution. In that country, where textiles were a major source of wealth, a new method of manufacturing was started, called the domestic system. Merchants would distribute large quantities of wool to be spun and woven by the people who wished to earn money by working in their homes. The merchants then paid the people for their work and sold the cloth at a profit.

In the mid-1700's, James Watt invented the 1st workable steam engine. This invention created a new source of power, which led to the invention of a machine that could spin several threads at once. Then a mechanical loom was perfected for weaving the thread. The machines made large quantities of a product quickly and cheaply — mass production. The merchants who had grown rich from the domestic system began to buy the new machines. They built factories and employed workers to run them.

In the late 18th century, James Hargreaves invented a mechanical spinning machine called the spinning jenny. His invention grew from his concern about how hard his wife and daughters had to work to spin their increasingly large quotas of thread. The women in his family were delighted, but his neighbours became fiercely jealous of the "unfair" competition and ran him out of town.

Machines were also invented for making other products. The making of the machines themselves became a major industry, which required large amounts of iron. Charcoal had always been used to smelt iron ore, but iron workers now discovered that iron ore could be smelted much more efficiently with coal. Consequently, the mining industry grew with the need for coal and ore. A method was discovered for making steel from iron, and much stronger and more accurate machines could be made. Manufactured goods and raw materials had to be transported to and from factories, which led to the growth of the shipping industry, railroads, and new roads. Then the telegraph was invented, quickly speeding up the communications industry.

Factories created many new jobs, but they also replaced people with machines. People came from far away to work in the factories and crowded into the new towns. They worked long hours, often in dangerous conditions, for little money. Workers began to rebel, forming groups that were later called labour unions. Eventually, laws were passed to correct many of the harsh working conditions, and the unions gained strength.

The consequences of yanking women and children out of the home to tend these huge, dangerous, and implacable machines in the mills caused devastating social problems. A factory is the antithesis of being "compatible with child rearing" on every point.

The Gender Divide of the Work Force

The most widely held job for men in 1996 was truck driver, while for women it was sales clerk, proving that the jobs men and women do are as segregated as they were in the 1950's.

Census figures show that, although women have streamed into the paid work force in increasing numbers, 32% still hold a job in a top-10 list that includes cashiers, nurses, teachers, office clerks, babysitters and receptionists.

Women are also much more concentrated in part-time jobs than men. In 1995, 12% of female employees worked part-time, usually in jobs that tended to be low-paid and for fewer hours than they wanted, compared to 4% of men.

When it came to full-time work, 4.6 million men worked full-time, averaging 45.7 hours a week, and 3.1 million women worked full-time, averaging 40.8 hours a week. [41]

Highest and Lowest Paying Occupations [42]

Census figures (in constant 1995 dollars) show incomes fell

5 Highest	Men	Women
Judges	$128,791	$117,707
Specialist Physicians	137,019	86,086
GPs and Family Physicians	116,750	81,512
Dentists	109,187	71,587
Senior Managers★:		
Ranges From	90,391	47,323
To	102,971	58,463

8 Lowest	Men	Women
Sewing-Machine Operators	20,664	17,340
Cashiers	20,557	16,977
Artisans and Craftpersons	20,555	13,565
Bartenders	18,899	14,940
Harvesting Labourers	18,683	14,465
Service Attendants	16,520	14,947
Food and Beverage Servers	18,052	14,271
Babysitters, Nannies	15,106	12,662

★ *Depending on industry*

Women Climb Wage Ladder

More women joined the ranks of the 25 highest-paid professions between 1990 and 1995, led by female school principals and lawyers.

While women held 17% of the jobs with the fattest pay cheques at the beginning of the decade, they have joined the 25 top professions in mass numbers over the past few years, filling 22% of those jobs on average by 1995.

At the same time, however, women continued to dominate the lowest-paying professions in equal numbers as 1990, holding 68% of those jobs. [43]

Top 10 Occupations in 1996, by Gender [41]

Male		Female	
...uck Driver	222,795	Retail Sales Clerk	339,025
...tail Sales Clerk	215,345	Office Secretary	311,835
...nitor/Caretaker	185,035	Cashier	235,585
...tail Manager	179,645	Registered Nurse	220,625
...rmer	176,985	Accounting Clerk	219,895
...les Rep	131,225	Teacher, K-Gr.8	187,070
...ehicle Mechanic	127,185	Waitress	176,310
...aterial Handler	119,135	Office Clerk	173,175
...rpenter	112,965	Babysitter	134,560
...onstruction Labourer	104,110	Receptionist	118,985

Women's Work: A Tradition with a Reason

One thing that women typically imparted to their children was language. Consequently, facts about women, their work, and their place in society have survived in considerable quantity. Consider that for thousands of years, women sat together spinning, weaving, and sewing, because of their responsibility for breast feeding. The only other task that fit with rearing children was preparing food. Food and clothing were what societies around the world came to see as the core of women's work.

This image held until the 1960's, when baby boomers began to refuse to accept the gender stereotypes. In *The Feminine Mystique*, author Betty Friedan noted that women were sending a message that the seemingly idyllic life of puttering around the home in a subservient role in the suburbs was more likely to induce a feeling of loneliness and low self-esteem than joy and contentment.

According to StatsCan, in 1966, 43% of women aged 26 to 35 had full- or part-time jobs. Ten years later, the participation rate climbed to 65%, and by 1986, the figure had nearly doubled to 78%.

The changing self-concept of women extended to education. By 1990, women were awarded 56% of all bachelor's and first professional degrees granted by Canadian universities, up from 25% in 1960.

For all the progress women have made in recent years, however, suggestions that we are approaching a state of gender parity are premature. Even though the gender-based wage gap has narrowed modestly over the past decade, by 1997, women working part-time still only earned 2/3 of what men earned. For full-time/full-year workers, the wage gap narrowed slightly to about 3/4 of what men earned.

Men also still dominate the higher earnings groups and make up a relatively small portion of workers in the lowest earnings categories. In 1994, 1.3 million men earned $50,000 or more annually, compared to 275,000 women. The majority of women remained in the lowest earnings categories — 3/4 earned less than $28,000 per year in 1994.

A recent study of 776 Canadian companies found that women made up only 5.5% of board members and 7.5% of company officers. It was also revealed that 57.5% of publicly traded companies had no female directors at all, while 52.2% had no women as top executives.

Even when women are successful, they suffer from "burn-out," according to author Susan Faludi in *Backlash: the Undeclared War Against American Women*. "Behind the news, cheerfully and endlessly repeated, that the struggle for women's rights is won, another message flashes," she writes. "You may be free and equal now, it says to women, but you have never been more miserable."

Demographer David Foot notes that many women are under stress because, like their ancestors, women are the ones who most often take on the job of caregiving. "Many of these women had children later in life than was the norm in past generations. Meanwhile, people are living longer. All these elements increase the chances of someone being responsible for both children and parents at the same time."

The term for this phenomenon is "sandwiching." A 1994 StatsCan study found that twice as many women as men were both working full-time and caring for an elderly relative. "Because women are more likely to be sandwiched than males, sandwiching is an important reason why more women haven't risen to senior positions in their careers," Foot says.

Meanwhile, a 1994 national survey conducted by the Angus Reid Group found that almost half of all working mothers agreed that "if I could afford to, I would stay home with the children." The same survey found, however, that 2/3 of all adults believed "It is not possible to support a family on a single income."

Average Income for 1990 and 1995

In constant 1995 dollars

City	1990	1995	% change
Calgary	$65,430	$63,586	-2.8
Edmonton	59,154	56,090	-5.2
Halifax	57,937	54,241	-6.4
Hamilton	62,945	60,899	-3.3
London	61,362	58,671	-4.4
Montreal	56,418	52,795	-6.4
Oshawa	65,639	62,101	-5.4
Ottawa-Hull	68,726	64,243	-6.5
Regina	58,688	56,844	-3.1
Saint John	52,215	49,138	-5.9
Saskatoon	54,424	53,196	-2.3
St. John's	56,140	52,054	-7.3
Sudbury	60,901	57,109	-6.2
Toronto	71,180	64,044	-10
Vancouver	63,769	60,438	-5.2
Victoria	59,086	59,585	0.8
Windsor	59,321	62,244	4.9
Winnipeg	55,414	53,759	-3

Understanding Productivity

Productivity is the ultimate determinate of the health of an economy; its importance cannot be exaggerated.

The Index of Economic Freedom [44]				
Rank	Country	1998	1997	1996
1	Hong Kong	1.25	1.25	1.25
2	Singapore	1.30	1.30	1.30
4	New Zealand	1.75	1.75	1.75
5	Switzerland	1.90	1.90	1.80
5	United States	1.90	1.90	1.80
7	Taiwan	1.95	1.95	1.95
7	UK	1.95	1.95	1.95
10	Ireland	2.00	2.20	2.20
12	Australia	2.05	2.15	2.10
12	Japan	2.05	2.05	2.05
14	Belgium	2.10	2.10	2.10
14	Canada	2.10	2.10	2.00
17	Austria	2.15	2.15	2.05
17	Chile	2.15	2.25	2.45
20	Netherlands	2.20	2.00	1.85
24	Germany	2.30	2.20	2.10
24	South Korea	2.30	2.45	2.30
27	Norway	2.35	2.45	2.45
35	France	2.50	2.50	2.30
35	Italy	2.50	2.60	2.70
39	Argentina	2.60	2.65	2.65
44	Philippines	2.65	2.80	2.90
53	Israel	2.80	2.80	2.90
62	Indonesia	2.85	2.85	2.85
85	Pakistan	3.20	3.10	3.05
88	Mexico	3.25	3.35	3.35
96	Brazil	3.35	3.35	3.45
104	Russia	3.45	3.65	3.50
117	India	3.70	3.70	3.75
120	China	3.75	3.80	3.80
147	Iran	4.70	4.20	4.20
147	Vietnam	4.70	4.70	4.70
153	Iraq	4.90	4.90	4.90
154	Cuba	5.00	5.00	5.00
154	North Korea	5.00	5.00	5.00

Measures 156 countries scoring on the following economic factors:
• Trade policy • Taxation • Monetary policy
• Banking • Property rights • Regulation
• Black Market • Wage and price controls
• Government intervention in the economy
• Capital flows and foreign investment

The productivity of an economy refers to the average amount of goods and services turned out by each worker (or by a combination of labour, machinery and raw materials) in a particular time. Productivity can be increased by improved technology or by better education.

Increased productivity has come to mean more for less. Economist Peter Drucker explained that the application of knowledge to work had made factories 3.5% to 4% more efficient every year for many decades until there was little work left to be done. In 1924, 74 hours of labour were required to produce 100 bushels of wheat. By 1960, it was 12, and by 1986, it was 7.

Improved productivity through technology is exemplified by the fact that sales of industrial robots continue to rise. The most striking growth has been in Germany, where the number rose by more than 40% in 1995 and 1996, and South Korea, where sales increased at an average rate of 47% from 1991 and 1996. Japan still has more robots than any other country.

In the 1950's, Toyota began experimenting with a new approach to production—different from mass production — called "lean production." The principle combines new management techniques with sophisticated machinery to produce more with less. Lean production, "combines the advantage of craft and mass production, while avoiding the high cost of the former and the rigidity of the latter."

Concurrent engineering, as it has come to be known, is based on the principle that everyone affected should participate as early as possible in development to ensure that each department's needs are taken into consideration before production standards are set. The notion of continual improvement is called *kaizen* and is

considered the key to the success of Japanese production methods. The team-based model creates greater efficiencies by encouraging workers to become multiskilled. Unlike the older corporate model, Japanese teamwork attempts to push decision-making authority as far down the managerial ladder as possible.

The Japanese production model also places a high priority on what is called "just-in-time" production. This idea came from a visit to the US by Taiichi Ohno of Toyota in the 1950's. Ohno was far more impressed with America's supermarkets than with its auto plants — the speed and efficiency by which they kept shelves stocked with exactly the products customers desired in just the amount needed: "We hoped that this would help us approach our just-in-time goal and, in 1953, we actually applied the system in our machine shop at the main plant." The US manufacturing philosophy, on the other hand, is based on "just-in-case" production needs.

Another example of how this works is explained by Michael Hammer and James Champy in their book, *Re-engineering the Corporation.* Before re-engineering at IBM Credit, requests for financing had to go through several departments. Afterward, the time it took to process a request was reduced from 7 days to under 4 hours.

Wal-Mart also owes some measure of its success to its pioneering role in harnessing new information technologies. Data gathered by scanners at the point of sale are transmitted directly to suppliers, who, in turn, decide what and how many items to ship. The process eliminates purchase orders, bills of lading, large inventories, and reduces clerical costs. Companies that have re-engineered to reduce the number of management levels include Eastman Kodak (from 13 to 4) and Intel (from 10 to 5).

Canada's Economic Ranking Drops

Canada has a long way to go in terms of increasing productivity. Despite abundant natural wealth, to stay on top requires world-class human resources and an innovative culture. Unfortunately, Canada has dropped to 14th from 9th in an international ranking of economic freedom released by the Vancouver-based Fraser Institute and 46 other like-minded research organizations.

Hong Kong placed 1st on the list of 115 countries, followed by Singapore, New Zealand and the US. Canada tied with El Salvador, just behind Malaysia, Philippines, Australia, and Panama — tied for 10th place. Algeria finished last.

The report said Canada won high marks for low inflation, low tariffs and a sizable trade sector. But it said high levels of government spending, "are looking more like those of the European welfare states and less like the US." This shows up at the pump where gas is 80% more expensive in Canada (see chart).

The Conference Board of Canada also reported that we are falling behind other countries in the international race to improve productivity. Canada's real output per person is slipping, exporters rely too much on an under-valued currency, and young people "face dismal job prospects."

Unit labour costs, a measure of competitiveness that combines productivity, growth and wage costs — are growing faster in Canada than the US. Canada's GDP per person was 2nd only to the US among industrialized countries until it was passed by Japan and Norway. Germany would have surpassed Canada as well had it not been for unification. Canada's growth of GDP per capita in 1997 and 1998 will match that of the US, but fall short of 5 other countries it used for comparative purposes.

In 1995, the US manufacturing labour-productivity advantage over Canada was more than 40%, compared to a gap of 23% in 1985. Some of this can be blamed on labour laws, which tend to impose a higher cost on employers and reduce the flexibility of labour markets. Minimum wages tend to be higher, hours of work (including overtime) and severance rules more stringent, and labour laws more conducive to the formation and retention of unions.

The report chided Canadian manufacturers for being slow to adopt new technology, and singled out education and training as key weak spots. Canada's high school dropout rate is too high, and too many students are consigning themselves to low incomes by not taking the right subjects. Demand for graduates in business

and science is growing steadily, but enrolment in these fields is stagnant.

Although Canada has a high proportion of post-secondary graduates, our literacy skills are only average. **Because high literates earn twice as much as low literates, lack of education is a low-income "life sentence."**

In contrast, Canada has jumped to 4th place in the 1997 Global Competitiveness Report published by the World Economic Forum. In 1996, Canada ranked 8th. If the 2 most competitive economies — Singapore and Hong Kong — are dropped because of their small size, Canada ranks 2nd, behind the US but well ahead of Japan, Germany, France, Britain and Italy.

The WEF defines competitiveness as "the ability of a national economy to achieve sustained high rates of economic growth" on the basis of suitable polices, institutions and other characteristics such as the quality of the workforce.

The IMF also says Canada will have the fastest economic growth among the G-7 countries in 1998, an improved rate of job creation, an unemployment rate of 8.8%, low inflation, and the smallest budget deficit of any of the G-7 countries.

The Cost of Productivity

Worker stress has reached nearly epidemic proportions in Japan. The government has even coined a term, *Karoshi,* to explain the pathology. A spokesperson for Japan's National Institute of Public Health defines karoshi as "a condition in which psychologically unsound work practices are allowed to continue in such a way that disrupts the worker's normal work and life rhythms, leading to a buildup of fatigue in the body and a chronic condition of over-work accompanied by a worsening of pre-existing high blood pressure and finally resulting in a fatal breakdown."

Worldwide, computerized technology has accelerated the pace of activity at the workplace, forcing millions of workers to adapt to the rhythms of a nanosecond culture.

Ann Finlayson's *Naming Rumpelstiltskin* laments the drive by business to increase the productivity of the workforce. "Companies have been 'reengineered' as though they were pieces of machinery. Workers, like the inanimate objects they manufacture, may be 're-organized,' 'redirected,' or 'reoriented' at will. Corporate hierarchies have been 'restructured,' 'flattened,' 'de-layered.' Workers have been 'de-hired,' 'de-selected,' 'severed.' Entire industries have been de-jobbed."

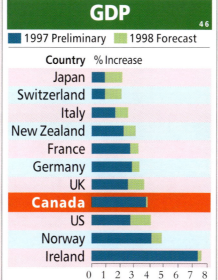

Gassing It Up 45

International gasoline prices per litre in selected locations for 1997

Location	Price
Caracus, Venezuela	$ 0.19
United States (average)	0.32
Bogota, Colombia	0.45
Canada (average)	**0.58**
Tokyo, Japan	1.32
London, England	1.53
Paris, France	1.54
Hong Kong	1.88

GDP 46

■ 1997 Preliminary ■ 1998 Forecast

Country	% Increase
Japan	
Switzerland	
Italy	
New Zealand	
France	
Germany	
UK	
Canada	
US	
Norway	
Ireland	

0 1 2 3 4 5 6 7 8

Canada: A Big Loser in Per Capita GDP

Canada ranked dead last when the Ottawa-based Centre for the Study of Living Standards compared per capita GDP — the paramount measure of a country's standard of living — in 13 OECD countries between 1989 and 1996. We were the only ones to record a decline.

Only Sweden, with no change, came close to matching our dreadful record. The best showing belonged to Norway, although it owed most of its 22.3% increase to North Sea oil revenues. Next came Japan and the Netherlands at 13.5% each, and Denmark at 12.3%. In the middle of the pack were Austria (10.6%), Belgium, Germany and Italy (around 9%), and the US and UK (around 6%).

The Centre's data also showed Canada's absolute level of per capita GDP fell from 2nd to 7th place. In 1989, our per capita GDP was 18% lower than that of the US; by 1996, it was 23% lower.

In productivity growth, Canada's total output for every employed person grew 4.3%, but 11 other countries did better. Again, Norway led the group with a 23% gain, followed by Denmark at 18%. Sweden, Germany, Italy, Austria, Belgium and the UK posted increases of between 11% and 15%, and Japan and France about 10%.

When comparing the 2 lists, the Netherlands was near the top of the 1st and at the bottom of the 2nd because the Dutch boosted their economy not through efficiency, but by adding jobs.

The curious thing about both lists is the strong advances put up by the big European economies despitetheir deplorable records in job creation.

Germany, France,the UK and Italy lost a total of 1.9 million jobs between 1989 and 1996, while Canada added about 600,000.

It appears that in Europe, workers are getting real wage increases because those with jobs have managed to prevent those without from putting downward pressure on wages. Of course, that means the unemployed stay that way and have to count on government for support.

Back of the Pack 91

Percentage change in real GDP per person 1989-96

Country	Percentage Change
Norway	22.3
Netherlands	13.6
Japan	13.5
Denmark	12.3
Austria	10.6
Belgium	9.4
Germany	9.2
Italy	8.0
France	6.4
United States	6.2
United Kingdom	5.9
Sweden	0.0
Canada	**- 0.4**

-5 0 5 10 15 20 25 %

Working Time to Buy a Big Mac

How many minutes do you have to work in order to buy a Big Mac? According to statistics calculated by the Union Bank of Switzerland, a worker in Tokyo leads the way at 9 minutes. At the other extreme, a worker in Caracas, Venezuela, must clock 117 minutes before earning enough to buy the burger. The bank made its calculations — a nifty way of comparing differences in the productivity of labour in different countries — by dividing the price of a Big Mac by the average net hourly wage in cities around the world.

The comparison also reflects different tastes around the world. For example, if a kilogram of bread is used instead of a Big Mac, it would take 14 minutes in Tokyo and 36 minutes in Caracas to earn the bread. In Shanghai, bread is not a staple food, so it takes 143 minutes to earn the loaf, and just 75 minutes for the Big Mac.

Minutes of Work to Buy a Big Mac (Q2-97) 47

Tokyo
Hong Kong
New York
Sydney
Canada
London
Paris
Singapore
Johannesburg
Lisbon
Bangkok
Mexico City
Manila
Budapest
Jakarta
Moscow
Caracas

0 20 40 60 80 100 120

The Dogma of Work and the Cult of Leisure

Supporters of shorter work weeks insist that this will create new jobs and leave workers with more free time. In 1932, a US Senator introduced a bill calling for a shorter week as the "only practical and possible method of dealing with employment." Much to the surprise of the country, the Senate passed the bill, mandating a 30-hour week for all businesses engaged in interstate and foreign commerce, but it failed to pass the House.

More recently, a movement was started in France to shorten the standard work week to 35 hours from 39. Legislation passed in the fall of 1997 that will take effect on January 1, 2000, is intended to significantly reduce France's unemployment rate.

Europeans already have a tradition of longer vacations and fewer working hours. In 1992, the average German put in 1,519 hours a year and received 40 days of paid vacation. Americans work an average of 1,857 hours a year while Japanese workers log more than 2,007. This contributes to the fact that European labour is 50% more expensive than either US or Japanese labour.

In Canada, a 1994 federal advisory group recommended the work week be cut and paid overtime limited. Even labour's position is for a gradual move to 30-hour weeks, starting with a cut in overtime. If such policies were phased in gradually, they could create jobs as well as reduce stress and the potential for accidents.

Job sharing can provide workers with the best of both worlds. The Royal Bank has 1,100 employees sharing jobs, the largest of any Canadian corporation. Job sharing first appeared in the US in the 1970's, and since that time, the number of Canadian collective agreements with such provisions rose from 3% in 1986 to 12% in 1993.

The United Steel Workers are considering shorter hours as a way of sharing in improved productivity – in other words, so none of them lose their jobs. Volkswagen became the first global corporation to move to a 30-hour week when the company and its workers accepted the idea as an alternative to layoffs.

But nobody wants reduced hours without a payoff. Big business is reluctant to hire new workers because it is more expensive to train them than to get extra work from established workers. In recent years, employers have used overtime as an alternative to maintaining a larger workforce to save on the costs of providing additional benefits. In 1997, factory overtime in Canada averaged 6-8 hours a week, one of the highest levels ever recorded.

In addition, trying to create jobs by reducing paid overtime is often a lost cause, according to the conclusions of a StatsCan study. It would hardly cut the unemployment rate, the study says, because the skills of many unemployed Canadians do not match those of people on overtime. Even more significant is the fact that most Canadians who currently work overtime do not want to give up the money, adding fuel to the continuing debate about the usefulness of work redistribution.

Canadian futurist John Kettle estimates that if all the work to be done in Canada today were allocated evenly over the workforce among those currently working and those looking for employment, our work week would average barely 30 hours.

If people are reluctant to shorten the work week, then what about a flexible work force? As demographer David Foot says, "Some people are working more hours a week than they would like, while many more can't find any work at all. Some people work full time although they would prefer semi-retirement, while others, still full of health, energy and talent are forced to retire at 65.

"A flexible workforce is one whose participants, rather than staying in 1 occupation with 1 employer for life, move easily between jobs, employers, and industries. It's also a workforce that allows its participants both to begin and to end their working careers gradually, and that provides plentiful opportunities for retraining. A final advantage is that the part-time senior worker is available to train and act as a mentor to the newcomer."

What people want may be a moot point, since many experts agree that a shorter work week is inevitable. As author Ann Finlayson writes, "Sooner or later, the scenario goes, technology will reverse the ratio of work and leisure: We will spend less time working because there will be less work to be done." The wave of re-engineering is not a temporary phenomenon, but part of a major restructuring of our economy.

"One way or another, more free time is the inevitable consequence of corporate re-engineering and technology displacement," according to author Jeremy Rifkin. "The dramatic productivity gains of the 1st stage of the Industrial Revolution in the 19th century were followed by a reduction of work hours from 80 to 60 hours a week. Similarly, in the 20th century, as industrial economies made the transition from steam technologies to oil and electric technologies, the steady increases in productivity gains of the computer and the new information and telecommunications technologies, a growing number of observers are suggesting the inevitability of reducing work hours once again to 30 and even 20 hours per week to bring labour requirements in line with the new productive capacity of capital."

Productivity Gains

As governments and industries realize that productivity gains resulting from new technologies have led to a rise in unemployment, they will have to reduce working time in order to maintain and create jobs. Governments might also consider extending tax credits for shifting to a shorter week and hiring additional workers.

Meanwhile, although we may seem to be working harder and longer hours, the reality is that we have more free time now than people have had at any point in the past 30 years.

Two American researchers tracked 10,000 people who kept time diaries every 10 years since 1965. They found that every age group, including working couples, has more free time now than they did in the past – largely because they are doing less housework, working fewer hours and retiring earlier.

A study by StatsCan found remarkably similar results. Canadians on average have 5.7 leisure hours a day with men getting 2 more hours a week than women. When women take a full-time job, they cut the number of hours they spend on housework from 29 to 17 a week. On the other hand, the study found 70% of baby boomer women with children felt under stress because they did not have enough time — as did 18% of female retirees.

The Angus Reid Group found that 65% of workers say their jobs are very or somewhat stressful, while 2% say that they are on the verge of a breakdown. More than half say they simply have too much to do in too little time, while another 1/4 blame their stress on balancing work and family.

About 20% of the working population — mostly entry-level employees and middle-managers over 40 — feel trapped in dead-end jobs, are less likely to be upgrading their skills and also report high stress levels. Most people who report they are stressed "have a sense their lives are out of control."

The Importance of Work

If people are so stressed and feel they do not have enough time for other things in life, then how come they cannot be convinced to work fewer hours?

For the individual, "work is at the centre of a normal life," says American economist Edmund Phelps in his recent book, *Rewarding Work*. But why is this so? One reason is that jobs provide mental stimulation, as workers solve problems and learn how to do new tasks well or old tasks better.

Another benefit of work is that the loss or lack of a job can be unhealthy. There is considerable research about the damaging health effects, including premature death, as a result of the loss of a productive role in society. Work fulfills their desire to have a place in society.

As Rifkin says, "Redefining the role of the individual in a society absent of mass formal work is, perhaps, the seminal issue of the coming age."

Workers Lose Taste for Shorter Hours

StatsCan reports that 6% of paid workers, mainly women, would prefer a shorter work week, even if it meant a pay cut. However, this is down from 1987, when 17.3% of Canadian workers said they were interested in a shorter work week, which may doom job-sharing programs.

StatsCan discovered that 66% of workers want to keep their current work week and 28% want more hours and more pay. Already, 14% of Canadians work an average of 6 hours of paid overtime each week. In 1996, there was a jump of 50,000 workers moonlighting when more than 700,000 Canadians held a 2nd job. The mind shift that has occurred since 1987 may be due to a growing insecurity over jobs, a stall in wage increases and growing competitiveness.

The survey also showed that 24% of workers had access to flexible work in 1995, up from 16% in 1991. Women with preschool children were slightly more likely to have flexible hours, at a rate of 28%.

The proportion of Canadians who usually work Monday to Friday, 9 to 5, remained almost the same. In both surveys, 60% of workers said their usual work week was Monday to Friday. Nine-to-fivers dropped to 68% from 70% in 1991, but more than 2 million Canadians, or 18% of the labour force, are now self-employed.

> *In the general population today, about one-third of people suffer severe levels of psychological distress, much of it caused by workplace-related stress.* [48]

Working Hours Shrink

Because of the industrialization of work and the elevation of life expectancy, the part that work plays in our lives is diminishing. In primitive times, people spent 33% of all hours of their lives working. In more recent traditional agrarian culture, the proportion of work hours shrank, but only to 29%. By 1900, it had shrunk to 24%.

During the past half-century, the amount of time we spend working has dropped by almost 50%. Today, the average person works less than 14% of the hours that he or she lives. During this period, the average work week dropped from 70 hours to 37 hours.

The earliest public pension plans were initiated in Europe during the late 1880's. In 1870, about 80% of men 65 and older worked. By 1986, it had dropped to less than 15%.

The proportion of the years of his life that an average Canadian male spent working declined from 67% in 1900 to 60% in 1970, and is expected to drop to 56% in the 1990's, leaving a dramatic 44% of life to spend on other activities of choice.

In the future, education will not just be a preparation for the practical aspects of life or for job advancement, but will be used to make life richer, especially in the 2nd half. Lifted by the coming Age Wave, a new leisure lifestyle focused on a flexible balance of recreation, play and continued intellectual growth and learning will emerge.[49]

> **2.5 billion:** *The number of people on earth who have never used a telephone.*
>
> **3.5 billion:** *The number of people on earth who have never touched a computer.*

Wired or Unplugged: Luddites and Neo-Luddites

Imagine if the early days of the automobile industry had to deal with a powerful buggy-whip producers lobby. Because the car would make the horse-and-carriage industry obsolete, buggy-whip producers would demand legislation to protect them from the technological developments leaving them behind. A pro-labour group would likely request government restrictions — such as government-financed retraining — claiming the sanctity of the jobs of buggy-whip makers.

People who hate technology are called "Luddites" after Ned Ludd, an invented English labourer of the early 19th century. Fearing that new labour-saving equipment would make his job unnecessary, he destroyed it.

Luddism actually arose among the weavers and spinners in the 15 months between November, 1811, and January, 1813. These men were not simply anti-technology, but were fighting to maintain their livelihood and standard of living. Their way of life was

Ned Ludd's "maddened men, armed with sword and firebrand... rushed forth on errands of terror and destruction."

threatened by the machines that could turn out cloth and lace in quantities they could not hope to match. As a result, these skilled craftsmen were replaced primarily by their wives and children, who worked long hours for low wages on the factory floor.

Whole villages became impoverished, and resentment of the machines — and their owners — grew. Armed men began to appear, swearing to bring down the machines and the system that created them in the name of the mythical "Ned Ludd."

Two factory owners were assassinated and more than 1,200 machines were destroyed. In the end, government sided with industry, and British justice was harsh — 2 dozen men were hanged, a similar number were sent to prison, and more than 50 were shipped to the penal colony in Australia. The story of the Luddites shows how industrialization led to the poverty depicted in the social commentary of Charles Dickens, and how the protests set the tone for future unionist reforms.

Today's Luddites use legislation and bureaucracy, not physical force, to destroy technology. For example, in 1998, the federal government decided to continue staffing 27 BC lighthouses despite the unqualifed success in automating the other lighthouses. While lighthouse automation technology will not revolutionize the world, **it exemplifies the neo-Luddite belief that governments should protect the obsolete status quo at the expense of innovation.**

This philosophy can damage the economy by giving government more control over what succeeds or fails. More importantly, if innovators were discouraged from developing new processes — stagnation would result.

Once, even the wheel was new technology. Our history would be much different, and much darker, if a wheel-smashing Luddite was frightened of that development. In the fast-paced information age, it is common to label anybody who hates computers or technology a "Luddite." It has become synonymous with an unthinking, blinkered approach to technology and "anti-progress." What most people forget is that there was a time when Luddites were all too real, and their brief reign of terror was not aimed solely at technology, but at the way in which technology changed their society.

> *These machines were an advantage to the proprietors, inasmuch as they obviated the necessity of employing a number of workers, who were left in consequence to starve. You now call these men a mob. But this is the mob that labour in your fields and mills, that serve in your houses, that man your navy and your army, and whom neglect and calamity have driven to despair.*
>
> — *Lord Byron, 1812, regarding Luddites*

Neo-Luddites

"Neo-Luddism" is a recent movement by a wide array of social critics examining technology's impact on social relationships in our culture. The parallels between our "information age" and early industrial Britain are strong. Technology has changed the way we work, learn, and interact with one another, changing long-standing social structures along the way. The computer chip has created new and rewarding ways of work, but it also means a sharp decrease in the need for skilled labour.

There are signs that a young underclass is growing in this age of "shrinking expectations," and there are fewer job listings that do not involve some computer experience. This reminds us of the conditions that prevailed in a previous era of transition and may help us make better technological choices. With time, "Luddism" may no longer be a term of derision, but refer to wisdom in the face of unfettered technology.

Today, other nations throughout the world are going through their own industrial revolutions. The change from an agricultural to an industrial economy can now take place rather quickly. Modern industry has raised the standard of living in many countries, but it has also created many serious problems. Factory work is often dull and unrewarding, and educated workers want more responsibility. Too many people are still crowding into the cities. Waste products of factories have polluted the air and the water. Industry and governments everywhere are aware of these problems, however, and are using scientific methods to improve the kinds of lives people can have in a modern, industrial society.

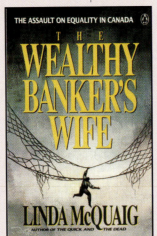

Canada's Neo-Luddites

Maude Barlow, political-activist, author, media commentator and chairwoman of the super-nationalistic Council of Canadians, promotes herself as an advocate for social justice. She joins ultra-left wing journalist and author Linda McQuaig in correctly identifying many of the elements of the emerging class struggle, only to fritter away her arguments with a vocal but extremely naive understanding of economics.

Barlow, McQuaig and their ilk are the Ned Ludds of today; they believe that they can stop globalization and the forces unleashed by information technology with rhetoric and social action. But McDonald's, Wal-Mart, Taco Bell, and Home Depot are indications that the Americans already have invaded. Unitel has become AT&T Canada, Disney markets the RCMP image and even that venerable Canadian institution Tim Horton's has US owners. The US accounts for 70% of our English TV programs and 96% of our feature films.

Barlow and McQuaig miss the point — as they try to defend us from the Evil Empires of Change. Sure, the US has direct investment of over $120 billion in Canada, but Canadians also have more than $80 billion invested in the US. In the decade since the bilateral free trade agreement, the ratio of US to Canadian investment has plummeted from 8:1 to its current 1.5 :1. Americans hold about $30 billion in Canadian stocks, but Canadians hold $45 billion in US stocks.

The reality is that, for better or worse, Canada and the US have integrated economies and those economies are going to become even more integrated in the near future.

We are dominated by aspects of the mega-economy of the US, but Canada does have a positive trade balance with the US and the rest of the world (we sell more abroad than we buy). The US, on the other hand, has a massive, permanent negative balance of trade (they buy much more abroad than they sell).

There *is* a widening gap between the Haves and Have-Nots, and that gap is even bigger, deeper and much more dangerous than the Barlow-McQuaig forces comprehend. Liberals and other socialists still think that they can redistribute wealth through the tax system, but the reality is that the number of "taxed at the source" workers is declining rapidly as self-directed workers evaporate into the underground (black) economy. (See page 137.)

This gap between the Haves and Have-Nots desperately needs attention, but neo-Luddites cannot hold back the unstoppable globalizing forces unleashed by the Information-Age revolution any better than their namesakes could hold back the Industrial Revolution.

It simply will not work to try to apply nationalistic solutions to the borderless reality of the global marketplace.

Trudeau's Legacy: A View from the Right

The federal government attempted to... define Canada vis-a-vis the US by its more generous, i.e., extravagant social programmes. The policy has proved to have completely failed in its objectives and to have been overwhelmingly unaffordable. Trudeau left Canada... the only country in the world to have effectively outlawed private medicine, and current wisdom blames successor governments for the healthcare disaster created 20 years ago. — *Conrad Black* [50]

The transnational corporate conspiracy to destroy human rights in the name of unfettered global capitalism is a busy operation.
— *John Barber, The Globe and Mail* [51]

Home-Based Businesses: Pajama Collar Workers

Home "offices" are not a new phenomenon. Before industrialization and the advent of factories and offices, people operated a business and lived in the back or on the 2nd floor of that business. Rural areas, especially, have a long tradition of residents' sewing, raising rabbits, or making honey alongside their mates.

But over the last decade, the small office-home office (SO-HO) sector has been mushrooming. Today, 2.5 million workers — or 18% of the labour force in Canada — are self-employed. Every 4th household contains a home-based business.

"The home will once again become your castle – rather than just a place to park your butt every night and sleep," says Dr. Paul Tinari, founder and nominal head of the Pacific Institute for Advanced Study.

Tinari joins others in predicting that workers will regroup in the home, where they will use technology to create new roles for themselves as highly specialized information brokers. The school-work-retirement pattern will be replaced by a cycle of work and training.

"Technology has impacted the ability of small businesses to be successful, in many ways more than large business." [52]

What we are starting to see is a fragmentation of what would be called "conventional" companies. Some projections estimate that, in the next decade, less than 50% of the total Canadian workforce will be engaged in full-time, salaried employment settings.

A lot of this can be attributed to corporate downsizing and government layoffs, technological innovations, more women in the workforce, and a shift to a service economy. Many Canadians have been displaced from the traditional workforce and an increasing number have been forced to create their own jobs. Self-employment represents more than 75% of the net gain in employment between 1990 and 1995, and most of the increase has been driven by the lack of alternatives in terms of decently paid, permanent work. During the downsizing that followed the recession, self-employment grew by 9.4%, while hiring, by comparison, increased by only 2.3%.

Surprisingly, though, StatsCan identified that, while 20% started a home office after failing to find employment, 42% said they opted for self-employment because they enjoyed the independence. And, while only 2% of men chose self-employment so they could work at home, it was 6 times as high for women (13%).

For many displaced older workers and well-educated younger workers, unemployment has meant an opportunity for success. Inventive people are anticipating and fulfilling needs, realizing that there are thousands of jobs that need doing — it just takes the entrepreneurial spirit to take advantage of this new knowledge-based economy.

As a matter of fact, in the past 6 years, people who work on their own, selling services to companies, have outnumbered the people who start new businesses 3 to 1. About 90% work in the rapidly growing service sector.

Another reason for the rise in home-based businesses is that companies and governments are increasingly relying on part-time and contract workers. By 1997, the number of temporary jobs has grown to include about 12% of Canadian employees, up from 8% in 1989 and 9% in 1994. [53]

Companies are realizing they can avoid expensive payroll taxes by hiring contract workers. Employers are not required to pay CPP or EI premiums or other benefits, such as disability and life insurance for employees classified as contract workers. In effect, contracting out allows large corporations to "breach an understanding with Canadians that has stood us in good stead for half a century: that employers have an obligation to contribute to the future well-being of their employees as part of doing business in Canada," says author Ann Finlayson. [54]

Do What You Love; Love What You Do

Contract work is a 2-way street. Employers may not pay for benefits, but contract workers can claim more deductions and pay less tax.

The self-employed eliminate the commute, drop expensive business lunches, and say good-bye to parking problems and grooming needs. Productivity also increases — you gain time and make better use of hours.

A reader poll conducted by *Home Computing* magazine revealed why people work at home: 72% said autonomy; 56% said more variety; 43% said time for a change in life; 41% said a desire to do more interesting work; 35% said dissatisfaction with the corporate world; and 33% said a desire for more time with the family.

Whatever the reason, Canadians seem more than willing to take on the responsibility – 60% said that, given a chance, they would rather run their own business than work for someone else.

Those with enthusiasm for self-employment should consider the negatives also. Energy can sag as obstacles and tedium mount. Isolation and overwork are the norm, while people often discover they are

working harder and longer to earn a comparable income. For women, home work can also be more limiting — it is not a substitute for daycare. Behind the romantic image is the reality of people stressed out and working longer hours.

In 1995, the average income of the self-employed was 9% less than the average for paid workers. The flip side, however, is that 4.2% of the self-employed made more than $100,000, compared with only 1.1% of employees. In other words, the earnings of the self-employed are more "polarized."

Self-employment also means leaving behind the stability of a regular income to live from pay often based on projects. The added financial strain and long days often take a toll on personal relationships. Everyone wants to be his own boss, but not everyone wants a 50+ hour work week — and any time you take off is lost income.

Those who have been there warn that the self-employed have to have a good time-management plan. Self-discipline is crucial as you try to balance your personal and family life.

This may seem like a lot to consider, but it is essential for survival of the business. StatsCan reports that half of all businesses do not survive the first 5 years of operation, and only 1 in 5 start-up companies last 10 years. Businesses go bankrupt primarily because the people running them are not up to the task, and the firms lack the basic competencies to survive.

One alternative to consider is to own and operate a franchise. According to the Canadian Franchise Association, 80% of franchised startups are still in business after 5 years. Few small businesses can afford the national advertising, marketing skills and product development that is routine for large franchisors. The downside of franchising, however, is overpriced assistance at every level from franchisors who are more adept at selling franchises than selling a product.

Telework

For those unwilling to make the complete leap to self-employment, another alternative is telework, where staff remain part of a well-defined office culture, but stay in touch from home.

Work-from-home arrangements are becoming more popular, both for recruitment and for improving job satisfaction. This can be a way to compensate people for loss of raises and job security, while cutting their transportation and clothing expenses. In an analysis of Edmonton Telephones, a teleworking staff survey found that productivity and average time signed-in increased, absenteeism and tardiness decreased, and the average number of customer complaints decreased.

Companies also realize savings in real estate costs. IBM, for example, was able to eliminate several office floors when it restructured — more than 20% of its sales and service

organization now work in a mobile fashion.

Pollster Angus Reid warns that organizations that invested heavily in bricks and mortar have, "found themselves on a collision course with a basic new reality: location matters less and less." He cites, as an example, how the cheap, bilingual labour force of New Brunswick, in the words of economist Thomas Courchene, has created "a business solution rather than a location."

But telecommuting demands a leap of trust — there is a fear that out of sight means out of mind. Consequently, home workers outdo themselves just to prove that even if their feet are up on the couch, their thoughts are still very much on the job. Even so, some companies are reluctant to admit they have informal telework arrangements, fearing that they could be creating a monster.

Opportunities for Other Businesses

Home-based businesses and teleworking are creating opportunities for other businesses. Real estate developers are calling almost every project a "live-work development." A home office has become as essential as a living room. Builders are creating homes with separate entrances to the basement office, where there are roughed in amenities – built-in shelves and desks, sophisticated wiring, home studios, and teleport systems.

Big firms should take advantage of the rising popularity of trade shows and publications catering to the home-based market. There are also trade and community organizations, such as the Young Entrepreneurs Association ("young" refers to the age of the business), which run monthly meetings featuring experts in various fields.

Community resources centres are also important, providing a place to access information and resources, and allowing users to share pricey office equipment.

There is room for growth in businesses such as office supply "superstores," copy centres, mailbox services, voice mail and Internet service providers, professional telephone services, courier services (which offer later pick-ups because people do not work from 9 to 5), and computer companies that can do troubleshooting and repairs. All of these services give the SO-HO sector increased credibility, while keeping overhead costs low.

The major banks and other lenders have been on a small-business publicity blitz, too, realizing there is money to be made in providing a range of services to businesses and the people who own them. There has never been a better time for small and medium-sized enterprises (SME's) to find loans, investors or other sources of financing. Access to capital has traditionally been a major problem facing entrepreneurs, especially women, who are often rich in

ideas, but short on cash.

SME's are a hot economic growth sector: They are responsible for 50% of all private sector employment and most new jobs; and Canada's venture capital funds pumped a record $1.1 billion into existing high-growth businesses, including more than 200 start-ups.

While banks have been streamlining their lending

practices, there have also been changes to government programs, such as the Small Business Loan Act, and a transformation of the Business Development Bank of Canada's (BDC) role from a supplementary lender to a complementary lender.

The explosion in home-offices has resulted in a simultaneous one in software designed for those who work at home, as well as growth in multipurpose machines – those that combine fax, copier, printer and scanner. At least 70% of home-based businesses own a computer, printer and a fax; at least 43% are on e-mail; and at least 37% are on the Internet.

The personal computer market is expected to post double-digit growth through the year 2001, with shipments reaching 151.6 million units. Small businesses account for 80% of sales at PC Outlet — specializing in used computers and demos — since most people do not need the most current computer for word processing, using spreadsheets and accessing the Internet.

Insurance agents and brokers can also cash in on the self-employed, since most of them need to look after their own insurance plans. While most plans require the employer to buy a fixed menu of benefits, a more flexible alternative has come to the market for the self-employed to assemble

any combination of life insurance, accidental death, disability, vision, dental, and extended health.

Home-based businesses also require home business insurance since most homeowner policies exclude coverage for businesses carried on in the home. New policies protect equipment, certain liabilities, business records, business interruption, loss of cheques or securities, financial losses caused by inadvertently false statements in advertising, theft, and environmental damage.

Security businesses should experience growth, providing alarm systems to home-based businesses — especially those where confidential information is stored on the computer.

The self-employed will require experts on zoning by-laws — elements that could restrict the number of employees on-site, outside signage, structural additions, and hours of operation. A 1992 study of home-based businesses found that 40% did not know by-laws even existed that affected their business.

As Revenue Canada cracks down on the underground economy, home-based businesses will need the help of tax experts. When it comes to handling taxes for a small business, allowables and disallowables are not always apparent and should not be taken for granted.

Incorporation makes financing easier to secure, allows others to participate from an equity point of view and limits personal liability. Profit earned through an incorporated company is taxed, on average, at 23%. Earned outside an incorporated company, that same "profit" could be taxed at a rate of upward of 50%. On the other hand, administering an incorporated firm is much more complex than a sole proprietorship. It is also a good idea not to incorporate initially, since it would be better to incur early losses personally and put those losses against other income.

Sole proprietorships that report many years of losses may get special attention from Revenue Canada, however. StatsCan estimates that this unmeasured economic activity accounted for between 1% and 5% of the GDP, or at least $21 billion in 1992 — this means substantial unpaid federal, provincial and municipal taxes.

Self-Employed Men vs. Women

The rate of growth in self-employment has been stronger for women over the last 20 years than men, according to the Labour Force Survey. While men represented about 74% of the self-employed in 1976, they now represent 66%.

In many cases, men and women living together were either partners in the same business, or they were both self-employed. Almost 20% of the self-employed had a spouse who was self-employed in the same business. More than 33% had spouses who were paid employees. Self-employed men (40%) were more likely to be employers than women (25%).

If you consult enough networking experts, you can confirm any opinion.
— *Lucent's Laws of Networking*

Unions

What simple policy change would free up a sector of the economy worth $50 billion a year, lower costs, create economic opportunities and be an act of nation-building? Answer: require public institutions such as municipalities, schools and hospitals, in their purchase of goods and services, to stop discriminating against Canadians from other provinces.

In 1994, Ottawa signed the Agreement of Internal Trade (AIT) in order to lift domestic trade barriers that cost Canadians as much as $7 billion a year. Until 1998, though, the deal left out many businesses, including the so-called MUSH sector. BC still refuses to sign the agreement. (See page 172.)

By refusing to sign, BC has driven up costs, protected uncompetitive local industries and blunted the pressures that should have moved BC workers and businesses into those areas where they are competitive.

In Ontario, on the other hand, the Conservative government is interested in getting better value for taxpayers' dollars. When successor rights were in place, privatization was impossible, public sector union leaders invulnerable and taxpayers virtual hostages. Eliminating successor rights gave Ontario a means of curbing the insatiable demands of monopoly providers of public services.

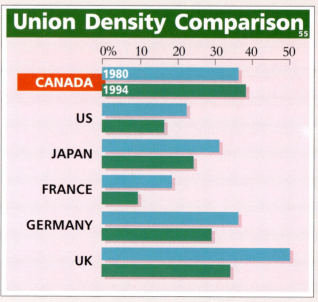

STUDENT   TEACHER   BOARDS   GOVERNMENT   TAXPAYER

DEWAR '97 OTTAWA SUN

> *I've never seen a torrent of anti-labour legislation equal to what I have seen in this government.*
>
> — **Gord Wilson**, *former president, Ontario Federation of Labour*

Two years of union frustration over government rollbacks of labour gains and cutbacks to social issues has the OFL communicating in lurid rhetoric.

Buzz Hargrove, president of CAW, promised that his union would be right behind the public sector unions in any strike action. Some union officials, however, are worried that members of OPSEU, who lost 5 weeks' pay during a strike in 1996, may not be able to afford to support further job action.

Similarly, the CEP is facing its first major cash crunch. The Ottawa-based organization is the 4th largest private sector union. The loss of members, downtime in the pulp and paper sector and steep costs associated with organizing and servicing small bargaining units have all contributed to the union's financial woes.

Kevin Hayes, senior economist with the CLC, said unions are facing pressures not seen since the beginning of the industrial revolution.

Political and economic change over the past decade have slashed the number of workers enrolled in trade unions worldwide by almost 50%. Part of the trend surfaced in former communist countries where workers had abandoned unions they were once obliged to join, but Western countries with long labour traditions such as Britain and France also saw a steep decline.

Only 164 million of the world's estimated 1.3 billion workforce — about 8.5% — belonged to trade unions in 1995, down from 16% in 1985. And only 14 of 92 countries surveyed had more than half the national workforce in unions.

The report recorded reductions of 77% in Israel, 55% in New Zealand, 44% in the Czech Republic, 21% in the US and 17% in Germany. In France, often viewed as a powerhouse of labour, the drop was 37.2%, bringing the percentage down to 9.1% — the lowest in Europe.

Despite the decline, the Finnish European Commissioner still considers the European market inflexible, compared with the US. "If it's raining in New York, you can always find someone on the street selling an umbrella," he said. "But if it's raining in Helsinki, you have to go to the 4th floor of a department store."

Are unions becoming obsolete? Queen's University professor Chaykowski writes that, "the foremost labour issue today is whether unions' time has come and gone... whether the very institution is becoming an anachronism."

Unions may not be losing their purpose, just shifting their focus. In any economy, any time that health and safety,

Union Density Comparison 55

	0%	10	20	30	40	50

CANADA 1980 / 1994

US

JAPAN

FRANCE

GERMANY

UK

fair treatment and good pay are of importance to most employees, but of less concern to employers, then there will be a demand for unions, according to Chaykowski.

In the end, it is probably the growing exposure of Canadian firms to the increasingly union-free US economy that poses the greatest threat to Canadian unions.

But to predict the demise of unions in Canada, however, would be at odds with the facts. Canadian unions are mounting an aggressive crusade for recruits. The CAW spends an average $4 million a year trying to sign up new members; the Steelworkers union has earmarked about 18% of its budget to bringing in new workers; and CUPE plans to increase its budget to $1 million.

"Our strategy is to go back to our roots; do what we did decades ago," says Richard Bensinger, organizing director of the American-based AFL-CIO. In the wake of a vigorous dismantling of labour laws during the past few years, some Canadian unions believe they now face many of the same daunting challenges that have ravaged the labour movement in the US.

They are also bidding to organize the small-business sector as well as branch plants of multinationals — where they can learn much from their American counterparts' attempts to organize.

The Steelworkers opened an institute to train youth to become organizers modelled on the AFL-CIO's school. The BC Federation of Labour launched a similar program in 1997. Unions are also trying to build links with other labour groups and churches to educate their communities about perceived unfair practices by local employers.

> *We are no longer engaged in business unionism where workers treat their membership like an insurance policy... somewhere along the way we had forgotten much of what made us successful. We had become too bureaucratic and technocratic.* — Stan Marshall, CUPE

This reflects the roots of trade unions, when following WWI, the demands for social justice were no longer held in check. Some entrepreneurs and political leaders were disturbed by the implications of the 1917 Russian Revolution and were quick to interpret labour demands as a threat to the established order. The result was the bitterest industrial strife in Canadian history.

In 1919, with a labour force of 3 million, almost 4 million working days were lost because of strikes and lockouts. The best-known of that year, the Winnipeg General Strike, began as a strike by construction unions for union recognition and higher wages, but quickly broadened to a sympathy strike by other workers in the city. Businessmen and politicians feared a revolution. After 5 weeks, the strikers accepted a token settlement, but the strike was effectively broken.

Will unions succeed in their bid to grow again? Catherine

Unions in the New Economy

The terrain for unions has shifted profoundly. There is a need to become more competitive and flexible, but unions have, for the most part, been reactive.

Despite a trend toward union decline among Western economies, the Canadian labour movement continues to be strong. In the US, overall union density (the proportion of paid employees who are union members) has declined to about 15% from 30% in the mid-1960's. But in Canada, union density has remained within the 30% - 40% range.

Overall Union Density		
United States	1960's	30%
	1998	15%
Canada	1960's	30%
	1998	38%

Union coverage ranges from a low of 30% in Alberta to highs of 45% in Quebec and 47% in Newfoundland. Union proponents say they continue to deliver workplace justice and raise the wages of their members above those of comparable workers — by about 10% to 20% in Canada.

Detractors, however, say unions constrain companies from pursuing productivity-enhancing work practices, create losses through strikes and reduce competitiveness.

Ultimately, unions have a redistributive role to play in the economy. Has the nature of work changed so much that unions will simply wither — or have they begun to adapt themselves to the Information Age?

In many industries, technological advances mean firms must continually adapt. This drives further changes in work organization and employee skill requirements. While new technologies enhance productivity, they often require greater flexibility, meaning changes in work rules and organization.

Wages remain a concern, but non-wage costs — payroll taxes or training — have become more critical. Rather than hire new employees, some firms have opted for requiring existing employees to work longer hours. Others have shifted to non-standard forms of employment — part-time or contract employees — to reduce labour costs and take advantage of the flexibility.

The "King" of a flexible labour force is McDonald's, now the target of a Canada-wide campaign by the QFL to unionize as many restaurants as possible. Two Montreal-area restaurants were about to be unionized by the Teamsters, but the outlets were closed and 60 employees lost their jobs. Currently, about 1,050 McDonald's restaurants in Canada employ about 70,000 people.

Much of our existing labour regulation is geared towards the traditional worker, so unions need to find new ways of organizing and representing workers who are not attached to a traditional type of work location. Currently, union density among part-time employees is only 22%. The broader policy challenge is to provide effective protection for workers who are not covered by unions and who fall outside the scope of conventional labour market policies.[56]

Swift, president of the Canadian Federation of Independent Business (CFIB), is skeptical. "People are suspicious of old institutions and unions are one of them. Our economy is taking off like a rocket right now, and it's usually a bad economy that drives people to be radicalized." Surveys have shown that workers are happiest in small, non-union shops, and smaller workplaces are more difficult to organize, which suggests unions' success is likely to be marginal at best.

Generation X-ers, however, may be in the process of creating a 3rd wave of unionism. Canadian unions have been gaining an increasingly large presence in the service sector as workers — many of them just beginning their careers — seek greater job security.

The banking sector has become a target because high profits and technological change are seen as threats to job security. Citizens Bank employees got union certification at the country's 1st "virtual bank;" a hospital established New Brunswick's 1st unionized Tim Horton's; a Windsor Wal-Mart became the 1st to unionize in a chain that has defeated all unionization attempts since it was founded in 1962; and a Vancouver Starbucks reached a contract with its workers, the only unionized employees in the coffee retailing giant. The 1st McDonald's in North America was unionized in BC in the summer of 1998.

At Suzy Shier Inc., a Montreal-based chain with more than 400 shops, a 22-year-old tried to organize a union, feeling that bosses did not respect workers. Organizing and then hammering out a contract took close to 2 years, and a deal was signed in the spring of 1997.

Unions have had some success at big stores — The Bay, Sears, Marks & Spencer, The Brick and Wal-Mart — but breakthroughs in smaller outlets are few and far between. Workers at the trendy Limité chain unionized, but the company shut down the stores shortly thereafter, and the workers never did get a contract.

About 73% of public sector employees belonged to a union in 1997, constituting 43% of the country's total union membership. Newfoundland and Quebec have the highest unionization rates; Alberta has the lowest.

Although the CAW lost members due to plant closings and downsizing, the union maintained its size by merging with other unions, expanding to represent workers in aerospace, fisheries, airlines, rail, restaurants and hotels. Auto workers now represent less than half of total membership. Two-thirds of dues-paying members are in Ontario but the union has members in every province and territory.

WELL, AT LEAST HE DELIVERED HIS RESPONSE QUICKLY AND ON-TIME...

MANAGEMENT

Airbus Industrie of France a few days later.

In the US, the 1997 walkout by 185,000 UPS employees was the biggest American labour upheaval in 25 years — a signal of gathering unrest and disenchantment with the mechanisms that have created prosperity across North America.

American labour experts say the UPS strike crystalized simmering unease about the global economy. It also underlined a dramatic change in labour union strategy. The evaporation of manufacturing jobs cost unions both membership and clout, but they have only recently begun to embrace the cause of the unskilled and low-paid workers at the bottom of the economic pile.

According to the US Labor Department, the economy has grown more than 18% since 1989, while wages and benefits have increased only 2.8%. Skilled white- and blue-collar workers registered a 10% increase in wages between 1975 and 1995. In the same period, the unskilled and lowest-paid workers' incomes fell by 22%.

The International Confederation of Free Trade Unions contends that globalization is destroying jobs. Women — especially those in textile industries in Southeast Asia and Latin America — are increasingly suffering the worst abuses. Their perception is that governments are afraid of missing the benefits of world trade and are increasingly willing to "do the bidding of big business."

Meanwhile, companies have pressed for extra labour flexibility to cut costs, improve global competitiveness and jack up profits. But the trend does little for workers who seek job security and want to start families or buy houses.

In general, women have been picking up the slack for declining union membership among men. In 1997, 45% of union members were women, compared with 20% in 1967.

Although powerful, the CAW's influence does not always work. Hargrove publicly urged Air Canada to buy Boeings rather than Airbuses to replace its 747's, or 15,000 jobs would be lost. Air Canada was not impressed, and the company announced a deal for $1.8 billion with

University Faculty Unionize

Pro-union forces garnered 65% support from the faculty association at the University of Western Ontario to form a union in the spring of 1998.

Voted by a 2-1 margin in favour, full- and part-time professors at the London, Ontario-based institution say they want more control over course load, research and advancement.

They unconvincingly assert that the action was not motivated by salaries or benefits.

Technology Takes the Skill Out of a Job

M.B Wilson has spent his life in movie theatres. Growing up in rural Ontario, he worked in his father's theatre, doing all the things there were to do — cleaning, selling tickets, working the concession stand, and eventually running the projector. In those days, that was a dangerous side of the business because the film was highly flammable.

Like almost all of us, he has worked through technological change. One kind of bulb became another, and eventually the old film reels and complex projectors evolved into a kind of industrial-sized VCR. When M.B. began his career, there were 3 people working in a projection booth, including the re-winder and the projectionist. Then there were 2 people and finally, it was a 1-person operation. Early in his career it was an 800-hour training program to become a projectionist. Lots of different things could go wrong. The projectionist's job was to do preventative maintenance and to know how to fix things when they broke down.

M.B. has worked in Toronto for Cineplex Odeon Corp. for 22 years, has been an active union member since 1969 and served as the Business Manager of his local chapter. He has always considered himself a loyal company employee. In 1996, M.B. was making $21.26 an hour — a pretty good wage for a man with a limited education. He was accustomed to the fact that he often had to work 7 days a week to get in his 40 hours, but it was the business he knew.

For more than 10 years, however, the union has incessantly refused to acknowledge that technological advancements have profoundly diminished the scope of responsibility of the projectionist. Technology advanced, and the projectionist's job was simplified. Cineplex Odeon argued that "Projectionists earn a disproportionate wage for performing a job that is no longer considered highly skilled."

By 1996, Cineplex Odeon, which operated 1,556 screens across Canada and the US, was feeling the competitive pinch that many companies feel in this era of "right-sizing" (in 1997, they posted a loss of almost $87 million, including a more than $64-million charge associated with the sale or closing of up to a dozen money-losing theatres). So they decided that the projectionist's task had become much simpler, and was no longer worth the $20+ per hour and offered a new wage scale of about $14. When the union predictably balked, M.B. and other projectionists were escorted out of their work by private security guards and the company and the union became enmeshed in a labour dispute that resulted in a lock-out. The dispute was settled on company terms, after a lockout of more than 20 weeks.

The new standard for Cineplex Odeon is that, in theatres with 3 or fewer screens, there are no projectionists. Theatre managers, their own jobs having become computer assisted and thereby less time-consuming, have also become a casualty of technological change — they are given a 2-week training course and double as the projectionists. Theatres with 4 or more screens use a projectionist as a 1st-line trouble shooter, backed up by $6.65 an hour ushers who serve as film "threaders."

If something goes wrong in the theatre, the chain will give patrons their money back. According to M.B., the company would rather run the risk of giving refunds or vouchers for future visits than continue to pay the projectionists' higher wages. After all, he says,

> *The concession stands are where the theatres really make their money and, even if patrons get their money back for the movie, they do not ask for a refund on the popcorn or candy bars already in their hands.*

Ultimately, Cineplex Odeon reduced the value of the job, which is true of many jobs today. For M.B., his salary was cut from about $50,000 to a rate that will earn him slightly more than $29,000. He was also expected to perform cleaning and maintenance tasks in the theatre (though the new contract rules out cleaning toilets).

▷ COUNTERPOINT

In a case of "what goes around, comes around," after a merger of Cineplex with US cinema giant Loews, virtually all of the Cineplex executives have lost their jobs (with CEO Allen Karp as the sole survivor). In the words of one industry observer, "They got rid of the big salaries and kept the grunts."

Potpourri

"Mad as a Hatter"

Lewis Carroll's Mad Hatter was a victim of the beaver hat's popularity. In the early 19th century, hat makers, looking for a way to use cheaper furs than the popular beaver, developed a way of turning rabbit fur into a relatively good quality hat-making felt. They used salts of mercury diluted in nitric acid, referred to as a "mercury carrot," to break down the keratin coating on rabbit fur that prevented it from felting properly. The finished rabbit hats were close in quality to beaver, and much cheaper. But there was a drawback: inhaling the fumes of this mixture led to a condition known as "hatter's shakes," an uncontrollable palsy that also affected the eyes and speech. In the final stages of hatter's shakes, the afflicted hatters went mad, the victims of a mercury-induced psychosis.

Canadian "Sweatshops"

You talk to retailers and other people about it, and they say, "Well, you know the economy's global now and we have to compete." Is this how we're going to do it — a race to the bottom for the worst kind of conditions? [57]

The face of the textile industry is changing in Canada. Garments once produced in factories full of hundreds of workers who laboured a set number of hours for at least minimum wage, are now made by thousands of (mostly female immigrant) homeworkers who eke out a living under substandard conditions and for well below the minimum wage.

Legally, employers of homeworkers must have a permit from the Ministry of Labour, and workers must be paid a premium of 10% above minimum wage to account for the use of their home, must receive vacation pay, and must be visited regularly by a ministry inspector. But this often is not the case.

Many blame the change on the FTA, since more than 30,000 jobs in the garment industry have disappeared in Canada since the deal was signed in 1988. Although factories closed and corporations moved businesses to the Third World, small orders continue to be made in Canada through subcontracting and homeworking. This allows flexibility for retailers and adds the marketing touch of a "made in Canada" label – something consumers believe is an ethical alternative to the sweatshops of Asia and Central America. [58]

Sophisticated computers will likely displace humans in the same way that work-horses were eliminated by tractors.
— Wassily Leontief,
Nobel Prize-winning economist

Toronto vs. Calcutta

To compare Metropolitan Toronto with Greater Calcutta, we would have to apply the following conditions:
• Take out 90% of Toronto's wealth and natural resources.
• Pour in the entire population of Quebec and Ontario.
• Throw in inhabitants who come with 18 fully developed languages, with a following of Hindi (35%), Bengali (10%), English (2%), and the related forms of mass media.
• Invite all the major religions and sects in the world with a following of 75% (Hindus) to 25% (Muslims, Christians, Sikhs, Jains, Buddhists, Zoroastrians, Jews, etc.), many of whom have intermingled and grown up together for many generations.
• Throw in several wars, border clashes, massacres, streams of refugees, secessionist terrorism, natural disasters and food crises.
• Include uni-political modelling and economic interferences by the major powers, and the single-minded commercial interests of multinational and financial institutions.

And then, monitor these conditions for 50 years and see what happens!

More and more workers are displaced by new technologies and set adrift in an economic sea with fewer lifeboats to rescue them.
— Jeremy Rifkin

More than 100,000 children live on the streets of Calcutta.

Choppers, Caulkers, Coopers and Colliers: Jobs of the Past

In the 1950's, Newfoundland had 13,600 "swilers" — the name given to those who worked in the seal harvesting process. There are almost none today.

Over the years, the world of work has lost thousands of types of jobs. Since World War II, at least 8,000 occupations have disappeared and more than 6,000 have been created. **Choppers** were workers who handled wool prior to the introduction of the mechanized loom; **caulkers** filled the seams between the planks on wooden ships, before their jobs went the way of the wooden ships themselves; **coopers** built barrels — the only functional method of storing goods — until their jobs vanished with the advent of glass and metal containers; and **colliers** (coal miners) were replaced by efficient, mechanized mining equipment.

In 1906, 85% of Canadians were involved in agriculture; today, we are a big exporter of farmed goods, with less than 3% of our population feeding us all. In the 1950's, 73% of people were involved in manufacturing; today, it is down to 15%, and it looks like in the long-term industrialized countries will drop to around 10% to 12%.

Our evolution from an agrarian society into an urban, industrialized, trade-oriented nation was a rapid one. Between 1896 and 1926, we enjoyed an export boom that transformed our economy. Burgeoning new industries — chemicals and electrical equipment, pulp and paper, automobiles and aluminum — pushed Canada into the wider world and also provided an abundance of new jobs.

Although the Industrial Revolution ultimately led to the mass-creation of high-value jobs and made most of us prosperous, **it took more than a century for the transition to work out.** Moreover, there were terrible social costs before things got better. Industrial production also required punctuality — the ordering and sequencing of hundreds of thousands of workers. In fact, according to pollster Angus Reid, "the frustration of English industrial workers with the indignities of factory work were as likely to lead to smashed clocks as to smashed machines."

Today, the worldwide surplus of at least 850 million workers will continue to increase as the population grows and we get better at using the information technology that will make us more productive.

US Steel, for example, used to have 120,000 employees, yet 16 years later they had increased productivity with only 20,000 employees. At the turn of the century, a modern rolling mill will produce as much steel in a day as a mid-century mill produced in a year. General Electric, another example, reduced worldwide employment from 400,000 to fewer than 230,000 over 13 years, while tripling its sales. Obviously, in many industries, we will need fewer

and fewer workers, which means the inevitability of permanent mass underemployment and unemployment.

The 2 models that we can see are Europe, with high wages and benefits but also high unemployment, and the US, with low unemployment but with many workers who earn meagre wages with few benefits.

While the number of jobs in North America has been growing robustly for the past 15-20 years (1.3 million new jobs in Canada in the last 10 years), the real concern is that there are fewer and fewer "good" jobs — those that pay enough for a reasonably comfortable lifestyle. The purchasing power of the average income has fallen by about 20% in the last 20 years — nearly 20% of the 13.7 million workers who have "McJobs" earn less than what StatsCan defines as below the "Low Income Cut-Off" (LICO) level. Almost half of 15 to 24-year-old workers hold full-time jobs that pay less than the LICO level. The decline in purchasing power has been the principal force behind grown children returning home and the explosive growth of 2-income households. Nearly 75% of all couples aged 20 to 55 now both work full time, up from 33% just 30 years ago.

Nationally, according to the Centre for the Study of Living Standards, the average Canadian worker earns about $600 per week — $30,000 a year, or about $16 an hour. At the bottom end of the earning scale are the people — many of them part-time — in the 2 worst-paying industries: retail and the myriad establishments in what StatsCan calls the "accommodation, food and beverage industry." In the hotels, restaurants and bars, the average worker earns a mere $240 per week — $6 an hour — or less than 40% of the national average. Retail workers are not much better off. Their $360 weekly check — $9 an hour — is about 60% of the national average. **Sadly, the McJob "clerk" is Canada's most prevalent job designation.**

Two-thirds of workers today are involved in some aspect of the service industry. By 2000, 44% of people will be involved as information workers. Of all the new jobs that will be created in the next 10 years, 90% will be created in the service and information sector — the information sector will obviously pay better wages.

Too Many Lawyers

The Canadian Bar Association fears that the biggest problem facing its profession is that there are just too many of them. Canada has almost 50,000 lawyers working in private practice — not including the more than 17,000 working in government, education or   for corporations. Students currently considering law should understand that, even after working hard through university, facing an arduous year of articling and writing the bar exam, their toughest task may be finding work. **Lawyers rank ahead only of politicians with respect to perceived status.**

We thought we knew the rules, but increasingly they no longer apply. And with this transformation, our path to the future has become obscured. — *Angus Reid*

The result is going to be increased productivity and greater job insecurity in every country of the world.

Unfortunately, something went wrong in Canada's manpower planning, and we are currently short about 12,000 Information Technology workers, with the prospect that this shortage will continue to increase.

We live in a society increasingly divided between a prosperous technocratic elite and an immense population of lower-middle-income service drones. For Canadians, our way of life began to change in 1989, when everything began to "downsize"—governments, corporations, unions, paycheques, and job opportunities. Since 1990, although the Canadian economy has grown, on average, by just over 2% per year, the wages of the average worker have dropped by about 5% when taking inflation into consideration. For workers in the bottom 20% of the economy, things are even worse — their wages have dropped by 19%. Kirkpatrick Sale, in *Rebels Against the Future*, warns that, if the economic wizards are right about the long term, the short term is upon us with a vengeance, producing one of the most severe periods of dislocation since the 1930's. As author Nuala Beck says, however, "Few people have the stomach or the desire to go back to the times when social safety nets did not exist, to the Dirty Thirties, when millions of Canadians roamed the country in search of food and shelter."

Paul David of the Center for Economic Policy Research at Stanford University forecasts that by 2010 to 2015, levels of general prosperity and upward mobility in the US will equal or surpass those experienced during the 1950's and 1960's. But for Canada, unable to keep pace with the US, this still means we are facing up to 20-25 more tough years ahead before things turn around.

Michael Hammer, the author of the widely celebrated book *Reengineering the Corporation*, said that, "Reengineering takes 40% of the labour out of most processes. For middle managers, it is even worse; 80% of them either have their jobs eliminated or cannot adjust to a team-based organization that requires them to be more of a coach than a taskmaster."

Basically, contemporary organization structures dictate that only about 1 of 3 managers in the Industrial-Age paradigm have a viable role in the Information-Age paradigm. This painful transition is the core of the most potent resistance to organizational change. It means that managers have to learn to move from the command and control tradition to the contemporary organization paradigm where they are working coaches.

Their resistance is understandable, given that this new paradigm decimates huge number of managers. Economist Peter Drucker first targeted middle managers as expendable in the knowledge economy in his 1993 book, *Post-Capitalist Society*. "They relay orders downward and information upward," he writes. "When information becomes available, they become redundant."

The new economy demands a more efficient, more flexible, technologically oriented workforce — equipped with degrees and credentials, one that communicates on the Internet and works in teams. By 2000, more than a billion people across the world will be users of personal computers — a dramatic increase from 450 million in 1994.

The pace of technological change is so fast now that we must be prepared for a worker to change not only jobs, but entire skill sets, 3 or 4 times in a lifetime.

In the 1950's and 1960's, a person could choose to do something new, exciting, and innovative in life but could also choose to say, "That's not for me: I am going to play it safe. I am going to stay in my home town and have a nice comfortable career in a salaried job." That 2nd choice no longer exists for the vast majority. Some may mourn the loss of "the good old days" of lifelong jobs, but others see this as an opportunity to lead a more varied and interesting life — full of the challenges of lifelong learning. As in the discussion about paradigm shifts (see page 2), do we see the old hag, or can we see the young woman in the picture?

Gallup reported that 2/3 of Canadians expect the next generation will be worse off than they are, but "turmoil of transition" is not the whole picture. Some industries will be winners and some losers, and you will be further ahead if you apply yourself in an industry/profession that has a vibrant future.

YES, IT'S BEEN A ROUGH JOB MARKET FOR ME...

FIRST, I WENT TO WORK FOR A FOREST COMPANY...

...BUT WE RAN OUT OF TIMBER.

...THEN I GOT A JOB AS A COMMERCIAL FISHERMAN...

...BUT THE SALMON DISAPPEARED

...THEN I TRIED A JOB AS A GOVERNMENT CLERK...

MINISTRY

...BUT THE GOVERNMENT DOWNSIZED

...SO I THOUGHT I'D GIVE THE RETAIL SECTOR A GO...

Eaton's

Over $100 million worth of Prozac — an anti-depressant — sold each year in Canada, making it one of the most heavily prescribed drugs.[59]

More Stress

With the workplace changing — and the nature of work itself changing — stress, not downsize or outsource is the single word that captures the human dimension of the workplace today. No wonder people are concerned about their futures when the very concept of a "permanent" job is being challenged on all fronts, and job security is considered a perk of days gone by. Studies find that people are sleeping less, have insufficient time with their spouses and families, constantly feel behind on their work and are hounded virtually day and night by an internal pressure that says, "hurry." Finding the path to success is difficult when the traditional signposts no longer stand.

People need to discern what they have control over and what they do not. Where you do have control in this changed market is in what you do as a worker, knowing that even if this company does not appreciate you, the next one will see what you can do.

Part-Time and Temporary Employees

While full-time, salaried positions are on the decline, corporate Canada's passion for part-timers is growing. According to a poll for *Report on Business* magazine, nearly 50% of Canadian companies now employ part-time workers, up from 41% in 1994 and 35% in 1989. Between 1982 and 1990, 3 of every 4 new jobs in Canada were full-time. Since 1990, just 1 in 4 has been full-time. This movement is not surprising, given that part-time employees earn 20% to 40% less than full-time workers doing comparable work. Part-timers now make up 30% of the average firm's total workforce, more than triple the 1989 level. Among companies with more than 250 employees, 69% used part-timers; among firms with fewer than 10 employees, it was 44%.

Almost half the jobs created in Canada in the last 20 years have been "non-standard" — part-time, temporary, or contract positions — now accounting for about 30% of all employment. Most of these jobs are without pensions, benefits, or job security. The impact has been felt mostly by young Canadians, with 45% of employed 15- to 24-year-olds holding part-time jobs in 1995, up from 21% in 1976 and 33% in the late 1980's. The situation is similar in the US, where it is estimated that more than 35% of the work force will be "contingent" workers by the turn of the century. In the Netherlands, 33% of the workers are part-time, in Norway more than 20%, and in the UK nearly 40%.

Meanwhile, "temping" may be the job model of the future. The surge in temporary and short-term employment is outpacing other forms of job growth. Manpower Inc., a temp agency with 1.6 million employees worldwide, has become the biggest private-sector employer in North America with 827,000 employees.[60] A study published by the Canadian Council on Social Development estimates that there are now more than 1 million Canadians in some form of temporary employment.

Temps provide a "peripheral" work force that can be hired quickly during business upturns and easily dismissed when they are no longer needed. This is not necessarily all bad, since individuals with specialized skills and expertise have the advantage of shifting from 1 potentially lucrative contract to another.

One major downside is that the legal protection for temporary workers falls short of that available to those in permanent jobs, with the Employment Standards Act not requiring the same notice of termination, maternity leave or severance pay. Economist Jeremy Rifkin calls these non-standard workers "the new reserve army," since their labour can be used and discarded at a moment's notice and at a fraction of the cost of maintaining a permanent work force.

How Bad Things Were:

1997: 30,000 applicants apply for 50 Alcan jobs.

1985: IBM reached its employment peak — 406,000 — double what it is in 1998.

COMOROS

REUNION

MADAGASCAR

Gene-Spliced Vanilla Costs 100,000 Jobs

Two US-based firms announced recently that they had successfully produced vanilla from plant-cell cultures in the laboratory. Currently, more than 98% of the world's vanilla crop is grown in the small island countries of Madagascar, Reunion and Comoros. With the new gene-splicing technologies, researchers produce commercial volumes of vanilla in laboratory vats, eliminating the bean, the plant, the soil, the cultivation, the harvest, and the farmer.

While natural vanilla sells on the world market for about $1,200 per pound, the genetically-engineered version can sell for less than $25 per pound. The result? **More than 100,000 farmers in the 3 vanilla-producing countries are expected to lose their livelihood over the next few years.**

Vanilla is not the only product that will be affected. A Dutch study estimates that 10 million farmers in the Third World may lose their jobs as laboratory-produced sweeteners begin invading world markets. The tragedy is that many Third World nations rely solely on 1 or 2 export crops. Biotechnology will bring about the collapse of many national economies dependent on labour-intensive crops.

The Real Cost of Unemployment[61]

Society generally tends to underestimate the magnitude of the costs of unemployment because most are invisible. They think that the costs only amount to transfers to the unemployed through employment insurance and social assistance programs. While unemployment is certainly costly to the unemployed worker who suffers a loss of wages, it also causes a loss of production for society as a whole, which means a loss of income for everyone.

In reality, employment insurance and social assistance benefits represent only the tip of the iceberg. All of the additional revenues, such as extra company profits and additional taxes that could be generated by the production of goods and services, are the hidden part of the iceberg.

During times of unemployment, everyone suffers. Even those who have jobs lose in 2 ways: The weekly average of hours worked is lower (less overtime, or full-time workers become part-time) and the proportion of well-paid jobs decreases. Businesses also lose heavily due to lost returns on capital. And governments are hit hard through loss of direct and indirect taxes, and expenses for employment insurance.

Inefficiencies abound in businesses, unions and government when there are labour surpluses. Companies have no interest in stabilizing their workforces to reduce the turnover rate, while anti-inflationary policies (like those in Canada), create financial pressure due to the weakness of domestic and external demand. Costs may be reduced due to competition in the labour market for existing jobs, but businesses which should adopt competitive conduct based on innovation and quality, rather than costs, invest little in training and do not commit themselves to innovative strategies.

Unions take a defensive stance as attempts are made to reinforce rules protecting jobs. While full employment is conducive to greater flexibility and efficient management of human resources, unemployment creates resistance to organizational change (reducing the number of classifications, broadening job descriptions, demanding greater versatility) and technological change.

Unemployment also has a significant social and economic impact on society: increases in delinquency, criminal behaviour, general degradation of health, multiplication of suicides, discrimination, dependency, poverty, and economic insecurity. It further blocks attempts to achieve economic goals such as growth and balanced budgets.

There is increased discrimination against various groups (young people, disabled workers, immigrants), implementation of employment equity is difficult, and older workers (55+) either remain unemployed much longer when they lose their jobs, or feel pressured into early retirement, thereby lowering the relative income of seniors.

Endemic unemployment increases income disparities, too, as the new economic environment emphasizes non-standard jobs and new labour management practices. It also leads to an increase in the average duration of unemployment. Scarce government funds are then spent on programs aimed at getting the long-term unemployed back to work, when they should be spent on preventative steps like on-the-job training.

Governments review social security programs during times of high unemployment and generally make them more selective and less generous. The result is further segmentation of the labour market, institutionalization of high rates of unemployment, and increasing economic insecurity.

Private investment in various sectors of the economy is also discouraged; future generations therefore receive a smaller inheritance in the form of economic infrastructure. When employment does not grow enough to absorb surplus labour, financial solutions (like reducing spending and increasing taxes) only make the deficit worse by slowing down the economy and hindering job creation.

In order to bring unemployment down without creating excessive inflationary pressures, a strategy encompassing active labour-market and regional-development policies, as well as a negotiated incomes policy should be implemented. This type of economic regulation of employment — social regulation — depends on the cooperation of governments and the private sector, represented by business and labour organizations, which must jointly share responsibility for its orientation and administration.

> *The factory of the future will have two employees — a dog and a person. The person's job is to feed the dog, and the dog's job is to make sure the person does not touch anything.*
> — *Warren Bennis*

Best Practices

The Factory of the Future

The factory of the future will also have fewer managers. Already, at Japan's LTV-Sumitomo plant, the job categories have been reduced from 100 to 3. The new classifications are "entry-level," "intermediate," and "advanced." Workers have been taken off hourly wages and put on salaries. New self-managing teams have been given greater control over the shop floor, significantly reducing the number of managers on the payroll.

At the Victor Company, also in Japan, automated vehicles deliver camcorder components and materials to 64 robots which, in turn, perform 150 different assembly and inspection tasks. Only 2 people are present on the factory floor. Before the introduction of intelligent machines and robots, 150 workers were needed to make the camcorders.

In terms of agriculture, although nearly 50% the people on the earth still farm the land, technological changes in the production of food are leading to a world without farmers. One can only imagine the consequences for the 2.4 billion people who still rely on the land for their survival.

> It is better for all of us to be at work some of the time than for some of us to be at work all of the time while others are not at work at all. [62]

Unemployment: **The Past**

The 1st compulsory national unemployment insurance program in Canada was established in 1940, funded jointly by employers, employees, and the federal government in response to an unemployment rate that rose to 20% during the Great Depression. While answering the needs of the jobless, the program also reinforced a philosophy that a compassionate society believes that helping the unemployed is a shared responsibility, just like health care and education.

Unemployment: **The Present**

Big layoffs have been a part of the Canadian economy for a long time, but the idea that we are experiencing a greater threat now of permanently losing our jobs is simply a myth. According to StatsCan, from 1978 to 1993, the number of workers permanently laid off each year varied little. In 1982, the worst year of the recession, 1,205,000 people got pink slips. In 1989, when the economy was booming, the number was 1,137,000. With another recession underway in 1991, it was 1,284,000. In other words, there has been little difference in the number of people laid off in each of the last 20 years.

In fact, the proportion of workers who were permanently "separated" from their employers fell during each recession because fewer people quit — they stayed put because they could not find other work. No matter how strong or weak the economy, the proportion of workers who leave their jobs remains at around 21.5% on average.

What is different, according to StatsCan, is which groups were affected by the layoffs.[63] The health, education and welfare sectors incurred a 19% increase in layoffs during the 1990's recession as compared to the 1980's recession. Additionally, the layoff rate was higher for men, for workers under 35 and over 55, for low-income earners, and for those working for small companies.

The hiring rate, on the other hand, is much more volatile. Of the 16 years covered in the study, the hiring rate went from a low of 14% of total employment in 1982, up to about 26% in 1987-1989, dropping down to 18% in 1991-1993. Although employers are not hiring, they seem to be buying the services of the self-employed, which could explain why self-employment has accounted for 3/4 of the net employment growth in Canada since 1989.

It is important that people dispel the myth that they are likely to lose their jobs, since job anxiety can be a self-fulfilling prophecy. When people are worried about losing their jobs, their confidence in the economy erodes, consumer spending declines, businesses lose sales and — they have to lay off workers.

Natural Rate of Unemployment

The natural unemployment rate is a term used to define the lowest unemployment rate without inflationary pressures (See page 73.). The rate increases with high unemployment benefits, long-term social support, high minimum wages, restrictive labour rules, unionism, non-privatized business, and interventionist governments. These factors drive up costs and create inflexible labour markets as well as conditions in which many of those who lose jobs find it more rewarding to stay home and collect benefits.

The Bank of Canada considers 8% unemployment as full (non-inflationary) employment. The US, with lower taxes and few labour restrictions, considers 5% as full employment.

Sometimes, the guidelines introduced to reduce unemployment actually reinforce interventionist strategies that increase the natural rate of unemployment. Left to its own devices, the economy tends to create jobs.

In the EU, for example, 12 of the 15 governments are left-leaning social democrats, leading economists to predict that European unemployment will remain at 10+%, despite improving economic conditions. The late 1990's European jobless rate hovered around 12% — with France, Germany, Italy, Spain, Ireland and Finland having the highest rates.

In contrast, the British unemployment rate dropped to around 5% — the lowest in more than 17 years. The number of Germans out of work set a post-war record — about 10% in the west and approaching 20% in the east. What is particularly chilling is that, in some towns, there are more unemployed than in 1933, when the Nazis were elected.

The OECD warns that, even if growth increases in the EU, countries that refuse to see the merits of flexible labour markets will pay dearly. Where it is most costly to fire someone, fewer workers will be hired. Where wages and benefits and taxes and hours of work limit an employer's right of choice and return on investment, less money will be spent on job creation. Where governments control, the private sector will continue to be handicapped.

Extreme environmental regulations are also a factor, along with tax rates that destroy incentives and heavy debt loads that reduce investment. More than 46% of the unemployed workers in Europe have been without jobs for more than a year — compared to the US, where the number is only 6%.

Europe's "job killers" — especially taxes and unions — are also problems in Canada. Our effective tax rate (direct and indirect) is 50%; if the government lowered our taxes, it would stimulate economic growth, competitive advantage and employment growth. Trade union participation accounts for much of the gap between Canadian and US unemployment rates — both in terms of what are considered natural rates of 8% and 5%, and for the performance gap between the 2 economies. In 1960, each country had a 30% unionization rate; today, the US rate is only 15% while the Canadian rate has grown to 38% (See page 63.).

> Contrary to John F. Kennedy's often quoted comment, "a rising tide lifts all boats," the economic tides of the last 15 years have not lifted all boats. Since 1985, the correlation between economic growth and wage growth has disappeared.

The Real Rate of Unemployment

Many experts believe that the unemployment figures hide the full extent of the labour surplus Canada currently faces, since as many as 7% have simply left the labour force because they have abandoned hope of finding a job. Another group of unemployed has retreated to the safety of post-secondary education because they could not find jobs. Some believe that Canada's "unofficial" unemployment rate — measured by pre-recession workplace-participation standards — is 13%, or even higher.

In Japan, which claims an unemployment rate of 2.5%, if the high number of discouraged unemployed workers and unrecorded jobless is added to the totals, the figure might be as high as 7.5%.

Officially, according to StatsCan, Canada's unemployment rate has not been as abnormally high as the fearmongers would have us believe. The national unemployment rate for the 10-year period between 1987 and 1996, averaged 9.5%; the unadjusted rate in September of 1997 was 8.2% — the lowest in 7 years. While keeping in mind that a high participation rate (the percentage of people over 15 who are seeking work) is positive, the rate ranged between 65.3% and 67.5% during the last 13 years. In July of 1997, it was 66.9% — the highest in 7 years and only 0.7% below the historic high of the 1989-1990 "boom."

By world standards, Canada has an excellent record in recent job creation. At the end of 1997, Ontario and Prairie Provinces had unemployment rates of 7.7%, while Quebec and the Atlantic provinces had unemployment rates of 12%.

The fearmongers would also have us believe that our youth unemployment is disproportionately high — with a rate of 17%, it is almost twice the national average of the entire labour force. In reality, Canada has had more than 400,000 unemployed youth in 15 of the last 20 years, including more than 600,000 in 1983. **The 1997 rate for youth, as a ratio of all unemployment, was 1.68 — virtually the same as it has been for the last 50 years.**

Immigration and Unemployment

Despite the fact that the recent recession reduced the availability of jobs for everyone — particularly the young and inexperienced — we already had an abundant supply of labour due to the fact that the entire baby boom is present in the labour force at the same time and the federal government has increased immigration levels to 250,000 per year. This immigration level, by far the highest per-capita level in the world, further increases the supply of labour and adds to the downward pressure on wages.

Canada allows immigration at a rate roughly double the other two major immigrant-receiving nations — the US and Australia. Canada also accepts 4 times the percentage of refugee claims as the average of the other 16 refugee-accepting countries.

Our extravagant and disjointed immigration policy adversely impacts the job market. A coherent immigration policy would dramatically increase the proportion of qualified immigrants in relation to the growing number of "family-class" candidates. (See page 42.)

> *Entrepreneurship is critical to job creation because only through the creative thinking and risk taking of hundreds of thousands are we going to extricate ourselves from the corner the new economy has painted us into.* — Angus Reid

Unemployment: **The Future**

The economy created 300,000 jobs in Canada in 1997, and is forecast to do even better in 1998. The reasons for job creation include improved outlook for business, non-residential investment, new house construction, and export growth.

Even with this upbeat news, economist Jeremy Rifkin predicts that "redefining opportunities and responsibilities for millions of people in a society absent of mass formal employment is likely to be the single most pressing social issue of the coming century."

The advent of new technology, coupled with re-engineering, will continue to reduce skill needs of the workplace. Most formal work will pass to machines, while the value of labour will become unimportant in the production and distribution of goods and services. Andersen Consulting estimates that in just one service industry — commercial banking — re-engineering will mean a loss of 30% to 40% of the jobs over the next 7 years.

The old rule was that a good education equals a good job, but now most professions have surpluses — lawyers, doctors, teachers, and dentists. Resident dieticians have been replaced by large-scale catering services. Internal competition within professions is increasing because of technological advances, such as software replacing accountants.

The good news is that, as our society ages, growth of the workforce will slow down. The supply of capital will increase, wages will rise and interest rates will come down. Capital will become cheaper, increasing the incentives to invest in new technology as an alternative to increasingly expensive labour.

Early in the new millennium, however, the baby-boom echo will mean another increase in the number of young workers in the job market.

Employment Growth

64

Cumulative growth of employment by class of worker

— TOTAL EMPLOYMENT
SELF-EMPLOYED
EMPLOYEES

(1000's of Workers: -400 to 1,000; years 1990 to 1997)

Canadian Natural Unemployment Rates*

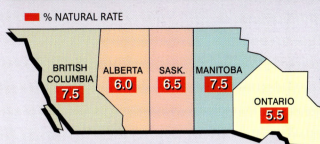

■ % NATURAL RATE

BRITISH COLUMBIA **7.5**

ALBERTA **6.0**

SASK. **6.5**

MANITOBA **7.5**

ONTARIO **5.5**

QUEBEC **10.5**

NEWFOUNDLAND **16.5**

NEW BRUNSWICK **11.5**

NOVA SCOTIA **10**

PRINCE EDWARD ISLAND **11**

*Defined as the lowest rate consistent with stable inflation

Using a technique developed by analysts at the US Federal Reserve Board, the natural unemployment rate is defined as the lowest rate consistent with stable inflation.[65] It is seen as the true measure of the degree of structural unemployment in a region and can be influenced by demographics, education levels, worker mobility and reliance on seasonal unemployment.

Across Canada, this rate varies from a low of 5.5% in Ontario to a high of 16.5% in Newfoundland. Canada's overall rate has fallen from 8.5% in the 1980's to 7.5% in the 1990's, but the actual unemployment rate is still stuck at almost 9%. Quebec and the Atlantic provinces all have natural unemployment rates of more than 10% because they have fewer university graduates, rely heavily on seasonal jobs, and have relatively more young people — whose jobless rate is higher. Ontario, on the other hand, has a highly educated labour force, a well-diversified economy, and high-technology growth areas.

The Prairie provinces have seen their jobless rates fall below the natural unemployment rates and, as a result, widespread labour shortages and strong wage pressures have emerged. All 3 provinces cured their unemployment problems not by make-work projects, but by eliminating their deficits, launching debt repayment programs and implementing tax-relief measures.

BC's rate of 7.5% is significantly higher than neighbouring Alberta's 6.0% because of greater reliance on seasonal industries, militant trade unions and government policies that are unfriendly to business. A vivid example of this government interference is the minimum wage, which has risen 40% since 1991, under the NDP governments of Mike Harcourt and Glen Clark. BC's minimum wage is $7.15, compared to Alberta's $5.00. The adverse impact of BC's interventionist policy resulted in a 16.5% youth unemployment rate contrasted with Alberta's 10.7%.

Unemployment is not a coast-to-coast problem — there is a national shortage in marketing, design, engineering, computer programming and oil and gas technology.

Okun's Law

Calculating the "hidden part" of unemployment was pioneered in 1962 by US economist Arthur Okun. By running a series of statistical tests, Okun concluded that each percentage point above 4% in the unemployment rate equals a 3% reduction in the real GDP. For example, if the unemployment rate rose from 4% to 5%, the GDP would drop by 3%. *That ratio of 1:3 between variations in the unemployment rate and production is called Okun's Law.*

Okun specified that potential production corresponded to what the economy could produce while maintaining stable prices and free markets. A 4% unemployment rate represented the natural rate of employment (or, the rate without increasing inflation). Many economists believe that the natural rate of unemployment has increased. In Canada, for example, it was 5% between 1973 and 1976, rising to 8% in 1987. Finance Minister Paul Martin believes that Canada's jobless rate could drop to US levels without triggering inflation, but his own officials argue that our richer social programs and less mobile work force will keep unemployment higher and that once the rate falls below 7%, inflation will pick up. Whether we follow Okun's Law or not, the unemployment rate is never zero. There are always jobless, either because they are looking for better jobs or because market fluctuations are reducing employment in one sector while increasing it in others. (This is called frictional unemployment.)

As the unemployment rate goes down, the increase in employment is more than proportional because an improving economy also creates jobs for those who were previously absent from the workforce; average hours worked increases, as does productivity. With this in mind, although Canada spent "only" $13.7 billion on employment insurance in 1995, the effective indirect costs of unemployment in 1997 were approximately $140 billion (17.5% of GDP), or more than $9,000 per taxpayer. [61]

Comparative Unemployment Rates [66]

Country	Unemployment Rate (%)
Japan	3.3
Luxemburg	3.4
Austria	4.4
US	5.3
UK	7.1
Portugal	7.3
Australia	8.8
Belgium	9.5
Germany	9.6
Canada	9.7
Sweden	10.9
Ireland	11.6
France	12.5
Finland	15.0
Spain	21.7
OECD average	7.5

0 2 4 6 8 10 12 14 16 18 20 22 24

TAGS: The Atlantic Groundfish Boondoggle[68]

The scope of the impact of the Atlantic groundfish moratorium, initiated for an indefinite period in 1994, was unprecedented in recent Canadian economic history. Some 40,000 workers were affected, most living in areas already experiencing high unemployment and low economic growth.

At the time of the closure, the government introduced The Atlantic Groundfish Strategy (TAGS), a $1.9 billion program designed to train fishermen away from the sea. The highly criticized program was scheduled to conclude in May of 1998, but a government review observed that the potential termination of the program was causing a great deal of anxiety. It was extended to August of 1998, giving the government more time to devise a replacement plan.

About 79% of the TAGS clients categorized as "heavily reliant" reside in Newfoundland. Total TAGS benefits paid into the province in 1995 were $265.3 million, compared to provincial social assistance expenditures of $244.9 million during fiscal 1995-96. **The "payroll" for administering the program in Newfoundland is greater than that of any local private sector employer!**

Financial hardship is nothing new to people involved in the Atlantic fishing industry, although it has taken many a long time to accept the bitter reality that their livelihood is lost forever. As far back as 1933, a Newfoundland Royal Commission concluded that, "Employment between September and June is at best available to only 4,000 to 5,000 men, and that for only part of the time." In 1993, the Cashin Task Force said that, "By itself, the fishery cannot provide a good living to all who partake. It could not do so when the resource was at its peak, and emphatically cannot do so today."

When the moratorium was introduced, fishers and plant workers believed that the government had a moral and legal obligation to provide income support, since it was responsible for mismanagement of the fishery. Most believe the fishery failed because government scientists did not have the backbone to stand up to bad political decisions, and that the Department of Fisheries and Oceans distorted research and intimidated scientists into silence. Ill-informed spokespersons also conveyed false information to the public, emphasizing the role of seals and cold water — not overfishing — in the cod's collapse.

The federal government, however, did commit almost $2 billion to a program that provided vital assistance to thousands of individuals who would otherwise have suffered financial hardship, but subsequently has been sharply criticized for creating a plan that supported people, but did not put them back to work.

There is strong consensus that the TAGS clawback should either be eliminated, made equivalent to the EI clawback or amended to operate on a sliding, or graduated scale in order to provide greater incentive to work beyond the $26,000 income level. Most TAGS clients view the clawback as a disincentive to work and as contributing to a "stay-at-home" culture.

Many believe that the government should support mobility incentives for those opting to leave because there is virtually no demand for real estate in many of these communities, and many are forced to simply walk away from their homes. In some Newfoundland towns, there has been an out-migration of as much as 30%, eroding the tax base and leaving behind villages of seniors.

Retraining may be difficult, however, for the more than 26% who are over the age of 50, and the further 18% who are between the ages of 45 and 49. There are serious implications, too, for the approximately 72% who have not completed high school, and especially the 40% who have completed less than a grade 9.

Consequently, there is strong support for an early

> *The vast majority of those affected agree with the principle of a training program, but feel there should be more of an effort link training to real employment opportuni — even if it requires training for jobs outside the community or the province*

retirement and licence buyout scheme, although one of the biggest problems with TAGS was that it did not fairly take into account age as well as years of experience in its criteria. As a result, many who had only worked in a plant for 5 years were able to access an early retirement package simply because they were old enough, while many others who had 25 or 30 years' experience did not qualify because they had not reached the age threshold.

In addition, very little capacity was removed in the 1st TAGS licence buyout initiative. Fishers felt the buyouts did not reflect the true value of the licences and did not provide a favourable allotment for small boat owners.

Whatever the government decides to do, more than 11,000 people remain very dependent on TAGS benefits. Battle lines have already been drawn between Newfoundland Premier Brian Tobin, federal Finance Minister Paul Martin and Fisheries Minister David Anderson. While Ottawa appears ready to ante up an additional $150 million over 2 years, Tobin is demanding much more, and Anderson is concerned over the deteriorating state of the West Coast salmon fishery — opening the door to some East-West reciprocity.

How long should the federal government be on the hook for the closing of the fishery? Many fishers have decided that it will be a case of "money or fish" and that if the government decides not to continue support, they will take their boats and fish again, whether it is legal or not.

Ending the Persistent Myth That Governments Can Create Productive Jobs

More than 1.5 million Canadians, or about 9% of the labour force, could not find work in the 1997-1998 boom. Even worse is the plight of our young people: 1997's jobless rate for Canada's youth with some high school education was 22.9%, and 14.7% for those with a high school diploma.

"When the prospects of an entire generation are threatened, the foundations of Canada's future economic and social health are endangered," warns Al Flood, Chairman of CIBC and Chairman of the Ottawa-based lobby group, the Business Council on National Issues. "Canadian business has a responsibility to take an active role and join with government and education to try to find a solution."

To count on Ottawa to put people back to work, however, is a mistake. The private sector is the key mover in job creation, while Ottawa should concentrate on creating the conditions for people to find "work" rather than creating "jobs."

> *While the educated and successful no longer put much stock in an active role for government, the less fortunate want government to "fix" things.*

How Not To Create Jobs

Government is just beginning to get public finances under control. If governments cannot be trusted to count fish — can they be entrusted with larger projects? People are skeptical, and rightly so, about government intervention making much of a difference.

The problem is that, not only has government tried to "create" jobs on its own, but it has meddled in ways which only make the jobless situation worse.

A number of harebrained "job creation" programs have failed miserably. Take, for example, Ottawa's $90 million "jobs for youth" scheme. This was chicken feed when spread out over 3 years, the numbers being helped were small, and the cost per job was high.

Canada Infrastructure Works was promoted as creating thousands of jobs. In Ontario, 611 projects were financed, creating 10,000 jobs. Ontario was the last to sign onto the program, as it felt that some funds had not been well spent.

The Liberals would like to spend a lot of money on public works, but for all the billions diverted into the infrastructure program, it created no more jobs than would have been created under the debt-reduction alternative — the same number as if the money had never been spent.

BC has some fundamental problems, related mostly to the government's policies on taxation and redistribution of wealth. New private-sector investment is virtually nil,

> *Politicians are eunuchs in the harem of the global information age.*
>
> 68

while the provincial government discourages new investment with its high rate of taxation.

Let us never forget the Atlantic Groundfish Strategy (TAGS), conceived as a 5-year, $1.9 billion effort to support idled fishery workers and get many of them out of the industry. But its generous terms attracted thousands more than expected, eventually leading the government to shut down TAGS in 1998 rather than 1999. (See page 74.)

Imagine if the TAGS concept had been applied to Canada's prairie farmers. Then, instead of giving away the fertile prairies to settlers and railways, the government would have kept all the land and made it accessible to everyone. With a signal from Ottawa, everyone would rush out and plant during the government-defined planting season, and only plant where others had not, and only plant up to the government-dictated maximum. Then, these "seasonal" workers would be eligible for unemployment insurance during the off-season.

Hibernia: Jobs @ $172,400

Ottawa gave $1 billion in grants and $1.7 billion in loan guarantees for the Hibernia oil project, whose initial construction and subsequent equipment purchases were among the most expensive in the world. The federal government's 8.5% share means that Ottawa, to some extent, began recouping its investment the moment production started. But the potential payback of Ottawa's grants is trickier to evaluate — taxpayers will get the money back in 20 years with little or no interest. The grants have already been written off. This $1 billion translates into a subsidy of $172,400 for each of the 5,800 jobs created at the peak of construction in 1995.

From another perspective, former New Brunswick Premier Frank McKenna said the federal government should stop giving grants to Atlantic Canadian businesses and use the savings to stimulate businesses in the region with lower tax rates. Over the past 2 decades, Atlantic Canadian businesses received more than $1 billion in direct grants and forgivable loans to help them get started or expand in a bid to create jobs in the economically depressed region. But the 4 Atlantic provinces are now looking at eliminating all federal subsidies and replacing them with an appropriate taxation system — one that rewards success rather than failure.

> *When all is said and done, there is a hell of a lot more said than done in the halls of government.*

The Real Way Governments Can Create Jobs

Hopefully, most politicians now know there is really nothing they can do about unemployment in the short term, and that they are likely to do more harm than good by trying. We have 30 years of inflation and a $600 billion AFD to thank for that insight.

To create a million jobs over a 4-year mandate, however, is an easy target when the economy is going well — and our economy should be able to do so, almost regardless of what the federal government does. Hence, government's role is not to actually spend money to "create" jobs, but to create the right atmosphere for the economy to grow and the private sector to prosper.

In its 1997 budget, government finally seemed to be getting the right idea, promising to help create the conditions to help stimulate job creation and ensure that Canadians are equipped to take advantage of the opportunities presented by a rapidly changing economy.

High interest rates generated by the huge debt and, until recently, the enormous deficit made countless investment projects unprofitable. By eliminating the deficit, the government helps to reduce interest rates and keep inflation low. This, in turn, has an impact on job creation: Canada finished 1st in employment growth among the G-7 in 1997, creating more than 300,000 jobs.

Get Out of the Way of the Private Sector

Business analysts believe that government regulations make it impossible for Canadian companies to function efficiently. A Chamber of Commerce survey suggests that many companies are still not hiring because of excessive government regulation and taxes. One in 10 said they plan to move at least part of the business outside Canada within 2 years as a direct result of federal legislative and regulatory policies. Payroll taxes, corporate taxes, tax compliance, oppressive labour laws, and a lack of skilled workers are listed as the main impediments to job creation.

Most entrepreneurs just want government to get out of the way. Cut taxes, they say, and they will be able to expand and create more work. **Reliable statistics constantly show that countries with the highest tax rates also have the highest unemployment.**

Government action must concentrate on creating a climate for economic development; not on specific industrial projects that are better left to the private sector.

Privatization is viewed as the alternative to taxation and bureaucratic lethargy. — Angus Reid

Policies that Create Jobs

Canada's film industry is an example of a sector that is best nurtured by incentives, rather than trade barriers and restricting foreign ownership. Lower tax rates and fewer restrictions are more likely to promote companies to invest here and to employ Canadians.

Employers, aware of the fixed costs of hiring, respond to an increase in demand by increasing overtime. The government's New Hires Program, however, means that those who are eligible paid virtually no employer premiums for new employees in 1997, and will receive a 25% reduction in 1998.

Producing and selling Canadian products and services around the world means more and better jobs for Canadians. **Every $1 billion in new exports is estimated to create up to 11,000 jobs in Canada.** Consequently, the government is working to encourage trade — Team Canada trade missions, free trade agreements, tariff reductions, increased lending capacity of the EDC, and increased international investment in Canada through Investment Partnerships Canada. Through Technology Partnerships, the government invests in research and development in key growth sectors such as aerospace, IT, biotechnology and environmental technologies.

The federal government provided $60 million to French pharmaceutical company Pasteur Merieuxa for a $350-million research program in Canada. The company anticipates the new investment will create 250 to 300 direct jobs and another 250 spinoff jobs. Vaccines could bring as much as $10 billion in royalties over the first 10 years, out of which the government would get a share.

The government is also beginning to invest in on-the-job training and skills development and programs that make it easier for people to find "work." They have increased the limits on the transfer of tuition and education credits, and increased the contribution and lifetime limits for contributions to RESP's.

The government and industry should be working harder to address the potential of a severe shortage of skilled trades workers which could plague Canada's auto parts companies in a few years. The education system and attitudes towards such jobs must be changed as well, because parents discourage their children from going into training programs and instead want them to grow up to be professionals — lawyers, doctors and accountants.

Small business, which has been responsible for most new job creation in Canada in the last decade, can get a boost from government in many ways. The Business Development Bank of Canada made more than $1 billion in loans and loan guarantees to more than 5,600 small businesses in 1996. The 1-year, $50-million extension to the Residential Rehabilitation Program supports home renovation for low-income Canadians — a major part of the small business sector.

s a society, we have been living beyond our heans, on borrowed time, borrowed money, and finite resources.

— Ann Finlayson, *Naming Rumpelstiltskin*

Bankruptcies

More Canadians are going broke, as an unprecedented 80,000 Canadian consumers declared bankruptcy in 1996 — up 22% from the previous year, which was in turn up 22% from 1994. Yet, fewer than 2,000 people a year went bankrupt in the late 1960's. The 1996 total works out to 3.41 bankruptcies for every 1,000 working-age Canadians, which StatsCan defines as those 15 and older.

The average consumer bankruptcy rate for the 1990's is 2.68, more than double the 1980's pace of 1.23. All told, there is a wide range of rates: Alberta's is 6.5 times that of P.E.I. Clearly personal bankruptcy is a growing trend and one that continues. But if you think the state of the economy is mostly to blame for the financial failure of individuals, you have to deal with some puzzling aspects to these numbers.

Canadians are the biggest users of debit cards in the world on a per capita basis. In 1995, we averaged 45.9 transactions per person, compared with 36.9 in the US and 25.2 in the UK. More than 200,000 retail outlets across Canada accept debit cards. Their use will hit 1.3 billion in 1998, and 1.5 billion in 1999. There are also 250,000 banking terminals in use and that should grow to 400,000. In addition, **annual spending charged on Visa and MasterCard grew from $4 billion in 1977 to $61 billion in 1994.**

"I don't see bankruptcy rates going down for the next few years, not as long as people are buying like they are," says Gib McMullen, executive director of the Credit Counselling Service of Ottawa. Some say that, although more households today may have both spouses working, people should not complain so much because it is mostly their own doing — they are simply living beyond their means.

The general rule was that it was OK to borrow money for a mortgage, a car, or to contribute to an RESP or RRSP, but borrowing money to buy disposable goods or to support lavish lifestyles is not OK. But not all debt is due to frivolous purchases — some analysts believe that the underlying causes of bankruptcies are widening income gaps between rich and poor. Debt is incurred simply to maintain living standards.

In addition to spending a lot, Canadians do not seem to be good "savers." The extended period of low interest rates may have the dual effect of reducing the financing costs of

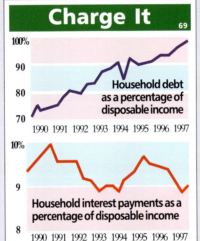

Charge It [69]

Household debt as a percentage of disposable income

1990 1991 1992 1993 1994 1995 1996 1997

Household interest payments as a percentage of disposable income

1990 1991 1992 1993 1994 1995 1996 1997

Consumers have been ringing up debt as the cost of borrowing has come down. Total household debt hit $504 billion in the 3rd quarter of 1997, up from $325 billion in 1990, while the average household debt is $64,000 compared with disposable income of $67,000. The savings rate has dropped from 11.5% of total disposable income in 1990 to 1.5% in 1997. But if the economy takes a downturn or interest rates rise, there could be a flood of personal bankruptcies.

big-ticket items and dampening the enticement of households to save. Savings rates declined to 1.7% in the 1st quarter of 1997. This is the lowest rate of household savings since 1947, the date for which savings rates were 1st calculated. Consumer credit rose to $132.6 billion in March, 1997, which is 5.3% greater than the level observed in September, 1996. Meanwhile, growth in disposable income has remained modest.

The savings rate is an increasingly controversial benchmark these days, however. Many economists — and the Bank of Canada — are discarding the standard measure of savings in favour of some new ones that carry a quite different message: Savings are not only relatively high, but quite stable as well.

The usual measure of savings — what people put away as a percentage of after-tax income — looks grim. After going as high as 18% in the early 1980's, the savings rate dropped to 10% until 1993, and then began a steady plunge, accompanied all the way by predictions that it could not go lower.

The simplest method, used by economists at the Royal Bank and Nesbitt Burns, works like this: Add up the value of the stocks, bonds, life insurance policies and pension plans of all Canadians and then subtract what they owe in the form of mortgages, consumer credit and other loans. The resulting figure is their net financial assets, which StatsCan estimates annually. From 1 year to the next, the change in those assets represents the total flow of new savings. Now divide that figure by after-tax income.

Suddenly, the savings picture brightens considerably. The 1966 savings rate was really 11.9%, not the 4.6% shown by the standard measure. The 1995 rate was 13.2%, not 6.9%. One economist estimates that the 1st quarter 1997 rate was closer to 10% than the reported 1.7%. Even the Bank of Canada has shifted to a more complex variation on this measure. It puts the 1996 savings rate at 17%, up from 12.3% in 1995.

But what about commercial bankruptcies? In a special report on California's Silicon Valley, the *Economist* argued that the region's spectacular growth has been driven more by its culture than by the economics or technology of computer hardware and software. Among the 10 "vital intangibles" cited, the 1st was its tolerance of failure.

In Europe, bankruptcy is stigmatized; in some countries, it disqualifies people from starting another company. In Silicon Valley, on the other hand, bankruptcy is treated like "a dueling scar in a Prussian Officers' mess." In that light, perhaps we should be celebrating, not lamenting, a higher failure rate by Canadian companies. It may simply be a sign of entrepreneurs learning lessons they can use when they try again.

Average Household Income 70				
In constant 1995 dollars				
	1960	**1985**	**1990**	**1995**
Husband-wife families	$55,945	$55,957	$61,053	$58,763
Male lone-parent families	46,133	43,738	45,557	40,974
Female lone-parent families	27,370	26,697	29,652	27,721

Historically, however, punishment used to consist of being sent to debtors prisons; an antiquated legal process which meant it was a lot easier to get someone's attention by throwing him in jail. Even if you got the person to court, there were no legal means of forcing him to pay. So, after you won the court case, you just put him in jail again and held him there until he could find some money or belongings that he could use to satisfy the debt he owed you. And, as we see in Charles Dickens' works particularly, people were constantly sent to prison, and they could not get out because they did not have any money or any goods. It was quite possible to stay there indefinitely.

In contrast, these days, under a federal bankruptcy law rewritten in 1982, it takes debtors about 9 months and $1,275 in fees to gain a clean slate.

Poverty

It is getting harder for Canadians to work their way out of poverty, according to a study by Canadian Council on Social Development. Quite simply, many jobs do not pay high enough wages to provide even full-time workers with sufficient income to adequately support their families.

Dual-income households saw their after-tax pay, adjusted for inflation, shrink by 2.4% from 1989 to 1995. The average income fell to $53,876, with higher income taxes the main culprit. Single-income families fared even worse. Real disposable income plummeted to $40,121, down 9.6%.

StatsCan studied 1995 incomes of households with 2 partners — married or common-law — and found 60.5% relied on 2 people to bring home income. On the flip side, about 22% of households had only 1 bread winner, a number that has held steady for the last few years.

Some people think mothers should get paid to stay at home; others think it is time for the government to get back into the business of helping parents cope. Many parents cannot afford quality daycare.

Meanwhile, poverty rates have continued to rise steadily, even though the last recession ended in 1991. The National Council on Welfare's annual report on poverty, *Poverty Profile 1996*, says that poverty rates reached 17.6% in 1996, meaning that more than 5 million people were living in poverty. Child poverty jumped to a 17-year high at 20.9%, representing 1.5 million children. By far the most poverty-stricken were single mothers under 25, with a rate of 91.3%, or 58,000 women.

The increase in poverty rates coincided with the federal government's replacement of the Canada Assistance Plan with the Canada Health and Service Transfer – and a cut of almost $3 billion from transfer payments to the provinces for health, post-secondary education and welfare. Total incomes of the poorest 20% dropped significantly from 1995, at the same time that the richest 20% got richer.

How StatsCan Defines Poverty and Low Income

There is a debate over the use of Statistic Canada's Low Income Cut-Offs as poverty lines, even though the agency has clearly stated, since their publication began, that they are not.

Proposed poverty lines have included, among others, relative measures (you are poor if your means are small compared to those of others in your population) and absolute measures (you are poor if you lack the means to buy a specified basket of goods and services designated as essential). Both approaches involve judgmental and hence ultimately arbitrary choices.

Poverty is intrinsically a question of social consensus, at a point in time and in the context of a given country. In Canada, political powers have not expressed their views. Provincial welfare rates (which vary considerably) have never been designated as placing recipients on one side or the other of poverty. In the meantime, StatsCan cannot measure the level of "poverty."

For many years, StatsCan has published a set of measures called the Low Income Cut-Offs (LICO). These are quite different from measures of poverty. They reflect a consistent and well-defined methodology that identifies those who are substantially worse off than the average. Of course, being significantly worse off than the average does not necessarily mean that one is poor.

In the absence of politically sanctioned social consensus on who should be regarded as "poor," some people have been using the StatsCan low income lines as a de facto definition of poverty. But they certainly do not represent StatsCan's views about how poverty should be defined.[71]

TODAY WE PAY TRIBUTE TO BENNY SACKS. A MAN WHO DIED PENNILESS

A MAN WITH AN IMPECCABLE SENSE OF TIMING.

The Hidden Costs of the Poor

Poverty is the worst form of violence. — *Gandhi*

90% *of families led by single mothers under 25 in Canada are poverty-stricken.* [72]

The number of poor people in Canada (below the poverty line) has increased from 1 million to 1.5 million in the last 6 years. The situation is getting worse. According to a study by the Canadian Council on Social Development, the average poor family became 6% worse off in the 10-year period between 1984 and 1994. Using a "market-poverty" index (the number of people whose work incomes did not raise them to the poverty line, multiplied by how far they fell below that line), the study concluded that poverty for the market poor got 6% worse.

In addition, more than 500,000 Canadian families relied on public income supports to keep them above the poverty line in 1994. Without those government transfers, the number of poor Canadian families would have jumped by 56% that year.

The market poor in Ontario were hit the hardest, although Ontario had the lowest percentage of market poor families. The market poor index for New Brunswick fell 30% and is surpassing Nova Scotia and the other Atlantic provinces in terms of raising people above the poverty line.

The causes of poverty vary across the regions, but there are 3 basic reasons: low wages, unemployment and periods of time spent outside the work force.

Across Canada in 1994, 450,000 families with 1 adult working were market poor and 100,000 families with both adults working were market poor, because many jobs simply do not pay high enough to provide full-time workers with sufficient income.

Poor Children in Canada

The number of parents of these children who are experiencing long-term unemployment has increased by 47%. A child is considered to be living in poverty if the family is spending more than 55% of its income on food, housing and clothing — a limit known as "the low income cutoff." **In 1998, 1.5 million children lived within this definition of poverty, an increase of 500,000 since the House of Commons unanimously passed a resolution 10 years ago to eliminate child poverty by the year 2000.**

Since the 1989 resolution:
- the number of poor children has increased by 58%
- the number of parents of these children who are experiencing long-term unemployment has increased by 47%
- the number of parents of these children who living in unaffordable rental housing has increase 48%
- the number of parents of these children who earn less than $20,000 per year has increased by 45%
- the number of parents of these children who require social assistance has increased by 68%.

It would take a 10-fold increase in National Child Benefits — $7.1 billion — to solve this problem.[73]

The Hidden Cost of the Poor: **Healthcare**

Poverty leads to illness; when you put people in situations of extreme stress, when they do not eat well, when they live in poor conditions, they have more health issues.

If you want to avoid a heart attack, strive to attain the highest social class possible and get a job where you are free to make decisions. Research findings from Russia, Europe and the US all underline the importance of socio-economic status in heart health.

Meanwhile, shrinking social services benefits are making welfare recipients sick. For example, in Alberta, in 1993-94, the province spent $68 million on 2.4 million prescriptions for 92,000 welfare recipients and participants in programs for the severely disabled. Three years later, $64 million was spent on 2.2 million prescriptions for 63,000 in the programs.

A report entitled the *Economic Burden of Illness in Canada, 1993,* showed the total costs of all ailments across Canada stood at $157 billion — the equivalent of 22% of our GDP, or $5,450 for every man, woman and child.

This number will rise as AIDS cases begin to take their toll. The number of people worldwide with full-blown AIDS has hit 1.64 million and is growing steadily at nearly 20% a year, according to the UN health agency. But the official count is just a fraction of those believed actually to have AIDS, so the agency estimates that the reported AIDS cases are only about 20% of the actual number. On that basis, the World Health Organization (WHO) estimated there were actually 8.4 million AIDS cases worldwide by the end of 1996.

The agency said the US accounted for 581,429 cases and Canada had 14,836. Europe has had 191,005 reported cases, Africa has recorded 576,972 and Asia 70,949. Of people with AIDS, 82% in the US are male, and 91% in Canada are male.

Although we may consider poverty-related health care problems bad in Canada, it is near-luxury to the rest of the world in which **"a decent toilet or latrine is an unknown luxury to half the people,"** according to a recent UNICEF report.

An additional 300 million people have been deprived of adequate sewage and toilet facilities since 1990, bringing the current total to a chilling 3 billion citizens of our world who live in what UNICEF calls "medieval" conditions. Just 1% of the 1 million people in the Nigerian city of Ibadan have sewer connections, while every public latrine in the Dharavai slum of Bombay has to serve about 800 people.

UNICEF estimates that to provide minimum access to sanitary facilities worldwide would cost an estimated $68 billion over 10 years, or just 1% of global arms spending over the next decade. Authorities fail to recognize this as a viable investment, even though the alternative will be to pay for higher medical bills and lost productivity. Remember that less than a century ago, the average life expectancy in the slums of Liverpool was 35 — primarily because of the diseases created by poor sanitation.

If the nation were now to pick one age group for special economic treatment because it was so poor and had bleak prospects for the future, statistics show that this group would not be the old, but the young.

49

The Hidden Cost of the Poor: Education

Poverty-related hunger, violence, illness, domestic problems, and deprivation all take a major toll on a child's ability to learn. Canada's poorest children are more than 3 times as likely as the richest children to be in remedial education classes, according to StatsCan. The richest pupils are almost twice as likely to be in gifted classes as the poorest, while the poorest children are twice as likely as all pupils to repeat a grade.

The findings speak of what has become almost an unmentionable in Canadian society: an entrenched class system. Our ideology tells us we are a democratic, egalitarian, free society that is basically classless, but the reality is that different opportunities exist. Poverty is a huge disadvantaging force in our society, and it is getting worse.

Extra financial support for Canada's poorest schools is starting to pay off in some areas, while others are just too swamped by a tidal wave of social problems to accomplish much more than crowd control. Schools cannot alleviate poverty, but they can do a lot to alleviate some of the stifling effects of poverty, particularly in the area of literacy. Schools can provide simple essentials, such as breakfast, books and a quiet place to do homework.

Many children are not getting the support they need to be fully ready for school. It is also clear that when kids get to school, we are not doing a good job. We presume readiness, but kids who do not show it tend to fall further behind.

"If you're depressed, no matter how much you love your child it's going to be difficult to get enough emotional energy up to cuddle the child or read to the child. It may even be difficult to find the energy to make the child a meal." [74]

Parental support and high expectations are more crucial to school success than family income, but poor people do not have the wherewithal to provide their children with the opportunities and stimulation that middle-class children enjoy as a birthright.

"Rich kids can focus on their education," says one 16-year-old boy, who has 2 menial-pay jobs to support himself. "When you're poor, you get wound up over personal issues."

Researchers say there is no single remedy to improve equality of opportunity, but some factors are clear. A lot of it is about having a common curriculum with agreed standards and being clear about what is supposed to be mastered at different ages. Teachers need to be explicit about what is expected.

Scientists increasingly believe that failing to stimulate a child's mind in the early years will have a lasting neurological impact that could impair his or her ability to reason, articulate and even make friends. The first 6 years of life lay the groundwork for adult competency, and it is very short-sighted to not invest in children before this age. The scientific evidence for this is compelling.

"It's bad public policy," concludes the head of the University of Toronto's Childcare Resource and Research Unit. "We cannot solve the problem of poor kids doing badly in school unless we do something about early-childhood development programs. And in that respect, Canada as a country is moving backward."

In contrast, in France, where publicly funded nursery school is available to all children between 3 and 5, census data have shown that the longer children are enrolled in pre-school, the lower the incidence of repeating Grade 1, no matter the socioeconomic background.

I wept because I had no shoes, until I met a man who had no feet

The Hidden Costs of the Poor: Housing

Ottawa wants to know how many homeless people live in Canada. This is not a population that is easy to track, but it is important to get accurate numbers about who is homeless and how they got that way in order to start working on solutions and prevention.

University of Regina sociology professor Tracy Peressini, who has done extensive research on the subject, believes close to 1 million people are homeless in Canada today. In Metro Toronto alone, about 3,500 people — including 600 families — are living in homeless shelters. Ten years ago, the average length of stay for a family in a shelter was 11 days. The average length of stay today is 90 days.

Meanwhile, the Canadian Mortgage and Housing Corporation (CMHC) has adopted a harder line at the same time it has come to negotiate the devolution of the federal social-housing portfolio. For social-housing advocates who fret about an increasing shortage of subsidized housing for low-income people under the provinces' stewardship, this is no coincidence. For Ottawa, the more social-housing projects CHMC can cull, the less funding it will provide to the provinces over the course of the agreement. Ottawa currently is involved in funding 656,587 units of social housing across Canada, a little more than 10% of them in co-ops.

To avoid becoming "homeless," many Canadians are turning to their families. According to StatsCan, more than 65% of 20 to 24-year-olds are still living with their parents. A 1996 Angus Reid survey found that 25% of Canadian adults expect their parents to be living with them, while some couples that might have split up a decade ago now recognize that the consequences often involve poverty.

Discrimination and violence against women are major causes of malnutrition.

More than 200 million children in developing countries under the age of 5 are malnourished, contributing to more than half of the nearly 12 million under-5 deaths in developing countries each year.

Kofi Annan, United Nations Secretary-General, warns that, "Malnourished children often suffer the loss of precious mental capacities. They fall ill more often. If they survive, they may grow up with lasting mental or physical disabilities."

The tragedy of this "silent emergency" is that the worldwide crisis has failed to grab the public's attention. Make no mistake, there is an emergency, the crisis is real, and its persistence has profound and frightening implications for children, society and the future of mankind.

Failure to heed the alarm is perplexing, particularly since malnutrition is not confined to the developing world. Holes in the social safety net and widening income disparities in many industrialized countries are also taking their toll on the nutritional wellbeing of children.

In the US, researchers estimate that more than 13 million children — more than 1 in 4 under the age of 12 — have difficulty getting enough food. More than 20% of children in the US live in poverty — more than double the rate of most other industrialized countries.

Malnutrition is a crisis of epic proportions — a crisis about mass death and disability not only of children, but about maternal mortality due to nutritional deficiencies and about the hopelessness and the social and economic costs. It is not only a consequence of poverty, but also a cause.

Countries in Latin America and East Asia have made gains in reducing child malnutrition, but the overall number worldwide has grown. While half of South Asia's children are malnourished, 1/3 of Africa's children are underweight, with the nutritional status of children worsening in several countries on that continent.

Malnutrition can take on many forms, including protein-energy malnutrition, iodine deficiency disorders, and deficiencies of iron and vitamin A. They often appear in combination, serving up a 1-2 punch to their hapless victims.

Malnutrition takes a heavy — and tragically preventable — toll. Of the nearly 12 million children under 5 who die each year in developing countries, the deaths of more than 6 million are either directly or indirectly attributable to malnutrition.

But malnutrition is about more than mortality. It affects all of society when malnourished children experience a lifetime of disabilities and weakened immune systems and lack learning capacity. Motivation and curiosity are dulled, play and exploration are reduced, and mental and cognitive development are lessened as these children refuse to interact with their environment and their caregivers.

Here are some of the consequences:
• Iron deficiency anemia in infancy and early childhood can delay psychomotor development and impair cognitive development, lowering IQ by about 9 points.
• Low-birthweight babies have IQ's that average 5 points below those of healthy children.
• Children who were not breastfed have IQ's 8 points lower than their breastfed counterparts.

It is appalling, wasteful — and criminal — that the depletion of human intelligence is almost entirely preventable. This "shrinking" of human brain capacity has further consequences, too, in worldwide productivity levels.

In 1990, the loss of social productivity caused by nutritional stunting and wasting, iodine-deficiency disorders and deficiencies of iron and vitamin A — all symptoms of malnutrition — amounted to almost 46 million years of productive, disability-free life. Vitamin and mineral deficiencies can cost some countries more than 5% of their GDP in lost lives, disability and productivity. For Bangladesh and India, this meant a loss of $18 billion in 1995 alone!

The intellectual toll of iodine deficiency is taking its toll in the republic of Georgia, where its widespread recent detection is estimated to have robbed the country of 500,000 IQ points in the 50,000 babies born in 1996.

Iron deficiency has had its effects, too. The WHO estimates that more than 2 billion people — mostly women and children — are iron deficient, and that 51% of children under the age of 4 in developing countries are anemic.

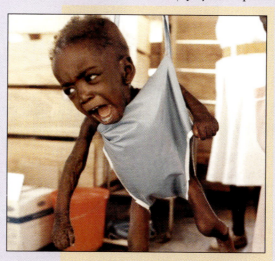

Anemia is a factor in the pregnancy and childbirth complications that kill 585,000 women annually.

Woman's Lifetime Risk of Dying from Complications of Pregnancy	
Country	Risk
North America	1 in 3,700
Europe	1 in 1,400
Latin America/Caribbean	1 in 130
Asia	1 in 65
Africa	1 in 6

UNICEF: **A child under age 5 dies of malnutrition every half second!**

> *If you look closely you will see that almost **anything that really matters** to us, anything that embodies our deepest commitment to the way human life should be lived and cared for, depends on some form — often many forms — of volunteerism.*
> — Margaret Mead, *anthropologist*

Sculpture at United Nations Plaza, New York City

Crime Costs:
Organized and Disorganized Crime

It costs $46 billion a year to deal with crime in Canada — more than we spend on education.[76]

A convicted murderer once told *Newsweek*, "We, the imprisoned, are America's shame. Millions of people in this land languish wasted, under-achieving... I say to you, the smug and contented: Watch out... Our numbers are enlarging, our costs are rising swiftly. Building bigger and better... prisons does not begin to resolve the reasons behind the problems and the madness."

What he was saying, and others would agree, is that society should take care of the root causes of crime, or we will all suffer the consequences.

"If a window in a building is broken and is left unrepaired, all the rest of the windows will soon be broken," criminologist George Kelling writes in *Fixing Broken Windows*, a philosophy on crime prevention that is getting much of the credit for the reduction in crime in New York City. "One unrepaired window is a signal that no one cares, and soon the entire area becomes rundown and... vulnerable to criminal invasion." (See page 235.)

Increased Unemployment = Increased Crime

This approach is also attracting interest as many teens turn to a life of crime and violence because of rising unemployment and loss of hope. This, in turn, has increased crime in more and more communities, especially in those areas hardest hit by the transition from a manufacturing to an information-based society.

In a study conducted in the US, researchers found that a 1% rise in unemployment results in a 6.7% increase in homicides, a 3.4% increase in violent crimes, and a 2.4% increase in property crime. The study also showed a striking correlation between growing wage inequality and increased criminal activity.

In Canada, crime costs are approaching $50 billion a year, but much of this could be avoided through the use of proven crime prevention and rehabilitation programs, according to the National Council for a Crime-Free Canada. They say that the most potent anti-crime measure neutralizes the root cause of crime: stress in the community.

An *Atlantic Progress* story calculates the payoff of theft in Canada. In 1996, only 1 in 3 — or 400,000 — break-ins were reported to the police. "The bad guy will get at least several hundred dollars for his effort. His chance of getting caught and charged is only about 12%."

Residential break-ins are generally on the rise throughout Canada, with thieves breaking into 1 in every 50 homes throughout the country in 1996. BC has the highest break-in rate and is also the hardest hit in terms of motor vehicle theft. StatsCan researchers note that youths between the ages of 12 and 17 accounted for 40% of the people charged with residential break-ins.

The overall crime rate, however, fell by 5% in 1997. It was the 3rd year in a row that the crime rate dropped. In the same year, the rate of violent crimes fell by 3%, while the murder rate fell to just over 2 per 100,000, the lowest in 25 years. And youth crime was down 6%.

But in the meantime, Metro Toronto had a 30% increase in Criminal Code offences between 1984 and 1994 — greater than the increase in population. And for Canada as a whole, the crime rate in 1994 was 8% higher than it was in 1984, and the rate of violent crime was 49% higher.

Demography and Crime

According to Demographer David Foot, the dramatic rise in violent crime between 1984 and 1994 was largely due to the number of criminals reaching an age when they are more likely to commit a violent crime. The slight dip that began in the early 1990's will continue as the large group of baby-boom criminals moves out of its violent years. "Different kinds of criminal behaviour by different age groups are more important than slight shifts in the overall crime rate."

An area of concern is the potential increase in youth crime, as the large group known as the "baby-boom echo" enter their crime-prone years. What is particularly worrisome is that teenagers are becoming more violent, and a leading criminologist fears that "an alarming absence of morality" among some of this generation could lead to a plague of serious teenage crimes.

Homicide Rates

In an article printed in *The Economist*, the rise in population was noted, as well as improvements in how crimes are reported. In 1984, there were 662 homicides in England and Wales. But there were also almost 50 million people living in England and Wales at that time. That is a murder rate of 1.35/100,000 population. By comparison, the 1985 Uniform Crime Reports show North Dakota with a murder rate of 1.0, and South Dakota with a murder rate of 1.8. This places England and Wales between the lowest and the 2nd lowest murder-rate states in the US.

Canada is the only nation in the western hemisphere whose homicide rate is as low as that of Europe. Canada's rate is roughly 5% that of Mexico or Colombia; 25% that of the US; equal to that of France or New Zealand, yet triple the rates of the Netherlands and Norway.

LOCO-MOTIVE.

A STUPID REASON TO COMMIT A CRIME

WILEY'S DICTIONARY

Biker War

Biker gangs have been fighting over Quebec's multi-million-dollar drug and prostitution trade, but most of the victims so far have been sympathizers and drug dealers. However, in 1995, an 11-year-old boy was killed and, as gang tensions rise, chances increase that more innocent people will be hurt in the crossfire.

Law officers define motorcycle gangs as a key part of organized crime — with virtually no distinction between what each does. Forty of the 62 members of Toronto's Para-Dice Riders, for example, have criminal records, including murder.

Quebec's nasty turf war could spread to the nation's capital as the Outlaws, the only biker gang operating in Ottawa for years, have formed an alliance with the Rock Machine.

Hells Angels, meanwhile, want to form an alliance with a Toronto gang in order to set up a coast-to-coast network. Ontario is the only populous part of Canada without an Angels clubhouse, and Toronto is the country's richest market for illegal firearms, drugs, smuggled cigarettes and liquor.

The Angels' BC arm is its richest, due to the fact that Vancouver is considered the centre of North American drug trafficking. With a major port, a relatively unpatrolled border and established gangs of every stripe.

Vancouver has become Canada's drug and crime capital.

On Canada's east coast, the RCMP and Halifax regional police are battling to keep the Angels out of their city — also considered a strategic drug-importing location. Police are hoping raids will produce enough evidence to chase the organization out of the city. Halifax and other isolated harbours around Nova Scotia are used to smuggle drugs. The province's sea coast is seen as a strategically viable "platform to the world" of international crime.

Provincial and international differences in cigarette and alcohol taxes have created a phenomenal smuggling problem, further fuelling the gang problem. Smuggled liquor in Ontario accounts for 11% of the $5.9 billion alcohol market. In BC, the province estimates its lost tax revenues from smuggled cigarettes is between $100 million and $125 million a year.

The biker battle promises to get more deadly, too, as the Rock Machine courts a vicious European group. Although Canadian gangs wage their wars mainly with handguns and dynamite, gangs in Europe have stepped up the battle to

Hells Angels in a Montreal Funeral Parade

> **The number of police officers in Canada has doubled since the 1960's, while Criminal Code offences reported to police were 5 times greater.**
>
> 77

include an array of sophisticated weapons stolen from military arsenals.

Spurred by growing public discontent, police swept down on the Hells Angels club headquarters near Quebec City in 1998 and seized the property under Canada's new anti-gang law. Under the law adopted by Parliament in May of 1997, police can search and seize a property if it can be demonstrated that the location was being used to organize criminal activities.

Provisions in the new law also include the use of peace bonds designed to target gang leaders, the right to gain access to income-tax information related to gang activity and stiffer penalties regarding the use of explosives.

Non-Biker Criminal Gangs

In addition to biker gangs, Canada has seen an increase in new ethnic-based criminal groups. Across Toronto, rival Tamil gangs are competing for lucrative criminal enterprises that include fraud, drugs and weapons sales, robberies, burglaries and extortion. Their bloody clashes have been fought with weapons that have included assault rifles, shotguns and semi-automatic handguns.

Winnipeg, however, is the country's gang capital — home of up to 1,800 gang members. One of the city's most notorious gangs has initiated a home page condemning the "approved, concentrated and systematic abuse of aboriginal people by the justice system." The Manitoba Warriors call themselves a traditional fraternity and their jailed members political prisoners.

The festering situation across Canada has turned into a political problem, with local mayors, provincial officials and police experts all clamouring for legislative action.

The provinces have concentrated on increasing their powers to shut down biker bars for liquor violations and giving municipalities more powers to use zoning bylaws to get rid of unwanted gang hangouts.

Others suggest that the best way to crack down on gangs is the same way gangster Al Capone was finally caught — tough enforcement of income-tax laws. The tax authorities have their noses everywhere, so why not in the business of the gangs?

No matter what route of action the government takes, something has to be done before the problem advances beyond control. In Colombia, called "the most savage country in the world per capita," there were 27,000 violent deaths in 1996. In a country where narco-trafficking appears to be the only viable industry, the central government is weak, and the President has been accused of financing his election campaign with cartel money.

Growing Prison Population

Jail — Brazilian style

The number of inmates in Canada has never been higher. On any given day there are about 34,000 adults in jail. With rising prison populations and rising costs, governments in Canada are joining an international trend towards privatizing prisons, with Nova Scotia going ahead with the country's 1st attempt at private prison management. In New Brunswick, a US company has won a contract to design and build a young offenders facility that will be leased back and operated by the province. And Ontario is poised to become the 1st jurisdiction in Canada to have privately operated adult prisons. Privatized prisons can take many forms, ranging from a private company managing on behalf of the government to the more extreme example of turning prisoners into a captive labour force for a prison corporation.

The Fraser Institute says that privately run prisons offer great benefits for "both taxpayers and inmates," with the average costs up to 15% lower than a government facility. Profit is a powerful incentive to reduce waste and increase productivity, but critics argue that prisons and incarceration are not issues to be judged by a balance sheet.

In the US, independent research has shown that privately managed prisons continue to perform well in most areas in comparison with the public sector. The cost difference between privately managed prisons and comparable publicly managed prisons has narrowed since privately managed prisons have taken on more commitments and the public sector has made efficiency savings.

North America had no private correctional facilities until 1984, when a Tennessee suburb gave a contract to the Corrections Corporation of America (CCA) instead of to a government agency. Since then, private-sector prison building and management has become an international growth industry. CCA had 1997 revenues of almost $700 million. Seventeen private correction management firms have received contracts for 119 facilities: 6 in Australia, 6 in the UK and 106 in the US.

Canada cautiously entered the private-sector prison market after the Nova Scotia government picked the Atlantic Corrections Group as the "preferred supplier" for procurement bids for some aspects of the province's correctional system. A preferred supplier is in charge of negotiating a series of contracts to define, design, implement and operate a solution to an identified problem.

Dave Peters, president of the Nova Scotia Government Employees Union, is nervous that Canada is considering a move towards privatized jails. He toured a series of private correctional facilities in the US and saw overcrowded inmates and underqualified guards.

Peters found that private prisons often cut back on social services for prisoners, such as substance abuse treatment programs, as well as reducing pay for guards. With 65% to 75% of prison costs consisting of employee salaries and benefits, modern prisons are being designed by the private sector to be less labour intensive. Low pay, poor benefits and extended working hours due to understaffing results in high turnover for prison guards which, in turn, leads to companies settling for less-than-prime candidates for guard jobs.

Others argue that the profit-making impetus of the private sector is such that it may be in its own interest to create demands even in the absence of any real need. If private prisons are successful in reducing the number of repeat offenders and deterring others from committing similar crimes, they in effect reduce the supply of profit-producing "customers."

But supporters of private prisons claim that such abuses also are rampant in government-run jails. For example, the largest contributor to the California gubernatorial campaign was the correctional officers union. After being elected, the governor became an active supporter of California's 3-strikes law, which flooded California's jails with prisoners. Besides, supporters say that private prisons make up less than 2% of all correctional facilities in America and lack the clout to lobby government for harsher laws.

Tougher laws are not even needed. Between 1980 and 1993, the prison population of the US increased by 188%. This increase was directly linked to the War on Drugs. In 1980, about 1 of every 15 convicts entering US state prisons had been sentenced for a drug-related offence. By 1992, that figure was roughly 1 in 3.

To cope with the expanding inmate population — which topped a million for the 1st time in 1995 — US corrections officials built 213 state and federal prisons between 1990 and 1995. Despite the building boom, state prisons operated at an average 3% over capacity and federal prisons at 24% over capacity.

According to some, **a much better suggestion for how to deal with crime is to rethink what constitutes a crime and what does not. The unholy trinity of vices — drugs, gambling and prostitution — should not be illegal.** Stamping out vice crimes is almost impossible, while statutes against them mostly net small-time offenders.

Money and energy saved from not enforcing vice crimes could be better spent on going after real criminals — murderers, rapists and large-scale thieves. It is a radical proposition, but a much more humane, cost-effective and Canadian alternative to turning prisons over to corporations.

It costs $100,000 a year to incarcerate a young offender.[76]

No Evidence For Gun Prohibition

Gun prohibition advocates frequently point to British and Canadian crime rates as proof that gun restrictions dramatically reduce criminal activity. For example, the murder rate in Britain in 1984 was 1.35 per 100,000 population and the Canadian rate in 1981 was 2.68, while the US murder rate in 1985 was 8.2. Can these differences be an indication of gun control at work? Or are we comparing apples and oranges?

For such comparisons to be valid, the countries need to have similar cultural values and legal systems. In other words, are British and Canadian people intrinsically more or less likely to commit rape and murder than their American counterparts?

If you ask the average white Canadian about the origins of our culture, as likely as not, the answer will be "England." But if you ask other segments of our diverse population, you may get more cosmopolitan answers.

Another area of cultural difference may be the kinds of people that immigrate to Canada. Before the American Revolution, it was common for minor criminals to be transported to British North America — "troublemakers" who refused to subscribe to the preferred religion in much of England and continental Europe.

In the case of Canada, there is yet another selection process. Many Canadians are descendants of those Americans who, in 1776, remained loyal to the King and chose not to live under a government of "traitors."

What about our supposedly shared legal system? Again, beneath the similarities are many differences. Just this century, Canada's *Charter of Rights and Freedoms* dramatically extended the rights guaranteed to defendants in criminal actions.

Taking these cultural and legal differences into consideration, the numbers are simply not persuasive that gun control alone is responsible for lower crime rates. In the US, 63% of homicides are committed with firearms. If we assumed that firearms were freely available in Britain as they are in the US, assumed that none of the murders would be done with firearms in preference to other methods (an unlikely assumption for premeditated murders), and assumed that no one successfully used a firearm for self-defence (another bogus assumption), the murder rate in Britain would still only be 2.1 per 100,000 population — lower than almost every US state.

Claiming the very low British rape rate is a result of gun control laws is not true, either, because firearms are used in rape only 7% of the time. Even adding 7% to British rape rates, they would still be lower than the safest part of the US and lower than 12% of US rates as a whole.

Some Canadian gun prohibitionists claim that Canada's murder rate is as high as it is because our proximity to the US causes "gun diffusion." The Maritimes have the lowest homicide rates in Canada, and Newfoundland (0.68) has the lowest rate of all. Quebec's rate (2.93) was lower than Alberta's (3.43), and BC has the highest provincial rate (4.02). However, the NWT and the Yukon have the highest rates of all (11.57 and 4.57 respectively). The Territories also have Canada's highest rate of increase; while in the US, the highest increase is in the major metropolitan areas.

This discrepancy may reflect differences in the locations of the socially alienated populations — America's blacks in urban slums and Canada's native people in the North.

If US gun diffusion is a cause of murder in Canada, the effect must be overwhelmed by other factors, because the NWT, with absolutely no contact with the US, has a much higher rate than the Yukon, which directly borders Alaska. Alberta, bordering Montana, has a murder rate 17% lower than Montana and 11% higher than Idaho. We could also compare Alaska's murder rate (9.7 in 1980) with the NWT (11.57) and the Yukon (4.57), or compare Washington's murder rate (5.5 in 1981) with BC's murder rate (4.02 in 1980). These differences are not always in Canada's favour, as you would expect if gun laws were the main factor.

Finally, crime rates are very multi-factorial. Gun availability could be argued as a factor, but evidence suggests that it is not a major factor, and something more persuasive than a few random crime rates needs to be documented.

Having said this, international analysts warn that illicit groups and the spread of arms will replace hostile states as the greatest risks to security. **Cheap guns are a bigger threat to peace than nuclear weapons, and global criminal networks operate freely across national borders.** The globalization of markets and the shrinking scope of state activities have helped expand the scope of gun-runners and illicit business networks.

These analysts are calling on governments to seek ways to control the spread of small arms such as the AK-47 automatic rifle (a weapon that probably caused more deaths than any single weapon since its invention 50 years ago) and to help strengthen states such as Russia, where organized crime is flourishing.

COUNTERPOINT

Small Arms, Big Impact

A recent report by the Worldwatch Institute says that the proliferation of small arms around the world is the cause of as many as 90% of the deaths in contemporary conflicts. Some countries, including the US, have as many or more firearms than people. Public and private arsenals continue to swell as the unrestrained annual production of millions of small arms join those already in circulation. The availability of these firearms is "like lighting a match near a fuel tank" at a time when unemployment, poverty and social inequity have made people desperate. If a sense of security is to be obtained by reliance on firepower, then one can never have enough of it, says the report. **Ironically, the more heavily armed a society is, the more insecure it may come to feel.**

Prison Labour

Since the early 1800's, conflicts have arisen over the use of prison labour in Canada, whether it is seen as a means of off-setting the cost of incarceration, or as a form of rehabilitation of the inmates.

By 1977, a Parliamentary Subcommittee recommended improved inmate training, the establishment of a national prison industries corporation, the introduction of inmate incentive pay and bonuses, and enlisting the full cooperation of business and labour in moving toward increased inmate work opportunities.

Today, CORCAN, a special operating agency responsible for the employment and work-related training for prisoners in federal penitentiaries, operates 32 individual production sites with annual sales upwards of $30 million.

Some inmates even operate computers for CORCAN, allowing the agency to schedule production, take orders, bill customers, and plan raw material and manufacturing supply. Not only does training on PC's reduce costs by allowing prisons to be more self-sufficient, but it helps inmates obtain marketable skills and consequently reduce recidivism — the percentage of inmates who *return* to the prison system.

In Ontario, prisoners pick up garbage and plant trees along the province's highways as part of their sentence. In 1996, more than 860 kilometres of provincial highways were cleaned up at what the ministry termed "minimal cost."

The use of prison labour also has a long history in the US. With 1.12 million people behind bars — an incarceration rate 2nd only to Russia and 4 times the rate in Canada — US prisons are packed. To keep prisoners busy and increase revenues, prisons across the country are expanding prison industries.

In a California prison, prisoners making blue work shirts earn about $60 for an entire month of 9-hour days. Those refusing to work are moved to disciplinary housing, lose canteen privileges, and lose the "good time" credit that reduces their sentence. In addition, these prison-made goods are exported overseas — the sort of "slave labour" for which human rights groups have strongly criticized China.

Regardless of such qualms, hundreds of thousands of American prisoners produce goods for sale to the government and for the open market, private companies contract with prisons to hire prisoners, and private prisons employ inmate labour for private profit, either for outside companies or for the prison operators.

Critics charge that inmates are exploited, the jobs provide few real skills, and prison industries throw prisoners into direct competition with civilian workers. Prison labour is proving highly competitive, however, as businesses discover that, in prison, no one calls in sick and inmates do not take vacations.

In Lockhart, Texas, a private prison receives $31 per day per prisoner from the state. From that money, they must provide housing, guards, electricity and everything else to run the facility. Whatever is left over is profit. Adding prison industries to the mix can help the bottom line.

The Lockhart facility currently houses 3 private companies, including 1 with a completely new factory assembly room, built to specifications by prison labour. Meanwhile, the factory closed its plant in Austin, laid off 150 workers and moved all the equipment to Lockhart, where it pays prisoners minimum wage. The prison then takes about 80% of inmate wages for room and board, victim restitution and other fees.

The Texas AFL-CIO considers this kind of prison labour "absolute indentured slavery." This explains why the trade union movement has been among the most active opponents of private prisons and prison labour in general. In a few cases, unions have successfully fought prison industries. In Ohio, a car company hired prisoners to assemble Honda parts; negative publicity and pressure eventually forced the company to eliminate the contract.

Some union officials, however, have worked with prison administrators and reformers to establish meaningful training programs. For example, since 1978, the electrical workers and the local building contractors have trained 6 San Quentin inmates each year as apprentice electricians. Of the inmates who continued the program after release, 90% stayed out of prison.

San Francisco runs an innovative jail labour program that helps keep order and rehabilitates less-skilled prisoners. They also reopened a long-abandoned agricultural field and set up a small farm where inmates grow specialty fruits and vegetables, which then are sold to local restaurants.

Such efforts avoid the exploitation of captive labour that is typical of profit-driven prison industry programs. Prisoners do need training, skills, and experience to help them compete, while civilian workers and businesses want guarantees that their jobs will not be taken over by profit-hungry prison industries. **As long as society remains hell-bent on packing the prisons, meaningful work programs that actually prepare inmates for life on the outside are worth a try.**

Good Ol' Days

In 1885, Texas forced mostly black inmates to haul granite for building the new state capitol, but the union of skilled granite cutters union strongly objected and boycotted the building project, forcing the contractor to import scab cutters from Scotland.

Prison labour led to the Tennessee Coal Creek Rebellion in 1891. When coal owners locked out unionized miners and used convicts to work in the mines, miners stormed the convicts' stockade and freed the prisoners. The company gave in, rehiring the miners and halting the use of convicts.

By the early 1900's, most states banned prison contract labour as the public became aware of the brutal conditions facing prisoners and the corruption of prison officials who took bribes to provide inmate labour to selected companies.

However, although the infamous chain gangs of the South were abolished in the 1950's, they recently were reestablished in Alabama and Arizona.

The Costs of Substance Abuse in Canada

$18 billion, or 2.7% of GDP, represents a very conservative estimate of the cost of substance abuse in Canada. The actual cost is probably significantly higher.

The impact of substance abuse on society is an issue of vital importance, yet there is very little available information that links this impact to economic indicators such as Gross Domestic Product.

To address this issue, in May 1994, the Canadian Centre on Substance Abuse (CCSA) organized an international symposium on the Economic and Social Costs of Substance Abuse and released a study. The investigation was not a study of the budgetary impact of alcohol, tobacco and other drugs on governments, but of how the costs related to society as a whole.

With certain exceptions, the major direct costs were the tangible, external costs of substance abuse — those costs borne by those other than the abuser, including the abuser's family. The costs for the users to purchase alcohol, tobacco and illicit drugs were not included. Nor were transfer payments, such as welfare benefits to people disabled by substance abuse.

The use of alcohol, tobacco and illicit drugs involves benefits as well as costs. For example, the *moderate* use of alcohol is associated with decreased levels of coronary heart disease at low consumption levels. The net number of deaths from coronary heart disease attributable to alcohol is negative, i.e., more deaths are prevented than caused by alcohol.

Intangible costs — death, pain, suffering and bereavement — are viewed as significant, even if they cannot be quantified in dollar terms.

It is estimated that 6,701 Canadians lost their lives as a result of alcohol consumption in 1992. The largest number of alcohol-related deaths were as a result of driving accidents. Alcoholic liver cirrhosis accounted for 960 deaths, and there were 908 alcohol-related suicides. Many of these deaths involved relatively young people. Because of the high incidence of deaths and suicides, the number of potential years of life lost was high: 186,257.

In regard to alcohol-related illness, the total number of hospitalizations in 1992 is estimated at 86,076. **These individuals spent a total of 1,149,106 days in the hospital.** The greatest number of alcohol-related hospitalizations resulted from accidental falls, alcohol dependence syndrome and motor vehicle accidents .

The total number of tobacco-related deaths in Canada was estimated at 33,498 in 1992. The largest number were from lung cancer (11,704), representing 35% of all such deaths. Tobacco-related heart disease accounted for 6,762 deaths, while chronic obstructive pulmonary disease accounted for 5,816 deaths. Almost 70% of those who died from tobacco-related causes in Canada were men.

Mortality resulting from illicit drug use is relatively infrequent compared with alcohol and tobacco-related deaths, but since illicit drug deaths tend to involve younger victims, they tend to be sensationalised.

The total number of deaths related to illicit drugs in Canada was estimated to be 732 in 1992. Of these deaths, 88% involved males.

Ross Rebagliati, Whistler's Marijuana Poster Child

Suicide accounted for 42% of illicit drug-related deaths.

The Costs

- Alcohol accounts for more than $7.5 billion (40.8%) of the total costs of substance abuse. The largest economic costs of alcohol are for lost productivity due to illness or premature death, for law enforcement and in direct health care costs.
- Tobacco accounts for $9.56 billion in costs — or more than half (51.8%) of the total substance abuse costs. Lost productivity due to illness and premature death accounts for more than 2/3 of these costs, and direct health care costs due to smoking account for 1/3.
- The economic costs of illicit drugs are estimated at $1.37 billion. The largest cost is lost productivity due to illness and premature death, and a substantial portion of the costs are for law enforcement. Direct health care costs due to illicit drugs are estimated at $88 million.

Because treatment, law enforcement and productivity expenses constitute the bulk of the costs associated with alcohol, it is reasonable to conclude that the majority of alcohol-related costs could be avoided, as could the economic costs.

Although a substantial portion of the costs associated with tobacco use is avoidable, ex-smokers still have an elevated risk for several disorders, such as lung cancer.

Illicit drug costs also are largely avoidable. The vast majority of illicit drug-related deaths are due to suicide, poisoning, and assault. The relatively small proportion of mortality due to drug-related AIDS (less than 10%) would persist, but most illicit drug mortality would cease if the misuse of illicit drugs ended.

In total, 40,930 deaths in Canada were attributable to substance abuse in 1992. This represented 21% of total mortality for that year, with smoking-related deaths alone accounting for 17% of the total. Potential years of life lost due to substance abuse constituted 23% of the total years of life lost due to any cause — 16% due to tobacco, 6% due to alcohol and 1% due to illicit drug use. The number of hospitalizations due to substance abuse constituted 8% of total hospitalizations and 10% of the total days spent in hospitals for any cause.

The total estimated value of lifetime earnings of people who die prematurely each year from substance-related conditions ranges from $7.17 billion to $12.35 billion.

The Case for Legalizing Marijuana

Groups ranging from the Canadian Police Association to the Addiction Research Foundation have urged Ottawa to decriminalize marijuana. **The Canadian Bar Association has been advocating the decriminalization since 1976; while the Police urged Parliament in 1993 to remove possession from the Criminal Code.**

In 1996, Canadian police made 30,000 arrests for marijuana offences. More than 25 years since a Royal Commission recommended decriminalization, the Criminal Code remains in the throes of "Reefer Madness" — insistent that possession and use of marijuana is a serious and dangerous problem for society.

In 1998, British *New Scientist* magazine created a stir when it accused the WHO of suppressing a Canadian-Australian comparison study of cannabis and legal substances, which **confirmed that cannabis is safer than alcohol or tobacco.** They said the WHO feared the study would give ammunition to the "legalize marijuana" campaign.

Meanwhile, an Ontario Provincial Court judge ruled recently that a 50-year-old Toronto resident could cultivate and use marijuana to alleviate the symptoms of his severe epilepsy.

Canada has become a mellow nation where even the middle-aged believe that smoking marijuana should not be a crime, according to a CTV/Angus Reid poll. A full 83% said that marijuana should be legal when used for health

OH CA-NA-BIS!

purposes. A majority now believe marijuana should not be a criminal offence, a dramatic change from the 39% who held that view just 10 years ago.

Those in favour of decriminalization argue that marijuana is not addictive, does not lead to criminal behaviour and rarely leads to the use of harder drugs.

Winnipeg's Cash Crop

Canada has joined Colombia and Nigeria in earning the dubious distinction of being declared a "source country" for drugs by the US Drug Enforcement Agency.

Manitoba has become a net exporter of marijuana, with more locally grown drugs seized in Winnipeg in 1997 than in any other Canadian city except Vancouver. Police confiscated $11 million worth of weed, compared with Vancouver's $26 million. In Toronto, a city with 5 times the population, police came up with only about double the amount of pot seized in Winnipeg. **The size of the marijuana industry in BC is now double the size of the logging/lumber industry and equal to the pulp and paper industry. At an estimated $2 billion, it is 7 times the size of the salmon economy.**

Despite decriminalization recommendations of a Royal Commission and a variety of law enforcement agencies, solid data that it is less dangerous and costly than alcohol and tobacco, the will of a majority of the people is being ignored by all politicians *because they lack the courage to address the issue.*

Restorative Justice

We should change the name of our justice system from "Criminal" to "Restorative." This would clarify the purpose, how it should operate, and provide a measure for its success.

Retribution leads to increased fear and retaliation. In a restorative system, the primary focus would be on the need for healing. Ideally, an offender voluntarily would recognize the injustice, make significant effort to restore damages where possible, make the changes to prevent injustice in the future, and voluntarily be accountable to others for keeping agreements.

A restorative system would use cooperation over coercion when possible and encourage the offender to decide voluntarily to become cooperative. If the offenders refuse to cooperate, they would move to the coercive side.

When actions on both sides are tested as to whether or not they are respectful, reasonable and restorative, then the whole system will be restorative.

An eye for an eye only ends up making the world blind.
— *Gandhi*

Retribution

What we have now is a throwback to the Biblical "eye-for-an-eye" system. People have developed an insatiable demand for tougher criminal laws, longer prison sentences, mandatory life sentences for repeat offenders, more and prompter executions, and harsher forms of detention. Public insecurity is "looking for blood," and the quest for rehabilitation has given way to punishment and revenge.

To the cheers of many, Ontario created its 1st boot camp for young offenders — a military-style set-up and strict discipline facility — at a time when other jurisdictions are closing theirs down. Studies have shown that boot camps have no lower rates of recidivism than any other facility.

We try to teach people responsibility by sending them to prison — where they have no responsibility. To teach them to be peaceful, we send them to a place that is ruled by violence. To teach about *positive* influences, we send them to a place without positive influences.

Although our prisons are rated better than those in the US and Third World countries, they are still more violent and crowded than most in Europe. Prisons are filled with routine rapes and beatings, rampant drug use, and murder — with people living or dying by a strict code. Corrections Canada admits the occurrence of, on average, 5 murders, 15 suicides, 6 hostage takings, and hundreds of inmate fights and assaults each year in federal prisons.

The nature of correctional institutions means that people are not sentenced to a loss of freedom, but doomed to a term of terror and pain. The viciousness of prison life actually works against rehabilitation. Advocates for prison reform say penal institutions corrupt non-violent inmates and make them more effective criminals once they are released.

"If you take a tomato and put it in a bog, it comes out rotten," says one ex-con.

A highly publicized law aimed at keeping dangerous convicts behind bars until the end of their sentences has failed miserably to predict those most likely to re-offend, according to a study. The findings mean that the public would have been safer if those convicts deemed most likely to re-offend had instead been released and those released early had been kept behind bars.

Canada's incarceration rate, 130 per 100,000, is the 4th highest in the industrialized world — behind Russia's 558, the US's 529, and South Africa's 368.

Canada should look to countries such as the Netherlands, where reducing incarceration rates meant regarding drugs as a health problem. Finland de-emphasized imprisonment, reduced penalties for offences such as theft and impaired driving, set parole eligibility earlier and increased the use of suspended sentences. Finland also decided to stop jailing juveniles, in the belief that prison was only recruiting teenagers to criminal careers.

But it is no easy feat to move Canada from its centuries-old penal system towards the kind of community projects that have proved successful in other countries. Attitudes about crime rates and the ability to curb them must be changed before the corrections system can be reformed.

People who are unable to pay fines, who need treatment programs or have committed lesser offences should not be jailed. Penitentiaries should be reserved for the offenders no one wants to see on the streets.

Surely alternatives to prison sentences would also help loosen the backup of tens of thousands of criminal cases jamming the courts, which threaten to repeat a recent crisis when cases were thrown out due to delays.

Some changes are being made. In federal penitentiaries, a new law cuts months and even years off the time prisoners must serve before being moved into halfway houses on day parole. The legislation changed day parole eligibility rules for inmates who: were serving their 1st term in a federal prison, were convicted of a non-violent offence, and who convinced parole board officials that they were not likely to commit a violent crime before the expiry date of their full sentence.

Inmates who meet the criteria can now be released on day parole to a halfway house after serving 1/6 of the sentence, or 6 months, whichever is longer. Previously, they were not eligible until they had served 1/3 of the sentence, less 6 months.

Incarceration is not always the answer. On the whole, Canadians believe that protection of the public and rehabilitation of offenders are of higher priority than punishment as goals of incarceration.[78]

Our jails and prisons create career criminals out of petty incompetents.

Alternative Justice

A variation of restorative justice known as "pre-charge diversion" is gaining life in the Canadian justice system. In a typical case, a woman who was caught stealing cosmetics was sent to a volunteer agency instead of criminal court. The woman, her case worker and the victimized store all made proposals for her punishment, while 3 local citizens were approached for their ideas.

In the end, instead of winding her way through criminal court, the young woman was forced to arrange and attend 15 job interviews, undergo aptitude testing at a local college, research the effects of a criminal record on women her age, spend 40 hours cleaning cages at an animal shelter, and spend 30 hours helping out at a breakfast club for schoolchildren.

Changing Public Attitude

When a British television talk show broadcast live from a prison, the station was inundated with complaints that the prison was too clean, too well decorated, and too bright, that the prisoners had too many possessions, and that they should not have been allowed recreational activities.

With attitudes like this, prison officials must impress upon the public that prison is a very costly and often destructive response and that harsher sentences do not lead to safer communities. In Brazil, the release of 45,000 inmates convicted of non-violent crimes could save enough money to build 18,000 homes for the poor. The imprisonment of a woman serving a sentence for stealing 2 packages of disposable diapers cost $20,160.

In Britain, despite a drop in crime rates, the adult male prison population has doubled in the past 5 years and continues to rise at a rate of 10% annually, the number of female inmates is increasing by 20% a year, and young offenders increase by 30% annually.

Finland, on the other hand, made a concerted policy beginning in the 1970's to slow down its incarceration rate. Since then, judges have reduced the length of sentences for non-violent crimes, while increasing the proportion of inmates sentenced to community service. Parole was extended so that now 99% of inmates are released under the program, politicians do not campaign with promises of tough anti-crime measures, and the media rarely sensationalise crime or lobby for tougher sentences.

Consequently, the number of prisoners in Finland has dropped from 120 per 100,000 in 1978 to a recent low of 60 per 100,000.

Aboriginal Justice

A recent Royal Commission concluded that aboriginals are over-represented in the courts and prisons across Canada. Currently, 13% of inmates in federal prisons are aboriginals, even though they are less than 5% of the Canadian population. In Saskatchewan, aboriginals now account for 74% of all admissions — 7 times their share of the provincial population.

It is clear that the current European-style system, which emphasizes punishment, does not work for these people. Aboriginals take a more holistic approach, focussing on healing and working with the offender in the context of the community. Consequently, the Commission recommended that an aboriginal justice system be created, including a separate Criminal Code.

The Commission also pointed out that aboriginal crime is linked to the experiences of colonialism, which has "undermined the social, cultural and economic foundations of aboriginal peoples, including their distinctive forms of justice."

Compared to non-natives, aboriginals are more likely to be arrested, less likely to have adequate legal representation, less likely to understand court procedures (for linguistic and cultural reasons), more likely to plead guilty, less likely to be granted bail, and more likely to be given prison sentences.

Legal experts have concluded that there is nothing in Canadian law that would preclude a separate justice system. After all, Canada already exhibits legal pluralism in its incorporation of the Civil Code of Quebec.

The 1991 Task Force on the Criminal Justice System proposed that numerous changes can be made relatively quickly to the existing system to make it more sensitive to the needs of Aboriginals.

The Correctional Service of Canada has added sweat lodges to many of its institutions and has encouraged native spiritual leaders to minister to inmates.

The most well-known tribal court is operated by the New Mexico Navajo, a justice system that functions well and is strongly supported by the tribe.

However, there are no Aboriginal communities of that size in Canada.

An example of a tribal court that is working well with smaller communities is the North West Intertribal Court system (in Washington State), which shares an aboriginal judiciary among 16 different tribes, involving communities of 200 to 500 people.

One concern with Native self-government, however, is that it could violate highly valued human rights norms, such as life and health, sexual equality, and non-discrimination. The question of what, if any, Charter requirements might be imposed *a priori* upon aboriginal systems of justice is a complex and murky issue.

Circle of Justice

The aboriginal method of justice known as "sentencing circles" are now used in several Canadian provinces. Trials are still held the conventional way, with a judge and testimony under oath. Although the judge still has the final say, local leaders advise him about the impact the criminal has had on the community and have a say in meting out punishments.

Sentencing circles are seen as an experiment, as a way to help the judge make sentences much like using pre-sentencing reports prepared by probation officers. As such, the use of sentencing circles did not require any legislative change. "A judge can use any normal and legal means to find acceptable sentences," says Quebec Court Judge Jean Dutil, the travelling justice for the northern Quebec region of Nunavik, but he cautions that only some types of cases are appropriate. (For example, he would not use a sentencing circle for a sexual assault case.)

In the Yukon, where sentencing circles have been employed since 1992, a study of recidivism rates is just under way. People are committing fewer and less serious crimes, and the circles are pulling communities together to deal with things that are their responsibilities.

Traditionally, violence was rare in native communities. When a dispute arose, the individuals involved were responsible for finding a solution. If it could not be resolved, individuals were told to leave and come back when they were ready to live peacefully.

In the 1960's, however, the situation changed as more natives began settling in villages, where alcohol was more readily available. The violent crime rate in Nunavik is now nearly 600% higher than in the rest of the province. Many individuals go back and forth to jail, not receiving help.

Judge Dutil warns that the sentencing circles, "are not a panacea." But the hope is that more constructive sentences will prevent criminals from re-offending.[80]

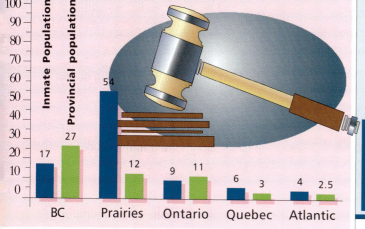

Aboriginal Inmates

[79]

Aboriginals as a percentage of federal populations across the country

Inmate Population / Provincial population

	BC	Prairies	Ontario	Quebec	Atlantic
Inmate	17	54	9	6	4
Provincial	27	12	11	3	2.5

I worry that we are losing our sense of collective responsibility, that we are losing our interest in the public interest.

The Problem Is Tribalism

Zambia vs. Goldman Sachs

What is the difference between Zambia and Goldman Sachs? One is an African country that makes $2.2 billion a year and shares it among 25 million people. The other is an investment bank that makes $2.6 billion... and shares it among 161 people.

The net wealth of the world's top 10 billionaires is worth 1.5 times the national income of the world's 50 poorest countries. The unprecedented shift from labour to capital is illustrated by the gap between the top 20% and the bottom 20%, which has increased from 30:1 to 78:1 over the last 25 years.[81]

Prejudice in the form of racism and sexism are systemic in Western society today, but the roots of both run much deeper than skin colour or genitalia. The heart of the matter is that almost no one likes anyone who is different. The root "-ism" that society must overcome is the belief that, if you are not "one of us," then you must be inferior. The intrinsic problem is tribalism.

The sexist says, "I am a man, and you are a woman (or I am a woman, and you are a man); you are not one of us and must be inferior." The racist says, "I am white, and you are black (or I am black, and you are white); you are not one of us and must be inferior." But the tribalist just says, "You are not one of us and must be inferior." That is the attitude that fuels hate, fear and violence in both the sexist and the racist. Almost everyone displays the behaviour without realizing that we all live on the planet Earth and, in fact, all of us are "one of us."

Tribalism May Replace Nationalism

Picture a world in the next century organized not around nation states but around a new form of tribes sharing the same culture and values. It is a world where you pledge allegiance not to a republic, but to a clan. That possibility is not too far-fetched when you take the current state of our fracturing world and overlay new information technologies and the new telecommunications infrastructure. After all, most of the conflicts the world is confronting today are intra-state conflicts. In the past few years, 30 to 40 deadly conflicts have been going on in various parts of the world. Here is how things conceivably could play out:

Canada no longer seems able to meld all the diversity within its borders into 1 harmonious whole. The "melting-pot" is not working out. As years go by, Canadians identify less with this nation and more with various subgroups based on ethnicity, religion or race. Canada not only has Quebec separatists, but dissenters in BC and people suggesting that Toronto and Vancouver will be city states in the new world order. Someone once said that Nigeria is not a country but a colonial legacy of 200 non-fitting tribes — and sometimes that definition seems equally applicable to Canada.

Meanwhile, now that the Cold War is over, the rest of the world is resuming its long-simmering ethnic rivalries. Nations from the former Soviet Union to Yugoslavia have broken apart into smaller countries. Separatist factions are mounting serious challenges to many nations — Spain, India, Cyprus, Sri Lanka, Morocco, Serbia and even the Scots in the UK. Conflicts existing around the world include Cyprus, East Timor, Georgia, Haiti, the Middle East, Kurdistan, Northern Ireland, and between Peru and Ecuador.

India and Pakistan have fought 2 wars over Kashmir and continue to be engaged in a tense military standoff. The 2 countries spend about $13 billion a year on defence and field a combined armed forces of 1.85 million. The dispute continues to be one of the world's most protracted and dangerous military conflicts. This regional conflict has taken on a higher urgency since both nations have tested nuclear weapons.

In Italy, stress fractures of north-south separatism creep across the country. While most major industries are in the north, many southerners live in poverty. The climate also affects the economic situation, as northerners keep much the same hours as Canadians, and southerners interrupt the day for 3-hour-long lunches and siestas. The idea of separation became much more concrete in the late 1980's with the founding of the Northern League, a political party whose aim is separation of north and south. More recently, a group of young men broke into one of Venice's best-known landmarks to unfurl a banner and declare themselves "soldiers of the Most Serene Republic of Venice."

The idea of the large nation state, grouping people together within geographic boundaries, does not seem to work anymore. We have organized that way for several centuries, but its usefulness may be running out. People now seem to identify more with those sharing a common culture or holding similar values.

People May Rely on "Tribes" for Education and Security

Digital technologies can enhance — or, depending on your perspective, heighten — tribal tendencies. They could allow people to connect with others more like themselves regardless of where they live in the world. Ultimately, they could allow people to formally organize themselves accordingly.

People are not necessarily born into the tribes, but they join them by adopting the values of each particular group. A person can even belong to several tribes for different reasons. These tribes could then carry out most of the functions that we now associate with nations or governments. Someone at the farthest outpost of the world could use the technologies for day-to-day contact and support from the larger group based far away.

They could get all the same news, entertainment and casual gossip, reinforcing their identities from afar. They could even rely on the group for all levels of education, much of their health care through advanced telemedicine, and even their personal security.

Tribal identities and affiliations could be so strong that no one would physically harm anyone else unless they wanted to incur the wrath of the entire clan. The tribal police of the future would travel the planet pursuing justice for their members, much as city gangs do today.

A Gated Community

In Dana Point, located in the "quintessential California" part of the state known as Orange County, the wealthy live behind guarded walls, while the immigrants who tend their lawns, live outside the gates. Roughly 1/3 of the 6-square-mile coastal city is sealed off behind 17 walled — or, in local parlance, "gate-guarded" — communities. Behind the guard booths, the gates and the long walls, the red tile roofs of these grand homes sit at the ocean's edge.

Right in the town centre sits a Latino neighbourhood.

Now a microcosm of the ethnic tension in California, Dana Point was not always this way. But development brought hundreds of low-wage jobs, and whites and blacks were not interested in the work. In Southern California, low wages mean Latinos, both legal and illegal. Residents of Dana Point learned too late that capital demands a supply of cheap labour, importing this labour makes it hard to deal with the consequences.

Gradually, those who worked hard all their lives to buy their dream homes found their neighbourhoods becoming more dangerous. It was drastically different from the town many white residents had come to when they fled Los Angeles and bought $250,000-$500,000 dream homes. Crime, centred around Latino gangs, is their biggest fear.

These days, between 30% and 40% of the city's major crime happens in Lantern Village, the part of town which is home to more than 2,200 Latinos.

Meanwhile, hard-working, law-abiding immigrants — just wanting to better their lives — were being told to get out and stay out. "The reason the rich go gated is because they feel safe," explained one Latino. "To me, they're afraid to learn. They're afraid to realize the truth. The truth that we are all human, and we all have to stick together."

Nationwide, however, the trend is not good. We are seeing the birth of a de facto oligarchy — as many as 4 million people live in walled communities. The isolation of these developments will only increase, too, as generations of children grow up in them and accept their reality. In Third World countries, for example, the rich have lived behind walls for generations and, removed from reality, they cannot see why wars start against them.

Tribalism and fear of others have fuelled a lot of misery in the history of the world. Hopefully, people like those in Dana Point will ultimately discover that they have more similarities than differences.

In much the same way, Canada's concierge-guarded high rises are really just gated vertical communities designed to separate the wealthy occupants from the unwanted poor.

Languages

Esperanto

Long before the dominance of English, Russian physician Ludwik Zamenhof created the best-known universal language, known as Esperanto, in a book in 1905. Meaning "hopeful," Esperanto is now used by more than 100,000 people; it is relatively easy to learn for people accustomed to French, Italian, Portuguese, or Spanish — the Romance languages.

The Universal Esperanto Association was founded in 1908; it currently has memberships in 83 countries and national and professional associations, and holds an annual Congress.

Perhaps the obsession by Quebecois and Catalans to preserve their own language and culture is not so paranoid. The worldwide number of languages, once estimated to be 10,000 to 15,000, now stands around 6,000 and is falling. Linguists predict that half will be extinct within the next century, and say that at least 100 are down to a single native speaker.

The Death of Languages		82
LOCATION	LANGUAGES	ENDANGERED
Alaska and the Soviet North	50	45
Russia	65	45
United States & **Canada**	**187**	**149**
Australia	250	225
Meso-America (& Mexico)	300	50
South America	400	110
All the Americas	900	300
World	6,000	3,000

English: The Universal Language

Languages die because of the influence of more common languages, such as English, a process aided by modern communications and easy transportation. **In France, the Education Minister says that English, along with computers, will be a fundamental part of the future, so the French people must learn to embrace both.**

"We must no longer look at English as a foreign language," he says. "We must no longer speak of a battle against English. That is something that is completely obsolete." France has been waging war against the intrusion of English and other foreign languages since at least 1539, the date of a decree ordering that justice be administered in French.

Oral speech is 150,000 to 100,000 years old, judging by fossil evidence. For comparison, writing was first invented a mere 5,500 years ago, and a widespread, standardized sign language for the deaf was developed only in the last century.

Worst Practices

The Genocide the World Ignores

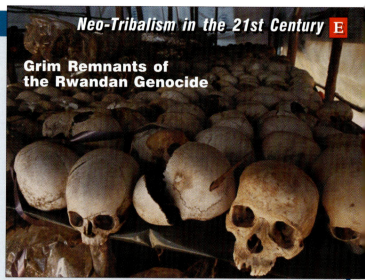

Grim Remnants of the Rwandan Genocide

Rwanda, a tiny land-locked country in Central Africa, was turned into a slaughter house in 1994 when up to a million Tutsis and moderate Hutus were killed by extremist Hutus. (Hutus make up about 85% of the population and Tutsis 14%.) The killings finally ended when a Tutsi-led army, the Rwandan Patriotic Front, invaded from neighbouring Uganda and routed the government forces.

Lives could have been saved, however, if the UN had given its peacekeepers more troops and a mandate to intervene, according to Canadian Major-General Roméo Dallaire, who headed a small peacekeeping force before and during the slaughter. But, he says, it is too easy to blame the UN, which is not a sovereign country; rather, it is "us," and therefore everyone is implicated.

UN Secretary-General Kofi Annan agrees, saying that the UN tried to embarrass the international community into action, but the political will to send a force did not exist. The US and other key member countries balked when asked to beef up the peacekeeping force. A well-equipped UN brigade of 5,000 could have saved hundreds of thousands of lives, but by the time the troops arrived, the killings had already taken place. General Dallaire eventually had fewer than 300 men and was powerless after Belgium withdrew its forces when 10 of its men were killed.

General Dallaire says that, if instead of reducing his force, the UN had decided to send reinforcements and change his mandate from one of peacekeeping to one where offensive operations could have been done, the international community could have slowed down the killings or stopped them altogether. Even before the genocide began, Dallaire warned the UN of the Hutu plans for the genocide, but his force was ordered not to intervene. They were later ordered out of the country.

General Dalliare remains haunted by the failure of the UN mission — even though his personal courage in dodging shells and braving crossfire to meet the Canadian Air Force Hercules transport plane that flew twice daily from Nairobi with supplies helped convince the Canadian government not to abandon the mission.

Not only did the international community not respond, but France delivered huge consignments of weapons to Hutu authorities in Rwanda, even after the massacre of the Tutsi minority began in April, 1994. This included an order for $15.7 million worth of heavy machine-gun and mortar ammunition: 12,000 shells and 20,000 mortar rounds. The last delivery was flown in on July 18, 1994, after France had dispatched a UN-mandated peacekeeping force to the area.

The Rwandan tragedy ultimately prompted Canada's push at the UN in 1997 to create a large, well-equipped rapid-reaction multi-national force that could be deployed anywhere in the world to combat ethnic or other conflict. The Security Council has yet to endorse the idea, but it is high on the agenda of Annan and his deputy, Canadian diplomat Louise Frechette.

Meanwhile, those who led the genocide fled for Zaire (now the Democratic Republic of Congo) and Tanzania, taking with them 2 million Hutu refugees. Late in 1996, a Zairian rebel force backed by the Rwandan army destroyed the refugee camps and sent the Hutus home to Rwanda.

Instead of seeing this as an opportunity for peace, the armed Hutus intensified their efforts to destabilize the government from inside Rwanda, with the support of at least some elements within the population. Since returning, Hutu rebels plunged Rwanda's northwest into guerilla war. No matter what the army did, the rebels' low-grade onslaught continued.

And the killings continue. Rights groups claim that the army has committed massive atrocities against civilians, burning houses, massacring civilians and wreaking havoc in an effort to root out the insurgents, a notorious militia known as the Interahamwe.

The Dem. Rep. of the Congo

Uganda

RWANDA

Burundi

Tanzania

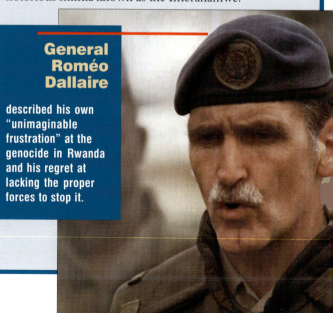

General Roméo Dallaire

described his own "unimaginable frustration" at the genocide in Rwanda and his regret at lacking the proper forces to stop it.

The Information Revolution and The Death of the Nation State

Ian Angell — The Copernicus of the Information Age

His vision of the New World Order that will follow the death of the Industrial Age is stark and anarchistic. He foresees a widening gap between the Haves and the Have-Nots, a collapse of the liberal social-welfare agenda and the slow, but certain, demise of the Nation State, which will be replaced by a darker-than-Orwellian vision of a world ruled by the economic elite through corporations.

According to Professor Ian Angell of the London School of Economics, we are on the verge of an Information Revolution that is taking us out of the Machine Age into a new dark age. Angell predicts that, as markets become global and the workplace gives way to cyberspace, only the elite will have anything to offer to the world's economies. There will be mass unemployment for the unskilled and a slow death for the nation state. Corporations will take over and a tiny elite will defend itself from dispossessed masses.

A new order is being created by telecommunications. Information super-highways will enable everyone in the world to "talk" to everyone else. Information technology with international travel is changing political governance and its relationship to commerce. Companies are global-izing, chasing spot markets in cyberspace. The costs of over-coming time and space no longer buffer the impact of cheap labour.

Unhindered by national barriers, corporations will be truly global. They will relocate, physically, fiscally and electronically, to where the profit is greatest and the regulation weakest. The global company no longer supports the aspirations of the country of its birth. To remain competitive, it can no longer afford to carry a large and over-priced inventory of a national "people product" of varying value and quality.

It is no accident that companies are downsizing, delayering and outsourcing. Routine production jobs can be performed by robots or exported anywhere on the globe, so wages will converge worldwide to Third World levels. "Social Dumping" is also dragging down wages for service work, a sector which is itself being increasingly automated. In 1994, the International Labour Organization claimed that there were 800 million sub-employed people in the world. **Job losses are not the result of some temporary downturn but are the result of structural changes — as profound as when agricultural workers left the land for the cities.** Now work is leaving the office and the factory for cyberspace.

The idea of a job, born with the Machine Age, is changing beyond all recognition. The very nature of work, institutions, society, and even capitalism, are mutating. Work is becoming increasingly casual and part time among the mass of workers. Released from a single location, companies are free to ring the death knell of unions. Middle management, too, is under threat, with companies firing more than a quarter of them. The motto for everyone is "add value or perish."

Politicians will never learn that technology is the problem, not the solution. Today, productivity is delivered by a technology needing only a few machine minders. National economies can no longer grow themselves out of unemployment. Growth is created by entrepreneurial knowledge workers, not low-grade service and production workers. **Members of the knowledge elite, just 10% of the world's population, will see their incomes skyrocket as corporations compete for their services.**

Talent, entrepreneurship and innovation are diviners of economic success. The role of the state is to nurture, propagate and supply quality human raw material. Government is merely the supplier at the bottom end of the value chain. If a state cannot produce a quality "people product" in sufficient quantities, then it must scour the globe for elite knowledge workers.

Politicians must find ways of attracting global employers in order to employ the locals. If the state maintains a greedy populist stance, then the entrepreneurial and knowledge aristocracy will move on to more agreeable locations, leaving the country economically unviable. The power in global economic forces means that **the tax burden is irrevocably moving away from the elite on to the shoulders of the immobile.** Governments are impotent as they face a triple whammy: substantially lower tax revenues, increased social security payouts, and the need to support "deprived areas."

The liability of an uneducated and aging population is another problem. Whole sectors of society who previously felt their future secure can see it slipping away. The slow redistribution of wealth that has occurred over the last centuries is being rapidly reversed. The rich are getting richer and the poor poorer. At the bottom of the heap, we are witnessing an expanding underclass.

The state must behave as an economic institution, a national firm judged against the new economic circumstances. **No state has an automatic right to exist.** Government, like every other enterprise, will have to survive on the efforts of an elite few. Democracy will degenerate into being the means of governing the immobile and dependent service workers. The big political question of the coming decades is how to find a socially acceptable means of dismantling democracy.

Who will defend us? Globalization has shown the myth that the state is good and global corporations are bad is a morality tale told by tax collectors. The world belongs to the global corporation.[68]

> *National security has been replaced with concerns such as the environment and trade as the preoccupation of nation states.*

> *The honourable term for mediocre is, of course, the word "liberal."*
> — *Nietzsche*

Definition of Nation State

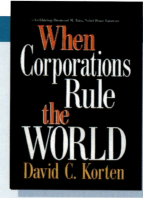

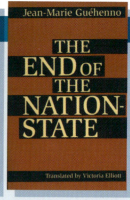

The world is made up of about 200 nation states of various sizes and forms of government, according to the most recent count by the United Nations. A majority of these places are not nation states in the strict meaning of the term, but survivors of older, cruder forms of political life. Nigeria, for instance, is not so much a country as a colonial legacy of 200+ incompatible tribes. Nevertheless, these nation states all share 2 essential characteristics — each covers separate portions of the earth's surface, and each has a government whose claim to speak for it is recognized by most other governments.

A nation state is a place where people feel a natural connection with one another because they share a language, a religion, or something else strong enough to bind them together and to make them feel different from others. It is the politics of the first person plural, and its government can speak for its people because it is part of the "We."

The Legacy of Modernism

It was little more than 200 years ago that men invented the nation state as a better way of organizing the business of government. No government, unless it is prepared to rely entirely on brute force, can do its job properly in the modern world if the people it governs do not have a clear-cut sense of identity that they share with the government — unless, in other words, they both are part of the "We."

Known as the modern era, this lasted exactly 200 years, from the fall of the Bastille in 1789 to the fall of the Berlin Wall in 1989. The scientific reasoning of modernism excluded, on principle, everything that could not be seen, measured, and empirically analyzed. Modernists genuinely believed that science would answer all questions and that the application of scientific principles would solve all social problems.[83]

Over the past 50 years, however, nation states have become less dominant, less independent and, in a way, less separate than they were in their prime. The separation between our political order and the realities of today has become too great. Although the science and technology of modernism led to a standard of living beyond the wildest expectations of our ancestors, it did not make everyone happy. Modernism has given way to the ideology of post-modernism, which argues that truth is not so much a discovery but a construction. Truth is relative, dependent on the individual's experience and culture. And, while modernists valued unity, post-modernists value diversity. Modernists looked for universal frameworks of knowledge; post-modernists question all established systems.

Just at the point in time when the idea of the nation state 1st began to crumble, the Balkans had to construct their new legitimacy — allowing their collection of "communities" to form all the more rapidly. Consequently, the collapse of Communism in Eastern Europe has given way to bloody conflict between ethnic groups. Even the unity of the Canadian culture is challenged by Quebec's separatists and the pluralistic diversity afforded new immigrant groups.

Global Forces Affecting Post-Modern Nation States

The rise of new global forces has noticeably tamed the nation state's old feeling of confident independence. Three powerful forces — political, technological and economic — converged simultaneously in 1989 during the fall of the Berlin Wall, and globalization was the fruition of that union.[78]

• One force eroding the nation state's autonomy is that a far bigger share of the world's capital is owned by multi-national companies operating freely across national borders. Now, since markets can transfer cash anywhere at the push of a button, it has changed the rules for policy making, introducing what sometimes seems like a sort of direct international democracy.

Global companies have begun to eclipse and subsume the power of nations. Transnational enterprises have increasingly usurped the traditional role of the state, and now exercise unparalleled control over global resource, labour pools and markets. The largest global corporations have assets exceeding the GDP of many countries. The nature of commerce is changing as we move from the Industrial Age to the Information Age and from the land to cyberspace; **geographically bound nation states suddenly find themselves increasingly irrelevant and without a clearly defined mission.**[85]

Multinationals must be sufficiently grounded in their local networks, however, and sufficiently "linked" to the other units of their enterprise to act out fully their roles as distributors within the companies. Like Gulliver in Lilliput, they are bound by thousands of little, nearly invisible cords, where only the rare individuals who still have the memory of another age can sense the reality.[84]

> **As the heirs of the Age of Enlightenment, we are inheritors with amnesia.**[84]

Non-Proportional Representation: 1997 Federal Election

Just as in the 35 previous general elections, Canadians have found their votes wasted, their political will distorted, and themselves being governed by a party supported by a minority of voters. Failure to create a system of proportional representation means that all votes are not equal — it took 31,233 votes to elect a PQ MP; 31,817 votes to elect a Liberal MP; 41,501 votes to elect a Reform MP; 67,733 votes to elect an NDP MP; and 121,287 votes to elect a Conservative MP.

Drugs: A Transnational Economy

The economy of drugs — with revenues estimated at $100 billion — is a good illustration of this bypassing of states by transnational gangs that are far more powerful than some states.

• A 2nd force is the changing face of national defence. For at least the 1st part of the coming century, very few countries will have the technology to ward off enemy missiles, which can be aimed at anywhere from anywhere else on earth. Without alliances beyond the nation state, each country will be vulnerable to such attacks.

In the era of post-modernism, we will never know the concentration of violence created by the world wars. No nation today is capable of mobilizing such gigantic forces around an idea. The great bloodbaths of the 20th century were made possible by the blending of the absolute power of a nation state and of a "religion" — nationalist, national Socialist, or Communist — that gave it direction.

• A 3rd force is the globalization of knowledge. As people in different countries have the means — through television, the Internet, and increasingly cheaper phone service — to know more about one another, the similarities will become more apparent and the distinct edges more blurry. In addition, we have passed from a network of navigable waterways and railroads to an infrastructure of air transport and telecommunications that has profoundly upset the notion of geographic distance.

The rise of fast computers and cyberspace (the widespread electronic networks connected via satellites) means that people who know how to exploit these systems can know virtually everything happening in the world moments after it happens — something which helped bring about the end of the Cold War.

Post-Modernist Canada

Canada is like Great Britain in that our insularity has from the outset afforded us a well-defined territory, and we do not have the same value for the notion of territory as the nations that have had to fight to establish their boundaries. We have taken our "We"-ness for granted.

Now, however, the security of the post-war Keynesian economics is gone, replaced by a realization that Canada is so integrated into the global marketplace that much of our economic fate lies beyond our grasp. When borders become meaningless, any attempt to stimulate demand dissipates quickly.[78]

In the new era, our cultural Maginot Line has been overrun. Historically, the CBC played a valued, if somewhat peripheral, role still in gathering issue-oriented Canadians around their radios, but CBC television, at least in English Canada, is becoming increasingly marginalized, to the point of irrelevance.[78]

*...he balance of power in world politics has shifted in recent years from territorially ...ound governments to **companies that can ...am the world with no regard for the local economies in which they operate**.[86]*

Alternatives to the Nation State

One suggested alternative to the nation state is to group people around the world according to a shared ideology. With the disappearance of communism, some people believe that countries would no longer have any serious differences of opinion over politics and economics, and we would all fall together nicely under a global government. The end of the Cold War was not the end of all ideological argument, however. Countries have long quarrelled, and will continue to quarrel, about many things besides ideology. We need look no farther than Israel, Bosnia or Serbia to know that the world remains explosively divided. In other words, we are far from a universal republic. What is coming into being is not a global political body but an apparently seamless fabric, an indefinite growth of interdependent elements.

Another alternative to the nation state is based on economics. Free trade, under protection of the new WTO, shows that the nation state can obey a global set of rules. But countries draw a line between the pooling of economic autonomy and the pooling of political and military power. That is why even the most miraculously smooth-running free-trade regime will not inevitably glide forward into a global political unity.

A 3rd suggested alternative is the idea that various groups of today's nation states, wanting to belong to something stronger, will gather together into big new entities, each speaking for the culture or civilization of its component parts. The problem with the civilization-unit theory, however, is that the component parts of even the more plausible ones are still profoundly reluctant to surrender their separate identities.

We are entering into the age of open systems, whether at the level of states or enterprises, and the criteria of success are diametrically different from those of the institutional age and its closed systems.[84]

*The disappearance of the nation carries with it the **death of politics**.[84]*

The European Union Prototype

Only in Western Europe is there any seriously conceived plan to dissolve existing nation states into something bigger. The countries of the European Union have come very close to the line that separates the pooling of their economic life from the merging of their politics.

The desire to be strong is a powerful force in politics. But not as powerful as the feeling that "we" are different from "them." That is one reason why a growing question mark floats over Europe.[87]

Habits of the heart shape our behaviour.[88]

The Threat of War Between the Haves and Have-Nots

"The world is breaking down into 2 tribes," says Keith Bezanson, president of the International Development Research Centre. "There are the included and the excluded. Unfortunately the number of excluded is rising quickly, and those who are included are becoming a very select group."

The statistics that demonstrate the growing inequality between the world's "Haves" and "Have-Nots" are quite staggering. **The 1996 United Nations Development Report found that economic decline or stagnation has affected 100 countries, and the incomes of 1.6 billion people have been reduced. In 70 of these countries, average incomes are less than they were in 1980 — and in 43 countries less than they were in 1970.**

The world has become economically polarized both between countries and within countries. The US has one of the greatest income disparities — and the most billionaires. What is particularly troubling is the number of billionaires who have addresses in developing countries, and the connection between wealth and power in much of the developing world. More than half of the world's billionaires come from Asia, Latin America and the Middle East – 23 in Asia live outside the traditional economic centres. There are billionaires in Mexico, Colombia and even in Ecuador.

The assets of the world's billionaires exceed the combined annual incomes of countries with 45% of the world's population. According to the UN Report, the net wealth of the world's top 10 billionaires is 1.5 times the GDP of the world's poorest 50 countries — China among them. The Report also calculated that the gap between the world's poorest 20% and its richest 20% had more than doubled, from 30:1 to 78:1 over the last 25 years. In 1972, the average US CEO made 44 times as much as the average worker; by 1992, the gap was 222:1.

> **Excessive pay for CEO's is the mad cow disease of North American business.**[89]

One company attempting to address this issue is Citizens Bank, whose President and CEO became the 1st bank boss with a salary cap — 10 times that of its average employee. This means she will likely pull in between $250,000 and $420,000, compared with the $3.9 million haul of the Bank of Montreal chief, and the $4.2 million take of Newcourt Financial's CEO.

Obviously, the banks are doing well, but despite the expectation that income distribution would equalize as the economy grew stronger, StatsCan says that the gap between the country's Haves and Have-Nots has widened. Canadians are getting richer, on the whole, but their wealth is not being spread out evenly. The top 20% snagged 41% of the country's total income, while the bottom 20% received 6%.

In the US, a study found that the average income of the poorest 20% in Washington, DC, had fallen over the last 20 years to $5,290 — the lowest in the country. In contrast, the richest 20% of DC families enjoy average incomes of $149,510, or 28 times larger than the poorest 20%.

Washington's poor are the poorest in the US, its rich are the richest, and the gap is the greatest, but it reflects a national trend — even though the economy has grown robustly in recent years. In 44 states, upper-income families have gotten richer and the poor have become poorer since the late 1970's.

Other statistics report 40 states where the gap between the highest-income and the middle-income families was larger than it had been for any state during the 1970's. Nowhere 20 years ago did the wealthiest 20% make more than 10 times the poorest 20%, but today 30 states have top-to-bottom ratios of 10 or greater, with the average disparity across the US having grown to nearly 13.

While there is a widening gap between the rich and poor *within* countries, the gap *between* countries also continues to grow, as statistics show that rich countries are giving less to poor countries. The Reality of Aid, an annual assessment published by Action Aid, points to a decline in aid-giving of 9% in real terms between 1994 and 1995. The big donors — Japan, the US, Germany and France — all confirm that the slide will continue.

Do not forget, too, the importance that income disparity places on health and well-being. Nowhere is this more relevant than in the fight against AIDS. Experts say it is immoral to describe as "manageable" a disease that is only manageable for a fraction of the wealthiest 10% of its victims. Despite expenditures of about $18 billion a year, not enough has changed in the countries that are home to 90% of the epidemic. Indications are growing of division between those countries and the wealthier ones, where people with AIDS are far fewer and resources far greater. (See page 38.)

About 90% of the 23 million people currently infected with HIV live in developing countries. The rates of infection will not peak until the year 2010 in 19 of the hardest-hit countries, most of which are in sub-Saharan Africa. By 2020, AIDS will be the largest single killer of adults in their prime in developing countries, responsible for half of all deaths from infectious disease.

Average total family income by quintile, constant 1996 dollars[23]					
Year	1st	2nd	3rd	4th	5th
1993	$17,486	$33,095	$48,521	$66,487	$110,185
1994	17,935	34,234	49,803	67,570	111,398
1995	17,882	33,741	48,864	67,144	112,822
1996	17,334	33,564	49,310	68,063	114,874
%Change	-3.1*	-0.5	0.9	1.4	1.8

* % Change 1995-96

The Security Industry

Americans alone now spend more on personal security than the budgets of the F.B.I. and all US police agencies combined. The security industry employs nearly 2 million men and women – more than served in the US army at the height of the Cold War.

Technology for the Rich

Technology also plays a role, as the world's rich and poor can be described as the information Haves and Have-Nots. While 90% of all Internet hosts are in North America and Western Europe, 80% of the people of the world still do not have access to phone service. **Manhattan (population 1.5 million) has more phone lines than in all of sub-Saharan Africa (population 522 million).**

Jeremy Rifkin warns, "Information and communications technologies and global market forces are fast polarizing the world's population into 2 irreconcilable and potentially warring forces — a new cosmopolitan elite of 'symbolic analysts' who control the technologies and the forces of production, and the growing number of permanently displaced workers who have little hope and even fewer prospects for meaningful employment in the new high-tech global economy."

Author Kirkpatrick Sale warns that not only are new technology and globalization producing a growing gap between rich and poor, but they are, "sowing the seeds of political instability." (See page 237.)

Angus Reid agrees, saying that, "The rich are sick of sharing. The middle class is desperately trying to cling to the middle of the ladder, despite all the broken rungs. Its members (and many of its former members) spend a lot of time trying to determine who is most responsible for doing them in — corporations, governments, governments in concert with immigrants, governments in concert with the poor, and so on."

Rifkin continues: "A new form of barbarism waits just outside the wall of the modern world. Beyond the quiet suburbs, exurbs, and urban enclaves of the rich and near-rich lie millions upon millions of destitute and desperate human beings. Anguished, angry and harboring little hope for an escape from their circumstances, they are the potential levelers, the masses whose cries for justice and inclusion have gone unheard and unadvised."

Already, France has experienced explosions of public anger in a country with an unemployment rate over 12% and youth unemployment as high as 30% in some parts.

Poverty is certainly a relative term when examined on a global scale, but we need look no further than Haiti to witness the effects of devastating poverty on civil unrest. (See page 34.) In Russia, where the economy has collapsed, people are getting poorer, and crime is running rampant. While Russian life expectancy has plunged to levels far below those of other industrialized countries, organized criminals are penetrating all levels of local and national governments, threatening the entire country with a tidal wave of banditry and corruption. As an example, a Siberian city elected a mayor with a long criminal record for robbery, car theft and fraud. The mayor and his gangster cronies run the city as their personal fiefdom — ordering contract killings, evading taxes, intimidating residents and engaging in racketeering.

The neighbourhood cannot be good for any if it is not good for all.[90]

Neo-Nazis

Besides political turmoil and social unrest, the inequities in the distribution of wealth could lead to increasing xenophobia and even anarchy. In the US, in early 1998, 2 men were charged with possessing anthrax. One of the accused, who has long been active in the racist, Idaho-based Aryan Nations sect, bragged of plans to attack the New York subway system with enough bubonic plague to "wipe out the city."

One FBI expert predicts that, "this kind of thing is only going to escalate." Not only are the number of hate groups on the rise but so is their virulence. Before the Oklahoma City bombing in 1995, the FBI had fewer than 100 open investigations into domestic terrorism; now there are more than 900.

In Germany, a neo-Nazi movement is growing, particularly in the east. It is no coincidence that the movement has flourished, because the fall of the Berlin Wall has led to great change and unease. The neo-Nazis attract the poor, the young, the unsure, the disconnected and the disaffected. Youth gangs have terrorized towns, driven foreigners out of homes and jobs, and ethnically cleansed villages.

In 1998, in 1 eastern German state that has an unemployment rate of almost 25%, a right-wing extremist party known for its xenophobic and anti-Semitic views recently scored a shocking breakthrough by attracting 13.2% of the popular vote in the state election. The Deutsche Volksunion ran a campaign urging the expulsion of foreigners and a return of the death penalty. Half of its supporters are the young unemployed.

We are in a state of crisis. The human population is exceeding the carrying capacity of planet Earth by leaps and bounds.
— *Michael Tobias, World War III*

• He was some mother's darlin'
• He was some mother's son
• Once he was fair and once he was young...[92]

Repairing the Safety Net

Social Assistance: The Roles of Government

To understand what role we think government should play in ensuring the well-being of its citizens, we need to examine historically the excessive amount of power and responsibility our society has given the state. Ottawa's Caledon Institute for Social Policy defines the basic models of economic organization in the West.

• The "coordinated market capitalism" (CMC) model is one in which national institutions cooperate on many of the most important economic decisions, including the business-labour management of social programs.

• The "neo-liberal model" is one in which the state uses its powers to keep the markets — particularly the labour market — as free of any interventions as possible,

The CMC countries include most of Europe, Japan and most of the emerging Asian countries. The neo-liberal countries spring from the Anglo-Saxon tradition and are primarily English-speaking. This tradition began when the Roman Empire collapsed in Britain, the centre of Anglo-Saxon culture, and allowed for the growth of mercantile powers to the point that they became substantial powers in their own rights, able to challenge the feudal powers.

Without constraining feudal power, the mercantile class grew stronger in England than elsewhere on the continent. With the 1st stirring of capitalism in the 1700's, it was the mercantile class of England that led the charge, and Anglo-Saxon cultural values spread wherever the English dominated. The motto of the American colonies — **"In God We Trust" — was not about religion, but about not trusting the state.** Canada was also created by mercantile capitalists, who needed a central administration. (See Mercantile System, page 229.)

Capitalism, in the view of Freudian philosopher Herbert Marcuse, is not only an economic system, but also a philosophy of life that takes for granted that all human problems are open to technological solutions. Marcuse believed that this "technological rationality" creates uni-dimensional and non-critical thought, where we incorrectly take for granted that social institutions must be organized in ways that exploit rather than nurture human beings and natural resources.

Creating the Welfare State

The welfare state (state-mediated redistribution of wealth) developed after WWII at a time when industry was absorbing the de-ruralized workers. This solution was reasonably effective then, but does not work today. While Canadians adopted measures in the 1950's and 1960's — such as Old Age Security, a universal health plan and the Canada Pension Plan — to ensure that no Canadian would lack the basic necessities of life, today the situation has changed. Most Canadians were proud of these programs — and now young Canadians are being told that they must be self-sufficient because "the state" can no longer afford to look after them.

According to author Ann Finlayson, it is critically important that we understand how radically the 1990's ideology of "self-sufficiency" will alter the traditional relationship between the state and the individual — particularly at a time when, **even as one of the richest countries in the world, we are willing to tolerate what the UN has identified as the 2nd highest rate of child poverty in the industrialized world.**

Back in the 1960's, however, the role of the federal government began expanding into all kinds of areas — influenced by the theories of British economist John Maynard Keynes. (See page 228.) He believed that government should use its taxing and spending powers to lessen the negative effects of business cycles, reinforcing the notion of the centrality of the state. It followed that, if the fiscal and monetary powers of the state could be used to soften the worst effects of the business cycle, then surely it could be used to lessen social hardships.

Government Transfers

In 1993, the country's 3 levels of government spent almost $95 billion transferring money to people. Social spending shot up from 9.6% of the GDP in 1989 to a peak of 13.3% in 1993 before falling back to 12% in 1996. In 1997, it dropped further to 11.5% as the economy continued to expand. In contrast, during the 1970's, the average social spending was 7.5% of the GDP.

Almost 47% of government transfers are aimed at seniors, up from 41% in the 1980's and 36% in the 1970's. As Canada ages, that tilt will become even more pronounced. By 1995, more than 3 million Canadians received social assistance, while 20% of all Canadians — including many seniors — lived below the poverty line.

What is the government's responsibility to people caught in the welfare trap — the poorly educated, multi-generational welfare recipients, single women with children, and those with emotional problems?

Alberta, in an attempt to steer people away from the system, overhauled its programs in 1993, cutting welfare rates and making it more difficult to apply, concurrently placing more emphasis on education and job training. The result was a dramatic drop of 60% in case loads — from 94,087 in March, 1993, to 39,506 in April, 1997.

But for those left on the welfare rolls, life remains grim. About half of those remain there for reasons related to mental or physical health.

> *Our technological ingenuity in inventing things to do to people, in the cause of health care, has long since outstripped our communal ability to pay for them.*[93]

Health Care

In 1966, the Medical Care Act created Canada's medicare system — a tribute to the perceived benefits and healing powers of sharing communal wealth. But, in the words of pollster Angus Reid, medicare is starting to look "crumbly around the edges."

In 1980, Canadian governments spent about 6% of the GDP on health care, rising to 7.5% in 1993, and 9.2% by 1996. Despite spending more on health care than most other advanced countries (Britain at 6% and Japan at 6.5%), we are not getting a better health system in return. (The US spends 13% of GDP on a system that still leaves the bottom 10% without coverage.) **Health care spending in Canada has doubled between the mid-1980's and the mid-1990's, with no evidence that we are healthier as a result.**

Some of the problems driving up the cost include a large number of hospital beds — the more beds available, the more patients will be admitted to fill them — and a high ratio of doctors to patients, creating unnecessary consultations, procedures and prescriptions. Some analysts claim that as much as 30% of all medical procedures are unnecessary.

These wasteful practices are symptomatic of a fee-for-service system that contains a built-in incentive for doctors to do unnecessary procedures and consultations. It rewards doctors who maximize the number of patients they see and penalizes those who take the time to explain and discuss health problems with their patients.

Despite what critics say, we can no longer afford our expensive health care system, and the obvious way to reduce costs would be to create a 2-tier system. As our society ages, our population will put an even greater strain on the system, so the pressure to enlarge the 2nd tier of the health care system will intensify in the years ahead. Some Canadians who are unwilling to wait for elective surgery already go to the US to buy procedures there. Why not open the market here, and plow the profits back into the system? **Look for the for-profit health care sector to be a growth industry.** Canadians themselves are not even as opposed to user fees as they once were, realizing that our system will deteriorate in the face of underfunding.

Foreign Aid

For decades, Canadians had a reputation as leaders in helping developing countries, but this is no longer so. Canadians, in fact, are paltry supporters of the planet's poor, with government under public pressure to help its own. A report published by international aid agencies found that Canada had slipped below the middle of the list of donor countries. In the post-1993 scramble to balance its books, the liberals in Ottawa slashed aid by 40%, far deeper than other federal programs.

Canada's foreign aid budget is now $1.8 billion (60% of it "tied aid" that must be spent on Canadian goods and services), a lowly 0.3% of the country's GDP. That falls short of our highest mark of nearly 0.5% in 1990 and our one-time pledge of 0.7%.

Haiti is now the single largest recipient of Canadian foreign aid, yet the country is worse off today than when we began our effort in 1994; corruption flourishes at every level of the government in this poorest nation in the hemisphere. (See page 34.)

The dilemma for charities is that Canadians tend to open their wallets when there are crises, but programs that are preventive and inventive are always struggling.

UNICEF, the international charity set up to feed and vaccinate hungry children after World War II, has 40,000 volunteers in Canada. It is best known for its Halloween penny collection, which now raises $3.3 million nationally, about 20% of its total revenues.

Service clubs have stepped in and become major players in supporting international causes. The Kiwanis Club has pledged to raise $100 million for salt-iodization programs in developing countries. (Lack of iodine is the principal cause of mental retardation.)

The Rotary Club has pledged $400 million to eradicate polio, a preventable disease that cripples 150,000 children a year. The Lions Club has spent more than $200 million to eliminate blindness caused by vitamin A deficiency, which affects 250,000 children a year.

Gambling

One way governments have been raising funds to pay for all of our social programs is through gambling — casinos, lotteries and slot machines. This is morally wrong. Gambling tends to prey upon the weakest members of society; while it may rake in millions of dollars initially, it actually costs society in terms of lost productivity and health care. Around 5% of the people in casinos suffer disastrous losses, and they are 6 times more likely than others to commit suicide.

Charities, which are seeing contributions from governments, corporations and individuals dwindle, are caught in this moral dilemma. When Toronto City Council decided to fight the province over charity casinos — the public had voted overwhelmingly against them in referendums in the municipal election — a coalition of fundraising groups that were losing funding accused the City Council of saying "no to charities and yes to crime."

> *Government was elected to protect its citizens, not become the house.*

185

VLT's: The Crack Cocaine of Gambling

A Nova Scotia Supreme Court judge has ruled that the province shared some of the responsibility for a woman who became addicted to video lottery terminals and stole nearly $14,000 from the local Legion to support her gambling habit. The judge said her addiction was assisted by the government and that society must realize that, if VLT's are allowed, then more crime is sure to follow.

Despite examples such as this — horror stories of blown savings, destroyed marriages, bankruptcy and suicide — it took a tremendous amount of public pressure to stop the Ontario government from placing thousands of VLT's in racetracks, permanent charity casinos and bars. This would have made it the nation's biggest VLT operator, generating revenues that would rival the $700 million annual profit of its liquor monopoly.

This is just the latest in what has been called a "tidal wave" of institutionalized gambling that has swept North America. Although lotteries and casinos were illegal in Canada until 1969, and slot machines and VLT's as recently as 1985, governments themselves seem to have quickly become addicted to something that was once considered a moral and social evil.

The attraction of large sums of money from gaming is just too appealing for governments to resist. As Donna Laframboise of *The Globe and Mail* put it so eloquently, "This gambling trend is about governments who have begun to believe their own lottery advertising: that one gets ahead not by hard work and careful planning, but by seeking pots of gold at the end of rainbows."

In Ontario, what started as a $100 million-a-year flirtation with lottery earnings in 1975 could balloon into a $5.4 billion annual revenue generating industry by 1999, once slot machines and mini-casinos are established. On average, provincial governments raise $4.5 billion a year — or 2.7% of revenues — from gambling.

Lottery revenues may have soared, but the social service contributions have not kept pace.

Paying a High Price

The goldmine is getting cleaned out as society pays the price for profits. Besides being excessively punitive to the underclass, it is an inefficient way to raise revenues, and gambling creates an added drain on the criminal-justice and health care systems.

The Alberta government, for example, took in about $625 million from all kinds of gambling in 1996, and is only putting $3 million back into addiction treatment for what statistics indicate could be as many as 160,000 problem gamblers. Experts estimate that every problem gambler drains $20,000 a year from society in terms of family counselling, addiction treatment, bankruptcy proceedings and lower work productivity. That translates into a cost of $3.2 billion a year to raise that $625 million in Alberta alone.

The Harvard Medical School conducted a study on the prevalence of problem gambling, and discovered that 1% of adults and 6% of teens are compulsive gamblers, and an additional 3% are problematic gamblers.

A study by the Washington Centre for Pathological Gambling says that every problem gambler can adversely impact between 10 and 17 others — family, friends, employers, community groups and government. The costs can take the form of family breakups, unpaid loans, unproductive workers and higher demands for social services.

In Alberta, a 1997 study found that more than 1/3 of the province's gambling revenues comes from the 5% of the population who are problem gamblers.

Proponents say a compromise could be reached by having VLT's run only 4 hours at a time, or run only 3 or 4 days a week. Many admit, however, that it is probably a mistake to ever have them in bars and lounges; "if a person is in a bar every night, there's already a problem."

> *Gambling... relies disproportionately on the addicts, on people who are unable to control their urge to gamble. **This is a money tree whose roots go deep in human misery.***
> — Jim Gray, Chairman,
> *Canadian Hunter Exploration & leading VLT critic.*

Ironically, liquor and tobacco are subject to far stricter regulations than gambling — the Ontario casinos and the Montreal casino are open 24 hours a day, 7 days a week.

One reader of *The Toronto Star* summed it up in a letter to the editor, saying that the "proud assertion that the Ontario casino industry has created some 30,000 jobs and brought in billions of dollars in revenue is much like asserting that the alcohol industry creates — directly or indirectly — hundreds of thousands of jobs for police, ambulance drivers, paramedics, nurses, anaesthetists, surgeons, physiotherapists, undertakers, cemetery operators, etc., and, as a result, produces billions and billions of dollars in economic benefits."

Niagara Falls' mayor "wins" at VLT!

A Call to Alms[94]

*The present system is rooted in the 19th century view of **charity,** the concept of the rich giving to the poor, not the modern concept of helping people.*[95]

Canadians may like to think of themselves as generous people, but the fact is that they are not; median level of giving among Canadians is a measly $150 annually. Factoring in inflation, Canadians give less to charity today than they did in 1984, and the number of people making donations has fallen steadily since 1990. Only about 1/3 of the taxpayers actually make donations that they claim as a tax deduction. It is a far cry from the days of tithing, or what in Quebec was called *la dime*, 1/26 of the harvest or 2 weeks' pay.

At the same time, **the voluntary sector delivers services worth more than $3,000 per citizen.** For example, if you have ever had surgery, gone to the opera, had a child enrolled in amateur sports, studied English or French as a second language, watched public television, attended university, gone to a place of worship, had a family member with a serious illness or played with your kids at a playground, you have benefitted from "charity." Charity today is far removed from the notion of alms for the poor, as Canada's voluntary sector delivers a vast array of health, social, cultural, educational, recreational and spiritual services.

Big Business

roadkill-drjobs.com

The voluntary sector employs more than 1.3 million Canadians, 1 in every 11 jobs. Charities pay out salaries and benefits of more than $40 billion a year; most of the other $50 billion that passes through the sector goes to program delivery (65%) and administration (15%); they are repeatedly touted as a principal growth area in the so-called "new economy." In addition to paid employees, more than 1.6 million people do volunteer work for charitable organizations every month, a contribution valued at $12 billion a year to the economy. More than $90.5 billion passes through the voluntary sector each year — the equivalent of the GDP of British Columbia — and governments are "off-loading" more programs every day. This approach of government expects more from charities with less funding, and is driven more by wishful thinking than thoughtful policy.

Until recently, little attention was paid to other benefits of doing good, namely the sector's contribution to prosperity, as a source of economic activity and key contributor to social stability. This informational and policy void is troubling, and becomes more so when you realize that the voluntary sector is struggling for recognition and respect at a time when it is increasingly expected to fulfill society's desire for collective assistance.

Big Assets

Registered charities own equipment and buildings ranging from the Optimist Club halls to the volunteer ambulances that form the foundation of community activity or a lifeline to the outside. The value of those assets is conservatively estimated at $109 billion.

Consider that the voluntary sector has revenues that are 3.5 times the value of all crops and livestock. Charities in Canada have revenues about 8 times as large as the transportation sector. Yet, while there are ministers for the agriculture and transporation there is no Canadian Charities Commission.

Impact of Government Cuts

If there has been a positive impact of government cuts, it has been to awaken this sleeping giant to the fact that it is being marginalized. The charitable sector is realizing that if it is going to survive, it has to start flexing its muscle and mobilizing its army of volunteers. The 1st step has been to increase its visibility and to begin demanding a place at the table as governments and corporations reshape the social and economic agenda.

In building a social welfare system that is the envy of much of the world, Canada has chosen to fund most basic services through tax collection, while contracting out much service provision to community-based groups.

Unfortunately, many politicians today conveniently ignore the 1st part of the equation, promoting the fiction that charities can miraculously fill the gap if we all dig a little deeper. The truth is that we have to lower expectations or make tough choices about our priorities as a society. After long ignoring the voluntary sector, governments suddenly have grand expectations. We cannot continue to off-load costs at the expense of social justice. Yet, as the voluntary sector increases its profile and carves out its rightful place in the public policy framework, Canadians and their elected leaders must grapple with a host of difficult issues.

Charity is far removed from the collection plate and the tin cup. It is about building an inclusive, caring community. Just as we are willing to invest in traditional infrastructure, so should we be willing to make a commitment to organizations that uphold our values of compassion, social justice and generosity.

Ethnic/Religious Giving

As the face of Canada changes, so does that of its donors, creating new opportunities and new challenges for fundraisers. For example, there is a very strong tradition of giving in many Eastern countries, particularly to support social services, health and education.

Direct mail, the most successful fundraising tool in mainstream Canada, is a bust in the Chinese community. Door-to-door canvassing is equally frowned on. But public events, like fundraising banquets and walkathons, are very popular. In the Indo-Canadian community, on the other hand, mail or phone solicitation is considered rude, but door-to-door canvassing is an accepted practice. Canada's aboriginal people are among the country's most generous donors.

The religious basis for giving is often overlooked. Many religious groups practice some form of tithing.

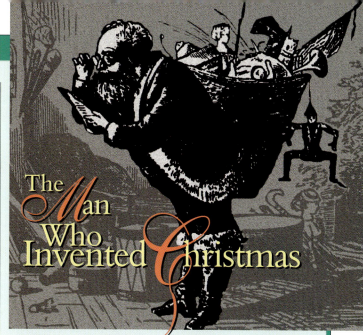

Fundraising

Despite all the letters, phone calls, pleading advertising, special events, and the lottery tickets and merchandise being sold for charity, only 11% of the voluntary sector's revenues come from fundraising. The vast majority comes from taxes. **For every dollar donated, the government contributes $5.80 to charitable organizations.** The result is that in this age of downsizing and budget balancing, fundraisers have to increase donations by $6 for every dollar the government cuts, just to keep services at their current level.

In Canada, the most successful form of fundraising by far is direct mail. It accounts for $1 out of every $5 raised and serves a key "prospecting" function — identifying donors who support the cause and will give in other ways.

Monthly donations really give a bang for a buck. As an added bonus, monthly givers, many motivated by environmental reasons, are removed from mailing lists.

The United Way and its popular payroll deduction plan has an uncertain future, even though in 1996, Canadians donated $252 million to the United Way/Centraide, making it the country's most formidable fundraiser. But it gets the vast majority of its money from work place giving; disappearance of giant factories and the trend towards working at home bode poorly for its continued success. Corporations are also taking a greater interest in their own charitable and volunteer activities. Rather than glibly signing on to the United Way, an increasing number are doing their own workplace campaigns. Baby boomers and Generation Xers also dislike workplace giving. They have a certain disdain for well-established agencies and want hands-on control to designate where their money will go.

The most popular form of fundraising is special events, an approach used by 2/3 of charities, although they account for less than 15% of money raised from the public. The problem with special events is their unpredictability.

Product sales are a mainstay of many groups, but it is an expensive and inefficient way to raise funds. The money-maker tends to be the manufacturer or wholesaler. Increasingly taking the place of product sales are alliances with businesses.

While an irritant to many, phone solicitation can be lucrative. The trick again is calling on people who already have given to the cause. Cold calls, where telemarketers phone randomly, have a deservedly poor reputation for being the preferred method of fraud artists.

As discussed on pages 102-103, charities have long turned to gaming as an easy source of money, but they have become increasingly dependent in the 5 years since governments began seriously budget cutting. More than half of non-religious charities now raise a significant porition of their revenues from gambling.

Three-quarters of charities receive unsolicited donations, accounting for $1 out of every $10 raised. The vast majority of donations come in the form of bequests. Less than 5% of people leave money to a charity in their will, making this an area of great opportunity.

> **Unlike Americans, super-rich Canadians are particularly stingy.**

The Man Who Invented Christmas

Christmas at the beginning of the Industrial Revolution was not the booming commercial season it is now; that all changed with Charles Dickens and his publication of *A Christmas Carol* in 1843. He, more than anyone else, invented the modern celebration of the season.

Christmas for Dickens had only the very smallest connection with Christian dogma or theology. He aspired to a religion of the heart that transcended sectarian dogma, and found it in the celebration of Christmas.

In a more general sense, Dickens' Christmas was a tool in the battle against the drabness of English industrialism: In fighting for Christmas he was fighting for the old European festival, for that trinity of eating, drinking and praying.

By contrast to this ferocious good cheer is a frequently dark and troubling undercurrent. Dickens' Christmas stories contain some of his most powerful attacks on the injustice of corrupt institutions and the grinding poverty of the working classes. He reminds us that those 2 great virtues of Christmas, charity and mirth, are the weapons to beat these cold and brutal forces.

Dickens' very real concerns for the poor and the labouring classes were demanding more and more of his time. He planned to write a pamphlet to be called *An Appeal to the People of England on Behalf of the Poor Man's Child*. But, happily, he changed his mind and decided to channel his anger into a Christmas story which would last forever.

The story is familiar enough: Ebenezer Scrooge, a coldhearted miser who despises Christmas, is visited on Christmas Eve by ghosts. They take him into his past and his future to reveal the causes and consequences of his selfish life. He awakens on Christmas morning, frightened out of his wits and determined to change his ways. He realizes at last that, as the ghost of his former business partner had told him, his real business was not a matter of trade, but of the common welfare... charity, mercy, forbearance, and benevolence.

Scrooge is the embodiment of all that concentration on material power and callous indifference to the welfare of human beings. His conversion, moreover, is more than the transformation of a single human being. It is a plea for society itself to undergo a change of heart. Whether the Christmas visions would or would not convert Scrooge, they convert us. All of which is doubtless true enough and accounts in part for the enduring nature of the book.[96]

The Roles of Corporations

Canadian corporations have a reputation not only for conservative giving habits, but for being miserly. Record profits have served to underline that image, while the percentage of those profits that corporations donate to charities has declined. Corporate Canada gives only about $1.2 billion to charities annually. Fewer than 5% report charitable contributions to Revenue Canada, and **more than half the 3,200 Canadian corporations with assets of more than $25 million do not give a penny to charity.**

The 5 big banks have served as a lightning rod for critics of philanthropy. Among them, they gave a total of about $50 million in 1996 — less than 1% of their profits. While certainly not an impressive figure, the banks are among the country's most generous corporate donors.

Lots of Room to Grow

Some corporations are recognizing that charitable giving is not so much an expense as a strategic investment. In addition, corporate citizenship entails myriad responsibilities, social and economic — from promising employability through to community health. A Harvard business professor argues that the factors that are important for cities to attract and retain business are "magnets and glue." The magnets are the usual business stuff such as low taxes, good transportation, a skilled work force, but the glue is the social capital — social agencies, sports groups, cultural institutions and a sense of community.

Promoting Volunteers

Businesses are learning that donations can come in the form of freeing up employees to be active in social causes. Employee involvement is good for morale, for the community and for the company — especially if it is one of the few contributions that a cash-poor company can make.

Chevron Canada created one of the country's most active employee volunteer programs, in which employees can take paid leave to do volunteer work. At Flint Canada, a construction firm, an impressive 75% of head office staff volunteer regularly, and the company pays for the training of those who want to improve their skills.

Socially responsible companies also attract more business. Research has found that 80% of consumers "decided to do business with a company because of its community involvement" and 74% "chose not to do business with a company or buy products from companies" that were not acting in the best interests of the community.

The success of Canadian Pacific has always been linked directly to the health of communities along the railway. In 1883, William Van Horne made CP's first donation, $2,000 for construction of the Winnipeg General Hospital. In recent years, the tradition has continued as each CP Hotel has been paired with a shelter for battered women, providing furniture, bedding, toiletries and volunteers.

> *Business is jumping into education with both feet because they're scared. They realize there is a link between social infrastructure and their future prosperity.*[97]

Canada's Biggest Corporate Donors [98]

Company	$ Donated (millions)
Royal Bank of Canada	$17.0
CIBC	16.5
Bell Canada	13.3
Imasco Ltd.[53]	10.7
Bank of Montreal	10.0
Imperial Oil	6.3
Scotiabank	6.0
Noranda	4.8
Glaxo Wellcome Inc.	4.6
Nova Corp.	4.0
Merck Frosst	4.0
Power Corp.	4.0
Shell Canada Ltd.	3.5
Toronto-Dominion Bank	3.5
Canadian Pacific	3.0
Bombardier Inc.	3.0

The notion, however, that businesses give to conservative, risk-free causes is increasingly being challenged. An analysis found that, among 143 corporations surveyed: 28% give to education (almost exclusively post-secondary); 22% to social service charities; 21% to health organizations; 12% to arts and culture; 8% to civic causes, and 4% to environmental projects.

Quebec software firm Tecsys Inc. invests more than $100,000 annually in a school for high school dropouts, spends at least 10% of company profits on educational causes, and makes a free summer camp available to a number of community groups.

Molson Co. Ltd. raised eyebrows years ago when it became the country's biggest corporate sponsor of AIDS groups. However, the highest per capita beer sales are in gay bars, and 3 of the 5 biggest bars in Canada are gay bars, so the commitment makes good business sense.

> *In 1946, the US government allowed corporations to write off charitable contributions up to 5% of profits, and that figure has now been raised to 10%.*

Canada has no tradition of philanthropy.

The Roles of Benevolent Organizations

A Supreme Court challenge is underway to establish new rules for deciding what constitutes a charity in Canada. Critics argue that the current law is incoherent and woefully out of date, since the criteria now used by Revenue Canada to determine charity status are based on the Statute of Elizabeth of 1601 and the Pemsel case of 1891. There are about 5,000 applications for charitable status annually, of which 2/3 are approved.

As a society, we have to ask ourselves, is something a charitable organization, or a de facto government agency that is not accountable in the same manner as public institutions? The question is as pertinent for para-governmental institutions like universities and hospitals, which, technically at least, are charities. Between them, teaching and health-care institutions account for 58% of "charitable" revenues, but less than 5% of charities.

Another little-analyzed fact is that the charitable sector is clearly dominated by religious institutions. Almost 2/3 of individual donations in Canada go to religious institutions, making them the biggest beneficiaries of tax credits for giving. Churches, temples, mosques and the like are also granted exemptions or discounts on property taxes.

A controversial aspect of Canada's regulation of the voluntary sector is the restriction placed on advocacy. In an era where governments provide funding for various groups to advocate on behalf of consumers, charities still risk losing their status if more than 10% of their receipted donations are spent on advocacy.

Mostly Small-Time Players

A Supreme Court case could have dramatic repercussions for a sector that handles $90.5 billion annually, employs more than 1.3 million people, and relies on 1.6 million volunteers a month. The 75,000 registered charities across the country fit into 6 principal categories: advancement of religion, health, education, relief of poverty, culture or other purposes that benefit the community. The charity status allows organizations to carry on business without paying taxes, and they can also issue tax-refund receipts for donations.

Best Practices — **The 5% Club**

The "Minnesota Tradition" is alive and well in Minneapolis, Minnesota, an economic powerhouse and home to 32 of the Fortune 1000 companies. In 1998 unemployment was 1/2 the US national average (2.7%), the city has a budget surplus of $2.8 billion and manages to maintain relatively generous social programs. The notion of corporate philanthropy encouraged 147 businesses to join the Keystone Club of the Greater Minneapolis Chamber of Commerce, promising to donate at least 5% of pre-tax, domestic profits to charity. Another 90 corporations pledged at the 2% level. The philosophy here is that the best return businesses can get on an investment is to spend on children by providing a decent education and keeping them out of poverty. They have calculated that, for every dollar they spend on children today, society will save 6 dollars in the long run.

As in society in general, there is an unstated class system within the charitable world. Half have revenues of less than $50,000, and fully 80% have revenues of less than $250,000. Almost 2/3 of charities have 1 or no employees. The big charities (the 10% with revenues of more than $1.5 million), on the other hand, are not only the most adept at getting government funds, they also scoop up 75% of the donations. For example, the Canadian Red Cross Society has revenues of $500 million and more than 7,000 full-time employees. While it has another 2 million volunteers and raised $34 million in donations in 1995-96, 90% of its revenues came from government.

Monitoring Abuses

Fundamental decisions about politically charged issues like advocacy are difficult to make without basic information about the activities of charities and without an infrastructure to facilitate its collection and dissemination. The UK has created an independent, government-funded body called the Charity Commission. This commission is not only responsible for the registration of charities, but for making information available to the public. At a time when we are all being bombarded with fundraising appeals, a similar clearing house for factual data would be most welcome, especially in a country where regulation is virtually non-existent (Alberta is the only province that has legislation designed to curtail abusive fundraising activities) and where unethical groups cannot hide behind the secrecy provisions of the Income Tax Act.

A Portrait of Canada's Charities 94						
Type of charity	No. of each	% of total number of charities	Revenues ($ billions)	% of revenues from government	% of revenues from donations	Employees per charity
Places of Worship	25,458	35.6	$5.3	1.6	72.6	56,000
Hospitals	978	1.4	27.5	65.6	0.9	468,000
Teaching Institutions	2,642	4.5	23.5	69.7	3.6	278,000
Public Foundations	3,466	4.9	4.7	46.3	29.4	48,000
Private Foundations	3,356	4.7	1.5	20.2	42.2	6,000
Community Charities	34,285	49.5	25.5	49.3	14.8	465,400

The Roles of Individuals: The 3rd Sector

Dubbed "the 3rd sector," French social scientists attempted to clarify the distinction between the social economy and the market-exchange economy. The social economy is not measured in terms of sales and revenues, but in the indirect economic gains — the number of handicapped persons cared for at home and not in hospitals, or the degree of solidarity among people of different age groups in a neighbourhood. Canadians may not be generous with their cash, but in any given month, an estimated 1.6 million are working, without remuneration, in soup kitchens, blood-donor clinics, sports leagues, hospitals, libraries, schools, seniors' homes and art galleries. Consider, for example, that 80% of Canada's firefighters are still volunteers.

About 27% of adults across Canada do volunteer work for an established organization, averaging 190 hours a year. Half as many again regularly do informal volunteer work, like shoveling a neighbour's driveway. Two-thirds have jobs, the most active age group is 35-45, and women are more likely to give their time.

Motivation

The nation's schools, colleges, hospitals, social service organizations, conservation and environmental protection groups, animal welfare organizations, neighbourhood advisory councils, volunteer fire departments, and civilian security patrols are "all creatures of the 3rd sector." Author Jeremy Rifkin adds, however, that appropriate incentives will need to be put in place to encourage people to contribute in some way to the 3rd sector, warning that the new group of high-tech international workers is likely to retreat from civic responsibilities in the future. These workers will prefer not to share their incomes with the country as a whole.

Incentives could include legislation to provide millions of unemployed with meaningful work in community service, tax deductions for every hour of volunteer time given to legally certified, tax-exempt organizations, social wages as an alternative to welfare payments, benefits for those willing to be retrained and placed in jobs in the 3rd sector, and salary scales similar to those in the public sector.

As government expanded in the 1950's and 1960's, it encompassed tasks that used to be the responsibility of the community, to the point that people became too reliant on government agencies. Now that governments are cutting back, people are going to have to start taking part in community service again.

Tax Incentives

There is renewed pressure for the Canadian government to do what the US government has done for more than 60 years — allow expenses incurred in the course of doing charitable work to be deducted from income taxes. As governments cut back their own funding, it is important that they encourage people to get involved in volunteer organizations, and this certainly would help.

Thanks to better tax breaks, for example, Canadians dug deeper into their pockets in 1996 to help charities. A total of 5.5 million taxpayers donated $4 billion — an increase of 11.5% over the previous year.

Dollar for dollar, government investment in programs designed to complement and support the volunteer sector have proven to be among the most cost-effective means of providing social services in local communities.

Community Charities Broken into Types
94

Type of charity	No. of each	% of total number of charities	Revenues ($ billions)	% of revenues from government	% of revenues from donations	No. of Employees
Social Service	10,317	5.8	$8.800	59.5	12.9	165,000
Health	3,180	4.5	6.400	54.4	17.9	102,000
Education	4,158	5.8	3.500	46.0	7.7	89,000
Religion	3,978	7.3	2.700	9.7	27.2	38,000
Benefits to Community	5,238	7.3	2.500	52.0	11.2	71,000
Arts & Culture	3,187	4.5	1.900	57.0	7.0	n/a
Libraries/Museums	1,615	2.3	1.300	58.0	9.0	n/a
Recreation	2,573	4.5	0.656	50.0	18.0	n/a
Other	1,087	n/a	0.107	1.4	65.9	400

National Service

National service — the enlisting of young volunteers to participate in community service programs — has been called "an instrument of developing human values." Supporters point to the benefits to those who are served, to those who serve, and to society at large, saying that well-run programs yield services with a value higher than the cost of the program.

Many see a strong relationship between national service and human rights, women's rights, environmental protection, economic development, population, and understanding among races. Participants emerge with more awareness of the needs of others, greater employability, and a much clearer sense of their career options and interests. Says one proponent, they "learn skills, work habits, safety practices, cooperation, and pride in a job well done. They acquire decision-making abilities; self-esteem; self-confidence; self-discipline; social maturity; new attitudes to authority, family, community; and new understanding between ages, races, ethnic and linguistic groups."

The CCC: Camp William James

At a global conference on national service, the keynote speaker spoke of national service as a rite of passage. He had been a student volunteer in a 1940 US national service experiment called Camp William James, which was associated with the Civilian Conservation Corps and supported by President and Mrs. Franklin D. Roosevelt. "The sacrifices it inspired, the nobility of its purposes, the diversity of those who were participants: men and women, black and white, educated and uneducated, rich and poor, a cross-section of youth in American society. That was Camp William James," he recalled. "When I retired about 12 years ago and looked back at my life, I realized that was the pivotal experience. I would have been a different person if I hadn't participated in Camp William James."

National service is so popular internationally that there has been a call for the United Nations to consider creating a UN passport for international volunteers. In developing countries, youth service is seen as a valuable tool in the preservation of traditional cultures. Even in North America, traditional cultures have benefitted, such as the Seneca Nation of Indians in New York State which was given a grant for a project in which young adult volunteers served as personal health aides to tribal elders. At the same time, the elders served as mentors to the young people, passing along their traditional culture and language.

The idea of national service is currently enjoying a renaissance, as budgets limit social services resources from governments, and young people search for job skills and experiences during times of higher youth unemployment.

Volunteering is more powerful than casting a vote. It allows you to mold your community and your country in a very real way.[99]

Canada World Youth

Canada has also offered a variety of national service opportunities to its young people for years. Since its creation in 1971, Canada World Youth has allowed more than 14,000 young people (ages 17 to 20) "to participate actively in just, harmonious and sustainable societies." CWY and its partner organizations work together on international education exchange programs, 7 months in length, with half the time spent in Canada and the other half in an exchange country in Asia, Africa, Latin America, or the Caribbean. Participants perform volunteer service in fields such as agriculture, community work, education, and the media, and in the process learn about other environments, cultures, and values, work toward mutual understanding, and contribute effectively to the development of their communities.

Another program offers opportunities for summer jobs that provide both work skills and work experience. Student Business Loans provides financial assistance to young people with entrepreneurial drive to develop their own jobs by giving loans for the summer. Summer Employment/Experience Development (SEED) offers wage subsidies to employers who otherwise would not create summer jobs for students. These work orientation workshops, combined with on-the-job experience, encourage participants to continue their education or seek specific skills training.

Katimavik

Approximately 20,000 young Canadians participated in Katimavik from its founding in 1977 until its demise in 1986. Katimavik's main objectives were:
- To help in the personal development of Canadians between the ages of 17 and 20,
- To serve Canadian communities,
- To stimulate environmental awareness, and
- To give young Canadians a greater understanding of their country.

Participants met these objectives through travel and service in 3 different regions of Canada; through living in 13-member group homes, where they assumed household chores and responsibility for meals; through study that complemented their practical experiences, and through working with dozens of different people as they served their host communities.

Canadian University Service Overseas

Founded in 1961, Canadian University Service Overseas (CUSO) is an independent development organization working in partnership with Third World people to improve their lives both socially and economically. CUSO provides technical advisers, project funds, and administrative support to groups in the Caribbean, Africa, Asia, Latin America, and the South Pacific, and places skilled Canadians in Third World postings and funds development programs. It focuses on projects that are locally controlled, sustainable, and sensitive to the environment and to women's issues.

Environmental Youth Corps

Both Ontario and British Columbia inaugurated Environmental Youth Corps (EYC) programs in 1989. They employ persons between the ages of 15 and 24 to work on environmental projects and to learn new skills in the process. EYC members generally serve for 2 to 6 months. Each provincial government engages more than 1,000 young people per year in EYC projects.

US: AmeriCorps

A volunteer citizen service known as AmeriCorps is working to "prepare America for the 21st century as they work to guarantee all Americans the opportunity and conditions to make the most of their own lives and to help those who need and deserve it with a hand up." Since 1993, 100,000 young adults of all backgrounds between 18 and 24 have earned help paying for their education in exchange for a year of service. Volunteers meet community needs with services that range from housing renovation to child immunization to neighbourhood policing. Currently, more than 25,000 members serve in more than 430 programs across the country, which is overseen by the Corporation for National Service.

Volunteers in AmeriCorps VISTA (Volunteers in Service to America) serve in a low-income community with a sponsoring agency to develop new programs, recruit and train volunteers, write grants and organize fundraisers and media campaigns. AmeriCorps State and National Direct members are sponsored by national, state, and local nonprofit organizations. In order to meet the specific needs of the communities they serve, local AmeriCorps sponsors recruit and train AmeriCorps members themselves.

AmeriCorps has not been without detractors, however. Some Republicans in Congress believe that young adults who receive a modest living allowance and up to almost $5,000 in education vouchers for completing 1 year of service should not be paid to volunteer. Distinguishing between voluntary and mandatory service is one of the thorniest issues surrounding national service. For example, physicians and other health professionals in the US who received federal support for their education are required to serve in needy areas for 2 to 4 years.

Also in the US, the Federal Work-Study (FWS) Program provides on- and off-campus jobs for students with financial need, letting them earn money to pay education expenses. The program encourages community service and work related to the chosen course of study. The FWS salary is at least the federal minimum wage but may be higher, depending on the type of work and the skills required.

France: Collective Utility Works

In France, in an attempt to reduce the number of unemployed youth, the country launched the Collective Utility Works. Under the program, more than 350,000 young people are paid a monthly salary by the government in return for performing work in either the public sector or the non-profit 3rd sector.

UK: Community Service Volunteers

In Great Britain, Community Service Volunteers (CSV) has been operating since 1962. CSV places volunteers ages 16 to 35; each serves for a period of 4 to 12 months, and in return each is given pocket money as well as food and lodging.

Volunteers work with the homeless, the elderly, young offenders, and the handicapped. Some work on projects enabling severely disabled people to live independently, while others provide 24-hour care, relieving people who are caring for family members or others. The cost is covered by central and local governments, trusts, foundations, companies, and the projects where CSV's serve.

In its first 30 years, the program has demonstrated both the uniquely positive, cost-effective impact of non-professional volunteers and the value to young people of volunteering. "London Action," for example, places substance abusers for whom all other forms of treatment have failed — 69% overcome the habit because having others depend on them gives them a purpose. Young Offenders join CSV for their last month of sentence, with half staying on with CSV, although they are free to leave. Another 20% are offered employment on their projects.

CSV hopes that someday every high school graduate will want to give a year of service and government will have the wisdom to enable them to do so.

Zimbabwe: National Service Act

National Service in Zimbabwe is governed by the National Service Act, created originally in 1976 in response to the intensified Armed Liberation War as a means of providing forced recruitment for the war effort. With the advent of independence and the continuing improvement in regional security, the military objective became of little significance. The government, however, recognized the need to continue with the scheme, but with a shift in emphasis from the military to the economic sphere.

The current objectives of national service in Zimbabwe include the following:
* developing leadership qualities and skills;
* promoting national unity through shared experiences;
* instilling a spirit of selflessness, patriotism, and community consciousness;
* enabling the appreciation of the merits of individual and collective involvement without financial rewards;
* creating an awareness of the importance of conserving natural resources;
* imparting a variety of basic skills; and
* providing career guidance.

The young people undergo training in their preferred disciplines. Interspersed with the training are community service programs in which they are involved in national development projects such as construction of dams, building of schools, land reclamation, and conservation. In the process, they acquire skills in areas such as plumbing, carpentry and building, while the combination of work and experience makes it easier for them to find work.

Deficit and Debt: National Debt

National Debt is the total money owed by a government to its creditors. It is part domestic and part external. Domestic debt is held by citizens of the country, while external (or foreign) debt is held by foreigners, including international banks, individuals and other governments. The recent Asian economic quagmire, for example, was deeply rooted in the imprudent use of borrowed *foreign* money.

The national debt is also part direct and part indirect. Direct debt is that portion owed by the national government itself. Indirect debt is that portion owed directly by public enterprises or crown corporations but guaranteed by the government. The government must repay (or negotiate an extension for) its direct debt when it comes due. With indirect debt, the central government is called on to pay only in case of a default by an institution whose loans it has guaranteed.

Provinces in Canada borrow large sums of money without central government guarantees, and these amounts are not considered part of the national debt.

In virtually all other countries (except the US), regional and local governments are financed by the national government; if the central government borrows for this purpose, then that debt makes up part of the national debt. This difference in practice makes it difficult to accurately compare the national debt of Canada to countries other than the US.

The national debt totals published by the government include only direct debt, narrowly defined. It is more realistic, however, to count both the direct and indirect debt, since national governments may be responsible for a large indirect debt. For example, in the US, the collapse of a large segment of its savings and loan banking industry in 1989-1990 cost US taxpayers about $150 billion.

A Canadian comparison to the US S&L bailout is Ontario Hydro debt. The provincial crown corporation has obligations estimated as high as $50 billion; however this obligation is not included in either the federal or provincial acknowledged debts.

It will need to be paid eventually but no provisions for payment have been made.

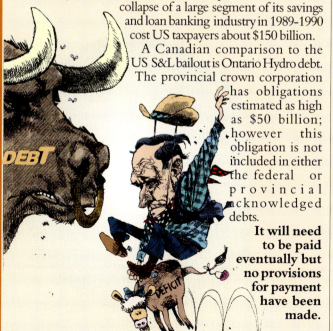

> *In advanced capitalist countries, national debt is primarily domestic. In Third World countries, national debt is typically external, the creditors being large international banks and the governments of richer nations.*

Growth of National Debt

Over time, the size of the national debt increases in nearly all countries undergoing economic development. This has been evident at least since the Industrial Revolution. Debt creation, taxation and money creation are the major mechanisms used by governments to finance expenditures.

When a government chooses to spend money that it does not have, it can create the money by printing new currency as Russia did causing hyper-inflation in late 1998, it can levy higher taxes or it can borrow the money and increase the debt. **Borrowing is simply deferred taxation.**

The Burden of the National Debt

Although social benefits arise from a properly managed government debt policy, real burdens also are placed upon government and society by the need to administer that debt. Advocates of a balanced budget contend that by financing through borrowing, the government forces current spending to be paid by citizens in the future. Today's imports will probably have to be paid for with the earnings from exports in the future. Similarly, a large *external* debt can push a government into bankruptcy, because a government obviously cannot print money in the foreign currencies that may be needed to repay foreign creditors.

Most economists agree that higher taxes tend to lead to a fall in private consumption, while debt finance tends to lead to a fall in private investment. In effect, with a fixed amount of money to be lent, if the government acquires a greater share by running a deficit, there will be correspondingly less for private businesses to borrow. It is then said that government debt has "crowded out" private borrowing.

A common scenario is that government debt simply increases the cost of borrowing money for the private sector. This translates to a higher cost of goods and results in a net reduction in national productivity.

Acknowledged Federal Debt (AFD)

As of 1989, the Federal Government acknowledges *only* $583 billion in debt. This number is a sham that is inconsistent with standard accounting practices or with the financial policies of most other developed nations. As we will see in this chapter **the true obligations of our governments, *i.e.*, we the taxpayers, equal substantially in excess of $2 trillion — more than triple the AFD.**

EVOLUTION OF A FACT
WILD GUESSES CAN BE TRANSFORMED INTO BUSINESS FACTS THROUGH THE MIRACLE OF COMMUNICATIONS.

STEP ONE: WILD GUESS
I DUNNO... IT COULD BE ANYWHERE FROM ONE TO A MILLION.

STEP TWO: RUMOUR
THEY SAY IT COULD BE A MILLION.

STEP THREE: FACT
EXPERTS SAY ONE MILLION.

How To Measure the Federal Debt

Federal debt can be measured in several ways. It is sometimes expressed as a percentage of GDP, or perhaps as a net federal debt. The table on this page represents these measures over the last 50 years.

Debt as a percentage of GDP is a useful measure because the burden of a debt is most important relative to the income of the debtor. For example, if an individual owed $100,000 to creditors, he would be in financial peril if his annual income were only $30,000. But if his income were $1 million per year, then the debt is clearly more manageable.

Another problem with measuring federal debt is how to account for inflation. A $100 debt in 1940 was more of a burden than a $100 debt today. To make an accurate year-to-year comparison, we need to adjust the numbers to reflect changes in the general level of prices. In recent years, the debt has been rising very slowly because of a low inflation rate.

If we look at debt only, all we know is that the level has been rising since the 1970's. We gain no sense of how the burden of the debt has changed over time. However, if we filter out the effects of inflation and examine the size of the debt relative to the economy, then we get a much different impression.

The History of Our Debt

The Canadian federal debt was 5% larger than the entire economy at the end of the World War II; at the same time the US debt was 28% larger than its GDP. The *relative* size of the Canadian debt shrank until the late 1970's, when it began to increase.

The relative size of the debt decreased after WWII, even though the government continued to run budget

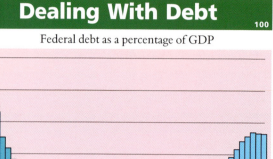

Dealing With Debt 100

Federal debt as a percentage of GDP

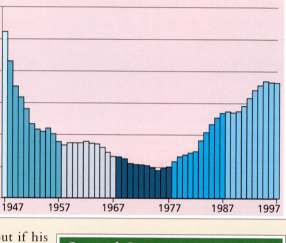

General Government Net Debt 101

Expressed as a % of GDP, National Accounts Basis

COUNTRY		DEBT/GDP	%
Japan	1988		18.3
	1998		18.7
France			14.2
			42.5
UK			23.7
			44.5
US			37.8
			49.9
Germany			21.3
			50.6
Canada			**37.7**
			63.5
Italy			90.8
			110.6

0% 20   40   60   80   100

deficits. This is possible when the economy is growing faster than the size of the debt itself. Conversely, budget deficits were small during the Great Depression, yet the relative size of the debt grew considerably because the economy shrank during that period.

While the US has the largest central government debt in the world, relative to the size of its economy, the debt is much smaller than that of several other industrialized economies, including Canada.

In addition, some nations with larger relative debts, such as Japan, had faster GDP growth rates than the US. It does not necessarily follow that a large public debt precludes a growing economy.

Composition of the Debt and Interest Payments

Nearly all of the federal debt consists of bonds issued and sold by the Bank of Canada. The securities are issued in a variety of denominations and maturities. A small portion takes the form of savings bonds and currency.

Interest payments on the federal debt have grown along with the debt itself, currently running at more than $40 billion a year on the AFD. This is more than 37% of what is spent on **all** federal program spending and approximately equal to the total annual revenue of the Ontario provincial government and about what the country spends on education. (See page 114.)

Operating vs. Capital Expenditures

Many people believe that the government finances should be run like a business, and the IMF tries to impose those standards on nations that want to qualify for loans. The accounting methodology of Canadian governments is quite different from that of the business world and is *less transparent* than most other nations.

Generally-accepted accounting practices separate a firm's expenditures into 2 categories: operating and capital expenses. Operating expenses, such as labour and material costs, are deducted directly from a firm's net revenues when computing profit or loss. Because capital equipment is useful to the firm well into the future, only a portion of its purchase cost is considered a current expense. This is called amortization and reflects the fact that a machine that is useful for 5 years is only partially used in a given year. Consequently, current expenses for the firm are considerably lower than if the firm were to deduct the entire cost in the year in which the equipment was purchased.

The federal government counts almost all expenditures in full during the year when the purchase was made. If the government had used private accounting methods, then it would have had budget surpluses even during the large deficit era of the early 1980's. Despite the many examples of clear government waste, it still turned a "profit."

> *In the 1960's,*
> *28¢ of every dollar was*
> *spent by governments;*
> *that grew to 52¢ in 1989.*

Holders of the Canadian Federal Debt
Total Debt: $583 Billion

Holders	%
Held by Government	35.5
Federal Agencies & Trust Funds	27.6
Federal Reserve Banks	7.6
Held by the Public	64.5
Commercial Banks	5.5
Money Market Funds	1.6
Insurance Companies	5.0
Other Companies	4.5
State & Local Governments	6.6
Individuals	6.7
Foreign & International	18.6
Other Miscellaneous Investors	16.4

> *Canadians have $194 billion*
> *invested abroad,*
> *and foreigners have $188 billion*
> *invested here.*

COUNTERPOINT

Implications of the Debt: Government Debt Is Not a Problem

If standard accounting conventions are not used, the financial data is severely contaminated.

Those who are not concerned about the size of government debt, notably *The Globe and Mail*, contend that regardless of how the debt is measured, its size and implications are grossly misunderstood. The most widely held misconception is that the large debt means the government is going bankrupt. As difficult and counter-intuitive as it may seem, this is not a possibility, for these reasons:

1. **Refinancing.** When a bond matures, the government does not retire that portion of the debt; instead it issues a new bond to acquire the funds to redeem the maturing debt.

2. **Taxation.** Unlike individuals or companies, the federal government has the ability to levy taxes.

3. **Creating Money.** The government can either print new money to pay the maturing bonds, or "monetize" the debt, which is to say the Bank of Canada will buy the new bonds.

4. **Debt Denominated in Dollars.** The US debt is denominated entirely in US dollars, but the Canadian debt has been denominated in foreign currencies.

In the business world, firms almost never seek to reduce their debt burden to zero. Instead they refinance those debts as they come due.

Are We Really Mortgaging Our Children's Future?

Another conservative perception of budget deficits and the federal debt is that they shift burdens from one generation to another. Higher deficits and debt increase the government's annual interest payments, which will be shouldered by future taxpayers. But ultra-liberal economic beliefs contend that this argument ignores the fact that a debt is also a credit.

While a bond represents the debt of the government, it is also someone's asset. Therefore, higher deficits and debt today translate into higher interest payments for future generations. Retirement of the national debt would "*only*" be a gigantic payment from taxpayer to taxpayer.

If a government project is financed with tax revenues, then the people at whom the tax is directed effectively pay its cost. If it is financed with debt, then the borrowed money is diverted from other current projects. If it is financed by printing new money, then the increased money supply will cause the average level of prices in the current economy to be bid upward, and the government will be able to bid the needed resources away from other projects. Again, only current resources are used.

The same is true for today's government financing choices. Regardless of the size of the debt and the deficit today, the economy's current potential output is strictly determined by the economy's current productive capacity, not by how government finances its expenditures.

Substantive Concerns About the Federal Debt

Another concern over the effect of the deficit and debt is its effect on income distribution. Because most domestic holders of the debt are upper-income families, the bulk of interest payments go to them. This means that tax revenues are collected from lower and middle-income groups and then paid to upper-income groups. In this way, **the national debt worsens income equality.**

Also, higher interest payments on the debt require higher taxes. This adversely affects incentives to work, innovate and invest. Thus, the debt shifts the burden from this generation to the next in the form of slower economic growth.

Almost 20% of the Canadian debt was held by foreigners. Interest payments to them drain purchasing power from the economy and reduce the general level of demand for goods and services.

Most economists believe that large deficits drive up interest rates, causing private investment to be lower than if the deficit did not exist — reducing the productive capacity of the future economy. This is another way the burden of current deficits is transferred to the future.

Finally, there is the concern that rising interest payments squeeze the federal budget so much that worthwhile programs cannot acquire funding. This concern is genuine when the debt is growing at a faster rate than the economy. If the economy is growing faster than the debt, then interest payments will take a smaller share of the budget. If the economy is growing more slowly than the debt, then the reverse will be true, causing prices and wages to fall.

Conclusions

Some of the popular concerns about the debt are clearly misplaced. There is no likelihood that the Canadian federal government could go bankrupt, and there is an appreciable shift of the burden of the debt from this generation to the next. But other substantive issues are at stake. The income redistribution effect in favour of upper-income groups is real, and can only be offset by costly transfer programs. The adverse impact on personal incentives is also very real and has a substantial adverse effect on the rate of economic growth. **The external debt effects are significant in the long run and should be of great concern.** The crowding-out effect cannot be offset by public investment. However, the budget-squeezing effect is minimized when the economy grows faster than the debt, which has actually been the case since 1993.

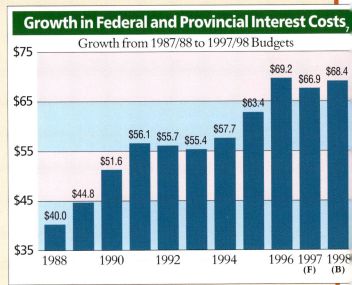

Growth in Federal and Provincial Interest Costs

Growth from 1987/88 to 1997/98 Budgets

1988	$40.0
1989	$44.8
1990	$51.6
1991	$56.1
1992	$55.7
1993	$55.4
1994	$57.7
1995	$63.4
1996	$69.2
1997 (F)	$66.9
1998 (B)	$68.4

Mergermania

A frenzy of mergers of giant companies has dominated business news as we move into the end of the century–Citybank/Travellers, Chrysler/Daimler, SBC/Ameritech, and Nova/TransCanada are big news because of their size. CNR acquired Illinois Central to create a seamless link all the way to New Orleans. PetroCan has sold its propane interests creating a company with a 70% market share. Newcourt Financial has vaulted to the position of the world's 2nd largest non-bank financier by acquiring AT&T Financial. Conrad Black's companies have moved closer to controlling the Canadian newspaper market with the acquisition of the *Financial Post*. (Now the *National Post*.)

Consolidation is another phenomenon occurring in the business sector that may have influenced the bull market pressures that drove share prices above their fundamental values — Magna, the Ontario-based auto parts giant, is a prime example of a company that has systematically integrated dozens of smaller competitors. Laidlaw now dominates consolidation in ambulances and school buses after a period of leading the consolidation in the waste management sector. Barrick plans to further consolidate gold producers. Vancouver-based Loewen Group and Service Corp International have damaged themselves by competing to consolidate cemeteries and funeral homes.

No one seems too concerned about these mergers and acquisitions. They are just part of the fabric of globalization. But the merger proposals of Royal Bank-Bank of Montreal and CIBC-Toronto Dominion has excited everyone from Paul Martin to CAW's Buzz Hargrove to neo-Luddite activist Maude Barlow. (See pages 58 and 120.)

Global supervision of the world's major financial systems, originally proposed by Canada at the 1995 Halifax G-7 meeting, is considered by many to be essential for stability of the international financial system; concern about this issue has been growing since the 1997 Asian and 1998 Russian and Brazilian financial crises. However, any potential for external control over the Canadian economy excites some factions of nationalistic activists. (See page 173.)

COUNTERPOINT

A minority of economists contend that current deficits have no effect on interest rates, and therefore have no effect on investment. Their arguments contend that since this is true, then there is no crowding-out effect, and burdens cannot be shifted in this manner. They argue that even if crowding-out exists and reduces current private investment, it is offset by the benefits of public investment.

Government Finances: Understanding 1971-1994

Throughout the 1990's, government deficits and debt have become a matter of concern for Canadians. Despite this national preoccupation, a basic understanding of government finance remains out of reach for many. Basically, debt levels in Canada are extremely high, and they continue to grow despite the elimination of the federal and most provincial deficits.

he federal debt alone represents 73% of GDP (one of the highest in the world), ith the total federal, provincial and municipal tax-supported debt topping 111% of GDP.

Debt-GDP ratios compare the size of the debt to economic activity. This is a useful measure because the economy ultimately sustains the costs of the debt through taxation.

AFD-GDP ratios in Canada, including the provinces, exceed 100%. This means that the debt has become so large it has surpassed the annual value of all goods and services produced in the economy.

As long as debt continues to grow faster than the economy, the debt-GDP ratio cannot be reduced. For the past 15 years, growth of the debt has continually outpaced economic growth. Growth in the debt may have slowed, but so has growth in the economy. Deficits increase when the economy slows, pushing up debt and increasing the amount owed.

The notion of debt being the government's problem is popular, but it is a myth. Debt does not cost governments — it costs taxpayers. In 1998, each Canadian owed about $20,000 in AFD — or $80,000 for each family of four. In addition, with some Canadians unable to carry their portion because they are too young or unemployed, the debt burden falls on those 50% who submit personal income tax returns.

Taxpayers are also liable for other debt. This includes the debt of crown corporations that today finance their own debt, but may not always be able to do so. Governments also owe unfunded public pension plan liabilities estimated to be $1.2 trillion. (See page page 120.) When these amounts are added together, the Canadian public sector's total current and contingent liabilities exceed $2 trillion.

Because governments have borrowed so heavily, huge sums of tax dollars are needed today just to cover the *interest* on outstanding debt, let alone to pay down any principal. During the 1971-1994 period, interest payments were the fastest-growing expense for every level of government. The growth in interest costs outpaced spending on health, education and welfare. Interest also outpaced growth in revenues.

Interest on the federal debt ate up 37¢ out of each tax dollar. In 1995, Canadians paid almost $73 billion in taxes to the federal and provincial governments to cover the *interest* on public debt.

This left 63¢ of every tax dollar to pay for social programs, but Canadians demand more than 63¢ in services. This demand forced Ottawa and the provinces to spend $1.25 for every $1 they received in taxes. In other words, Canadians received an extra 25¢ in services for which they did not pay; they just put the services on the government charge account.

But here's the catch to charge accounts — you eventually get the bill, with interest. Because the government borrowed billions of 25¢ pieces, more money was needed just to pay the interest.

Debt that grows faster than revenue (or the GDP) cannot continue indefinitely. Sooner or later, either most taxes will go towards interest or taxes will have to rise substantially. The only way out is to cut spending.

If budgets are to balance, Canadians must find ways to begin paying for the services that governments provide them. Otherwise, debt will continue to accumulate and, with it, higher and higher interest payments.

Canada's massive debt burden is the result of continual overspending for 25 years. Deficits peak during economic recessions, but their chronic presence indicates a structural, rather than purely cyclical, imbalance between revenue and expenditure.

Most Canadians do not understand that when governments run deficits, they are really borrowing money on behalf of individual Canadians and their families. It is Canadian taxpayers and not the government who are ultimately responsible for any debt that accumulates.

Deficits are really tax increases that are being postponed.

Beyond the Balanced Budget: Alternatives to Increased Taxes

There are only 3 sources of deficit reduction: (1) tax increases; (2) spending cuts; and (3) economic growth — which expands the tax base.

About 75% of the deficit reduction to date has come from increased revenues provided by a rebounding economy. When the economy grows, government revenue grows as incomes increase. Spending also decreases as fewer Canadians draw on social support programs such as EI. Most of the federal effort — the economic growth portion and also part of the cuts portion — may only be reducing the cyclical deficit. This part of the deficit is created by economic slowdown and recession. But, there is also a significant structural component, which exists in both buoyant and depressed economic conditions. Clearly, a significant portion of the savings recorded in 1996-1997 will not occur in the future if the economy takes a downturn.

In the past 2 years, spending cuts accounted for only 45% of the decline in the deficit. Another 45% came from stronger growth and the net effect of lower interest rates. Higher taxes contributed the final 10%.

About $5 billion worth of the deficit was vaporized in 1997 by the proceeds from privatizations despite the financially responsible view that all proceeds from privatizations should be applied to debt and not spent as part of operating expenses.

Despite the net reduction in program spending, Ottawa's total spending continues to grow. This has occurred because of the increasing costs of paying interest on a larger debt.

Personal income tax is the federal government's primary revenue source, but Ottawa also collects taxes on a variety of goods and services, as well as premiums for EI and CPP.

Most of these taxes have increased. EI premiums for each $100 of insurable earnings have, until recently, gone up. CPP premiums have also increased. The GST (implemented in 1991 to replace the Manufacturers Sales Tax, or MST) generates almost $4 billion annually in taxes.

Although the federal government has taken steps to lower its general corporate rate, some provinces have increased their rates. With respect to the small business tax rate, 7 of the 10 provinces have lowered their rates, while BC, Alberta and Quebec have slightly increased theirs.

Corporations today are paying more taxes. In 1986, the total federal and provincial corporate tax bill represented 21% of corporate profits. In 1996 corporate taxes represented 31% of profits. Some argue that corporations should pay even more tax, but **corporate tax is a myth; it is, for the most part, really passed on and paid by consumers through their purchases.**

Provincial sales and commodity taxes have also increased in the 1990's — 5 of the 9 provinces with sales taxes have increased their rates. In Saskatchewan, the sales tax rate has almost doubled from 5% to 9%. Many provinces have also expanded the list of goods and services to which their sales tax apply.

Cigarette taxes have also jumped considerably, although 4 provinces have joined with Ottawa to lower their rates in an effort to stop smuggling. Fuel taxes have increased in all provinces.

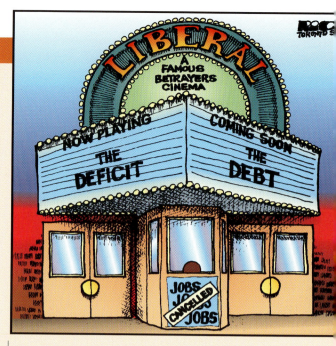

Missing the Point on the Deficit

Public concern about the deficit and debt has dwindled to its lowest level in 5 years as Canadians encourage governments to spend more on health and education — only 16% of Canadians cited the deficit or debt as an issue that "should receive the greatest attention from Canada's leaders." [103]

The will to address deficit and debt is crumbling as governments and a largely naive media continue to chatter about the **mirage** of a fiscal dividend from having a budget surplus.

Hidden Taxes and The "Real" Price of Gasoline

While people gripe about the price of gasoline and accuse the oil companies of collusion and price fixing, in reality **the pre-tax price of gasoline is cheaper than at any time this century.** The seemingly high cost is a vivid example of the insidious nature of indirect taxes on the price of consumer goods.

StatsCan published a report on gasoline prices, converting gallons to litres and all prices into inflation-proof 1995 dollars, in order to accurately compare the prices from one year to another. The report showed that the price of a litre of gasoline in 1957 was about 56¢, dropping to a low of 45¢ in 1972, hitting a high of 71¢ in 1985, and has been on a steady downward trend since. (See page 53 for international comparisons.)

Recently, gasoline has been as low as 47¢, which converts to 45.5¢ in 1995 dollars, or the same price as 1972 when the price of gasoline was at its lowest point.

More importantly, the before-tax price is even lower. If the government excise and sales taxes were collected at rates that prevailed 30 years ago, the price of gasoline could be 20% lower than it is. The combined federal-provincial tax rate in the 1980's was about 25%; today, it's above 45%.

If we paid taxes at the 1980's rates, gasoline would cost only 40¢ a litre — directly comparable to the price of gasoline in the US.

What to Do With the "Surplus"?

For the 1st time in almost 30 years, the federal government has a balanced budget. A "surprise" surplus happened in 1997. Now, the debate has begun over what to do with this new-found money.

Ottawa has promised to put 50% of any surplus towards new spending. Liberal politicians are looking for ways to spend our money, dividing a pie that does not exist. But all the talk is about spending on "hot" issues such as health, education and social services — responsibilities that clearly belong to the provinces.

Some analysts suggest that the government reduce federal taxes and let the provinces decide how to spend that money, allowing them to set spending priorities to suit local needs, demographics and ideological preferences.

Business leaders would prefer that the government put a stop to *any* big spending plans, and concentrate 1st on reducing the debt and cutting taxes. The Business Council on National Issues, representing the chief executives of Canada's 150 largest corporations, warned that the government is sitting on a "tax time bomb."

Statistics from the OECD showed Canadians paid 13.9% of GDP in income taxes in 1996, versus a G-7 average of 9.6% — almost a 45% premium.

Tax burden has definitely grown heavier for Canadians over the past 15 years through the de-indexing of income-tax brackets, higher excise taxes, higher income tax surtaxes, and the sharply increased CPP contributions.

Taxes could be cut in 1998 and beyond because Ottawa is continuing to run a budget surplus. The economy, despite a series of economic woes in foreign economies, is stronger than it has been for almost 10 years, real incomes have declined, salary and wage increases have been curtailed by a 9% unemployment rate, and Canadians deserve to be rewarded for eliminating the deficit since taxes went up originally to fight the deficit.

The Reform Party has pushed for broad-based tax cuts. But most Canadians seem relatively indifferent to paying some of the world's highest taxes. In a 1997 poll, Canadians emphasized that the surplus should be spent on debt reduction first. Canadians have bought into a metaphor of paying down the mortgage, with 47% in favour of reducing the debt, 33% wanting to cut taxes, and only 13% voting for an increase in spending.[103]

According to Angus Reid, "many of us have been left feeling that the country has lost its bearing, and maybe its soul as well."

Tax cuts could come in the form of reductions in the GST, income tax and EI premiums. The cost of cutting GST could be offset by an increase in consumer spending.

Instead of cutting taxes, however, the government makes the sleight-of-hand argument that by balancing the budget, the growing economy will reduce the debt-to-GDP ratio, which is projected to drop to below 60% of GDP within 4 years.

A Tale of Two Bridges

The MacDonald and MacKay Bridges have been the key links across Halifax Harbour since they were built in 1954 and 1969.

To construct the MacKay, and to retire the construction obligation on the MacDonald, the financially unsophisticated Halifax Bridge Commission borrowed the equivalent of $25 million in German marks. When the loan came due, in 1973, the Commission refinanced it with another foreign-dominated loan, this time — Swiss francs. The 1973 global oil bounce created an exceptional disaster in the international monetary system costing Nova Scotia taxpayers a foreign exchange loss of $15 million on the Swiss-denominated loans.

The loan, still in Swiss francs, was routinely "rolled-over," hopeful that the mounting foreign exchange losses would simply evaporate. This delusion lasted until 1981, when the authorities finally faced reality and renegotiated the loan in Canadian dollars. At the beginning of 1998, the 2 bridges, including subsequent improvements, are still shouldering a debt of $76 million! [104]

Living With The Sinking Loonie

Canadians should understand that the decrease in the value of the loonie is not something created by currency speculators, but rather the direct result of clearly identifiable, specific flaws in our economic behaviour. Most knowledgeable economists understand that raising interest rates, such as the 1% increase in August of 1998, will only compound the problems and damage the already fragile economy.

Raising interest rates would be akin to amputating the legs of an overweight person in a desperate attempt to reduce excess weight — it would reduce the weight, but it would severely handicap the individual and do nothing to address the root of the problem of being overweight. **There is no good quick fix, and, in this case, doing nothing is better than doing something wrong.** The systemic problems are broader than the standard litany of deficit, debt and tax reduction.

While the vilified international currency traders, those "25-year-olds in red suspenders," clearly compound the loonie problem, they are simply exploiting basic flaws in our economy. Currency speculation contamination should eventually be minimized with the introduction of some form of the proposed "Tobin Tax." (See page 123.)

Core Economic Problems

1. Too Much Government — Between 1960 and 1995, the cost of services provided by governments, as a % of GDP, decreased slightly in the US, while in Canada the costs of these services increased 46%.

2. Too Much Trade Union Inefficiency — In 1960, trade unions represented about 30% of the labour force in both the US and Canada. Today, the US rate has dropped to 15% and the Canadian rate, with 40+% of the membership in the public sector, has grown to 38%.

3. Too Many Taxes — The direct and indirect tax bite of Canadian governments is significantly higher than the US. The various methods of measuring this difference all contain acknowledged flaws; one of the higher methods, the one chosen by the Reform Party, puts the Canadian tax premium at 143% of the OECD average rate.

4. Low Productivity — The per capita GDP in the US is about 40% higher than the Canadian per capita GDP. This point is probably not really a cause for our poor economic performance as much as it is a symptom of the 1st three causes.[105]

1998 Federal Program Spending	**109 billion**
1998 Federal Interest Payments	**41 billion**
1998 Federal Surplus	**3 billion**
1998 Total Federal Revenue	**$153 billion**

IMF PREDICTS BOOM IN CANADIAN ECONOMY...

A Time for Action

Until we get off our butts, increase our productivity and demand more accountability (and fewer services) from our politicians, we are going to pay the price through a continuing decrease in the value of our currency — 65¢ is not the floor if we continue to implement flawed economic policy and counter-productive union controls.

Two of the excuses that appear most often as explanations for our poor economic performance are our resource-based economy and the Asian flu. While there is obviously an adverse economic impact from the Asian financial crisis, one that will overhang the market for years, it is, at best, a lame cover-up for core flaws of business that would rather ship raw or semi-finished resources than find ways to enhance the Canadian portion of the value add to these natural resources.

The Reality: The US$.65 Loonie

By and large, the 1999 market has the loonie properly valued in respect to the US$. And the low exchange rate does have at least one positive side in that it contributes significantly to our high trade surplus.

In the longer run it is helpful to our languishing balance of payments because it will dampen imports and other foreign spending. But, in the big picture, this argument really just tries to make lemonade out of a lemon economy.

Paul Martin: Canada's One-Trick Pony

There are well-deserved kudos to the successful attack on the deficit led by Finance Minister Paul Martin, but he is a classic example of a "one-trick pony." With an education limited to philosophy and law, he is a vivid example of Bentley's 2nd Law of Economics: The only thing more dangerous than an economist is an amateur economist!

With his sights set on the PM's job, he keeps ducking opportunities to make a difference — failing to reform old-age benefits, for example, will waste billions that we need for other more relevant issues.

An Overview of Financial Services

The Impact of Interest Rates: It is a truism that higher interest rates slow the economy, while interest reductions tend to stimulate it; however, high real interest rates are necessary to stimulate high real savings and satisfy the stronger demand for credit. The budget is particularly sensitive to these pressures: A 1% increase in rates that lasts for 1 year represents a $1.5 billion increase in interest costs.

The Money Market is a general term covering lending instruments with maturities of 1 year or less. These instruments include Treasury bills, bonds with less than a year to maturity, notes issued by private corporations, and tradeable certificates of deposit. Together, these securities have a highly liquid value of about $300 billion — half in Canadian government treasury bills.

The Canadian Bond Market is more than $500 billion, about 20% more than the capitalization of Canadian stock markets. Daily volume on the secondary bond market is more than 3 times the volume of Canada's stock exchanges combined. This market reacts poorly to uncertainty. Total outstanding debt on the world's bond markets, consisting primarily of domestic markets, stands at about US$25 trillion, which means that Canada represents only 2% of the world bond market.

Canadian financial institutions are naturally the largest bearers of Canadian bonds, and form something of a captive market. However, to diversify risk and increase yields, these institutions are placing a growing portion of Canadian savings abroad. Canadian bonds are seen by foreign investors as a substitute for US bonds. Canadian bonds are considered riskier because of debt, political uncertainty, and small market; they therefore demand higher interest rates.

Currency Trading: The spectacular volume of currency trading has little relation to the needs of international trade. Speculators can exacerbate the movement of capital, and they might even be able to touch off such movement. But they cannot exploit a weakness that does not exist.

Banks: Even with the significant financial sector consolidations in Canada over the last 10 years, our banks are still being dwarfed by consolidation in larger markets like the US, the UK, Germany and Japan. For example, there are single banks in Japan and the UK that are bigger than the Big 6 in Canada combined.

Insurance Companies: With assets of $500 billion, Nippon Life is the world's largest life insurance company, 10 times larger than Canada's biggest, Manufacturers Life, and twice as large as the American giant, Prudential.

In Japan, a country where appearances must be protected at all costs, cooking the balance sheet — known as "window dressing" — has become an art form as esteemed as the traditional Ikebana flower arrangements.

Pension Funds: BCE manages the pension funds of its subsidiaries Bell Canada and NorTel. With assets of $8.5 billion, it is Canada's 8th largest pension fund, and the only *private* entry in the country's top 10.

Gold Reserves Overhang the Market 106

Central banks hold huge reserves of gold. Some countries (in bold) have been selling their reserves and fears that others will follow have been driving the price of gold down. Starting in 1980, **Canada was the 1st central bank to sell off its gold reserves.**

Canada's Gold Reserves

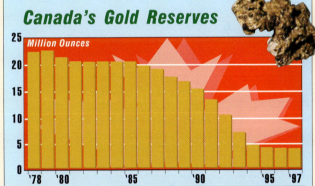

Million Ounces ('78 – '97)

Central Bank Gold Holdings (billions of $)

	1980	1990	1997
All countries	955.6	939.0	891.9
United States	264.3	261.9	261.7
Germany	95.2	95.2	95.1
Switzerland	83.3	83.3	83.3
France	81.9	81.9	81.9
Italy	66.7	66.7	66.7
The Netherlands	43.9	43.9	27.1
Belgium	34.2	30.2	15.3
Japan	24.2	24.2	24.2
Portugal	22.2	15.8	16.1
Austria	21.1	20.4	9.3
Canada	**21.0**	**14.8**	**3.1**
Britain	18.8	18.9	18.4
Spain	14.6	15.6	15.6
Australia	7.9	7.9	3.2
Sweden	6.1	6.1	4.7
Developing countries	141.7	152.4	156.6

Lying About the Size of Government Debts

Foreign Debt

During the 1980's, Canadians' foreign investments were about 37% of GDP; their liabilities to foreigners were 74% of GDP. By 1997, our foreign investments had surged to 61% of GDP.

Our liabilities to foreigners increased comparably. Most of the increase occurred between 1989 and 1994, when foreigners added about $29-billion a year to their holdings of Canadian bonds and another $5-billion worth of treasury bills.

Federal Debt

Like the spurious AFD of $583 billion that the press loves to print endlessly, *The Globe and Mail* writers continually use $102 billion as Ontario's acknowledged debt. This debt is dramatically understated because it omits "other" debt, unfunded pension liabilities and liabilities of Crown Corporations. In 1998, Ontario alone paid almost $9 billion in interest on debts.

The chart below gives a more accurate perspective including $56 billion in "other" debt, $40 billion in unfunded pension liabilities and $93 billion in the debt of Crown Corporations. Even these much larger amounts show provincial debts at a staggering $436 billion. A vivid example of the distortion is that while Ontario shows $31 billion in Crown Corporation debt, the actual obligations of Ontario Hydro alone have surged past $40 billion and may end up being as high as $50 billion. (See page 162.)

Ontario and Quebec have obligations that the taxpayers will eventually pay of 3 to 4 times their annual operating budgets. **This is the equivalent of individuals having debts totalling 6 to 8 times their after-tax income.**

Until taxpayers demand real financial transparency and the use of generally accepted accounting practices at all levels of government, we invite the serious kind of understatements of liabilites that in a publicly traded company would result in delisting by the stock exchange and probable jail terms for the misrepresenting managers.

Restructuring

The Alberta success story is covered on page 163, and Ontario has made exceptional progress in dealing with its deficit since the Harris Common Sense Revolution started in 1994. In 4 years, the province has cut 10.6% of the record-level spending of the NDP government and has cut provincial income tax to the lowest of any province at 45% of the federal tax (Alberta is close at 45.5%).

But the cost of cuts is expensive because of what economists call restructuring charges — spending more to spend less — primarily severance payments for laid-off public sector workers in the MUSH sectors. **The 1997 restructuring costs, budgeted at $900 million, actually cost provincial taxpayers $2.3 billion.**

Bank Mergers: A 1997 Perspective

Populist static has been raised about mergers of the big banks in the fall of 1998, by various anti-business groups, the Competition Bureau and the Finance Minister. The message a little over a year earlier was both encouraging and correct for the economy in the long run.

In a July 1997 report, the Task Force on the Future of the Canadian Financial Services Sector concluded that the government policy that the "big shall not buy big" has no legislative basis and that any proposed merger between 2 (or more) Schedule I banks should be assessed only on its merits especially where such transaction would have a positive or negative impact on the capacity of the institutions to adopt innovative technologies. They recommended that Competition Bureau review could proceed simultaneously with consideration by the Finance Minister.

This interim report concluded that the **"Task Force believes that mergers that can be shown to increase competitiveness, enhance innovation and benefit customers will—over the longer term—contribute to great economic growth and greater employment opportunities for Canadians than we would otherwise enjoy.** But in the short run there will most likely be transitional impacts that result in job loss."

This report is remarkably consistent with the enlightened fall 1998 report by the McKay Commission.

Federal & Provincial Government Debt in Canada, 1997/98 (billion of $)

102

	Direct Debt	Other Debt	Tax Based Debt	Pension Liability	Sub Total	Crown Debt	Total
Federal	$610,289	★	$610,289	★	$610,289	★	$610,289
BC	$11,603	$12,147	$23,750	$3,427	$27,177	$7,617	$34,794
AB	$14,833	$5,032	$19,865	$4,981	$24,846	★	$24,846
SK	$7,923	$1,155	$9,078	$3,628	$12,706	$3,489	$16,195
MB	$6,598	$2,885	$9,483	$2,570	$12,053	$5,068	$17,121
ON	$108,481	$6,050	$114,531	$8,856	$123,387	$30,867	$154,254
PQ	$79,589	$26,273	$105,862	$11,158	$117,020	$42,200	$159,220
NS	$8,283	$908	$9,191	$770	$9,961	★	$9,961
NB	$4,565	$405	$4,970	$1,200	$6,170	$3,014	$9,184
NFD	$4,498	$857	$5,355	$2,795	$8,150	$1,000	$9,150
PEI	$851	$1	$852	$240	$1,092	★	$1,092
TOTAL	$857,513	$55,713	$913,226	$39,625	$952,851	$93,255	$1,046,106

The Failure of Confederation Life

Rod McQueen's 1996 book, *Who Killed Confederation Life? The Inside Story,* reads like a compelling mystery novel. It chronicles the birth-to-death experiences of one of the country's great companies and abounds with lessons as our financial institutions grow and compete in the global marketplace. The long-term costs will be felt for years, as the international community regards all Canadian financial institutions with well-founded scepticism and cynicism.

Confederation Life was founded in 1871, 2 years before the North-West Mounted Police (now the RCMP). After 123 years, however, it was no more. The institution launched by John Kay Macdonald suffered an ignominious death; greed, stupidity and sloth were the culprits.

The tragedy is that Confed did not have to fail. In the absence of leadership from Ottawa, the industry, or Confed itself, a malaise set in that translated to: If nothing is achieved for long enough, there is nothing left to do but pull the plug. "Everyone lost the zeal to find a collective solution," said a key player in the failed rescue mission. "They [the industry CEO's] all went home to their collective camps to preserve whatever they had."

There's not all that much new in the world of why financial institutions fail: bad management, accidents, the world changes.

— Grant Reyber, Chairman, CDIC

"We created the illusion of increasing prosperity, while actually creating a sharply increasing debt."

The Seeds of the Collapse

In 1957, the federal government passed a protectionist bill to mutualize insurance companies. Ownership changed from a few families to the policyholders, a cooperative view seen as the best way to prevent foreign takeovers.

In 1990, the Canadian Life and Health Insurance Compensation Corporation (CompCorp) was created to administer a compensation fund, should a company become insolvent. New rules meant that insurance companies could use aggressive guidelines to arrive at liability figures. Any "extra" funds could be used to finance leasing companies or banks. This arcane mathematics would be at the heart of Confed's disaster.

What resulted was a system rather like the national debt. Just as governments and society became addicted to spending and allowed deficits to pile up, Confed thought it could consume its internal funds and create businesses without worrying about cost or eventual repayment. Confed issued more than 700 notes totalling more than $76 billion. Of that amount, less than 2% was ever paid off: the rest was merrily rolled over for another day, the never-never land of non-payment.

• A subsidiary was set up in Barbados to handle dental and health claims. It grew to look after 30% of the sector and saved an estimated 50% of running a similar operation in Canada.

Confed, was, in effect, printing its own money. Now, where else to put it?

• In 1986, Confed joined York-Hanover Developments Ltd. to buy the upscale stores and condos of Hazelton Lanes in Toronto for $40 million. (By 1995, York-Hanover was bankrupt — costing banks, pension funds, and individuals on 4 continents $3 billion.)

• Confed entered the murky world of derivatives — little understood and potentially fatal. (Futures trader Nick Leeson ran a derivatives portfolio unchecked in Singapore, bringing down the UK's venerable Barings Bank in 1995.)

• Newcourt Financial, the leasing company, was spun-off prior to the collapse of Confed and is now the world's 2nd largest non-bank source of financing. In August 1993, no longer controlled by Confed, Newcourt repaid $200 million in advances owed.

Winners and Losers

• Three years after the collapse, individual Canadian investors were able to get their money. About 40,000 clients recovered $1.1 billion in group and individual savings annuities.

• The policyholder losses included $275 million that the industry pumped into CompCorp, plus $175 million in losses by those policyholders above the CompCorp limits, and $800 million in losses by US policyholders.

• Fees paid mostly to lawyers and liquidators totalled $125 million in the first 2 years. These vultures were the only winners — the gravy train of a lifetime.

• Some institutional investors lost huge amounts, for a total of $157 million. The biggest loser was the Province of Ontario — $100 million of taxpayer money.

No Ownership of Political Failures

As for the Ottawa politicians and lackey bureaucrats, never has so little been done by so many in the sorry service of their country. The unwillingness of insurance CEO's to put up the money for Confed's rescue package, coupled with Finance Minister Paul Martin's categoric unwillingness to provide a "modest" $150 million bridge loan can be argued to be the "nail" that lost the shoe, that lost the horse, that lost the war. But ultimately Confed was also the victim of something else — no one cared enough to save it. In all the tragedies to hit Canada, Confed is just about the only seismic event that has not been subject to government hearings or a Royal Commission.[107]

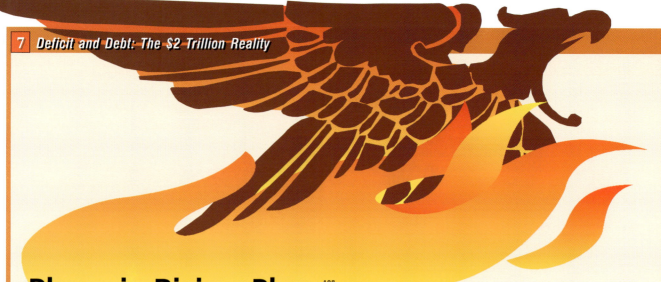

Phoenix Rising Plan: [108]

An Executive Summary

Phoenix Rising presents a unique solution to the deficit/debt problems that plague many modern governments, including Canada. It is unique from any of the standard offerings, daring in that it involves an undertaking by the financial community on a scale unheard of to date, and radical in that it requires a drastic alteration in the way that we deal with modern government. It is also conventional as it is merely an adaptation of standard business practice, commonplace in that almost every week some business uses this approach, and prudent because it terminates a common problem before it becomes too serious.

The Total Debts of Canadian Governments

For the governments of Canada, this plan proposes an equity underwriting of up to $840 million which will be used to pay down the entire acknowledged indebtedness of the government, both Federal *and* Provincial. The equity that will be used is a 30-year stream of tax revenues "bundled up" such that the new instrument will have sufficient present value to replace the principal indebtedness of the governments. The new instrument would be called the Canadian Phoenix Trust. Shares in the Trust (hereafter "Phoenix Trust Units" or "Phoenix Trust") would be exchanged for current government indebtedness on a dollar-for-dollar basis at market value. It is therefore a replacement of the existing debt — both acknowledged and unacknowledged — with prospective tax revenue "equity."

The plan begins with the self-evident proposition that the Government of Canada is in a severe financial condition. It calculates that the "negative drag" on the Canadian economy imposed by the excessive debt load amounts to roughly 2.5% of the total Gross Domestic Product. Its elimination would result in an increase in the GDP of approximately $140 billion. This number has been approximated by economists Diane Bellemare of the Universite du Quebec and Lise Poulin-Simon at Laval University in their study, *What Is the Real Cost of Unemployment in Canada?* (Canadian Centre for Policy Alternatives), who estimate that the Canadian GDP would be at least $110 billion higher if the unemployment rate for Canada fell to its structural lows of the 1950's. The difference between the 2 determinations of the current GDP shortfall lies in the degree to which the "multiplier" effect would cut in. In either scenario, the payoff would be profound in terms of growth, employment, the concomitant decline in social costs, the increase in tax revenues, and consequently the elimination of any balance of the deficits themselves.

Conventional ways of dealing with the "deficit crisis" in North America comprise 2 experiments: "Reaganomics" (cut taxes and grow your way out), and "Mulroneyism" (raise taxes, cut expenditures). Both have failed horribly. Paul Martin, the current finance minister, has been much more successful somewhat because his discipline has been better but mostly because of a hyper-buoyant economy, especially the impact of interest rates at a 30-year low.

The 1st country that has directly and successfully beaten down its **deficit**, but not its **debt**, through massive spending cuts over the past 10 years, is New Zealand (See page 9.) However, it has experienced virtually no real growth in GDP for almost a decade, and a huge increase in unemployment, which only now is beginning to abate.

Given these experiences, this plan has taken a fresh look at the problem, not from the point of view of dealing with the deficit, but rather by dealing with its underlying cause, the exponentiating debt.

The solution requires a paradigm shift. *Phoenix Rising* is a plan to eliminate the accumulated **debt** through sale of assets to reduce the debt to either zero, or at least to manageable proportions. The challenge has been to find sufficient assets to sell, as the balance sheet of the governments do not contain enough "hard" assets to even begin to pay down the $2 trillion we owe. However, governments do "own" the right to tax. It is the sale of a modest amount of this right for a fixed period which is the basis of *Phoenix Rising*.

The details are as follows:
• The federal government and its provinces sell the rights to a future stream of tax revenue to a tax-free trust. The size of that stream should be large enough to create a present value of up to $840 billion, the total of all *direct* government indebtedness. The units of the trust would be swapped for existing government debt obligations. The words "up to $840 billion" are used advisedly, as the plan calculates that an adequate job could be done by retiring as little as half of the debt.

• Assuming a 3.5% nominal growth rate in GDP and a 4.5% tax-free discount rate, it would require about 4.2% of GDP annually over a 30-year term to service and retire the $840 billion of equity trust units so created. For 1997, with a Canadian GDP of approximately $840 billion, the trust would have received approximately $35.6 billion.

• Monies paid into the trust would come from existing tax revenues. As the current cost of servicing the current debts is approximately $60 billion (and rising), there is an estimated immediate saving of roughly $28.9 billion in debt servicing costs. Monies that go to the trust not only pay the service costs, but also retire the full debt.

• The trust would be similar to a mortgage in which blended payments of interest and principal are paid out every year. The units can be subdivided and modified to meet the varying needs of investors as to term, maturity schedules, and income versus capital gains.

• Security for the trust would consist of a flat 4.2% of the GDP of the country for 30 years (assuming that all government indebtedness is retired), which means that the annual amounts paid in would grow in direct relation to the growth of Canada. Should Canadian GDP grow faster than 3½%, holders of the trust units would realize capital gains that could be very substantial. Should interest rates remain low, further gains would be realized as the required discount rate declines. The trust is also inflation-protected as the GDP growth assumption is in nominal dollars (not adjusted for inflation.)

With debt-free government balance sheets, Canada could expect not only much lower interest rates and faster growth, but also a firming dollar, thereby making this an attractive investment option in foreign markets. The elimination of debt would permanently enhance Canada's debt rating, resulting in lower interest costs, improving the climate for innovation, investment, and the overall long-term growth rate of the Canadian GDP. With strong growth, and the budgetary savings that flow directly from the conversion, deficit would turn to surplus and permit lower tax rates in the years ahead. History shows that economies with a reducing level of taxation exhibit much higher growth rates than those with rising taxation trends.

A return to growth and prosperity would provide a new sense of national purpose, pride, and confidence, coupled with a renewed faith in government.

The Phoenix Plan Approach to Solvency

Stephen Hawkings said that he feared his readership was in inverse proportion to the number of equations that he used, so he promised to keep them to a minimum. Except for a single formula in common usage for determining the present value of a common stock, *Phoenix Rising* emulates Hawkings' technique, although it provides more numbers in the appendices for those who are interested. While the techniques that are used to determine credit (or "solvency") strength are mathematical in nature and are applicable to any entity with a balance sheet, the current debt/deficit problems of our governments are so severe and well-publicized that it is unnecessary to delve into the actual approach that we use.

There is a deep insolvency at work within the estimated balance sheet of the Federal Government of Canada (and the US). The implications are that:

• Debt growth in the government balance sheet has a natural and mathematical tendency to compound, and compound at a rapid rate.

• The economic potential of Canada is being crippled, as the debt service requirements consume the nation's capital resources.

• There is a trend in this country towards more (government-induced) inflation, a lower purchasing value for the Canadian currency, higher structural levels of unemployment, and, ultimately, a collapsing dollar with rocketing interest rates.

The *Phoenix Rising* approach to analysis proposes a way to end these problems through the total elimination of government indebtedness and hence the deficit. While the approach is radical *for governments*, it is commonplace in that corporations use varying forms of this approach all the time.

While the advantages are many, the principal one is the speed with which it can be implemented and the expected effects will accrue. This radical approach is vital as the economy and our governmental balance sheets have been on a collision course — and the downward pace is accelerating.

The complete contents of the Phoenix Rising Plan, like all other items showing this icon are available at the RoadKill web site.[108]

The major economic function of all governments is the redistribution of wealth.

The Tobin Tax

Nobel prize-winning Harvard economist James Tobin first proposed a "currency transaction" tax in 1972, targeting the money exchanging hands in international currency markets. His objective was to ensure that governments had more scope to manage their own economies.

He was not trying to stop capital from moving, but simply to curb speculators in order to prevent them from wreaking havoc with national currencies and from wielding too much power over national governments.

To do this, Tobin advocated imposing a small tax whenever money was exchanged from one currency to another. His was the 1st proposal to impose a tax (0.2%) on the $1.8 billion moving around the globe daily in currency exchanges. Shared revenues from that source would slow capital movement and allocate revenues to member governments. This would have the effect of discouraging short-term, in-and-out investments, while not really affecting more desirable long-term investments.

Now approaching 80 and still teaching at Yale, it appears that Tobin is not being heard as globalization continues unabated, and his great idea might die with him.

Jubilee 2000: Forgiving Third World Debt!

Jubilee Time

This petition is part of the Jubilee 2000 campaign led by religious, environmental, labour, women's and student organizations.

Biblically, the jubilee year was one year after the "space of the 7 sabbaths of years"– the 50th. It was a year-long celebration to commemorate the Jews' liberation from Egypt. During this period, slaves were freed, lands were returned to their original owners, agricultural work was halted, and debts were cancelled.

The year 2000 has been targeted by Jubilee 2000 as the goal for debt relief for the world's poorest countries. National campaigns are operating in Australia, Austria, Canada, Germany, Ireland, the Philippines, South Africa, Sweden, the UK and the US.

The poorest countries struggle because their governments are forced to make debt repayments with limited resources required for the basic needs of the people.

PETITION

We, the undersigned, believe that the start of the new millennium should be a time to give hope to people living in poverty. We must put behind us the mistakes made by both lenders and borrowers and cancel definitively the crushing international debt of impoverished countries burdened with high levels of human need and environmental distress.

• We call upon the leaders of the richest countries, the commercial banks, International Monetary Fund, the World Bank, regional development banks and other international financial institutions to write off these debts by the end of the year 2000.

• We ask these leaders to cancel the debt in a way that benefits ordinary people and without conditions that perpetuate or deepen poverty and environmental degradation.

• We ask them to work with governments and civil society to prevent recurring cycles of destructive indebtedness.

Mexico, Morocco, Peru and the Philippines were reduced by about 35%. However, the Brady Plan was only advantageous to countries with developing incomes who had large commercial debt.

The World Bank and IMF

International financial institutions are governed by member nations. If the debtor country does not make payments on time, it is considered "off track" and will not receive loans from other members. Under the 1996 HIPC (Heavily Indebted Poor Country) initiative, countries reduce their debt over a period of about 6 years, to a level determined to be "sustainable." However, HIPC requires strict economic policy measures, which have sometimes had negative effects on poor countries and their environments.

Effects of the Debt

Cancelling debts of poor countries potentially serves everyone. In our world, problems of any one country can affect people everywhere:

• People living in poverty need the resources that are being used for debt payments. Increasing debt means that less funding is a available for social and economic development within the country.

• The environment is affected by debt payments that must be made in the creditors' currencies. One way to generate hard cash is by exploiting mineral resources and cash crops, including agriculture, fish stocks and forests. Inadequate protection of these natural resources harms everyone.

• Rich countries are affected by the debts of poorer countries in a variety of ways. Most obviously, poorer countries have less money to buy goods and services from other countries. Poverty encourages emigration, potentially bringing with it the communicable diseases that are the result of poor sanitation and lack of medical resources.

Norway's Challenge

Norway, flush with North Sea oil, has called for deeper debt cancellation for the poorest countries and has challenged countries like Britain and Switzerland to do the same. Norway plans to write off debt over and above debt relief that is negotiated internationally. In essence, Norway will promise to cancel debt owed by severely and moderately indebted low income countries, but only after the debtor has gone through the HIPC Initiative or other international debt relief process.

The Brady Plan

Through the US-initiated Brady Plan of 1989, commercial banks reduced the debt owed by some debtor countries, with the remaining debt guaranteed by governments and international financial institutions. In essence, the Brady Plan shifted risk from the commercial creditors to public ones. Overall, debts of Argentina, Brazil, Costa Rica,

The Costs

Without debt cancellation, the great majority of highly indebted poor countries will never be able to pay off their foreign debts. In this condition they cannot attract private investment. A definitive debt cancellation could hardly make them less creditworthy. In fact, it is likely to make them more attractive to private sector investment.

• Many of the original borrowers were corrupt dictatorships which have now been replaced by more democratic governments.

• Debtor countries have paid a huge price already.

• In their uncreditworthy condition, they cannot attract private investment desperately needed for development.

The Pension Plague: History of the CPP

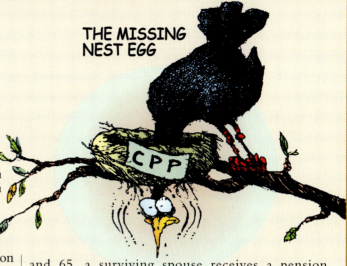

THE MISSING NEST EGG

The Canadian Pension Plan was introduced in 1966 to provide all members of the labour force with retirement income, as well as death and disability benefits. It covers all employees and self-employed persons between 18 and 70 with employment earnings, except residents of Quebec, which has a separate plan.

The CPP is financed by compulsory contributions from workers and their employers and interest on accumulated reserves. Workers contribute a percentage of their earnings between a basic exemption and the maximum. Employers pay an equal amount. Self-employed people contribute at the combined rate. Currently, 10 million Canadians contribute, and more than 3.5 million receive benefits. In 1996, the CPP paid $17.5 billion in benefits.

Excess contributions in any given year go into the reserve fund and earn interest. By law, the money can be used only for benefits or for investment in the form of loans to the provinces.

Full benefits are provided at age 65, calculated according to the number of years a person has worked and contributed to the plan, and on the salary or wages earned. Pensions are fully indexed to reflect inflation, so that the annual pension is equal to 25% of the average of the contributor's pensionable earnings adjusted for wage growth. The calculation excludes periods of disability or child-rearing, and disregards 15% of a worker's lowest years of earnings (up to 7 years).

Canadians between 60 and 64 can apply for a pension at a reduced benefit rate (6% is deducted for pensions beginning at age 64, 12% for those beginning at age 63, and so on). The pension remains at that level permanently, subject to indexation. Canadians can also continue paying into the system up to age 70, boosting the benefit by 6% for each year worked after age 65.

A disability pension is provided to participants who are unable to work due to a physical or mental condition, and is payable until age 65 or until recovery. To be eligible, the person must contribute for at least 5 of the last 10 years, or 2 of the last 3. The amount of disability benefit paid is based on a flat-rate and an earnings-related portion, equal to 75% of the pension the contributor would have received at age 65. Disability benefits paid in 1996 were $3.3 billion.

Each child of a contributor who receives a disability pension is also entitled to a benefit, as long as the child is under 18, or between 18 and 25 and attending school full time. In 1996, these payments totalled $329 million.

The death benefit is a one-time payment to, or on behalf of, the estate of a contributor. It amounts either to one-half of the pension payable in the year of death or 10% of the maximum pensionable earnings, whichever is less. Payments in 1996 equalled $250 million.

The surviving spouse's pension is a monthly pension paid to the spouse of a deceased contributor. Between ages 45 and 65, a surviving spouse receives a pension consisting of a flat rate and an earnings-related portion. The pension is also paid to a spouse under 45 who has dependent children, or who is disabled. A spouse between 35 and 45 who is not disabled and who has no dependents receives a pension reduced for each month that the survivor was under 45. After age 65, the spouse is entitled to a pension equal to 60% of the pension entitlement of the deceased. Contributions in 1/3 of the contributory period are required for the surviving spouse and children to be eligible. In addition, each child of a deceased contributor is entitled to an orphan's benefit as long as the child is under 18, or is between 18 and 25 and is attending school full time. Payments for these benefits in 1996 were $2.3 billion.

The 4-Pillared Retirement System

Pillar 1: Tax-funded minimum income support

Pillar 2: Mandatory CPP/QPP

Pillar 3: Voluntary employer pension plans and RRSP's

Pillar 4: Additional wealth accumulated in home equity and other savings and investments

The major problem is that the CPP/QPP is grossly underfunded and federal government policies seriously hamper the ability of individuals to provide for their own retirement. At its core, the existing policies increasingly favour seniors to the detriment of lower-income workers and spenders at the expense of savers.

To re-balance the 4 pillars and to make Canadians pension adaquate, some ACPM recommendations are:
• The findings of the recommended regular 5-year review of the retirement income system should be widely disseminated to Canadians in understandable language.
• Governments and their agencies (e.g., StatsCan) should be encouraged to turn out data and research on the retirement income system that will better inform Canadians about their retirement income system.
• Canada's education system should design and teach life cycle financial management courses at the high school level.
• Canada's financial services sector should better inform customers about the basics of pension and investment economics.[110]

Ponzi Schemes

You and I Would Go to Jail if We Did What the Government Does

A Ponzi scheme is one in which the confidence man promises unrealistic payments to investors to entice them. The early investors do very well, and word spreads. However, because the con artist does not invest the money he receives, he has to find increasingly large numbers of new investors. Eventually, the numbers catch up with him and the scheme collapses, although often he will have absconded with his gains.

Private Ponzi Schemes Are Felonies

Canadian Government pensions — federal, provincial and municipal plans — are run as Ponzi schemes. The trust funds, admittedly inadequate, are not assets to begin with. They have never been invested in anything. The taxes collected by the government have been spent, and IOU's have been placed in the "trust funds." The government can raise funds to repay these IOU's only by selling bonds or taxing citizens. Because the funds have never been invested, but only spent, they depress investment and inhibit economic growth — the source of governmental income.

Hence, what is owed eventually, as in all Ponzi schemes, outstrips the government's ability to tax or borrow. If these pension programs (some of which lack even IOU's as a foundation) increase at the current combined rate of 7%, while the GDP increases at a projected 2.5%, they will equal the GDP by the year 2050 — nothing would be left for any other purposes.

In fact, the 2050 date vastly understates the problem. As the multiplier differences between GDP and entitlement take effect, investment and production would be choked off, reducing jobs and tax collections enormously. Built-in increases in payments, resulting from accelerating increases in entitlement payout, would have a catastrophic impact on the population, with only a small chance of correcting the debacle, even in part.

What is essential is that nonproductive entitlement not become an increasing percentage of the GDP.

Charles Ponzi and His Scheme

The origin of the Ponzi scheme goes back to 1920. During that year in Boston, Charles Ponzi set up a plan by which he promised to pay investors 50% profit on their money in just 45 days.

Gullible people poured money into his plan. But he could not earn enough on the money to deliver the rate of return he promised. So when someone wanted to withdraw his principal and interest, Ponzi simply paid from money received from new investors. Eventually he could not meet the demands for repayment, and his scheme collapsed.

He ended up going to jail for 3½ years.

The Unions Too

An actuarial report filed by the Canadian pension fund of the Labourers International Union shows that it should have assets of almost $1 billion, but is reporting assets of just over 50% of that amount, resulting in an unfunded liability of over $400,000.

This means that if the fund had to meet its existing obligations it would only be able to cover 53¢ on each dollar owed. Since the report was filed in early 1996, a union source states that the situation has worsened and the fund's ability to meet its existing obligations has slipped below 50¢ on each dollar owed.

The vice-chair of the pension fund admits that the fund has serious financial difficulty but states that it is not due to bad management and investments.

He blames the unfunded liability on declining pension premiums paid into the plan on behalf of working members.

In the late 1980's, employers paid premiums on behalf of 35,000 members, but only 19,500 are working now, while benefits paid out are increasing. This is only the tip of the iceberg on underfunded union pension plans.

PROPOSED CRIMINAL CODE CHANGES TO DEFINE 'CRIMINAL ORGANIZATION' AS ANY GROUP, ASSOCIATION OR BODY CONSISTING OF FIVE OR MORE PERSONS, FORMALLY OR INFORMALLY ORGANIZED AND HAVING AS ONE OF ITS PRIMARY ACTIVITIES COMMISSION OF AN INDICTABLE OFFENCE...

GENTLEMEN, ONE OF YOU WILL HAVE TO GO!

Government Pensions:
The Great Intergenerational Heist

Canadian Government pensions are run as Ponzi schemes. The Canadian Pension Plan (CPP) is a pay-as-you-go system, which is just an attempt to avoid the real descriptor — **unfunded.** This means that contributions made by workers each year are paid out to retirees. With only minimal pre-funding in the CPP Account (equal to about 2 years of benefits), the CPP relies on the continuing ability of each working generation to pay for the pensions of preceding generations. Historically, this system has worked because more workers have contributed to the plan each year than there have been pensioners collecting benefits.

Canada's population is aging, however. The percentage of people over 65 will almost double over the next 35 years — from 12% today to 23% by the year 2030. Currently, there are approximately 5 workers for every retired Canadian; in 30 years the ratio will be 3 to 1; and in 50 years it will 2.5 to 1. Expenditures will continue to rise steadily as a share of the economy as long as the proportion of retired Canadians receiving CPP benefits keeps increasing. This is why governments are now taking a fundamental look at the CPP to ensure that it can continue to play a key role in providing income security to Canadians in retirement.

The Impending Crisis:
The Changing Dependency Ratio

Four main factors now drive the CPP towards crisis: changing demographics, changing economic conditions, benefits enrichments and the growth in disability benefits.

Canadians are getting older, living longer and a shrinking pool of working Canadians will be asked to support a growing number of retired people. Actuarial types call this the dependency ratio. Essentially, this compares the size of Canada's working-age population with that of the "dependent" population outside of the workforce — those younger than 20 or older than 65. In 1995, for instance, there were roughly 1.5 people of working age for every dependent person.

The trouble looms in the year 2030, with the dramatic increase in the number of workers for every dependent Canadian. An aging population adds a twist: Per capita, governments spend about 3 times as much on seniors as they do on youth, once you include the Old Age Security pension, medicare, education and the like.[5]

Hence, a variation of the dependency ratio, called the expenditure ratio, adjusts for that difference. In 1995, this ratio was roughly 2.9:1, meaning that the cost of supporting a single dependent youth or senior was effectively shouldered by 2.9 Canadians of working age. By 2030, that cost will be borne by fewer than 1.9 working people.

Economic growth has also slowed down considerably since the CPP was introduced. With slower growth in labour productivity and the labour force, total wages and salaries are growing much more slowly. In addition, real interest rates have increased substantially — from 2% in the 1960's to more than 6% in the 1980's and 1990's.

Further, the CPP original intent has been corrupted as a number of specific enrichments to the CPP have been introduced since its inception. Full indexation of benefits to changes in the cost of living were introduced in 1975. Other major enrichments include the payment of survivor benefits, dropping the retirement and earnings test, the introduction of a child-rearing drop-out provision and an increase in disability benefits.

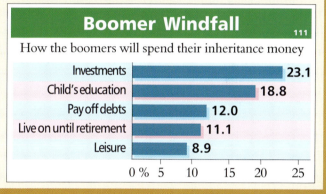

Boomer Windfall 111

How the boomers will spend their inheritance money

Investments	23.1
Child's education	18.8
Pay off debts	12.0
Live on until retirement	11.1
Leisure	8.9

0 % 5 10 15 20 25

> *I don't believe in relief at all. I'm probably the most right-wing person you've ever met. I believe that you should look after yourself... I think that we have ruined the calibre of our people with handouts.*
>
> — Roy Thompson,
> *when he was in charge of dispensing relief*

The year is 2020 and after contributing for over 45 years, Bob turns up to ask for his CPP benefits...

I ♦ GOVERNMENT OF CANADA

Disability Benefits

The number of Canadians collecting disability benefits under the CPP has increased substantially. In addition, Canadians are collecting these benefits for longer periods of time. Although measures were put in place in 1993 to improve the plan's administration and guidelines, which have helped to curtail the growth of disability claimants, the CPP still paid $3.3 million in disability benefits in 1996.

The last actuarial report projects the cost of the CPP to increase from the current 5.6% of contributory earnings to 14.2% in the year 2030 in order to maintain the current system. The architects of the CPP expected costs to rise to only 5.5% by that time. That future generations will be unable or unwilling to pay contribution rates in the 14% range is a serious concern — especially inasmuch as this tripling of contribution rates will have no corresponding increase in benefits. If a 14.2% contribution rate had been in effect in 1995, employees at the average wage of $34,900 a year and their employers would each have contributed $2,236 — instead of $850!

The key issue facing the federal and provincial governments is how to spread the cost of the CPP more fairly and equitably across generations. The average contributor born in 1911 receives $48 in benefits for every $1 in contributions, which is a rate of return of 31.1%. A baby boomer born in 1948 still will receive over $11 for every dollar contributed, or a return of 9%. Under the Chief Actuary's assumptions, a person born in 1988 will receive just over $5 for every dollar contributed. Taking into account inflation and possible future changes in policy, today's young people will be looking at very small or possibly even negative real returns. It is estimated that people who retire in the year 2006 will collect $1.44 for every dollar that they put into CPP, but those who retire in 2026 will only collect 64¢ for every dollar they put in. **They would clearly be better off to save on their own.**

The CPP also lacks fairness when compared province to province. Alberta, for instance, has a younger population and a higher rate of participation in the labour force. This means that Albertans pay more into the CPP than they will ever get out of it, subsidizing the plan by at least $500 million a year at the current contribution rate. Provinces have the right to organize their own pension plans, which is tempting when we see that the Quebec Pension Plan has done better than the CPP because of a better investment strategy and a tighter rein on disability benefits.

Some of the inefficiencies of the current system are related to its political administration, which has tended to enhance benefits without increasing contributions. Youth will always be a voting minority and thus will always risk having the benefits of older generations enhanced at their expense.

There are a number of concerns about the overall efficiency of the CPP, relating both to the efficiency of the system itself and its secondary impacts on Canada's economic performance. When growth rates exceed interest rates, a pay-as-you-go system is more efficient. These were the conditions that prevailed at the time the fund was established, but they appear now to have been a historic anomaly. Current and future economic conditions will see interest rates exceeding growth rates and therefore call for movement to a defined contribution, funded plan. Such a

11

system would generate more income for all Canadians.

Another source of inefficiency is the spiraling costs of the disability portion of the plan. The Auditor General has pointed to cost overruns in the neighbourhood of $100 million. Disability incidence rates tend to increase during recessions, and the benefits have become a disguise for early retirement in many provinces, particularly in Atlantic Canada. The pay-as-you-go system transfers these costs onto younger workers.

The funding mechanism is another source of broader economic inefficiency. The CPP relies on a payroll tax, half of which is picked up by employers. This tends to increase the cost of labour at a time when Canada's youth are experiencing an unemployment rate of 15-20%. By further increasing the cost of labour, the CPP will contribute to higher levels of unemployment, creating a further burden on future generations.

Unemployment is a key reason why poverty rates among youth and young families have increased significantly in recent years. **Although there are still poor seniors (particularly single women), in relative terms Canada now has a bigger problem with child and youth poverty.**

Since 1989, the poverty rate among working-age people has increased from 11.8% to 15.5%. Even more starkly, child poverty levels now hover around 20%. Current economic realities have led to income insecurity for both young people and seniors, making transfers between these groups less likely to increase overall income security.

In addition to exacerbating unemployment, the CPP reduces private savings. Lower levels of savings will reduce the capital that future generations have to work with, lowering productivity and incomes.

The Road to Reform

Canadian governments have been strongly committed to the CPP since its beginning and remain so; but this strong statement of support needs to be reinforced with a plan of action that will rescue the CPP from its current crisis and set it on the road to fiscal health.

Under legislation, the federal and provincial governments are required to review the CPP every 5 years. As part of the current review process, governments released a *Federal, Provincial, and Territorial Information Paper for Consultations on the Canadian Pension Plan.*

The Certified General Accountants' Association of Canada (CGA-Canada) offered comments in response to the Information Paper, supporting 4 guiding principles with respect to pension reform — fairness, equal opportunity, equity of access and security (see page 129).

Reviewing the Canada Pension Plan — CGA[113]

The Certified General Accountants of Canada (CGA-Canada) believe that Canadians who want the CPP retained must first demand changes in administrative performance and accountability so that the CPP is not vulnerable to the political temptations that have produced today's crisis. An estimated 53% of men and 82% of women starting their careers at age 25 will require financial assistance at retirement — only 8% of men and 2% of women will be financially secure. Certainty and security are necessary conditions for encouraging a healthy and stable planning environment. A proper fix for the CPP will avoid further erosion of the system. The CGA-Canada recommends that:

• Governments ensure that the burden is shared by those who will, or have already, benefited in excess of their relative contributions.

• The CPP move immediately to a steady-state funding approach with a contribution rate of no more than 10% to be phased in by the year 2000.

• Changes in benefits affect present pensioners and those nearing eligibility, including moving the CPP towards a pure pension plan and away from a social welfare instrument, with elements that are not pure pension features reduced, eliminated or funded elsewhere.

• CPP reserve fund be invested in capital markets by financial institutions operating under a transparent mandate.

• The earnings exemption be removed from the CPP or, conversely, no benefit be paid with respect to the exempted amount, discouraging employers who hire part-time workers in order to avoid payroll deductions.

• The disability benefit be removed from the CPP; it could be a supplement to the social security system paid out of general tax receipts. If governments decide to keep disability benefits, then reducing CPP benefits to take into account Workers' Compensation is appropriate.

• CPP benefits be periodically adjusted to account for rising life expectancy. In addition, an adjustment should be made to those currently collecting benefits.

• The move towards a higher retirement age be avoided, but if it is necessary, Canadians should be given a reasonable transition period.

• The drop-out provisions be reduced or eliminated; or in the case of the child-rearing, funded elsewhere. If not, the general drop-out and child-rearing drop-out provisions should be combined for a maximum that is lower than at present.

• Partial indexing be considered, for present pensioners as well. An adjustment may be the only way of recovering from present pensioners some of the benefits that exceed what they paid.

• Administrators make systematic and timely adjustments in response to actuarial studies to maintain the long-term financial viability of the CPP.

• Self-employed individuals be provided with greater tax assistance on what normally would be the employer share of contribution.

The Opposition's Alternative

The Reform Party, incensed with the Liberal commitment to maintain the CPP in its present form, offers another solution. Reform's plan includes more careful targeting of benefits to lower-income seniors, expanding rather than restricting the RRSP system, shifting younger workers onto a super RRSP system with mandatory contributions (comparable to the Chilean model explained on page 134), and introducing a program of broad-based tax relief.

This plan would provide higher benefits at lower costs while maintaining intergenerational fairness and taking 300,000 low-income seniors off federal income-tax rolls altogether.

The proposed huge increases in contributions to CPP/QPP (thinly disguised tax increases) have the effect of confiscating $100 billion over the next 20 years. It presumes that the government can be more successful in investing the money than individual Canadians. It is a misguided attempt to deal with the quagmire of unjust tax rules, misconceptions, inequities and restrictive regulations that plague the pension system. The net result frustrates the ability of Canadians to save for retirement.

Relieving Pension Headaches

With premiums rising by 73% and future benefits cut by 1.6%, the benefit-cost ratio is much greater for today's seniors than today's youth. In addition, the increase in payroll taxes will impact negatively at a time when unemployment continues to be a concern.

One problem is the result of not raising the retirement age. In the 1920's, Canada chose a retirement of 70 when the average life expectancy was 61. By 1951, a pension was available at 65, when life expectancy had grown to 68½. When the CPP was introduced, life expectancy was 72, and today it is 78. Calculations have shown that even with modest productivity growth, an increase of 2 to 3 years in the retirement age would cover the increase in retirees.

The US recently raised eligibility for pensions. Those retiring in 2015 will have to be 66 and those retiring in 2025 will have to be 67. The law was passed early enough to give those affected time to plan their finances accordingly.

The most worrying feature of Canada's legislation is the use of premiums to create a new arms-length agency to invest the funds in a portfolio — which is expected to grow up to $76 billion within 10 years. Much of the money will end up in the Canadian stock market and will compete with the current crop of mutual and pension funds. But selling those assets to pay pension obligations will have a negative impact on the price of the stock. Therefore, as all the boomers retire, the fund is likely to experience capital depreciation of its assets.[114]

The massive debts of the various governments combined with enormous unfunded pension schemes represents the greatest robbery in the history of the country. The older cohorts are scheduled to receive a comfortable retirement and leave the bill for the baby boomers and later cohorts.

CGA's Reform of the CPP [185]

- Privatize, or at least partly privatize, the CPP.

- Fully fund the plan, which would require a significant rise in contribution rates, but be offset by the benefits created by privatization.

- Service the current unfunded liability of the plan, but amortize it over a long period of time to mitigate the intergenerational inequity of the transition generation having to "pay twice."

- Pay out benefits already accrued in the CPP in the form of "recognition bonds" to the mandatory RRSPs.

- Create a mandatory RRSP contribution rate of 4.8%, a contribution to service the unfunded liability of 2.9%, and a continuing contribution for death and disability insurance of 2.2%, for a steady-state contribution rate of 9.9%.

- Transfer the investment risk — and the control over risk-return decisions — from the government to individuals, with the Seniors Benefit acting as a safety net for lower-income households.

- Raise the RRSP contribution limits to $27,000 from $13,500 to re-establish equity for the self-employed and others who are not part of a public or private pension plan.

- Re-index investment and capital gains taxes for inflation.

- Repeal the 20% foreign investment rule on RRSP's.

The Alberta Pension Exception

Under Premier Ralph Klein, legislation has been enacted that requires Alberta MLA's, if elected after 1989, to make arrangements for their own pensions.

Opting Out

In opting out, Reform MPs are making a pact with taxpayers. When they have the chance to put in a plan, there will be no grandfathering. There will be no "trough regular" and "trough lite." They will take every legal step necessary to cut benefits that were not adequately contributed to by members of Parliament.

In the summer of 1998, some Reform MP's broke ranks and trotted up to the troughs with the others.

Creating Gold-Plated Pensions for MP's: Bill C-85

Liberal Chief Whip Don Boudria made a career of misrepresenting the MP pension plan to Canadians and bad-mouthing the National Citizens' Coalition for exposing it (and him). NCC president and former Reform MP Stephen Harper suggested that the NCC be invited to make a submission on Bill C-85.

The NCC was not invited to the hearings, nevertheless, some fairly harsh comments were made by others "more friendly" to the liberal perspective on MP pensions.

The History of the Plan

Up until 1993, the plan said the members would contribute 11% and the government would contribute 11%. What was missing was the extra 40% to pay for the systematic underfunding of these benefits. In 1993, they made up that difference, which was in the order of $200 million. The matching contribution principle that was involved in the MPs' pension plan until 1993 was a sham.

According to a managing partner of KPMG Management Consulting, **the proposed pension plan is about 7 times more generous than a typical public sector plan and 4 times more generous than a typical private sector plan.** The pension benefit, the 4% per year of service, is about double that available in the public and private sectors.

In other sectors you can typically retire and receive a pension when your age plus years of service equals 85. Plus, in the public sector, pensions tend to be indexed on average by about 2/3 of inflation. It is quite rare in the private sector to have indexing and then only during retirement. Full inflation protection is too expensive and unheard of except for very senior executives of very large businesses. If you want full indexing, you just have to accept less pay to pay for it.

Finally, the maximum pension for MPs is 75% of the best 6 years' earnings. For others, it is 70% typically, but it takes 35 years to earn it, compared to 19.

So what's the justification for gold-plated MP pensions? The main argument seems to be that members are being compensated for interruptions in their careers. StatsCan, however, says that the average length of stay with an employer these days is now only 7 years, not much different from the average tenure of an MP. So length of service *per se* might have been a good reason at one time but it certainly is no longer.

It makes some sense to compensate MPs for career interruption, but not by paying a much higher pension for 25 or more years. The appropriate way is to pay a severance or a re-establishment allowance.

Why is this man Smiling?

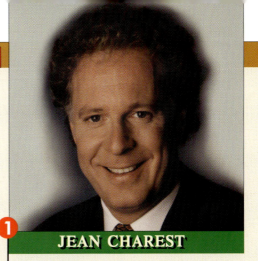

JEAN CHAREST

One of Ottawa's most outrageous scams has made former Federal PC leader, now Quebec Liberal leader, Jean Charest, a very rich man. Assuming he lives until 75, he will collect a bloated, fully indexed pension. Regardless of cost of living increases, his pension will automatically compensate for *any* level of inflation. **It should be repugnant to every taxpayer that at 40, this politician has qualified for millions from his relatively brief public service.**

Public servants deserve to be rewarded as well as the average worker, but the entire public service pension system is scandalously out of touch with the benefits of those paying the bill.

Eighty-seven others, including Lucien Bouchard and Audrey McLaughlin, qualify for this plan that will cost taxpayers $124 million.

Former Reform MP and current NCC president Stephen Harper (see page 130) has been a vocal opponent of the plan ever since the NCC made it an issue.

In 1984, the Conservatives promised MP pension reform and never delivered. Finance Minister Michael Wilson wanted to proceed, but members of his own caucus shouted him down. The current minister also tried to bring about some significant reforms that were ultimately thrown out of the caucus and cabinet.

During debate on the bill, the chief government whip asserted there was nothing wrong with this plan. What he did not mention was the source is exclusively tax dollars and the majority does not come from MPs' pay cheques.

Most of the outflows have yet to come and the inflows are to cover the future liability streams. In his report published in 1991, the Chief Actuary pointed out the plan had only $27.9 million in assets to cover about $182.7 million in liabilities.

During hearings on MP pensions, the government met behind closed doors. So much for more open government. So much for government with integrity.

Several government members also indicated they believed even a 9% contribution level is too high. Obviously it is not nearly high enough. A plan with matching contributions would provide a reasonable retirement income and save the taxpayers a bundle.

What rubs salt in this wound is that the **MP's have voted $200 million so that their pension plan would be fully funded while the rest of us are left with a severely underfunded CPP**.

What Is a "Normal" Pension?

Normal for most Canadians is *no* employer pension plan at all. According to StatsCan, as of 1992 only about 48% belonged to an employer pension plan. About half were in the public sector. Although 44% of all pension plan members have some form of indexing, in the private sector less than 12% have any automatic protection from inflation, and full protection of the kind offered to MP's is virtually unheard of, even in the public sector.

While the bill gives MP's a benefit rate of 4% per year of service, 98% of all pension plans have a benefit rate less than half that generous. No other Canadians have this benefit.

How Hard Do MPs Actually Work?

Few MP's play any real legislative role. Most vote with the party no matter what, whether they have read the bill or not. If that is the way the government believes the House of Commons should work, maybe MP's are regional sales reps for their parties.

The Top 10 MP Scofflaws [115]	
Upon retirement from office, assuming these MPs live only 75 years, this is what they will receive — *Assuming NO inflation!*	
1. Jean Charest, PC	$4,525,537
2. Brian Tobin, LIB	$3,907,507
3. David Dingwall, LIB	$3,660,930
4. Svend Robinson, NDP	$3,556,546
5. Bill Blaikie, NDP	$3,380,406
6. Sergio Marchi, LIB	$3,105,143
7. John Nunziata, IND	$2,734,328
8. Sheila Copps, LIB	$2,551,223
9. Andre Ouellet, LIB	$2,636,953
10. Don Boudria, LIB	$2,152,672

Brian Tobin

John Nunziata

Sheila Copps

Seniors

There are an estimated 3.6 million seniors (people 65 and older) in Canada, representing 12% of the population, up from 10% in 1981 and 5% in 1921. **Two-thirds of all those who have lived beyond 65 in the history of the world are alive today** and, for the first time, there are more Canadians over 55 than under 15. The senior population will continue to grow rapidly during the next several decades. StatsCan has projected that by 2016, 16% of all Canadians will be seniors, rising to 23% by 2041.

Two hundred years ago, a child born in Canada could expect to live to 35. A century later, life expectancy was only 50. In the decades since 1900, Canadians have added 28 years to average life expectancy — a child born today can thus expect to live to be almost 80. In a little more than 200 years we have experienced more than a doubling in life expectancy.

As the population ages, however, the number of people with dementia is expected to triple by 2031. The prevalence of dementia, a progressive illness in which memory and judgment are impaired, increases with age. The most common type is Alzheimer's, which accounted for almost 2/3 of all dementia cases in Canada in 1991. As institutional costs rise and family care givers face competing demands for their time, Canadians will be challenged to find solutions for the care of those suffering from dementia.

Pollster Angus Reid says an aging population is going to hit the health care system like a "battering ram." According to a physician friend of his, "we have the 'go-go's' (65 to 75) who are healthy enough to live life to the fullest, the 'go-slow's' (75 to 85) who can still lead relatively active lives, as long as they get to bed by 7:30 p.m., and the 'no-go's' (over 85) who are often disabled and require nursing care."

In addition, changing family structures — increased divorce and re-marriage, the proliferation of common-law conjugal relations and sharply declining fertility rates — may have a profound effect on future care of the old. Because life expectancy is lower for men, chances are that a woman will be present to take care of a male partner who has a disabling health problem. But if a widow falls ill, there may be no partner around to look after her needs.

More than half of those who work care for elderly family members, and of that group, 60%

report extreme stress and conflict in trying to balance work and family. The report predicts the number to rise to 77% by 2001.

Meanwhile, many more Canadians are choosing — or being forced into — early retirement. A StatsCan study shows that Canadians are retiring 2 ½ years earlier than they did between 1976 and 1980. The percentage who retired after 64 fell, while those retiring before 60 more than doubled. One exception was among self-employed people, who are retiring at almost the same age.

The fortunate, who worked for a long time for a company or government agency, built up considerable pension entitlement. The less fortunate are pushed by downsizing and find themselves without work at an age when job opportunities are scarce.

As a rule, people working for governments, public utilities and schools tend to retire earliest (59.8 years) because of generous pensions. Some large companies, which underwent severe downsizing, had median retirement ages of only 57.8. In 1975, 68% of Canadian men between 60 and 64 had a job; by 1991, the figure had plummeted to 44%. It has since fallen to under 40%. In the Netherlands, the ratio fell from 62% to 21%.

Many of the older unemployed simply abandon their job search and opt for self-employment (a euphemism for "not working") or quasi-retirement. If you are over 46 and unemployed, you will face the same obstacles as someone 62.

The country that can harness the talents of its older population, however, will have the competitive edge economically, with the added benefit of enhanced quality of life for its older citizens. Too many employers believe that older workers lack the stamina required for many jobs. There is also a belief that older workers should step aside so that younger people can have their jobs.

In contrast to earlier times, today's older workers are boldly exercising their right to keep working. As a result, increasing numbers of legal fights will erupt over age discrimination, retraining, seniority, and other work-place issues. In addition, the growing power of the New Seniors is also becoming a political fact of our time.

When the boomers advance into their 50's and 60's, they will set the political agenda and dominate election outcomes.

John Glenn, America's first man in space, returns aboard the shuttle, at age 77.

The Age Wave is Coming[49]

The senior boom, the birth dearth, and the aging of the baby boom are coming together to create a massive demographic shift, one which author Ken Dychtwald refers to as the "Age Wave." It is forecast to peak in the early decades of the new century as the baby boomers reach their 50s, 60s, and 70s.

Most of us tend to think of seniors as decrepit non-contributors, but Dychtwald and co-author Joe Flower identified 6 myths that we need to abandon in updating our perspectives on the New Seniors. Four of these impact the future of work:

Myth 1: People over 65 Are Old.

There are neither biological nor psychological reasons to connect the number 65 to the onset of old age. German Chancellor Otto von Bismarck picked the 1st official retirement age in 1889, when he established the world's 1st state system of social security. He chose the biblical "three-score and ten" (70), but self-serving bureaucrats later reduced that to 65. **Most Western countries — including Canada — follow this century-old concept, even though life expectancy has jumped radically**.

Myth 2: Most Older People Are In Poor Health.

The myth that age automatically means decrepitude leaves little room for such people as diet-and-exercise guru Jack LaLanne. Throughout his life, LaLanne has celebrated aging by demonstrating that, with proper care and maintenance, the human body has remarkable powers of resilience. His spirit is captured in his observation that most people "die at 40 and they bury 'em at 70. Who wants that?"

Myth 3: Older Minds Are Not as Bright as Young Minds.

Of the 3.6 million Canadians over the age of 65, only 10% show any significant loss of memory, and fewer than half of those show any serious mental impairment. Chances are that if you continue to challenge yourself, your sharpness and understanding will increase with age.

Myth 4: All Older People Are Pretty Much the Same.

When we look beyond the myth, there is no age group more varied in physical abilities, personal styles, tastes and desires, or financial capabilities than the older population.

The 25 Most Longevous Nations[49]	
% of population over 65	
1. Sweden	18
2. Norway	16
3. United Kingdom	15
4. Denmark	15
5. West Germany	15
6. Switzerland	15
7. Austria	15
8. Belgium	14
9. Italy	14
10. Greece	14
11. Luxemburg	14
12. France	13
13. East Germany	13
14. Finland	13
15. Hungary	13
16. Netherlands	12
17. Spain	12
18. United States	12
19. Ireland	12
20. Bulgaria	12
21. Portugal	12
22. Faroe Islands	12
23. Uruguay	11
24. Czechoslovakia	11
25. Canada	**11**

A Portrait of Seniors in Canada

• There have been particularly rapid increases in the number of people in the very oldest age categories in Canada. In 1995, there were almost 350,000 people 85 and over, representing 1.2% of the population: double the figure in 1971 and six times that in 1921.

• Many seniors have a chronic health condition as diagnosed by a health care specialist. In 1995, 81% of all non-institutionalized seniors and 95% of those living in an institution had such a problem.

• The incomes of seniors have risen faster than those of people under age 65. The average income of people 65 and over in 1994 was 16% higher than the figure in 1981, once the effects of inflation have been accounted for. In contrast, there was almost no change in the average income of people aged 15-64.

• Women make up a relatively large share of the senior population, especially in the very oldest age range. In 1995, 58% of all people 65 and over were female. Women also made up 70% of the population over 85.

• The large majority of seniors live at home. In 1991, 92% of all people over 65 lived in a private household. Over half (61%) lived with members of their immediate family, while 8% lived within an extended family and 2% lived with non-relatives.

• A substantial proportion of seniors, however, live alone. In 1991, 28% of all people over 65 lived alone, compared with just 8% of those 15-64. Senior women, especially those in the very oldest age groups, are particularly likely to live alone. In 1991, 38% of all senior women, and 53% of those over 85 lived on their own.

• Among seniors, women have average life expectancies considerably longer than men. A 65-year-old woman in 1991 could expect to live another 20 years, on average, 4 years longer than the figure for a man this age. However, only 1 year of this 4-year difference was expected to be free of disability.

Modern Maturity — the grandmother of all popular 50+ magazines — surpassed *Reader's Digest* and *TV Guide* to become the magazine with the largest circulation in America, with 18 million subscribers and an estimated 30 million readers.

The Canadian Association of Retired Persons (CARP) represents 370,000 of Canada's 7 million over the age of 50. It provides active advocacy for seniors and publishes *CARP News*, with bimonthly coverage of topics such as health, money and travel that are of particular interest to seniors.

Studies show that once people pass their 50th birthdays, they tend to feel 10 to 20 years younger than their actual ages.

Best Practises

Privatization of the Pension Plan in Chile

While people may not approve of Mr. Pinochet's methodology, the end in his case, justified the means.
— *Peter Munk,*
CEO, Barrick Gold

Bankrupt state-run pension systems are haunting the world. The pay-as-you-go system has destroyed the link between effort and reward, while fewer workers are supporting more retirees.

In 1980, Chile replaced a government-run system with a privately administered, national system of Pension Savings Accounts. By 1995, pensions in the new private system were 50% to 100% higher and the resources amounted to 40% of GDP. The privatization has been so successful that Mexico, Argentina, Peru, Colombia, El Salvador, Bolivia, Uruguay, and Venezuela have begun similar reforms. Latin America is setting the pace for reform, and the World Bank predicts that 30 countries will follow in the next few years.

Under Chile's system, what determines a worker's pension is the amount of money he accumulates during his working years. Neither the worker nor the employer pays a social security tax. Nor does the worker collect a government funded pension. Instead, he automatically has 10% of his wages deposited by his employer each month in his own PSA. (This applies only to the first $22,000 of annual income.) A worker may contribute more if he wants to retire early or obtain a higher pension.

Competitive Private Pension Fund Administration companies (AFPs) manage the PSAs. These companies are subject to government regulation, and each operates the equivalent of a mutual fund.

The PSA plan allows for individual retirement preferences. Computers calculate the expected value of a worker's future pension, based on the money in his account, and the year in which he wishes to retire. He can then adjust his deposits. Worker contributions are deductible for income tax purposes, and the return on the PSA is tax free.

A worker who has contributed for at least 20 years, but whose pension fund is below the legally defined minimum, receives that pension from the state once his PSA has been depleted. Those without 20 years of contributions can apply for a welfare-type pension.

Workers can continue working after retirement, or choose to take early retirement. Upon retiring, a worker may purchase an annuity from any private life insurance company, or leave his funds in the PSA and make programmed withdrawals.

The system solves the problem of an aging population because the workers do not pay for the retirees. The problem of unfunded pension liabilities also does not exist.

The PSA system is independent of the employer, is fully portable, and helps create labour market flexibility.

Public pension liabilities in many industrialized countries are between 60% and 150% of GDP – Canada's pension liability is more than double the acknowledged federal debt.[116]

In Chile there were 3 basic rules in defining the new system:
• The government guaranteed those already receiving a pension that their pensions would be unaffected.
• Every worker was given the choice of staying in the old system or moving to the new system.
• All new entrants to the labour force were required to enter the PSA system.

The financing was complex, using 5 methods to finance the short-run fiscal costs:
• State pension obligations were offset by the value of state-owned enterprises and other types of assets.
• A temporary transition tax was implemented.
• Roughly 40% was financed by issuing government bonds.
• Financing was an incentive to reduce government spending.
• Economic growth substantially increased tax revenues.

More than 90% of Chilean workers who ha been under the old system are in the new system. Given a choice, workers vote for the free market.

The decision to create the PSA system first, then privatize the state-owned companies, gave workers the benefits from the increase in productivity of the privatized companies.

The capital market became more efficient and experienced growth. The vast resources administered by the AFPs encouraged the creation of new financial instruments while enhancing others . Since the system began to operate, the average real return on investment has been 13% per year. The new system is also widely credited with increasing Chile's savings rate to 29% of GDP. Pensions under the new system have been significantly higher too, reducing poverty by increasing the size and certainty of pensions, and by promoting economic growth and employment.

Fighting "Financial Sin"

When the price of copper collapsed in 1997, how did Chile — whose main export is copper — manage to avoid the fate of its counterparts in Asia? "We don't live in financial sin," said Chile's finance minister. Chile's success includes strong fiscal discipline, cautious debt management and a tightly monitored banking system open to foreign investment. Chile has also had a balanced budget for 11 years and has maintained a cautious approach to foreign debt.

Tax Reform: Efficiency of Taxation

Modern governments can spend more money for 2 reasons: the spread of the money economy and the development of efficient systems of taxation. Taxation has become much more efficient over the years because of better communications technology, improved information processing, and cheaper enforcement costs. In the time of Louis XIV of France (1638-1715), more than half of all tax revenues were spent on the costs of collecting the taxes. In contemporary times, such costs have been reduced to, at most, a few percent.

Revenue Canada, with 45,000 employees, is the largest agency in Canadian government. It is interesting to note the the US equivalent, the IRS, has *only* 102,000 employees to collect taxes from 10 times as many taxpayers.

> **Why does Canada need more than 4.5 times as many tax collectors per capita as the US?**

Because of the ability to tax almost limitlessly, government debt has become relatively risk-free. Lenders are more willing to accept government debt, so governments can borrow at more favourable interest rates. A government may go into debt for capital projects, to build schools, roads, dams, and other projects for the social infrastructure. Like a family's house, these investments are expensive initially, but deliver their services over a long period of time. It is therefore reasonable to finance these expenditures through public debt. Many debates over a balanced budget reflect this connection between national debt and the welfare state. Public debt management is thus part of public policy concerning economic growth and the business cycle.

Marginal Personal Tax Rates 118

Comparing marginal **federal** tax rates in 1995 with annual production wages in G7 countries

Germany	
Canada	
France ('94)	
UK	
Italy	
US	
Japan	

0% 10 20 30 40 50 60

Inequity of Progressive Taxation

Progressivity means that those with low incomes pay a lower percentage of their earnings in tax than others. However, if taxation is very progressive, government borrowing can be more costly for them than raising taxes, because government borrowing drives up interest costs and higher interest tends to benefit the wealthy.

Once called a source of growth, "progressive income tax" was studied by Cambridge economist J.E. Hausman, who determined it was the cause of declining productivity. One hidden cost is that in Canada, top marginal rates run from 53% to 56%; in the US the rate is 46% to 48%. The most important difference is that the top Canadian rate kicks in at $59,180 in income versus about $280,000 in the US. The problem this creates is that many industries have trouble recruiting top executive talent to high-tax Canada.

Canada has 3 basic federal tax rates. In 1994, roughly 6.4 million taxpayers did not have enough income to pay federal tax; another 7.3 million had taxable income less than $30,000 and paid the lowest rate of 17%; 4.7 million had income between $30,000 and $60,000 and paid a marginal rate of 26%; and 1.6 million had income over $60,000 and paid the top rate.

Bracket Creep

Since 1986, however, taxpayers have had no protection against inflation. Take the example of someone who earned $30,000 last year and paid 17% in total federal income tax. If that taxpayer receives a 2.5% wage increase this year, just to match inflation, he or she will not have the same real income. The $750 increase in income causes "bracket creep," meaning that the new income of $30,750 will be taxed at a higher rate, resulting in an increase in taxes that will exceed the income increase *after* the cost of living adjustment. This has become an annual tax increase *by stealth,* eroding the value of basic tax exemptions, taxing gains, and pushing Canadians into higher tax brackets. Between 1994 and 1997, the non-indexation of the tax system has driven tax revenue up by $4 billion a year.

Bracket creep has effectively made the low-to-middle-income earners pay the highest marginal rates of all. The accounting firm KPMG calculates that bracket creep since 1988 has allowed Ottawa and the provinces to collect an extra $353 a year from minimum wage workers. By one government estimate, for each additional $1 earned, these workers lose 75¢. The reason for this astonishing situation is not just that Canada has high federal and provincial rates, but that people at this income level also find their benefits — child tax credit, GST credit and provincial drug coverage — clawed back.

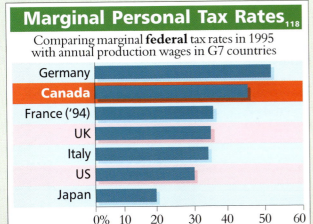

REVENUE CANADA

EMPTY YOUR POCKETS

OF ALL REVENUE CANADA AGENTS, RALPH WAS THE BEST...

Cutting the Top Rate to Zero

Libertarians, who view taxation as theft, have put forward the radical idea of cutting the top income tax rate to zero. They contend that this will trigger incentives and improvements in the lives of everyone — including and especially the poor.

Under the current system, the size of your income is always of significance in determining your tax bill, and the more you earn, the more it matters. By contrast, a zero top rate would end a mass of calculations and claims and counter-claims and deceptions concerning the exact size of large incomes, both from those making the incomes (claiming they are smaller), and from the tax gatherers (arguing that they are larger). Instead, you could concentrate entirely on making and spending more money.

If Canada were to make this change, there would be a huge influx of high-earning foreigners and returning tax exiles, and a far larger influx of low and middle-income Canadians into the ranks of the high-income Canadians. The people earning below a certain amount, wondering if it is worth working any harder (knowing that as soon as they reach a higher income level they will be hit with more taxes), would suddenly stir themselves. Young people wondering if a life of hard work will be worth the effort, could decide in far greater numbers that it is. Even the poor might decide to try to climb to the top rate bracket.

If high earners do more, lower earners get pulled up the income ladder to do jobs that the high earners are now too busy to do. The increased spending and investing of high earners creates more chances for the people below, and hence more spending by them.

Dividends 26%

Capital Gains 32%

Regular Income and Interest 42%

119

A top-rate-of-income-tax-equals-zero regime would massively intensify all such effects, making life less of a struggle for low-income earners. Government income would probably go up, too, as boosting the number of middle-income earners and encouraging all of them to try to get into the highest bracket would probably more than compensate for the loss of income tax revenue from the relatively few top earners who now pay a far greater amount per head. As for justice, the rich are not those who *earn* lots of money, but those who *have* lots of money. Denying those who work hard the extra rewards they are earning is itself unjust. Inequality and injustice are 2 completely different and often opposite things. If all of our lives are improving, do we really care that the lives of richer people are improving even more? [120]

Indexed Income Taxation

186

Deindexation, which began in 1986, punishes lower income workers who are taxed at the source. (See Bracket Creep, page 135.) Consequently, the 1990's has been a period of stagnant and falling real incomes for Canadians, who have seen the share of income taken by the government rise almost 9%, from 23% to 25%. Deindexation has propelled 1 million low-income taxpayers — whose incomes were previously regarded as too low to tax — onto the tax rolls. In addition, almost 2 million other taxpayers have been pushed from the lower to the middle tax bracket — with a marginal rate increase from 17% to 26%, an increase of more than 50% — while 600,000 more have been bumped from the middle to the upper tax bracket, with no real increase in income.

While every Canadian pays the same **federal** income tax rate, there is a growing gap in the provincial income tax bite. (See the chart to the right.) We can disregard the NWT rate because the territories are heavily subsidized by Ottawa, but the comparison between Alberta and BC is very dramatic — over 8% of the federal rate.

This partially explains the boom/bust difference between the 2 economies and explains why the Ontario government has given a high priority to cutting its tax rate which dropped to 45% just after this chart was created.

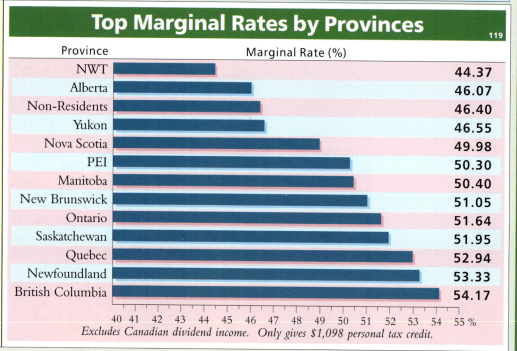

Top Marginal Rates by Provinces

119

Province	Marginal Rate (%)
NWT	44.37
Alberta	46.07
Non-Residents	46.40
Yukon	46.55
Nova Scotia	49.98
PEI	50.30
Manitoba	50.40
New Brunswick	51.05
Ontario	51.64
Saskatchewan	51.95
Quebec	52.94
Newfoundland	53.33
British Columbia	54.17

40 41 42 43 44 45 46 47 48 49 50 51 52 53 54 55 %

Excludes Canadian dividend income. Only gives $1,098 personal tax credit.

The Underground Economy

As the government eats up regular income with taxes and inflation, more and more people are joining the underground economy and doing business tax-free. They are becoming what author Adam Cash calls "Guerrilla Capitalists," people who are practicing free enterprise in what they consider an unfree society.

Feeling the squeeze of governments at all levels who continue to raise taxes and spend beyond their means, millions of ordinary Canadians at all economic levels are fighting back — not by protesting and writing letters to their MP's, but by actually disobeying the law by not reporting income and by falsifying their tax returns.

They consider the "black market" merely the real market driven underground by government controls, and include everything from moonlighting, bartering, evading price controls and rationing, to smuggling and dodging the regulations and taxes that hamstring the "mainstream" economy — and more.

> e Government has been compelled to levy
> axes which unavoidably hit large sections
> of the population. The Italian people are
> isciplined, silent and calm; they work and
> know that there is a Government which
> governs, and know, above all, that if this
> overnment hits cruelly certain sections of
> the Italian people, it does not so out of
> caprice, but from the supreme necessity
> of national order.
>
> — *Benito Mussolini, Italian Prime Minister, 1923*

StatsCan's ultraconservative estimate is that this unmeasured activity accounts for up to 5% of the GDP, or $40 billion — an amount that implies substantial unpaid federal, provincial and municipal taxes. Other estimates goes as high as 15-20%. In its study, StatsCan warned that the murky world of cash-only bargains hidden from the tax collector is too large a problem to be ignored.

This is becoming a growing concern for Revenue Canada, particularly since 75% of the new jobs that have been created are in self-employment, which leads to the underground economy. The self-employed are not exactly highly motivated to run and pay taxes to the federal government for work for which they are paid in cash. The temptation to do other things with that money, as more people move into self-employment, means the underground economy will grow. And as the underground economy grows, the taxes of people with regular jobs that are taxed "at the source," will have to increase to pay for the loss.

Although Revenue Canada has relatively little difficulty with tax compliance on the part of wage and salary earners, it does have problems with businesses that receive contract payments. In its 1998 budget, the federal government laid out plans to tighten the net around this activity. These plans included federal departments and agencies issuing information slips for contract payments made after 1997, the same for Crown corporations after 1998, and making mandatory after 1998 the construction contract reporting system 1st introduced in 1995. Revenue Canada's compliance specialists found "a very active underground economy" in the construction sector. (See page 138.)

Smuggling

Another area of concern for the government is smuggling — especially the smuggling of alcohol and tobacco. While federal and provincial taxes had forced up the legal price of a carton of cigarettes to nearly $50 in Quebec in 1994, tobacco smuggled primarily from the US sold for roughly half the legal price. At the time 75% of the cigarettes consumed in Quebec and 40% in the whole country were contraband. Even the chief of the Quebec Provincial Police had to warn his officers against smoking smuggled tobacco.

When the federal and Quebec governments reduced the taxes on a carton of cigarettes by $20, smuggling dropped by 80% to 90% in the province. Unfortunately, other provinces that did not cut their own tax rates — or not as much as Quebec — began complaining about interprovincial smuggling.

Obviously, the smuggling networks were not dismantled — and they began switching to other lucrative markets. Industry sources estimate Canadian taxes on liquor products amount to 83% of the retail cost, twice the average US level of taxation, which has led to alcohol smuggling equaling 15% to 25% of the legal market. Other popular smuggled products include perfume and firearms — on the rise following legislation aimed at disarming Canadians.

This development of smuggling networks has had a negative impact on government revenues during the past few years. Total revenues from alcohol and tobacco started falling in 1992, dropped by 7.9% in 1993, and created a revenue shortage, especially at the federal level.

Smuggling has become so popular that there are even books available on the subject, such as *The Complete Book of International Smuggling*, and *Sneak It Through: Smuggling Made Easier* by Michael Connor Finn. Mr. Finn, a defence investigator, tells the secrets of successful smugglers — which goods sell well in which countries, what customs agents look for, counter-surveillance measures, and how drugs are smuggled. Connor explains how to improvise large and small stash areas where no one

> *Hundreds of thousands of otherwise honest people...*
> *have withdrawn their consent to be governed by escaping in the*
> *underground economy.* — *Paul Martin, Finance Minister*

will look, and provides instructions and illustrations for transforming ordinary items into secure, made-to-order hiding places. He even includes chapters on security evasion, airdrop techniques and improvised landing strips.

As we know, however, the underground economy is not all full of drug dealers and other criminals. Millions of ordinary, otherwise law-abiding citizens do business without a licence, keep their income "off the books," keep 2 sets of books, invest unreported income, skim money from above-ground businesses, look for "loopholes" in tax laws, multiply "business" deductions, and falsify deductions. Does anyone who uses a cleaning lady pay in anything other than cash? While some believe what they are doing is morally right — fighting back against government wastefulness and tax laws that discriminate against the "little guy" — others truly believe government agents and Revenue Canada act like "Big Brother." They insist that Revenue Canada can obtain confidential bank records, analyze checking accounts and acquire information from banks and governments in order to "Al Capone" someone — nail them for income tax evasion.

"While Canadians may be morally justified in resisting state intrusion by retreating in the underground economy," warns author and economist Pierre Lemieux, "the danger is that these justified cheating habits against government may well spread to other fields."

> *"Confiscatory taxes and galloping regulation destroy public morality."*
> — *Pierre Lemieux, economist*

Excessive User Taxes

Excessive airport-related government taxes are ultimately passed along to the travelling public in the form of higher ticket prices, airport fees and service costs. Many of these charges place Canada at a competitive disadvantage to airports in the United States. An airplane leaving Vancouver can pay as much as $4,000 in fuel taxes, while a similar plane flying from nearby Seattle pays only about $210.

These indirect taxes get passed on to every traveler in the form of higher ticket costs.

Palmieri's Law of Collective Incompetence 107

Put a group of successful, experienced, and intelligent politicians (or businessmen) in a panelled room, call them a committee or a board of directors, and their individual level of intellectual acuity and moral courage will immediately plummet to the lowest common denominator.

"It's another demonstration of the extent to which boards of directors peopled by individuals — who in their own right are successful and even shrewd businesspeople — can, when they assemble in a boardroom, lose 50% of their IQ points..."

The Underground Construction Industry 121

An 18-month study into underground economic activity in the construction industry for Human Resources Canada found that those operating in the underground economy are abusing and undermining social programs such as EI, welfare and workers' compensation, and that once they get into the world of cash deals, skimming and barter, it is hard to get out.

The study also found that the underground economy in Canada's $92 billion-a-year construction industry — mostly through home renovations — is not only flourishing, but growing.

The "underground" workers often pad their untaxed wages with social program payments, earning more than workers on legitimate construction jobs, undermining the governments' ability to fund those same social programs. The trade-off is that these same workers can put their future financial security at risk, accepting less than legitimate working arrangements under which employment insurance premiums are not deducted, workers' compensation is not provided and there is no protection against dangerous or unhealthy working conditions.

The lure of working underground — where otherwise legitimate activities are hidden, and not taxed or regulated — is mainly economic, although some cite factors such as politics, an inverted sense of self-righteousness, and various forms of socio-cultural motivation. Willing participants include not only consumers looking to save a few bucks, but in some cases major financial institutions and building suppliers.

The underground economy hurts legitimate businesses, unable to compete with prices undercut by as much as 30% by avoiding taxes and other regulations.

Some accuse politicians of "turning a blind eye" because the problem is too pervasive, and others admit that buyers are unlikely to blow the whistle because the work is not necessarily of lesser quality.

"Zapping"

It is the computer-age technique that permits retailers — especially restaurants — to delete certain non-traceable cash sales from the receipts that they report to Revenue Canada.

The widely practised predecessor system was called double tapping and took the owner/manager more time as he or she had to re-run the tape of the day's sales again to eliminate the receipts to be hidden.

See, computers really do save work! In both cases the purpose is to skim off selected cash receipts in order to understate profits and thereby avoid taxes.

It is estimated that restaurant zapping costs Quebec $385 million a year in lost tax revenues.

Creating a National Retail Sales Tax:
Taxing Consumption Rather than Productivity[122]

The national debate over taxation should no longer be a question of *whether* to alter our current tax system or not, but *how*. In recent polls, 68% of respondents say they believe the current federal income tax system is unfair or very unfair. This broad consensus is bringing politicians to begin considering change.

> *No one could have imagined the vast impact the federal income tax would have on their children, grandchildren and future generations of Canadians.*

Creation of the Income Tax

The Canadian income tax is a 20th century invention that was created to pay for the 2 wars that we had fought for Great Britain. The program was so successful at the federal level that it did not take long for the provinces to adopt the scheme. The Fathers of Conederation believed, correctly, that taxing individuals on their private income was economically imprudent. The absence of an income tax, which is a tax on productivity, had allowed our economy to grow and individuals to prosper for more than a century.

The original income tax legislation affected only higher-earning individuals and excluded the general labourer. Because those originally income-tax-exempted labourers are "taxed at the source" they now carry an unfair portion of the income tax. The original income tax law was simply worded, the tax return consisted of only a few pages; The entire tax code now requires thousands of pages, and has become so complex that it requires millions of Canadians to seek professional help, not to mention an enormous bureaucracy to enforce and administer it.

In addition to the billions needed to operate Revenue Canada, we must add the immense costs of complying with the complex tax code.

> *Massive amounts of our national wealth are consumed merely by measuring, tracking, sheltering, documenting, and filing our annual income tax returns.*

The income tax system is especially unfair because it hits hardest at those least able to afford it, making payroll deductions before the earnings are even received. It is too complex, resulting in penalties for people who cannot even understand the laws. Income taxes are a drag on the economy, too, discouraging personal savings and investments, and reducing the competitive ability of businesses because the taxes are built into the cost of goods and services.

The total negative impact of tax-compliance make-work costs Canadian business more than 400 million hours *every year* — effort that has to be diverted from increasing productivity. Taxes on labour discourage production improvements by taking away the personal fruits of our labour and drastically reducing our take-home pay. Various eminent economists estimate the marginal excess burden of income taxes on labour to be in excess of 30% of the taxes collected. That is, for every dollar raised in income taxes, the cost to our society in lost production is more than 30¢ of the dollar taken from the private sector.

Sales Tax Reform

Since its inception in 1924, federal sales tax (FST) reform has been debated. However, other than study and criticism, little action has been taken. Industry and tax specialists view it as a fundamentally flawed system that became increasingly complex in the 1970's when Revenue Canada permitted numerous exemptions and provisions to ameliorate some aspects of the tax that diminished Canadian competitiveness.

Sales tax reform did not become a high priority until the 1980's. In 1987, the government proposed options for replacing the FST, including a federal-only value-added tax (GST). This system provided flexibility to exempt and zero-rate selected goods and services.

While the GST was uniquely federal, nothing in its design would have precluded provinces from joining with the federal government in a single system of administration. After its implementation in 1991, the government promoted a national sales tax at regular meetings of both the federal and provincial Ministries of Finance.

Arguably, the greatest impetus towards a national sales tax came in 1993 with the election of a federal Liberal government, whose policy platform made direct reference to the GST. Specifically the policy Red Book stated that:

"A Liberal government will replace the GST with a system that generates equivalent revenues, is fairer to consumers, reduces the paperwork for small business, reduces the underground economy, and is harmonized with the provinces."

This Red Book approach is populist in its rhetoric but is, if fact, highly discriminatory. The GST, PST and HST (Harmonized sales tax — the blended rate of GST and PST implemented in Newfoundland, Nova Scotia and New Brunswick in 1997) are the most equitable taxes that Canadians pay — they are based on consumption and are applicable to everyone. **The GST cannot be beat for efficiency, and it does not play favourites.**

> *The two most important things in the world are truth and honesty. If you can fake them, you've got it made.* – Groucho Marx

A Fair And Simple Consumption Tax

Canada was founded on hard work and independence, yet we attempt to tax every dollar people earn, and that is not fair. Under the current system, wage and salary income is taxed when it is earned. Then, if a portion of the wage or salary income is saved or invested, the resulting benefit is taxed again. If the investment is sold for a gain, that "capital gain" is taxed. Corporate income is taxed before it is distributed to shareholders as dividends and is taxed again as income to shareholders. In some jurisdictions, when the taxpayer dies, estate and gift tax hit the investment.

Any new system of taxation must fairly and efficiently distribute the burden of funding our government, promote economic growth, present less of a compliance burden, and offer every Canadian better economic opportunity.

There are Canadians who are dedicated to replacing the current system with a National Retail Sales Tax (NRST), with no exceptions and no exclusions, on all new goods and services at the point of final purchase for consumption. The NRST would tax only what individuals choose to spend, giving workers absolute control over how much tax they pay and when they pay it.

The proposed NRST would apply a 25% tax to the sale of all *new* consumer goods and services. The tax would be collected from the consumer by retail businesses, who would receive a small fee for collection. Used items would not be taxed, and neither would business-to-business purchases for the production of goods and services. The NRST would replace all federal income taxes, including capital gains, corporate income, self-employment, and estate and gift taxes — and replace them with a single-rate tax collected only once at the point of final purchase. The NRST would close all tax loopholes, abolish Revenue Canada, and **15 million individual taxpayers would never again file tax returns.**

The NRST is not a flat tax, which some people advocate. With a flat tax, a large part of the burden would remain hidden, individuals would still file an income tax return, the payroll tax would be retained and income tax withholding would still be with us. Notwithstanding the honourable intentions of flat tax proponents, income tax reform has been less than a success in the past because people have concentrated on reforming the income tax when they should just get rid of it entirely.

Supporters of the value added tax (VAT) find virtue in the fact that it allows multiple rates and exemptions. However, the NRST was deliberately developed without exemptions and multiple tax rates since they are complex, non-neutral, unfair and reduce economic growth. In addition, multiple rates and exemptions have led to the development of one of the most costly and damaging byproducts of our current tax law, special interests groups.

Although a 25% tax may sound high, most people are already paying this much or more, but the taxes are hidden. For most Canadians, this would be far less than the percentage they are forced to pay now under income tax, which can exceed 60% when federal and provincial income taxes are combined with existing GST, PST and/or HST. The taxes embedded in the goods we buy already adds 20% to 30% to the cost of goods and services. Today, federal taxes and compliance costs are hidden in the price of everything we buy — from clothing to medicine. When those hidden costs are eliminated, the retail price consequences of a 25% NRST are dramatically reduced.

Since the consumption and user taxes would be more visible than existing income taxes, and given the current state of voter distrust and disaffection for government, this factor of transparency can be viewed as a political advantage of this method of taxation. The amount of the consumption tax would be explicitly stated on the sales receipt, not hidden in multiple layers as taxes presently are.

As an example, in Denmark a business tax return for reporting sales tax is a post card with only 3 lines on it. Thus, this revised form of taxation would be far less expensive to administer than an income tax. Studies in Sweden, the UK, Portugal and Australia found that **consumption and user taxes cost significantly less to administer than income taxes.**

A consumption tax is also a more reliable source of revenue than income tax because, even though people may lose their jobs and their incomes, they still consume by either borrowing funds or using savings.

In the US, research supported by The National Tax Research Committee at 11 major universities and research centres across the country shows that the NRST would: be fair, simple and efficient; provide a progressive system of taxation; lower individual taxes and effective tax rates; expand economic growth and new job creation; increase global competitiveness; and encourage savings, investment and capital formation.

A recent Tax Foundation study shows that the *direct* federal and provincial tax on a single wage earner with an income of $30,000 is approximately 27%. With the NRST, that same wage earner would pay only 25% in taxes on *new* items consumed.

There is no doubt that Canadians would be better off under the NRST. Every taxpayer would be subject to the same sales tax rate with no limited exceptions and exclusions.

Most economists consider that it is really the employee *who pays the matching employer portions of CPP/QPP and EI withholding taxes through* lower wages.

Fairness

Throughout the history of our country our citizens and government have had an objective to increase every Canadian's chances to achieve economic independence by providing greater opportunities to share in our country's growth and prosperity. The NRST would help us achieve this goal.

Comparing Tax Bills: Canada vs. the US Total Tax Bill

123

Salary	Type of household	Toronto	Calgary	New York	Houston
$420,000	Married, non-working spouse, mortgage, 2 children	$201,600	$182,840	$139,160	$113,960
140,000	Married, non-working spouse, mortgage, 2 children	57,820	53,900	38,080	29,540
84,000	Married, non-working spouse, mortgage, 2 children	28,980	28,000	19,600	14,560
140,000	Married, working spouse,* mortgage, 2 children **Each spouse earning $70,000*	46,900	46,060	41,020	32,480

Our current tax system is unfair because it is highly responsive to political influence on behalf of special interest groups. Average taxpayers, without the means or organization to influence tax policy, are at a clear disadvantage. Under the NRST, there are very limited exceptions and exclusions — and no loopholes to be exploited by special interests. Under the NRST, all taxpayers would have an equal voice.

The NRST Is Fair to Retailers and Provinces. Retailers would play a key role in collecting the NRST, but they would not carry an unfair burden. Retailers in almost every province already collect provincial sales taxes, and the NRST would simply be integrated into that existing process. Retailers and provincial agencies would each be paid 0.5% for collecting the federal portion of the sales tax. Everyone would benefit from increased consumer spending and the ability to operate free of payroll taxes, income taxes, and the complexity and overhead that go with them.

The NRST Is Fair to Seniors and Low-Income Wage Earners. The NRST rebate system would ensure that senior citizens and low-income wage earners would receive a monthly rebate to offset the taxes they pay on essentials like food and medicine. Those living below the poverty line would pay no federal taxes at all and would take home 100% of their paychecks. Tax-deferred retirement accounts such as RRSP's and RESP's would no longer need to exist and money already in these accounts would not be taxed upon withdrawal.

While most people can see the strong economic advantages of replacing the income tax with consumption and user taxes, some have argued that there is something unfair or regressive about consumption taxes. This argument is based upon the belief that consumption taxes place a disproportionate burden on low income citizens who use a higher than average percentage of their income on consumption. Actually, consumption taxes are proportional, meaning that those with higher disposable income consume more and in turn pay more in taxes. If they live a conspicuous lifestyle, they pay for it with higher taxes. If they save or invest their money, we all benefit from the higher economic growth and job creation rates.

> *Canadians are governed by tax laws that they cannot understand, and that are needlessly burdensome, intrusive, complex, costly and often invisible.*

Simplicity

A fundamental notion of fairness is that citizens should be able to comprehend the laws that affect them. However, current tax law is beyond the comprehension of most taxpayers, including many of those who devote their entire professional lives to it. The current tax codes fill thousands of pages; the regulations covering implementation of the tax codes thousands more and court rulings on income tax regulations occupy additional thousands of pages. The current tax systems are so complicated that taxpayers spend an estimated $50 billion yearly to comply with them.

Businesses and individuals waste hundreds of thousands of hours on income tax compliance activities per year. That is a staggering burden and a drag on the economy which adds precisely nothing to that all-important productivity growth or national competitiveness — the 2 most vital elements in increasing wages and living standards. The NRST would reduce compliance costs by as much as 90%.

Despite broad agreement on the importance of small business to the economy, under the current tax system, small corporations bear a compliance cost burden at least 27 times greater than the largest corporations. In 1992, as a group, small businesses had to spend a minimum $724 in compliance costs for every $100 it paid in income taxes.

Businesses must use complex tax accounting rules to keep track of income, inventories, types of expenses, depreciation, tax basis for assets sold, various pension and deferred compensation rules, and various employee benefits and payroll taxes, including CPP/QPP, healthcare and EI, and file the necessary accounting and information returns. The cost of complying with all these rules drives producer prices up and makes Canadian products less competitive.

The simplicity of the NRST means that tax planning is now within the reach of the ordinary taxpayer who can choose when and whether to pay income taxes by deciding when to make purchases and whether to buy *new* or *used* products.

The NRST Would Abolish Revenue Canada by reforming the process. With provinces collecting the NRST, just as they collect provincial sales tax now, there would no longer be any need for Revenue Canada and its complexity. The declining need to collect import taxes and duties could be transferred to the Ministry of Industry.

The NRST Also Makes Tax Evasion More Difficult. Tax evasion is a major and growing problem in today's income tax system. In 1996, for example, the Finance Ministry hired an extra 63 auditors to conduct an additional 829 sales tax audits. They discovered $11.6 million in taxes owing, an average of almost $14,000 per company. Unlike the income tax, which encourages tax evasion, the NRST could cut tax evasion to virtually zero, capturing a portion of the money that now goes unreported and untaxed. Tax crooks are endlessly creative; in Quebec, the restaurant industry is being investigated for concealing millions of dollars of income through a special software program. A blackmarket program called a "zapper" rigs the electronic cash till, producing false sales figures significantly lower than they really are. (See page 138.)

The income tax system actually encourages people not to report all of their income. Because taxes are not being collected on any of the money earned in the underground economy, the tax rates of those with incomes taxed at the source must pay much higher rates. With a revised system, all people pay a fair share, because they all spend money. Even criminals and tax evaders, whose earnings currently go unreported and untaxed, would be subject to sales tax when buying cars, boats, jewellery, or other merchandise.

Under the NRST, only the retailers who collect tax would file tax forms, reducing the total number of "filers" by about 90%. That would make monitoring more efficient and enforcement more manageable.

> *Canada's corporate taxes are the highest in the 27 countries surveyed. From the point of view of business looking for a cheap home, that is Canada's weak point.*
>
> — *The Intelligence Unit,* The Economist

> *The average after-tax family income in 1996 was $45,032, representing a loss of 5% in purchasing power from 1989. This average family paid a record $11,597 in direct federal and provincial income taxes — an increase of 4.2% over the previous year. The income decline continued in 1997.*

124

Efficiency

In addition to the taxes on income that we pay, we also pay the cost of payroll and corporate taxes that are embedded in every product that we purchase. **Businesses pass their tax costs on to consumers in the form of higher prices.**

But the burden to the consumer does not stop there. We also pay for the cost of complying with the income tax codes that have become so complicated that it is estimated that taxpayers spend over 27.2% of total income tax revenues and more than 3% of the GDP in order to comply with them.

The twin burdens of time and money required for record keeping, tax form preparation, calculating and funding estimated payment schedules, and tracking income and expenses would be eliminated. The NRST would generate the same amount of revenue as the current tax system, but at a much lower cost.

The NRST Is Revenue-Neutral. The NRST plan would not deprive the government of *needed* funds, or citizens of needed programs. Extensive, independent economic research shows that the NRST would generate net revenue equal to the current tax systems. It would be good for taxpayers, business and the economy.

Economic Impact

The NRST Would Generate More Savings, Investment, Jobs, and Growth. Taking home 100% of every pay cheque would give each wage earner more money to spend, save, and invest. Low marginal tax rates and elimination of the tax bias against investment would stimulate economic growth — creating more and higher-paying jobs — and raise the living standards for everyone. Investment in people (education and training) also would not be taxed.

Slow economic growth and economic stagnation have a disproportionately adverse impact on low-wage earners. These families are more likely to lose their jobs, are less likely to have the resources to weather bad economic times and are more in need of the initial employment opportunities that a dynamic, growing economy provides. The income tax retards economic performance by creating a significant bias against saving and investment through double, triple and even quadruple taxation. **Virtually all economic models project a much healthier economy under the NRST.**

The NRST Would Make Businesses More Competitive. Eliminating corporate and payroll taxes would dramatically reduce the cost of producing goods in this country. Canadian businesses would become more competitive both at home and abroad. And, as the cost of doing business falls in Canada, we would become a more attractive place for Canadian and foreign companies to do business and locate facilities — bringing in jobs and investment.

Canadian businesses must become more competitive, especially because less developed regions of the world are lowering their rates of corporate tax in order to attract investment to their regions. In a survey of more than 60 countries around the world by KPMG's International Tax Services group, the developed countries of the OECD and the EU have an average corporate income tax rate of about 37%. Considering federal taxes alone at about 45%, Canada's average federal corporate rate ranks 4th highest among OECD countries, after Germany, Italy and Japan. Provincial corporate taxes add 45-55% of the federal rate. In contrast, Latin America and some countries in the Asia-Pacific region have average rates closer to 30%. **Under an NRST system, however, businesses would pay no corporate taxes — a tough rate for other countries to match.**

The NRST Would Dramatically Increase Investment Levels. Compared to levels that are achieved under the current income tax system. Increased savings would stimulate investment and productivity, and the economy would grow more rapidly, creating demand for workers and improving job opportunities. Because taxes on capital would be removed, foreign capital would flow into Canada, creating businesses and jobs. Canadian products competing abroad would be free of the 30% hidden costs of taxation — while an NRST would be collected on foreign products sold in Canada. **After implementation of the NRST, yearly real investment would initially increase by 80% compared to the investment that would be made under present law.**[125]

Under the NRST, Interest Rates Would Drop. When the tax on interest is removed, the lender can charge less because he no longer has to compensate for taxes paid on interest earned. In addition, once savings and investments are no longer taxed, then Canadians will be encouraged to save more, creating a larger pool of funds in lending institutions, and causing the borrowing of funds to drop.

> *An average producer price reduction of up to 30% is predicted after adoption of the NRST. Falling producer prices would allow retailers to maintain profit margins, while reducing retail prices to consumers.*
>
> 125

The NRST Summary

The NRST would:

- Repeal the federal and provincial income taxes, including capital gains taxes.
- Repeal corporate and self-employment taxes.
- Repeal all payroll taxes, including CPP/QPP and provincial health care taxes.
- Repeal any estate and gift taxes and the threat that they would be introduced in jurisdictions where they currently do not exist.
- Make the collection of income taxes unconstitutional.
- Provide a universal rebate equal to the sales tax paid on essential goods to ensure that no Canadian living below the poverty line pays taxes on necessities.
- Impose a flat 25% tax inclusive rate on the purchase of new goods and services in Canada.

The NRST would not:

- Cause prices to rise.
- Decrease government revenue.
- Unfairly burden the poor or elderly.
- Unfairly burden retailers.
- Be structured as a VAT.
- Provide tax loopholes on any kind of consumption.

A tidal wave of taxpayer demand for a simpler, fairer, more efficient, and less intrusive system of taxation is building daily. The NRST would deliver these benefits to the Canadian people and more — more government accountability for taxpayer dollars, a tax system that is less susceptible to being manipulated by special interests and perhaps most importantly, tax relief for those who are most in need. In addition, as our population ages and a greater number of people are retired, there will be fewer taxpayers and government will have no choice but to move from taxation of labour income to taxation of capital income.

"The current system of income taxes has depressed real personal incomes and results in slow growth and unemployment. Since the poor are the ones most vulnerable to this unemployment, I would argue that a seemingly fair and progressive income tax is, in the argument, really unfair and regressive." [126]

Mission Impossible: Taxing Internet Commerce

Governments, worried about how to ensure that consumption tax is applied and enforced on Internet sales, are looking at forcing software manufacturers to devise a way to track on-line sales. Analysts predict that by the year 2001, Canadian shoppers will spend $13 billion on products bought over the Internet, potentially generating $2 billion in GST. Worldwide Internet sales could reach $420 billion by the year 2001 — this represents a lot of potential tax revenues.

Germany is pushing for the adoption of a worldwide effort to effectively track and tax sales of music, movies or software downloaded digitally, as well as the sales of goods bought on-line but delivered through the post or other services. Another option is for international parcel-delivery companies to automatically calculate and add VAT payments for products ordered on-line. The WTO, meanwhile, recently reached an agreement to bar governments from collecting tariffs on goods delivered over the Internet — at least until they meet again late in 1999.

The reality is that a tax on goods or services that are delivered to a global market over the Internet cannot be effectively administered.

High-Tech Shortage

While Ontario's high-tech industries estimate creating up to 56,000 new jobs over the next five years, only 14,000 potential new employees will graduate from the province's universities.

Part of the problem is that Ontario's universities have a shortage of spaces for new students in computing science and electrical engineering — last year it was just 2,745 places — forcing the schools to turn away many students with 85-90% averages. The University of Toronto, for example, turned down 3 students for every student accepted in engineering in 1996.

Another problem is the province's funding formula, which provides just $7,000 per student in undergraduate engineering and upper-year honour science courses. Industry members argue that the funding should be raised to $14,000 per student due to the high cost of technology needed in such courses.

Pacific Salmon

The outlook for the salmon-fishing industry on Canada's West Coast looks very grim, with predictions of even fewer fish and significant job losses. A study conducted on the once lucrative industry found nearly 8,000 jobs were lost in 1996 because of poor salmon returns and severe increases in the cost of federal fishing permits.

> *"The inescapable conclusion is that unless radical reductions occur this year in the Alaskan fisheries, the upper Skeena coho stock is doomed."*
> — Glen Clark, *NDP Premier of BC*

According to a federally funded but independent advisory council, lack of trust and information sharing among federal and provincial and industry interests is holding back new strategies to save the increasingly endangered fisheries on all coasts.

> ### Caring and compassion really mean socialism, wealth confiscation and redistribution.
> —Conrad Black, 1992

> ### Welfare is immoral because it increases population and therefore promotes starvation.
> —Thomas Malthus, 1798

The Brain Drain

Even though unemployment numbers improved by early 1998, the rate was basically double the unemployment rate for the US. The MUSH sectors were functioning at sub-par levels as politicians battled union-based resistance to logical restructuring because of the accompanying shifts in funding patterns. **The climate encourages the best and brightest to leave the country.**

The low dollar has a generally positive impact on our foreign trade and balance of payments. However, when coupled with over-regulation, monopolistic traditions, lack of funding for research and development, and one of the world's highest tax rates, it becomes the prime ingredient for a growing exodus of Canada's elite workers to the US and elsewhere.

The US is also soaring ahead in research grants. A director of the Medical Research Council of Canada notes that hundreds of medical experts are being forced to head south because of funding cuts to research. A 5-year research grant in the US, for example, is set at $280,000 per year. In Canada, a typical new grant receives about $65,000 a year for 3 years. University leaders are warning that this "brain drain" is drawing the intellectual life out of Canada, and an infusion of dollars for research and training is vital to stanch the flow.

Federal government grants by the Council dropped to $221 million in 1997, from $248 million in 1994, and from as high as $300 million in previous years. **For every million-dollar cut, 160 full-time support staff jobs are lost..**

Before government cuts for medical research in 1994, scientists who frequently published in journals were most likely to receive continuing grants. Gradually, the support has shifted to those with patents that can be exploited commercially. However, there is reason for cautious optimism in the Canada Foundation for Innovation's potential for new research jointly funded by government, universities and industry.

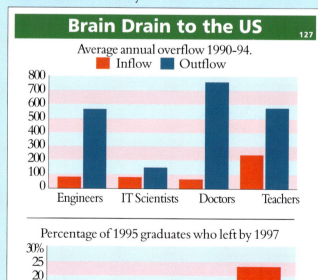

Brain Drain to the US

Average annual overflow 1990-94.
■ Inflow ■ Outflow

Engineers — IT Scientists — Doctors — Teachers

Percentage of 1995 graduates who left by 1997

College Diploma — Bachelor's Degree — Master's Degree — Doctoral Degree

Our High-Tech World: Exploring the Future

The Japanese first embraced labour-saving technology in the 1960's and 1970's when they were trying to compensate for labour shortages caused by the low birth rates of the 1940's. Today's companies are adding machines instead of labour, resulting in improved productivity but also increased unemployment.

The history of work has been, in part, the history of the worker's body. Production depended on what the body could accomplish with strength and skill. Techniques that improve output have been driven by a desire not only to decrease the pain of labour, but also by the intentions of employers to escape dependency upon that skill that only the labouring body could provide.

Skilled workers historically have been ambivalent towards automation, knowing that they could be the bodies it would augment or replace. The progress of automation has been a result of a transfer of knowledge from man to machine, and it has, in turn, further enabled those transfers.

Information technology will continue to diminish physical effort, and it will replace a variety of experience-based skills. Many workers are appropriately concerned that new technologies will replace them; while it is true that computer-based automation continues to displace humans (a process that has come to be known as *de-skilling*), the technology simultaneously creates pressure for a profound *re-skilling*.

Good Jobs, Solid Careers

The purpose of this chapter is to explore the bright side of new technologies that will create a demand for highly specialized information workers who are rewarded for their ability to manipulate the evolving tools of the knowledge society. The speed of change due to technology shifts is staggering, but with it comes some unique opportunities that may be unfamiliar to you.

The world's first fully functional computer (ENIAC), built in 1943, weighed 30 tons, had 18,000 radio tubes, 70,000 resistors, 10,000 capacitors, 6,000 switches, and was 40 ft. by 20 ft. by 20 ft. It was not nearly as smart as the chip in today's coffee pots, managing about 3 additions per second. Improvements resulted in the launch of the IBM 360 in 1964, which could perform about 100,000 additions per second, cost $4-5 million, and required a squadron of technicians to maintain it.

In 1955, one megabyte of digital memory cost $550,000. Today, one megabyte of digital memory costs about $5. A former Intel engineer, who invented the microprocessor in 1971, predicts that the maximum number of transistors that can be practically designed into a semi-conductor "cube" using *existing* silicon manufacturing technology is 10 trillion. The Pentium currently contains 3.1 million transistors, churns out more than 100 million bits per second, and is smaller than the size of a stamp.

ENIAC, 1947

In 1998, the PC market is expected to grow 19%, with shipments approaching 85 million units. The market will continue to post double-digit growth through the year 2001, with shipments exceeding 150 million units.

Like the advancement of the computer, the Internet and its creation of cyberspace has radically changed our world. Five years ago, the average person had not heard of cyberspace. He or she had some vague sense that it had something to do with computers or the Internet. Cyberspace is a dimension where distance does not exist — the distance between Toronto and London, Ontario is no different than the distance between Toronto and London, England. At the time of the Industrial Revolution, it took 2 years to get a message from England to Australia. Now it takes seconds. *The Economist* concluded that, **"the demise of distance as the key to the cost of communicating may well prove the most significant economic force shaping the next half century."**

The application of Information Technology (IT) creates jobs. In the US, about 40,000 more *microchip technicians and machine operators* are needed by 2002, according to a coalition of semiconductor manufacturers. At least 10 makers of the microchips that store and process data are looking for people to staff 38 new plants across the US. *Computerworld* magazine estimates that, considering the number of companies demanding more sophisticated technology systems and the burgeoning Internet industry, the US could face a shortage of IT professionals for the next 6 to 10 years. Competition for employees with computer skills means companies are offering better compensation packages to keep their computer specialists.

Canada's shortage of IT professionals is even more acute than the US's shortage and will be much more difficult to solve because education, caught up in its own transformation, remains largely unresponsive, taxes here are the most pernicious in the OECD and the plummeting value of the loonie reflects our inability to compete with the more productive economies.

New Developments

• The US Energy Department announced that it, in partnership with the private sector, has produced electricity from gasoline through a new method that yields twice as much useful energy per litre as a car engine does, and with pollution 90% lower. Such a car would be refilled with energy in minutes from the pump at the corner gasoline station and get double the gas mileage of a comparable car with an internal combustion engine. The method uses a fuel cell, a device 1st used by NASA for the Apollo moon program, that makes electric current by combining hydrogen and oxygen from water. A new generation of ultra-clean vehicles could be introduced without having to replace the existing network of refineries, pipelines, trucks and service stations. (See page 150.)

• Tragoes, which has a partnership with a European software company called Infobank, plans to sell its encryption and back-office software to companies that want to set up electronic "storefronts." This foundation will allow businesses to sell anything from documents to music videos on-line without fear of copying. A user would download a piece of software that would handle the encrypted item, decoding it when necessary and keeping track of how many times it had been used. The system is known as "superdistribution." Tragoes believes that the Internet is leading to the kind of digital economy where people no longer pay for ownership, only for use.

• Philips announced for sale in Canada the 1st non-computer Internet access. It is a box about the size of a laptop computer that sits on top of a TV and is controlled with a handset. It means that now, if you want to explore the Internet, you do not have to go through a computer. This will change the Internet from the domain of the hackers to mass accessibility. *Wired* predicts that **everyone** will be on the Internet within 30 years.

• Scientists are predicting that within 20 years virtually every aspect of farming will come under the control of computers, including monitoring, analyzing and making recommendations in every conceivable area of farm management. A robotized sheep shearer is likely to be fully operational by the turn of the century, part of the fully automated "farm of the future."

Technophobia

Most of us remain a little befuddled by this technology. If you are over 40 and even if you can surf the Internet, you probably cannot program your VCR. Even the most technically proficient in our midst have remarkably little idea about the monstrous economic forces that are propelling the expansion of technology. We are addicted to speed and the faster we can do things, the more things we *need* to do.

IT Growth: 1992 to 1997

IT jobs doubled between 1992 and 1997, with 139,000 jobs in 1992 and 267,000 jobs in 1997. In 1997, 4 out of every 10 programmers were ages 25 to 34, yet only 20% of newly hired workers were under 25. As a result, most of the growth in employment has been among workers old enough to have previous work experience.

The popular image of the workaholic computer programmer is not supported by StatsCan data: The growing market for programmers has not created longer work weeks. In fact, programmers worked an average 38.8 hours a week in 1997, about an hour less than in 1992. Programmers were also no more likely than others to work overtime or to hold a second job.

In late 1997, computer programmers and systems analysts earned, on average, about $300 more per week than workers overall ($843 compared with $577). But they earned slightly less than other workers in the occupational group that includes the natural sciences, engineering and mathematics.

Programming jobs are found mainly in Canada's metropolitan areas — especially Toronto, Ottawa-Hull, Montréal and Vancouver, which accounted for 171,000 of the 267,000 jobs in 1997. Ottawa-Hull had the highest concentration of IT workers in 1997, totalling more than 5% of all employed persons in the region.

Between 1992 and 1997, Ontario added the most jobs (+58,000), a growth of 90%. Despite what we read in newspapers, the increase in Atlantic Canada was lower than in the rest of the country. Of the 128,000 computer programming jobs created between 1992 and 1997, almost 70% were in the business services industry, which supports the perception that contracting out has increased.

Iridium

Iridium is a satellite-based, wireless personal communications network designed to permit any type of telephone transmission — voice, data, fax, or paging — to reach its destination anywhere on earth.

The Iridium constellation of 66 interconnected satellites orbiting 780 km above the earth will simplify communications for users who need the features and convenience of a wireless hand-held phone for worldwide use. (www.iridium.ca)[128]

India: The Next Software Superpower?

Bill Gates of Microsoft calls India, with a population of a billion people, the next "software superpower." This is remarkable for a country that, despite having a nuclear capability, is chronically short of electricity. Power outages have long been a fact of life in India — 78% of households are not even connected to electricity.

This did not stop the Indian computer and software industry from bringing to the country the US-based Comdex, the world's foremost IT exhibition company. The exposition, which was Asia's largest, brought the latest in software products and solutions, hardware and components. Trade delegations from the US, Taiwan, Japan, Singapore and South Korea, among others, participated in the show, which helped to bridge the awareness gap with Indian technology.

Previously, a product launched in the US took 6 months or more to reach India. Today, products are launched concurrently with North America. The president of the Manufacturers' Association of Information Technology says that, inasmuch as Indians constitute 17% of the world population, the domestic IT industry should target achieving 17% of the global market share by leveraging the intellectual power of its people.

The Comdex tie-in helped to take the message to the world that India is a country of opportunity in the IT sector, and that the time is now to invest and set up a manufacturing base. In the 1995-96 fiscal year, the IT industry reported sales of $2.8 billion, and exceeded $4 billion a year later. By the turn of the century, sales are expected to reach $14 billion and could go as high as $20 billion.

There is growing awareness of IT in India, but the financial market has to develop to create the necessary ambience for solid growth. With its enormous brain power, India should take its place as one of the most powerful countries in the world, possibly driven by information technology.

Historian Paul Kennedy asks, however, whether countries like India can, "take the strain of creating world competitive, high-tech enclaves ... in the midst of hundreds of millions of their impoverished countrymen."

Indians are raised on two unquestioned truths: that Indian (or Hindu) civilization is superior to most (probably all) others, and that any foreign power that begins to take on imperial shape will sooner or later threaten India. To the latter we might add a corollary: that most (if not all) of India's problems are caused by somebody else.[129]

The Chip on India's Shoulder

India's decision to resume nuclear testing is less an act of self-defence than one of self-assertion. A proud nation that has fallen far short of its potential, India desperately wants to show the rest of the world that it matters.

"A nation as large and capable as ourselves must make its impact felt on the world arena," the leaders of the Hindu nationalist Bharatiya Janata Party (BJP) proclaimed in their election manifesto before coming to power in March of 1998.

India suffers from a profound inferiority complex. In fact, it probably has less economic-diplomatic power than Canada, a country with 3% of its population. In the BJP's world view, India is facing not 1 but 2 evil empires: Islam, represented by Pakistan, Iran, Afghanistan and the other Islamic states to India's west; and the white, Christian, capitalist empire of Europe and North America. BJP's recent success has revived anti-Muslim and anti-foreign resentments.

India must look homeward first. Instead of railing at international corporations, it must unleash the productive forces of its overregulated, corruption-ridden economy. Instead of spending billions on new weapons, it must improve the scandalous condition of its poor.[130]

Dialing the Internet

In 1997, USA Global Link Inc. became the 1st company to launch global phone-to-phone Internet service. It expected to service 5 countries, impacting directly on the $112 billion international telephony market. The launch was slower than expected, but this application of existing technology will put international telephone calls into cyberspace.

Users need not have a computer or pay subscription fees. Instead, touch-tone phones transform analog signals to digital signals and transmit via the Internet to any phone worldwide, saving users 80% to 90%.

For this to work, a customer calls Global Link's 7-digit telephone number for Internet access. A voice message is heard, telling the caller to enter the international number to call. Once the number is dialed, the call is completed. The call, routed over the Internet, does not trigger international tariffs because it is technically seen as a local call, not an international one.

Computer Use

The number of people using personal computers around the world will increase from 450 million in 1996, to more than 1 billion by 2000.[131]

Millions of jobs around the world will be destroyed by the Internet, but new technologies will eventually create many replacement jobs — but radically different ones than the jobs that are being lost.

Governments need to expect and allow markets to breakdown barriers to Internet commerce even though the result will be job turmoil and displacement comparable in impact—but much faster in terms of transition time—to the upheaval of the Industrial Revolution.

Canada's High-Tech Role in the Global Economy

Demographer David Foot says that a fundamental link has always existed between demographics, technology and employment: In a society with a lot of workers, labour is in abundant supply and is cheap. Consequently, Canada fell behind older countries such as Germany and Japan in adopting new technologies between 1965 and 1985. "It wasn't because we were Luddites," Foot explains, "but because we were younger and had more labour and less financial capital than those countries ever did." Instead of installing robots, Canada found jobs for its young people — a strategy that preserved social harmony, but did not increase productivity.

Closing the Gap

By 1995, when more personal computers than televisions were purchased for use in Canadian homes, it was time Canada started to catch up on the technology front. Almost a quarter of Canadian households are now accessing the Internet, while most of us have at least some computer knowledge and are eager to learn more. In 1985, only 15% of Canadians were using computers at work; by 1996, the number was 55%. In addition, information technology is growing by 15% to 20% a year as software becomes a vital part of running everything from telephone systems, bank machines and photocopiers, to automobiles, refrigerators and VCR's.

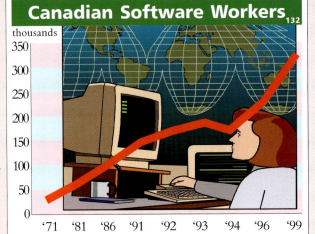

Canadian Software Workers 132

thousands: 350, 300, 250, 200, 150, 100, 50, 0

'71 '81 '86 '91 '92 '93 '94 '96 '99

Canada is now considered the most wired country in the world on a per capita basis. At the point in time when the US had 28,470 networks — or series of computers linked to the Internet — Canada had 4,796; on a per capita basis this means that the US had 114 networks per million population and Canada had 192. Following Canada and the US are Australia (110), France (37), Britain (24), Germany (22), and Japan (15).

Competing for Skilled IT Workers

Information Technology industries in Canada are desperate for qualified workers. In a late 1997 survey of high-tech companies, 88% of 220 respondents said their companies faced a shortage of skilled workers. The Software Human Resource Council — an Ottawa-based research group jointly funded by industry and government — estimates that there were 15,000 vacant programming jobs in Canada. Several sources estimate shortages as high as 30,000 or more by the year 2000.

The shortage of skilled workers is due to the fact that the industry is growing faster than expected, that about half

the graduates in computer science, software and related fields are hired by major information technology users (banks and governments), and there is already a shortage of about 190,000 workers in the US, so American companies are aggressively recruiting in Canada. The US, with the world's largest economy, has been growing rapidly, adding 1.5 million jobs annually between 1992 and 1997, while Canada was suffering through the worst bout of long-term high unemployment since the Great Depression.

The Brain Drain

The attraction to head south is hard to resist, too, given that expatriates in the US believe that their salaries would be nearly 20% lower if they returned to Canada. When you add the "extra" Canadian taxes and consider the exchange rate, the perceived gap climbs to a whopping 50%. For outstanding candidates, US recruiters have offered up to a year's salary as a signing bonus — an attractive incentive to recent graduates with huge student debts.

From 1985 to 1996, the number of Canadians moving south on temporary work visas more than doubled, and most of the increase took place after 1990. More than half of those who left were professionals with visas obtained under the 1993 NAFTA rules. Now, work visas for the US take only 3 to 5 days to process when the applicant is from Canada, compared with as many as 8 weeks for job seekers from other countries. As many as 60% of those Canadians on the visas get permanent working papers, or green cards, signifying permanent US residency within 2 years of arrival, meaning that the annual totals underestimate the cumulative effect of the exodus.

Few Women Entering IT

One of the most glaring reasons for the IT shortage is the small numbers of women taking up the discipline. Women in computer science programs in North America represent approximately 15% or less of total enrollment. Females seem to be turned off by the mistaken idea that computers are associated with asocial, isolated work for "nerds," without realizing that computers are in everything and IT professionals work with the end users, with training programs, and in management. Male or female, industry executives say that too few Canadian students are enrolled in post-secondary computer programs, and that we should be doing more to entice students to go into the technology field.

Foreign Workers Needed

The owner of an Ottawa-based high-tech recruiting company travels to India regularly to attract skilled workers for companies such as NorTel, Newbridge Networks, Corel, and Cognos. He says that with today's high youth unemployment, companies generally do not like to have to recruit in India, but the alternative is to poach from one another, driving up salaries, and doing little to add to the supply.

Meanwhile, Canada's high-tech sector launched a major overseas recruiting drive in 1997, hoping to hire 3,000 foreign software workers by July of 1998. The organizers, who hope this will be an annual event, aim to recruit highly skilled but underpaid programmers from 11 cities in Europe, Asia, Africa, and South America.

Pressed by the IT industry, the federal government relaxed immigration laws to allow between 1,500 and 3,000 qualified foreign software developers into Canada in 1997. The government fast-tracked applications of foreign high-tech workers to enter on "temporary" work permits because the shortage of skilled workers will adversely impact growth in this important sector. The primary sources for these workers are India, Pakistan, Malaysia, and South Africa.

Wanted: IT Executives

Canadian software companies are scouring the globe especially for executives to make up for a shortfall of talent in a still-maturing domestic industry. Globally, veteran high-tech executives are in extremely short supply. Canadian companies have to cope with their own particular disadvantages, including remoteness from the centre of high-tech activity and difficulty matching the big paycheques and lower tax rates in the US.

Missing the High-Tech Boat

The Information Technology Association of Canada (ITAC) says that the current skills shortage means that companies will either have to curb their own growth, rely increasingly on foreign workers, or transfer more of their activities to countries such as Ireland, India, Singapore, and Malaysia. According to ITAC, there are more than 15,000 IT firms with $60 billion in revenues, $16 billion in exports and 350,000 employees in Canada.

High-Skill/High-Wage Jobs for the Non-Degreed 133

CRAFTS & CONSTRUCTION
- construction drafting
- construction project manager
- heating/air-conditioning technician
- plumbing, pipe-fitting technician
- precision welding
- specialized carpentry and installation
- specialized interior finishing/install

HEALTH OCCUPATIONS
- dental assistant
- dental hygienist
- emergency medical technician
- home health aide
- licensed practical nurse
- medical laboratory technician
- medical record technician
- optometric technician
- radiology technician
- surgical technologist

MANUFACTURING
- computer-controlled equipment operator
- equipment operator
- drafting technicians
- electronics engineering technician
- electronics lab technician
- engineering technician
- manufacturing systems operator
- manufacturing technician

SERVICE OCCUPATIONS
- accountant
- agribusiness sales
- automatic office manager
- commercial design
- computer graphics specialist
- criminal justice and corrections
- data processing manager
- fire fighter
- law enforcement/protection
- library technician
- paralegal
- professionally trained chef

TECHNICAL SERVICE, REPAIR AND INSTALLATION
- specialty auto mechanic
- airframe mechanic
- avionics repair technician
- biomedical equipment technician
- computer systems install/repair
- eletromechanical repair technician
- telecommunications install/repair

Canada is clearly missing a unique opportunity to develop excellence in the Information Age. Montreal's Eicon Technology Corp., for example, lost 10 of its best workers to the US in 18 months, leading to delays of up to 6 months in the release of new products, the loss of millions in revenues, and raises of as much as 20% to keep its remaining employees. There is no point in attracting new industry or encouraging growth of existing companies if there is a shortage of workers.

We have a huge worker shortage in a key growth area at a time when we have a surplus of 35,000 qualified teachers. **Canada could easily "create" an additional 30,000 IT specialists in 2 or 3 years if we had the political will and leadership to make it a national cause.** Such a CyberSkills Program could cost a fraction of what the federal government is budgeted to spend each year on highly questionable "manpower" programs.

While most Canadian high-tech companies feel that the growing shortage of key skilled workers will hamper the growth of their businesses, they are doing very little to train their employees, according to the Canadian Advanced Technology Association (CATA), an industry trade association. Canadian firms are spending on average only 1.5% of revenues on training — not nearly comparable to many other western countries. The failure to make provisions for training is ultimately an industry problem, but it would nevertheless be an obvious area to invest federal/provincial training funds.

IT Boomers

• **Northern Telecom** — a global corporation based in Ontario — has 68,000 employees throughout the world, including 22,000 in Canada — a favoured location for expansion because of R&D tax credits.

In the late 1980's, only 45% of NorTel's employees were classified as knowledge workers. Today, it is 77% in Canada, and the figure in Ontario exceeds 80%.

NorTel alone already recruits about 25% of all Canadians with undergraduate degrees in electrical engineering and computer science, and 30% of the masters and doctoral graduates.

• **Newbridge Networks Corp.** of Kanata, Ontario is also set for expansion with plans to accommodate another 3,000 to 4,000 workers by the year 2001. This would represent, at a minimum, a doubling of the local workforce of the high-tech company.

• **Bell Canada**, meanwhile, recently launched its own software research and development lab to create new services for the country's largest telephone company. Creation of what will be Canada's 2nd largest privately owned R&D complex is in response to the need for innovation in the face of customer needs and the threat of greater competition from giant global telecommunications alliances. Bell already owns a 30% stake in Canada's largest private R&D complex, Bell-Northern Research Ltd. (NorTel Technology). Bell's parent company, BCE Inc., owns 51.3% of NorTel.

Education and Training

Educators assert that there is no "quick fix" solution to the shortage of skilled workers in the IT industry. Universities, incapable by nature and philosophy of being able to respond to the market, say that they are already functioning well beyond capacity in the disciplines that groom their students for the IT sector.

A 1998 commitment by the Harris Government in Ontario to make $150 million available to universities for IT-related education was labeled as a "sellout" to industry by senior administrators and academics, who assert that universities exist to promote knowledge and not to pander to business. (See page 207 for more on these medieval institutions.)

To educate more students would require more resources, including staff — but universities are finding it difficult to attract qualified faculty when they are competing with more lucrative offers from industry. At McGill's department of electrical engineering, 25% of faculty teaching positions were vacant at the end of the school year. A professor at Waterloo says that industry, by hiring away *all* of the qualified people, does not leave those needed to teach, "in a sense is killing the goose that lays the golden eggs" and pointed out the need for industry to come forward with endowments.

Waterloo, considered one of the top facilities of its kind in North America, attracts more than 100 US companies to its campus in search of programmers, even though only 200 students earn undergraduate degrees in computer science each year.

One institution willing to answer the call from industry, the University of New Brunswick, has teamed up with Sun Microsystems, DMR Consulting Group, NorTel, and N.B. Telephone Co. Ltd., to develop Canada's first business-degree major and part-time certificate program in electronic commerce. A master's degree program in EC began in September of 1998.

The largest producer of new IT graduates is not a university, however. The Information Technology Institute — a publicly-traded company with programs in Halifax, Moncton, Ottawa, and Toronto — is generating 1,700 graduates a year with its 9-month, $22,000 programs. The program is not intended as sufficient background for advanced software engineering tasks or R&D. Typical careers for ITI grads are consulting, network administration, application development and sales and marketing.

Canadians are among the most wired people on Earth, ranking 4th in Internet usage despite a small population.[134]

Net Registration

Registering an Internet domain name — that part of an e-mail address that comes after the dot — is going to get easier with the transfer of control of the volunteer ".ca" administration to a not-for-profit entity that will charge a fixed price.

Since 1987, free domain names have been given out by a volunteer registrar based at the University of British Columbia. With the growing popularity of the World Wide Web, however, the current system has restricted individuals and organizations to one domain name, and an applicant had to wait a week while the request was reviewed. Consequently, businesses have been paying $140 to register .com or .net domain names in the US, where their applications are processed immediately and they are allowed to register as many names as they want.

Meanwhile, a bloc of global and national companies and cyberspace bodies recently set up a new structure for registering addresses on the Net, expanding the number of domains and bringing competition to the lucrative domain name business.

Energy of the Future

As the automobile industry attempts to develop energy-efficient and pollution-free vehicles, the answer looks like it might be found in the once-exotic fuel cell, a source of energy that propels cars fueled by hydrogen and water. A world leader in the development of this technology is Vancouver's Ballard Power Systems Inc., which has teamed up with Germany's Daimler-Benz to build a prototype minivan that has a range of 240 km.

Fuel cells convert hydrogen and oxygen into electricity and water without combustion. There is no pollution and the cells waste little energy. Unlike batteries, which store and release energy, fuel cells produce electric energy directly. Fuel cells have been supplying energy to spacecraft since the 1960's, but earthly applications for the masses are still a number of years away.

In Ballard's fuel cell, the hydrogen and oxygen are fed into opposite sides (the anode and cathode) of a tiny box or cell separated by a membrane. The presence of platinum on the walls of the anode side causes the hydrogen to split into electrons and positive hydrogen ions. These ions squeeze through the membrane and unite with oxygen on the cathode side to form pure, clean water. The electrons left on the anode side pass through an electric motor, which generates about 1 volt of electricity. When enough fuel cells are stacked together, they produce enough electricity to drive an electric vehicle or power a factory.

Today, about 100 small commercial power generators are in operation around the world, while a handful of experimental buses and vans are in use in the US, Canada and Germany. A large system was tested at a power plant in California, and fuel cells are turning waste gas into electricity at a municipal landfill in Connecticut.

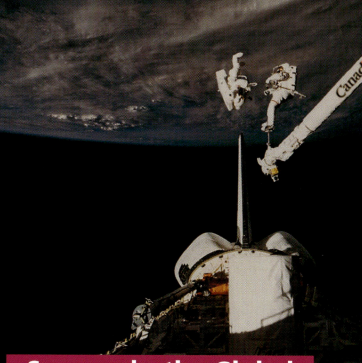

The Cashless Society

Will Canada be the world's 1st cashless society? Smart cards — or electronic cash — are catching on in Canada. Billed as a replacement for cash, smart cards are embedded with a computer chip into which a user can electronically load cash value from their accounts and then use to make purchases.

Once the cash value runs out, instead of throwing the card away, consumers reload it using a compatible telephone, pay phone, or bank machine. Because there are many more pay phones than bank cash machines, this is very convenient for consumers. It also delights banks, as ATMs are expensive to install and require a very high level of maintenance.

Smart card systems currently are being tested in Guelph, Kingston and Barrie, Ontario. Once the system rolls out across the country in late 1998 and is completed in 5 years, Canadians are expected to adopt the smart card quickly; we have a history of being open to new banking technology. On a per capita basis, Canadians use debit cards 10 times more than Americans. The Guelph project is the only electronic cash system in North America to utilize telephones and is also the most comprehensive implementation of electronic cash worldwide.

Merchants are pleased because there is no need for phone authorization of purchases; customers do not have to enter personal identification codes to debit accounts; and merchants do not have to wait for cheques to clear, or need to count and sort notes and coins. This should slash credit card fraud, too, as the computer chip replaces the magnetic strip.

The card will soon have the ability to store different currencies on the same card, an invaluable asset for the traveller. It will become a convenient and secure means of payment over the Internet as well as becoming compatible with cellular telephones. Each card also stores details of the last 10 transactions, helping track spending and preventing disputes between customers and merchants over the amount of money exchanged.

The Guelph test is being conducted by Mondex International Ltd., a British-developed system that is 51%-owned by MasterCard and represents close to 90% of the Canadian financial services marketplace. Other systems being tested include Visa Cash, developed by credit card giant Visa International Inc., and Exact, the Canadian version of a system called Proton developed by a consortium of Belgian banks.

A Wireless World

By 2002, 40% of Canadians will be wire free. The copper wires that carry phone service are destined to become history. The minute that the cost of wired and wireless become the same, there will be no reason other than the massive investment in copper infrastructure, to have a tethered phone. Wireless capabilities will grow quickly after September 1998, when Iridium, a system of 66-globe-spanning satellites goes into service. This will make it possible to place a wireless phone call from anywhere in the world. (See page 146.)

Success in the Global Aerospace Industry

Canada's aerospace industry has achieved notable success since it was privatized a decade ago, and it has the key elements that are needed for it to continue to be a strong competitor in the future.

Canadian aerospace companies have grown by 50% over the past 10 years, more than any other member of the OECD. The private sector has poured billions of dollars into this sector in order to create industry leaders, and it was done with minimal direct government involvement. The industry's contributions to the Canadian economy are significant: 54,000 highly paid jobs, 70% of sales exported, and $1.5 billion invested annually in R&D.

One challenge facing Canadian aerospace companies in the global market is the level of government subsidies. Compared to support by many foreign governments — which can be in the 60% to 90% range — the Canadian Government's support, through the Technology Partnerships Canada Program, while significant, is more modest than the support programs of most of the competitor nations.

Montreal-based CAE Inc. — the world's largest supplier of aircraft flight simulators — is seeing its business grow as military budgets around the world have stabilized or are expanding.

Along with Spar Aerospace, Bombardier and its Canadair and de Havilland aircraft divisions, CAE has helped Canada's aerospace sector grow to become one of the largest in the world. CAE is the industry leader in military flight simulation, supplying 60% to 70% of the global market, and had a backlog of orders of $890 million at the end of fiscal 1997.

Most of CAE's contracts are for helicopter trainers, and it recently signed contracts with Britain, Germany and Australia. It also built flight simulators for the Malaysian Royal Air Force and its Russian-built MiG29 fighters.

Dolly

George and Charlie

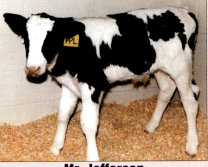

Mr. Jefferson

Tadpole at Bath University, England (1997), with a headless clone; scientists created the frog embryo without a head, a technique for growing organs and tissue for transplant.

BioTech: Hello, Dolly!

The nuclear-transfer technology made famous in the cloning of Scotland's Dolly the sheep and Polly, the world's first transgenic lamb, is advancing so that scientists are now using it to develop pharmaceuticals using farm animals — or "pharming" — and to treat diseases in humans. Experts are worried, however, that laws banning the practice of human cloning could limit research in other areas of cloning.

Researchers, who cloned calves George and Charlie in Texas, see cloning as a step that could lead to the mass production of drugs for humans in cows' milk. The process could also lead to the ability to produce cells that can be transferred into humans to treat diseases such as Parkinson's and Alzheimer's.

The American Society for Reproductive Medicine created carefully worded legislation banning human cloning, while keeping in mind that cloning is a term that is widely used to mean many different procedures.

Problems with anti-cloning legislation occur with research insitutes such as the Cornell Medical Center in New York, which is trying to understand the cause of serious chromosomal defects. In the process, researchers transfer nuclei from damaged adult human cells into immature healthy eggs. This technique, if perfected, could be used by anyone else to apply to produce human clones.

Meet Mr. Jefferson

Using a technique similar to that used to produce Dolly and Polly, PPL Therapeutics cloned a healthy Holstein calf, born on President's Day in the US.

Unlike Dolly, "Mr. Jefferson" is not transgenic (carrying a human gene) and was not produced by taking the nucleus out of a cell from an adult animal, but was produced by nuclear transfer from a fetal cell.

This opens the way to producing transgenic cows using nuclear transfer technology — taking the nucleus out of a cell from the mammary gland of an adult animal and fusing it, using an electrical current, into another egg cell from which the nucleus has been removed.

Hope for Amputees

Researchers have found a breed of mice that grow back amputated parts of their bodies, which could be a model for tissue regeneration in mammals. These mice do not close their wounds with scar tissue like other mammals, but with normal skin and fur. Typically, only amphibians such as frogs are able to regenerate their complex body tissues and parts. Scientists are now looking for the genes involved in the unique regeneration process.

British scientists, meanwhile, have created a frog embryo without a head, a technique that may lead to the production of headless human clones to grow organs and tissue for transplant. The technique could be adapted to grow human organs in an embryonic sac living in an artificial womb. The 2 techniques could then be combined so that people needing transplants could have organs "grown to order" from their own cloned cells.

Scientists have also discovered that monkeys make new cells constantly in an area of the brain used for long-term memory. If humans do the same, it raises hope for treating Alzheimer's, Parkinson's, and injuries from stroke and trauma.

In other medical advances, Scotland's cloned sheep were genetically engineered to carry a human gene for the production of a blood clotting agent to help hemophiliacs, and to produce a human protein used to treat cystic fibrosis.

Who Says Scientists Lack a Sense of Humour?

Dolly the sheep got her name from country singer Dolly Parton. "She was derived, as you know, from mammary cells and the people who were looking after her could not think of a more impressive set of mammary cells than those that belong to Dolly Parton."[135]

ALTHOUGH AN ADVOCATE OF MODERN SCIENCE, THERE WERE TIMES THAT WILBUR WISHED THEY HAD NEVER IMPLANTED HUMAN GENES IN LAMBS...

GIN

Patenting New Forms of Life[136]

While governments are singling out biotechnology as a job-creating industry, the idea of genetic manipulation has raised a considerable number of moral and ethical questions.

Biotechnology is the creation of new or altered life-forms called "transgenic" and includes plants, animals or geneplasm. "Transgenetic" is the term used when a foreign gene is introduced into an organism. The resulting DNA has been changed, and these changes may be transmitted to any progeny.

Are these new species? This is currently being debated even as transgenetically altered foods, plants and animals are being created.

Beyond any moral considerations, public health risks can be extremely high. Transferred genes have the potential to cause allergic reactions, even fatal ones. These transferred genes may also increase resistance to antibiotics.

Some publicly "known" transgenic organisms include: tomatoes, genetically altered to take twice the normal time to ripen; and salmon, genetically modified to grow quickly to 40 times their normal weight. Some of these transgenic foodstuffs are already making their way to our supermarkets.

Meanwhile, multinationals are gaining more control of commercial plant breeding. Patenting is now being used to prevent living organisms — including seeds from the world's chief crops — being copied. By granting such broad patent protection, governments are approving the idea that living creatures are equal to manufactured inventions and subject to the same exploitation.

The bulk of the raw genetic material used in western companies' laboratories is derived from farms and forests in developing countries. But the local farmers — whose knowledge of the domestic, commercial and medicinal uses has been handed down from generation to generation — will not benefit from these patents. To some then, the multi-nationals have "plundered" the knowledge of the indigenous people.

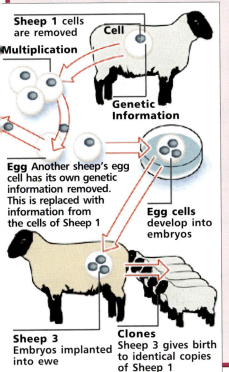

Sheep 1 cells are removed **Cell**

Multiplication

Genetic Information

Egg Another sheep's egg cell has its own genetic information removed. This is replaced with information from the cells of Sheep 1

Egg cells develop into embryos

Sheep 3 Embryos implanted into ewe

Clones Sheep 3 gives birth to identical copies of Sheep 1

AgraTech

Chemical and plastics giants are joining the mad rush to try to design better food, snapping up seed companies, crop patents and biotechnology concerns.

One executive says that plant biotechnology will turn out to be "the next Silicon Valley." Estimates put the consumer market for low-fat designer foods and other genetically engineered crops growing from today's $30 billion to as much as $500 billion a year over the next 20 years.

Genetic alterations kill pests or allow plants to withstand high-grade herbicides. A genetically altered potato, for example, is designed to kill its main predator, the Colorado potato beetle. This means that someday farmers may be able to do away with the vast quantities of raw materials, manufacturing waste and fuel consumed each year to apply insecticides on potato fields.

To date, the Canadian Food Inspection Agency has approved 34 genetically altered vegetables and grains for use, including canola, corn, tomatoes, cotton, potatoes, and soybean. Nearly 20 million hectares of genetically altered produce were planted in 1998 in Canada and the US — a tripling of the growth in the 2 years that these seeds have been on the market.

Scientists see the next stage in development as enhancing the flavour of protein-rich crops or the quality of their oils or their abilities to produce medically attractive chemicals. This is 3 to 5 years away.

Future developments could include nutritional advances such as oils that form lower cholesterol and even proteins or hormones that may help with arthritis, hormonal cancer and menopause. Currently, scientists are working on a potato with reduced water content (which will absorb less fat when fried), a floating rice that can withstand floods, and a caffeine-free coffee bean.

The 3rd stage of the biotech revolution will move food crops into textile or industrial-strength materials, such as biodegradable plastic made from corn. This brings us back to the chemical companies, many of whom see that the technological skills developed in the chemical and plastics operations overlap with genetic and agricultural research.

For example, St. Louis-based Monsanto Co. split off its chemical arm into a separate company so it could devote more of its energies to developing healthier crops — and the leading edge pharmaceuticals that may grow out of them. In 1997, agricultural products provided 42% of the company's $7.5 billion in sales, compared to 32% from pharmaceuticals.

Chemical companies are rubbing their hands in glee at crossover applications and are developing dedicated farm markets. Monsanto produces Roundup Ready soybeans and Roundup Ready canola to work only with its well-known Roundup herbicide — and charges a special "technology fee" per acre for the package.

Roundup sales have been increasing by more than 20% annually. By linking it with specifically tailored seeds, the herbicide has been given an added boost just a couple of years before its US patent protection is scheduled to expire.

Medical Advances

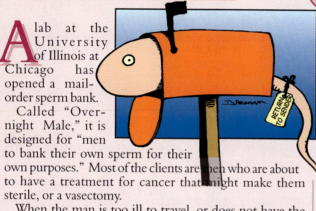

A lab at the University of Illinois at Chicago has opened a mail-order sperm bank.

Called "Overnight Male," it is designed for "men to bank their own sperm for their own purposes." Most of the clients are men who are about to have a treatment for cancer that might make them sterile, or a vasectomy.

When the man is too ill to travel, or does not have the time, the lab sends him a "kit," including a preservative solution, a container with a tamper-proof seal, and packaging to have it couriered back to Chicago the next day. The rest, as they say, is easy.

Scientists believe that this ability to freeze sperm, embryos and everything else eventually, could change the entire process of procreation, just the way agriculture changed survival and wheels changed mobility.

HANDS OFF MY DNA!!

Molecular Nanotechnology

The principles of physics... do not speak against the possibility of maneuvering things atom by atom.[137]

Manufactured products are made from atoms. The properties of those products depend on how those atoms are arranged. If we rearrange the atoms in coal we can make diamonds. If we rearrange the atoms in sand (and add a few other trace elements) we can make computer chips. If we rearrange the atoms in dirt, water and air we can make potatoes. Today's manufacturing methods are very crude at the molecular level — primarily the ancient practices of casting, grinding and milling.

It is like trying to make things out of Lego blocks with boxing gloves on your hands. You could push the Lego blocks into great heaps and pile them up, but you could not snap them together the way they are designed to fit.

In the future, nanotechnology, used to describe many types of research where the characteristic dimensions are less than about 1,000 nanometers, will let us take off those metaphorical boxing gloves. We will be able to snap together the fundamental building blocks of nature easily, inexpensively and in almost any arrangement that we desire. This will allow us to fabricate an entire new generation of products that are cleaner, stronger, lighter, and more precise.

The exponential improvements in computer hardware capability are built on 50-year old technologies, and there is a fairly widespread belief that these technologies will serve us for another 10 years. Beyond that period, we will have to develop a new manufacturing technology that will let us build inexpensive computer systems with molecular elements interconnected in complex and highly idiosyncratic patterns. Nanotechnology will allow us do this.

Precise positional control is frequently used in normal macroscopic manufacturing today; the need for molecular-level positioning leads to an interest in molecular robotics, i.e., robotic devices that are molecular both in their size and precision. These molecular-scale positional devices are likely to resemble very small versions of their everyday macroscopic counterparts. These systems are able both to make copies of themselves and to manufacture useful products. If we can design and build one such system, the manufacturing costs for more such systems and the products they make (assuming they can make copies of themselves in some reasonably inexpensive environment) will be very low.

The idea of manipulating individual atoms and molecules is still a relatively new concept — we need to apply, at the molecular scale, the concept that has demonstrated its effectiveness at the macroscopic scale: making parts go where we want them to go by being able to put them where we want them to be!

Discontinuous Futures and Disintermediation

The effects of the information age are far-ranging, especially in terms of the job market. Technology has eliminated whole categories of jobs — particularly those that traditionally have been the "middlemen." Music, movies and software are all common digital products that consumers buy through retail intermediaries, but any of these can be delivered on-line by new intermediaries, such as multimedia and software delivery services. Tickets for such things as theatre, concerts and travel are really intangibles: They can be handled by on-line information brokers. Insurance policies, mortgages, stock and bonds are also intangibles that can be "delivered" electronically by transaction brokers, another new class of intermediary.

Is there a need for a wholesaler in the process if a retailer can buy from an on-line catalogue? Is there a need for a retailer if the consumer can buy directly from the manufacturer? Following are some examples of sectors of our economy that likely will find themselves victims of "disintermediation."

The Financial Sector

• In 1997, Toronto Stock Exchange (TSE) got wired; that means no more of those "strange" guys on the trading floor, shaking their heads and doing these fancy hand signals to one another.
• The networks of brokers and agents who sell insurance products will vanish, because most of the functions they provide — particularly with respect to similar products can be provided electronically, or with less manual intervention than is needed by the existing system.
• Real Estate is not immune, either, as the Internet has become a 1st rate real-estate catalogue. Buyers surf through listings, view properties, (including virtual reality tours), and exchange e-mail messages with vendors.
• In April of 1997, Dutch financial services giant ING became the 1st financial institution to launch an aggressive push into the $90 billion-a-year Canadian consumer banking business with an electronic or "virtual" bank.
• The Toronto Dominion bank subsidiary Green Line — the country's largest discount stockbroker — is offering price comparisons to its 500,000 clients and the general public over the telephone and the Internet. Vector Intermediaries, Green Line's "partner" has an interactive price quotation service on the Internet and sells insurance through some Wal-Mart stores.
• Britain's Direct Line Insurance entered the market in 1995, basing its business entirely on direct sales that eliminated brokers. It now has 25+% of the UK market.
• Leeds, England, is home to the world's leading telephone-only bank. First Direct is an extremely successful branchless banking operation that has attracted the attention of bankers around the world.
• Deloitte & Touche's financial services group estimates that in the US 450,000 banking jobs will disappear over the next decade, including half of all the bank teller jobs.

This is only the beginning. It is predicted that electronic transactions will oust branch visits as the main way Canadians bank by 1999, but no single method will dominate, according to an Ernst & Young survey. Debit cards are predicted to be the most popular banking method in 1999, accounting for 32% of transactions; computer banking, whether through the Internet or a direct connection, is projected to account for 5.5% of transactions, quadruple its share in 1996; telephone transactions will nearly triple to 10.5%; and face-to-face visits are to fall sharply as a percentage of transactions to just 31% of the total, from 45% in 1996. At a minimum, that means that banks will need 35% fewer tellers.

In Canada, though, most redundant tellers are not being fired, but are being retrained and relocated as the banks scramble to sell every other financial service imaginable.

The Retail Sector

Personal computer manufacturer Dell has captured 3rd place in the overall Canadian PC market with build-to-order and direct distribution. It does not build a computer until it knows it has a buyer. Once the unit is built, it goes directly to the owner, rather than to a reseller. That eliminates the middleman and allows the Texas-based company to shave between 7% and 12% off its costs.

The US "big box" retailing chains deal directly with the manufacturer, crushing the buying power of smaller operations and, of course, eliminating the middlemen wholesalers. Like middle management, wholesalers are becoming increasingly redundant in the age of instant electronic communication. Since 1989, the wholesale sector has dropped more than a quarter of a million jobs. Economist Jeremy Rifkin predicts that, "by early in the next century, most wholesaling, as we have come to know it, will have been eliminated, a victim of the revolutionary innovations in electronic transmission control and coordination."

The use of electronic bar codes and price-scanning equipment have made cashiers more efficient, and therefore, fewer of them are needed.

The Entertainment Sector

The music industry is looking to the Internet for a lift. With consumers already ordering compact discs from various web sites, and music companies increasingly using the Net for new music previews, the industry envisions transmitting music digitally, directly to personal computers, which would let consumers make their own discs.

Sony registered as a trademark the term "Netman" (evoking its revolutionary Walkman and Discman personal stereos) for such applications as a hardware device that would allow users to download music from the web for playback later and eventually transfer it to recordable discs.

On-line music distribution will transform how music is sold. Record companies will abandon the costly process of pressing CDs in massive factories and shipping them to stores. The possibility of eliminating the middleman has retailers worried, making record companies cautious.

Blockbuster announced plans to launch an electronic-distribution system that would enable retailers to make compact discs in their stores without the expense of maintaining an inventory. However, the plan was dropped in 1995, after record companies balked, citing concern over royalties and copyrights. **The issue is not technology, which is already here. The problem is that record companies have huge investments in compact-disc plants and are worried about anything that would break their control of the business.**

Through technology, new silicon-age musicians — referred to as "synths" — can produce the sounds of multiple instruments without compromising the quality of the work; costs are slashed and profit margins are improved.

Intermediation

Mediators are the "middle" businesses that have traditionally been the link between the creators of the goods and services and the consumers. They are the wholesalers, brokers and agents that occupy such roles as banks and other financial services, insurance brokers, travel agents, stockbrokers, real estate agents, telephone companies, radio and TV stations, newspapers, hydro wholesalers and automobile agencies. Intermediators are also the retailers who have linked the creators of goods and services with the end customers. The alliance between Newcourt Credit Corporation and Dell Computers to provide lease financing to buyers is a very representative example of how traditional channels of intermediation (banks) have been ruptured by alternative channels.

In academic jargon, the economy is ripe for what might be called "disintermediation." For those in this middle ground of commerce, the message is much simpler and much scarier — joblessness. "The speed with which things are moving on the Web is stunning, and punishment is proving to be swift for those who don't understand this," says Don Tapscott, author of *The Digital Economy*. Traditional agents, brokers, distributors, and wholesalers — and even many retailers — *anybody* who performs these customary intermediation functions ought to be doing some very serious career planning.

Disintermediation

The rate of disintermediation, the elimination or replacement of the traditional "middle man," is exploding. This rate governs the ability of firms to choose between providing a service themselves or using a 3rd party service provider. If you can access the Internet directly through a bare-bones Internet service provider (ISP), you simply do not need AOL Canada, Prodigy or any other "value-added" middleman to do it for you.

Disintermediation has the potential to impact almost every type of business. **Many of today's thriving companies will find their businesses replaced by players that do not exist yet.** Technology pundits say that direct, speedy and inexpensive Internet connections between buyers and sellers are making traditional middlemen obsolete. Some will adapt by assuming new forms that add value to transactions in nontraditional ways. Others will simply disappear.

The notion of linking up customers and suppliers dates back to the 1960's with the introduction of American Airlines' Sabre electronic reservation system, points out digital guru Don Tapscott. What is new, he says, "is that more transactions, more commerce, more human interactions are happening on the public infrastructure of the Net." It should not be a surprise to learn that that much of the future of business lies on the Internet and its successor systems.

Cybermediaries

Numerous researchers suggest that a changing information environment will bring about the development of entirely new businesses. The "Cybermediary" is where the development of new technology actually makes it cheaper to go through new, non-traditional intermediaries.

The potential for turning businesses upside down is enormous. For example, instead of customers going out searching for mortgages, they are posting their requests on the Internet so lenders can come directly to them. The Internet is direct marketing in reverse, with the customer coming to the business. With new direct media, customers will only come to the organization that can create an offer that is valuable and relevant to them.

These changes will reduce marketing costs and should result in lower prices, thus allowing more people to afford a particular service or product, while existing customers will get more for the same amount of money.

It also means that there is an enormous amount of room for new kinds of creativity to be unleashed.

Will you be a disintermediator or one of the disintermediated?

Reintermediation

Reintermediation is creating new value between producers and consumers. As commerce, learning, health care, and most things become digital, users are drowning in data. There are a thousand new TV channels, a hundred thousand new services, millions of new databases, and a billion users, but not until structure is added to data can you get information.

"Data mining" is the developing alchemy of adding context, analysis, synthesis, editing, and new services to convert meaningless data into valuable information.

The CRTC's landmark ruling opened the door to full competition between telephone and cable TV companies effective January 1, 1998. While the implications of this decision had been anticipated for some time, the massive capital investments in these infrastructures will take some time to sort out relative competitive advantages. We can be very sure that there will be continued shake-ups in these traditionally stable and highly profitable industries in the next 2 years.

The relatively recent deregulation of long-distance telephone services has given Sprint's Candace Bergen more air space than most of us appreciate. But we can take heart in the realization that long-distance services are just at a very temporary plateau. The 1998 "break-through" Sprint rate of $20-a-month for unlimited calling in Canada is only a preview of the $20- a-month unlimited calling in the *world*. If you can reach anyone in the world via Internet e-mail for only a nominal local access charge (1998 ads offer *unlimited* Internet access for as low as $169 a year), what is the economic logic behind the decreased but still relatively high charges for international telephone calls? USA Global Link has raised $500 million to offer international telephone calls using the Internet. Can other reintermediaters be far behind? (See page 147.)

If your business card says, "Digital, Electronic or Online Commerce," you're on the right track.

Hydro Privatization

Directions for Change: Charting a Course for Competitive Electricity and Jobs in Ontario sets in motion a legislative and implementation schedule aimed at introducing a fully open, competitive electricity market.

The Ontario White Paper is actually quite reminiscent of the famous white paper on power privatization **produced by the Thatcher's UK government in 1988**.

roadkill-drjobs.com

The POT* Busters
*(Plain Old Telephone)

Most of our homes now are wired with what is known as "twisted pairs," which have limited capacity for delivering information. To use an analogy, twisted pairs might have the capacity of a sidewalk, while some new technologies have the capacity of a multi-lane superhighway.

This has great significance for the Internet. Currently, most small Internet service providers still use POTS (plain old telephone service), which can be fairly slow, inasmuch as most people are connected at 28.8 kbps. The main options for the future will likely remove the speed limits on the Internet.

• **ISDN (Integrated Services Digital Network):** ISDN is a special phone line that has 2 channels, each running at 64 kbps, which can bond together to give 128 kbps service. Bell Canada already offers 2 ISDN services, one for home use and the other for business.

• **ADSL (Asymmetric Digital Subscriber Line):** ADSL is a dedicated phone line with 3 channels — 1 for telephone calls, 1 for sending data (up to 640 kbps) and the 3rd to receive data (eventually reaching 52,000 kbps). ADSL is currently undergoing testing and was available in some areas in late 1998.

• **MMDS (Microchannel Multipoint Distribution System):** Through MMDS, users transmit to the Internet across the phone line (at 28.8 kbps), but download at 10,000 kbps via microwave from an antenna attached to a satellite dish installed on a roof or window.

• **Cable Television:** Cable was originally designed for 1-way use only — to deliver TV signals. To handle 2-way traffic, it will need a major upgrade to fibre optics, but this will make it super fast (up to 10,000 kbps in the future) and permanently connected to the Internet. Rogers Cable had the service available to 1.5 million homes at the end of 1998.

• **Powerline Telephony:** This technology lets homeowners make phone calls and access the Internet at high speeds via the electric outlets in their walls. The system can transmit data at a speed of more than 384 kbps over regular electrical lines. The advantage is that existing power lines can simultaneously transmit both electricity and a phone call — their frequencies are different so they do not interfere with one another. The technology is well suited for the power grids in Europe and Asia-Pacific, but is currently too expensive for North America.

• **CAnet2:** This network is part of a $60 million project being developed by the Canadian Network for the Advancement of Research, Industry and Education (CANARIE) that will create a nationwide service with an effective speed about 100 times faster than the POTS — an electronic multi-lane Trans-Canada highway. Universities and research institutes will be 1st online, followed by teaching hospitals, to provide such services as distance learning and tele-medicine. The lessons and technologies will be quickly transferred to the main Internet afterwards.

Privatization: Global Trends

In 1996, privatization worldwide amounted to an all-time high of $88 billion — with a record-breaking $68 billion raised in OECD countries alone. In 1997, privatization rose to more than $100 billion.

Since 1993, OECD privatizations predominantly have been made through public offerings in the capital markets, as opposed to trade sales to strategic investors. Although international investors continue to play a significant role, domestic investors have become increasingly important buyers. Privatization-related public offerings have been evenly balanced between retail and institutional investors in the past 3 years.

In the UK, $19 billion worth of privatization occurred between 1988 and 1995 under the Tory government; new Labour Prime Minister Tony Blair has promised to continue the process — perhaps even more aggressively. Germany has privatized more than $11.5 billion worth of industry, most of it in the post-1989 consolidation with East Germany. Argentina has privatized $6.5 billion worth of industry, Australia $6 billion, and even Communist China has privatized $1.5 billion with a commitment to do much, much more.

The government of the state of Sao Paulo in Brazil has been making a flurry of asset sales, which could bring that state as much as $23 billion over the next 2 years. It recently auctioned off its 41% stake in an electrical distribution company for $2.2 billion, and before that, 2 consortia paid more than $4.2 billion — a price 80% above the bidding floor — for 2 privatized distribution companies.

Why has privatization become so popular? Basically, many governments have come to realize that they should not be in business. Can you imagine if the Ontario government announced that it had taken over the auto parts industry? We know this does not make sense, given that auto parts giant Magna International already does a highly profitable business, and we do not need government creating auto parts. So what makes electricity, liquor, broadcasting, or anything else run "better" as government-owned businesses?

As countries around the world are beginning to see, removing inefficiencies due to monopolies and government interventions not only makes things run better, but adds significantly to their GDP.

Canadian governments have had their fingers in too many private pies. For more than 100 years, governments felt that the best way to serve the public good was to create a public institution. "So pervasive was this pattern," explains pollster Angus Reid, "that by 1990, more than 200,000 Canadians were employed by Crown corporations and not-for-profit organizations owned or directly supported by one or more levels of government." Lately, however, most Canadians have found that governments have grown "bloated and stale." [78]

> *No Government* should ever provide services that compete with the more efficient *private sector.*

Union Resistance to Privatization

When the Conservatives came to power in Ontario in 1995, they did so on a platform that promised privatization of a number of crown assets. The "Common Sense Revolution" promised that the government service would be downsized by 15%. Unfortunately, 3 years later, the privatization secretariat was frustrated with bureaucratic attempts to stall its plans. One of its roadblocks has been a key clause in the government's contract with the 60,000 employees who belong to OPSEU requiring that the government use "reasonable efforts" to ensure that when a service is contracted out to a private employer, the government workers now providing the service keep their jobs with the new employer. In a dozen attempts to contract out services, arbitrators have ruled that the government had failed to use "reasonable efforts."

The government had to abandoned further attempts to privatize services and has not appealed any of the other arbitrators' rulings. Instead, it drafted legislation to eliminate the "reasonable efforts" clause and allow itself the unrestricted right to contract out services.

Stalled privatization plans include those for TV Ontario, a provincially-owned television outlet that receives more than $50 million a year from the Ontario government. Several ministers and key government advisors opposed changes that would upset supporters of TVO, arguing about the heritage perspective of the importance of public television in "shaping our society."

Another target was the Liquor Control Board of Ontario (LCBO) — the world's largest liquor retailer. While consumers in most other provinces can buy alcohol from the corner store, consumers in Ontario must make an extra trip to the LCBO and be served by staff earning significantly higher salaries and enjoying better benefits than if the operation were run privately.

The BC Contrarians: While Ontario is trying to go one direction, BC is going in the opposite direction. In 1997, the province became co-owner of the financially troubled pulp and lumber maker Skeena Cellulose Inc. The government committed $270 million to the commercially non-viable mill, prolonging its life and costing taxpayers an estimated $450,000 per job at the mill to save the jobs for a very limited period.

> As gruesome as the Ontario Hydro story is (see page 162), the per capita obligations of New Brunswick Power are even more outrageous than those of Ontario. NBP has obligations of $4 billion that do not appear on the province's balance sheet. Each NB taxpayer is on the hook for about $5,300 while each Ontario taxpayer is obligated for a *mere* $4,000.

> *The cost to taxpayers of getting out of the patronage-tinged airport deal with Pearson Development Corp. could easily exceed $1 billion over the next 20 years.*

*The next 3 pages provide profiles of **winners and losers** in Canada's slow move to deregulation and privatization.*

Private Funding of Public Works

North America's first electronic toll road — Highway 407 north of Toronto — is for sale by the Ontario government, although it was already built and is being maintained by a private consortium. The money for the 1st part of the 407, which will cost $2.5 billion by the time the entire project is finished, was borrowed by a Crown agency, which gets the toll revenue from the road and assumes the risk that tolls might not pay for its building and maintenance. The road was to be privately financed, but the province funded construction because it could borrow money at a lower rate.

Privatization would mean the consortium that takes over the road from the province would raise the money for the extensions from capital markets and assume the financial risk. Whoever buys the road — possibly for $2.5 billion — will get to keep all the toll money and taxpayers will no longer have to worry about paying for the road or being saddled with any debt for the proposed extensions on both ends.

The 4-lane highway now rolling out between Moncton and Fredericton is the latest project to show that, when it comes to major public works, the private sector can do it better. New Brunswick set up a company that will build and run 195 km of toll highway connecting its 2 largest cities — and the road will be built in 4 years, rather than the 14 years it was projected to have taken if the money had to come from the provincial budget. Construction has already begun, and financiers are selling about $525 million in bonds to pay for the road. The companies that won the right to build did so for $170 million below the nearest competitor.

Prince Edward Island's Confederation Bridge — its 1st permanent link to the mainland — cost $1 billion to build, but was put together by a private consortium.

This notion of privatization of infrastructure is not new. One of Canada's most picturesque and famous bridges — Vancouver's Lions Gate Bridge — was built with beer money from the famous Guinness family of Ireland. (See page 117 for a view of government inefficiency in bridge building.) The BC government has invited the private sector to come up with plans for a toll bridge to replace the deteriorating 60-year-old landmark. A new crossing is expected to cost between $250 - $300 million. One downside to private funding is that no one can raise money cheaper than the government.

The R$_x$ for Pharmaceutical Research

Pharmaceutical research in Canada has soared 300% in the last 10 years, thanks to a "friendlier" environment created by our federal government. Bill C-22, the controversial patent-protection legislation passed in 1987, has prompted pharmaceutical companies to increase their drug research dramatically — to the tune of $665 million in 1996.

Twice as many Canadians are enrolled in clinical trials as there were 7 years ago: 35,000 patients investigated 140 drugs in 1996. These clinical trials are not only a boon for the industry and a shot in the arm for academics and physicians faced with government funding cuts, but also good for the ill patients, who get treated with leading-edge therapies and an expanding variety of drugs.

Canada has a long way to go, however, to make itself the most attractive host for this global activity. The US is still considered faster to conduct clinical trials because of fewer regulatory barriers. Canada's Health Protection Branch is hopeful that, before the end of 1998, it can reduce the 60-day review process to 45 days for trials of high-risk drugs, 15 days for low-risk drugs and instantaneous approval for drugs already widely tested.

Importance of Funding R&D

If the government is serious about improving Canada's future and producing a climate for job creation, it must raise spending in areas that improve our capacity for innovation, provide leadership, and stimulate and encourage the innovation process. In a knowledge-based economy, it is brainpower that generates the ideas that create new high-tech companies and produce good jobs.

Funding must also be maintained for university-industry research partnerships to develop new technologies. The Natural Sciences and Engineering Research Council and the Medical Research Council have been hit hard by budget cuts at a time when they are trying to attract the best and brightest post-graduate students.

There is now a tremendous need for many more highly qualified researchers, a growing dependence by industry on university basic research for new ideas, and rising costs to research.

Deregulation Works

Without long-distance competition, you would be paying 48¢ a minute for calls across Canada instead of today's average price of 17¢. Long-distance rates have traditionally heavily subsidized residential local rates. With competition, local rates are moving towards what it costs to provide residential service.[138]

Successful Programs

The Industrial Research & Assistance Program provides advice and technology development funding to small and mid-size companies. Without more money, the IRAP says that good projects from innovative companies will be turned down.

The Technology Partnerships Canada program, which provides repayable funding to companies in the aerospace, biotechnology, environmental and other growth industries, is another area that could use increased funding.

Best Practices

Canada Dominates Open Skies

The open skies agreement of 1995, which deregulated air travel across North America, has seen Canada's 2 major airlines dominate cross-border air travel.

Montreal-based Air Canada, which has doubled its network of flights to US cities since the agreement, now accounts for nearly as many cross-border flights as all the US airlines put together. Canadian Airlines of Calgary, with its "gateway to Asia" in Vancouver, now serves twice the number of US cities it served in 1994, and its transborder revenue has climbed to $310 million — 5 times what it was before open skies.

Air Canada, with its "Fortress Hub" in Toronto, launched dozens of new routes as soon as the agreement took effect. It gambled on the new 50-seat Bombardier Regional Jets, which can operate on marginal routes at a fraction of the cost of traditional aircraft, allowing the airline to move into new markets until it built up enough traffic to purchase bigger planes.

The feared invasion by giant US airlines never happened and, regardless of who won the battle for the transborder skies, both sides agree that they are happy with the way open skies has turned out. The agreement has been a boon for travellers and businesses, more than 40 new services have been launched from Toronto to the US, traffic has risen by 31%, and it has brought the economy billions of dollars and thousands of jobs.

Riding on its success in Canada, a unit of the **Vancouver International Airport Authority** is part of a consortium that won the rights to build an extension to an airport in Chile and manage the terminal. The contract includes building a terminal, constructing a control tower, developing the cargo and "land side" of the airport, and looking after customer service, ticketing, food services and other functions.

Worst Practices

Canada Post

A national dinosaur waiting for privatization is Canada Post, which continues to have a public monopoly on 1st class mail. It processed 10.9 billion pieces of mail in 1996, which means that millions of Canadians still rely on the mail even if they have e-mail or a fax machine. Postal strikes disrupt cash flows, render post-based businesses risky, and stop millions of dollars of potential transactions from taking place.

Politicized postal rates do not cover the true cost of running a universal letter service at a uniform national rate, which helps explain why has Canada Post suffered total losses of $1.5 billion since 1982.

Its 1996 mandate review found that Canada Post engaged in unrestrained competition with the private sector. It was called a "vicious competitor," unfairly leveraging its publicly financed monopoly infrastructure to support its non-monopoly businesses (e.g., its 75% interest in Purolator Courier, formerly Canada's largest private service). And its collective agreements with its unions were found to be "what is arguably the most uncompetitive and inefficient labour agreement currently in place in North America."[139]

The union has been very successful in fighting both privatization and flexibility in its contract. Since 1967, Canada has seen 11 national postal strikes, including 2 fought after privatization, which had guaranteed that 482 post offices would remain open. While management tries to create efficiencies, the union still insists on such ridiculous practices as allowing letter carriers to return to a Canada Post facility for lunch, rather than take their breaks while out on their routes.

The Canada Post Logo

A federal crown corporation, which has tried for years to foster the image of a private corporation, is putting Canada back into its logo.

Canada Post, which was a federal department until it was made a crown agency in 1981, decided, following its 1996 review, to change its current red and blue logo of just Mail/Postes to Canada Post/Postes Canada.

The post office now wants to emphasize that it is a federal crown corporation and has a presence in almost every Canadian community. The last logo change in 1989, was a "quick change" and cost taxpayers $30 million. This time they believe that a "phased" approach can hold the cost to *only* $8 million.

ROADKILL ON THE **INFORMATION HIGHWAY**

Success With Nav Canada

The federal government is recouping more than $1 billion in user fees and taxes from the national airline industry as it transfers operation of Canada's airports from Transport Canada to private-sector, non-profit corporations. Until recently, the government was spending $250 million a year to run airport operations; now, it stands to make $250 million in "annual profits," giving Ottawa an net gain of $500 million every year.

The government is also withdrawing the RCMP, forcing airports to hire private security agencies at a cost of between $20 million and $25 million a year. Also sold was the air navigation system to Nav Canada, a not-for-profit corporation owned by the aviation industry, for $1.5 billion (although the deal was called a $1 billion subsidy for the industry by the Auditor-General, who said that Transport Canada's own financial advisors valued it at $2.4 billion). The sale to Nav Canada means that the tax on airline tickets will be cut by as much as $25 since the tax was collected originally to pay for the air traffic control system.

Sweden Post Gets Wired

After losing its monopoly of mail delivery services in parts of Sweden, the national postal service is negotiating a deal with Netscape Communications to create a national Intranet covering the whole country of 8.8 million people.

Sweden Post, wanting to become a major player in Internet services to compensate for the loss of any traditional business, is reportedly paying an initial fee of roughly $10 million for Netscape's browser and server software to offer Swedish households and small businesses Intranet and Internet access services.

These will include a single "white pages" facility covering all households, as well as electronic mailboxes, electronic shopping, Web access, Web publishing facilities and the ability to set up secure electronic trading outlets. Sweden Post would manage e-mail services like it already manages paper-based mail services, although households without networked computers would receive e-mail either as separate faxes or printed messages. There is a logistical — and perhaps legal — problem, however, if Sweden Post decides to assign e-mail addresses similar to the recipient's street address, which could violate the 1995 European data protection directive. While resourcefulness is commendable, there is a serious flaw in wanting to grow Sweden Post.

> **Governments should never provide services that compete with the more efficient private sector.**

International Comparisons

Internationally, reform of the electricity industry is under way in numerous countries, including Australia, the UK, Norway and Latin America.

Those calling for complete privatization of Ontario Hydro point to how the Thatcher government broke the British power system into several parts and sold off the pieces, or even how US and Canadian regulators have already ended Bell's long-distance monopoly.

Victoria was the first Australian state to privatize its utilities and to introduce competition into its electricity market. It has now sold $22.5 billion worth of its electricity assets, using the proceeds to cut state debt.

Closer to home, Pennsylvania recently switched to a competitive electricity market. More than 40 companies have been licensed to sell power to homes and businesses, which are expected to reduce rates by at least 15%

Hydro-Quebec, meanwhile, plans to build new hydroelectric dams and transmission lines to carry its electricity into the US and Ontario markets. With its low-cost hydroelectricity, Hydro-Quebec is well positioned to crack these markets under deregulation.

The Spirit of Hong Kong

Hong Kong is influencing China, and not the other way around, as up to 4 million jobs, half of China's central-government positions, will be lost when it streamlines its civil service and privatizes many state-owned enterprises.

Considered the most drastic shakeup of resilient bureaucracies in the world, the restructuring includes cutting 15 of 40 ministries. Most of chopped ministries have control over state-sector industries, which will be privatized to form publicly traded companies.

Other reforms, overwhelmingly approved by the People's Congress in March of 1998, include a $45 billion recapitalization of China's 4 commercial banks, increased spending on infrastructure and major job cuts for virtually every large industrial sector. Plans are also underway to rid the state-owned enterprises of incompetent managers, stressing business acumen over Communist Party loyalty.

Revitalizing China's state-owned enterprises is considered the most difficult task because of the potential social unrest arising from the inevitable layoff of tens of millions of workers. Even so, the economic and trade commission vice-minister seems undaunted: "Currently, state-owned enterprises employ some 75 million people. If we downsized the work force by 1/3, they could still operate normally. If we cut 50%, it would be even better."

Australia Sells Airports

The Australian government plans to sell 15 regional airports – the largest single airport sale undertaken in the world, in terms of the number being offered – which could yield between $400 million and $500 million. This follows on the heels of a recent sale of the Melbourne, Perth and Brisbane airports, which sold for $3.37 billion, exceeding expectations by $1 billion. International interest in the sale is intense, with more than 60 airport and basic industry companies expected to bid.

The End of Ontario Hydro

Ontario Hydro's problems are replicated, to a large degree, in all provincial hydro crown corporations.

The insolvent crown behemoth known as Ontario Hydro is in for a major overhaul, following a government paper calling for the restructuring the entire power industry.

The government realized that ending the monopoly is the key to creating new jobs and an economy that is attractive to investors, providing lower costs while safeguarding a reliable electricity supply, and restoring financial soundness.

North America's biggest electric utility, which generates about 95% of Ontario's electricity, has been plagued by problems in recent years, which are the legacy of its monopoly. Power costs have been increasing, there have been environmental problems, poorly trained personnel, lazy managers, a huge backlog of maintenance, even substance abuse, and **the utility is notorious for high wages and excess staff.**

Hydro has been fighting against a breakup; the province has been under pressure from the business community, municipalities and even some environmental groups to open the market to competition.

The cost of electricity influences the price of products and the ability of companies to create jobs. The total annual electric bill for the province currently amounts to almost $10 billion, with the average household spending nearly $1,000 annually. Competitively priced electricity is especially important for Ontario's export-oriented industries in its core manufacturing sectors.

New technology and low fossil fuel prices will allow large industrials to produce their own power more cheaply. Electricity rates are falling due to large surpluses, particularly in neighbouring US states — and producers are anxious to gain access to captive high-paying customers.

Although Ontario Hydro has a high dependence on nuclear plants, which generate over half the province's electricity, its reactors are performing far below industry standards. In 1997, 3 plants achieved a 56% performance rating, based on factors such as power production, unplanned automatic reactor shutdowns, safety systems, employee accident rates, and radiation exposures. While Hydro sets a performance target of 60%, the American average is 80%.

Demand for electricity collapsed in the recession of the early 1990's, prompting restructuring of the nuclear division. **The 1,100 nuclear workers who were laid off were given severance packages averaging $105,000.**

Downsizing compounded the problems, as the utility suffered a brain drain, and repairs were either performed haphazardly or not at all.

The nuclear division problems are very costly; in 1996, Ontario Hydro reported a $6.3 billion loss — the largest in Canadian corporate history.

Hydro also introduced a nuclear recovery plan — costing in excess of $11 billion. Hydro officials estimated it would take an 11% increase in rates to cover the cost of the recovery program and pay down its $38 billion debt.

Long-term debt has more than doubled since 1980, and interest payments amount to well over 1/3 of total revenues. In business, write-offs occur because of unexpected changes in market conditions. In Hydro's case, they also reflect a record of poor decision making.

The government plans to open competition in 2000. Its plans include: establishing an Independent Market Operator to act as an impartial manager of the system; separating monopoly operations from competitive businesses; and providing the Ontario Energy Board with an expanded mandate to protect consumers.

Under this proposal, 2 new companies would succeed Ontario Hydro: The Ontario Electricity Generation Corporation, which would take ownership of Hydro's generation assets; and the Ontario Electric Services Corporation, which would handle the other electricity businesses, including transmission, operating, distribution and retail contracts.

On the competition start date, Ontario Hydro's transmission grid and the wires would become common carriers with posted prices, in much the same way that telephone lines and gas pipelines became common carriers when those industries were opened up to competition. Similar to the development in the telephone sector, the "wires" businesses — or monopoly parts of the industry — would be operated in a way that is fair to all participants. All generators, including those outside Ontario, would be able to compete.

The government has also developed a plan to put the proposed new companies on a sound financial basis and to advance the public discussion about potentially stranded debt. This includes considering the sale of an equity stake to a foreign utility.

In 1996, a government report called for not only the dismantling, but also the logical privatization of Hydro. Hydro has been able to borrow extravagant amounts of money by sharing the province's credit rating, but it still conducts its affairs in secret and enjoys the unique status of being an unregulated utility.

> When it is all over, the debts of Ontario Hydro could exceed $50 billion, an amount equivalent to the national budget for education or the total annual budget for Ontario. If this happened in the private sector, people would go to jail — at Ontario Hydro, they just get large severance packages and fat pensions.

Best Practices

The Alberta Advantage:
Out of the Business of Being in Business!

When Alberta Premier Ralph Klein is done, his province will have fewer services, greatly reduced waste, a stronger work ethic and lower taxes. After imposing a 5% wage rollback on health care workers and a 20% reduction in municipal grants, Klein escalated the war against Alberta's multi-billion budget overrun. In 1994, provincial debt **(excluding pension liabilities)** was $8.3 billion. By 1998, the debt will be eliminated. Standard and Poor's upgraded Alberta's credit rating to AA+ in 1997. **Alberta now has the best overall credit rating among the Canadian provinces.**

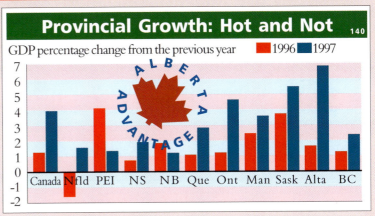

Provincial Growth: Hot and Not
GDP percentage change from the previous year ■ 1996 ■ 1997

Creating a Smaller Government

These wage rollbacks and cuts mean that Alberta's employees in the MUSH sector will be fewer in number and not so highly paid. Because most of this sector receives more than 90% of its funding from the province, the cuts could net between $400 million and $700 million a year. By 1997, the government was 1/3 smaller than 4 years earlier and only slightly larger than in 1971.

Schools will be cheaper to operate and managed by fewer administrators, with fewer optional courses and offering extra-curricular activities only if local taxpayers decide to pay for them.

The good news is that, as the Alberta government shrinks in size, the province creates more jobs. As one of the leanest governments in the country with few, if any, programs designed to artificially create jobs, in 1997, Alberta led Canada in job growth, while its GDP also led the country in growth at 6.5% versus 3.8% nationally.

The Health Care Challenge

The biggest challenge remains health care, which still constitutes 1/3 of the provincial budget. The government's plan calls for fewer rural hospitals and more community health centres, and hospitals will require the right to charge user fees for more of their services, limiting needless visits. Many of Alberta's 177 hospital boards have been consolidated.

Most of the participants at a health care roundtable favoured bringing in user fees and making seniors pay for medicare premiums. But this goes against the Canada Health Act, which dictates that provincial governments must adopt national health care standards. However, most analysts expect the federal government will eliminate these transfers and be completely out of the business of funding health care soon.

Alberta currently has 27 community health centres, or units. These units have no acute care beds but offer a wide array of services. Unlike hospitals, which conduct about 90% of their services within the building, health units provide only about 25% to 30% of services on site. All health units have staff paid to look after patients within the home,

allowing hospitals to cut expensive beds. It costs less than $500 *a month* to care for a patient at home, compared to $350 to $400 *per day* in a hospital. Alberta still has 4.3 beds per 1,000 residents, 30% more than BC.

Most community centres are almost entirely staffed by nurses and physiotherapists who earn 1/3 to 1/6 of a doctor's pay. Over the past decade, the number of doctors in Alberta has increased by 40% while the population has grown by only 9.5%, and payments to doctors have almost doubled since 1982.

Tax Reform

But all the coming reforms will have less effect on the economy if the province retained its existing tax system, which is not competitive or attractive to investors. For this purpose, the Alberta Tax Reform Commission was appointed to determine what mix of taxes is most appropriate. Until it was undercut by Ontario in 1998, Alberta had the lowest provincial income tax rate. (See page 136.)

The Commission examined the long-term decline in Alberta's oil and gas revenues, which fell by 114% between 1985 and 1993. The Alberta Heritage Savings and Trust Fund currently totals over $12 billion.

Some critics insist that Klein never had the mandate to make the drastic cuts he made, since he only received 44% of the vote. Alberta's municipalities have banded together against the government's tax reform commission, while about 250 municipalities and school districts announced their united opposition to the elimination of the machinery and property tax.

The Alberta Association of Taxpayers predicts that the knee-jerk complaining from unions and municipalities will only reinforce popular support for spending cutbacks. "Most people are already tired of the whining."[141]

Balanced budgets are now the law, ensuring investor confidence and strong economic growth for the future.

Potpourri

Tribalism in the Global Community: The Demise of the Family Unit

The basic unit of human society is not the nuclear family. Our notion of the basic family unit arose from the economics of the Industrial Revolution and reached its zenith during the economic domination of modernism in the 20th century. The basic human unit is the tribal community, in which several extended families mix and mingle, sustain and support each other, and establish close relations with other nearby communities, setting up a far-reaching network of social and economic interdependence between and among tribes. For example, The League of the Iroquois provided local power to tribes and federal power to a joint council in which each tribe, regardless of size, had an equal voice.

Another example are the Mennonites and Amish, who take what little they need from modern society's offerings while turning their backs on the rest. The world, in turn, pays the occasional polite visit but usually leaves these gentle people in peace. As one member says, "Don't feel sorry about our way of life. It's a great way of life and it's satisfying. There's so much love in the families here." People, not states, make a nation.

The nuclear family is in decline, and it is not the consequence of something as simple as the breakdown of family values. As we move from Industrial Age to Information Age — from Nationalism to Globalism — the critical weaknesses of the family unit are exposed. In a world that embraces tolerance and pluralism, traditional peoples may be assured survival. In a global economy, we are all traditional peoples.

The 2000 Bug: A Recession Time Bomb

Business leaders in Canada and around the world could trigger a global recession unless they get to work on beating the Year 2000 computer bug.

At midnight on New Years' Eve, 1999, the 2-digit year code on many computer clocks will change from 99 to 00 — but many computers will assume 00 is the year 1900. This could cause massive computer failures unless the software programs are rewritten.

Regardless of what happens in Canada, the entire world must take the problem seriously or else everyone will be in trouble. The worldwide cost of the problem has been estimated at $840 billion.

Worst Practices — Pakistan: Swords or Schools?

Faced with the reality of a nuclear arms race with India, Pakistan's scarce resources are being diverted from the social to the military sector — a troubling thought for its 140 million residents, who add another 4 million to their ranks every year.

Together with India, the 2 countries spent $98 billion on defence from 1990 to 1996, while spending only $16.8 billion on education. About 80% of Pakistan's central spending now goes to debt service and defence, while **per capita spending on education, health and social services is a mere $7 per person per year.**

Meanwhile, 1 in 5 children do not enter 1st grade, and nearly 1/2 do not complete the primary level. In overgrown villages across the country, most women do not practice birth control, the majority of residents do not enjoy municipal water and are therefore subject to using groundwater contaminated with chrome from the local tanneries, a single doctor may serve as many as 30,000 people, and there may be no functioning government schools, working hospitals or paved roads.

South Asian Education Crisis

South Asia, which has more school dropouts, more illiterates and more unemployed graduates than any other region in the world, is on the brink of a great disaster as it enters the next millennium, thanks to its "education emergency." Although Sri Lanka, the Maldives and parts of southern India have achieved near universal literacy, the rest of the region (India, Pakistan, Bangladesh and Nepal) accounts for about 1/2 of the world's illiterates.

The situation is even worse for girls, who are less likely to attend school there than anywhere else in the world, or even if they do attend, they spend about 1/3 as much time in school as boys.

The 1998 Human Development in South Asia report calls for a regional freeze on military spending to finance enough new schools and teachers to reach the goal of universal primary education. More than 1/3 of teachers have no formal training, 40% seldom show up for work and most are paid less than domestic servants. In India, Pakistan and Bangladesh, the average teacher is paid less than $50 a month and is often recruited according to ethnicity, caste or political leaning.

In Pakistan, a recent government report found that state-run primary schools, on average, cost 80 times as much to build as those constructed by communities. Operating costs in community-run schools were also about 1/2 those in government-run schools.

The report calls for an urgent effort to hire and train 2.1 million teachers to reduce South Asia's pupil-teacher ratio from 60 to 1 — the highest in the world — to something more in line with sub-Saharan Africa (45 to 1) and East Asia (28 to 1).

The History of Trade

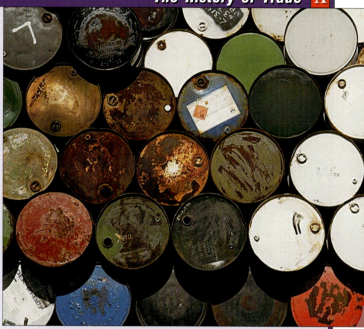

O ne of the most significant human commitments of the last half of this century has been to economic growth and trade expansion, and we have been spectacularly successful in accomplishing both," writes international development expert David Korten in his book, *When Corporations Rule the World*. Global economic output grew from \$3.8 trillion in 1950 to \$18.9 trillion in 1992, and total exports exploded from \$308 billion to \$3.6 trillion. Korten says this means "that, on average, we have added more to total global output in each of the past 4 decades than was added from the moment the 1st cave dweller carved out a stone axe up to the middle of the present century."

Mercantilism

Mercantilism was the economic system that began to emerge as the feudal system disintegrated. A scheme was needed that would accommodate the urgent need to:
- consolidate the power of central governments,
- control the rapidly increasing industrial and trade sectors, and
- accumulate wealth to finance the constant wars of the period.

Consolidation of power included the control of coinage (money), the formulation of national policies to regulate industry and trade, and the ability to plan and pay for inland transportation improvements. Mercantilism met these goals with its emphasis on the accumulation of precious metals for coinage and restrictive import limitations to foster local industrial development.

The regulation of the industrial and trade sectors was accomplished by imposing strict controls on the emigration of skilled workers and the exportation of technology. It also led to the establishment of quality control efforts, such as guild standardization and government inspection. (For more on the mercantile system, see page 229.)

The need to finance war came from the pervasive conviction that war was a normal and rational apparatus of national policy. Mercantilism, with its emphasis on colonization and the accumulation of precious metals, indulged this political dogma.

Mercantilism evolved into a complex system of both internal and external policies, but bullionism — the "gold standard" of the 19th and 20th century — was the fundamental rule. The goal of each nation was to increase its stock of precious metals by achieving a favourable balance of trade. It was seen as a zero-sum model in that no nation could gain anything, except by making others lose as much, or, in the extreme, by preventing them from gaining it. Whatever activity that tended to accumulate money or bullion in a country added to its wealth; whatever sent the precious metals out of a country impoverished it. If a country possessed no gold or silver mines, the only enterprise by which it could be enriched was foreign trade. The result was a complex series of tariffs and monetary restrictions.

This protectionist orientation produced a decrease in trade that resulted in the informal establishment of the 1st "modern" trade alliances — Spain and Portugal against the British-Dutch alliance. The British and Dutch forged a coalition capable of funding the naval power required to lower protection costs, leading eventually to the 100 years of the *Pax Britannica* — 1815-1914. (See page 184.)

In 1776, 3 events occurred that, taken together, ensured the end of colonization as a viable economic strategy:
- The publication of *On the Wealth of Nations* by the Scottish economist Adam Smith (incorporating much of the preceding thought of David Hume) engendered the theory of "*laissez-faire et laissez passer*" — literally, let happen what may, or non-interference.
- The American Revolution created an economy that was to prosper as a new entity, largely self-sufficient and with a strong belief in the principles of Adam Smith.
- The far-reaching introduction of James Watt's steam engine became the hub of the Industrial Revolution, and mercantilism proved incompatible with the industrial economy.

While mercantilism equated money with wealth and power, people began to realize that money, as money, satisfies no want, and that wealth is really — in the words of John Stuart Mill — all "useful or agreeable things which possess exchangeable value."

The degeneration of mercantilism was arrested by the French Revolution and the Napoleonic wars, but as soon as political and financial order were restored, Great Britain moved decisively away from mercantilism and swept the slate clean of industrial regulations, guild controls, bans on emigration, restrictions on machinery exports and protectionist tariffs. The other major European countries followed this example with eagerness as the 1st free trade era came into being around 1860.

This experiment was momentary, however, as the worldwide depression of the 1870's induced tariff wars and a rebirth of protectionist sentiments, resulting in increased international tension and stirred-up nationalism.

Trade in the 20th Century

WWI (The Great War)

WWI was, to a great extent, caused by trade complications. Of course, nationalism and factionalism, both of which were encouraged by protectionism, played dominant roles.

In particular, the land concessions and reparations of the Treaty of Versailles ensured both political and economic chaos would ensue. The eminent economist John Maynard Keynes published *The Economic Consequences of the Peace* in 1919, decrying "the absurdity of the reparations."

The Great Depression

The extreme American isolationist tariffs during the 1920's inflamed and prolonged the Great Depression, preventing the world trade that was necessary for the payment of both war debt and reparations. The hyper-inflation of Germany's Weimar Republic was a direct result of the failure of world trade, leading to the ascendancy of Hitler.

On the other side of the world, the Japanese had already adopted their answer to isolationism and depression by invading Manchuria in 1932. It was an unfortunate precedent, which soon followed in Europe.

World War II

The impact of World War II on world trade was both devastating and cleansing. By the end of the war, tremendous advances in transportation and an unprecedented surplus of merchant shipping set the stage for a new era in trade. Unfortunately, only a single developed economy remained intact — the US. Under the sponsorship of the only surviving economic goliath, preparations for the restoration of world trade were made before the end of combat.

Bretton Woods

In July of 1944, the rural New Hampshire resort of Bretton Woods was selected as the site for a series of meetings designed to lay out the economic blueprints for post-war recovery. Representatives of the US, UK, Russia, Canada and 40 other nations created an accord that led to the establishment of the International Monetary Fund, the World Bank, and the International Trade Organization (ITO), which later evolved into the General Agreements on Tariffs and Trade (GATT) — the most important legacy of these historical negotiations.

The ITO

The International Trade Organization (ITO), founded by the Havana Charter of 1948, was designed to ensure fairness in world trade, resolve disputes between members, and institute coverage for the emerging markets in services and intellectual property rights, as well as direct investment. The US sensed threats to its national sovereignty and believed that the ITO would have too much intervention power and refused to join. Without its membership, the ITO expired quietly.

The GATT

The Nature of GATT

The failure of the ITO left the GATT, originally intended only to be an interim secretariat for international trade negotiations, as the major international body promoting world trade for almost 50 years. GATT acted as a channel for multilateral negotiations on a variety of international trade practices, including tariff and quota policies.

GATT was never a conventional organization; it was merely an arrangement for discussions between members. Its strength stemmed from the concept of Most Favoured Nation (MFN) status, a policy that every member nation was entitled to the same trade conditions that applied to any other member's "most favoured" trading partner. This excluded the possibility that 1930's-type trading blocs would emerge to fractionalize world trade.

Three Major Defects:

• Membership was restricted to Western nations with the exception of Japan. Even though it *included* the great preponderance of the world's economic power, it *excluded* the majority of the world's population.
• A censured country could not be punished because effective enforcement power was not available.
• It failed to include provisions for evolving trade issues such as trade in services, intellectual property rights and trade-related investment.

Consequences of GATT

Despite the inherent defects of its structure, GATT was an amazingly productive pact. It resulted in a dramatic lowering of tariff barriers during the postwar period, and international trade flourished. The most constructive impact of GATT was on tariff reduction, which fell from about 40% during the 1930's to around 5% by 1980.

The WTO

The Genesis

The limitations of GATT had long been recognized when preparations began for the 1994 Uruguay Round of multilateral trade negotiations. These talks resulted in the signing of the *Marrakesh Protocol to the General Agreement on Tariffs and Trade 1994,* which systemized the entity known as the World Trade Organization (WTO). Members agreed that:
• Trade and business should take into consideration standards of living, full employment and growth of real income. Trade must also allow for the optimal use of the world's resources in accordance with sustainable development, while protecting and preserving the environment.
• Efforts should be made to ensure that developing countries share in the growth in international trade in proportion to the needs of their economic development. This included reducing tariffs and other barriers to trade and eliminating discriminatory treatment.

Members resolved to develop an integrated, more viable and durable multilateral trading system encompassing the GATT, past trade liberalization efforts, and the results of the Uruguay Round of negotiation. To preserve the basic principles and to further the objectives underlying this multilateral trading system, the WTO was established.

The hectic process of installing a new bureaucracy, finding a politically acceptable Director-General, and implementing "the 24,000 pages of agreements that are the framework of the WTO" began. It did not go smoothly. It took 4 months to seat the 1st Director-General, Reanto Ruggiero, primarily because of US fears that the Italian would exhibit a pro-European bias. In addition, despite claims that the WTO would not infringe on member nations' sovereignty, it took more than a year for members to "bring their laws into compliance with the membership requirements of the WTO," as dictated by Article XVI of the Agreement Establishing the World Trade Organization.

Structure and Procedures of the WTO

The WTO complex is located in Geneva and is governed by a twice-a-year, 1-country/1-vote conference of the member nations. It has a typical bureaucratic structure, comprised of operating bodies of representatives that meet as required to take action on disputes submitted by various sub-committees.

Dispute Resolution Procedures

The Dispute Resolution Body is the most marked difference between WTO and the old GATT. When a member nation feels that it has a cause for action against another member, it may request that a Dispute Settlement Panel be established. The panel is composed of 3 members appointed from a pool of "well qualified governmental and/or non-governmental individuals." Panels are required to complete their hearings and present their report within 6 months. In addition, panels must give preference to developing countries.

A standing Appellate Body — composed of "persons of recognized authority, with demonstrated expertise in law, international trade and the subject matter of the covered agreements generally" — hears appeals from panel cases.

The only sanction authorized by the WTO is for the aggrieved party to "request authorization to suspend concessions or other obligations under the covered agreements to the 'guilty' member."

Despite the lack of teeth in the enforcement sanctions, the dispute resolution process is very active.

WTO Strengths and Weaknesses

Strengths:

• The dispute resolution mechanism allows small and/or developing economies the opportunity to obtain a fair hearing without being subject to threats of linkage or reprisal. This makes the refusal of any major nation to abide by a WTO ruling politically unacceptable and **brings some degree of parity to international trade for the 1st time in history.**

• It encompasses intellectual property rights, which were not addressed under GATT. These are particularly relevant for an international agency because "intellectual property exists only as a creation of law; there are no intellectual property rights in countries where the law does not provide for them."

• It is vigilant in preserving its focus on trade to the exclusion of non-trade matters such as labour standards.

Weaknesses:

• Many members hold fears regarding the loss of national sovereignty.

• In an understandable effort to achieve fairness, it does not have a mechanism for weighting the influence of a member proportionally to the size of the member's economy.

• The relative unenforceability of its conflict resolution decisions merely allows an aggrieved member to institute retaliatory sanctions in a sector in which it may or may not have any leverage.

• Neither Russia nor China is a member. Russia has been unable to meet the requirements for membership while China is unwilling to comply.

• The development of such regional trading blocks as the NAFTA, the EU, APEC, MERCOSUR and The Confederation of Independent States (former USSR) reduces the role and influence of the WTO.

• Insistence on food self-sufficiency in developing members is both economically and environmentally unsound. The inappropriateness of this policy is illustrated by the fact that Indonesia is destroying its tropical rainforest in order to create arable land for the cultivation of rice and soybeans, while the US pays farmers to *NOT* grow these staples. This policy is a fundamental violation of the concept of "comparative advantage."

• There is insufficient liberalization of foreign direct investment. Neither the agreement on Trade-related Investment Measures, which applies to goods, nor the General Agreement on Trade in Services, which applies to services, "grant foreign investors 'national treatment' — the right to be treated as well as local firms." This issue is being addressed by the Multilateral Agreement on Investments. (See page 173.)

The WTO is the 1st truly worldwide trade organization. It has successfully succeeded the GATT accords and completely overshadows the ineffectual trade regulation attempts of the United Nations. Although highly politicized, the WTO is the closest thing to a democratic international organization that the world has ever seen.

If the WTO can avoid attempts to polarize it into a "developed nations" versus "developing nations" forum and the perception that it seeks to establish economic domination by undermining the sovereignty of its members, it has the potential to play a pivotal role in the advancement of the human condition.

The ultimate test of the viability of the WTO will be its ability to move from decisions made in "smoke-filled back rooms" to the new standard of transparency.

Key Events in Canada-US Trade Relations

The differences and aspirations of these very separate societies can be traced back to the American Revolution in 1776, when Canada allied with Britain on the losing side.

• During the War of 1812, Canada became the site for what was a dispute between Britain and the US. Canadian forces turned back attacks from Americans 5 times. US forces burned what is now Toronto and, in retaliation, the British burned Washington. These attacks cemented the attitude among Canadians that they *will not* be Americans.

• By 1817, relations between the countries were friendly enough that the Rush-Bagot Treaty was signed, declaring that the border should never again be armed. To this day, it remains the world's longest undefended border (9,000 km).

• The 1897 Yukon Gold Rush attracted 50,000 Americans to take part in the prospecting of Canada's north.

• Free Trade with the US 1st reared its head in 1911 when Prime Minister Laurier lost the national election because of his pro-trade platform. The opposition won on the promise of "No truck or trade with the Yankees."

• The US refused to join The League of Nations in 1918 because Canada was allowed to join on its own, independent from Britain.

• By the late 1930's, Canadian Prime Minister Mackenzie King was growing tired of British interference and wanted to take advantage of the power and growth south of the border. US President Franklin D. Roosevelt encouraged relations with Canada.

• In 1936, Roosevelt visited Quebec, becoming the 1st US President to visit Canada.

• Four years later, Roosevelt pledged to support Canada in the event of an attack. Mackenzie King, then signed an agreement that tied our defensive future to the US.

• Following the war, Mackenzie King grew wary of the US and abandoned Free Trade talks. *Time* magazine published an economics article calling Canada the 49th state, while King wrote in his diary that he was afraid of US absorption.

• By the 1950's, C.D. Howe, Canada's US-born "minister of everything" was Prime Minister Louis St. Laurent's right-hand man. The 40's and 50's saw huge foreign investment in Canada; by 1957, Americans controlled 70% of the capital of the petroleum and natural gas industry and 90% of the auto industry.

• During PM Diefenbaker's reign from 1957-1963, he challenged extensive US investment in Canada. His nemesis was President Kennedy, who visited Canada in the 1960's and became angry at Canada for trading with Cuba. Considerable conflict followed the Cuban Missile crisis.

• Liberal PM Pearson, styling himself as a friend of the Americans, was accused by Diefenbaker of being a US puppet while leading Canada from 1963-1968.

• Relations with the US chilled under PM Trudeau from 1968-1984. Questioning Canada's relations with the US, he went to Washington in 1971, and complained about US tariffs on Canadian exports. In 1972, President Nixon returned the visit and faced anti-US demonstrations. Trudeau later announced that Canada must diversify with other countries to avoid excessive influence by the US. He established Petrocan and the National Energy Board because, by 1972, the energy industry was 99% foreign owned. The Board lasted only 4 years due to an undermining American influence.

• Under Conservative PM Mulroney, from 1984-1993, the tide turned again with a return to pro-American policies.

• In 1987, the Free Trade Agreement (FTA) between Canada and the US was signed and implemented on January 1, 1989.

• In December of 1992, the North American Free Trade Agreement (NAFTA), which included Mexico, was signed.

The Importance of Free Trade

Although Canada is the 8th largest trading nation in the world, the US alone accounts for 80% of our total exports (roughly half of our GDP) and 70% of our imports. On the other hand, while we are the largest buyer of US exports, we do not take a dominant share of them, nor is the US economy nearly as export-dependent as ours.

Since the 1965 auto pact, Canada has become more intimately interconnected with the US than ever. Free trade has created an integrated market — with Ontario a more important player in the US economy than any single state except California. Clearly, Canada needs free trade more than the US needs us. As pollster Angus Reid recounts in *Shakedown*, "Lester Thurow, one of America's top economists, is even more direct on this subject. Speaking to the Municipal Finance Officers Association in Muskoka in 1995, Thurow said bluntly: 'You Canadians are pygmies. If all of Canada were an American state, it would rank 5th or 6th in GDP terms. Yet you think trade decisions will be made in Ottawa. They'll be made in Washington.'"

This kind of arrogance — whether true or not — plays into the hands of protectionists such as Heritage Minister Sheila Copps. She could not help the Canadian magazine industry, however, when the WTO ruled that excise tax and postal subsidies were unfair trade barriers. on imported US split-run magazines. These editions, filled mainly with US content, compete for Canadian advertising dollars.

In his book *1967: The Last Good Year*, Pierre Berton expresses how Canadians have wrestled over free trade for more than 130 years: "This longtime Canadian dilemma goes back beyond the Reciprocity election of 1911 to the Canada 1st movement that followed Confederation... How cozy should we get with the Americans? How much of the country's resources can we afford to peddle to foreigners? How can we accept Yankee dollars and Yankee institutions and still retain a measure of independence? These composed the great Canadian quandary the politicians talked about, the journalists wrote about, and the people argued about in 1967. Thirty years later, they still do."

> *The boundary separating your nation from mine is no more meaningful than the equator — a line on maps, devoid of meaning.*
> —Jacques Maisonrouge
> US head of IBM World Corp.

Free Trade Is Not Free of Costs

Canadians have to learn that they cannot have it both ways. Sure, the gains from trade for Canadians in general are paid for in part by individuals who have lost their jobs. But the most insecure jobs are those that exist because of trade barriers.

The C.D. Howe Institute's Daniel Schwanen isolated the influence of the FTA from larger economic trends — such as globalization, technological change, currency movements and the business cycle — to explain the dramatic growth in Canada-US trade between 1988 and 1997. Despite the fact that currency movements made Canadian goods cheaper for other foreigners than for Americans, it was Canada-US trade that grew fastest.

The US, with an added 18% price advantage from the Canadian dollar's fall, doubled its imports from Canada. But Europe, where the extra currency advantage was 35%, increased its Canadian purchases by only 37%. Furthermore, growth was greatest in those sectors liberalized by the FTA. The volume of Canada's exports to the US increased 133% in the newly liberalized goods, but only 48% in the rest.

Canada is also better off because there are fewer trade disputes, and they involve products like wheat and salmon, which in trade terms are worth only tens of millions of dollars a year, compared with 2-way trade flows of more than $1 billion a day.

And those who worried that investors would disappear discovered that, while other foreign countries' foreign direct investment (FDI) in Canada remained at historical levels, US FDI has boomed in Canada since 1988.

Between 1965 and 1990, when the total volume of world trade doubled, trade between Canada and the US more than tripled. Reid writes that, "As impressive as these gains were, they do not come close to matching the increases recorded since 1990." Cross-border trade today is worth $400 billion annually.

It seems that, despite the initial backlash to the FTA, most people realize it makes an important contribution to Canada's continued prosperity. The downside is that even though the US may be the biggest market in the world, relying so much on the success of their economy is dangerous, somewhat like having a business were most sales are to a single customer.

The success of the FTA for Canada, and the need to find additional trading partners prompted the government to sign more free trade treaties. Since signing NAFTA — which included Mexico — in 1992, Canadian exports increased 34% in the first 3 years.

Robust World Trade

World exports grew by 9.5% in 1997, up from 5% in 1996. It was the 2nd best performance since the rate hit 11.8% in the boom year of 1976. The US and Canada, meanwhile, grew by 10.5% in 1997, against 6% in 1996, while imports grew by 12.5%.[142]

An Economic Car Bomb

There are far too many factories producing vehicles around the world. Industry experts say that worldwide capacity is 70 million vehicles — 32% more than consumers are now buying — and will reach 79 million by 2002. This will create an excess capacity of 18.5 million — equal to the number of vehicles produced by General Motors, Ford and Toyota in 1997.[143]

By the year 2002, global overcapacity will create an estimated 88 surplus plants.

Every nation insists on tariffs and other trade barriers to protect a home-grown auto industry. The higher the protective barriers, the more companies are forced to build uneconomic ventures. The global push to put an auto plant in every political backwater, though, is costing consumers billions in bloated wage, investment and operating costs.

Meanwhile, auto makers worry that the global surplus in cars will undercut prices — good for consumers but bad for manufacturers and dangerous for economies that are overly dependent on that sector.

In Canada, for example, more than 1/3 of our exports — about 1/4 of our GDP — is in the automotive sector, which has been under Free Trade agreements since the 1965 Canada-US auto pact. Under the original agreement, General Motors, Chrysler and Ford can import vehicles duty free. Other manufacturers, except Volvo, must pay the import tariff, giving the Big 3 a competitive advantage, but penalizing consumers with what is seen as a blatantly hidden and unfair tax.

The 6.7% Canadian tariff on vehicles imported from outside North America cost consumers $460 million in 1997 and could cost another $1.2 billion over the next 3 years.[144] This affects the 68% of vehicles sold in Canada that are imports.

The auto industry kept Ontario from sliding deep into a recession during the early 1990's and is now an $80 billion-a-year business — about the size of Ireland's GDP. One in 6 jobs in southern Ontario now relies directly or indirectly on the auto sector. Aurora-based auto parts giant Magna International Inc., for example, now has 47 plants in the area and employs almost 13,000 people.

Of the vehicles made here, 88% are exported, most to the US. These plants are now among the most efficient in North America because of high-tech improvements in productivity and good management. Despite fears of plant closings, Honda and Toyota plan to expand.

When the auto industry does well, everyone does well, including the government.

Protectionism vs. Free Trade

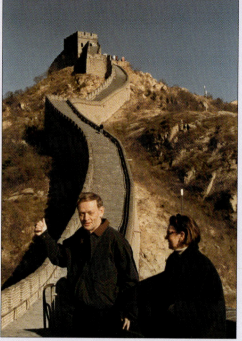

"Trade has long been the lifeblood of empire," wrote the *International Herald Tribune*. "Flourishing commerce helped underpin the Pax Romana and the supremacy of Victorian Britain. American dominance in the late 20th century rests as much on leadership of the open world trading system as on military power." The *Tribune* argued that US trade leadership over the past 50 years brought unprecedented prosperity to Americans and to millions of others around the globe, helped win the Cold War and made the US the world's largest and arguably the most competitive trading nation.

So why are people still fighting against free trade and pushing for protectionism? It is true that trade liberalization hurts some industries and some people (mainly the unskilled), but as the moderate US social policy group, The Democratic Leadership Council, said, "It is simply unfair to elevate the interests of industries or groups threatened by international competition above the interests of workers in exporting industries; of consumers; of communities that benefit from foreign investment; and of [everyone] who benefits from steady growth, low unemployment and low inflation."

Not since the Roman Empire have trade and travel been so unfettered. EC'92, NAFTA, GATT and the WTO are models for other areas seeking borderless trade, such as APEC in the Pacific Rim and MERCOSUR in South America. The FTA and the NAFTA have been so good to Canada (see page 168) that the government is busy pursuing further trade liberalization. In 1997, Canada and Chile signed a full free trade agreement, modelled on NAFTA, and Canada is currently negotiating a trade and investment cooperation agreement with the MERCOSUR trading bloc — made up of Brazil, Argentina, Paraguay and Uruguay.

Unfortunately, signing and implementation of a sweeping Free Trade Area of the Americas (FTAA) deal may be delayed because the US could not get fast-track authorization for the April, 1999, Summit of the Americas, when 34 North and South American leaders are due to kick off the hemispheric free trade talks in Santiago, Chile.

US President Bill Clinton has lost the fight with Congress for "fast track" authority — a procedural issue that would have allowed his administration to enter new trade deals and then put those agreements to a "yes" or "no" vote in Congress. Without this authority, Congress can amend trade deals at any stage of negotiations. And a coalition of left-wing Democrats, right-wing Republicans, isolationists, labour unions and other special interests oppose fast track, mainly for fear that further trade liberalization will undercut American jobs and wages.

Some corporate leaders in the US, who were once the most enthusiastic advocates of free trade, are now complaining that the global economy is producing more cars, computers, clothes and other consumer goods than people are willing to buy.

If the US loses the political momentum for free trade that all post-war presidents have been able to call on, the *Tribune* says they "will have carelessly hastened the day when the Pax Americana goes the way of its illustrious Roman predecessor."

One of the most awesome permanent fortifications ever built is the Great Wall of China — about 4,000 kilometres long.

Worst Practices
Churchill Politics

We have seen protectionism at its finest in Churchill, Manitoba. The 68-year-old port on Hudson Bay — 2,000 km north of Winnipeg by rail — had been a chronic money loser since the 1970's, until it was bought recently from the federal government by Denver-based short-line operator OmniTrax. The privately held firm, which also bought a 850-km rail link to the south from Canadian National, upgraded the port facilities with financial help from the federal government, to increase the volume and types of commodities the port can handle. Churchill shipped a record 750,000 tons in 1976, before slumping to 50,000 in the 1988 season.

In its 85-day season in 1997, the port shipped 401,000 tons of wheat, barley and oats to Brazil, Turkey, Mexico, Nigeria, and Ethiopia. (For more about the politics of the Manitoba economy, see page 179.)

Early in this century, Woodrow Wilson proclaimed himself a **"citizen of the world."** *Unfortunately, the years that followed produced violent divisions of nationality and ideology. But a new century brings with it the rebirth of Wilson's vision. Global citizenship may well be within our grasp.*[145]

How Vietnam Lost the War

Although the Vietnamese won the war, they have lost the peace to their old enemy — the US.[146] Market capitalism, foisted upon the Vietnamese by the World Bank and IMF and willingly accepted by its own Communist politburo, has negated all the heroic efforts of the Vietnamese to liberate themselves from the French and American imperialists. Capitalism has shattered the primarily agrarian economy, made "wage slaves" of the urban workers, concentrated power and wealth in the hands of a mostly corrupt and selfish bureaucracy and Chinese entrepreneurs, alienated the masses, and set the country on a course toward chaos.

The decay of the Communist regime in Vietnam is part of a pattern of disappearance of communism worldwide one of the great vanishing acts of history. Genuine socialism — state control of the means of production and distribution — has not succeeded for long anywhere in the world.

Nations have to evolve, within the limits of their own cultural patterns, in order to succeed in creating a fair distribution of wealth — or risk social disintegration. To gain the benefits of the victory that the Vietnamese won from the French and Americans, they now have to find a means to depose the corrupt, self-serving Communist regime, and create an accountable government.

Worst Practices

Sweden's Economic Implosion

Sweden is a "worst practices" example of an extravagant case of giving too many benefits. No nation in the world has more epitomized the concept of cradle-to-the-grave socialism in the decades after World War II.

By the 1990's, the country had become a land of oppressive taxes (63% of GDP, compared with about 50% for Canada and 31% for the US) and the consequent economic calamity. Swedish living standards, once the highest in Europe, had fallen behind those of France and Italy. In the 1990's, Sweden's public debt doubled, unemployment tripled, and the budget deficit increased 10-fold to 10% of GDP in 1994 — worst among all of the industrialized nations.

The government elected in 1994, facing this 5-alarm fiscal emergency, began cutting programs with abandon, including welfare, pensions, health insurance, unemployment, family assistance, and child allowances. Result: the budget deficit fell to 3.5% of GDP in 1997. Additional cuts of 4% of GDP were scheduled over the next 3 years.

Worst Practices

Korea Wears Out a Good Idea

Although South Koreans dislike the Japanese and many still resent Japan's colonial occupation (which lasted from 1905 to 1945), no other country has imitated Japan as closely.

When South Korea began to industrialize in the 1960's, it followed the Japanese method: choose a few key industries to be your economic champions, lavish cheap loans and other subsidies on them, encourage them to sell aggressively overseas, and protect them from foreign competition. General Park Chung-hee, South Korea's president from 1961 to 1979, even built an economic situation room next to his office to monitor the country's progress.

South Korea leaped into the ranks of developed nations faster than any other country, tripling the size of its economy every 10 years after 1960 and raising the average income of its citizens from $100 to $10,000 a year.

Unlike many Japanese and most North American multinationals, however, the South Korean conglomerates — known as chaebols — were into everything, rather than focusing on 1 or 2 chosen fields. Daewoo, for example, made cars in Korea, TV sets in Uzbekistan, home appliances in Russia, and plywood in Burma. The chaebols also borrowed heavily for their growth sprees, accumulating debt-to-equity ratios of 4 to 1 or 5 to 1, compared with less than 2 to 1 in the US.

Japan hit a wall in 1990 when the stock market crashed, property values plummeted; the economy, once the envy of the world, has been stagnant ever since. Without heeding the warning, the Korean chaebols continued to expand. As recently as 1995, Samsung announced plans to quadruple its sales to $200 billion by 2001. Instead of preparing for bad times by concentrating on what they did best, Samsung and other chaebols continued to diversify.

With growth as the national religion and the Japanese model its bible, South Korea was headed for a national disaster. It now finds itself an international beggar, crawling to the IMF for billions in aid.

Meanwhile, the Japanese government's slow reaction has meant that its 8-year-long economic crisis continues to get even worse. Its banks are buried in bad loans, its currency is under pressure, and its stock market is faltering.[147]

Restrictions on Foreign Investments

Canadian pension fund investors who curse the 20% foreign investment limit will be interested in the conclusions of an OECD study, which explores the economics of foreign investment regulation for pension funds.

The study organized the data from 23 developing and developed countries between 1986 and 1993, to determine the validity of the argument that foreign restriction policies stimulate growth of domestic capital markets. Surprisingly, it found there was "a weak negative correlation" between a country's total pension fund assets and the growth rate of its stock markets.

Even if there is some evidence to support keeping pension assets domestic, "The home bias generally observed in pension fund investment should translate into sufficient potential demand for domestic financial assets so as to deepen markets and develop the institutional infrastructure," the study concludes.[148]

Exports Top Internal Trade

Canada's internal trade has expanded far more slowly in the 1990's than its exports abroad, according to a StatsCan study entitled *Interprovincial Trade in Canada; 1984-1996*. While our exports grew at an average annual rate of almost 11% between 1990 and 1996 — increasing from $161 billion to $293 billion, interprovincial trade grew at a mere 2.8%, "inching ahead" to $160 billion from $141 billion. Between 1984 and 1990, both forms of trade grew 3.5% a year.

Ontario was the only province to record a surplus in each of the 13 years covered by the study. Nova Scotia was the only province to record "persistent and sizable" trade deficits both with other provinces and the rest of the world.

Exports were powered by a strong US economy, a falling Canadian dollar, free trade agreements with the US and Mexico, and a lowering of trade barriers worldwide.[149]

AIT:
Battling Inter-Provincial Trade Barriers

The Agreement on Internal Trade (AIT) was signed in 1994, promising to end non-tariff barriers to trade between provinces in everything from government procurement to sales of local beer. Coming on the heels of NAFTA, it seemed a rational next step. What was the logic of free trade between Canada and Mexico if there was none between Alberta and BC?

But the AIT is just a toothless set of doctrines. Since 1994, for the most part, the provinces have discriminated against one another in purchasing decisions and in bidding against one another for investment, all in the name of jobs for the local economy.

This nonsense costs us twice — both as consumers and as taxpayers. These trade barriers cost us at least $7 billion annually. It is estimated that inter-provincial trade barriers cost the average family of 4 a total of $1,000 annually on goods and services.

The real roadblocks to an enforceable deal have been highest on both coasts — in BC, which thinks it does not get its fair portion of federal business, and in the Atlantic provinces (principally Newfoundland and New Brunswick), which have aggressively wooed businesses in competition with other provinces.

While first ministers have made the time to address the unity issue, their resolution to remove inter-provincial trade barriers is proven to be nothing but political rhetoric.

In the end, Ottawa and all the provinces except BC agreed in February 1998 to end interprovincial trade barriers — including a key chapter on the MUSH sector.

Business groups, notably the Canadian Chamber of Commerce, pressured the provinces to drop the requirement that they must have unanimous consent before concluding further deals under the AIT, but were not impressed by the conclusion of the agreement. The Chamber said that all governments involved deserved a failing grade for missing deadlines and lacking the political will to get the job done.

Where Do *Barbie Dolls* Come From? [150]

The phenomenon of globalization is perfectly illustrated by the results of a recent analysis by the *Los Angeles Times* of the contents of a doll marked "Made in China" and selling for $9.99 in the US. The doll was found to contain only 35¢ of Chinese value added. In reality, more than $8.00 of the selling price remained in the United States in the form of paint (shipped to China where the doll is assembled), shipping, transportation, and wholesale and retail trade.

Thus, a country that stays out of the loop (for example, by forbidding the entry of "foreign" products, services, investors, or technology) exposes itself to tremendous costs for its domestic firms and workers. There are no entirely "foreign" goods anymore — an observation that applies increasingly to services and investments as well.

Multilateral Agreement on Investment (MAI)

The MAI is the Charter of Rights and Freedoms for corporations.

The much-delayed MAI was designed to be a pact that would require governments to treat foreign corporations in the same way as domestic ones. For Canada, it would largely resemble investment provisions already agreed to in NAFTA.

Critics call it "NAFTA on steroids" because they say it takes the worst provisions of that agreement, magnifies them and applies them to a whole new host of countries. Defenders, however, say the MAI would bring order to a chaotic investment world — a world which currently has more than 1,300 bilateral investment agreements, with no symmetry or standards.

The MAI is supported by those in favour of the free exchange across all borders of goods, services — and money. To economic nationalists, environmental groups and unions, however, it means a diminishing of sovereignty.

Under the MAI, foreign corporations would be allowed to actually *sue* countries before an international tribunal if they believe the country's demands present unfair trade practices. These tribunals would determine compensatory monetary damages or any other form of relief on the basis of the terms of the treaty itself rather than on the national laws of the country in question.

The Treaty talks come at a time when foreign investment in Canada has nearly doubled since 1986, and flows of foreign direct investment (FDI) have grown nearly 3 times faster than the trade in goods and services since 1980. Ottawa estimates that each $1 billion in foreign investment in new plants results in 45,000 jobs. One Canadian job in 10 is derived from FDI.

According to an editorial in *The Globe and Mail*, "the fact that Canada, a high-cost, high-tax jurisdiction, is a net recipient of FDI helps to put the lie to the notion that this money flows only to low-wage jurisdictions and contributes to a 'hollowing-out' of our economy."

To its supporters, the MAI would protect Canadian investment abroad — including investments through mutual funds, RRSPs or pension funds. *The Globe and Mail* also argues that trade benefits everyone because it "is a positive-sum game: benefits for one side are not won at the expense of the other."

MAI's scope would be limited by exceptions, however. Countries are allowed to refuse to apply the deal to specific sectors, although critics argue that the wording is problematic because it will limit the ability of the government to take actions to protect a number of key governmental functions.

Culture

One "hot-button" sector Canadians fear losing control over is culture. Under proposed MAI rules, government subsidies to promote Canadian culture, Canadian content rules for radio and television, and restrictions on foreign ownership of broadcasting would no longer be permitted.

Labour And Environmental Standards

Another concern is the policing of environmental and labour standards. Business lobbies and trade experts say this falls under the jurisdiction of the UN and its ILO, rather than in trade and investment deals. But attempts to include labour code and environmental standards into MAI are gaining attention, including a clause that requires foreign investors to adhere to the yet-to-be-defined "core labour standards." Business is afraid that Canada and the other countries will sign the MAI before labour rules are clearly spelled out.

Others fear that foreign corporations will use the treaty to deliver services such as welfare, health and education. MAI dictates that when a crown corporation, public utility or other government enterprise is privatized, it must be offered to tender to all the private-sector investors of all the member countries.

Nationalism Sinks the 1998 Talks

Other critics call the MAI nothing more than a "charter of rights for absentee landlords," charging that foreign investors and multinational corporations set up shop in countries where they have no roots or loyalty.

Ultimately, these disagreements and a huge pile of requests from 29 countries seem set to bury the Treaty. Canada alone has 52 pages of reservations dealing with agriculture, cars, energy, financial services, transportation, aboriginals and social services. And Canada has insisted on leaving culture out of the deal, either for Canada or for all of the OECD countries.

Europe is arguing over its attempt to have itself designated a Regional Economic Organization — which would allow European nations to discriminate against foreign investment on the grounds that it is 1st liberalizing rules from within. And the Americans are still arguing over investment in Cuba.

After 3 years of talks, negotiators have missed another deadline and have not set a new one. There is also a move, led in part by Canadian Trade Minister Sergio Marchi, to move the talks from the mostly rich, industrialized countries of the OECD to the more diverse WTO. Such a move could kill the deal altogether, since there is no start date yet for the next round of WTO talks — and the last round took 7 years to complete. Besides, more than 80% of worldwide FDI originates from OECD countries, and any agreement should meet OECD standards.

Many are starting to believe that it might be better to drop out of the negotiations now, because so little is left of the original liberalizing of investment rules. The MAI will eventually pass, but 1998 was just was not right time.

Globalphobia:

On the political left, labour, human rights and environmental organizations oppose trade deals with lesser developed countries.

On the right, status-quo protectionists and short-sighted neo-Luddities increasingly clamour to slow the pace of change.

Corruption: An Extreme Inhibitor of Economic Growth

Conviction is growing that corruption is damaging to global business development. The Berlin-based NGO Transparency International (TI) publishes a Corruption Perception Index (CPI) to demonstrate this concern. The OECD has adopted explicit recommendations on anti-corruption actions as a result.

The agreement includes action to end tax deductibility for foreign bribes and to criminalize bribing of foreign officials. All 29 members of the OECD are working towards enforcing a law making it a criminal offence for a corporation to pay bribes in a foreign country and to begin immediately to abolish tax deductibility.

TI was founded in 1993 to curb corruption by supporting global integrity systems; it now has more than 60 Chapters worldwide. The index it publishes is based on surveys undertaken by a variety of prominent organizations.[151] The rank relates solely to the results drawn from a number of surveys — a perfect 10.00 would be a totally corruption-free country.

The ranking is designed so that countries that are perceived to be the least corrupt are given the highest scores. Denmark, Finland and Sweden emerged in top place, while, for the 2nd year running, Nigeria finished last.

As a summary of polls, the index provides insights into perceptions, which have an impact on how private companies operate in the rest of the world. By drawing on a Gallup poll, for the 1st time, the CPI also included a viewpoint from *within* countries, making the index less biased against developing countries than when it was compiled only from perceptions of foreigners.

Only 52 countries qualify for inclusion on the list because a minimum of 4 surveys is required. Given that there are almost 200 sovereign states, it is certain that other countries may be more corrupt, but there is not sufficient information to rank them all.

The CPI has had a salutary impact on national politics in many countries and is shaping public opinion. It is a measure of lost development opportunities, inasmuch as a recent study has shown that a rise in corruption levels from that of Singapore to that of Mexico is equivalent to raising the marginal tax rate by more than 20%. A point increase in the marginal tax rate reduces foreign direct investment by about 5%.

Corruption Perception Index [151]			
Rank	Country	1997 Score	1996 Score
1	Denmark	9.94	9.33
2	Finland	9.48	9.05
3	Sweden	9.35	9.08
4	NZ	9.23	9.43
5	Canada	9.10	8.96
6	Netherlands	9.03	8.71
7	Norway	8.92	8.87
8	Australia	8.86	8.60
9	Singapore	8.66	8.80
11	Switzerland	8.61	8.76
12	Ireland	8.28	8.45
13	Germany	8.23	8.27
14	UK	8.22	8.44
15	Israel	7.97	7.71
16	US	7.61	7.66
18	Hong Kong	7.28	7.01
20	France	6.66	6.96
21	Japan	6.57	7.05
23	Chile	6.05	6.80
24	Spain	5.90	4.31
26	Belgium	5.25	6.84
30	Italy	5.03	3.42
31	Taiwan	5.02	4.98
32	Malaysia	5.01	5.32
34	South Korea	4.29	5.02
36	Brazil	3.56	2.96
39	Thailand	3.06	3.33
40	Philippines	3.05	2.69
41	China	2.88	2.43
42	Argentina	2.81	3.41
44	Venezuela	2.77	2.50
45	India	2.75	2.63
46	Indonesia	2.72	2.65
47	Mexico	2.66	3.30
48	Pakistan	2.53	1.00
49	Russia	2.27	2.58
50	Colombia	2.23	2.73
51	Bolivia	2.05	3.40
52	Nigeria	1.76	0.69

The impact of the index was perhaps greatest in Pakistan, where many people believe that the index contributed to the downfall of Benazir Bhutto's administration.

In Malaysia, the Prime Minister labeled the index another example of Western "cultural imperialism." However, a delegation of the Malaysian Anti-Corruption Agency was sent to learn the mechanics and methodology of the index. The government then started an anti-corruption campaign — pointing to the index as the reason why all Malaysians needed to counter corruption.

In Argentina, the public debate led to a dispute between the government and TI. The Minister of the Interior said the index, "conveys a lie, is unjust and absurd." Later, members of government met with TI Argentina to express the conviction of the government: a dedication to fight corruption.

OECD Bribery Deal

The OECD has put together a deal to be implemented by the end of 1998 to criminalize bribery. It is hoped that doing so will reduce the damage it does in the Third World, such as in African countries where governments conduct business with the company willing to pay the highest bribe.

The Convention on Combating Bribery of Officials in International Business Transactions makes it an offence "to bribe to obtain or retain business or other improper advantage." The convention lays out the general outline, but leaves the details up to the members, who will monitor one another.

Currently, many companies decide what is right and what is wrong by "the front-page test" — asking executives if they would be comfortable reading about their actions if they were featured in the newspaper the next day.

Globalization and International Trade Agreements

Don't protect it, promote it!

As was mentioned earlier in this chapter in the History of Trade (see page 165.), the General Agreement on Tariffs and Trade (GATT) was drawn up by 23 countries in 1948. The Agreement was originally part of a draft charter for the failed International Trade Organization (ITO).

The "Havana Charter" of the ITO contained not only the GATT, which governed trade, but also wide-ranging rules relating to employment, commodity agreements, restrictive business practices, international investment, and services. GATT itself, a large list of negotiated trade concessions and rules of conduct, entered into force in January, 1948 (as GATT 1947). The rest of the Havana Charter was never ratified, primarily because of opposition in the US Congress.

For the following 50 years, the ever-expanding group of Contracting Parties to the GATT (128 when the World Trade Organization was created) treated it as if it were in fact a permanent commitment, rather than the provisional agreement it really was. The tiny secretariat associated with the Havana Charter continued to act as secretariat to the GATT. Eight "rounds" of negotiation, counting the original, reduced tariffs and struggled to produce rules to govern international trade.

Most of the rounds dealt with tariff reduction only, but as tariffs came down, non-tariff barriers went up. The Kennedy round (1964-1967) came to agreement on anti-dumping. The Tokyo Round went further, dealing with subsidies and countervailing measures, technical barriers to trade, import licensing procedures, government procurement and other non-tariff areas of concern. These agreements, however, were signed by only a few of GATT's Contracting Parties (mainly OECD members).

The most recent round, the Uruguay Round, was the most comprehensive of any, lasting over 7 years and creating a legal institution — the World Trade Organization (WTO) to replace the provisional GATT. As a body of law, the WTO embodies the GATT 1994 (as well as several other non-goods-related Agreements) and has a single dispute settlement mechanism to cover all the various Agreements. Unlike the case with the GATT, all WTO Members automatically committed to all of the Agreements, with only a few minor exceptions.

The WTO joined the FTA and the NAFTA in breaking new ground for Canadian trade in areas such as protection of investment, the movement of business and technical personnel, access to government procurement, and trade in some services. Some have interpreted Canada's vigorous pursuit of these new issues as a departure from traditional policy, which had concentrated on negotiations on commercial barriers such as tariffs and quotas.

But the expanded scope of trade policy can be seen as the dynamic response of Canada and other countries to the phenomenon of globalization. It is based on the view that a wider range of formal economic relations among trading partners is required, in case any country should see its desirability as an investment location diminish and its standards of living jeopardized.

Globalization was not, for the most part, created by governments. Rather, it can best be described as the result of a large number of actors in the private sector tapping new opportunities stemming from technological changes that reduced the costs and increased the potential reach of transportation, telecommunications and financial transactions. In turn, these have permitted the emergence of a new international division of tasks and new investment opportunities through networks of suppliers, customers, ideas, and investors that transcend national boundaries.

Nevertheless, responsibility for the perceived negative effects of globalization is often laid at the door of governments that have actively promoted their respective country's participation in this loop through domestic regulatory reforms and international trade agreements. In particular, some people see globalization as meaning a loss of independence by their national governments vis-à-vis both other governments and the private engine of globalization — the multinational enterprise (MNE). Globalization's institutional incarnation, free trade, is often seen as the ultimate example of governments letting outside actors dictate economic and even social outcomes.

Free trade agreements such as the FTA, NAFTA, and WTO forbid countries from discriminating against the goods, services, or businesses of their trading partners; in exchange, they receive the same treatment from other member countries. Such agreements also establish some minimum reciprocal standards of market access by, and treatment of, foreign nationals (for example, zero tariffs, and no expropriation without compensation).

Chilean Trade

In July 1997, the Chilean senate gave final approval to an historic free-trade agreement between Chile and Canada. The agreement immediately swept away tariffs on about 80% of trade between Canada and Chile and will phase out the rest over the next 18 years. Chilean officials say that the treaty will increase bilateral trade, which is currently about $670 million, 5-fold over the next decade. The agreement is expected to create jobs in both countries and provide duty-free access for 75% of Canadian exports. It will also eliminate an 11% Chilean import duty on industrial and resource-based goods over the next 5 years.

EU Trade

The European Union reached deals with Canada and the US on safety standards covering $45 billion (US) a year in trade. Products tested and approved for sale in Europe will automatically be considered ready for sale in Canada and the US. The agreement paves the way for harmonization of North American and EU standards.

The Noticeable Export Gains of "Invisibles"

Some exports, we cannot see. With good reason, statisticians sometimes call them "invisibles," because they consist of a wide range of things that cannot be seen but are very real commercially, such as business services and rights for which fees and royalties are paid. Canada's exports of these items have been soaring in recent years. You might be surprised to discover just what kinds of things we are getting good at selling to foreigners.

Since 1990, Canadian exports of architectural and engineering services have increased almost 5-fold, royalties and licence fees paid to Canadians by foreigners have almost tripled, and exports of computer services have more than doubled.

Compared with the almost $400 billion in goods we will export in 1998, our $20 billion in exports of all commercial services looks rather puny, even if it is twice what we earned in 1990. And while we ran a $41 billion surplus in goods in 1997, we had a $4 billion deficit in business services.

Our top export is insurance, almost $4 billion worth of it in 1997. It has grown rapidly from $2 billion in 1990, but not fast enough to keep up with imports of insurance, which hit over $5 billion in 1997. Clearly, insurance is increasingly becoming a hot trade item as Canadian companies exploit their specialties abroad and foreign insurers try to win Canadian customers.

The next-biggest category of exports is communications services — everything from couriers to the most sophisticated forms of telecommunications, like teleconferencing and electronic data exchange. This category was worth about $2 billion in exports in 1997 and is one in which we usually run a surplus.

Third on the list is research and development, which counts everything done by Canadian scientists and other researchers who worked for foreign clients. It was worth $1.7 billion in 1996, up from $700 million in 1990. Canadian companies are much less inclined to buy their R&D from abroad. We have run surpluses in this category since 1985.

The 4th ranked export item is something StatsCan calls architectural and engineering services, which brought in revenues of almost $2 billion in 1997, a huge leap from $330 million in 1990. This is an area where Canadians are clear world-beaters. We consistently run surpluses in this category, sums that amounted to more than $1.1 billion in 1996 and 1997.

Computer services are another hot growth area. This covers the design, engineering and management of computer systems and includes the production of original software. This area brought in more than $1.2 billion in 1997, compared with $500 million in 1990. Again, we sell more than we buy from other countries. In 1997, the surplus in computer services amounted to $300 million.

Canada's Economic Ranking

Canada dropped to 14th spot from 9th in an international ranking of economic freedom released by the Vancouver-based Fraser Institute and 46 other like-minded research organizations in other countries. (See page 240.)

The report said Canada won high marks for its low inflation, low tariffs and sizable trade sector. But it said high levels of government spending, "are looking more and more like those of the European welfare states and less like the US."

Asia-Pacific Economic Cooperation (APEC)₁₅₂

Formed in 1989 with 12 members, APEC imposed a 3-year moratorium on new members after admitting Chile as the 18th in 1994. Referred to as "economies" rather than countries – in order to allow Taiwan and Hong Kong to participate without drawing opposition from China – APEC's members had a combined annual income of more than $15 trillion, accounting for approximately 55% of the world's total income and 45% of international merchandise trade in 1995. APEC's developing members saw their average annual per capita GDP rate grow at 7% over the past decade – double any other region in the world. All of APEC's members agreed in 1994 to commit themselves to free and open trade and investment by 2010 for developed members and 2020 for developing members. Future members could include Colombia, Ecuador, India, Macau, Mongolia, Pakistan, Panama, Peru, Russia, Sri Lanka and Vietnam.

1995

Country	Population (millions)	Population growth (%)	Life Expectancy (M-F years)	GDP $ (billions)	GDP $ per capita	Imports $ (billions)	Exports $ (billions)
Australia	18	1.2	75-81	473	26,208	86	74
Brunei	0.3	2.8	73-76	7	23,855	3	3
Canada	30	1.1	74-81	804	27,132	236	269
Chile	14	1.6	69-76	83	5,824	22	22
China	1,200	1.5	68-72	1,043	868	185	208
Hong Kong	6	2.1	75-81	199	32,186	275	243
Indonesia	193	1.8	61-65	266	1,372	57	64
Japan	125	0.5	77-83	609	13,580	189	175
Malaysia	20	2.6	70-75	109	5,446	109	104
Mexico	92	2.2	70-76	427	4,648	102	112
New Zealand	4	1.4	73-79	73	20,076	19	19
Papua New Guinea	4	2.3★	56	7	1,624	2	4
Philippines	69	2.3	63-66	101	1,470	3	25
Singapore	3	2.4	74-79	112	37,422	174	166
South Korea	45	0.5	77-83	609	13,580	189	175
Taiwan	21	0.9	72-78	361	17,415	156	145
Thailand	58	1.5	68-72	224	3,836	99	79
United States	263	0.6★	72-79	9,940	37,772	1,080	817

★1996 data

The Sanctions Dilemma

The basic fact about unilateral trade sanctions is overwhelmingly obvious: They do not work. In fact, they are counterproductive. Long-standing US sanctions against Cuba, Libya, Iraq and Iran seem to have perpetuated the regimes they were designed to topple. They are unwieldy, hard to enforce, can be circumvented by unscrupulous companies willing to take the risk, and usually deemed a failure.

"My experience with sanctions has convinced me that they don't work — unless you are trying to make life miserable for the general population of a country without any concern for the long-term consequences," maintains Retired Canadian Major-General Lewis MacKenzie, who was the 1st UN forces commander in Sarajevo in 1992. "They were a failure in Yugoslavia, and in Iraq, if anything, they have solidified the population's contempt for the West."

Tariffs and quotas, the traditional forms of trade restraints, are less damaging to trade than sanctions. Unlike tariffs, which protect domestic industries from foreign competition, sanctions undermine the position of multinational companies in international trade by prohibiting doing business in the targeted countries.

Unilateral trade sanctions have also grown rapidly and changed in nature. Once a Cold-War tool applied to the Soviet Union and Cuba (in 1988) sanctions became a way to retaliate against countries that refused to open their markets. Today, sanctions are an instrument with which the US attempts to coerce changes in the political, social and religious policies of other governments.

US legislators are sponsoring new laws that would apply trade sanctions against countries in which there is religious persecution. While they have in mind Syria, Sudan, China, and Russia, the list of potential "violators" is almost limitless.

The US has become almost feckless in its use of unilateral sanctions, by 1 count, imposing 61 sanctions against 35 countries over the last 4 years. Rather than convey moral force, these sanctions make the US appear capricious and inconsistent.

Sanctions are often the outgrowth of intense pressure from well-organized domestic political groups with ethnic, cultural, environmental, human rights or religious grievances against a foreign regime. Harvard University and other self-righteous universities banned Coke from their campuses for selling cola in Burma, even though such sanctions are against the WTO rules.
• Unions want trade sanctions against countries that offend US labour standards.
• Greens want sanctions applied to countries that violate environmental standards.
• Human rights groups want sanctions imposed to combat political oppression.
• Anti-terrorist groups want to punish Syria, Iran and the Sudan for their alleged support of terrorism.

Many are not content for the sanctions to apply only to US companies, but also want to target every company in every country that trades with the offending nation through such legislation as the Helms-Burton Law that threatens Canadian and other non-US companies who do business in Cuba.

Despite a recent loosening of the US sanctions against Cuba, officials see no prospect of any major reversal in the 35-year-old US economic embargo. Ottawa and the EU have pressured the US to use engagement, rather than isolation, to bring about change in Cuba. There is also a new undercurrent of support for US engagement, with many Cuban-Americans rethinking the embargo. In addition, the visit by the Pope to Cuba in 1997 created room for people to act in contravention to Cuban leader Castro.

Critics of the embargo say it has failed to weaken Castro while wreaking havoc on ordinary Cubans. Canada blames the US embargo for impoverishing the Cuban people and promoting the rise of prostitution as ordinary Cubans try desperately to get hard currency.

The National Association of Manufacturers (US) study tends to agree, saying that trade sanctions hurt the people, not the government. Sanctions are as deadly as bombs, according to Iraqis. Where once Iraq's people indicated, at least in subtle ways, how they despised President Saddam Hussein, the years of the embargo have turned their ire against the enemy outside.

When UN Secretary-General Kofi Annan concluded a 1997 agreement with Iraq, the last paragraph of the deal mentioned what Iraqis want the most — the lifting of sanctions the UN imposed after Hussein ordered the invasion of Kuwait in 1990. Medicines and food are in short supply; 30% of the country's children younger than 5 are malnourished; in a country of 23 million, 1,000 children die from malnutrition each week — all primarily as a result of conditions created by the sanctions. Despite the sanctions, 7 Canadian companies signed more than $1 billion in purchase orders with the Iraqi government in 1997 to provide humanitarian aid to the embargoed nation, including 1,000 pre-fabricated houses, medical supplies, livestock and seed potatoes.

Linking trade to human rights can also cost domestic jobs, according to a forum on Asia-Pacific, because countries are overwhelmed and angered at Westerners dictating and imposing their values on them. An American study found that the US lost 250,000 jobs and reduced exports by $20 billion as a result of trade sanctions.

On the other hand, sending military equipment to a country such as Indonesia sends a political signal that we are not critical of how they use their armed forces. Indonesia's military is regularly used to put down unrest and has been engaged in a brutal campaign that has claimed thousands of lives in East Timor since 1975. Even so, in 1996, Canada authorized 5 export permits valued at $32 million for the sale of military equipment to the southeast Asian giant. (See page 179.)

If economic sanctions do not work, past experience has shown that sports sanctions can carry greater weight and are more difficult to get around. That was the case with South Africa under apartheid, which was banned from taking part in international events; it also could have worked against Nigeria, if it had been banned from participating in the 1998 World Cup soccer competion.

Arms Trade

Hardly anyone noticed in June of 1996 when a group of Nobel Peace laureates, led by former Costa Rican president Oscar Aria, issued an appeal for an "International Code of Conduct" on arms sales. From California to China, arms manufacturing means jobs, big incomes and prestige.

Arms selling, like war, will not go away. But like any dangerous occupation, it needs rules. As the global free trade in weapons hits the fast track, such rules are getting harder to imagine by the day.

The cash-starved government of Russia believes foreign arms sales are the only way to keep production skills alive and expertise inside the country, but it has fallen to 3rd place in the global $31.8 billion arms trade. Russian military sales were $4.6 billion in 1996, or about 14.5% of the total market. Britain was 2nd, with $4.8 billion (15.1%); the US, to no one's surprise, was in 1st place, with a whopping $11.3 billion.

The US is responsible for 44% of all weapons deliveries around the globe. In 1996, US companies sold roughly $20 billion worth of military products abroad.

As arms dealer to the world, the US House of Representatives adopted a restrictive "code of conduct" that attempts to legislate international morality by imposing a ban on US sales of airplanes, tanks, trucks and high-tech arms to non-democratic countries guilty of human-rights abuses. A co-sponsor of the bill said this would send a message that the US "intends not just to be a military and economic superpower but a moral superpower as well." He went on to say that, "The Cold War is over. It is time for us to have a new code of conduct that puts democracy and human rights ahead of a fast buck in selling weapons to the dictators around the world who repress people and violate the very principles which this country is supposed to be all about."

In fact, however, US President Bill Clinton is moving in the opposite direction, announcing the resumption of US arms sales to Latin America due to the strong lobbying of the very powerful Industrial-Military Complex. Such sales were banned by President Jimmy Carter in 1977 during a period of upheaval, military strong-arm tactics and violence in many Latin countries.

Clinton supporters argue that not only are arms sales in the US national self-interest — being an arms dealer amounts to a great deal of money and hundreds of thousands of jobs — but refusing to sell military equipment to undemocratic countries does not deny them what they want. They will simply buy elsewhere.

In the former Yugoslavia, for instance, NATO troops seized 4 truckloads of weapons from the police — known supporters of Bosnian Serb president Radovan Karadzic. Diplomats suspect Karadzic's supporters were trying to intimidate and mount a coup against their rivals in the NATO-backed moderate Serb government of Biljiana Plavsic. Karadzic, you may recall, was indicted for his role in the racial cleansing in Bosnia.

In any case, the Latins have continued to arm without support from the US. Peru, for instance, bought a squadron of Russian-made MiG's last year.

Latin democracies are currently racing one another to feed the hunger of their restless militaries, depleting treasuries of funds otherwise needed for the region's grave social problems. Chile may be pro-democratic and doing very well in many aspects of economic growth, but it is just a decade since it was ruled by an extreme right-wing military dictator. The sale of state-of-the-art F-16 fighter planes to Chile will mean that the generals in Argentina will "need" similar toys, which means that generals in Brazil will be next and right on down the line until El Salvador — the region's poorest country will "need" them, too. What a terrible waste of money when so much is needed for education, health care, and so on.

Small Arms

Many arms-control and human rights experts say a small-arms ban would need to be matched by restrictions on sales of heavier military equipment to regimes that use tanks, artillery and military planes to suppress their citizens.

Canadian Foreign Affairs Minister Lloyd Axworthy wants the coalition of middle powers, peace groups and international humanitarian non-governmental organizations that made the land mines treaty possible to take on the problem of the proliferation of small arms.

The 1st step may be to restrict small-arms shipments into conflict zones. Later, the small-arms trade could be "suffocated" with restrictions on weapons manufacturing. But the suppliers — countries like France — will be loath to give up the revenue from these sales, according to Project Ploughshares. (See page 241.)

Besides, small arms, like the cheap but deadly Kalashnikov automatic rifle, are readily available on black markets in Central African, Southern Asian and Latin American hot spots. In the past 4 years, 85% of US arms sales to the Third World have gone to undemocratic governments.

Small arms are not just proliferating in countries with undemocratic governments. More than 500 million small arms — military-style assault rifles, hand grenades and land mines — are in circulation worldwide today, and fully *half* are in the US, according to a new report from the Worldwatch Institute. That means a weapon for every man, woman and child in America.

OH... ALL RIGHT. ALL RIGHT... WE WON'T SELL ANY MORE LAND MINES. WE DON'T WANT ANYBODY SAYING WE DON'T HAVE A HEART...

India

India had much to celebrate as it marked its 50th birthday last year. The very survival of such a wildly diverse country, with 16 official languages and 5 major religions, is a kind of miracle. Its survival as a democracy is doubly miraculous.

Life expectancy has doubled to 60 years, but half the country's billion people still can neither read nor write. Almost half of the children do not reach Grade 5, nearly half of rural children never go to school at all and more than half of children under age 4 are undernourished.

In fact, in at least 2 critical development categories, literacy and infant mortality, India's figures are no better than those of sub-Saharan Africa, the world's poorest region. In Ganjam in the state of Orissa, the infant mortality rate of 164 per 1,000 live births is worse than in any nation in the world!

As a result of these failures, tens of millions of lives have been abbreviated and hundreds of millions blighted.

India spent more on a single purchase of 20 Russian jet fighters a few years ago than it would have cost to educate all the 15 million girls who were out of school.

Military Sales to Repressive Governments

The US may have bought 21 advanced MiG-29 warplanes from the former Soviet republic of Moldova to keep them out of Iran's military arsenal, but the US joins Canada in being guilty of selling arms to Indonesia, a country with 1 of the world's most repressive anti-human rights records, according to Amnesty International and Human Rights Watch. Not only does that prove that "undemocratic" is a subjective term for the world's arms dealers, but it speaks volumes about our value systems. Indonesia invaded the former Portuguese colony of East Timor in 1975; by some accounts, more than 1/3 of the people of East Timor have been killed in organized genocide since Indonesia seized the area and began settling Indonesians there.

Canada's official policy on military exports is to "closely control" such exports to countries "involved in or under imminent threat or hostilities," and to control exports to countries "whose governments have a persistent record of serious violations of the human rights of their citizens, unless it can be demonstrated that there is no reasonable risk that the goods might be used against the civilian population." This was not enough to stop Axworthy from approving the sale of $1.6 million worth of military goods to Indonesia in late 1996.

At a time when Canada has pledged to be a "more responsible player in the global military goods market," exports to such countries as Algeria, Indonesia, China, India and Turkey have increased. While total exports declined from $463 million in 1995 to $459 million in 1996, the share of exports that went to low and middle-income countries jumped from 8.6% to 14.5%. In addition, the percentage of exports sent to non-NATO countries and those not in another group that includes Australia, Western Europe and Saudi Arabia increased to 18.5%. (Military exports to the US, which account for most of Canada's defence industry output, are not included because they are not subject to permits.)

Canada's military exports to Third World countries engaged in internal conflicts also increased significantly, including Algeria, where the military-backed regime has been accused of complicity in civilian attacks, and Indonesia, which since 1975 has waged a despotic military occupation of the former Portuguese colony of East Timor.

CF-5 Sales

In an apparent contradiction in Canadian foreign policy, Canada has sold 13 modernized F-5 fighter jets to Botswana.

The poor country, whose air force used to consist of 2 old propeller-driven warplanes, has been building up arms in a political power play with purchases of used tanks and other military equipment from Britain and the Netherlands. The addition of the jets adds an alarming dimension to the situation of a country whose borders are circled by conflict.

Canada's fleet, built in the 1960's, was rebuilt and mothballed in 1995, when the government began marketing the jets at South World Arms shows, especially in Africa. A contract with Botswana was finalized in 1996 for a value of $84 million. Only 13 of the original 72 were sold, 11 are incomplete and 48 are in storage and waiting for disposal, prompting speculation that another deal with another African country could be in the works.

The government naturally wished to keep the deal quiet, which is not surprising given that Foreign Affairs Minister Lloyd Axworthy has become a regular peacenik, promoting a worldwide ban on land mines. It also flies in the face of the peace-building and conflict resolution that Axworthy proclaims as a solution to African problems. The kicker is that the company doing the modernizing and servicing of the jets is Winnipeg-based Bristol Aerospace — located in Axworthy's Manitoba riding.

IF NUKES ARE OUTLAWED, ONLY OUTLAWS WILL HAVE NUKES

IRAN

NUKES DON'T KILL PEOPLE, PEOPLE KILL PEOPLE

IF YOU WANT TO TAKE AWAY MY NUKES, YOU'LL HAVE TO PRY MY COLD, DEAD FINGERS OFF 'EM

179

Potpourri

Interdependency:

The Aztec Two-Step, The Asian Flu, The Russian Bear and The Brazilian Mardi Gras

CEO of failed Yamaichi Securities resigns in shame.

Former CEO of one of South Korea's largest conglomerates trains to be a waiter.

Financial Firefighting: Canada's IMF Commitment

Canada has answered the call and pledged increased support for the IMF, the agency which recently promised billions to bail out collapsing Asian and Russian economies.

Canada's support includes: a quota increase, which will raise our subscription from $8.4 billion to about $12.4 billion; bilateral agreements, expected to address Canada's ability to respond to requests for additional aid from specific countries more nimbly (this type of support was turned down for Thailand and Indonesia initially, but Canada eventually agreed to contribute an extra $1.4 billion for South Korea); and new agreements to borrow — intended to allow the IMF itself to borrow more from participating countries in times of emergency.

To ratify an increase in IMF funding requires 85% of the votes of its members — but the US has almost 18% of the vote itself, giving it a blocking minority. In the US, the Senate appropriations committee approved the additional funds, but attached strict conditions, including the restriction that the $20.3 billion for reserves could not be released until the IMF agrees to further open its books and toughen requirements on borrowers.

The total outstanding loans of the IMF have grown from about $20 billion in 1980 to over $80 billion in 1997.

To meet growing demand a new credit line was created from 25 countries who will commit an additional $70 billion. Canada's share is $3 billion or about 4% of the total in new commitments.

IMF's Largest Rescue Packages

153

Country	Year	Billions
Brazil	1999	40*
Russia	1998	27
South Korea	1997	32
Indonesia	1997	17
Thailand	1997	6
Mexico	1995	25

*Anticipated — Billions (0 10 20 30 40)

The Nature of War

We Stand on Guard for Thee

The Old Paradigm:
Men make war because war makes men.

What attracts us to war? Why do we so enjoy forming large armed groups and spilling the blood of others? Author Barbara Ehrenreich has a theory that the origins of war have their roots in our previous status as prey. Man's transformation from prey to predator, which took millions of years, was a stunning victory, but we still think like prey.

Man was once one of the choicest items in the food chain. Terrified of carnivores, he spent almost his entire time on Earth being torn apart and eaten by them, inducing a state of terror that is doubtless still imprinted in our genetic code.

According to Ehrenreich in her book, *Blood Rites: Origins and History of the Passions of War*, this explains why we stick together in groups for safety. It also explains our custom of burying the dead, depriving predators of an easy meal, and refusing, even in death, the label of prey.

War has a rhythm of revenge, adds Ehrenreich. It is the most imitative, contagious activity there is. Someone offends us. We retaliate. They retaliate. Only in human war could this happen, she explains, because animals do not retaliate.

But the greatest modern war-starter is nationalism, she says. It flourishes despite the fact that most nations are mongrels: Britain has its Scots and Welsh; Spain has the Basques and Catalans; most African nations are inventions of a civil servant with a ruler; and the US is a hodgepodge. Pedigree does not matter, though; it is the idea of nation that thrills people.

Patriotism is just the most extreme form of nationalism, which Ehrenreich says is a religion that worships war. War now defines manhood, too. Men make war because war makes them men.

WWI: A Costly Crusade of Nation-Building

Putting Canada's losses of more than 66,000 during World War I into perspective — the US really has nothing to compare. *On a proportional basis*, Canada suffered more casualties in WWI than the US did from its Revolutionary War through the war in the Persian Gulf. (See chart on page 185.)

How the Great War Myth Forged Canada

Referring to his book, *Death So Noble: Memory, Meaning and the First World War*, Jonathan Vance eloquently says, "This book is about memory. It is about constructing a mythic version of the events of 1914-1918 from a complex mixture of fact, wishful thinking, half-truth, and outright invention, and expressing that version in novel and play, in bronze and stone, in reunion and commemoration, in song and advertisements."

In spite of their actual cause and conjectured design, our rational nature compels that all wars be remembered as meaningful. Great importance must be attached to the mayhem to cover the usually pointless, ignorant and inhumane acts committed in the name of some god, belief or for the sake of some rather real or imagined political entity. Vance bountifully documents the myriad myths about Canada's involvement in World War I.

One of Canada's foremost myths camouflages the truth: "Canada's progress from colony to nation was by way of Flanders." The colossal number of casualties of the Canadian Corps had to be conceived as beautiful, and the dead seen not as *losing* their lives but *giving* them.

He observes that, "Having accepted that the war had been a crusade in defense of Christian principles, people simply could not conceive that 66,000 soldiers descended into oblivion after dying in a righteous cause." Of all Canadians who went into WWI, 28% were wounded; 10% were killed.

WHY CAN'T WE ALL JUST GET ALONG?

BECAUSE WE'D ALL BE OUT OF A *JOB*, THAT'S WHY!

The Boer War:
Our Adventure in Imperialism

The contingents that went from Canada to participate in the South African War of 1899-1902 were the effect, not the cause, of Canadian imperialism. Yet the war did what perhaps nothing else could have done in proving the existence of this imperial sentiment: igniting sensitive pride in the Empire from seeing the position of the motherland in Europe threatened by a possible combination of hostile powers.

Offering troops to the Imperial Government had no precedent. During the Crimean War, nothing had been done by the disorganized provinces except the voting of a sum of money for widows and orphans and the enlistment of the 100th Regiment. During the Sudan War, in 1885, a small body of Canadian volunteers and voyagers, paid from Imperial funds, had gone up the Nile.

More important, however, as a factor in this and other developments of an imperial nature, was the work done by the Imperial Federation League in Canada during the years following 1885. The indirect effect of the League's work in England and in Canada became visible in many directions and strongly aided development along imperial lines.

The British Empire League in Canada passed a resolution declaring that the time had come for all parts of the Queen's dominions to share in the defence of British interests, and the Saint John *Telegraph* — a strong Liberal paper — declared that "Canada should not only send a force to the Transvaal, but should maintain it in the field." *The Montreal Star* sought and received telegrams from the mayors of nearly every town in the Dominion, approving the proposal to dispatch military assistance to fellow subjects in South Africa.

The mayor of Belleville, Ontario, represented the general tone of these multitudinous messages in the words: "It is felt that the Dominion, being a partner in the empire, should bear imperial responsibilities as well as share imperial honours and protection." This new and important departure from precedent and practice was evidenced by the announcement that a Canadian contingent had been accepted by the Imperial Government and was to be dispatched to South Africa.

There was no active opposition to the proposal, except from a segment of the French-Canadian press. However, the feeling of the country generally was too fervent to permit this obstacle having anything more than an ephemeral and passing influence. And any opposition that might have existed among French Canadians assumed an essentially passive character.

The 1st contingent of 1,000 men steamed down the St. Lawrence from Quebec on October 30, 1899. Every village that contributed a soldier to the contingent also added to the wave of popular feeling by marking his departure as an event of serious import. To quote the Minister of Militia and Defence: "This was the people's movement, not that of any government or party; it emanated from the whole people of Canada." This was the 1st time in history when Canadians and Australians fought side by side with British regular troops.

Canadian troops defend The Empire in South Africa.

Meanwhile, public feeling in Canada seemed to favour the sending of further aid, but it was not until some of the earlier reverses of the war took place that the offer of a 2nd contingent was accepted, and once again the call to arms resounded throughout Canada. The 1st troops had been infantry; the 2nd were artillery and cavalry.

It was decided to send 1,220 men, together with horses, guns, and complete equipment. A 3rd force of 400 mounted men was recruited in the following month and sent to the war fully equipped. Field Marshal Lord Roberts, shortly after his appointment to South Africa, cabled his expression of belief that "the action of Canada will always be a glorious page in the history of the sons of the empire."

The Royal Canadian Regiment saw much service and experienced much deprivation; they shared in all the important battles and revealed to the world in a moment the unity of sentiment and imperial loyalty that had been developing for years in the backwoods and cities of Canada and in the bush and the civic centres of Australia. **Canada appeared to take its proper place in the defence system of the empire.**

Individual incidents of bravery were numerous in all the regiments; and the losses by death or wounds, and the suffering from a variety of diseases, were great. The actual achievements of the men themselves in steadiness, discipline and bravery reveal ample reasons for considering the participation of Canada in this war as a profound event in its history. Additional contingents went from Canada for a total of 8,372 men, and many individual Canadians achieved distinction for their valiant efforts. Terms of peace were signed at Pretoria on May 31, 1902, and the rejoicings in Canada were marked by an enthusiasm tempered only with the memory of the 224 gallant Canadians who had lost their lives in the struggle.

Few Canadians today would offer support for such a military adventure as the Boer War because the paradigm has shifted — we share a much different world view than that of the nation 100 years ago.[154]

Vimy Ridge: A Turning Point in WWI

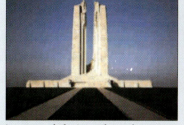

Between April 9th and 12th, 1917, Canadians attacked the Germans at Vimy Ridge. This area had been held for 4 years by German forces; it secured their path to the mines and factories in the Douai plain, from which they drew strategic wartime resources.

France had tried to capture Vimy Ridge twice and failed; Britain had attempted once and also failed. Consequently, Canadian victory was one of Canada's crowning wartime achievements, culminating in the capture of more than 4,000 German prisoners.

Vimy Ridge was a natural defensive area, which had been fortified by an elaborate trench system and underground tunnels. Canadian strategy involved the creation of a detailed, full-scale replica to practice their offensive movements. In addition, aerial reconnaissance of the area provided detailed information about German defences.

Canadian troops dug tunnels under the Ridge, allowing the Canadians to move as close as possible to the German defences, and, once the battle was underway, to transport the wounded to safety.

The on-ground Infantry attack was preceded by a 3-week-long artillery bombardment that involved 1,000 guns. Canadian guns shelled German trenches and defensive positions on the Ridge with great accuracy.

The Infantry attack — 100,000 strong — began on April 9th, 1917. The Canadians crossed the greasy, crater-ridden No-Man's Land, laden down with equipment and pelted with freezing rain and sleet. As they advanced under a shower of shells, fresh troops continually took over the lead; by mid-afternoon, the Canadian Divisions had captured most of Vimy Ridge.

By the next day, Hill 145 was captured, and by April 12th, the Canadians controlled the entire area. The Canadians had captured more ground, more prisoners and more guns than any other "British" offensive in the war to date. In the end there were 10,602 Canadian casualties and 3,598 dead. This is a high and tragic number, but it must be seen in the context that 200,000 Canadians, British, French and Germans were buried on the Ridge from earlier, unsuccessful attacks. **Many consider the charge on Vimy Ridge a turning point in Canada's march towards "nationhood."**

The Korean "Conflict":

This 3-year United Nations "police action," as it was labeled, cost the nation 1,771 casualties—including 516 deaths. July 27, 1998 marked the 45th anniversary of the 1953 Korea Armistice Agreement.

Dieppe:
A Costly Failure

On August 19, 1942, hundreds of Canadians were killed during the Dieppe raid.

The 6,000-strong amphibious attack, named Operation Jubilee, on this English Channel port was led by about 5,000 Canadians, many of them young volunteers from small towns and farms across the country.

The raid, Canada's bloodiest day of the war, began to go wrong from the start. The vanguard was spotted by a German naval convoy as the invasion force crossed the channel. The landing craft arrived late, and the tanks bogged down on the pebble and shale beaches, leaving the Canadians defenseless. Only a few of the Canadians made it into the town, where they were quickly killed or taken prisoner. There were 1,466 casualties, including 880 dead. Almost 1,900 were taken prisoner. Although the raid failed, the town was liberated 2 years later by Canadian troops.

The "Unknown Canadian Soldier," drawn in 1942, was thought to have been killed at Dieppe.

Pax Americana

Pax Romana 27 BCE - 235
Pax Britannica 1815 - 1914
Pax Americana 1945 -

For 2 centuries the political left has been expounding the obsolescence of war in terms of the spread of democracy and the pacifying power of commerce. However, as Donald Kagan observes in his book, *On the Origins of War*, "Over the past 2 centuries, the only thing more common than predictions about the end of war has been war itself." Kagan says that, "Statistically, war has been more common than peace, and extended periods of peace are rare in a world divided into multiple states." Given what Kagan calls "ubiquity and perpetuity" of war, the 1st duty of political leadership is to continue to fund the military for the federal government's foremost responsibility — defence based on the premise that **"peace does not keep itself."**

Sir Michael Howard, a British military historian, writes that military power has 3 functions: deterrence, coercion and reassurance. The last may be most important because it determines the environment within which international relations are conducted.

Reassurance provides a general sense of security that is not specific to any particular threat or scenario. The role played by the dominance of the British Royal Navy in the 19th century is an example. The coalition against Napoleon was held together until the victory at Waterloo — Napoleon's final defeat in 1815, and the Congress of Vienna that followed, reestablishing European borders in a way that was not excessively punitive to France and resulted in the subsequent Pax Britannica, which lasted precisely 100 years.

The Pax Americana, which began in 1945, embodied non-punitive settlements against the Axis powers and has the potential to last for at least another 100 years. Like the Royal British Navy of the 19th century, it will cost money, but it will cost significantly less than war, which our experience should tell us could be the alternative.

A Single Superpower

From the end of WWII until the implosion of the Soviet Union, the world was split into 2 armed camps: an East-West conflict of superpowers.

Strategic planning used to mean thinking about how to deter an attack by the Russians, but the Russian military is now in such chaos that nobody even knows the exact number of soldiers in uniform. The most visible of the Russian army's many problems is lack of money. With Russia suffering economically and its military strength waning, Russian President Boris Yeltsin even visited China to bury the last vestiges of a border hostility that has soured relations for 300 years.

Is America the only remaining superpower, or has Russia been replaced by China? Despite what American pro-defence analysts would have us believe, the chart on this page illustrates that China has nowhere near the military might of the US. Reminiscent of the singular power held by the British in the 19th century, **we have entered the era of Pax Americana.**

For Canada, strategic planning in this new environment means budget cuts, and figuring out how to cope if the government suddenly asks the military to take on a new peacekeeping mission or help during a natural disaster. Purchases of capital projects are being deferred, half the military installations have been closed and the air force is mothballing many of its fighter aircraft.

But even with budget cuts, the Department of National Defence is still one of the most expensive operating departments in the federal government. The spurious assertion that the Canadian Forces remain an "insurance policy" against the risk of war is nothing more than wishful thinking.[191]

Many would agree that DND needs a "transformation strategy" for the 21st century — for further adapting forces from the Cold War era to the security threats that are likely to face Canada and its allies 20 years from now.

Superpower Statistics

155

Category	The United States	China
GDP	$7.2 trillion ($US)	$560 billion ($US)
Military budget	$263.9 billion	$31.7 billion
Strategic nuclear weapons	7,150	149
Long-range strategic bombers	178	0
Ballistic missile submarines	17	1
ICBMs	580	17
Aircraft carriers	*11	0
Modern tactical aircraft	4,450	**697
Transport ships	205	55
Transport aircraft	1,070	484
Helicopters	7,925	513
Attack submarines	78	61
Active-duty personnel	1,483,800	2,935,000
Population	265,622,400	1,210,476,000

*Plus one refit   **Including many of Korean War vintage

Rusting Russian sub:
military obsolescence

In the US, Pentagon war planners have been told to include in their list of potential targets states that could launch chemical or biological weapons. Using the phrase "defence of the homeland" to capture its idea, the National Defense Panel recommended that a military geared toward planning for wars abroad look also to what can be done about the risk of smaller assaults on America itself.

That mission is becoming more important as more nations hostile to US interests acquire weapons of mass destruction and the means to deliver them, and the superpower conflicts give way to local conflicts — with the US acting as referee.

One example is Turkey, which is beginning the process of "integrating" the occupied part of northern Cyprus, the location of a regional arms race with both Greeks and Turks bankrupting their treasuries to acquire high-tech weapons. As Turkey's paymaster and armourer, Washington has a right to demand that Cyprus be given its own fair chance to share in an expanded Europe instead of becoming prisoner of an expansionist Turkey.

US F/A-18 Hornet in the Gulf: military arrogance

Towards a New Nuclear Strategy

Under Pax Americana, shifting military responsibilities include a change in the role and importance of nuclear weapons. Protracted nuclear war is no longer part of the planning agenda. For the 1st time since 1981, the US has made a change in its nuclear weapons planning and has agreed to further reductions in its arsenals. But the nuclear issue is not dead; even though treaties have been signed and thousands of bombs destroyed, thousands more are still in place. The 1998 nuclear tests by India and Pakistan compound these issues.

Since US President Bill Clinton signed the Comprehensive Test Ban Treaty, public expectations are high that America and others will freeze and dismantle their bombs, not upgrade them. But the US Energy Department has been caught in a $5.6 billion program to upgrade and modernize existing weapons. Washington is playing with political fire if its push for ever-better bombs undermines the spirit of the treaty.

Nuclear weapons remain the cornerstone of US defence policy. Even while old bombs are being demolished, the Pentagon is planning "sub-critical" underground tests to make sure its remaining arsenal is effective and to learn how to design reliable and "survivable" nuclear weapons. This continues despite the fact that **the annual cost of keeping the US nuclear strike capability is estimated at $50 billion, or about 5 times our defence budget.**

Canadians are not blameless in the nuclear arms race. Although we have never made or dropped an atomic bomb, we have supported and contributed to the US nuclear weapons program in many ways and have benefitted from its protection. It seems clear that our Candu reactor technology was instrumental in the advancement of Indian nuclear technology.

The Latent Russian Danger

And in Russia, the 1998 economic implosion could mean a greater reliance on nuclear weapons. There is also a danger that its aging nuclear weapons could be fired by accident, according to a German study. The report said problems with early warning systems have led to the practice of keeping nuclear weapons in a permanent state of alert, meaning they could be launched at the 1st signs of a real or imagined attack.

Cash-strapped Russia has called upon its former foes in NATO to help assess the problem of dismantling its creaky fleet of rusting nuclear submarines. This is an intricate problem faced by other countries, including the US, but Russia's financial circumstances and the fact that it has the largest number of mothballed subs (156) creates a bigger environmental threat. (See photo on page 184.)

Just 16 of the 156 retired subs have been fully disassembled so far, with another 100 scheduled to go out of service by the year 2000. More than 60% of the mothballed submarines still have fuel in their reactors, threatening to unleash radioactive waste that could bring environmental ruin.

Nuclear disarmament obviously has its difficult consequences, but those who want to see the end of these horrific weapons are winning small victories. For example, while Canada led efforts to broker a global treaty on the ban of land mines, Australia is leading a worldwide agreement on nuclear disarmament.

US Casualties in Principal Wars 156	
War/Conflict	Battle Deaths
Revolutionary War (1775-1783)	4,435
War of 1812 (1812-1815)	2,260
Mexican War (1846-1848)	1,733
Civil War - Union (1861-1865)	140,414
Civil War - Confederate (1861-1865)	*74,524
Spanish-American War (1898)	385
World War I (1917-1918)	53,402
World War II (1941-1945)	291,557
Korean Conflict (1950-1953)	33,651
Vietnam Conflict (1964-1973)	47,378
* best estimate – authoritative data not available **Total**	**649,739**

Anyone can become angry, but to be angry with the right person, to the right degree, at the right time, for the right purpose.
— *Aristotle*

Nuclear Non-Proliferation Treaty

At the 1995 Nuclear Non-Proliferation Treaty Review and Extension Conference, which marked the 25ᵗʰ anniversary of the 1970 Nuclear Non-Proliferation Treaty (NPT), Australia worked to achieve an indefinite extension of the Treaty. Australia observed that indefinite extension would be effective in pressing existing declared nuclear weapon states to continue the process of disarmament; contain the nuclear aspirations of the so-called threshold states; and meet the interests of all the other parties to the Treaty who wanted to utilize its provisions to encourage peaceful cooperation.

In the end, NPTREC saw the Treaty given indefinite life. Of the 185 members of the United Nations, 175 signed the agreement. Of the 10 countries that were not party to the Treaty — Angola, Brazil, Comoros, Cuba, Djibouti, Oman, United Arab Emirates, India, Pakistan and Israel — only the last 3, driven largely by regional tensions and rivalries, are actual nuclear powers.

That same year, Australia led a request of the International Court of Justice to give its opinion on the question, **"Is the use of nuclear weapons in any circumstance permitted under international law?"**

Its objective was to determine the legality or illegality of the threat or use of nuclear weapons. Proponents of the illegality of the use of nuclear weapons argued that such use would violate the right to life, that the prohibition against genocide is a relevant rule of customary international law, and that any use of nuclear weapons would be unlawful in relation to the safeguarding and protection of the environment. Since the turn of the century, precedent has been set to prohibit the use of certain weapons, such as dum-dum bullets and asphyxiating gases.

The Introduction of New Weapons

While nuclear weapons may be winding down their usefulness, the defence industry is turning its attention to the development of new weapons.

The US Air Force announced plans to arm seven, 747 jumbo jets with photon lasers designed to shoot down enemy missiles. The YAL-1A laser, which will make bullets and missiles obsolete, is being hailed by the military as inexpensive and realistic.

Circling at about 40,000 feet outside of enemy airspace, the jets will be equipped with heat sensors to detect an enemy missile launch, track the missile and fire the laser once the rocket clears the clouds. The missile would be attacked when it is on an upward trajectory, allowing it to explode while still over enemy territory.

Lasers have been used for decades to guide bombs and aim weapons, but this is the first time they will be used as a high-energy defence weapon, combating missiles such as the Scud. The system will test in 2002, and be deployed in 2008 at a cost of more than $11 billion to develop, build and operate for 20 years.

In addition, the US military spent $84 million testing its most powerful laser (the "Miracle": Mid-infrared Advanced Chemical Laser) to determine its effectiveness in destroying satellites. The futuristic weapon is a by-product of Ronald Reagan's infamous Star Wars program.

Satellites have become a vital part of modern warfare, especially low-orbit spy and global-positioning satellites, which allow missiles and bombs to be guided with precision. The Americans are leaders in the extremely expensive business of intelligence satellites, which gave them a huge advantage during the Persian Gulf war because Iraq did not have any of these satellites.

The Americans are not alone in stockpiling new weapons. German, Spanish, Italian and British defence ministers signed a contract allowing production of the Eurofighter military defence jet. The contract commits the 4 governments to purchase 620 jets, worth $84 billion, with the 1ˢᵗ one ready in late 2001.

These costs are trivial, however, compared with those to follow: a multi-billion-dollar space war and arms race ignited by the US "superlaser" test. This "race" raises questions about supporting those who make it a priority to perfect the weapons to "win" the next world war versus those who want to stabilize the world based on shared knowledge and responsibility.

New Security Threats

While the world pushes for nuclear disarmament and questions the development of futuristic weapons, it is forgetting that some more sinister forces may threaten national security. The demise of superpower confrontation has also led to increased attention on local conflicts, often fought with low-tech small arms. Hundreds of thousands of surplus small arms and light weapons are gravitating towards regions of tension.

In the US, the Pentagon was warned by a congressionally chartered panel that it should pay more attention to such emerging threats as hit-and-run biological attacks on American cities (recall the arrest in early 1998 of 2 American biochemists who were caught purchasing the deadly toxin Anthrax, allegedly for release in the New York subway system), and ordered to broaden its list of potential targets to include those states that might use chemicals or biological weapons.

Among the recommendations made by the panel was that the military should devote $5 to $10 billion a year to develop a strategy with new weapons and war-fighting concepts to "hedge" against unforseen changes in global security.

Coincidentally, the UN believes that Iraq may have produced up to 400 tons of VX — theoretically enough to kill every person on the face of this earth. Who needs traditional weapons when one drop of this stuff will produce death in a matter of seconds?

In addition, *Jane's Intelligence Review* reported that Iraq still has the scientific talent and industrial base to build nuclear weapons. Iraqi defectors and sources close to the International Atomic Energy Agency have indicated the Iraqis still maintain an active nuclear weapons program.

Jane's also reports that Syria has a "distinct interest in acquiring weapons of mass destruction of its own."

Chemical & Biological Weapons

Between 1990 and 1995, the number of conventional heavy weapons held in military arsenals worldwide was reduced by 1/3. Compared to other types of weapons, the destruction of conventional weapons is not very costly. **However, only 1.2% of all weapon systems falling under the 1992 Conventional Forces Europe (CFE) Treaty have actually been converted.**

Although the US and Russia are the only countries with significant quantities, as many as 30 other countries must destroy chemical weapons.

Looking back over nuclear disarmament, the extent of the rollback is striking. By the end of 1996, all US and Russian intermediate-range ground-launched missiles had been eliminated, all naval tactical nuclear weapons had been withdrawn, as well as all nuclear artillery shells and land mines and nearly 1,700 strategic delivery vehicles and more than 5,600 of their warheads.

The generation of surplus is a paradox: reducing the number and even eliminating whole classes of weapons, but making more weapons available internationally. This is fostered by a lack of disposal technologies and insufficient policies to deal with surplus. The extent of disarmament has generated an enormous surplus, outstripping what facilities were designed to handle and placing a premium on upgrading storage capacity.

Researchers from the Bonn International Center for Conversion (BICC) have concluded that we are likely to see new surplus weapons emerging in large quantities. Establishing ways to dispose of surplus is necessary before the world can enjoy the benefits of disarmament.

Although the international trade in *new* weapons has declined, used weapons are increasingly available. The source of surplus weapons has diversified, with at least 41 different countries supplying secondhand major conventional weapons. (See page 178.)

Disarmament is constantly opening up new conversion opportunities and challenges. In a number of developing countries, reintegration of former combatants remains a major problem because of poor economic development prospects. Countries in the process of transformation struggle with converting their capacities in arms production and defence R&D for civilian use. Economic crises in these countries hamper conversion efforts, while downsizing continues to be delayed for political reasons or because of pressure groups.

In Western industrialized countries, large reductions caused by the end of the Cold War have now given way to smaller reductions, while in East Asia some countries are building up military sectors, generally parallel to the previous boom in their economies.

Thus, the trend of the "disarmament decade" has not been interrupted, but the pace has slowed down from 5% per year between 1991 and 1994 to 3% in 1995-1997.

The Peace Dividend

Those in favour of arms reduction say the savings in military expenditures could be used to:
- Hasten the conversion of military resources to peaceful purposes;
- Permit the allocation of additional funds for social and economic development;
- Register and eliminate offensive weapons development, production, deployment and sales;
- Address the dangers of armed conflict, the production and trade in arms, and the sale of arms that have indiscriminate effects, terrorism, violence, and crime;
- Destroy current stockpiles of land mines and promote mine detection and clearance technology.

Global military expenditures decreased by 30% between 1985 and 1995, when they amounted to about $1 trillion. The reductions were most pronounced in Europe, Russia, Africa, and Western Asia. These were the differences between expenditures during those years and the peak of $1.7 trillion reached in 1986.

People who assume that this "peace dividend" is spent on such things as social services will be surprised. The most frequent use is reduction of government deficits. In Germany, they became the investment in unification.

Reductions in military efforts also produce costs that partially offset the savings. This includes pensions, unemployment benefits, investment in base re-use, funds for weapons disposal, and the military's subsidized housing, education, health, transportation and food.

The substitution of defence spending by other kinds of spending — or by deficit or tax reductions — is a product of a regime's ideology, the timing of election cycles, the politics of interest groups and a country's political culture and institutions.

Relevant studies on "who pays for defence" have typically taken a zero-sum perspective on budgetary allocations. They assume that dollars spent for defence are readily transferable to programs enhancing popular well-being. Generally, recent and valid analyses have not shown such correlations. Budgets expand or shrink according to the perceived need for various expenditures and to the anticipated size of revenues. Officials may increase the budget by raising taxes or increasing the deficit; or by reducing taxes and deficits. Another alternative is to keep the budget constant, redistributing the funds within the constraints imposed by the overall budget.

In the US, defence and non-defence expenditures have increased simultaneously. Increases in the West German defence budget were accompanied by increases in the payroll tax for social security. In other words, higher military expenditures did not come at the expense of lower social expenditures. In a similar vein, South Korea used a surtax to finance higher defence spending.

The use of savings from military expenditures supports the view that a "peace dividend" exists, just not in the short run or detectable through reallocation within government budgets, but rather in the long run through increases in the growth of economies and the welfare of individuals.

NATO

Effective Solution to an Intrinsic Threat

The North Atlantic Treaty Organization (NATO) is a political and military alliance of countries in the Northern Hemisphere. Established in 1949, its current members are Belgium, Canada, Denmark, France, Germany, Greece, Iceland, Italy, Luxemburg, the Netherlands, Norway, Portugal, Spain, Turkey, the UK and the US.

Until the disintegration of the Soviet Union, NATO's principal focus was the maintenance of military capabilities sufficient to deter and, if necessary, defend against a military attack against its members. The Alliance also sought to improve relations with other nations through discussions on arms control, human rights, and various non-military forms of cooperation. **With the end of the Cold War, the Alliance is struggling, unsuccessfully, to justify its existence.**

NATO After the Cold War

NATO has made great strides in developing a posture that is more appropriate in reaching out to former adversaries to build a more peaceful, stable and democratic order. With the end of the Cold War, however, a need to justify the Alliance has arisen, especially because some enlightened countries have been reluctant to come up with funding. Other justifications have ranged from peacekeeping to peacemaking, and from crisis management to maintenance of stability, as well as emergency assistance and air-sea rescue.

NATO has significant military capabilities, as well as experience in the planning and execution of multi-national military operations. Since 1990, the Alliance has sought to focus away from the deterrence of a specific threat and towards addressing current and potential security challenges. This includes the development of NATO's new Strategic Concept (1991) and the ongoing discussions of Combined Joint Task Forces.

For some advocates, acceptance of new members — particularly former Warsaw Pact rivals – is the way to contain an unstable and potentially dangerous Russia. However, some feel as if the US is acting as though NATO is its exclusive preserve.

Many of NATO's former rivals are now eager to become full members of the Alliance, so NATO has pursued measures to integrate these countries into a pan-European security regime. The North Atlantic Cooperation Council (NACC), created in 1991, includes the 16 members of NATO and 22 other countries, including former Warsaw Pact countries and republics of the former USSR. Partnership for Peace is an Alliance initiative that offers all NACC countries, as well as members of the Organization for Security and Cooperation in Europe (OSCE — formerly the CSCE), the opportunity to participate in efforts to increase stability, consultation, joint planning and military exercises with NATO.

Canada is in favour of including these countries, but believes enlargement must avoid the creation of new divisions in Europe and minimize the risks of importing unresolved conflicts that could destabilize the Alliance.

Ineffective Solution to a Nonexistent Problem

Having said all that, **NATO now represents an architecture that is clearly obsolete.** Its continued existence is a redundancy foisted on members by the US and its parasitic defence industry. NATO and the Conventional Armed Forces in Europe Treaty confuse the natural roles of the UN and the OSCE. Many Russians, as well as other former members of the Soviet Union, harbour a negative attitude towards NATO, reflecting their concern of being regarded as its historical enemy.

Furthermore, security today means resolving conflicts — many of them centuries old — before they escalate into warfare, as in Bosnia. A key danger is the prospect for ethnic conflict.

Norway, Iceland, Denmark, Finland and Sweden are working with the US, Germany and the UK to help the Baltic states of Latvia, Lithuania and Estonia develop independent defence forces and a joint battalion for participation in peacekeeping operations.

Other threats do exist, such as the proliferation of weapons of mass destruction and their delivery systems, terrorism, drugs, money laundering and organized crime. In addition, unrest from economic deprivation and rising Islamic extremism threaten stability in the Mediterranean, with the risk of massive immigration to Western Europe and growing pressures on Western democratic governments. But these are EU concerns that do not require North American intervention, and **a less expensive alternative to NATO could be found.**

More importantly, NATO has proven to be ineffective in dealing with the problems created by the break-up of the former Yugoslavia, primarily by the cumbersome decision-making process that requires consensus. New NATO members will only cause further paralysis because of disparate national and regional interests.

The West did show sufficient resolve against Iraq during the Persian Gulf War. But we failed bitterly in Bosnia. In this case, instead of showing resolve, we preferred "diplomacy" and "consensus." As a result, a quarter of a million people were massacred. This was a horror that I, for one, never expected to see again in my lifetime. But it happened. Who knows what tragedies the future holds if we do not learn from the repeated lessons of history?

Margaret Thatcher, now Baroness Thatcher of Kesteven

Canada's Participation in NATO

Canada has contributed to NATO through naval operations, land and air commitments, participation in common-funded programs, personnel for headquarters and training facilities. Canada has also been a part of the CSCE/OSCE since its inception in 1973; is a signatory of the CFE Treaty; and its troops make up a substantial part of UN peacekeepers in the former Yugoslavia.

Canadian politicians remains strong supporters of NATO and *wrongly* believe it is a fundamentally valuable organization and a unique link between the security of Europe and North America. The benefits of collective defence, as well as NATO's experience in joint operations, are of enduring value. Multilateral cooperation also represents a way to pool national defence resources.

Some more enlightened Canadians believe, however, that NATO can make a greater contribution by providing other multilateral organizations (such as the UN) the military support they currently lack and playing a key role in the development of a more cooperative security regime in Europe.

NATO should become a more efficient organization in terms of budget and operating costs. Its bureaucracy must be reduced, and budgets spent only on activities that are relevant to the new defence environment.

Canada's perspective on NATO underpins the future of its symbolic peacetime Alliance commitments: 1 ship to the Atlantic Standing Naval Force plus 1 ship, on an occasional basis, to the Mediterranean Standing Naval Force; personnel to the Airborne Early Warning System; and personnel to various NATO headquarters.

In the event of a crisis, Canada would make available contingency forces to deploy on UN and other multilateral operations. This would entail forces not to exceed: a maritime task group, a brigade group, an infantry battalion group, a wing of fighter aircraft, and a squadron of tactical transport aircraft. Should a more serious crisis emerge, Canada would mobilize additional forces for the defence of Alliance territory, consistent with its obligations of the Treaty.

Canada's chief of defence staff, General Maurice Baril, is being deceptive when he says that Canadian forces can be deployed quickly if needed by its allies. This would include the deployment of only small advance units within the first 9 hours. **Larger units, such as a full battle brigade, could show up if given 90 days notice.**

Canada has been a long-standing contributor to NATO's defence infrastructure, but with the end of the Cold War and the recovery of Europe's economy, it should reduce its contributions. The complex security problems that confront the international community today defy easy solutions. Nevertheless, Canada believes that multilateral organizations — including NATO — should address these problems.

Getting Out of NATO

It is now time for Canada to declare that the "Emperor has no clothes," and withdraw from NATO and the CFE Treaty. Taking into consideration the new Russia-NATO agreement (*The Founding Act on Mutual Relations, Cooperation and Security between NATO and Russia*), signed in 1997, Canada should follow in the footsteps of France. Remaining in NATO is costly and members face $5 billion in new costs over the next 10 years.

In 1966, General Charles de Gaulle removed France's military commitment to NATO. France remains part of NATO, but not of the integrated military command. De Gaulle took this action because he felt that France did not have enough say in NATO's military decisions and French interests came 1st. This indicated that France would remain apart from any conflicts that America had with the rest of the world.

According to Peter Roberts, former Canadian ambassador to Romania (1979-83), Canada can learn from France. He says American interests have induced us to enlarge NATO to the East. This means that NATO armed forces will be able to come close to the Russian border. They will be on the borders of Belarus — unless, of course, Romania is invited to join NATO as suggested by Jean Chrétien. And if Romania joins, why not Ukraine? Why not ask Russia to join? Or is NATO there to protect us from the Chinese? If that is the case, then should we just ask them to join?

Pointing out the ludicrous nature of these decisions, Roberts highlights Russian fears of NATO, and asks us to remember that the former USSR lost 30 million citizens in WWII, and millions more lost arms and legs. As Canada opts out of NATO, we should politely say that we are friends and trading partners of Russians, and we have no interest in putting hostile forces on their borders to frighten them.

COUNTERPOINT   Let Them Use Our Skies

Canada continues to offer various training facilities to NATO. With high population density and congested airspace in Europe, many of these nations have limited opportunities to conduct suitable armoured or low-level flying training. By contrast, Canada, with its vast open spaces and sparse population, has many suitable training areas. Why not give NATO use of our airbases and skies in return for eliminating our planes?

Outlawing Land Mines

In a twist of fate, as Diana, Princess of Wales was killed in a tragic car accident, delegates were gathering in Norway to draft the final wording of a treaty banning the use of land mines worldwide. Diana had led a personal crusade against land mines. When she died, news agencies around the world trotted out recent photos and video footage of Diana visiting victims in Angola and Bosnia, thus raising the profile of this salient global issue.

Diana, however, came late to the cause. Relief agencies, as well as disarmament groups, had been fighting for years to ban these hideous weapons. The Mines Advisory Group (MAG), which currently administers 1,800 indigenous deminers around the world, was founded in 1990 by former British military engineer Rae McGrath, who also launched what later became known as the International Campaign to Ban Land Mines (ICBL) in 1991. Diana, however, brought a human touch to the problem. Suddenly, people around the world began feeling a collective shame.

Land Mines Are Designed to Maim

Land mines are a cheap and highly effective way of stopping armies from advancing and remain active for years or even decades. They are a small type of bomb planted just under the surface or on the ground, laid randomly and almost never mapped. Typically, they explode when someone steps on them or walks into a trip wire. Most are not made to kill people, just wound them by blowing off a foot or a leg.

An estimated 26,000 mostly innocent civilians are killed or maimed every year by land mines in former war zones around the world. Land mines kill 800 people a month, maim another 1,200, and worldwide it is estimated **there are 250,000 mine-related amputees**. UN agencies say as many as 120 million anti-personnel mines remain in the ground in 68 countries, many in former war zones such as Bosnia, Cambodia, Mozambique, Afghanistan and El Salvador. The largest land mine problems are in Angola, Egypt and Iran. In Angola, 1 of every 324 people has been killed or crippled by them.

The fear of mines keeps farmers out of their fields year after year, obliging poor countries to import food. Angola has some of Africa's best agricultural land, but about 1/3 of it is mined. It is the same story in Cambodia, where once-bountiful rice paddies have been abandoned, and years of wild growth now complicates the demining job.

> *We can...remove 100 million mines an arm and a leg at a time, or we can act.*
> — *Axworthy*

Canada's Key Role

Canada has now taken a leading role in the campaign to rid the world of land mines. Four years ago, Canada's foreign affairs department declared that Canada should take a strong stand and diplomatic risks to get global arms control talks moving.

Andre Ouellet, the foreign affairs minister who preceded Lloyd Axworthy, scratched out the prepared text of a letter being sent as a reply to one he had received on the horrors of land mines, and instructed staff to send a reply indicating he personally was in favour of a ban.

In November, 1995, he was asked at a conference on foreign aid if he would support a private member's bill tabled in the House of Commons advocating a ban; to the amazement of his audience, Ouellet said yes. Ouellet's remarks may have irritated then defence minister David Collenette, but it provided the impetus for a new era in Canadian foreign policy: using our moral force for humanitarian purposes.

Without the resources or reach to mount a global crusade, the Canadian government joined forces with an international coalition of 750 human rights groups, churches, aid agencies, children's advocates and veterans' organizations pushing for the abolition of land mines. They enlisted prominent figures to speak out against the scourge. A nucleus of veterans wounded in the Vietnam War also joined together.

Then, when a UN convention to limit the use of land mines ended in failure in 1996, Canada sponsored a conference to build solidarity among countries favoring a global ban.

In October of 1996, the Canadians asked like-minded countries to sign a complete ban on their own. Axworthy proposed a deadline of 2 years for a global ban on the production, sale, transfer or use of anti-personnel mines, which was signed in Ottawa in December, 1997.

From a small start, Canada's initiative ballooned. Britain's new Labour government got on board, then a change in political climate brought France into the fold. The treaty, which was drafted in Oslo, was endorsed by a coalition of more than 1,000 NGO's.

The Holdouts

Some of the world's largest military powers are holding out — including the US, Russia, China and India.

Canada designed the accord so that it can be signed at a later date without watering down the agreement now. In addition, China, once the world's biggest exporter of anti-personnel mines, said that it had exported no mines since 1995. Russia has also voluntarily agreed not to export land mines.

Perhaps the "holdouts" will feel more pressure to sign an agreement since the 1997 Nobel Peace Prize was awarded to the ICBL and its coordinator, American Jody Williams. Russian President Boris Yeltsin pledged his support for Williams' cause, but US President Bill Clinton was unmoved, prompting Williams to declare that he had "abdicated his role as commander-in-chief and let the military set foreign policy."

Meanwhile, the Canadian federal government ordered the army to proceed with the destruction of the last of its stocks. Only a small number — enough to allow soldiers to practice mine-clearance techniques — will be retained.

UN Secretary-General Kofi Annan praised the pact as a landmark in the history of disarmament. It was extraordinary for a substantive international agreement to be achieved — mostly through non-governmental effort — in the remarkably short gestation period of less than 2 years. No matter how many countries sign the accord, however, the world still faces the problem of cleaning up the mines that are already spread across the earth.

Hidden Killers [157]

Number of people killed, injured worldwide, annually:	**26,000, mostly civilians**
Number of mines worldwide:	**100 million in 68 countries**

Egypt:	23 million
China:	10 million
Cambodia:	10 million
Afghanistan:	10 million
Iraq:	10 million
Angola:	9 million
Bosnia:	2 to 3 million
Croatia:	2 million
Somalia:	2 million

Ratio of mines placed to mines cleared:	**20 to 1**
Estimated cost of mine removal around the world:	**$150 billion**

field, but the removal tools are "decades behind the skills and inventiveness of armaments industry scientists."[183] No single method is adequate, but given the right amount of money and international priority, a method for safe, mechanized removal should evolve.

An automated airborne detection system can cover 26 km² in 3 hours. Land mines containing metals can be detected by metal detectors, but most modern land mines are made with plastic explosives. Dogs can be trained to sniff, but their attention span is too short to do big jobs. Detecting heat emitted from the soil in the form of infrared radiation is another method, while ground-penetrating radar is another means. X-rays and gamma rays can also be used successfully to discriminate a land mine from surrounding soil.

The "Mine Guzzler," designed by Sweden's Bofors, is a 40-ton, tank-like machine built to plow fields, detonating mines; the German Mine-breaker 2000 is a 60-ton version with similar technology.

Bofors' "Mine Guzzler"

Using current technology, it will cost $150 billion and 24,000 lives to clear the mines presently deployed.

The Clean-Up Costs

In 1993, 80,000 mines were removed from the ground — while 2.5 million were planted. It cost $100 million to clear those 80,000, or roughly $1250 each. Solid technical and financial leadership from countries like Canada is needed if land mines are to be eliminated.

Canada was one of the 1st countries to help Cambodia start clearing its mines in 1992. There were 52 platoons of Cambodian sappers (deminers) working to remove up to 6 million land mines, and after 1 month they had cleared only 152 of some 2,600 mine-fields. Cambodian sappers earn a starting salary of $210 a month, a small fortune in 1 of the world's poorest countries.

It takes 30 of Canada's best-trained deminers more than a week to clear just 500 square metres, since the mines have to be detected and removed by hand in a laborious process. Canadian-trained deminers are considered among the best, but even so there are casualties. The International Red Cross estimates that, calculated on a global basis, 1 deminer is killed for every 5,000 mines successfully removed.

There are many ways to demine a

Nobel laureate, Jody Williams

Norway Sets the Standard

Norway was the 1st country to announce new funds for programs aiding land mine victims, pledging $150 million to be spent over 5 years. Canada has announced plans to match Norway's contribution. The US has led the world in the humanitarian disarming of mines, spending $215 million since 1993 with plans to raise this to $1.4 billion annually. Without money, the treaty is a shell, and all those mines will stay in the ground, waiting to blow off people's feet and legs. The legacy, however, "is the creation of a loose-knit worldwide coalition of activists who have forged relationships with governments and learned how to get things done," said activist Williams. "There are already plans... to monitor the implementation of the treaty, to ensure that stockpiles are destroyed, that deployed mines are removed within 10 years."

Smoke and Mirrors: A year after 126 countries signed the Ottawa accord, we are still losing ground. "More mines are being laid than are being lifted."
—UN Office for Humanitarian Affairs

Creating a Niche Military

A Global Role

The paradigm, or world view, on which the Canadian military operates is that of peacekeepers. But looking at their organization, the paradigm they continue to operate under is the Empire/Cold War paradigm — going back to when we sent troops to support the Boer War in South Africa through the Cold War when we needed to protect ourselves from attack by the Soviet Union. **We have built a military for a reality that no longer exists.**

If Canada is truly a global player with global interests, how can those interests be served most honourably?

In 1956, Lester Pearson helped to initiate the 1st real UN peacekeeping operation in response to the Suez crisis. Ever since, support for and participation in UN peacekeeping operations has played a prominent role in Canadian foreign and defence policy.

When the Soviet-backed Egyptian government in 1956 seized the Suez canal, Pearson's ability to rally support for a Canadian-led peacekeeping force stemmed from the reality that the world faced an intractable regional dispute that could spiral into a superpower conflict. By demonstrating the necessity of the peacekeeping model of conflict prevention, he won the Nobel Peace Prize and defined for Canada an influential international role that far out-stripped our military and economic resources.

The Trudeau agenda sought to avoid Canadian defence commitments abroad and instead placed emphasis on peacekeeping and issues such as nuclear disarmament and defence industry conversion. Then, when the Berlin Wall fell in 1989 and ended the 45-year-old East-West conflict that had split the world into 2 armed camps, our worldwide military commitments changed.

Today, Canada is the world's 8th largest economic power, with more than 50% of our GDP based on the export sector. Global security these days is largely economic; therefore, our economy not only assures us a place in the world's front ranks, but also calls upon us to be a player. Foreign policy is largely a question of recognizing where and how we can best advance our broadest interests, which most Canadians agree encompass global security, global well-being and global justice in a compatible and complementary fashion.

Canada's foreign policy needs to break out of its Cold War mould. The United Nations mantra that "we" live in an interconnected world where local events have global consequences is a convenient credo for a financially anemic, but bureaucratically bloated organization.

We need new leaders with the Pearsonian vision of Canada as a world player to get us out of ourselves and into the international community where our compassion, multiculturalism, pluralism and commitment to responsible democracy and human rights (flawed as they may be at times) can challenge other countries to change.

> *The quality of housing for the Canadian Forces comes out dead last in comparisons with the US, the UK and Australia.*

Leaderless Military in Disarray

Unfortunately, no one since Pearson has led our military with vision. **The military brass in Ottawa has been described as the most powerful lobby group in the country,** and to leave them in charge of military budget decisions is like having the fox guard the henhouse. Unified in 1967 under then National Defence Minister Paul Hellyer, the process was plagued by, as he puts it:

"...endless differences by way of 5-person committees... About 300 committees met for months to reach a consensus, which was usually rejected by 1 of the service chiefs who had veto power.

"With its unified service, Canada was on the cutting edge of military organization. Sweden decided to follow our example and sent a delegation to Ottawa to get more details — but the attitude they encountered was so negative that they changed their minds.

"How much of this re-emergence of fiefdoms was ambitious self-serving will never be known. Certainly the army's re-establishment of regional headquarters across Canada smacks more of job creation for generals than of military necessity. They have revived the worst of the pre-unification boondoggles. In fact, today's organization is very similar to the one that existed before unification, with all the planning, command and control problems that existed then. A thorough overhaul is needed."

Today, the 67,000 men and women in military uniform continue to be politically leaderless.

Canadian Regular Armed Forces Strength [158]

Year	Navy	Army	Air Force	Total Active Duty
1914	379	3,000	—	3,379
1918	4,792	326,258	—	331,050
1925	496	3,410	384	4,290
1939	1,585	4,169	2,191	7,945
1944	81,582	495,804	210,089	787,475
1950	9,259	20,652	17,274	47,185
1965	19,756	46,264	48,144	114,164
1990 *	—	—	—	87,976
1995	—	—	—	72,079
1996	—	—	—	63,656
1997	—	—	—	66,981

* *Since 1968, Canada's Armed Forces has been a single body composed of what had been a separate army, navy and air force.*

In March of 1997, then Defence Minister Doug Young approved 65 initiatives that would, among other things, raise pay levels, enhance the independence of military police and stabilize the annual military budget at $10 billion — up from its then $9.2 billion. He said he wanted to end further cuts to the Defence budget, to stabilize Defence spending and maintain uniformed strength at 60,000 officers and enlisted personnel.

But no one could have predicted Young's loss of his seat in the election that year, and his replacement by Art Eggleton as Defence Minister. The Defence job has rarely been a career builder — no minister has served a full 4-year term

MISSED!

SOMALIA

GENERAL ROT

Participation in UN Peacekeeping Missions

1947-48	Korea	1989-90	Namibia
1949-79	India-Pakistan	1989-92	Central America
1953-	Korea	1990-93	Afghanistan, Pakistan
1954-	Egypt, Israel, Jordan, Lebanon, Syria	1990-91	Haiti
		1991-	Iraq, Kuwait
1954-74	Cambodia, Laos, Vietnam	1991	Iraq
1956-67	Egypt (Sinai)	1991-94	Western Sahara
1958	Lebanon	1991-93	Angola
1960-64	Congo	1991-94	El Salvador
1962-63	West New Guinea	1991-92	Cambodia
1963-64	Yemen	1991-94	Former Yugoslavia
1964	Cyprus	1992-93	Cambodia
1965-66	Dominican Republic	1992-	Yugoslavia
1965-66	India-Pakistan border	1993-	Mozambique
1968-69	Nigeria	1992-93	Somalia
1973-79	Egypt (Sinai)	1992-93	Somalia, Kenya
1973	South Vietnam	1993-94	Somalia
1974-	Syria (Golan Heights)	1993-94	Uganda, Rwanda
1978	Southern Lebanon	1993-	Rwanda
1986-	Egypt (Sinai)	1994	Dominican Republic
1988-90	Afghanistan	1994-	Haiti
1988-91	Iran/Iraq	1994-	Cambodia

in the past 20 years — but the military will feel the loss of Young. His departure reintroduces instability to the system which, along with a lack of resources, is crippling the uniformed troops.

The DND has long been aware of the need for change. In an internal study last year, it concluded that the command structure in Canadian military and peacekeeping operations is often severely hampered by what it called "the CNN factor" — described as "a reluctance to make decisions because of political and press-related concerns."

Take the case of General Maurice Baril, Canada's Chief of Defence Staff, who got the coveted job because he is a do-nothing bureaucrat who was able to avoid doing anything wrong as opposed to a leader who might have, in the course of doing something, made a human mistake. In contrast to what the media and the Somalia Commission characterized as the horrific flaws in the chain of command that resulted in the wrongful death of a single Somali hooligan, **General Baril, along with UN Secretary General Kofi Annan, were key players in the inaction that led to the death of as many as a million Tutsis and moderate Hutus by Hutu extremists.**

In the highly proactive words of a real leader who has had his hands tied by the Annan-Baril cabal, Major General Romeo Dallaire hit the nail on the head when he said, "The international community is fundamentally racist, so, it ain't Yugoslavia, it ain't next door and not in our back yard, and so what if a million black guys in Africa slaughter each other."

The army is now in horrible disarray; the professional level of competence is on a downward curve, and the trouble is, there is no strong, coherent pro-defence constituency among the public. **The result is a shared sense that traditional military culture has become a relic of the past, leaving a vacuum.**

Eggleton, characteristically out of touch with reality, said that "it is time to turn the page in the history of the armed forces of Canada. It is time to reinstill the sense of pride that most Canadians have in our armed forces."

In the 20th century, Canada went to war because of commitments to its great power benefactors.

For Canada, the world wars were Britain's wars; the Korean and Gulf wars were US wars.

Making War or Making Peace?

Canadians need to decide whether the role of our armed forces is to preserve peace or make war. One difficulty is that combat soldiers are "asked to evaluate and make decisions in peace missions that they would not traditionally be asked to make" in times of combat.

If the military recognized its primary role was to be a peacekeeper, it could then provide a "seamless web" of peace training throughout a soldier's career, including sophisticated ethics courses and role playing that would teach soldiers how to deal with high-stress situations.

The new values reflect a decline in the importance of the warrior culture and the rise of a managerial culture that focuses on political constraints and budgets. The culture converges with the ethos of civilian society rather than the historical ethos of a separate warrior class. The emphasis should be more on policing than war-making, and defence policy should reflect that purpose in acquisitions and in personnel retention, selection and training.

Canada's politicians should focus the military on peacekeeping. Budgeting and acquisitions would be made far easier, and a clear message that Canadian soldiers are not primarily warriors would improve the confused morale of those who choose to remain in uniform.

Military training encourages soldiers to focus on the group rather than on individuals in order to achieve cohesion. While this sort of training "promotes motivation and appropriate behaviour in combat, it can also lead to an ever-widening gap with civilian society."

Peacekeeping and war are not discrete goals for the military. Canada's defence-policy establishment has shown a strong preference for peacekeeping in practice, if not in the allocation of resources. Politicians demonstrate this preference by scaling back their rhetorical and budgetary support for an armed force of warriors, and by regularly committing troops to peacekeeping missions.

How *Not* to Spend $10 billion

Finance Minister Paul Martin's budget called for the DND to spend a total of $9.9 billion in 1998, down from $12.8 billion in 1991. Nonetheless, DND's budget remains higher (after inflation) than it was in 1980-81 when the last budget build-up of the Cold War began.

There is no reason for DND to continue spending as much or more than it was in 1980. Project Ploughshares estimates that a more specialized Canadian Forces could perform the essential military functions that Canada requires with a budget as small as $7.5 - 8 billion per year. If Canada spent the same proportion of its GDP on defence as Germany, our budget would be closer to $7 billion.

Canada deserves more of a peace dividend; redefining the military is the core means to realizing that fully.

The main explanation for the government's seeming inability to make deeper cuts in military spending is its failure to live up to its Red Book promise to "reorient Canadian defence policy and procurement practices to emphasize the key priority of peacekeeping." Instead, the government took the position in its 1994 White Paper that Canada needs to maintain "multi-purpose, combat-capable sea, land and air forces." This means that DND is still attempting to maintain the unneeded full variety of its Cold War-era combat capabilities.

In early 1998, when war looked imminent between the US and Iraq, Eggleton remained out-of-step with reality when he said, "the objective of a multi-purpose, combat-ready force is very relevant today." The irony was that Iraq's threat — chemical weapons — cannot be countered with traditional weaponry. And while DND cries about budget cuts, it continues to make more capital purchases.

A new armoured reconnaissance vehicle called the Coyote is coming into service with an armoured personnel carrier cousin next on the assembly line. Then there is a program to put soldiers in state-of-the-art clothing and accessories. Next on the list will be a replacement for the weary Iltis — a Jeep-type vehicle that is the army's basic transportation — a project bound to run

Canada in the Gulf War

Canada's "participation" in a (potential) attack on Iraq was negligible, thanks to attrition, increasing obsolescence and deep cuts in military spending, senior military brass admitted.

Even though our contribution in the 1991 Gulf War modestly consisted of ground troops guarding an airport in Qatar, and a squadron of CF-18's flying uneventful combat air patrol, we could not even make this commitment now since our flying filling station — for deploying CF-18's over long distances — was grounded for lack of spare parts.

into tens of millions of dollars.

The effort to acquire Britain's 4 mothballed Upholder-class submarines is a clear example of DND's determination to maintain non-essential capabilities. The $610 million cost of acquiring these Edsels is just the beginning. Modifying to Canadian standards, basing, operating and eventually upgrading these vessels **will push the cost up to $5.4 billion over the next 30 years.** The Canadian Forces cannot afford to sink that kind of money into non-essentials, and neither can Canadian taxpayers.

As an example of some real nit-wit thinking, Vice-Admiral Larry Murray, when he was the acting chief of the defence staff, stated that the army and air force heads are behind the purchase and "agree that this should not be treated as a single service issue. We consider the Upholder acquisition a question of maintaining an essential defence capability for Canada."

Project Ploughshares argues though, that "it's a complete waste of money."

The vessels will replace the Canadian Navy's 3 obsolete Oberon-class subs, bought in the mid-1960's and due to be retired over the next 5 years. The 4 Upholders cost Britain more than $2 billion, were built in the early 1990's and have a remaining full service life of 30 years. Farcical military briefing notes cite the 1995 turbot dispute with Spain as a "good" example of the potential use of these subs.

Meanwhile, Canada has been forced to rent a US refuelling plane to get its fighter jets to Europe — something a former general calls an embarrassment for a country that prides itself on fulfilling NATO duties. Having grounded the last of the old Boeing 707's that used to refuel jet fighters in the air on long-distance flights, Canada will have to rent a tanker from the US Air Force to get its gas-guzzling CF-18's to Bosnia, to help enforce the no-fly zone. While on the 3-month mission — which also involves protecting NATO soldiers on the ground — refuelling will be provided by NATO aircraft.

The pressure for change from fiscal restraints, changes in the security environment, and technological innovation are sweeping through every corner of Canada's military; nowhere is this better exemplified than the Air Force.

Canadian Forces

	Regular Force	Reserve	Civilian	Total	Operating Budget (Thousands)
Air Force	13,500	1,650	2,600	17,750	$517,415
Land Forces	20,881	13,701	4,674	39,256	$637,282
Maritime Forces	9,669	4,000	5,591	19,260	$416,449
DND	66,981	25,500	30,500	26,237	$9,916,518

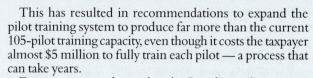

At one point in the 1950's, our Air Force operated a total of 3,290 aircraft. Today "the Air Force is... at the minimum level of its core capability." With military hardware wearing out, **only 83 of the Air Force's 123 CF-18 fighters were able to fly in mid-1998.**

In terms of resources, Air Command controls more than half of the Canadian Forces' base infrastructure and supports many Land and Maritime activities. At present, its facilities include: 14 wings; 11 minimally manned long-range radar sites; 36 unmanned gap-filler radars; 4 minimally manned coastal radar sites (currently being upgraded with a newer version of the long-range radars now installed in the north); and forward operating locations used for deployed NORAD fighter operations.

And then there's the recent nervous excitement by the Canadian government over the purchase of EH-101 military helicopters — just the latest in a series of confused decisions made by the feds on the purchase of major equipment — which are meant to replace the military's ancient Sea King helicopters. *The Globe and Mail*'s Jeffrey Simpson said that Cabinet ministers approach these decisions "as regional barons and political wheeler-dealers." It does not help that this is typical of how the Chrétien government operates, even at its highest levels.

> **It costs the taxpayer almost $5 million to fully train each fighter pilot.**

History points to examples such as the Avro Arrow — scrapped by the Diefenbaker government, the expensive refit and then scrapping of the Bonaventure, the Liberals' hesitation on purchasing the Leopard 1 tank, the Trudeau Liberals' decision to purchase the CF-18 maintenance contract fron Canadair in Montreal instead of the more-deserving Bristol in Winnipeg. As journalist Simpson pointed out, all this makes Canada look like a Third World country — scaring away potential future business.

Another situation where military money is misdirected is that the Air Force currently has a critical pilot shortage as they are leaving in record numbers to join commercial airlines. **The Force expects to be 250 pilots short by the end of this fiscal 1998** — the only time that it has faced such a shortage in its 64-year history, with the exception of WWII.

This has resulted in recommendations to expand the pilot training system to produce far more than the current 105-pilot training capacity, even though it costs the taxpayer almost $5 million to fully train each pilot — a process that can take years.

Desperate to stop the exodus, the Canadian military wants to offer bonuses of up to $75,000. Currently, military fliers' salaries peak at $65,000, while airlines pay as much as $125,000. The military is also spending "marketing" money — even though the overall size of the force has been reduced — trying to attract 4,000 to 5,000 people to cover normal attrition and reorganization.

Further, Canada's military, in a painful and protracted sexual harassment scandal, is now scrambling to attract more women. In 1989, a tribunal of the Canadian Human Rights Commission ordered DND to integrate women into the ranks — especially in combat roles — within 10 years. The only exemption was for submarine duty. Operation Minerva is the code name for a forces-wide attempt to make up for years of not being able to attract enough women into the services. While women represented 9.9% of the forces in 1989, 9 years later the increase was less than 1%, to 10.7%.

Canada's Top-Heavy Forces: Too Much Brass

About half of DND's budget covers payroll. In 1994-95, DND employed 72,670 regulars in its armed forces, 29,464 militia or reservists and 35,522 civilians. Plans are to prune these numbers to 60,000 military, 23,000 reservists and 20,000 civilians. This is not the logical answer, but the self-serving response to the military brass wanting to keep and expand their costly and out-of-date power base.

When large organizations 1st came into being, there were only two models — the church and the military. The Roman legions had squads of 10 headed by one leader, 10 squads headed by a centurion, and following the logic of that span of control of 10, it required 1,111 people to "run" 10,000 troops. In the old model, people were often unmotivated, often uneducated conscripts, and there was a lot of dissent — so they created extra managers.

With today's better-educated, better motivated all-volunteer forces, a different type of management is more appropriate. DND spends $11 billion a year — or the equivalent of the lifetime disposable incomes of 20,000 people — supporting *operational* costs of a military with more officers per capita than any other military in the world. We have more generals than we know what to do with. Canadian Forces has too many officers, some 17,534, or 23%. Only 14.5% of US and UK armed forces are officers. The least top-heavy is the US Marine Corps with only 10.7% brass.

Only 65% of our CF-18's can fly — even if we had enough pilots to do the job.

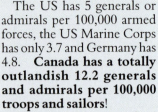

The US has 5 generals or admirals per 100,000 armed forces, the US Marine Corps has only 3.7 and Germany has 4.8. **Canada has a totally outlandish 12.2 generals and admirals per 100,000 troops and sailors**!

The answer is to chop the number of regulars and double the reservists. The militia is already the most cost-effective portion of the military budget. The time has come for Canada to abandon the notion of a large standing army, and have a large militia of citizen-soldiers. Italy and The Netherlands have militias that are double the size of their standing armies. **Canada is the only major industrialized country where the regular Armed Forces is 3 times larger than the reservists.** In the US, reservists are nearly the strength of the regular army. In many other countries (Germany, Belgium, the UK, Norway and Spain) there are significantly more militia than regular military personnel.

Besides culling the ranks, reservists should replace regulars because, when activated, their salaries and expenses are only 55% of the compensation given to regulars. Since WWII, reservists accounted for 3.3% of the person years paid for and produced 25% of the peacekeepers.

The fact that Canada's military is top heavy makes it far more expensive than it needs to be. The basic salary for a new recruit in the Canadian Forces is $15,708 a year. After 4 years, a private can be earning as much as $26,916. Corporals — by far the largest group of non-commissioned officers — earn $33,996 a year. About 25,500 (37%) of the troops fall into these 2 ranks.

Military wages were frozen in 1991; since then there have been reports of privates relying on welfare and charity to make ends meet. A DND study admits that poorly paid soldiers and sailors, forced to moonlight or line up at food banks, are among those most prone to family violence.

What has further "gutted" the regular troops is that, even though they have been waiting since 1991 for a pay increase, $4,000 bonuses were paid out to 498 generals, colonels and some lieutenant colonels last year. Minister Eggleton has insisted, however, that he wants to raise pay scales for all members of the Canadian Forces and civilian defence employees now that the government has eliminated the deficit.

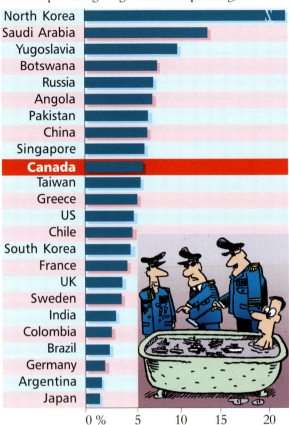

Defence Spending

As a percentage of government spending, 1998

North Korea	22
Saudi Arabia	13
Yugoslavia	9.5
Botswana	7
Russia	6.5
Angola	6.5
Pakistan	6
China	6
Singapore	5.5
Canada	5.5
Taiwan	5
Greece	5
US	5
Chile	4.5
South Korea	4
France	4
UK	3.5
Sweden	3.5
India	3
Colombia	2.5
Brazil	2.5
Germany	2
Argentina	1.5
Japan	1.5

Peacekeeping and Natural Disasters

We have a military failing in its preparation against threats that no longer exist. Canada's defence-policy establishment has a strong preference for peacekeeping, our world image reflects this, and the Canadian public has shown its appreciation and pride in a military specializing in peacekeeping and disaster relief.

Who was not touched by the sight of Winnipeg natives waving good-bye to soldiers who had worked to sandbag the city when the Red River flooded its banks in 1997? The soldiers said it touched their hearts, too, to know they were really appreciated. They were also called in during the famous ice storm in Ontario and Quebec in 1998. It is interesting to note that of the 15,000 soldiers called in to help, 4,000 were reservists.

And as far as peacekeeping goes, Canada is the only nation in the world that has participated in *every* UN peacekeeping operation. Our military does this beautifully, with an even-handed, efficient, progressive mentality.

In Haiti, Canada has provided offices and equipment to a special 90-member SWAT team approved by the UN Security Council to rescue other UN police in case of trouble. The special emergency team is part of an international civilian police contingent that remains on the island since the departure of Canadian and Pakistani troops. Canada contributed 700 of the 1,000 peacekeeping soldiers stationed in Haiti and, with their departure, our 2,000-member contingent in Bosnia remains as our lone large-scale peacekeeping force currently abroad. Canada has also been a major player in supporting the UN's plan to create a permanent international court for genocide and war crimes.

While the government's actions suggest it wants the purpose of Canadian soldiers to be peacekeeping, this constabulary role has not been formally institutionalized. The peacekeeping purpose should be made overt. Most important, the military should strengthen its ability to preserve public order against domestic threats and natural disasters. For this, Canada requires firm but measured ground troops whose methods and training dovetail with the blue-beret role.

International Criminal Court

In mid-1998, 120 countries, led by a Canadian chairman, Philippe Kirsch, approved an historic treaty creating the world's 1st permanent war-crimes tribunal, the International Criminal Court (ICC). The 50-year effort to create a court, based on the Nuremberg Trials set up to prosecute Nazis, will have jurisdiction to try cases of genocide, war crimes, crimes against humanity and crimes of aggression. The ICC will have jurisdiction over *contemporary* crimes but will not have any retroactive authority.

The Negatives of Peacekeeping

There is a downside to peacekeeping — particularly if Canada does not train its soldiers specifically for this role. When members of the Airborne were deployed to Somalia, the soldiers were not prepared for the task and that failure was costly to the Canadian reputation.

Peacekeeping is nerve-racking, too. About 1 in 5 peacekeepers comes home with some psychological consequences of the tour of duty, including depression, recurring nightmares and lack of interest in family affairs. A study suggested 15% probably had post-traumatic stress disorder when they returned home. It also showed that only about 3% had the condition before they went — matching the rate in the general population.

Creating a UN Legion

UN-directed military field operations have been dismal failures. The complex bureaucracy creates fuzzy mandates among incomparable sub-components that have consistently failed to act in a decisive manner. The inability to curb Serbian aggression in Bosnia or Kosovo is sad but pales in comparison to inaction in Rwanda (See page 94), Angola, Mozambique and the Sudan.

This has led to proposals to create a permanent standing force of approximately 44,000 troops divided into 4 brigades, and a field support structure to complement and augment member-state contributions to peace operations. Such a force would be under the direct control of the Security Council and would address the barriers to rapid deployment.

The proposed mechanisms to manage such a force tend to reek of bureaucracy, but the concept is not without merit. Key problems are establishing compatible communications systems and bridging language and military culture barriers.

Under the circulated proposal, all personnel would be volunteers from member states. Field officers would be recruited from individuals leaving national service. Such a force would be supported, at least initially, by officers seconded from active duty and located at 3 or 4 bases chosen to facilitate global reach. The total cost of such an operation would be about US$3.5 billion or about 0.5% of present global defence expenditures.

The Battle of the Medak Pocket

The Canadian army's biggest battle since the Korean War was the obscure 1993 Battle of the Medak pocket — a 16-hour combat in which a battalion fought a Croatian force to a standstill in the former Yugoslavia.

The Canadian battalion, almost half of whom were reservists, was reinforced by a pair of French army companies as they exchanged rifle and machine-gun fire at ranges as close as 150 metres, endured heavy shelling and mortar fire, and made their way through mine fields.

All told, 27 were killed or wounded in the Croatian army, 4 Canadians were slightly injured by shrapnel, and 16 civilians — whose bodies were picked up by the Canadians — were murdered.

Worst Practices

New Submarines for the Canadian Navy?

The decision to spend $610 million on 4 mothballed British Upholder-class subs, built in the early 1990's, is seen by the DND as necessary to maintain membership in the NATO "club."

The heads of the army, navy and air force have put aside their traditional rivalries to support the purchase of these expensive and unneeded toys. Former Defence Minister Doug Young and the current minister, Arthur Eggleton, warned of "grave penalties" if the deal did not go through. They argued that, "Canada's military commitment to NATO will be questioned if the purchase does not proceed."

This exceptionally lame reasoning is based on the Liberal government's 1994 Defence White Paper, which includes the requirement for combat-capable forces *including submarines*. Critics argue that these subs are dinosaurs of the Cold-War era and represent a complete waste of money. Like the standards of Roman Chariots (see page 10), the government is failing to stop and ask the zero-based question, "Why do we need submarines today?" DND briefing notes make the ludicrous assertion that the subs would have been of great value in Tobin's 1995 Turbot Fishing War with Spain! Would this also be equally, and as absurdly, true for BC Premier Clark's on-going Salmon War with the US?

There is no rational answer, other than to say that it will keep admirals (and generals) happy and will make sure that Canada can keep its commitment to NATO — a notion that has been (hopefully) discredited by your understanding of paradigm shifts and zero basing.

Myths: Why Canada Needs Submarines

Submarines are being operated, purchased or developed at a rate that, by 2000, will see some 49 nations operating well over 600 subs worldwide.

Without debate the best defence against a submarine is another submarine. The following statement has to be one of the most outlandish things ever said:

"The potential for escalation to hostilities between naval forces during the Turbot Crisis in 1995 was probably reduced by the deterrent value that Canada's submarines add to Canada's maritime forces."

—Vice-Admiral G. R. Maddison, Chief, Maritime Staff at National Defence Headquarters

Potpourri

HEY LOOK... IT SHRUNK...

SOMALIA

Manitob

*Why not fight war as hard
as wars are fought?
Why not defeat war?
It makes sense. We could win.
It would be the last good war.*[182]

Worst Practices

Coast Guard College Waste

The Canadian Coast Guard College is scrambling to cut costs and increase revenues after an internal review found it was spending $84,000 a year on each cadet.

With an $8 million annual budget, the college is overbuilt, overstaffed and spends about 5 times as much money to train students as comparable institutions.

The College, located in Sydney, Nova Scotia, has not enrolled any new officer cadets since 1996, as the Coast Guard fleet shrinks due to federal deficit cutting.

The review concluded that the cheapest solution would be to close the school and contract out teaching to other facilities.[160]

Worst Practices

The RCMP Does Not Want to Share "Toys"

The RCMP wants to spend $8.5 million on a fleet of 10 armoured vehicles so that it will not have to borrow them from the military, as it did during a standoff in BC in 1995. They have already entered into short-term leases on 4 of the vehicles. An RCMP spokesperson said that the vehicles are needed for a wide variety of applications, from rescue operations to crashing barricades.

This amount of money would purchase 8,500 computers for our schools, or any number of more important items for the social safety net. This is a dangerous precedent to set; what we do not need is more military equipment or the RCMP developing as a paramilitary force on its own.

Share your toys, kids, and let us put that money to better use.

The Most Important Advances in the 20th Century [161]

• The structure of the atom, quantum theory and relativity, which have provided the foundation for our understanding of atomic fission and fusion, the atomic and hydrogen bombs, the peaceful uses of atomic energy and our understanding of the nature of the universe.

• The discovery of penicillin, antibiotics and the structure of DNA, which have revolutionized medicine, helped create the new field of genetic engineering and are poised to provide humankind with solutions to many of its health and food problems.

• The discovery of the transistor and the development of semiconductor technology. This has driven the information age.

• The discovery of the laser and the amazing impact it has had on our lives, from eye surgery to "star wars" to the supermarket.

• The materials revolution – not attributable to a single scientific advance but encompassing the design and assembly of everything from plastics (we are in the plastics age – when it is foreseeable to have an automobile made out of plastic) to superconductors.

• The invention of the computer, which is closely related to the invention of the transistor and laser.

I worry that we are losing our sense of collective responsibility, that we are losing our interest in the public interest.[162]

The Impact of Our Antiquated Theories of Education

> The great country, the great society,
> the great community is, first of all,
> the well-educated country,
> the learned society,
> the community of excellence.
> The nation knows it, proclaims it,
> even rhapsodizes about it.
> Then it busies itself with other matters.
>
> — *Benjamin Barber*, An Aristocracy of Everyone

GRADUATION DAY

REAL LIFE 101

*If an unfriendly foreign power had attempted to impose on Canada the mediocre educational performance that exists today, we might well have viewed it as **an act of war.***

163

We have a 19th century agrarian paradigm for education – developed during the time of the little red schoolhouse. At the turn of the 20th century, 85% of the people were involved in agriculture, and the school year was designed around when they needed help on the farm. Consequently, these days we do not keep our children in school for as many hours as other countries. If you were going into business, would you design a company that had your bricks and mortar empty for almost half the year?

There is a massive failure in our school system. From 1966 to 1991, the composite score of grade 8 students taking the Canadian Test of Basic Skills — measuring performance in language skills and mathematics — dropped by 6.3%. Of high school graduates today, 30% cannot read simple English, and 36% cannot perform simple arithmetic. Canada's high school dropout rate of 30% is one of the highest in the industrialized world. Who is going to hire someone who cannot read simple English and do simple math? These are staggering numbers, given that we pay absolutely top dollar for our education systems.

We should zero-base the school system for the information age. The attempts at school reform have been both sorely disappointing and sadly predictable, and the problems extend well beyond crumbling infrastructure. If children had top-notch teaching staff, administrations that used funds efficiently, and effective curricula, maybe they would be doing all right. But they do not, and they are not.

It is ironic that the 1 academic credential that is proven to affect teacher quality — a bachelor's degree in the subject being taught — is not required by public schools. A Harvard professor has shown that the more a teacher knows of his subject, the better his students tend to perform.

Great Expectations:

The Need to Reform Canadian Education

High standards are not about curricular bells and whistles; they are about ensuring that high school graduates have the basic skills and knowledge to be productive workers and informed citizens. More than 80% of teachers think removing chronic misbehavers would substantially improve kids' education.

School officials slack off on discipline because they want to keep students in school, they do not want to lose the funds they receive on a per-pupil basis, and there is the fear of lawsuits from aggrieved parents. Disruptive students often go unchallenged for the same reason as bad teachers are not challenged — schools do not want to spend years in court defending their decisions.

Parental involvement is perhaps the most important determinant of a student's success in school. In many schools, parents are made to feel unwelcome by teachers and principals who are too busy, or fearful that parents will challenge their authority or the system.

Not just parents, but the entire community needs to get involved. Schools need an explosion in this kind of volunteer activity, particularly for labour-intensive services like tutoring. When a civil servant or an office manager or an engineer comes to school, students are exposed to worlds they might never have seen. There are retired and semi-retired people who have lots of wisdom. But it is the teachers' almost exclusive purview about what comes into the classroom, making it difficult to add these valuable resources.

There is a study about a frog and its ability to adapt in which the frog is put in a shallow pan over a burner, and the heat is gradually turned up. The frog, thinking it can adapt, will stay in the water until it dies, rather than jump out of the pan to save itself. This is a strong analogy for what is happening in our education system today.

Instead of adapt, adapt, adapt, we need to have a fresh start.

The real issue of education is developing human capital.

We expected less of our young people, and they gave it to us.

163

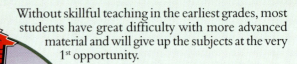

The good news is that virtually every young Canadian has access to basic education. Furthermore, we rank 2nd only to the US in the proportion of our population continuing to college or university. There is nothing wrong with our raw material. But we need to reform Canadian education in fundamental ways if we hope to make our way successfully into the 21st century.

The Economic Council recently warned that failure to correct the serious ills of our educational system would mean that **Canada's schools will graduate a million functional illiterates during the next decade** — a social and economic catastrophe for which there is no quick fix.

Eliminating Antiquated Concepts and Practices

We are teaching content, instead of teaching how to learn. Education's purpose is to replace an empty mind with an open one.

The illiterate of the 21st century will be those who cannot learn.

People have to be able to learn how to learn. To date what has passed for education reform is the equivalent of repairing a horse-drawn buggy rather than replacing it with a high-quality automobile. The key missing ingredient is the lack of political will to act in the face of a group of well-entrenched Luddite interests that are dedicated to defending the status quo.

Canada must get on course to create the human resources development that will lead to success in the demanding times ahead.

• **A national focus on basic skills plus science.**
The school curricula must become a national curricula with a focus on reading and writing literacy, numeracy, and computer literacy — contemporary versions of the 3R's. Additionally, there must be far greater emphasis on mathematics and science.

• **Demanding higher teacher qualification.**
The qualifications of science and math teachers in the elementary grades need significant improvement. One study found that in Japan, for example, these teachers are drawn from university graduates whose mathematical skills rank in the top quarter, whereas in North America, elementary school math teachers — notwithstanding many exceptions — tend to come from the bottom quarter of math and science skills.

> *The greatest myth is that once upon a time there was a golden age, a time when schools maintained rigorous academic standards, when all children learned, when few dropped out and most graduated on time. That golden age never existed but that doesn't mean it isn't a worthy goal.*
>
> — *Marguerite Jackson,*
> *Toronto District School Board*

Without skillful teaching in the earliest grades, most students have great difficulty with more advanced material and will give up the subjects at the very 1st opportunity.

• **Spending more time in school.**
The typical school year in Canada is only 170-190 days. The school year in Japan is about 240 days; in most European countries it is at least 225 days. The longer school year in most countries means that young people get at least 25% more basic education.

• **The need for national standardized testing.**
A basic fact of human nature is that the prospect of an examination creates greater motivation to consolidate and master the material. National standard testing in the core subjects of the high school curriculum *integrated with computer literacy* is imperative. And a common set of nationwide tests would provide the objective data needed to evaluate the performance of students, teachers and schools as well as the school systems.

Rigorous, broad-based testing is the norm in many countries, as it once was in ours. Most importantly, rigorous testing parallels the realities of a globally competitive world. Ekos Research found that 95% of those surveyed support national educational standards.

The US Foreign Service pays for the children of staff serving in Canada to attend private high schools at a cost of more than $10,000 per student. Why? Canadian public high schools in most provinces have no standardized tests, and it is difficult for their graduates to secure access to good American universities.

Once students face the world of work, they are required to meet standards of performance that are now being set by the best global competitors. We do our students a disservice by attempting to shield them from the reality of competition and high standards of performance.

• **Putting competition into the education system.**
It is unrealistic to expect that public schools will reform themselves. This is why there is increasing interest in putting some real competition into the system.

One way is to give parents much freer choice. As examples, Vancouver and Edmonton have had some positive experience with this approach. With freedom of choice, schools that succeed in attracting more pupils would be given greater financial support. Parental choice will only be effective if there is enough data — including broad-based test results — to evaluate and compare schools.

If we farmed today like we educate today, we would all be starving.

Problems and Tensions

These suggestions require substantial investment and profound changes in the role of learner and educator. Consequently, certain problems will need to be addressed, such as formal versus informal approaches to learning, real access in a climate of limited resources, and viewing education enterprises as a short-term businesses or as long-term strategic investments in people.

Barriers to Educational Reform

For our impatient society, perhaps the biggest difficulty is to set our mind to a task whose payoff is measured in decades, not in days or weeks.

Barriers to fundamental reform in education have been very well constructed. Public education has been fragmented among provincial jurisdictions and too many school boards. We face powerful institutional resistance from a system that is dominated by unions and bureaucratic administration and where too often seniority more than merit is the criterion for advancement.

The fundamental problems facing our education system are rooted in the very nature of our society. When both parents have to work, there is less time and energy to provide the necessary encouragement and supervision at home. The problems of child poverty and the single-parent household only complicate matters further. Our society has failed to deal honestly with the consequences of this reality. Instead, we have implicitly foisted far too many social responsibilities on our schools. In the process we have compromised their educational objectives and exceeded their professional competence and commitment.

Because it presents a defined institutional target, that in theory is subject to political control, the public school system has been the focus of most would-be reformers. However, to create a learning society — a society in which education is a life-long process — we must address each phase of human development. The crucial transition out of grade school is poorly managed, and the result is disillusioned dropouts who end up in dead-end jobs or on welfare.

Alternative Certification

Requiring education degrees for teachers makes as much sense as blackballing actors who did not go to acting school. It would be more sensible for public schools to hire teachers based on subject knowledge, enthusiasm, and ability. Some teacher training is necessary. As Jonathan Schorr wrote, "developing and executing a good curriculum is about as simple as composing and performing a good symphony." He suggests an initial training period should be short — as little as 8 weeks. Then, novice teachers should be joined with a mentor, or "master teacher."[164] Recruiting, training, and encouraging good teachers will go a long way toward improving public schools — but not far enough. *A key task is to get rid of teachers who are not doing their jobs.* But the tenure laws that govern public and denominational schools make firing teachers expensive and as painful as removing an impacted wisdom tooth.

The Uglier Task

Although police and school boards move quickly in cases of physical or sexual abuse, assessing and improving the performance of a dull or incompetent teacher is a time-consuming exercise. At best, a poorly performing teacher may be quietly shuffled off to another school, but the transfer usually takes at least a year.

If a principal rates a teacher "unsatisfactory," it provokes the wrath of the union. Throughout the country, unions use their formidable political clout to perpetuate the status quo. Bad teachers make for more work and less respect for the good ones. But the problem runs deeper than just bad teachers. Even good ones have no outside incentive to do the job well, because they cannot be fired or even seriously disciplined. Teachers do have a legitimate worry about principals abusing their power to hire and fire, so why not involve teachers in personnel decisions?

Canadian teachers teach as few as 172 days a year, but the average worker works at least 240 days. **Teachers are also paid a year's wages, but work a full 14 weeks less than the average worker.** Teachers are well paid, but why are they not doing their job?

For many teachers, the word "anemic" fits beautifully. The system grinds them down; it is not that they do not care, but somehow the system sucks the life right out of them. The 1st step towards a solution is to eliminate tenure. Offer new teachers a 1-year contract, then, if they do well, a 3-year contract, and after that, maybe 5-year contracts. And require general, subject matter, and solid computer competency exams as a condition of re-certification.[164]

Those in control have evolved remarkably effective tactics of self-preservation.

How Many of the Young Are Really Unemployed?

The Canadian Imperial Bank of Commerce says there are almost 500,000 jobless youth who are not counted in StatsCan data.

StatsCan does not include many 15- to 24-year-olds because, to be counted in the unemployed part of the labour force, a person must be *seeking* work, and these young people are not. This definition and measure of unemployment complies with the standards set out by the International Labour Organization and is used by all G-7 countries.

CIBC warns that policy makers should take into consideration the 225,000 dropouts, as well as the other 225,000 officially not counted as unemployed, who are no longer in school but are not actively seeking work.

However, if the official jobless rate did not include high school students in the 15-19 age group who are seeking work, but whose main activity is learning, the unemployment rate for 15- to 19-year-olds would drop from over 20% to about 8%.

Classroom Math 24

Ontario tops the provinces in money spent per student,
(1996 -97 data excluding capital costs)

	Elementary & Secondary Enrolment	Percentage Change Over 5 Yrs.	Total $ Spent Per Student
BC	608,667	+9.1	$6,074
Alberta	522,344	+5.7	5,265
Sask.	193,549	- 0.9	5.522
Manitoba	202,889	+0.8	5,749
Ontario	1,914,934	+3.2	6,915
Quebec	1,032,592	- 2.6	6,736
NB	125,018	- 5.0	3,757
NS	153,864	- 2.0	5,019
PEI	25,230	+2.7	4,482
Newflnd.	99,786	- 12.8	5,576

We Spend Enough on Education

In Canada, we spend as much money on public education as any nation in the world (about $55 billion annually) — **the highest per capita among the G-7 countries**. Our spending per student is more than 7% of our GDP. Despite being big spenders, our results are not better — and are frequently worse — than in many comparable countries. Our problem is that we have to spend our education dollars more effectively.

Research shows what common sense tells us: Money matters. Princeton researchers have shown that the more money spent on students' education, the higher their wages are likely to be in the future.[165] The "equalization" movement, pooling tax money at the provincial level for more equitable redistribution, is a step towards alleviating discrepancies in teacher salaries, school facilities, and supplies.

Lacking proper funds is not an excuse to do nothing now; many reforms, such as changing certification and tenure rules, would cost nothing. Part of the answer is to eliminate the kind of wasteful spending that has been tolerated:

• Cost of administration as a percentage of total school board expenditures has more than doubled since the early 1960's. **In Ontario, more than 40¢ of every education dollar goes to sustain non-classroom activities.** Meanwhile, students hold bake sales, sell candy bars and wash cars to finance field trips.

• Expenditure per student, during the past 3 decades, has increased more than 230%. Demographer David Foot says that, as the boomers passed through the system and were replaced by a smaller group, school boards failed to remove funds from the level with shrinking enrolment and pass the money to the next level, where enrolment was expanding.

At the post-secondary level, students who either drop out or take far too long to complete a degree squander scarce resources. Resources are also wasted on antiquated teaching methods and programs that are not needed in the real world of work.

Privatization — contracting out schools to for-profit companies — has not enjoyed notable success in Canada so far. But the idea of vouchers — giving parents the money to send their children to public, private or denominational schools is gaining momentum. It is no coincidence that the people who set the agenda choose private schools. But these prominent individuals, by neglecting the crisis in public schools, are guaranteeing that the conditions that made them flee the public system will last, and possibly worsen, for the next generations.

One solution is to restructure. School-level restructuring includes changes in teaching methods, curricular materials and/or assessment procedures. In contrast, district-level restructuring focuses on decentralizing decision making. Decisions about roles, resources and personnel are given to the schools. This is called school-based, site-based or local management. Whatever the approach, restructuring embodies the principle of local autonomy within provincial parameters.

Restructuring will not work, however, unless there is a true divesting of power. Concomitantly, resource distribution must be in proportion to the degree of devolution.

As society segregates further into privileged and disadvantaged enclaves, the need for public schools that work becomes even more urgent. The loss of public schools would be a severe one because they provide a common space where children of all backgrounds meet, interact, and learn to understand one another.

Results of the TIMSS for Grade 8 16

Rank	Mathematics		Science	
	Country	Score	Country	Score
1	Singapore	643	Singapore	607
2	South Korea	607	Czech Republic	574
3	Japan	605	Japan	571
4	Hong Kong	588	South Korea	565
5	Belgium (Fl.)	565	Bulgaria	565
6	Czech Republic	564	Netherlands	560
7	Slovakia	547	Slovenia	560
8	Switzerland	545	Austria	558
9	Netherlands	541	Hungary	554
10	Slovenia	541	England	552
11	Bulgaria	540	Belgium (Fl.)	550
12	Austria	539	Australia	545
13	France	538	Slovakia	544
14	Hungary	537	Russian Fed.	538
15	Russian Fed.	535	Ireland	538
16	Australia	530	Sweden	535
17	Ireland	527	US	534
18	Canada	527	Canada	531
19	Belgium (Fr.)	526	Germany	531
20	Thailand	522	Norway	527

Making a Successful Transition to Workplace From Classroom

Our school system pays too little heed to the 70% of students who are not bound for college. One of the most significant shortcomings has been a failure to connect the traditional school experience with the requirements of the working world. Too often, the school dropout is simply the unmotivated student who cannot see the relevance of school.

The real test of schools' success will be the preparation and the motivation they impart to this majority — the average students. Surely the way to engage this majority is to provide contemporary vocational education alternatives that are rigorous, relevant and respected. Justifiably renowned, the German dual-track system of apprenticeship is 1 of several successful models. In The Netherlands, about 1/3 of Dutch students enter vocation-oriented schools at age 14.

It will not be easy to erase the cultural bias in Canada, but unemployable university graduates are living testimony to the value of a stronger vocational orientation. We should start by boosting the quality of elementary and secondary education so that a university degree is no longer needed simply to provide an adequate base of intellectual skills. The vocational system could then be made challenging and equipped with sufficient resources.

While we have a jobless rate stuck near 9% in Canada, industry is crying out for people with high-technology skills. Canada's school systems are turning out legions of young people who are destined for chronic unemployment, while some of the country's best jobs in new technologies are going unfilled.

It is essential to expand the growing contacts between businesses and schools. Led by our increasingly relevant community colleges, co-op programs have made some solid progress. This is built on the successful university co-op movement, in which Canada now leads the world in per capita participation.

In the US, the corporate sector has become increasingly involved in funding educational initiatives and seeking input on matters of curriculum.

The problem is that for many years, unions and school management alike were opposed to co-ops. When students return to school from a work term, they can tell their teachers, "what you're telling us is wrong and does not reflect the current practices."

Some of the critical issues are seen at the high school level, where teachers have typically had no experience outside of the school system. It is a minority of Canadians who even go on to college, and in the high schools they are taught by people who "have very little idea of any path through life other than through a university."[184] Some institutions are coming to the conclusion that they need co-op programs for faculty.

In the old model, research was separated from development, an approach that is best replaced today with a formula of lively exchange between industry and academe.

We must also eliminate inter-provincial barriers in the areas of apprenticeship and professional licensing. These self-inflicted costs result in a much less efficient labour market and system of skills development.

Vision of Learners in the 21st Century
168

Modern technologies are having an increasing impact on our learning systems. The range of opportunities has narrowed as technology and global competitiveness divide the job market to low-level service skills needing little education and high-level technical and managerial skills based on post-secondary certification.

If we continue relying on existing assumptions, structures and labour-intensive ways of teaching and learning, and integrating technology into existing structures, already limited resources may decline, affecting learning quality and public confidence.

SchoolNet developed a Vision Statement on Learners in the 21st Century. The statement stressed the goal of education should be the application of knowledge, skills and attitudes for the benefit of society as well as the individual. And there must be a commitment by the community to provide adequate resources.

Interconnected Learning Communities

A new learning system for the future would involve changes in all the interconnected elements of the system:

- Structures are more varied with less emphasis on hierarchies.
- Government is based on the concept of participation of all members of the community in the decision making.
- Funding is diversified but equity is protected by sharing resources.
- Curriculum is built around learning outcomes, clearly defined knowledge, skills and attitudes, together with standards of expectation.
- Industrial design links outcomes to assessment and stresses both individual and cooperative learning.
- Assessment includes evaluation of prior learning and alternative forms of assessment.
- Institutions provide resources and services in a structured learning environment; attendance involves different forms of contact but not necessarily full-time physical presence, and learners may "attend" many institutions simultaneously.
- Some roles now filled by teachers are assumed by non-professionals and para-professionals.
- Technology expands access to learning.
- Research must enlighten policy and practice.
- Evaluation provides feedback on whether we are learning the right things, how well we are learning and the degree of match between learning services and learner needs.

```
C:\DOS.
C:\DOS\RUN
RUN\DOS\RUN.
```

Literacy for the Information Age

It is astounding that 42% of Canadian adults have limited literacy skills. Millions have a hard time with everyday demands of reading, writing, or using numbers. This is a big problem, particularly in the information age. You can survive in the service economy with limited skills, but you cannot flourish in the information economy.

Robert Logan refers to computing as the "Fifth Language," and that the central issue is the relationship between language and learning. Computing is not just a new technology or a new method of communication; rather, it is a way to process and utilize information and represents a new form of literacy.[169]

Literacy problems affect the economy in many ways. For instance, less than half of social assistance recipients had graduated from high school. In 1988, the unemployment rate for people with less than 9 years of schooling was 2 points higher than the national rate.

Meanwhile, even though almost 75% of organizations feel they have a problem with functional illiteracy, in 1991, they provided only 14 hours of structured training per year for their employees. And only 2% was literacy training. Canada's public spending on employment and training programs is 0.5% of our GDP, while Sweden, Germany and Denmark all spend at least twice as much.

International Adult Literacy Survey [170]

In the global economy, literacy has become a worldwide concern. Thus, 7 industrialized countries, including Canada, participated in a project to measure adult literacy skills.

For the International Adult Literacy Survey (IALS), Canada stands about average. The report showed that literacy skills at the low end have stabilized in Canada. As with other countries, there were still many whose literacy skills must be improved in order to give them the opportunity to fully participate in society.

Employment status continues to be strongly related to literacy skills. In addition, the correlation of educational attainment and literacy skill was confirmed. The IALS report also demonstrated that the difference between marginal and advanced literacy skills has an impact on a nation's economy.

As many regional economies in Canada move from a resource to an information base, and as new technology changes the face of employment, workers must have the ability to make major adjustments. Acquiring new skills and knowledge from printed material will prove essential in making those adjustments.

> **No nation** holds a monopoly on a technology, or on the uses of technology in education.[171]

> We should wire every classroom in the country to the Internet by the year 2000 – that is a rallying cry, like President Kennedy's 1960's promise to put a man on the moon by the end of the decade.

Cyber-Assisted Responsive Education[172]

Most people believe that a major transformation must take place in our education system, and that IT should be exploited as part of this transformation.

Logan's study of computers in education concluded that **our schools are part of the industrial-age paradigm, while teaching is being delivered by factory-like methods.** "Millions of schoolchildren are taught the same content in the linear sequential order guided by a uniform curriculum dictated by a centralized bureaucracy."[169]

Because of technological developments, the meaning of physical space has changed. A school principal can address students and the community over a cable channel. A professor can use video conferencing so that lectures may be shared among multiple sites.

It is clear that distance and space will have less and less meaning in the education of the future. Moreover, 1 of the largest impacts of technology on society is the tremendously increased need for life-long learning, as occupations, professions, and jobs constantly change.

The development of hypertext makes a perfect parallel to non-linear learning, where students can progress down multiple avenues of learning simultaneously.

Styles of Interaction

According to the Socratic style of teaching, teachers ask students questions in order to guide them to an understanding and rehearse their knowledge through "drill and practice."

The technology already exists, however, to support fundamental changes in teaching methods and to allow broad collaboration between groups of teachers and students even though they may be widely distributed in either space or time.

The overwhelming anecdotal evidence strongly supports the notion that group activities offer tremendous promise throughout traditional curricula, as well as part of more experimental interventions.

Communal and Corporate Credentialing

Confucius said learning (or education) has no limit (or ending). These days, the issue of life-long learning and continued education has never been more important.

Accredited educational institutions have earned the right to bestow credentials, but as technology has advanced, they have fallen behind in providing skills that new industry sectors require.

For example, universities and colleges should be capable of training students concerning "advanced computer operating systems," but many are not, because of the very rapid evolution of the computer industry and the tendency of institutions of higher learning to remain entrenched in outmoded technologies.

In many cases, commercial companies find it necessary

to take the initiative and provide training themselves. Consequently, Novell has created Network Management Certification, and Microsoft has created Windows Certification, a model followed by hundreds of high-tech companies. Corporations are continuing the trend of teaming up with educational institutions to design and offer degree programs *specifically* tailored to their employees.

As the information age advances, blurring old distinctions between corporate and formal education and between work and education, the role of advanced information technologies will increasingly be called upon to implement and enhance the education process. Network-based solutions will be needed because employees will become more widely distributed. And as the speed of change accelerates, old skills will constantly need upgrading, new skills will need to be acquired and the education process will need to be continued on an on-going basis. Traditional universities must recognize this paradigm shift and begin now to design the means to support industry.

Global Alliances

Some argue that IT is culpable for many of the distressing elements in our society. Nevertheless, there is now plentiful evidence that IT can be a powerful educational tool and a solution to many of the problems we are facing. For example, video conferencing can be viewed as a solution to not having enough teaching resources to cover a large number of distributed learners.

Even though numerous studies have shown the effectiveness of IT in an educational setting, not everyone is convinced that such technology is necessary in classrooms. Consequently, **teacher education in IT is an urgent necessity in teachers' colleges and universities.**

The Television Scenario

Canadian children and many adults watch an average of 4 to 6 hours of TV every day. Many argue that this makes TV a particularly effective educational tool.

Fierce competition between telephone and cable companies has resulted in an acceleration of experimentation in distance learning initiatives of all sorts. Some cable companies have also begun to make cable modems and connections to the Internet available over their systems.

The NC Scenario

A 1995 study found that more Canadian homes had more PC's than any other country in the world. Like US President Kennedy's rallying cry of putting a man on the moon in the 1960's, we should strive to make every *classroom* "wired" by the year 2000. The current goal is to wire every *school* by the year 2000.

A viable alternative to funding PC's is to consider network computers (NC's) — PC shells that do not have hard drives or floppy drives. Instead, they access a network server computer for their information and software. Like all technologies, NC's have their trade-offs, but this is an option worth testing. PC prices continue to drop rapidly, and it is now possible to buy a good, Internet-capable PC, for under $1,000. Software is much easier and less expensive to keep current than traditional textbooks.

The Internet Scenario

The Internet, which grew out of US government defence and research agencies, was 1st designed to be used for communications between research organizations, the military and universities. By 1998, the Internet had more than 2.5 million host sites and about 25 million users.

Many educators now anticipate that the Internet will itself become the major educational force around the world very soon. But, in 1998, students in only about 3-4% of the nation's classrooms have access to the Internet — something that must change immediately.

Conclusion

It is important to consider the inevitable integration of computer and telecommunications media and the implications of the proper interface between the wired and wireless world and the merging world of computer and communication devices in the consumer electronics marketplace. Canadian educators must:
• develop a new methodology of teaching and learning, meeting the challenges of education in the next century, and
• develop a user-friendly media creation facility and a methodology for faculty to produce teaching content in anticipation of non-linear and distance-less learning.

Singapore's IT Advantage

Singapore is earning a reputation as having the best work force in Asia. Its IT manpower grew 4.5 times in 10 years to 18,000 professionals by 1993, with a goal of reaching 35,000 by the year 2000.

The fact that the 1994 World Competitiveness Report rated it as number 1 for its computer literacy rate is no accident. Already boasting a labour force with a literacy rate of 89%, Singapore made the bold move of making its citizens computer literate as well. Schools currently have a computer ratio of 1 for every 15-20 students. By 2000, they hope to achieve a ratio of 1 for every 3. The country's goal is to connect every home, office and school with information technology.

It helps that Singapore is a very small country with only 2.8 million people. It also has a sophisticated infrastructure already in place. The government is luring foreign investment through tax breaks and employee training — and deregulating and liberalizing many areas of the telecommunications market. Adding to its competitive edge is Singapore's ideal proximity to the rest of Asia.

Sophisticated computers will likely displace humans in the same way that work-horses were eliminated by tractors.
— *Wassily Leontief,* Nobel Prize-winning economist

The University of Manitoba celebrates outstanding success... again!

For the third year in a row, students at the University of Manitoba were leading winners of Special Corporate Awards for Canada Scholars in Science and Engineering - winning 11 awards in total. Over the past three years, 46 of these prestigious awards have been won by U of M students. The closest competitor won 26 awards over the same period.

Special corporate awards provide up to $1,500 to the winning student and are based on an outstanding academic record and a demonstrated interest in the field specified in the award. Selections are made by a national panel convened by the Association of Universities and Colleges of Canada.

The following are the 1997 University of Manitoba winners of Special Corporate Awards for Canada Scholars in Science and Engineering:

Glaxo Wellcome Scholarship in the Biological Sciences

Nicole Baryla, *honors chemistry;*
Shikha Mittoo, *honors microbiology;*
Marcello Panagia, *microbiology;*
Tammy Leigh Stuart, *honors genetics;*
Stasa Veroukis, *biochemistry*

Pratt & Whitney Canada Award

Krystal Park, *electrical engineering;*
Natalie Rizkalla, *civil engineering*

AECL Research Award

Michael Potter, *mathematics and astronomy/physics;*
Cristina Spanu, *honors physics*

GE Canada Award

Krystal Park, *electrical engineering*

Governor General's Canada Scholarship in Environmental Engineering

Brea Williams, *civil engineering*

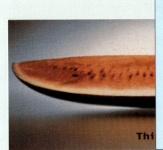

Seated (left to right): Michael Potter, Nicole Baryla, Mar...
Cristina Spanu, Stasa Veroukis, Natalie Rizka...

The Univer...

For more examples of successful U of M s...
or e-mail: bob_armstrong@u...

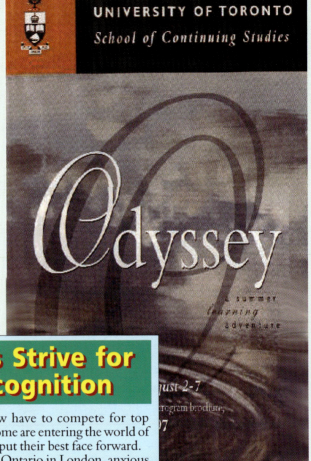

UNIVERSITY OF TORONTO
School of Continuing Studies

Odyssey

a summer learning adventure

...ugust 2-7

...rogram brochure,
...7

...ar@scs.utoronto.ca

Universities Strive for Brand Recognition

Canadian universities now have to compete for top students, and consequently some are entering the world of advertising and marketing to put their best face forward.

The University of Western Ontario in London, anxious to shed its party image, is running a targeted poster campaign in Toronto's subways, bus shelters and youth-oriented media, showcasing top-achieving students to send the message that Western attracts the best and brightest.

Western is a latecomer to a field 1st sampled several years ago by Montreal's Concordia University, which has run year-round ad campaigns in Quebec and Ontario for 7 years, featuring well-known graduates. Realizing the importance of brand recognition, other Quebec universities have joined the fray, including the University of Quebec at Montreal with a set of billboards.

Thi...

Universities: Ending the Medieval Paradigm

niversities have changed less in the last f-century than any other institution, with possible exception of the Catholic Church.
— *Stan Shapiro, Simon Fraser University*

Our universities and colleges — to whom we entrust the education of 1.5 million people — are in dire financial straits. This has persisted to the point where the quality of education has already suffered significantly. Too many of our brightest students have concluded that to maximize their educational opportunities, they must go elsewhere, usually to the US. This is an unacceptable state of affairs.

Most of the fault lies with the universities themselves because their tradition combines both the 19th century agrarian paradigm and the medieval model of scholarly learning. The antiquated tradition of academic regalia, for example, dates back to European universities in the Middle Ages, when caps, gowns and hoods were required for warmth in the unheated buildings. Canada's 1st university adopted these costumes in order to add colour to academic functions and to serve as visible reminders of the historic antecedents of intellectual pursuits.

Maintaining this tradition is typical of universities today, which have remained isolated from the economic realities of the world. Among other torments, unyielding faculty demands have made university administration one of society's most thankless tasks and has attracted some of the least creative "managers."

Professors at York University once enjoyed a "flexible retirement" package considered a sweet deal among universities. This allowed them to accumulate unused sabbaticals (earned at the rate of one for every 6 years' teaching) and get paid in cash instead

of taking them as paid leave, and to work beyond the usual retirement age. These professors also had the right to teach 1 course in each of the 6 years following retirement at a rate of $21,840 per course. At this rate, a professor retiring this year would still be eligible for almost 70% of pre-retirement income.

The administration, faced with tighter budgets, tried to reduce this costly benefit, offering instead the right to teach 1 course for 3 years following retirement at a lower rate of $10,600 — the same pay rate as regular part-time faculty. (Contrast this with Western, Waterloo and U of T professors, who do not have any automatic right to teach after retiring, and if they are invited back, at Western they are paid $8,000 to $10,000, at Waterloo $4,000 to $6,000, and at U of T generally $8,700 per course.)

The response from the York professors was to go on strike. If a business were faced with the same situation, it would discard the disgruntled senior workers and employ cheaper workers as replacements.

Universities might find it easier to follow business' lead if the antiquated concept of tenure — guaranteed employment to insure freedom of speech among university faculty — loses its power.

As budgets are cut and senior, expensive professors retire, they are increasingly being replaced by sessional lecturers. "These are part-timers hired on a 1-year contract for 1 course, often at a salary so ludicrously low that it would be pure exploitation except that the university can afford nothing better," explains pollster Angus Reid.

Meanwhile, a survey of deans and department heads found that universities are losing highly skilled people and gaining only entry-level replacements.

In the past 2 years, Canadian universities have lost about 1,300 faculty through early and regular retirement, departures to foreign universities and the private sector. In the next 4 years, new hires will only keep pace, at best, with departures.

The problem is that our indebted governments are no longer able to fund higher education as generously as they once did. Our institutions of higher education must also face up to the consequences of those bygone days when the government gravy train was under a full head of steam.

With predicable results, institutions are making do with less, resulting in the decline of educational quality. More post-secondary institutions should operate year round, which would allow others to close. Universities have become like breweries used to be in Canada: Every province must have 1, however costly, inefficient and unnecessary.

A major challenge facing post-secondary institutions is simply to obtain the revenue needed to deliver what is expected of them. It would be easier if they enjoyed the same philanthropic support as their counterparts south of the border. For example, the annual income per student at California's highly prestigious Stanford University from gifts and endowment exceeds $20,000. This dwarfs — by a factor of 10 or more — the amount from comparable sources in Canada.

For some reason, the pools of individual wealth in this country have never equaled the US's generosity toward universities. But now that excellence in education and research is increasingly seen as a key for economic success, it is hoped that philanthropic support of universities might increase dramatically. (See pages 107 and 108.)

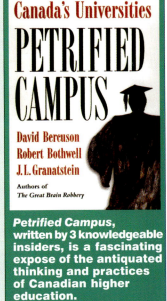

The Crisis in Canada's Universities

PETRIFIED CAMPUS

**David Bercuson
Robert Bothwell
J.L. Granatstein**

Authors of
The Great Brain Robbery

**Petrified Campus, written by 3 knowledgeable insiders, is a fascinating expose of the antiquated thinking and practices of Canadian higher education.
This section relies heavily on this source.**

In this regard, Canadians can be very proud of the Centres of Excellence programs established by Ottawa and some provinces. Realizing that successful innovation tends to be concentrated where a critical mass of research and research infrastructure can be brought together, the programs set up networks among a number of universities, hospitals and the private sector. The Canadian Institute for Advanced Research also has outstanding initiatives, which have shown us how to pool the best research talent across Canada into focussed programs that are tackling many of the most important economic, scientific and social questions of our age.

In addition, the federal government created the Canada Foundation for Innovation, an independent body designed to help renew infrastructure at post-secondary institutions and associated research hospitals. The Foundation will support innovative capital projects in the areas of health, the environment, science and engineering by creating new partnerships among post-secondary institutions, research hospitals, the business community, the voluntary sector, individuals, and provincial governments.

Leading-edge science and research requires leading-edge research environments. The capacity to carry out state-of-the-art research depends upon putting in place modern equipment, installations and communication networks.

Too Many Schools, Too Many Programs

With all the demand to cut budgets, universities are looking at amalgamating or even eliminating whole departments. The selfless search for discovery and devotion to learning that we traditionally expect of universities are no longer enough to support the existence of certain faculties. Some may argue that a good deal of study is a sheer waste of money.

Does anyone really care what happened in the 1st nano-second of the Big Bang, for instance? Is it worth spending billions on supercolliders to find out? Others say that any subject that helps us understand the human condition, or celebrate it, is worthy of the taxpayers' dollars. But who in our university system decides to reduce enrolments or close programs?

Carleton University sparked a campus furor when it announced plans to close some programs. The rationale was not because graduates did not get jobs. Rather, university officials said they needed to cut $5.8 million from the operating budget.

In Ontario, Premier Mike Harris set teeth on edge at the province's universities when he mused about their capacity to chop or change programs to meet the job demands of the economy. He also hinted at performance-based funding.

"Who is responsible for opening or expanding programs in other fields when there are significant shortages in computer science and software engineering?" Harris asked, noting that there are 10 PhD programs in geography and 6 in sociology. "With each individual university autonomous, my challenge to them is how do they collectively make decisions that will ensure a better distribution of courses that are more relevant to the next century?"

Critics of Harris' approach say that "relevance for the next century" is an oxymoron because relevance assumes pertinence "to the matter at hand," and education in the next century is a remote concern. They argue against the Harris premise and the "cult of marketability" — the present drift in higher education towards purposes having less to do with improving young minds than turning students into marketable commodities.

Of the university graduates today who are unemployed or under-employed, the Premier says they took the wrong courses — instead of computer science or engineering, they majored in history, languages, politics, sociology, or philosophy.

In addition to universities offering too many programs (and the wrong kinds of programs), the previously referenced government gravy train of the 1960's and 1970's caused us to end up with more universities and colleges than we need or can afford. And the assumption that the money would roll in forever created a system built on the idea that every university could offer every program.

Now, there is an urgent need to rationalize many overlapping programs in a multiplicity of institutions. A small country like Canada also needs to concentrate academic talent (as in the Centres of Excellence) in order to build the critical mass that is needed to achieve world-class standards.

In Nova Scotia, Dalhousie and the 6 universities in the Halifax area have been forced to form a "Metro Halifax Universities Consortium." In time, there will be a common course calendar, and eventually, a "University of Nova Scotia." Similarly, the province of Saskatchewan is beginning to contemplate merging the Universities of Saskatchewan and Regina.

University of Hawaii

To deal with the problems created by tenure, the administration and the professoriate at the University of Hawaii found a way to make the system work by introducing limited-term contracts. Responsibility was delegated downward to department chairs, peer-based standards were devised, and the review process was constructive.

Contrary to earlier fears, faculty were not written off as "dead wood," but were given an opportunity to improve their teaching and research capabilities on a case-by-base basis.

In the 1st review cycle, 245 faculty were reviewed. Some 15% decided to retire, partly influenced by the review. Of those reviewed, 70% had their contracts renewed, while 22% were judged to have deficiencies in teaching, research, or service that had to be corrected.

These deficient faculty were characterized as those in the mid-career slump, the aging faculty member, the alienated full professor, and the non-functioning professor — the types who poison the campus atmosphere and turn off students by the score.[173]

In Ontario, there will be a multi-tier system of higher education, with the research-intensive universities at one end and the community colleges at the other. In between will be a range of institutions: boutique universities, such as the University of Waterloo with its engineering and math, and Oxford wannabes, such as Trent; big, second-rank schools like York, serving the Toronto suburbs; and regional institutions, such as Lakehead University, meeting the needs of far-flung communities.

Some say that in the next decade, they fully expect to see the emergence of what will be recognized as "ambulatory care" universities to cater to the Canadian penchant for accessibility. At the same time, the "full-service" universities in the Canadian metropolises will attract the best scholars and get the lion's share of provincial funding for their libraries, buildings and courses.

In effect, the universities are at last beginning to go through the process that the private sector and the hospitals have had forced upon them.

Sliding Academic Standards

Not only have we created too many universities — and too many programs within each university — but standards vary widely among programs. At the University of Alberta, nearly 80% of the students in education scored grades equivalent to an A, while less than 40% of engineering students did.

Universities are also admitting too many unqualified students. Today's full-time student population is 5 times greater than it was 4 decades ago — even though the national population has only doubled. The part-time student enrolment has also doubled in the last quarter-century and, while thousands of students still drop out, it is harder than ever to fail. In some institutions, almost literally, the only requirement for a degree is to be present and to turn in the assignments.

Traditionally, admission standards have been used to identify those with the greatest chance of success; to guarantee equitable treatment for admission and scholarships; to certify that a student is qualified for admission to a specific program; and to ensure that the student has the education expected of a high school graduate. Now, however, admission standards have been engineered to allow almost anyone access to university.

Some universities teach and grade for the median student, but because a large part of the increase in enrolment came — and continues to come — from students at the bottom end of the academic scale, the median continues to fall. According to data from the OECD, 10% of Canadian university graduates are functionally illiterate, able to read only the simplest of texts.

Weak students do not seem to enjoy the university experience, either. Indeed, attrition rates among marginal students, thanks to the policy of open accessibility, are staggeringly high. Universities are not doing such students any favour by admitting them. Predictably, the drop-out rates are highest among the very students targeted in the push for accessibility.

One rationale was to open up the university to the historically disadvantaged — the immigrants, the poor, women and other historically maltreated groups. And the

result? At Carleton, 1 Ontario institution that made an effort for open door admissions, the student body remained surprisingly unaltered. According to a 1994 assessment, students were disproportionately male and middle class when compared with other institutions.

This issue is nothing new, as evidenced by a scathing indictment written for *Maclean's* magazine in 1961 by Professor William Cunningham at Mount Allison University:

"My conservative estimate is that 20 to 30% of the number now attending university cannot qualify as students," he writes. "The search for more money to provide for more 'students' is not the only or even the best answer to apparent university shortages. A rigorous exclusion of academic clods is another answer."

He goes on to say that, despite failure rates of more than 50% in required English courses, some students managed to reach 3rd year, although they were unable or unwilling to write sentences "equal to those of a good student in an elementary school." Prof. Cunningham adds that university curricula neglect the student's need for assistance in developing writing abilities, and too much time is wasted on students who are not really interested in mastering these skills. "Their goal is a degree; their hope is a lucrative job. Academic studies are a barrier, reluctantly approached, lowered and circumvented if possible," he writes.

He concludes by saying that there are too many students in university who have no right to be there because they lack the minimum attributes necessary to benefit significantly from the privilege they enjoy. "Let the universities take the example of the football coaches, and politely but firmly exclude the rest," he declares.

As evidence, consider the fact that 50% of the University of Saskatchewan's 450 1st year engineering students failed their calculus exam, as did 37% of those at the University of Manitoba.

> **Remember, it's not who you know in life that makes a difference ...but whom you know!**
> — Steve Forbes, Publisher

Acadia Advantage

Nova Scotia's Acadia University became the most wired educational institution in Canada when it launched the "Acadia Advantage" in the fall of 1997. Every incoming student was issued an IBM laptop; the campus was rewired so that students can plug into the Internet or the university from classrooms, lounges and residences; computer-related learning is now mandatory in every department at the university; and most departments now require students to submit work electronically.

Advantage students pay $1,200 more per year for tuition than the students who arrived before the program was launched, making Acadia's $5,055 annual tuition one of the highest in the country.

Creating Relevancy

Universities and colleges are the logical candidates to provide the retraining that workers need, but, as demographer David Foot says, "offering a course every Monday afternoon for 8 months is not going to help people who have to be retrained in a month."

Several universities are focussing on niche areas with wide appeal to business people. The strength of the University of Calgary curriculum is its entrepreneurial focus — the 90-minute lectures are designed to keep business people up to date on breaking business issues. At Dalhousie, the MBA program is offered in partnership with the Institute of Canadian Bankers. Customized programs are the hallmark of UBC's executive education programs, which run from 1 day to 2 months. McMaster found its own niche in the market by offering its easily adaptable series of shorter modules to businesses that do not have the time or the budget to send people on 3- or 4-day courses. Meanwhile, the University of Western Ontario opened a $20-million business training centre in Hong Kong in 1998.

Industry and Academia

The University of Toronto's management faculty features a joint venture with the Human Resource Professionals Association of Ontario, designed so students can acquire their accreditation either by attending week-long sessions or night school over a 2-year period. U of T's program is just one example of industry and academia teaming up to shape curriculum.

At the University of Calgary, a joint program with the Certified General Accountants Association will allow CGA students who do not hold a bachelors degree or want to earn an accounting-related degree in conjunction with their CGA studies to get a degree through the new bachelor of accounting science degree. U of C's engineering faculty spearheaded a similar program 5 years ago in its "engineering for the environment" program.

Distance Learning

While universities must make their course material more relevant, they must also make it more accessible. Experts predict distance education to expand dramatically, bringing higher education to even more people and at a more reasonable cost.

StatsCan reported that enrolment for distance education has been growing; between 1991 and 1993, it increased by 9%, in contrast to a 6% increase in traditional education.

Accessibility and affordability are going to be more important since it is estimated that 50% of jobs created in this decade will require more than 16 years of education/training. The predicted job market shift means that more Canadians will be at a disadvantage when trying to obtain employment unless they move to improve their education and training. For many of them, that will mean distance education.

The Partnership of Universities and Corporations

Industry and post-secondary institutions are increasingly seeing the involvement of business in education as a necessary tool for building the schools, minds and companies necessary for Canada to compete.

"Certainly, there are...people who are worried about the university becoming the handmaiden of industry," says a UBC spokesperson. "But the reality is that we wouldn't have achieved so much without such partnerships."

• UBC partnered with the environmental company Westport Innovations Inc. to develop a technology that reduces harmful emissions from diesel engines. UBC owns the technology, but has licensed it to Westport; UBC is also paid a royalty and owns shares in the company, although Westport has the right to exploit the technology. From its partnerships, UBC has created 71 companies, attracting nearly $634 million in private investment and creating 1,500 jobs in BC.

• Brock University in St. Catharine's, Ontario — the province's wine belt — launched the Cool Climate Oenology and Viticulture Institute in 1997 with the help of a $5 million investment from local industry and the federal and provincial governments. The industry benefits from having highly trained graduates, while the school is provided with state-of-the-art equipment.

• Hamilton's Defasco Inc. has set up links with several universities across the country, but primarily with local McMaster, in order to address the skills shortage of talented engineers, researchers and scientists with knowledge of the steel industry.

> *We have to build the brand. It's really crucial.*
> *— Richard Ivey School of Business, University of Western Ontario*

Marketing Canada's Business Schools

Canadian business schools are taking an aggressive stance in marketing their products, pouring more resources into differentiating their products in what has become a fiercely competitive environment. The schools are realizing that, as business increasingly globalizes, a new wave of managers has to follow suit.

There are 37 Canadian universities offering MBA or equivalent programs, compared with 700 in the US. Traditionally, Canadians have not marketed their product. Now, boundaries no longer mean much, and schools that cannot hold their own globally will not only lose international applicants, but perhaps some of our own best students.

Called a "cross-border battle for business brains," the education wars are being fought in the boardrooms of multi-nationals — not only the career targets of many business students, but the principal source of supply for lucrative business education courses.

EQ vs. IQ

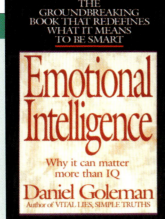

The term "emotional intelligence" was popularized by a 1996 book by Daniel Goleman, a Harvard psychology PhD and *New York Times* science writer. Commonly referred to as EQ, to contrast it with the familiar IQ, the term has its roots in the concept of "social intelligence," 1st identified by the educational psychologist, E. L. Thorndike, in 1920. He defined social intelligence as "the ability to understand and manage men and women, boys and girls — to act wisely in human relations."

EQ researchers Salovey and Mayer defined 4 primary components of EQ:
1. emotional self-awareness,
2. stress tolerance,
3. impulse control, and
4. interpersonal relationship.

When we think of brilliance we tend to think of high achievers who were wired for greatness from birth. However, this does not explain why some natural talent disappears in some and ignites in others. It seems that **the ability to delay gratification is a master skill**, a triumph of the reasoning brain over the impulsive one, a succinct sign of emotional intelligence.

What researchers have been trying to understand is how the EQ and IQ complement each other and how one's ability to handle stress affects the ability to put intelligence to use.

In the words of the director of the Organizational Learning Center at MIT, "People with high levels of personal mastery...cannot afford to choose between reason and intuition, or the head and heart, anymore than they would choose to walk on one leg or see with one eye."

If there is an anchor to EQ, it is a sense of self-awareness. Scientists refer to the ability to pull back and recognize the basic feelings of being mad, glad, and/or sad as "meta-mood consciousness." Meta-mood is a complex skill because emotions so often appear in disguises. A person in mourning may know he is sad, but he may not recognize that he is also angry at the person for dying.

The three R's remain important, but the ability to deal with individuals and groups may be even more important.

In Goleman's analysis, self-awareness is perhaps the most crucial ability because it allows us to exercise some self-control. The idea is not to repress feelings, but rather to be fully aware of them.

Anger and fear are 2 of the hardest impulses to control because of their evolutionary value in priming people to action. Anxiety also serves a similar purpose. The peril comes when excessive worrying blocks thinking.

IQ gets you hired, but EQ gets you promoted.

Perhaps the most visible emotional skills are the people skills like empathy, graciousness, and the ability to read a social situation. Harvard psychologist Robert Rosenthal developed a test to measure an individual's ability to read emotional cues. He shows subjects a film of a young woman expressing feelings, edited so that a nonverbal cue is blanked out. People with higher scores tend to be more successful in their work and relationships.

Like other emotional skills, empathy is an innate quality that can be shaped by experience. Empathy can also be seen as a survival skill. Researchers have found that children from psychically damaged families frequently become hyper-vigilant, developing an intense awareness to their parents' moods.

Goleman likes to tell of a think-tank manager, whose top performers were those workers who were good collaborators and networkers and popular with colleagues. They were more likely to get the cooperation they needed to reach their goals.

Executive leaders are discovering that attention to emotions has been shown to save time, expand opportunities, and focus energy for better results. Studies suggest that it is EQ, not IQ, that underpins many of the best decisions, the most dynamic organizations, and the most satisfying and successful lives.

Q-Metrics of San Francisco has discovered that EQ is learnable at almost any age. All of the EQ-related capacities — often overlooked in traditional management development and training — prove crucial to exceptionally successful work in leadership and organizations.

Goleman notes that there are practical applications in our everyday life for EQ. In addition to its use for hiring employees, it can increase marriage odds, and improve how parents should raise their children and how schools should teach them. Nowhere is the discussion of emotional intelligence more pressing than in our schools. Instead of constant crisis intervention, it is time for preventive medicine.

Students who are depressed or angry literally cannot learn. Children who have trouble being accepted by their classmates are 2 to 8 times as likely to drop out. An inability to distinguish distressing feelings or handle frustration has been linked to eating disorders in girls. If, as data strongly suggest, emotional intelligence determines how successful we become as human beings, it has major implications for our educational system.

The Marshmallow Test

An intriguing experiment tells of a researcher who gives 4-year-olds the option of having a marshmallow right away, or waiting until later, when they could then have 2. While some grab the treat immediately, others last a few minutes, and a 3rd group determines to wait. **By high school, those who held out and waited generally grew up to be better adjusted, more popular, adventurous, confident and dependable.** Those who gave in were more likely to be lonely, easily frustrated and stubborn, buckling under stress and shying away from challenges.

Community Colleges: Work-Relevant Learning

In pollster Angus Reid's book, *Shakedown*, 1 of the myths he dispels is that a good education necessarily means a good job. While Canadians with some post-secondary education earn over 30% more than the average Canadian worker, and those with a university degree earn about 50% more than those with no post-secondary education, even the well-educated are having a tough time finding a good job these days.

"Dentists, who could once expect 6-figure incomes within 5 years of graduation now struggle to find work," he explains. "In 1995, more Toronto dentists went bankrupt than in the previous 10 years."

He cites statistics that say, in 1986, Canadians were evenly divided on whether it was best for young people to learn a skilled trade or get a general university education. But by 1995, those favouring a skilled trade had increased from 39% to 56%, while supporters of a general university education were unchanged at 32%. Studies also conclude that high school students with average academic skills are being misdirected into universities, and then failing to either graduate or develop marketable skills. The belief that most jobs require a university degree is a future-limiting myth. By the year 2005, only 21% of the jobs will require a university degree.

Instead of cranking out an over-supply of over-qualified university graduates, society should direct students to vocational education programs, work-based training programs and apprenticeships, and 2-year post-secondary schools. Students themselves should focus on getting the skills needed to compete for higher-skill/high-wage occupations that do not require a university degree. Technical workers without a university degree will earn higher salaries than all university graduates, except those who find work in the professional ranks. And, as bizarre as it may sound, a well-trained chef will make more money than a PhD with no market-revelant skills.

Sheridan College: World-Class Animators

A star in Canada's community college system is Sheridan College, whose world-class animation centre is internationally renowned. Many of Sheridan's graduates have become leading players in Hollywood's computer animation ranks, while the firm whose software created the dinosaurs in *Jurassic Park* was founded by former Sheridan staff. Recognizing the value of Sheridan's program, the Ontario government has given modest tax breaks and seed money to the centre and has committed money and involved private-sector partners to incorporate the latest digital and multimedia technologies.

Sheridan has also acknowledged industry demand for people who have mastered 3-dimensional design and drafting — a talent that is in high demand, especially among auto makers and the aerospace industry. In Ontario, Sheridan is the only institution offering CATIA (computer-aided three-dimensional interactive applications) education as part of any engineering curriculum. Graduates with CATIA experience can expect 10%-15% more in starting salaries: Boeing Aircraft in Seattle offers a salary of $84,000 to people with at least 2 years' CATIA experience, and the auto industry insists that all of its suppliers and subcontractors submit work in CATIA form.

ISO 9000 Standards of Academia?

Joining the call from business to prepare market-ready graduates, St. Lawrence College in Eastern Ontario blazed a trail, becoming the 1st post-secondary institution in North America to register its academic unit to ISO 9000. The Geneva-based ISO (International Organization for Standardization) created 20 sets of standards by which an organization disciplines itself to determine how good a job it is doing. ISO registration required St. Lawrence, a college that is heavy in technology and health sciences, to analyze its programs and services from a user's perspective. After ISO, St. Lawrence enrolment went up 2.8%, while the rest of the Ontario community college system growth hovered at a stagnant 0.2%.

Market-Relevant Education

Both Humber College and Ryerson Polytechnic University are offering new travel-industry related programs in response to requests from the market. Industry analysts anticipate a growing demand for qualified professionals to handle eco-adventure tours — fast becoming a large component of the travel business. At Ryerson, students can take a 90-hour course leading to an examination and diploma that are recognized worldwide. The Humber course is aimed at people who want to extend their interest in travel into a business by designing and leading group tours.

Working closely with industry to turn out job-ready graduates is not sitting well with everyone, however. Predictably, the Canadian Association of University Teachers launched a global boycott of Tech BC, a newly launched institution that operates 7 days a week, offers no tenure (for now) to staff, and whose board of governors has the authority over business and academic decisions. At most universities, the faculty-controlled senate takes the lead on academic programs, making academic-program decisions for educational, not economic reasons. The CAUT argues that, "the new institution does not offer protections for academic freedom and institutional autonomy contained in other university statutes."

University-College Cooperation

Ontario's largest college and Canada's 3rd-largest universit have reached an agreement whereby some college students wi be able to graduate with a college diploma and a universit degree in 3 instead of 4 years.

Although the arrangement between Seneca College and Yor University is considered a breakthrough in post-secondar cooperation in Ontario, students in Alberta and BC have had long tradition of flexibility in moving between colleges an universities. The York-Seneca deal, which should become national model (currently restricted to the general arts an science program), requires students to study year-round spending alternate terms at each institution.

Paying the Tuition

University administrators and student groups complain that the growing student debt load is becoming an enormous problem. Cuts in government funding have caused the average debt of a post-secondary graduate to rise to $21,000 in 1996, from $13,000 in 1991.

According to StatsCan, in the past 10 years, the cost of university arts programs has doubled, outstripping a 37% increase in the cost of living. Nova Scotia is the most expensive place to study liberal arts: The average tuition is $3,737, compared with Ontario's $3,234 and Alberta's $3,211. The cheapest liberal arts tuition is in Quebec, where the provincial government has frozen fees at 1990 levels — only $1,726.

The Canadian Federation of Students (CFS) predicts that tuition will rise to $25,000 annually within 15 years. Already, they argue, university is losing its accessibility, with higher fees making it increasingly difficult for low-income students to get a post-secondary education. This is reflected in fewer university applications—down 2.5% in 1997. For decades, Canadians have viewed post-secondary education, like universal health care, as a birthright.

Meanwhile, key changes to the Ontario Student Assistance Program (OSAP), which provides loans to about 217,000 students, could add to student debt load. Under the changes, in order to assess financial need, students must report any earnings in excess of $600 (previously it was $1,700) as well as student and spousal assets (including cars worth more than $5,000); students also must take at least 60% of a full-time course load (up from 20%) and must pass at least 60% of their courses to remain eligible.

Loan Defaults: A Tempest in a Tea Pot

The elimination of OSAP grants 4 years ago also means that defaults on OSAP loans are expected to jump due to the greater number of student loans being made. The cost to the Ontario government (the taxpayers) of student loan defaults has quadrupled over the past 4 years. In all, Ontario students owe $99 million on 17,272 defaulted loans, more than double the number in default the previous year.

The federal government has compiled a list of 3,500 of its own staff members who have fallen behind on Canada Student Loan repayments, and it intends to demand that they begin repaying the outstanding debts. National Service is a viable method to to pay down school loans. (See page 109.) Despite all the noise being made, defaulters owe the federal government a paltry $28 million.

Problems with defaulters caused the CIBC to pull out of its lending contract with the province of Nova Scotia because it was too costly. (The CIBC is a major player in the federal government's Canada Student Loans Program.) Problems began when the program ended guarantees under which governments had been reimbursing banks for loans that went sour and replaced them with so-called "risk premiums," under which they are paid an annual fee, generally 5% of the value of the loans written in a given year.

Government's Role

Students and society each contribute to paying for higher education, but what is the fair share for each party? Our traditional assumptions about the public good and private gain of higher education need to be reassessed as reduced government subsidies are forcing individuals to pay for a larger share.

In Britain, the government is scrapping its long-standing tradition of free university.

This means that the 1.1 million full-time students at 90 universities, who now pay nothing for their schooling, must pay their own way or take out loans.

174

MY HUSBAND AND I HAVE TO PAY OFF OUR STUDENT LOANS BEFORE WE CAN HAVE A BABY. DO YOU THINK I'LL BE TOO OLD TO START A FAMILY AT 60?

In Canada, student fees accounted for only 25% of operating revenues of universities in 1995, up from 17% in 1975-1985. Since 1990, tuition fees have grown by 62%, compared to a rise of only 7% for the 1980-89 period. At the same time, however, government funding was 42.7% higher in 1995-96 than in 1981-82.

Every province and territory currently has measures to help avoid or reduce student debt, estimated to exceed $500 million annually. University administrators complain that government is not doing enough. They point out that the publicly funded University of Michigan gets almost twice as much federal funding as the similar-sized University of Toronto. While tuition in the US is higher, its universities have a much larger grant and bursary system because of private support.

A House of Commons committee, using out-of-date logic, recommended that the federal government institute a system of grants, awarded according to a formula that considers both the need and the academic merit of eligible candidates. The ministers agreed that Ottawa should pay its "fair share" of the costs associated with helping to reduce or make manageable student indebtedness.

Liberalized Repayment Schedules

The government has extended from 18 to 30 months the period of time during which students may defer payments on student loans. In addition, students will be able to choose a repayment schedule tied directly to income. Under the income-contingent repayment (ICR) scheme, a student makes no payments when his or her income is low. As income rises, the tax system collects payments automatically, tailored to each student's income. Proponents argue that ICR is fairer than the current scheme, cheaper, and much less open to abuse and default.

University graduates, on average, have lifetime incomes above those of the rest of the population and can afford to pay back their student loans, even given tuition increases. The economic benefits of education accrue chiefly to the student in terms of improved job and earning prospects. Therefore, some argue, correctly, that **the more the cost of their education is borne by the taxpayer, the more this represents a regressive transfer from the less well-off** (e.g. those with no university education or living in poverty or whose children will not attend university) to those who will be at the top of the income pile.

Through the CSLP, means-tested loans are available to a minority of students, and the interest is paid by the government during the course of studies and for up to 3 years after graduation. Repayment is made in the 10 low-earning years after graduation, and the program is essentially administered by the banks.

ICR, on the other hand, spreads repayment over a person's working life and is sensitive to rises and falls in income. Below a certain income level, repayment is suspended, all based on an objective formula. This spreads the risk of low-income non-payers across a bigger pool and eliminates the cost of attempting to target loans at particular groups. Costs are further lowered by using the income-tax system to collect payments.

Although total deregulation is not planned in the immediate future, colleges and universities will be free to set their own fees for graduate and professional programs where job opportunities for graduates are "virtually guaranteed and income after graduation is substantial."

At Queen's University, for instance, the MBA program already charges $22,000 a year in tuition, and the University of Western Ontario is proposing $36,000 as its MBA tuition by the year 2000.

While the CFS calls for a tuition freeze, critics say this will only exacerbate the underfunding problem and lead to a reduction in the quality of education. Others suggest government money might be better spent on cooperative programs with the work experience students say prospective employers value most.

Still, government remedies do not necessarily have to be as direct as subsidizing tuition fees. Government policy can have an impact before students even enter college or university, and long after they graduate. The federal budget changes have made it easier for families to create tax shelters for education savings. And the CSLP spends $192 million a year subsidizing interest on student borrowings — allowing full-time students to avoid paying interest while they are in school.

The Strong Case for Higher Tuition

While many Canadians are calling on the government to spend more on higher education, they leave tuition — the largest and most appropriate source of university revenue — almost untapped.

Although fees have increased lately, for years tuition represented a declining share of the cost of undergraduate education. In Ontario, it dropped from 38% in 1951 to less than 20% today; in Atlantic Canada, from 43% to 23%; in Quebec, from 35% to 14%.

Tuition is nothing more than a user tax. Yet, in the logic of politics, we have somehow reached the nonsensical conclusion that tuition must be kept low in order to protect universal access.

> *Experience in many countries has proven that access to university education is largely unrelated to the tuition charged.*

Disadvantaged students are very common at private US universities, despite annual tuition levels as high as $40,000. Those universities have set aside a portion of their increased revenue to fund scholarships for academically deserving students. **There is no reason why tuition in Canadian universities should not cover as much as 50% of the cost.** Even at that, the fee would be considerably less than the rates charged by many US institutions. Most importantly, students (or parents) who paid more would demand more — another healthy spur to excellence.

Universities have chosen to loosen their standards in order to boost enrolment — they mistakenly believe that they need students so they can maintain their revenues. Consequently, the university degree is being devalued, and the good students are being diluted by the hordes.

One problem is that students are drawn by peer pressure and antiquated family expectations into university programs that do not fit the information age — a tragic waste of resources to the individual, to society and to those of us who pay the bills. Students are flocking to universities. In 1975, for example, just 8.3% of Canadians aged 19 to 24 were in university. By 1995, that had grown to 18.6%. Also in 1975, there were 423,000 full-time equivalent university enrolments (made up of full-time and part-time students). By 1995, that figure had grown to 651,000, even though the population aged 19 to 24 had dropped by 9%.

Being realistic, it is probably too much to expect of either our universities or our politicians — to take the bold step of deregulation of tuition fees alone. We need some leadership and a concerted action from the taxpayers who pay the bill for the abuses of a medieval system and its Luddite administrators.

Subsidizing Foreign Students

Universities find international students financially attractive because they pay twice the fees of domestic students, but this is still a competitive price compared with institutions in the US.

Canadian universities have introduced advertising and marketing campaigns, new scholarships, and a new reliance on faculty and alumni to seek out desirable students. McGill has plans to increase its enrolment of international students to 25% of its undergraduates, and now U of T offers some spots in its dentistry program to foreign students for $21,000 a year.

With English clearly the world's premier 2nd language, English as a Second Language (ESL) programs, once an almost ignored sideline, are now growth centres. The new middle class in Asia and South America, who can afford to send their children for English training, like the fact that Canadian communities are safe and clean, and teaching standards are reasonably consistent.

Ecole des Hautes Etudes Commerciales in Montreal is one of many Canadian universities expanding its international connections to allow domestic students to go abroad and to recruit foreign students to come here. HEC is building reciprocal arrangements with institutions in 21 countries; today, 1/3 of the business administration students graduate with at least a semester of foreign studies.

"Canada is a sleeping giant," states HEC director of student services, Robert Bonneau. Both the European Union and the US have set targets to have 10% of their students study abroad, and institutions in Australia are following suit.

Some are calling on the government to create more scholarships and exchanges for Canadians to leave and for more foreign students to arrive here for their studies, arguing that 1/3 of Canada's jobs depend on exports, but fewer than 3% of Canadian college and university students study abroad. They also want Ottawa to spend $50 to $60 million a year by 2000 on international education.

In light of growing concern over the cost of higher education, the lure of foreign students for their higher tuition is wrong minded — they are still heavily subsidized by Canadian taxpayers.

Making the User Pay

In a popular television show, *Northern Exposure*, a brash New York medical student was forced to spend his 1st few years after graduation serving a small community in Alaska, the state that sponsored his education. It was a typical "fish out of water" story, but the idea of making students "pay back" the taxpayers who actually paid for their education is a very appropriate concept.

According to recent studies in Newfoundland, the tiny province is short at least 80 doctors. This is despite the fact that there is a medical school in the provincial capital. Now, doctors who stay in rural practices for at least 2 years are receiving hefty bonuses. Understaffed health boards in northern Saskatchewan and Ontario are also luring physicians away with promises of grants and subsidies.

> *Despite paying more, foreign students pay less than half the cost of their education — the Canadian taxpayer pays the balance.*

University Education Pays

A study done by a U of T economics professor shows that, on average, the annual after-tax rate of return for a bachelor's degree is 13.8% for males and 17.6% for females. He concludes that, "The biggest mistake that people make is saying they can't afford to go to university... The answer is you can't afford not to." [175]

In making his calculations, he estimated that fees make up 10% of the cost component, food and shelter 40%, and foregone earnings 50%.

Despite increasing tuition, his point is still valid because the wage gap between high school and university graduates has widened. He adds that **those who work part-time through school are making a bad investment of their time, if they end up taking 5 or 6 years to complete a 4-year degree.**

While having a university degree is no guarantee to participate in the good life, graduates do end up with better jobs and a richer life, and those without post-secondary education are on their way to dead-end work. A university education, at least in theory, teaches people to think, interpret information and solve problems in general terms.

Some experts still recommend that people pursue a broad liberal arts or science degree at the undergraduate level and then complement that with a specialized degree, although they also say that parents should recognize the value of trade schools as a viable alternative.

The bottom line is that kids should not be pushed into university if they feel it is not for them, but they also should not use the excuse that they cannot afford to go. If they really want to go, they can find a way.

The average income of a university graduate is 60%+ higher than non-university graduates; the unemployment rate for university graduates is about half the rate for non-university graduates.

Rates of Return [175]

Annual after-tax rate of return for a university education

	Males	Females
Humanities, Fine Arts	7.3%	14.8%
Social Sciences	12.8	17.0
Commerce	16.2	21.8
Biological Sciences	6.8	15.0
Maths, Physical Sciences	15.1	21.2
Health Professions	14.9	21.0
Engineering	16.0	19.8
Law	15.0	16.0
Medicine	20.8	19.7
All Bachelor Degree programs	13.8%	17.6%

Saving for an Education

With the annual cost of a year of university education now running around $9,000 — and expected to rise to at least $16,000 per year in a decade — parents are looking at different ways to save towards their children's education.

• One of the most popular options is a registered education savings plan (RESP). Self-directed RESP's are registered accounts set up with a financial institution in which you can make a wide range of investments, from GIC's to mutual funds. The major attraction of an RESP is that all investment income generated — including interest, dividends and capital gains — grows on a tax-deferred basis. RESPs are even more attractive now that the government has doubled the annual contribution limit to $4,000 a year per child, to a lifetime maximum of $42,000. Contributions can be made for up to 21 years, but the plan must be collapsed within 25 years of the starting date. Since January 1998, you have been able to withdraw income from an RESP if the plan has been in existence for at least 10 years and none of the named beneficiaries has started post-secondary education by age 21. However, if the plan has not been in existence that long, contributions would be returned without income.

• Another method is to set up an account in-trust with a financial institution (because an adult has to be responsible for providing the investment instructions and signing the contract on the child's behalf). An in-trust account is more flexible and allows for bigger contributions than an RESP. Once your child reaches the age of majority and assumes control of the trust, the money is his or hers. Interest and dividends are taxed in the hands of the donor (you), while capital gains are taxed in the hands of the child.

• A 3rd method is to use a savings account, GIC or Canada Savings Bond outside a registered plan. While this route is still popular, the experts agree that it has significant tax consequences. For instance, whenever an investment earns its return in the form of interest, the person who buys the investment has to pay the tax on the interest earned at his or her own marginal tax rate. Only the 2nd generation interest — earned through compounding — is taxable at the child's tax rate.

• A 4th plan is to use a cash-value life insurance policy, where a portion of each payment goes to pay for the insurance and the remaining money is invested on the child's behalf. The accumulated cash value grows on a tax-deferred basis; when the funds are withdrawn, generally only the portion in excess of the policy's cost base is taxable. This is an expensive plan because a portion of the money must pay the insurance premium, so less money is working to earn a return.

> *Canadians must either develop high skills or accept low wages.*

Worst Practices

Millennium Scholarship Fund

Among recent moves made by the federal government are enhanced tax incentives for parents to save for their children's education, and the $2.5 billion Millennium Scholarship Fund, which will begin assisting students in the year 2000.

Few of the many goofy political acts from Ottawa can match the Liberals' Millennium Scholarship Fund for pure audacity. As pure political showboating, it is a clear invasion of provincial jurisdiction, costly to administer and, most importantly, helps to camouflage the systemic problems in the higher education system.

> *The $2.5 billion millennium scholarship fund will work out to only $3,000 a student*

176

Professors As Academic Purists and Trade Unionists

There is a certain irony in the expectation that universities can help in the transition to the new work of the information age. With the possible exception of the Catholic church, no institution has been more resistant to change. The medieval paradigm defines the university as a contemplative setting where knowledge for its own sake is the goal. Since the end of WWII, emphasis has grown for the practical side of education; what has developed is a strained balance between the contemplative and the practical. Ontario's Spring, 1998, decision to invest an additional $150 million in the education of more badly needed computer and electrical engineers was strongly criticized by academics as "selling out to industry."

Once again we have left the fox to guard the henhouse. The faculty union, the CAUT, successfully defeated the attempt by BC to create a modern institution — The Technical University of British Columbia, not because the design was flawed or the need did not exist, but because it was going to be created without the traditional self-governance of an academic board and tenure to protect academic freedom. Self-governance and tenure are part of the politics of education, and their purpose is blatant trade-union protection of faculty rights, but they are anomalies in the diversity of our pluralistic society.

The core issue is whether or not it is legitimate for Canadian universities to cater to Corporate Canada, which is embodied in the Business Council on National Issues. Right-wing think tanks/political action groups such as the Fraser Institute, The C. D. Howe Institute and the National Citizens Coalition argue that we should not spend public money to create expensive non-applied knowledge — such as philosophy, whose graduates often end up as clerks at Wal-Mart.

Learning on the Job

Education must be a continuous and lifelong endeavour. Global competition has demonstrated the need for continuous upgrading of products, of services and, especially, of people. It follows that there must be far greater commitment to training and skills upgrading by employers in Canada. The present shortcomings are particularly acute in smaller businesses, though certainly not confined to that sector.

The most critical component of our learning system is the process by which on-the-job skills are created and upgraded. By and large, this has been a haphazard process in North America. For some reason, we have developed and retained a 19th century attitude that formal education and training are not complementary investments. We have left it almost entirely to schools and colleges to provide a stream of fully-prepared entrants to the workforce.

> **Workplace training in Canada is notoriously poor by international standards. Our system of vocational education is widely recognized as inadequate, particularly when compared with competitors in Europe and Asia. The advanced countries in Europe and Asia — especially Germany with its renowned dual-track system — spend at least 5 to 10 times as much per worker on training as does Canadian.**

Job Relevant Training: A Corporate Responsibility

The Toyota company in Japan views the fresh engineering graduate as almost entirely devoid of directly relevant knowledge. Of course, the new recruit is well equipped to learn, thanks to the rigours of the Japanese school system. In Japan, Toyota accepts as its responsibility the provision of an extended period of intensive *relevant* training to equip the newcomer for production responsibility. And thereafter, throughout the worker's career, the company will provide frequent intervals of formal training to continuously deepen and broaden that base of skills. The result in Japan, and in much of Europe, is a work-force that views continuous training and retraining as the lifelong norm.

The reluctance of many firms in North America to undertake more training is a fear that the investment will be lost if the employees leave, particularly if they leave to join a competitor. **(There is also ample evidence that what has passed for corporate training has little if any impact on productivity.)** The best-managed companies, however, understand that much retraining must take place on the job, whether through apprenticeship programs, mentoring, or other kinds of training.

San Francisco-based Q-Metrics, a company that has worked with thousands of executives, managers and other professionals to develop measurements of emotional intelligence and other dimensions of human intelligence at work, says that "a significant part of an organization's profitability is linked to the quality of its work life, which is based largely on trust and loyalty both within the organization and with outside people, such as customers and suppliers. Profitability is also linked to the way employees feel about their jobs, colleagues, and company." (See EQ, page 211.)

"Over the years working with business leaders and organizations, I've studied 3 driving forces of competitive advantage: building trusting relationships, increasing energy and effectiveness, and creating the future," says Q-Metrics chairman Robert K. Cooper. "Those EQ-related capacities are often overlooked in traditional management development and similar training."

Demographer David Foot argues that the flattened corporate structure — where employees move from a linear to a spiral career path and take on new duties and responsibilities — will not work unless management increases the re-education and retraining budget. "How can people take on new work they have never done before without education and training?" he asks. A lateral organization, on the other hand, needs to know people's job preferences, help them plan their career paths, and give them the training they need.

Companies with a reputation for excellent training inevitably attract more high-potential employees. They may also end up keeping a higher proportion, particularly if continuous training is part of an integrated program of career development. A study conducted in 1995 for the US Department of Labor by researchers at the Harvard and Wharton business schools and the Boston-based Center for Business Innovation concluded that **companies that invest in worker training are more profitable than those that do not.**

Despite this logic, the fact remains that most Canadian businesses continue to dramatically under-invest in formal training for their employees.

TECHNOLOGY AND INNOVATION
INNOVATION

COMPANIES ARE GENERALLY SLOW TO ADOPT NEW WAYS OF BUSINESS, ESPECIALLY IF IT MEANS A REDUCTION IN THEIR BELOVED PAPER.

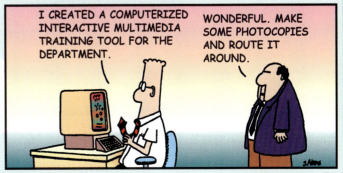

Government Job Training Simply Does Not Work

Investing more in "people, education and job training" is a common political lament. Logic says that more training for the underskilled would mean more, or improved, employment. The spurious argument continues that, since private industry cannot be expected to do this, it should be done at public expense.

Unfortunately, government training is as inefficient and heartless as the average bureaucratic agency and is not working. Even in programs that show marginal improvement, the costs rival those of expensive graduate schools. Consider the following:

• A US study revealed that the $5 billion Job Training Partnership Act had little or no effect on the average earnings of female youths and reduced the earnings of male youths. Specifically the study indicated that for those trainees under 21, "the training had no effect at all."

• The London School of Economics found that, after discounting those who would have found work anyway, "hardly any benefit remains from Britain's training schemes."

• A 1993 study by the US Department of Labor found that less than 20% of those who were retrained under federal programs for dislocated workers were able to find new jobs paying at least 80% of their former salaries. Even so, the White House is seeking more than $4.76 billion in federal funds to upgrade existing training programs and initiate new projects.

• The Australian Bureau of Labour Market Research study showed the results to be "so embarrassingly bad" that the Bureau was shut down. Even so, Australia is now investing more than $11 billion over 4 years in job training.

• When Alberta overhauled its welfare system in 1993, placing more emphasis on job and educational training, there was a dramatic drop of 60% in case loads. But, although about 2/3 of respondents found either full-time or part-time work, and 40% said job training helped them get a job, their employment earnings still only averaged $1,300 a month — not exactly catapulting them into middle-income brackets.

• A study for the Swedish parliament concluded that retraining might result in slightly improved chances of employment, but that it did so at a higher cost than simple job search advice.

In contrast, Germany's highly regarded dual-track education system that assigns apprentices to a combination of local employment and government-supported vocational schools is certainly a better, but still flawed, alternative. When market forces make these employees too expensive; they are replaced by lower-cost guest workers.

The bottom line is that **large-scale training/ retraining programs simply do not work.** Training initiatives must address global competitiveness and the need for highly-paid, high-performance employment. What is needed is a commitment on the part of business as well as to hire the people and to make sure that they receive the appropriate training.

The Better Training Solution

The answer is on-the-job training (OJT), in contrast to "out-of-a-job training," to bring improvements in productivity and wages. According to the US Economic Policy Institute, such training increases productivity twice as much as formal education or new technologies.

Research in the US, Germany, Scandinavia and the UK shows that OJT, even in minimum-wage jobs, produces greatly enhanced worker mobility. As an bonus, teachers tend to learn more about what they teach, so the workers providing the training also benefit as they share their knowledge.

Nowhere is this more evident than in the non-profit sector. For example, the Girl Scouts in the US have 6.5 million members with a paid staff of 6,000 — and 730,000 volunteers. The challenge in the for-profit sector is to manage the knowledge worker for better productivity. Non-profits have proven that this works best by having a "clear mission, careful placement and continuous learning and teaching, management by objectives and self-control, high demands but corresponding responsibility, and accountability for performance and results."

Paired with these strategies is the notion of training partnerships between schools and industry — natural outgrowths of traditional apprenticeship programs. In Japan, large companies recruit entry-level workers from high schools, who receive OJT to make them better workers. In Germany, 85% of non-college-bound students are enrolled in structured apprenticeship programs and assigned to a combination of local employment and government-supported vocational schooling.

The best approach is a job-referral system, coupled with some form of dual education, nurtured in a free-market reality. The waste of massive government funds on unsuccessful retraining schemes needs to end. The costs inevitably are passed along to business in the form of higher taxes and fees, creating further disincentives to compete in the increasingly global marketplace. Rather, competitiveness is the result of comprehensive, well-designed corporate training programs.

Who Makes It Happen?   170

Employees' share of adult education and training courses

Sweden	
United Kingdom	
United States	
New Zealand	
Netherlands	
Australia	
Switzerland	
Canada	
Ireland	

0% 10 20 30 40 50 60 70 80

> Upon the **education** of the
> people of this country,
> the **fate** of this country depends.
> — Benjamin Disraeli,
> British Prime Minister, 1874

> Without economic success, there is
> little chance to achieve society's
> social and cultural goals.

Lifelong Learning

There is an overwhelming need to create a Canadian society committed to lifelong learning — from cradle to grave. We know that today the economic health and prospects of Canada depend as never before on the *quality* and *relevance* of our human skills and knowledge. Growing wage inequality is simply the market signalling furiously to people to complete their education, get some training, and move into expanding fields with better relative wages.

And as we approach the 21st century, the truth of Disraeli's statement has taken on even greater significance. It has become a cliché, but nonetheless true, that ours is a knowledge-dependent economy. And, in a knowledge-based economy, we need people who know how to learn and who are committed to learning throughout their working lives.

This means that economic value, and the potential for greater productivity, depends upon the generation of ideas, the manipulation of information and the ability of workers to continuously upgrade their skills.

> **To succeed in such an environment,
> one must be capable of lifelong learning
> and great vocational flexibility.**

The present economic realities have only accelerated the inevitable process of adjustment in which businesses are forced to shed the hundreds of thousands of jobs that cannot survive Canada's cost structure in the face of more open competition.

Think of the unemployed auto parts worker with 20 years' experience, too young to retire; but what is he going to do with the next 20 or 30 years of his life? Have we equipped him with the basic learning skills needed to embrace complex new computer-based technology — skills that will have to be upgraded repeatedly throughout the balance of his working life?

Studies have shown that if you already have a university degree in Canada, the odds that you will take part in further education or training as an adult are 6.5 times better than they are for a person with grade 8 education or less. Canada ranks a disappointing 8th among comparably developed western nations (see chart, page 218).

The importance of education obviously goes beyond the dimension of economics; it is also a prerequisite for social and cultural vitality. Recent studies have even highlighted a positive link between one's education and one's health, regardless of income level. So by virtually every measure, the quality of our lives reflects the quality of our learning environment.

> **"Knowledge is power."**
> — Francis Bacon, 1597

Lifelong Learning as the Direction

There is an old maxim in strategic planning that says: "If you don't know where you're going, you'll probably end up somewhere else."

The learning process must be viewed as a system that extends from infancy until the end of one's life. It is a highly complex and interrelated process in which each phase creates the conditions for success or failure at subsequent stages. To develop the learning society that Canada needs in order to prosper in a world where knowledge rules requires a clear statement of the primary goals. We must begin to transform education with a clear sense of direction.

Our education system should prepare young people for lifelong learning, assist students to find information-age careers for which their aptitude, ambition and skills are well suited; and foster continuous development of the potential of the individual — intellectually and vocationally — throughout their adulthood.

Career Intelligence

"When I was growing up, my parents didn't think that much about my future other than wanting to see that I got good grades and went to college," observes Barbara Moses, author of *Career Intelligence: Mastering the New Work and Personal Realities*. She says questions about how to provide for children are among those she most frequently receives at her workshops. Some of her responses include:

• Computer literacy is important but technical skill alone is an inadequate focus.

• Children end up sharing their parents' anxiety about their progress in school and will pick up an obsession with grades.

• Too much emphasis on programmed learning can rob children of other life opportunities that are vital.

• By the same token, petitioning your children for career decisions very early may be a poor strategy. Ironically, in a fast-changing market, individuals "who have kept their options open may well be better positioned than their counterparts who were pushed to make lifelong career decisions at the age of 14."

• "Don't prepare for jobs, prepare for areas of competence." Parents should encourage the pursuit of personal passions, understanding that if children "follow their true interests and strengths, they are much more likely to attain satisfying work in the end, although it may not be in an area that they can currently envisage."

• Encourage children to develop their trade skills by: having them learn about making and saving money; telling dinner-table stories about business matters; using "take your child to work" opportunities; encouraging them to read business news; having them follow a stock or invest their own savings; and involving them in the day-to-day administration of the household budget.

Potpourri

Basic Facts About Canadian Education

Canadian Schools: JK - Gr. 12 [177]

Province	Elementary	Secondary
Newfoundland	367	128
PEI	52	18
Nova Scotia	385	146
New Brunswick	333	108
Quebec	2,285	751
Ontario	4,469	1,222
Manitoba	679	162
Saskatchewan	800	152
Alberta	1,409	377
British Columbia	1,566	429
Yukon	25	6
Northwest Territories	67	10
TOTAL	**12,437**	**3,509**

Community College Enrolment [178]

Full-time and part-time, the provinces and territories.*

Full-time Enrolment

Location	'91-'92	'92-'93	'93-'94
CANADA	**349,098**	**361,511**	**376,840**
Newfoundland	4,361	4,758	5,124
Prince Edward Island	1,225	926	985
Nova Scotia	2,653	3,375	3,787
New Brunswick	2,988	3,194	3,415
Quebec	163,768	169,583	176,928
Ontario	111,362	117,113	121,330
Manitoba	3,936	3,850	3,900
Saskatchewan	3,509	3,541	3,325
Alberta	25,464	25,323	25,183
British Columbia	29,288	29,304	32,270
Yukon	262	262	277
Northwest Territories	282	282	316

Part-time Enrolment

Location	'91-'92	'92-'93	'93-'94
CANADA	**216,748**	**177,640**	**181,040**
Newfoundland	180	233	167
Prince Edward Island	-	-	-
Nova Scotia	215	179	252
New Brunswick	48	42	64
Quebec**	60,954	22,060	22,060
Ontario	88,630	88,735	93,290
Manitoba	1,697	1,646	1,646
Saskatchewan	1,027	710	581
Alberta	16,768	16,764	16,764
British Columbia	46,667	46,709	45,709
Yukon	206	206	257
Northwest Territories	356	356	250

★ Includes related institutions such as hospital schools and agricultural, arts, and other specialized colleges.
★★ Decrease between 1991-92 and 1992-93 is due to the reclassification of some part-time enrolment to continuing education.

University Enrolment by Field of Study, 1994-95 [179]

Full-time

	Male	Female	Total	Master's	Doctoral	Diploma/Certificate
Arts/Science/General	27,635	37,341	64,976	279	412	2
Education	17,859	35,791	53,650	4,202	1,858	274
Fine/Applied Arts	6,534	10,838	17,372	1,225	270	36
Humanities	19,692	30,522	50,214	5,901	3,723	98
Social Sciences	69,698	87,748	157,446	14,823	4,778	600
Agriculture/Biological Sciences	14,443	21,588	36,031	2,881	2,159	48
Engineering/Applied Sciences	36,880	9,490	46,370	5,814	3,609	127
Health Professions	8,749	19,879	28,628	3,451	3,578	104
Not reported	9,013	10,877	19,890	46	27	9
TOTAL	**230,144**	**272,515**	**502,659**	**42,100**	**22,688**	**1 439**

Part-time

	Male	Female	Total	Master's	Doctoral	Diploma/Certificate
Arts/Science/General	10,478	18,301	28,779	204	95	258
Education	7,040	18,214	25,254	25,254	8,909	959
Fine/Applied Arts	1,794	4,299	6,093	478	57	1
Humanities	6,713	13,998	20,711	3,016	886	535
Social Sciences	29,704	48,461	78,165	9,702	1,183	2,244
Agriculture/Biological Sciences	1,902	3,047	4,949	579	213	12
Engineering/Applied Sciences	5,209	1,150	6,359	1,948	353	162
Health Professions	1,260	10,087	11,347	1,757	290	287
Not reported	22,010	33,749	55,759	159	30	18
TOTAL	**92,597**	**154,163**	**246,760**	**27,717**	**4,503**	**4,904**

Key Recommendations

Focus on causes not symptoms; on prevention not cure.

We must systematically examine both our often inappropriate over-dependence on the traditions of the UK, and in some cases France, and our counter-dependence towards the US. Substantial roots of our ineffectiveness in the transition to the new age are imbedded in these complex issues. We need to create a common vision for the future so that there is a populist will to change things that do not work.

The key to success in this endeavour is to continue to press for devolution and re-balancing. If you have framed a problem so that the solution requires any level of government to do something innovative and decisive, you have probably incorrectly defined the problem.

In this chapter, we present a broad range of recommendations for change — **there are items here that will offend every vested-interest group** and there are many that will elicit the protect-the-status-quo response, "There is no way we could make a change like that."

The reality is that it is our country and we have the option of making virtually any change if we can overcome special interest resistance and the economic ignorance that limits broader perspectives of thought.

Eating an Elephant: a bite at a time:

These 101 recommendations distill the myriad problems facing the country into do-able actions. By their nature they tend to run from mundane things that could be decided and done by bureaucrats in a day, such as eliminate the 1-cent coin, to things that would require constitutional change like forcing the amalgamation of the Atlantic mini-provinces.

It is important not to confuse the ease with which a change could be made with either its importance in the global economy of the post-modern world or in creating a more egalitarian environment.

These 101 recommendations, in many cases, go to the heart of revitalization of our country and if there is a single theme, it is doing things that will arrest the diminution of the middle class and the growing chasm between Haves and the Have-Nots.

What is most important is for us to wake up and see where the world is going so that we can make proactive choices rather than just being dragged along by the global flow.

Let's be in charge, to the degree practical, rather than spend our time tryng to defend lost causes.

A **Financial Reform:**
Systematically reduce debts and prohibit deficits.

B **Privatize Government Functions:**
Get the government out of the business of being in business.

C **Productivity Enhancement:**
Match US productivity by creating and implementing a robust national export policy.

D **Employment Reform:**
Combat unemployment and brain drain with policies that make Canada "job friendly."

E **Education Reform:**
Rebuild our education systems into a world-class enterprise with an emphasis on reducing economic ignorance.

F **Social Programs Reform:**
Abandon the defence of the mythical Canadian culture and promote and reward self-reliance.

G **Government Reform:**
Dramatically shrink the role of governments; eliminate unneeded regulation; make our governments lean, transparent and accountable.

H **Environmental Reform:**
Challenge the degradation caused by unsustainable levels of population growth and get serious about controlling pollution.

I **Pension Reform:**
Convert the CPP (and QPP) to bona fide pay-as-you-go investment plans.

J **Military Reform:**
Get out of the warrior business by being a world leader in demilitarization.

When and How to Sell Government Assets and What to Do With the Money

Timing of the sale of government assets should take into consideration what will be the best "deal" for the taxpayer. The government still owns 18% of Petro-Canada, for example, but the former crown corporation has gone from being the hated occupant of "Red Square" in Calgary to red hot. And those who invested in the $2.2 billion offering of Canadian National Railways in November, 1995, have been very well rewarded. The share value has skyrocketed, the number of employees has been slashed from 36,000 to 18,000 and the acquisition of Illinois Central has extended the track through mid-America to New Orleans. When the government sells its stake, it could mean hundreds of million dollars to reduce debt for the benefit of all taxpayers.

Selling crown assets and using the money for operations is similar to selling pieces of the family farm and consuming that money rather than using it to pay off the mortgage. **The proceeds from the sale of any public asset should, by statute, be used to reduce public debt.**

A Financial Reform:

Systematically reduce debts and prohibit deficits.

Using New Zealand *[p. 9]* as a best practices model, the sovereign credit rating can be improved through debt reduction, as follows:

1. Revamp the tax system to one based solely on consumption and user fees. *[p. 139-143]*

2. Create a transparent, fiscally-accountable system of government financial record-keeping by requiring TSE accounting standards for all federal and provincial governments. *[p. 9]*

3. Prohibit all governments from borrowing for operations without specific repayment times; limit amounts and require specific approval by parliament and the governors of the Bank of Canada.

4. Create a 30-40 year plan to pay off all government debt through the implementation of The Phoenix Plan. *[pp. 112,114,120,122,123]*

5. Limit the cost of all government services to 15% of the GDP.

6. Create powerful and independent governors for the Bank of Canada consisting of 8 non-political members appointed for 4-year terms such that 2 new members are appointed each year. Anyone who has held elected office or been an official of a political party is not eligible.

7. Require specific approval of all major federal capital expenditures by the new governors of the Bank of Canada.

8. Eliminate GST, PST & HST on all computer hardware and software to stimulate the growth of the market and the development of computer skills.

9. Adopt a "pay-as-you-can" version of Jubilee 2000 for Third World debt owned by the Canadian government and private financial institutions; underwrite a 50% reimbursement for banks that have made loans to foreign governments. *[p. 124]*

10. Get the government out of the gambling business and its imbedded costs (visible and hidden) that exceed the revenue they generate. Eliminate all VLT's. *[p. 103]*

11. Promote savings through home ownership by liberalizing RRSP withdrawals for 1st- time home buyers.

12. Promote savings through home ownership by allowing a tax deduction for interest paid on a primary residence.

B Privatize Government Functions:

Get the government out of the business of being in business.

The Country will be more competitive in the free-trading global economy as a result of the following:

13. Prohibit the federal and provincial governments from owning crown corporations, requiring them to be sold off through the equity markets or eliminated if they are not commercially viable. (*This includes Canada Post.*) *[pp. 9, 158-162]*

14. Require by law that any income from the sale of crown assets or rights is to be applied to the respective federal or provincial debt.

15. Cut the number of government employees at all levels by 25% over a 5-year period, primarily by attrition and outsourcing of services. *[p. 9]*

16. Eliminate the CRTC (Canadian Radio-television and Telecommunications Commission) and other unneeded regulation.

17. Treat the CBC as just another crown corporation; sell it in the equity market.

18. Eliminate the Canadian Wheat Board, a monopolistic remnant of WWII. *[p. 32]*

19. Close all provincially-owned banking institutions.

C Productivity Enhancement:

Match US productivity by creating and implementing a robust national export policy.

Productivity will be enhanced as the result of the following:

20. Create a Royal Commission-level economic task force to identify the factors that make US productivity (per capita GDP) more than 40% higher than Canada and create and implement a plan that will systematically correct those flaws over a 10-year period. *[p. 19,52,170]*

21. Introduce tax incentives for new exports.

22. Enforce the Agreement of Internal Trade (AIT) and eliminate all interprovincial trade barriers. *[p. 172]*

23. Make it a national priority to create IT professionals and the kinds of jobs that will encourage them to remain in Canada. *[pp. 148-150]*

24. Actively support the adoption of the Multilateral Agreement of Investments (MAI). *[p. 173]*

25. Lead the World Bank and IMF by imposing the Tobin Tax and pressing for the OECD to follow. *[p. 123]*

26. Move to #1 on the Transparency International (TI) Index of least corrupt countries. *[p. 174]*

27. Abandon the wardship mentality of being dependent on government; decisively promoting self-reliance. *[p. 33]*

28. Educate everyone about the trade-offs of a free market economy in our border-less world. *[pp. 57-58]*

29. Reduce the "natural rate of unemployment" to US-levels. *[p. 75]*

D Employment Reform:

Combat unemployment and the accelerating brain drain with policies that make Canada more "job friendly."

The systematic creation of jobs would be greatly enhanced by the following:

30. Prohibit public sector unions as counter to public policy interests. *[pp. 62-63]*

31. Establish the goal of full gender pay equity by 2010, recognizing that both higher pay for women and lower pay for men may be equally viable solutions. *[p. 50]*

32. Convert the Employment Insurance program to a non-governmental system run by business and the unions.

33. Prohibit closed shops (those requiring mandatory union dues payments by all workers) and replace them with the "right-to-work" (free-choice-of-affiliation) option.

34. Limit EI payments for seasonal workers to 6 months in any 4-year period and integrate relocation allowances into the basic structure of the system.

35. Invest 1% of the GDP in high-tech R&D. *[p. 159]*

36. Eliminate the financial advantage that a company receives in hiring part-time and contract employees by requiring proportional benefits for all employees.

37. Manage the shift to a shorter work week (to 32 hours over a 10-year period) to create more jobs by re-distributing the existing work. *[p. 55]*

38. Induce companies to shift towards a shorter work week with a tax benefit placing significant surtax on overtime hours, such as requiring double time above the mandated work week (See recommendation 37) up to 40 hours a week and triple time over 40 hours.

39. Automate all lighthouses: the amount of money is small but the symbolism is immense.

E Education Reform:

Rebuild our education systems into a world-class enterprise with an emphasis on reducing economic ignorance.

Revitalization will be the result of the following:

40. Re-engineer primary and secondary education with a focus on life/work skills for the Information Age.

41. Hold students and teachers accountable by rigorous standardized tests that correlate with what it takes to find work in the Information Age. *[p. 202]*

42. Eliminate religious separate school boards in all provinces; there is no reason why Catholics should have their own public-sponsored education in the multi-ethnic environment of the 21st century.

43. Reward the teaching profession for acting as agents for change rather than the guards of the status quo. *[pp. 200-201]*

44. Create a comprehensive approach to early-childhood development and learning, consolidate and coordinate services to improve school readiness.

45. Make it easier to get rid of non-performing teachers (and administrators) by putting them all on closed-end contracts with a maximum 3-year term. *[p. 201]*

46. Promote competition in education through charter and expanded private schools with education vouchers.

47. Lengthen the primary and secondary school year to a minimum of 225 days. *[p. 200]*

48. Require all teachers to be computer literate and promote integrated learning applications in all curricula.

49. Wire every classroom (not school) in the country to the Internet by the year 2000, and make Internet access readily available and free at all public libraries.

50. Replace the model of computer labs with computers in every primary classroom and individual computers at the secondary level.

51. Require financial management courses and entrepreneurial curricula at the high school level as key life skills.

52. Reduce direct government support of post-secondary education to 25% by the year 2010. *[pp. 213-215]*

53. Create incentives for families and students to start earlier to save more towards the cost of post-secondary education. *[p. 216]*

54. Reward high academic standards with loans for qualified students, based on financial need, to be repaid through National Service and scheduled, income-contingent debt pay-off.

55. Prohibit the federal government from using the Millennium Scholarship Fund; education is clearly a provincial responsibility. *[p. 216]*

F Social Programs Reform:

Abandon the defense of the mythical Canadian culture and promote and reward self-reliance.

Self-reliance will be the result of the following:

56. Create a poverty task force to identify and eradicate the causes of child poverty by the year 2005. *[pp. 46, 79]*

57. Shift the anti-crime focus away from retribution to prevention and restorative justice. *[pp. 85,88]*

58. Create a dynamic national service, allowing the unskilled to make a transition to the work world and university students to repay their tuition assistance. *[pp. 109-110]*

59. Implement the 440 recommendations of the Royal Commission on Aboriginal Affairs. *[p. 26]*

60. Enhance the rewards for corporate and individual philanthropy. *[pp. 106,108]*

61. Crack down hard on welfare abuse including on-reserve transfer payments to eliminate ineligible recipients. *[p. 33]*

62. Decriminalize non-violent acts including the growing, sale and use of marijuana. *[p. 5, 88-89]*

63. Offer greatly-enhanced financial assistance to medical-school undergraduates who agree to practice in underserved areas when they get their licences as doctors.

64. Eliminate the National Heritage Ministry and stop trying to defend a mythical, historical culture.

G Government Reform:

Dramatically shrink the roles of governments, eliminate unneeded regulation and make our governments lean and accountable.

Governments are inefficient at almost everything they do. We need fewer expensive government services which can be accomplished by the following:

65. Resign from the Commonwealth. *[p. 5]*

66. Declare Canada a Republic. *[p. 36]*

67. Amalgamate the 4 Atlantic provinces into a single province. *[p. 10]*

68. Introduce proportional voting.

69. Eliminate the term "of Commons" from the National Legislative Assembly (NLA): the term conflicts with our egalitarian culture.

70. Cut the size of the NLA to 120 members.

71. Create an elected Senate of 52 members (6 from each major province, 2 from each of the 4 Atlantic provinces, 2 from each territory and 2 from the Assembly of First Nations.) *[p. 10]*

72. Implement similar reductions in the size of provincial and territorial legislative assemblies.

73. Put an end to professional politicians with a combined political service limit of 10 years and a pension maximum of 1/3 of a full pension.

74. Appoint federal and provincial "Ministers" from non-political ranks; demand, through senate ratification, that they be competent to manage their specific files.

75. Eliminate the federal Department of Indian Affairs and Northern Development and transfer responsibility to provinces and territories, with financial support through block grants.

76. Eliminate the 1-cent coin; the copper penny costs 1.4 cents to produce and even the 1997 bronze-plated zinc replacement costs .7 cents. Using pennies costs more than their value in most transactions.

H Environmental Reform:

Challenge the degradation caused by unsustainable levels of population growth in Canada and in the world and get serious about controlling pollution.

Sustainability includes all actions that adversely impact the environment, such as the following:

77. Lead the cause of reducing the world's population to a sustainable level of 2 to 4 billion. *[pp. 37, 38, 69]*

78. Limit the Canadian population to 35 million people. *[p. 40]*

79. Set the goal of being in the bottom quartile (lowest 25%) of pollution levels for comparably developed countries. *[p. 44]*

80. Create and manage an invigorated, realistic immigration/refugee program that will reduce immigration (including refugees) to 0.3% of the population through 2005 and set subsequent levels consistent with holding the population at 35 million. *[p. 42]*

81. Allocate 50% of the immigration slots for economic contributors, i.e., the best "human capital" available.

82. Implement a "One Strike" rule for immigrants: loss of immigrant status and deportation for anyone convicted of a felony.

Fathers of Confederation, Charlottetown, 1864

THE MISSING
NEST EGG

CPP

I Pension Reform:

Convert the CPP (and QPP) to bona fide pay-as-you-go investment plans.

To create a financially viable and equitable pensions system, the following actions are recommended:

83. Implement a Chilean-type plan to replace the CPP/QPP. *[p. 134]*

84. Bring all government employees' pension plans — especially MP's — to a level consistent with the national average for private sector pensions.

85. Increase the CPP/QPP retirement age to 70 by adding 1 year to the current level every 2 years.

86. Raise the RRSP limit by 20% a year for 5 years.

87. Raise the 20% limit on foreign assets held by pension plans and RRSP's by 3% annually until it reaches 32% — and then eliminate it completely.

J Military Reform:

Get out of the warrior business by being a world leader in demilitarization.

The goal of changing our military to peacekeepers rather than warriors can be accomplished by the following:

88. Replace the DND with the new Militia and move the headquarters from Ottawa to a central location, reduce the number of active bases to 4 and cut the "defence" budget to $3 billion. *[pp. 192-195]*

89. Reorganize a new Militia to have 20,000 active troops and 40,000 reservists, limiting civilian support to 5,000.

90. Focus the smaller, reservist-intensive Militia on being peacekeepers and natural disaster protectors. *[p. 195]*

91. Withdraw from NATO. *[pp. 188-189]*

92. Create a single, 5,000-person, combat-ready brigade as a part of our UN commitment. *[pp. 8, 197]*

93. Eliminate the Navy and all ships, except those that would be transferred to the Coast Guard for search and rescue functions.

94. Eliminate the Air Force and move transport planes and a relevant number of helicopters to the Militia and Coast Guard.

95. Lead by example in ceasing all arms sales; *destroy* rather than sell all excess military equipment, including all arms that do not fit the new militia paradigm. *[pp. 178-179]*

96. Continue to lead the cause to outlaw land mines (The Ottawa Process) and to develop improved training and technology for removing them. *[pp. 109-191]*

97. Join Australia in leading the cause to eliminate the world's 30,000 nuclear weapons. *[p. 186]*

98. Eliminate military police and replace them with a contingent of 5,000 RCMP, serving 4-year, non-consecutive tours on "active" militia duty. Allow a maximum of 2 tours, at least 4 years apart, during a RCMP career.

99. Redesign the curriculum of the Royal Military Academy in Kingston to focus on peacekeeping, making it the world's best non-warrior military academy. Accept up to 80% of the students from other countries that want to share this focus, with no more than 5% from any one country.

100. Shut down the Coast Guard Academy and replace it with a 1-year program that can adapt bright engineers and computer scientists to be officers. *[p. 198]*

101. Cancel the deal for the British Submarines that will cost us $5.4 billion over their "useful" life. *[p. 197]*

Economics 101

> *If economists were doctors, they would today be mired in malpractice suits.*
> — **John Ralston Saul**

> *Trickle-down economics is "the doctrine that if the horse is fed amply with oats, some will pass through to the road for the sparrows."*
> — **John Kenneth Galbraith**

Economics is a social science that had its birth in 1776, when the Scottish moral philosopher Adam Smith published his classic *Inquiry into the Nature and Causes of the Wealth of Nations*. This book was the 1st to point out the nature of the economic system that was developing in the UK and continental Europe. It laid the foundation for all future study of the subject and provided the basic definitions of wealth and labour.

Thomas Carlyle, who also lived at the time of the Industrial Revolution, was representative of the way people for centuries had thought about economics. He referred to it as "pig philosophy," regarding the businessman's quest for profits as mere greed.

Productive and Non-Productive Labour

Labour that produces wealth is called productive. Much of society's labour does not create wealth and is called non-productive. Those who work in education, government, religion, athletics, some of the arts, and the military do not produce products. The cost of non-productive labour is paid for by taxes and other fees.

Non-productive labour does help to create wealth through purchase; payments go back into the productive labour sectors.

Three Types of Economic Management

Economies are always *managed* to the degree that there is a finite amount of everything.

(1) An economy may be almost totally planned, as it was in the Soviet Union. In a planned economy, the government sets all priorities, and the producers follow the directives handed to them.

(2) An economy may be almost totally unplanned, as it is in the US. The government does not mandate what will be produced or how it will be marketed.

(3) There may be a combination of planning and freedom, as is the case in Japan. In a partially planned economy, the government frequently encourages industry and helps with subsidies.

Unplanned economies depend on individual initiative, personal ambition and ingenuity, as well as political freedom. The prime control for unplanned economies is the marketplace — called capitalism, or the free market. Capitalism is self-regulating, occurring through the operation of supply and demand.

The complaint against unplanned economies is that wealth is unevenly distributed. A minority is rich, a significant minority is poor, and the great bulk of the population (the middle class) lives in reasonable abundance, depending on the economy. It is primarily this uneven distribution that planned economies hoped to solve.

Competing Political Systems

Capitalism since the Industrial Revolution has caused massive social dislocations that continue in our emerging global information age.

Capitalism is the only real economic system that has emerged in the world. It can be called a system because it embraces all of society and operates on its own terms. It does not need government or any other institutional framework to make it operate.

Socialism and communism are not true economic systems. Rather, they are political arrangements that attempt to do away with what are perceived as the worst features of capitalism.

In the late 20th century, the great economic issue was the efficacy of planned versus unplanned economies. The defining moment in the triumph of capitalism over communism is considered to be the fall of the Berlin Wall in 1989.

Inherent Complexities

Economies are primarily city-based and city-originated operations. This fact is camouflaged by a government when it issues reports on GDP. At any given time, 1 city or province may be prosperous, while another may be in decline and have high unemployment.

Clearly, the economies of modern industrial nations are complex and likely to break down. Governments play a large role even in unplanned economies through regulation, most of it meant for the protection of the public. All regulations affect the way businesses operate, often increasing costs and reducing profits. Other policies (taxation, budget deficits, and regulation of the money supply) affect how much money is available for people to spend on goods and services.

For centuries, economies have been subject to periods of prosperity followed by periods of decline. These "boom and bust" alternations are commonly called business cycles. In the late 20th century, all industrialized societies, through their governments, have tried to stabilize economies, keep them prosperous, and reduce unemployment. None of the these remedies has worked to the extent that was anticipated.

Keynesian Economics

John Maynard Keynes' major achievement was to understanding how government debt policy can help stabilize the cyclical tendencies of the capitalist economy and achieve a generally high level of growth, productivity and employment. Keynes' economic theories, most fully developed in response to the Great Depression, held that government attempts to increase revenues and decrease expenditures worsened rather than cured the problem of widespread unemployment and underutilized industrial capacity.

The cause of the Depression, Keynes believed, was insufficient demand for goods and services. Because of this, investors were unwilling to spend money on factories and equipment. The result was a downward spiral of employment and production: Workers were fired, so they could not buy goods; then investment fell more, leading to more workers being fired. The effect was predictable: Since individuals were earning less and buying fewer goods, they were paying less taxes. Government revenues, therefore, were *pro-cyclical,* increasing in economic upturns and declining in economic downturns.

The real misfortune, suggested Keynes, was that in depressed economic circumstances, governments reacted to the decline in their revenues by decreasing their own demand for goods and services. The policy of maintaining a balanced budget exacerbated the problem instead of contributing to its solution.

The correct policy, Keynes argued, was to have government spending be *counter-cyclical.* During an economic downturn, the government should increase its expenditures to compensate for the decline in private demand. Conversely, during an economic upturn, the government should decrease its expenditures to make room for productive investment and consumption.

Keynesian economic stabilization policy became the accepted orthodoxy in virtually all capitalist economies in the decades of the 1950's and the 1960's. Nevertheless, Keynes has remained a controversial figure, and his policy recommendations have come under heavy attack. Often this has centered on the implications for the size and growth of the national debt. (In other words, Keynesian policy may temporarily stabilize the economy, but at the expense of a growing public debt. Conservatives distrust national debt for fear of full employment and its concomitant increase in the relative power of labour over capital.)

The Keynesian position has been met with extreme hostility from economic conservatives, for whom extensive government economic activity and budget deficits represent inefficient and unjust interferences with the market economy. Such conservatives, most notably Milton Friedman, gained favourable reception following the worldwide economic crisis of the early 1970's. Keynesian economic policies had worked for 25 years (the mid-1940's to the late 1960's), but the high rates of inflation that accompanied the strong economic downturn of the early 1970's enhanced the credibility of anti-Keynesian theories. In any case, Keynesian policies may have to be supplemented by controls on capital flows in order to prevent politically motivated transfers of capital to other countries.

Three Economic Perspectives

Economics includes many specialized facets of economic functioning, such as public finance, monetary policy, international economics, industrial organization, labour, agricultural, growth and mathematical economics, and econometrics. In general, economics is divided into 3 subcategories:

Microeconomics (small) focuses on individual economic units, studying the behaviour of individual consumers, firms, and industries and the distribution of total production and income among them.

Macroeconomics (large) is the study of the whole economy and its interrelationships: total goods and services produced, total income earned, the level of use of productive resources, and the general behaviour of prices. (This area owes much of its development to Keynes.)

Development economics is concerned with the factors responsible for self-sustaining economic growth and the extent to which these factors can be manipulated by public or government policies. It is focussed on increasing production and finding the most effective use of resources.

Henry George (1839-1897)

American Henry George (1839-1897) best known for explaining the complex i layman's terms in books such as *Progress an Poverty,* a book that was outsold only by th Bible at the turn of the century. Althoug popular, George only had a superfici acquaintance with economic works an history, and his views on the real causes c poverty were somewhat at odds with th prevailing academic explanation. He ha endured poverty himself for many years; o his 1st visit to New York, George was shocked to learn that wealt was abundant, but it was not distributed. George established th *San Francisco Evening Post,* where he published his views o poverty and labour. He became so popular as a "man of the people that labour organizations backed his bid for Mayor of New Yor City in 1886, although he lost. Running again in 1897, he die 4 days before the election, but not before exclaiming, "I have neve advocated nor asked for special rights or special sympathy fc working men. What I stand for is the equal rights of all men."[18]

John Maynard Keynes (1883-194

A brilliant British economist, he held that governmer should use its taxing and spending powers to lessen th negative effects of business cycles. Keynesian economics wa as political as it was economic. It served to reinforce th notion of the centrality of the state. If the fiscal and monetar powers of the state could be used to soften the worst effects c the business cycle, why not lessen other hardships?

The security that Keynesian economics offered is gone replaced by a realization that Canada is now so integrated int the global marketplace that much of our economic fate lie beyond our grasp. When borders become meaningless, an attempt to stimulate business cycles dissipates quickly.

The Mercantile System
The Nature of Wealth

Everyone has some understanding of what is meant by personal wealth — either how much money we possess and/or how much our entire personal property is worth. It is more difficult, however, to describe the wealth of a nation.

The Mercantile System is a set of principles developed by economist Adam Smith and articulated by John Stuart Mill in *Principles of Political Economy*, which equated money with wealth and attempted to explain how national wealth was accumulated. According to Smith, activities that accumulated money or bullion (gold or silver) for a country added to its wealth. Countries without bullion enriched themselves through trade. Exports were encouraged because the goods were paid for in cash. Importing anything except bullion was regarded as a loss, other than raw materials to be re-exported at a profit.

To possess anything other than money was to possess that particular thing only: If you wanted something else, you had to sell it, or find someone willing to barter.

Thus, a government derived comparatively little advantage from taxes unless it could collect them in money. If it had large payments to make — especially for wars — no payment except money would serve the purpose.

> The **commerce** of the world was looked upon as a **battle between nations.**
>
> It was seen as a zero-sum model in that no nation could gain anything, except by making others lose as much, or at least preventing them from gaining it.

Like other things, money's worth is in its ability to acquire things. This leads to a distinction in the meaning of wealth. To an individual, anything is wealth that enables him to claim from others a part of their stock. To those who own the public debt, cancelling the debt would be no destruction of wealth, but a transfer of it: It is an element in the distribution, but not in the composition, of the general wealth. Wealth, then, may be defined as all things that possess exchangeable value. It is debatable, though, whether what are called "immaterial products" — natural or acquired power of body or mind — should be called wealth.

In earlier times, subsistence was preserved with little other labour than that of guarding livestock. Here began the inequality of possessions. In the nomad state, the successful had no other use to make of their surplus than to feed the less fortunate. The less fortunate, in turn, enabled the successful to divest themselves of all labour except that of government.

In communities, surplus food was usually torn from the producers, either by the government to which they were subject, or by individuals who established themselves as lords, by force or by other methods of subordination. The government seldom left much to the cultivators but enough to support life until another harvest. A large part of the plunder was distributed among the various functionaries of government and among the sovereign's lackeys. Commercial operations took place principally upon that part of the produce that formed the government's revenue.

These little communities lived in a state of almost perpetual war — a frequent cause was the mere pressure of their increasing population upon their limited land. The community often emigrated, expelled others from the land, or detained them to cultivate it.

What the less-advanced tribes did from necessity, the more prosperous did from ambition. The Romans always began or ended a conflict by taking a great part of the land to enrich their own leading citizens, and by coopting the principal possessors of the remainder of the land into the governing body. (See the map of the British Empire at its peak on page 12.)

In the new framework in which European society was cast, the population of each country was composed of 2 distinct nations — the conquerors (the proprietors) and the conquered (the tillers). Slavery had transformed itself into serfdom.

Any small provision a serf had was used to buy his freedom. Emancipated serfs mostly became craftsmen and lived by exchanging the produce of their industry for the surplus food and material that the soil yielded to its feudal proprietors.

Security of person and property grew slowly, but steadily. The arts of life made constant progress, plunder ceased to be the principal source of accumulation, and feudal Europe ripened into commercial and manufacturing Europe.

The countries that were richest made more use of their resources and obtained larger produce than others. From country to country, the condition of the poorest class varied, as did the proportional numbers and opulence of the classes that were above the poorest. The great empire of Russia was, in many respects, a scarcely modified copy of feudal Europe.

The manner in which wealth is distributed in any given society depends on its statutes. Though governments or nations have the power of deciding what institutions shall exist, they cannot arbitrarily determine how those institutions shall work.

Key References on Economics

Keynes, J.M. *The General Theory of Employment, Interest, and Money* (1936).

Malthus, Thomas. *Essay on Population* (1798).

Marx, Karl. *Capital* (Vol. 1, 1867).

Mill, John. *Principles of Political Economy* (1848).

Ricardo, David. *Principles of Political Economy and Taxation* (1817).

Smith, Adam. *The Wealth of Nations* (1776).

GEOPOLITICS 101

Geopolitics

It is the business of the future to be dangerous.
— Alfred North Whitehead

The concept of national "territory" is often so strong that people are prepared to die to protect their land. This combination of geography, politics and economics — or "geopolitics" — provokes powerful sentiments, which can result in deadly battles for control of territory and resources, fueled by differences of race, ethnicity or gender.

Geopolitics — derived from the German word "geopolitik" — means the study of the relationships of (1) geography, (2) environment and (3) economic and political development, power and policies of a country, particularly in terms of its international relations. In other words, a sovereign nation occupies a particular territory with physical features that partly determine viable forms of economic, social, political, and military organization.

Geopolitical theories and interpretations are based on geographic location, climate, or access to economic resources. They attempt to explain politics and economics by focusing on the importance of factors such as natural boundaries and access to waterways. Most theorists — particularly prior to WWII — believed that control of the sea was the key to world power. Others have noted that changes in temperature and humidity affect the behaviour and capacities of people. Still others believe that no state can become or remain a great power without secure access to huge quantities of fossil fuels and other natural resources.

International relations historically concerned conflict and cooperation, and tended to focus on the military might of a nation. Climate, topography, hydrography, and soil were all studied from the perspective of how they contributed to national power or influenced the national temperament. Nations 1st developed in temperate zones, although the physical features of each region influenced the density of settlements and the boundaries between nations. Rivers determined trade routes, the location of cities and the movements of armies. From the topsoil came the food to feed armies, and the subsoil provided the energy and minerals needed to fuel and build industry. Demographic variables also were examined with an eye towards calculating power — the larger the population, the larger the army that could be raised.

While geographic factors are important, initially too much causal weight was given to them. That is, early geographic theories explained too much about politics based on too few environmental variables. For example, it has been argued that Great Britain's inclination to expand was driven by its being an island nation. In contrast, Japan, also an island nation, had a history marked by isolation until the 20th century.

Even before the term geopolitics was coined, a number of important intellectuals wrote about the influence of geography on the conduct of global strategy. In the late 19th century, the American naval historian Alfred Mahan wrote about the importance of physical geography in the development of seapower in his study *The Influence of Seapower upon History* (1890). The road to national superiority, not surprisingly for the naval officer, was through naval expansionism.

The German geographer Friedrich Ratzel also wrote about the importance of the relationship between territory and the nation in the development of imperial strength and national power. In his book, *Political Geography* (1897), Ratzel, influenced by social Darwinism, considered the state to be a living organism engaged in a struggle for survival with other states. Like a living organism, the state needs to constantly expand or face decay and death. Ratzel's social Darwinism celebrated the German nation and German soil as superior to all others. Germany, he argued, should expand at the expense of "inferior" states to secure more territory for itself.

Technology has altered many geopolitical theories, however. Air transportation counters the importance of the sea, modern heating and cooling equipment negates climatic influences, and modern substitutes for raw materials lessen the importance of natural resources.

Imperialist Geopolitics

Geopolitics received initial acclaim based on the works of German army officer and political geographer Karl Haushofer. He believed that geography drove politics and that through geography, politics could be described in terms of discernible facts and provable laws that would in turn drive policy. Borders, rather than being constant, were seen as flexible depending on various national problems and priorities.

Geopolitical thought has its origins in imperialism, in the period leading up to WWII. All the world powers at the time had geopolitical philosophies marked by racist attitudes and beliefs, with the major rivalry between the British and Germans at the heart of both World Wars.

Coined originally in 1899 by a Swedish political scientist named Rudolf Kjellen, the word "geopolitics" has moved well beyond its original meaning. In the early 20th century, Kjellen and other imperialist thinkers defined geopolitics as that part of Western imperial knowledge that dealt with the relationship between the physical earth and politics.

Within this imperialist context, geopolitics 1st emerged as a concept and practice; it was a form of knowledge concerned with promoting the expansion of nation states and securing empires. All of the leading geopoliticians were conservative white male imperialists who sought to explain and justify expansion of their own particular country or, as they often termed it, their "race."

The writings of these men were full of arrogant pride: Their country represented the zenith of civilization; their way of life was superior to that of others; their ideals were the ideals of all of "mankind" or humanity. They thought in terms of continents and strategized in worldwide terms, labeling huge areas of the globe with names like "heartland" and "rimlands."

They also used multiple supremacist arguments: the supposed "natural" supremacy of men over women; of the white race over other races; of European civilization over others. One particularly nasty form of this twisted chauvinism was the ideology of the Nazi party in Germany; it celebrated idealized visions of "Aryan manhood" while persecuting what it labeled as "Jewish Bolshevism." The rhetoric led to murder as those who were corralled into the category "Jewish Bolshevism" were sent to their deaths in concentration camps like Auschwitz, Dachau and Bergen-Belsen.

After Hitler came to power in 1933, geopolitics became increasingly associated with National Socialism and Nazi demands for *Lebensraum* ("living space"), the doctrine advocating and justifying aggressive expansion in central Europe. Haushofer's contributions to German adventurism are clear, but when he objected to Hitler's planned foray into the Soviet Union, he was imprisoned in the concentration camp at Dachau.

The aggressive colonialism developed by the Axis Powers — the *Lebensraum* in Germany, the "empire" in Italian Fascist ideology, or the "co-prosperity sphere" in Japan — spawned a new twist to colonial doctrine aimed at the distribution of the world's colonial areas.

Cold War Geopolitics

The outbreak of a Cold War provided a new context and a new maturity for geopolitics, in terms of both theory and practice. Whereas imperialist geopolitics tended to emphasize the determining influence of physical geography on foreign policy, Cold War geopolitics connected geography so closely with ideology that it was difficult to separate the two.

The West became more than a geographical region; it was an imaginary community of democratic states that supposedly represented the very highest standards of civilization and development. Even historically "Eastern" powers like Japan and South Korea were part of this symbolic "West." The Soviet Union was represented as an "Eastern power," and Eastern Europe was known as "the Eastern bloc." All communist states were said to belong to the "Second World," as opposed to the "First World," which was, of course, the West.

During the later years of the Cold War, geopolitics was used to describe the global contest between the Soviet Union and the US for influence and control over the nation states and strategic resources of the world. Former US Secretary of State, Henry Kissinger, almost single-handedly helped revive the term in the 1970's by using it as a synonym for the superpower game of balance-of-power politics played out across the global political map.

Experts from both capitalist and communist countries defined a so-called "Third World" of poor and developing countries out of the rest that fit into neither camp.

Distinguished not only by traditionalism and underdevelopment, the Third World was a zone of competition between the West and the East. Both sides constantly evaluated and surveyed the strategic value of such regions as the Middle East, the Horn of Africa, southern Africa, Indochina, the Caribbean and Central America. The US even used Haushofer's ideas to justify its expansionist policies in the Americas as "manifest destiny."

Geopolitics became a game of superpower politics played out across the world map. Competing geopolitical experts designated spaces of the world as belonging either to "us" or to "them." In the rhetoric of the West, this meant the free world as opposed to the totalitarian world; in the discourse of Soviets, this meant the people's democracies as opposed to the capitalist and imperialist West.

Both sides were preoccupied with the "fall" of certain states to the enemy. This fear was particularly acute in the US after the "fall" of China to the Soviet camp in 1949. This soon spawned the anti-communist hysteria of McCarthyism. In turn, it helped produce the "domino theory," a form of geopolitical reasoning that designated countries as no more than potentially falling dominoes in a great superpower game between the communist East and the capitalist West. The domino theory marked the epitome of Cold War geopolitics as a type of power game that completely ignored the specific characteristics of places, peoples and regions.

Complex countries like Vietnam were no more than abstract stakes in the game. Tragically, the US ended up fighting in a bloody civil war in a country it knew very little about and whose real strategic significance was marginal. The Korean, Vietnam and subsequent Central American wars in the 1980's are vivid instances of the powerful effects and destructive consequences of Cold War geopolitics. The same can be said for the Soviet interventions in Hungary in 1956, Czechoslovakia in 1968 and Afghanistan in 1979.

New World Order Geopolitics

As a consequence of the end of the Cold War, symbolized by the fall of the Berlin Wall in 1989, international politics has experienced a crisis of meaning. The old defining East-West struggle evaporated, and no overall defining struggle of international politics has taken its place. Many experts, nevertheless, have tried to define what they claim to be the essential contours of the new world order. It is within these discussions that geopolitics is being renewed as an approach and practice.

Geopolitics has become popular once again because it deals with comprehensive visions of the world political map. In addition, it seems to promise unusual insight into the future direction of international affairs and the coming shape of the world political map.

Intellectual Edward Luttwak foresees a world where nation states continue to compete with one another, though now in economic rather than military conflicts. He stresses that trade conflicts between the US and Japan suggest a new West (US) versus the East (Japan) development in world affairs.

Luttwak's vision of geo-economics is strongly nationalistic, but other geo-economic visions stress the relative decline of nations and the importance of transnational flows and institutions. "Transnational liberalism" or "neo-liberalism" is a belief that the globalization of trade, production and markets is both a necessary and desirable development in world affairs. It is most notably articulated by the leaders of the G-7 industrialized nations (including Canada) and by neo-liberal economic experts in the IMF, the World Bank and the WTO.

In contrast to the optimism about globalization articulated by neo-liberals, the American neo-conservative political scientist Samuel Huntington stresses the power of transnational geo-cultural blocs, arguing that ancient civilization blocs underpin world affairs. Once obscured by the Cold War, they now are emerging again (e.g., Islamic fundamentalism).

For some, the end of the Cold War has created a world where the globalization of economic activity and global flows of trade, investment, commodities and images are re-making states, sovereignty and the geographical structure of the planet. For others, the "new geopolitics" describes a world no longer dominated by territorial struggles between competing blocs but by emerging transnational problems like terrorism, nuclear proliferation and clashing cultures.

For yet others, the relationship of politics to the earth is more important than ever, as states and people struggle to deal with environmental degradation, resource depletion, transnational pollution and global warming. For the environmentally minded, the new geopolitics is not geo-economics but ecological politics or ecopolitics.

Initially an issue of little thought, the environment has emerged as an object of considerable focus and concern. Connected with many other issues (e.g., over-development, explosive population growth and the widening gap between the Haves and the Have-Nots), the question of sustainable development has become the vortex of global debate. It is within this transition that the relationship between the earth and its inhabitants is being re-defined, and a new environmental geopolitics is being created.

The New Geopolitics

Classical geography used organic thinking as the justification for predation (i.e., countries are like animals; animals consume other animals; therefore states should consume other countries). The New Geopolitics recognizes instead that organic-ness refers to the transitory nature of nation states. Although countries may seem permanent, they are not immortal fixtures on the world stage. Countries can disappear because of intra-national as well as transnational processes.

Modern nation states are under stress from a host of forces, and perhaps the best example of intra- and trans-national tension exists in Western and Eastern Europe. The emergence of the EU has become the pre-eminent example of supranationalism, or shared sovereignty. Traditional functions of the state, including the setting of internal standards and external trade policy, have been assumed by a centralized political authority. In 1995, 11 of the 15 member countries of the EU even decided to make plans to introduce a single currency — the "euro." (See sidebar below.)

This integration and power transfer is by no means total, but it does provide evidence for diminished state authority. This is especially noteworthy, given Europe's violent history, a microcosm of which can be seen now in Eastern Europe. The localized conflicts within the former Yugoslavia and Soviet Union are only the most graphic examples of state disintegration based on sub-national political movements seeking to create new, smaller states from the old. In an era of such fluid boundaries, domestic and interstate conflicts become ever harder to distinguish.

The New Geopolitics, therefore, constitutes a recognition of multiple relevant factors; state security and survival now imply more than simply achieving sufficient military power. The Soviet Union was, after all, 1 of the world's 2 superpowers; its demise points out the importance of other, non-military factors. The New Geopolitics asks tough questions about why the nation state as an institution is experiencing such difficulties.

Clearly, a key force eroding the nation state's autonomy is the fact that a bigger share of the world's capital is owned by multinational companies that operate freely across national borders. These companies are usurping the traditional role of the nation state — with some generating assets that exceed the GDP of many countries. Increasingly, geographically bound nation states find themselves without a clearly defined mission. (See pages 95-96.)[79]

The Euro

In 1995, the 15 member states of the EU made plans to introduce a single currency, called the euro, worth around $1.50, which will gradually replace all EU national currencies. The euro will begin to be phased in on January 1, 1999, when 11 of the member countries will give over their monetary policies to the European Central Bank (ECB), and stocks, bonds, bank accounts, credit card purchases and bills will be measured in euros. From January 1, 2002, traditional national European currencies will begin to disappear. They will still be usable, but will be measured against the euro. By July 1, 2002, national European currencies will disappear altogether. The ECB, located in Frankfurt, will be headed initially by a Dutchman, Wim Duisenberg.

In
Austria
Belgium
Finland
France
Germany
Ireland
Italy
Luxemburg
Netherlands
Portugal
Spain

Out
Denmark
Sweden
UK

Unqualified
Greece

ANNOTATED BIBLIOGRAPHY
Recommended Readings

Adams, Charles (1993). *For Good and Evil: The Impact of Taxes on the Course of Civilization.* **New York: Madison Books.** American tax attorney Charles Adams combines tax scholarship and a libertarian view of history to explain the rise and fall of civilizations, from ancient Egypt to post-WWII USA. He relates how the Pharaohs collected taxes on everything but income (a modern innovation), and rebellion only took place as a consequence of perceived tax inequity. Adams goes on to tell how Rome fell because Emperor Julian's egalitarian taxes were corrupted and overturned by his greedy successors. Later, Adams explains, Enlightenment thinkers equated liberty with tax consent, and defined tax freedom as a "natural right."

Today, Adams believes that modern America is repeating the mistakes of earlier civilizations, including widespread anti-democratic tax "spying" and taxation without consent. Without reform, he predicts disaster, defining a good tax only as one that is accepted by its subjects and that promotes industry and privacy.

Adams, Michael (1997). *Sex in the Snow: Canadian Social Values at the End of the Millennium.* **Toronto: Penguin.** Written by experienced pollster and sociologist Michael Adams, this book draws on his 25 years of experience as President and co-founder of Environics Research Group Ltd., one of Canada's leading market research firms. It challenges the premise of David Foot's book *Boom, Bust, and Echo* with the simple declaration: "Demography is no longer Destiny." Adams tackles that quintessentially Canadian question: "What is Canadian?" and takes the reader on a journey through the new Canadian social landscape. Using data generated by Environics, Adams divides the Canadian population into "psycho graphic" geographical units, that ultimately indicate current and future trends. According to Adams, "Know better your neighbours, and you will better know yourself."

Arronowitz, S. & DiFazio, W. (1994). *The Jobless Future: Sci-Tech and the Dogma of Work.* **Minneapolis, MN: University of Minnesota Press.** This highly successful book by sociology professors Arronowitz and DiFazio goes behind the headlines to challenge the idea that a high-tech economy will provide high-paying jobs for all who want them. They argue that high technology will destroy more jobs than it creates, as fewer parts and fewer workers produce more product.

Well-researched and supported by statistics, *The Jobless Future* concludes that high-tech industries will create fewer jobs than those lost in the "smokestack industries," and that most of the new jobs will be in traditional occupations — clerical and factory work — with few in engineering or technology.

A must-read for those who are tired of self-satisfied statements from politicians and economists that the economic recovery has arrived, without noting that most of the job growth has been in part-time, low-paying work.

Barber, Elizabeth Wayland (1994). *Women's Work: The First 20,000 Years. Women, Cloth, and Society in Early Times.* **New York: W.W. Norton & Company.** How do we understand the contribution that the female workers of antiquity and pre-history made to civilization if most of what they produced has perished? Wayland-Barber attempts to tackle this problem and, drawing on data gathered from archaeology, literature and mythology, she documents the role of women in economic history.

Wayland-Barber's chapter on "The String Revolution" reminds us that emergence of fibre weaving was as important in the evolution and unfolding of human history as the harnessing of steam during the Industrial Revolution. This book firmly locates women's work to its rightful place in history.

Beck, Nuala (1995). *Excelerate: Growing in the New Economy.* **Toronto: Harper Perennial.** Beck, a Canadian economist, has employed the five-star rating system used by hotels and restaurants into a system of rating the hottest jobs in the new economic structure. Do you need to know which industries are thriving and growing in the '90s? Do you have a teenager in your midst who needs advice on where to focus his or her energies for the next 4 years of study? *Excelerate* tells you exactly which industry is the least or most volatile, based on a simple rating system.

Beck also applies her five-star rating system to the industries and sectors that are emerging and declining in the new economy. The result is a practical manual that guides us through today's ever-changing marketplace.

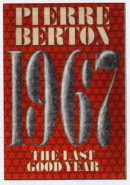

Berton, Pierre (1997). *1967: The Last Good Year.* **Toronto: Doubleday Canada Limited.** Prolific Canadian author Pierre Berton focuses on Canada's centennial year as a turning point for our country. We were a nation "in love with itself," according to Berton, examining new ways to approach Quebec, investigating the status of women, and enshrining in law new attitudes about divorce and homosexuality.

It was a year for Trudeaumania, which saw the launch of Women's Lib, Gay Pride and even Red Power.

Sprinkled with insightful profiles of significant figures — Judy LaMarsh, Lester Pearson, Marshall McLuhan, Glenn Gould — 1967 also marked the year that Canada's exultation gave way to a growing fear that the country was facing its gravest crisis. Berton points out that we are far better off today than we were 30 years ago, but there remains much hand-wringing because of the fear that the country we celebrated is in the process of falling apart.

Browne, Harry (1995). *Why Government Doesn't Work.* **New York: St. Martin's Press.** Libertarian Party US presidential candidate Harry Browne presents a realistic plan for cutting government and ending up with higher incomes, safer cities, better schools, and a more civil society. The author of numerous financial books says he is "sick of seeing government take almost half the national income and then dole it back to us as though we are children on an allowance." He shows why government fails so miserably at everything it touches, and how much better off we would be by making government much smaller. Some find it easy to discount this unique perspective, but it asks some excellent questions.

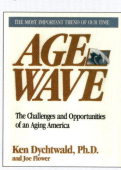

Carroll, Jim (1997). *Surviving the Information Age.* **Toronto: Prentice Hall Canada Inc.** Jim Carroll is the coauthor of more than 13 books, including the *Canadian Internet Handbook,* and is therefore able to bring an extensive and impressive list of credentials to this no-nonsense guidebook to the wired world.

Carroll guides his readers through some useful strategies for surviving in the information age, such as job hunting and how to think about computers. Importantly, Carroll notes that the boomers are the last generation to come of age without computers at their fingertips and need to overcome some basic fears of technology that the next generation of job hunters will not have.

Coupland, Douglas (1991). *Generation X: Tales for an Accelerated Culture.* **New York: St. Martin's Press.** Canadian Douglas Coupland's 1st novel is a hilarious salute to the generation born in the late 1950's and 1960's, known vaguely up to now as "twentysomethings." The 3 protagonists each quit "pointless jobs done grudgingly to little applause" and cut themselves adrift on the California desert. Each is underemployed, overeducated, intensely private and unpredictable. Like the group they mirror, they have nowhere to direct their anger, no one to alleviate their fears, and no culture to replace their anomie.

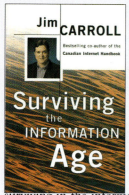

Dychtwald, Ken and Flower, Joe (1989). *Age Wave: The Challenges and Opportunities of an Aging America.* **LA: Jeremy P. Tarcher.** Written in 1988, *Age Wave* is a thorough analysis of the impact that demographics have had and will continue to have on the contemporary American social landscape.

The authors reexamine what it means to grow older in a world that is dramatically changing. In 1900, the average American life expectancy was 47; today it is more than 75 and this has profoundly impacted on how we work, play and do business. This is an important book about demography and its impact on our lives.

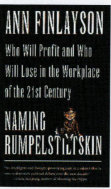

Finlayson, Ann (1996). *Naming Rumpelstiltskin: Who Will Profit and Who Will Lose in the Workplace of the 21st Century.* **Toronto: Key Porter Books.** Finlayson attempts to cast a different light on the 'job crisis' of the 1990's by naming Rumpelstiltskin — those "self-serving proponents of change" who have downsized Canadians out of work. Finlayson addresses the myriad ways in which technology has changed the nature of work and the way that we work, and attempts to displace the fear that we feel about our uncertain future by exposing her perspective on the underlying ideologies. Whether you agree with Finlayson or not, *Naming Rumpelstiltskin* is a thought-provoking book.

Foot, David K. and Stoffman, Daniel (1996). *Boom Bust & Echo: How to Profit From the Coming Demographic Shift.* **Toronto: Macfarlane Walter & Ross.** According to Foot and Stoffman, demographics is two-thirds of everything. To better understand demography, the study of human populations, *Boom, Bust & Echo* is an excellent starting point. Even if you do not believe in the inevitability of demographics, Foot and Stoffman build a convincing case for comprehending the impact that demographics has on our lives.

This book is an interesting overview of contemporary Canadian history and the economic and political forces that have propelled us to the point we are at today. If you want to fully comprehend the profound impact that the boomers have had on the post war economy. A very important book.

Goleman, Daniel (1995). *Emotional Intelligence.* **New York: Bantam Books.** *New York Times* contributor and former Harvard professor Daniel Goleman makes a fascinating and persuasive argument that our view of human intelligence is far too narrow. Drawing on groundbreaking brain-behavioural research, Goleman shows the factors at work when people of high IQ flounder and those of modest IQ do surprisingly well.

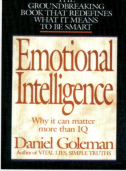

This "different way" of being smart is called emotional intelligence, and includes self-awareness and impulse control, persistence, zeal and self-motivation, empathy and social deftness. Goleman offers a new vision of excellence and a vital new curriculum for life that can change the future for us and for our children. (See page 211.)

Guehenno, Jean-Marie (translated by Victoria Elliot) (1995). *The End of the Nation State.* **Minneapolis, MN: University of Minnesota Press.** A number of books have been written about the impact of the printing press, literacy and the emergence of the modern nation state. However, *The End of the Nation State* examines the profound implications that the electronic information age has had and will continue to have on our legal and political systems.

Diplomat Jean-Marie Guehenno's book is a readable examination of the struggle that geographical communities will face as they are forced to continually redefine themselves in the information age. As we witness the emergence of the virtual community and borderless economic units, Guehenno forces us to rethink 19th century nationalism and the very concept of the modern nation state. One of the philosophical questions that Guehenno asks in this book is, "Can democracy survive in the new era of electronic information technology?"

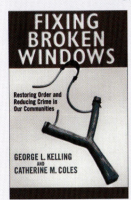

Kelling, George L. and Coles, Catherine M. (1998). *Fixing Broken Windows: Restoring Order and Reducing Crime in Our Communities.* **Boston: Free Press.** "Broken windows breed disorder," is based on a seminal 1982 *Atlantic Monthly* article. **Their concepts are credited as the basis that New York City used to make the city dramatically more livable. It has become a model for understanding the psychology of urban blight.** They call for community policing and contend that the aggressive protection of public spaces are the best crime-control options available. Three-strikes-and-you're-out is fine for baseball but not for crime prevention because it focuses on punishment rather than prevention. The authors make sensible suggestions for restoring law and order to the places where they no longer seem to exist. Their argument is aided immensely by real-life examples of how their "broken windows" strategy has reduced crime where it's been tried.

Two key insights inform the sort of preventive, community policing that Kelling and Coles advocate. First, citizens are less troubled day to day by the prospect of serious crime than by such highly visible minor threats as aggressive panhandling, public drunkenness, low-level drug dealing, and noisy commotions. Second, such seemingly petty offenses are directly related to more serious ones: those who commit them are often violent felons themselves, and when their lesser infractions are ignored, it suggests a general lack of concern on the part of the community and thus invites major infractions. The core of the philosophy is zero tolerance for the minor offenses with the proof that this will dramatically decrease serious felonies.

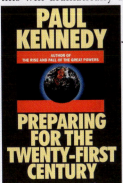

Kennedy, Paul (1993). *Preparing for the Twenty-First Century.* **London: Harper Collins.** Yale history professor Paul Kennedy digests and synthesizes a gigantic quantity of information on current developments in population growth, environmental change, biotechnology, robotics, communications technology and global financial markets to identify the winners and losers in the next century and tells us why. The author of the critically acclaimed *Rise and Fall of the Great Powers* reveals the challenges, the forces for change, and the preparations society must make in order to prepare for the 21st century.

Kirk, Janis Foord (1996). *SurvivAbility: Career Strategies for the New World of Work.* **Kelowna, BC: Kirkfoord Communications.** Janis Foord Kirk is a career columnist for *The Toronto Star* and is well attuned to the problems, questions and difficulties that face job hunters and employers in the tumultuous world of work in the 90's.

SurvivAbility is a primer that can help you locate your place in the new economy and strategize on ways to market your skills in the Electronic Information Age. Foord Kirk provides some useful tips and tools for job hunting today.

Kingwell, Mark (1996). *Dreams of Millennium: Report From a Culture on the Brink.* **Toronto: Viking.** University of Toronto assistant professor and *Saturday Night* contributing editor Mark Kingwell examines the disparate cultural phenomena — global warming, economic and democratic demise, Internet enthusiasm — that foster millennial anxiety and link us to other apocalyptic periods in history. *Dreams of Millennium* draws on pop culture, current events and historical parallels to show how millennial anxiety threatens to extinguish our faith in ourselves. In an eloquent and irreverent style, Kingwell argues that the brink tendencies manifested by popular culture are, in fact, inextricably linked to the impending end of the millennium. His insights include interviews with such visionaries as Concordia professor Arthur Kroker and U of T political scientist Thomas Homer-Dixon.

Korten, David C (1995). *When Corporations Rule the World.* **Hartford, CN: Kumarian Press / San Francisco: Berrett-Koehler Publishers.** This eye-opening book shows how the convergence of ideological, political, and technological forces is leading to an ever-greater concentration of economic and political power in a handful of corporations and financial institutions, separating their interests 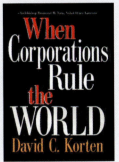 from the human interest, and leaving the market system blind to all but its own short-term financial gains.

Korten, founder and president of The People-Centered Development Forum, a global alliance dedicated to the creation of just, inclusive, and sustainable societies through voluntary action, explains why our survival depends on a community-based, life-centred alternative beyond the outmoded criticisms of communism and capitalism, and suggests steps to achieve it.

Kuhn, Thomas (1996). *The Structure of Scientific Revolutions,* **3rd Edition. Chicago: University of Chicago Press.** Described by the *New York Times* as "perhaps the best explanation of [the] process of discovery," physicist Thomas Kuhn's classic book — 1st published in 1962 — attempts to explain the history and development of science. His radical theory is that the "progress" of science is not a steady movement towards the truth, but the replacement of 1 model of thinking or "paradigm" by another. As he puts it, a "series of peaceful interludes punctuated by intellectually violent revolutions," and in those revolutions, "One conceptual world view is replaced by another." The highly-influential book challenges its readers to think about the history and philosophy of science; cultural and technological change.

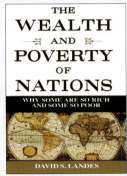

Landes, David S. (1998). *The Wealth and Poverty of Nations.* New York: W. W. Norton. Taking his cue from Adam Smith's 1776 treatise *The Wealth of Nations,* Harvard history and economics professor David Landes explores the 1,000-year, fascinating story of wealth and power throughout the world — the great successes and failures among the world's historic economies. From the failure of 15th and 16th century Spain and Portugal to reinvest their gold and silver loot in their own industries and agriculture, to the ignorance of modern-day Muslim Middle Eastern countries to tap into a huge pool of talent by discriminating against women, Landes chronicles the paths of winners and losers, the rise and fall of nations. Landes' goal is to demonstrate how we can relieve much of the world's poverty — and it is in our best interest to do so — by understanding the lessons history has to teach us, including the fact that the driving force behind economic progress has been "Western civilization and its dissemination of knowledge, the techniques, the political and social ideologies."

Lewis, T.G. (1997). *The Friction-Free Economy.* San Francisco: Harper Business. In this provocative book, T. G. Lewis investigates some of the unusual economic and business features of the digital age, examining this wave of technology and explaining where it will carry us. He argues that the friction-free economy is revamping economic theory for everyone, from high-tech companies to low-tech businesses like restaurants. The rise and fall of products in a very short time has become a requirement of the friction-free economy. Lewis says that products get better and faster as they get cheaper — inverse economics — which leads to Davidow's Law: A business must be the 1st in the industry to render its own products obsolete in order to maintain dominance. He also stresses the importance of "markets-of-one" — products that are narrowly constructed to serve just one consumer.

McRae, Hamish (1995). *The World in 2020: Power, Culture and Prosperity.* Boston: Harvard Business School Press. This acclaimed commentator and best-selling author sets out to determine which nations will experience economic growth and prosperity in the next century, and paints a competitive landscape where culture and values will be the new sources of advantage for the industrialized nations. McRae sees the "old motors of growth" — land, capital and natural resources — being replaced by more qualitative assets — quality, organization, motivation and self-discipline of the people. Everywhere, governments will take a less active role in the social and economic life of the nation, where the best predictor of success will be how a nation strikes a proper balance between creativity and intellect on one hand, and social responsibility on the other.

McQueen, Rod (1996). *Who Killed Confederation Life: The Inside Story.* Toronto: McLelland & Stewart. The bankruptcy and dissolution of Confederation Life was one of the most significant financial-sector failures in the world.

Rod McQueen artfully reconstructs the events leading up to this event in a book about finances that reads like a whodunnit.

When Confederation Life was seized by regulators in 1994, it was not only the 4th largest insurance company in Canada, but a significant part of Canadian history since it was founded in 1871. This is a well-researched book that reconstructs in detail the events and people involved in the collapse of a Canadian institution. (See page 121.)

Morton, Desmond (1994). *A Short History of Canada (2nd revised edition).* Toronto: McClelland & Stewart. Noted historian and entertaining storyteller Desmond Morton writes an absorbing book of Canadian history — from Sir John A. Macdonald to Brian Mulroney, from Jacques Cartier to Lucien Bouchard — in a lively, engrossing volume. Morton, the 1st Director of the McGill Institute for the Study of Canada, argues that to understand Canada today, we must know what shaped its past. He has succeeded in bringing together all the pieces of our history in a book that is both entertaining and informative.

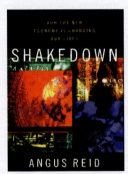

Reid, Angus (1996). *Shakedown: How the New Economy is Changing our Lives.* Toronto: Doubleday Canada Ltd. For 20 years, Angus Reid Group Inc. has been one of Canada's most important polling firms, conducting market and social opinion research for both private and public sector clients.

Shakedown is an in-depth look at some of the most significant and important recent economic trends. Reid ponders the emergence of the technical age and the impact of globalization, and poses the question, "Is the end of traditional work a landmark towards the demise of civilization as we know it?" *Shakedown* is an insightful and provocative account of future trends that should be on everyone's bookshelf.

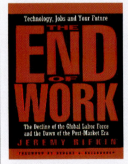

Rifkin, Jeremy (1996). *Technology, Jobs and Your Future: The End of Work: The Decline of the Global Labor Force and the Dawn of the Post-Market Era.* New York: G.P. Putnam's Sons. Economist Jeremy Rifkin argues that the world is changing in ways that have never before been seen in human history. As we witness the decline of traditional jobs we are witnessing an upheaval that is leading a trail of displaced and bewildered workers in its wake. What is the real impact of the emergence of computers, robotics and telecommunications?

This book attempts to grapple with some of the fundamental, philosophical concepts that inform our idea of the nature of work. Rifkin challenges us to think about the current era in terms of a positive social transformation that can enhance human history, not signify its collapse.

Ritchie, Gordon (1997). *Wrestling With The Elephant.* Ritchie, former right-hand man to chief negotiator Simon Reisman in the 1986-87 Canada-US free trade negotiations, details a fascinating behind-the-scenes story of the players and tactics in the Canada-US trade war. Dismissing former ministers as "mediocrities," portraying American negotiators as dishonest, unreliable and poorly prepared, and criticizing Canada's former ambassador to the US for pushing for a deal at any price, Ritchie unloads a scathing indictment of many of those involved in the process.

While believing that Canada is better off with a free trade agreement, Ritchie contends that its impact is hard to measure, although Canada remains highly exposed to US assaults on Canadian exporters and efforts to dismantle our cultural and other policies.

Robinson, Dr. John and Van Bers, Caroline (1996). *Living Within Our Means: The Foundations of Sustainability.* **Vancouver: The David Suzuki Foundation.** As humanity realizes how much it has inadvertently altered the world – and for the worse – in just a few short generations, *Living Within Our Means* explores how we will have to reorient our economies and cultures to return to a balance with the capacities of the Earth. Robinson, Director of the Sustainable Development Research Institute at the University of British Columbia, and Van Bers, an environmental consultant, present an overview of the ecological, social and environmental foundations of sustainability. They demonstrate the crucial links between these 3 systems, explore the ethical and spiritual necessities of life, the behavioural changes involved in a transition to a sustainable society, and conclude with suggestions for ways to measure our progress.

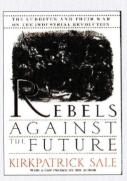

Sale, Kirkpatrick (1996). *Rebels Against the Future: The Luddites and Their War on the Industrial Revolution: Lessons for the Computer Age.* **Reading, MA: Addison-Wesley.** If it is true that we are doomed to repeat history unless we learn from our past mistakes and choices, then we can learn from the original technology backlash: the Luddite Rebellion. *Rebels Against the Future* examines the implications of new technologies on human ethics, communities and morality. This book takes us from the Unabomber back to the 1st technology backlash of the modern age, the Luddite rebellion of 1811.

Sale cautions against wholesale acceptance of new technologies as the answer to all of our problems. He reminds us that the current technological revolution needs to be tempered by an ethical and moral protest that can help us to understand fully the impact it will have on human communities.

Schwartz, Peter (1996). *The Art of the Long View: Planning for the Future in an Uncertain World.* **New York: Currency Doubleday.** What increasingly affects all of us is not the tangibles of life — bottom-line numbers, for instance — but the intangibles: our hopes and fears, our beliefs and dreams. Only stories, or scenarios, and our ability to visualize different kinds of futures

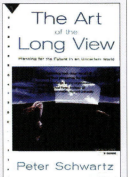

adequately capture these intangibles. Schwartz, one of the world's leading futurists, outlines the "scenario" approach, giving us the tools for developing a strategic vision within our businesses. He argues that scenarios are the most powerful vehicles for challenging our "mental models" about the world, and lifting the "blinders" that limit our creativity and resourcefulness. He describes the new techniques, originally developed within Royal/Dutch Shell, based on many of his first-hand scenario exercises with the world's leading institutions and companies, including the White House, EPA, BellSouth, Pacific Gas & Electric, Motorola, and the International Stock Exchange.

Strong-Boag, Veronica and Fellman, Anita Clair, editors (1986). *Rethinking Canada: The Promise of Women's History.* **Toronto: Copp Clark Pitman Ltd.** Until recently, Canadian history has focussed on the economic and political origins of the 2 founding cultures and on the winning of nationhood, while leaving in the shadows many groups of people, including most women.

Strong-Boag, who teaches history and women's studies at Simon Fraser University, and Fellman, who also teaches women's studies at Simon Fraser, have collected a series of essays on the history of Canadian women. They argue that historians cannot reconstruct a reasonable history of the Canadian people while ignoring the lives and participation of half of them, and that the history of women invites the rethinking of Canada itself. Even in areas in which they would seemingly not figure, such as the battlefield, we learn that women are part of the total picture. Since much of female experience has gone unrecorded, historians have had to tap unused, uncollected sources, including diaries, letters, recipes, songs, photographs, and oral testimony.

Swartz, Mark (1997). *Get Wired, You're Hired: The Canadian Guide to Job Hunting Online.* **Scarborough, ON: Prentice-Hall Canada.** Securing work in today's economy means rethinking old strategies and tried-and-true methods of self-marketing. *Get Wired, You're Hired* is an excellent resource manual for electronic-age job hunters. Swartz gives the reader a brief overview of how to utilize the new technologies as part of an overall work-search. There are excellent chapters that detail the proper way to fax or E-mail a resume in the information age.

This is a book you are going to want to keep beside your computer and refer to often.

Tapscott, Don (1997). *Growing Up Digital: The Rise of the Net Generation.* **USA: McGraw-Hill Companies, Inc.**

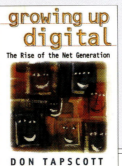

The man who coined the term "Net Generation" (or "N-Gen") – the approximately 88 million children born between 1977 and 1997 – goes to the source to not only downplay fears that new technology is making kids more antisocial and less intellectual, but to prove that kids are using it to play, build relationships and explore the world. While offering commonsense caution, Tapscott argues that society should harness this "force of social transformation" because, for the 1st time in history, children are more comfortable, knowledgeable and literate than their parents about an innovation central to society.

Tapscott further warns that governments are lagging behind in thinking about the implications of this new generation on policies ranging from cyberporn and the delivery of social services to the implications of the N-Gen on the nature of governance and democracy.

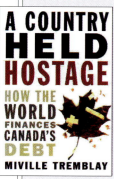

Tremblay, Miville (1996). *A Country Held Hostage: How the World Finances Canada's Debt.* **Toronto: Stoddart Publishing Co. Limited.** Tremblay, a senior financial reporter for the Montreal daily *La Presse*, takes readers behind the scenes to examine how Canada's staggering debt is financed. We meet the world's leading bankers, investment dealers, and institutional investors and learn what they think about our economic and political future, as foreigners nearly double the amount of assets they hold in Canadian public debt. This fascinating "whodunnit" takes readers on a journey to 21 cities, inside trading rooms, and to meet key players such as government borrowers, middlemen and creditors — most of whom have agreed to speak on the record for the 1st time.

Wilson, William Julius (1997). *When Work Disappears: The World of the New Urban Poor.* **New York: Alfred A. Knopf.** This Harvard social policy professor writes about the devastating effects that the disappearance of work has on individual, family and neighbourhood life in the urban ghetto. He explores the current loss of blue-collar jobs, the effects of the "suburbanization" of employment, the lack of locally available training and education, the lack of government and private support, and the attitudes of employers toward ghetto residents. Wilson, the acclaimed author of *The Truly Disadvantaged*, goes on to use stories of inner-city men and women to demonstrate that their desire and quest for success and a stable life are comparable to those of society at large.

One of America's most highly-praised and influential sociologists concludes with practical ideas to help both the urban poor and the middle class, defines a framework of solutions to get the jobless working again, and outlines training and jobs for new high school graduates.

Zuboff, Shoshana (1988). *In the Age of the Smart Machine: The Future of Work and Power.* **USA: Basic Books, Inc.** Zuboff considers the history of work as a history of workers' bodies. She argues that management's aims for technological development have been to reduce physical pain, and escape dependency on the knowledge of labourers' bodies. She warns that the automation of jobs can rob workers of their sentient bodies' skills, while increasing the distance between workers and management.

On the other hand, Zuboff explains that the same technology can "informate." It can empower ordinary working people with overall knowledge of the production process, making them capable of critical and collaborative judgements. Zuboff presents a case for choosing "information" over automation.

ADVOCACY GROUPS

Representative Organizations

Canada

The Alliance of Manufacturers and Exporters

The Alliance is a network of export business professionals, whose mission is to advocate to government on behalf of their members, to promote the development and implementation of advanced technology, and to deliver opportunities for training, education and professional growth. Their vision is to continuously improve the competitiveness of Canadian industry and to expand export business. The Alliance is Canada's senior trade association with offices across the country.

75 International Boulevard, Suite 400
Toronto, Ontario M9W 6L9
Phone: (416) 798-8000 Fax: (416) 798-8050
Email: national@the-alliance.com
http://www.palantir.ca/the-alliance/indexe.html

The Business Council on National Issues

The Business Council on National Issues was founded in 1976 as a non-partisan, not-for-profit organization. Its motto is ". . . to help strengthen the country's economy, its social fabric, and its democratic institutions".

Today the Council is made up of 150 CEOs from every sector of the economy. The Business Council has lobbied for liberalization of trade and investment policies, as well as for the development of progressive social policy issues. The Council is actively engaged in research, consultation and advocacy.

90 Sparks Street, Suite 806
Ottawa, Ontario K1P 5B4
Phone: (613) 238-3727 Fax: (613) 236-8679
Email: bcni@flexnet.com
Internet address: available early 1999

The Caledon Institute of Social Policy

Founded in 1992, The Caledon Institute for Social Policy is a private, non-profit social policy think tank that conducts social policy research and analysis. Their broad aim is to achieve concrete reform of social programs at all levels of government and of social benefits provided by employers and the voluntary sector. As advisor to the federal government, Caledon has played a key role in the reform of public pensions, child benefits, fiscal transfers to the provinces and programs for Canadians with disabilities.

An independent voice that does not depend on government funding, Caledon is supported primarily by the Maytree Foundation. The Institute has also received project funding from the Trillium Foundation to research social partnerships between business and non-profit organizations and from the Atkinson Charitable Foundation for a book on employment.

1600 Scott Street, Suite 620, Ottawa, Ontario K1Y 4N7
Phone: (613) 729-3340 Fax: (613) 729-3896
Email: caledon@cyberplus.ca http://www.caledonist.org

The Canadian Action Party

The Canadian Action Party is a coalition of concerned Canadians seeking to achieve a better balance between responsible government and the private sector. In particular they propose sharing a money-creation function between government and the private banks as was the case from 1940 to 1974. The leader of the CAP is Paul Hellyer.

99 Atlantic Avenue, Suite 302, Toronto, Ontario M1N 2X8
Phone: (416) 535-4144 Fax: (416) 535-6325
Email: cap-pac@istar.ca http://home.istar.ca/~cap-pac

Canadian Advanced Technology Association

The Canadian Advanced Technology Association is a multi-sector trade association for the technology industry, representing the collective power of more than 500 of Canada's leading-edge technology companies. CATA's mandate is to stimulate global growth through partnerships and by building entrepreneurial values. This is achieved through ongoing advocacy and monitoring of government policies, programs and activities.

CATA has directed its efforts towards the areas of R&D Investment Tax Credits, federal government procurements, tax changes impacting new technologies and Industry Canada's policies and programs. The Association also has on-line conferences and discussions to promote networking and the exchange of information.

388 Albert Street, Ottawa, Ontario K1R 5B2
Phone: (613) 236-6550 Fax: (613) 236-8189
Email: inquiry@cata.ca
http://www.cata.ca/cata.htm
http://www.technoskill.com
http://www.technogate.com

The Centre for the Study of Living Standards

The CSLS was established in 1995 to undertake research in the area of living standards. The objectives of the CSLS are to contribute to a better understanding of trends in living standards and factors determining trends through research, and to contribute to the debate on living standards by developing and advocating specific policies.

111 Sparks Street, Suite 500,
Ottawa, Ontario K1P 5B5
Phone: (613) 233-8891 Fax: (613) 233-8250
Email: csls@csls.ca http://www.csls.ca

The Conference Board of Canada

Founded in 1954, the Conference Board of Canada is the leading independent non-profit applied research organization in Canada. The Conference Board provides objective information and analysis on economic, management and public policy issues to assist more than 600 member organizations from business, government and other sectors to anticipate and respond to the increasingly changing global economy. The Board is committed to furthering Canadians' understanding of economic, management and public policy issues. The Board is made up of a number of research groups including; The National Business and Education Centre, The Business and the Environment Research Program, Financial Services Research and Economic Services and the Centre for Management Effectiveness.

255 Smyth Road, Ottawa, Ontario K1H 8M7
Phone: (613) 526-3280 Fax: (613) 526-5248
Email: marketing@conferenceboard.ca
http://www.conferenceboard.ca

Canadian Centre for Policy Alternatives

The Canadian Centre for Policy Alternatives was founded in 1980 to promote research on Canadian economic and social issues, and to monitor and study current trends that affect Canadians. Membership is open to both individuals and organizations. The CCPA attempts to demonstrate that there are alternatives to the business agenda of the government and other institutes by publishing research reports, sponsoring conferences, organizing briefings, and providing commentary on the issues of the day.

251 Laurier Avenue West, Suite 804
Ottawa, Ontario K1P 5J6
Phone: (613) 563-1341
Fax: (613) 233-1458
Email: ccpa@policyalternatives.ca
http://www.policyalternatives.ca

The Conference of Defence Associations and CDA Institute

The Conference of Defence Associations is a non-profit, charitable organization founded in 1932 to study problems of national defence as they pertain to Canada and to bring those problems to the attention of Canadians. The CDA also makes recommendations to the government of Canada through the Minister of National Defence and other appropriate channels, and promotes the efficiency and well-being of the Canadian forces.

The CDA Institute was established in 1987 as the charitable public information arm of the CDA. The CDA does government liaison work while the CDA Institute conducts security and defence research and presents it in a public forum. Individuals become members of the Institute rather than the CDA itself. CDA memberships consists of 13 service associations including the Royal Canadian Legion and the Royal Canadian Armoured Corps Association.

359 Kent Street
Ottawa, Ontario K2P 0R7
CDA Phone: (613) 236-1252 Fax: (613) 236-8191
Email: cda@istar.ca
http://home.istar.ca/~cda
CDAI Phone: (613) 236-5768
Fax: (613) 236-8191
Email: cdai@magi.com
http://home.istar.ca/~cda

Canada West Foundation

The Canada West Foundation is a non-partisan, non-profit organization that conducts research into the economic and social characteristics of the West and the North in a national and international context. The Foundation is in its 3rd decade of research and public education and plays an important role in conducting informed research on issues such as economic diversification, trade policy developments, natural resources, social services reform, agriculture and the environment.

630 3rd Avenue SW, Suite 550
Calgary, Alberta T2P 4L4
Phone: (403) 264-9535
Fax: (403) 269-4776
Email: cwf@calcna.ab.ca
http://www.cwf.ca

Canadian Chamber of Commerce

Founded in 1925, the Canadian Chamber of Commerce is Canada's largest and most representative business association. As the national arm of the grass-roots Chamber movement, its membership includes 170,000 businesses, local chambers and boards of trade across the country. The Canadian Chamber is Canada's business voice, bringing the concerns and views of entrepreneurs of all sizes to the federal government through public policy advocacy.

Delta Office Tower,
350 Sparks Street, Suite 501
Ottawa, Ontario K1R 7S8
Phone: (613) 238-4000
Fax: (613) 238-7643
Email: info@chamber.ca
http://www.chamber.ca

Canadian Institute of International Affairs

The Canadian Institute of International Affairs is a non-partisan voluntary organization. For almost 70 years CIIA has helped Canadians develop a better understanding of world developments and foreign policy, and of Canada's role in a changing world by providing a nationwide forum for informed discussion, analysis, and debate.

The Institute conducts extensive public education programs, including speaker series, symposia series, foreign policy conferences, roundtables and international briefing missions for senior executives to countries of vital interest to Canadians. The CIIA has 16 branches across Canada, and produces 2 quarterly publications, *Behind the Headlines* and *International Journal*.

Glendon Hall, 2nd Floor
Glendon College Campus
2275 Bayview Avenue
Toronto, Ontario M4N 3M6
Phone: 1-800-668-2442 or
(416) 487-6830
Fax: (416) 487-6831
Email: mailbox@ciia.org http://www.ciia.org

The Fraser Institute

The Fraser Institute was founded in 1974 as an independent, non-partisan organization dedicated to research and education. Its focus is on Canadian public policy issues, with a goal of achieving a society of economic and social well-being, based on free market, private property, individual responsibility and limited government.

The Institute is Canada's leading think tank, with 2,700 individual, corporate and foundation supporters in Canada, the US and 12 other countries. It is funded entirely from the contributions of members and the sale of publications. Its list of researchers has grown to more than 350 in 22 countries, 6 of whom have been awarded Nobel Prizes, who have contributed to 250 Institute books and thousands of articles.

626 Bute Street, 2nd floor
Vancouver, BC V6E 3M1
Phone: (604) 688-0221 Fax: (604) 688-8539
Book orders: 1-800-665-3558
Email: info@fraserinstitute.ca
http://www.fraserinstitute.ca/

The C.D. Howe Institute

The C.D. Howe Institute, formed in 1973, is considered Canada's most respected, non-profit, economic and social policy research institution. The Institute has its roots in the Private Planning Association of Canada (PPAC), which was formed in 1958 by business and labour leaders to undertake research and educational activities on economic policy issues. In 1973, the PPAC merged with the C.D. Howe Memorial Foundation to become the C.D. Howe Research Institute.

The objective of the Institute is to refrain from polemics and keep an open mind about finding solutions to difficult problems. It encourages support and input from a broad range of private sector groups and engages in substantive discussions with both federal and provincial governments.

125 Adelaide Street East
Toronto, Ontario
M5C 1L7
Phone: (416) 865-1904
Fax: (416) 865-1866
Email: cdhowe@cdhowe.org
http://www.cdhowe.org/

McGill Institute Study Canada

The McGill Institute for the Study of Canada was established in 1994 by the Bronfman family with a pledge of $10 million, which was to be matched by McGill University. The goals of the Institute are to promote a better understanding of Canada through the study and appreciation of our heritage, to provide understanding about Canada's economy, future and the benefits of pluralism and to breathe life into the field of Canadian Studies.

This is achieved through inviting distinguished Canadians to speak on a range of Canadian issues, offering five graduate fellowships in Canadian Studies and hosting student exchanges with the Centre for the Study of Canada at SUNY, Plattsburgh and Duke University, and offering interdisciplinary and experimental courses in Canadian studies.

3463 Peel Street
Montreal, Quebec
H3A 1W7
Phone: (514) 398-8346
Fax: (514) 398-7336
Email: ldarroch@leacock.lan.mcgill.ca
http://www.arts.mcgill.ca/programs/misc/info.htm

Movement for Canadian Literacy

The Movement for Canadian Literacy (MCL) is a non-profit organization that gives a national voice to literacy communities across Canada. It advises and works with the federal government on priority issues for those working to improve literacy.

458 MacLaren St,
2nd Floor,
Ottawa, Ontario K1R 5K6
Phone: (613) 563-2464
Fax: (613) 563-2504
Email: mcl@magi.com
http://www.literacy.ca

The National Citizens' Coalition (NCC)

The National Citizens' Coalition (NCC) promotes free markets, individual freedom and responsibility. Its supporters believe in "more freedom through less government." Founded in 1967, the NCC is non-profit, has 45,000 supporters and is independent of all political parties. Its publication *Overview* is published 6 times a year and is sent to supporters who contribute $135 or more annually. The NCC does not lobby politicians or bureaucrats, but speaks directly to Canadians through advertising campaigns in print and electronic media and the mail.

100 Adelaide Street West, Suite 907
Toronto, Ontario M5H 1S3
Phone: (416) 869-3838
Fax: (416) 869-1891
Email: national@citizenscoalition.org
http://www.citizenscoalition.org

Project Ploughshares

Project Ploughshares is a Canadian ecumenical peace coalition, founded in 1976 and premised on the biblical vision of transforming material wealth consumed by military preparations into resources for human development. Now a project of the Canadian Council of Churches, Project Ploughshares undertakes policy research, education, and advocacy programs to promote the peaceful resolution of political conflict, demilitarization, and security based on equity, justice, and a sustainable environment. Its membership of 10,000 is effective and has a broad influence as a network for the dissemination of information.

Institute of Peace and Conflict Studies
Conrad Grebel College
Waterloo, Ontario N2L 3G6
Phone: (519) 888-6541
Fax: (519) 885-0806
Email:plough@watserv1.uwaterloo.ca

http://watserv1.uwaterloo.ca:80/~plough/

International

Bonn International Center for Conversion (BICC)

The Bonn Center, established in April 1994, supports and promotes the shifting of human and military resources towards an alternative, civilian purpose. It resulted from an initiative of the German state government of North-Rhine Westphalia, in cooperation with the Investitions-Bank and the andesentwicklungsgesellschaft, the state of Brandenburg, Germany, and with the assistance of the United Nations. BICC operates as a worldwide clearinghouse on conversion projects and experiences, providing information, documents and consulting services for any organization or government involved in converting military resources to civilian ends.

The Director of BICC is Dr. Herbert Wulf.
An der Elisabethkirche 25
D - 53113 Bonn, Germany
Phone: +49-228-911 96 0
Fax: +49-228-24 12 15
Email: bicc@bicc.uni-bonn.de
http://bicc.uni-bonn.de

Club of Rome

The Club of Rome, founded in 1968 in the Italian city, is a group of scientists, economists, businessmen, international high-level civil servants, heads of state and former heads of state, who are convinced that the future of humankind is not determined once and for all and that each human being can contribute to the improvement of our societies.

In a world whose predicaments are far beyond the capacity of individual countries to solve, the Club of Rome has decided to adopt a global perspective, to seek a deeper understanding of interactions within the tangle of contemporary problems, to suggest effective solutions and to take a longer-term perspective in studies than governments do.

34 avenue d'Eylau, 75116 Paris, France
Phone: +33 1 47 04 45 25   Fax: +33 1 47 04 45 23
Email: cor.bs@dialup.francenet.fr
(Secretary General Bertrand Schneider)
http://www.clubofrome.org/

Global Water Partnership

The Global Water Partnership was formally established at a founding meeting in Stockholm in August 1996.

The Partnership is an international network open to all parties involved in water resources management, including governments of national countries, UN agencies, multilateral banks, NGO's, research organizations, the private sector etc.

The GWP's key objective is to support integrated water resource management programs by collaboration. It encourages governments, aid agencies and other stakeholders to adopt consistent mutually complementary programs and policies. It develops innovative and effective solutions to problems common to integrated water resources management and suggests practical policies and good practices based on those solutions.

GWP Secretarariat
c/o sida, S-105- 25 Stockholm, Sweden
Phone: +46 8 698 5000 Fax: + 46 8 698 5627
Email: gwp@sida.se

International Institute of Applied Systems Analysis (IIASA)

IIASA is an Austrian-based non-governmental research organization, originally founded in 1972 by 12 countries to bridge the gap between East and West through joint research in environmental, management and policy issues. Since the end of the Cold War, the Institute began to conduct policy research emphasizing the connections between regional and global interests, such as the impact of climatic changes on agricultural production, and the impact of the newly emerging economies of the former Soviet Union and Eastern Europe.

IIASA's annual budget is about $10 million, 75% of which comes from 15 member organizations in North America, Europe, and Asia, and contracts and grants from government ministries, with private foundations making up the balance. A staff of more than 200 includes 100 full-time research scholars, recruited from member countries employed on fixed-term contracts.

A - 2361 Laxenburg, Austria
Phone: +43 2236 80700 Fax: +43 2236 71313
Email: inf@iiasa.ac.at   http://www.iiasa.ac.at/

Transparency International

Transparency International (TI) is a non-profit, non-governmental organization whose mission is to curb corruption through international and national coalitions, and to encourage governments to establish and implement laws and policies against corruption. It aims to strengthen public support and understanding for anti-corruption programs and enhance public transparency and accountability in international business transactions.

TI was launched in 1993 in response to the mounting corruption that is taking place in many countries and has since generated worldwide interest among people who are concerned with the abuse of public power for private profit. TI's concern is a humanitarian one since corruption causes funds to be misappropriated, much of which was originally earmarked for schools, hospitals and other institutions to serve the needy. The money is often channeled into projects of negligible social value by officials receiving kickbacks.

Transparency International Italy (TI-It)
Offices: Via Zamagna, 19 - (i) 20148 Milan
Tel. 02 40093560
Fax 02 48706074
Email ti.it@ntt.it

World Economic Forum

Founded in 1971, the Forum is an independent, impartial organization with no political, partisan or regional interests. It is today the foremost international organization integrating leaders from business, government and academia into a partnership committed to improving the state of the world. Through global, efficient, direct, personalized and highest-level interaction, the World Economic Forum serves its members and constituents to define their agenda for action. The World Economic Forum is self-financed by membership fees and cost contributions for specific events. The core community includes 1,000 of the foremost global companies. The motto of the World Economic Forum is "Entrepreneurship in the global public interest."

53 chemin des Hauts-Crets
1223 Cologny/Geneva, Switzerland
Phone: +41 22 869-1212 Fax: +41 22 786 2744
Email: contact@weforum.org http://www.weforum.org

United States

Carnegie Endowment for International Peace

CEIP was founded in 1910 in Washington, D.C., as a tax-exempt organization that conducts programs of research, discussion, publications and education in international affairs and US foreign policy.

In 1993, the Endowment established a research centre in Moscow to promote intellectual collaboration between US and Russian scholars. The Endowment does not take an institutional position of issues of public policy and is funded from its own resources and non-governmental philanthropic grants.

1779 Massachusetts Avenue NW
Washington, DC, USA 20036-2103
Phone: (202) 483-7600 Fax: (202) 483-1840
Email: info@ceip.org
http://www.ceip.org/

Council on Foreign Relations

The Council on Foreign Relations was founded in 1921 by businessmen,bankers and lawyers, who were committed to linking America with the rest of the world. Its goals are to gain new insights into the rules and rhythms of international affairs and provide analysis for US foreign policy, to share these insights with others who have a stake in international matters, and to find and nurture the next generation of foreign policy leaders and thinkers.

The Council has a national membership of more than 3,300, and past members include almost all past and present senior US government officials, renowned scholars, business leaders, human rights activists and other non-governmental groups.

The New York-headquartered think tank is non-partisan and non-ideological, and its members meet regularly with world leaders. The Council has no affiliation with the US government and is financed solely by members dues, publication income, subscriptions, endowment income, grants and voluntary gifts. It is not a lobby group, but regularly makes its reports and publications accessible to the public.

Harold Pratt House, 58 East 68th Street
New York, NY, USA 10021
Phone: (212) 434-9400
Fax: (212) 861-1789
Email: communications@cfr.org
http://www.foreignregulations.org/

International Conference of Technology and Education

The ICTE convenes in the spring of each year at a location alternating between a site in North America and a site in Europe, with the goal of providing a forum to support and encourage the exchange of ideas and the sharing of information among those engaged in using technology in its various forms in the field of education. Approximately 1,200 delegates attend the Conference, representing technology-using educators from a wide range of higher educational institutions, state departments of education, ministries of education, and school systems worldwide.

The Conference promotes the idea that, "No nation holds a monopoly on a technology, or on the uses of technology in education,there are a great variety of ideas in the field of education."

PO Box 540579Grand Prairie, Texas 75054-0579, USA
Phone: (817) 534-1220
Fax: (817) 534-0096
Email: icte@icte.orghttp://www.icte.org

Worldwatch Institute

The Worldwatch Institute is dedicated to fostering the evolution of an environmentally sustainable society — one in which human needs are met in ways that do not threaten the health of the natural environment or the prospects of future generations. The Institute achieves this goal through the conduct of inter-disciplinary non-partisan research on emerging global environmental issues, the results are widely disseminated throughout the world.

1776 Massachusetts Ave., NW
Washington, DC, USA 20036-1904
Phone: (202) 452-1999 Fax: (202) 296-7365
Email: worldwatch@worldwatch.org
http://www.worldwatch.org

RESOURCES

Bibliography • Image Credits • Citations • Index • Website

Bibliography

Note: Books in bold type are in Appendix D: Annotated Bibliography.

Adams, Charles. (1993) *For Good and Evil: The Impact of Taxes on the Course of Civilization.* New York: Madison Books.

Adams, Michael. (1997) *Sex in the Snow: Canadian Social Values at the End of the Millenium.* Toronto: Penguin.

Angus, Ian. (1997) *A Border Within: National Identity, Cultural Plurality and Wilderness.* Montreal & Kingston: McGill-Queen's University Press.

Arronowitz, S. & DiFazio, W. (1994) *The Jobless Future: Sci-Tech and The Dogma of Work.* Minneapolis, MN: University of Minnesota Press.

Attali, Jacques. (1991) *Millennium: Winners and Losers in the Coming World Order.* Toronto: Random House of Canada.

Barber, Benjamin R. (1992) *An Aristocracy of Everyone: The Politics of Education and the Future of America.* New York: Ballantine Books.

Barber, Elizabeth Wayland. (1994) *Women's Work: The First 20,000 Years. Women, Cloth and Society in Early Times.* New York: W.W. Norton & Co.

Barlow, Maude and Campbell, Bruce. (1991) *Take Back the Nation 2: Meeting the Threat of NAFTA. Revised Edition.* Toronto: Key Porter Books.

Barnet, Richard J. and Cavanagh, John. (1994) *Global Dreams: Imperial Corporations and the New World Order.* Toronto: Simon & Schuster.

Beach, Charles M. and Slotsve, George A. (1996) *Are We Becoming Two Societies? Income Polarization and the Myth of the Declining Middle Class in Canada.* Toronto: C.D. Howe Institute.

Beck, Nuala. (1995) *Excelerate: Growing in the New Economy.* Toronto: Harper Perennial.

Bellemare, Diane and Poulin-Simon, Lise. (1994) *What is the Real Cost of Unemployment in Canada?* Ottawa: Canadian Centre for Policy Alternatives.

Bercuson, D., Bothwell, R. and Granatstein, J.L. (1997) *Petrified Campus: The Crisis in Canada's Universities.* Toronto: Random House of Canada.

Berton, Pierre. (1997) *1967: The Last Good Year.* Toronto: Doubleday Canada Limited.

Bridges, William. (1994) *Jobshift: How to Prosper in a Workplace Without Jobs.* Don Mills, ON: Addison-Wesley Publishing Company.

Browne, Harry. (1995) *Why Government Doesn't Work: How Reducing Government Will Bring Us Safer Cities, Better Schools, Lower Taxes, More Freedom and Prosperity for All.* New York: St Martin's Press.

Canadian Centre for Policy Alternatives / Choices: A Coalition for Social Justice. *Alternative Federal Budget Papers 1997: A Million Jobs... Economic Security. A Budget for the Future.* Ottawa: Canadian Centre for Policy Alternatives.

Carroll, Jim. (1997) *Surviving the Information Age.* Scarborough: ON: Prentice-Hall Canada Inc.

Connor, Michael. (1980) *Sneak It Through: Smuggling Made Easy.* Paladin Press.

Coupland, Douglas. (1991) *Generation X: Tales for an Accelerated Culture.* New York: St. Martin's Press.

Dickens, Charles. (1961) *A Christmas Carol.* London: Perpetua Books.

Dickens, Charles. (1958) *A Tale of Two Cities.* London: Dent.

Drucker, Peter F. (1993) *Post-Capitalist Society.* New York: Harperbusiness.

Dychtwald, Ken and Flower, Joe. (1989) *Age Wave: The Challenges and Opportunities of an Aging America.* Los Angeles: Jeremy P. Tarcher, Inc.

Ehrlich, Paul. (1975) *The Population Bomb.* Rivercity, MA: Rivercity Press.

Ehrlich, Paul R. and Ehrlich, Anne H. (1974) *The End of Affluence: A Blueprint for Your Future.* Amereon Ltd.

Ehrenreich, Barbara. (1997) *Blood Rites: Origins and History of the Passions of War.* New York: Henry Holt & Company, Inc.

Faludi, Susan. (1991) *Backlash: the Undeclared War Against American Women.* New York: Crown.

Fassel, Diane. (1990) *Working Ourselves to Death: And the Rewards of Recovery.* San Francisco: Harper.

Fellegi, Ivan P. (1996-97) *On Poverty and Low Income.* Ottawa: Statistics Canada.

Finn, M.C. (1983) *Complete Book of International Smuggling.* Paladin Press.

Finlayson, Ann. (1996). *Naming Rumpelstiltskin: Who Will Profit and Who Will Lose in the Workplace of the 21st Century.* Toronto: Key Porter Books.

Fleming, Robert J. and Glenn, J. E. (Eds.). (1997) *Fleming's Canadian Legislatures, 1997.* Toronto: University of Toronto Press.

Foot, David K. and Stoffman, Daniel. (1997) *Boom, Bust & Echo: How to Profit from the Coming Demographic Shift.* Toronto: Macfarlane Walter & Ross.

Francis, Daniel. (1997) *National Dreams: Myth, Memory and Canadian History.* Vancouver, BC: Arsenal Pulp Press.

Friedan, Betty. (1997) *The Feminine Mystique.* New York: W.W. Norton & Company.

Garvin, Andrew P. and Berkman, Robert. (1996) *The Art of Being Well Informed: What You Need to Know to Gain the Winning Edge in Business (2nd Ed.).* Avery Publishing Group.

Goleman, Daniel P. (1997) *Emotional Intelligence.* New York: Bantam Books.

Guehenno, Jean-Marie (translated by Victoria Elliot). (1995) *The End of the Nation-State.* Minneapolis, MN: University of Minnesota Press.

Hammer, Michael and Champy, James. (1994) *Reengineering the Corporation: A Manifesto for Business Revolution. Reprint Edition.* New York: Harper Business.

Kagan, Donald. (1995) *On the Origins of War and the Preservation of Peace.* New York: Doubleday.

Kelling, George L., Wilson, James Q. and Coles, Catherine M. (1996) *Fixing Broken Windows: Restoring Order and Reducing Crime in Our Communities.* New York: Martin Kessler Books.

Kennedy, Paul. (1993) *Preparing for the Twenty-First Century.* London: Harper Collins Publishers.

Keynes, John Maynard. (1995) *The Economic Consequences of the Peace (Twentieth-Century Classics). Reprint Edition.* Toronto: Penguin.

Kingwell, Mark. (1996) *Dreams of Millennium: Report from a Culture on the Brink.* Toronto: Viking.

Kirk, Janis Foord. (1996) *SurvivAbility: Career Strategies for the New World of Work.* Kelowna, BC: Kirkfoord Communications Inc.

Korten, David C. (1996) *When Corporations Rule the World.* San Francisco: Berrett-Koehler Publications.

Kuhn, Thomas. (1996) *The Structure of Scientific Revolutions (3rd. Ed.)* Chicago: University of Chicago Press.

Landes, David S. (1998) *The Wealth and Poverty of Nations.* New York: W.W. Norton & Co., Inc.

Leary, Timothy. (1994) *Chaos and Cyber Culture.* Ronin Publishing.

Lewis, T.G. (1997) *The Friction-Free Economy.* San Francisco: Harper Business.

McClelland, David C. (1967) *The Achieving Society.* New York: The Free Press.

McQueen, Rod. (1997) *Who Killed Confederation Life?: The Inside Story.* Toronto: McClelland & Stewart.

McRae, Hamish. (1995) *The World in 2020: Power, Culture and Prosperity.* Boston: Harvard Business School Press.

Mahan, Alfred Thayer. (1980) *The Influence of Sea Power Upon History, 1660 - 1805.* Englewood Cliffs, NJ: Prentice-Hall.

Malthus, Thomas Robert. (1985) *An Essay on Principle of Population.* Toronto: Penguin.

Meadows, Donella H. and Meadows, Dennis (Editor). (1972) *The Limits to Growth; A Report for the Club of Rome's Project on the Predicament of Mankind.* New York: Universe Books.

Morton, Desmond. (1994) *A Short History of Canada (2nd ed.)* Toronto: McClelland & Stewart Inc.

Moses, Barbara, Ph.D. (1997) *Career Intelligence: Mastering the New Work and Personal Realities.* Toronto: Stoddart Publishers.

Naisbitt, John and Aburdene, Patricia. (1990) *Megatrends 2000: Ten New Directions for the 1990's.* New York: William Morrow and Company, Inc.

Phelps, Edmund S. (1997) *Rewarding Work: How to Restore Participation and Self-Support to Free Enterprise.* Harvard University Press.

Reid, Angus. (1996) *Shakedown: How the New Economy Is Changing Our Lives.* Toronto: Doubleday Canada Ltd.

Rifkin, Jeremy. (1995) *The End of Work: The Decline of the Global Labor Force and the Dawn of the Post-Market Era.* New York: G.P. Putnam's Sons.

Ritchie, Gordon. (1997) *Wrestling With the Elephant.* Toronto: MacFarlane Walter Ross.

Robinson, Dr. John and Van Bers, Caroline. (1996) *Living Within our Means: The Foundations of Sustainability.* Vancouver: The David Suzuki Foundation.

Robson, William B.P. and Scarth, William (eds.). (1997) *Equality and Prosperity: Finding Common Ground (Policy Study 30).* Toronto: C.D. Howe Institute.

Sale, Kirkpatrick. (1995) *Rebels Against the Future: The Luddites and Their War on the Industrial Revolution: Lessons for the Computer Age.* Don Mills, ON: Addison Wesley Publishing Co.

Schwartz, Peter. (1996) *The Art of the Long View: Planning for the Future in an Uncertain World.* New York: Currency Doubleday.

Simon, Julian L. (1996) *The Ultimate Resource 2.* Princeton University Press.

Smith, Adam. (1979) *The Wealth of Nations : An Inquiry into the Nature and Causes.* Hammondsworth: Penguin.

Strong-Boag, Veronica and Fellman, Anita Clair, eds. (1986) *Rethinking Canada: The Promise of Women's History.* Toronto: Copp Clark Pitman Ltd.

Suzuki, David T. and McConnell, Amanda. (1998) *The Sacred Balance : Rediscovering Our Place in Nature.* Prometheus Books.

Swartz, Mark. (1997) *Get Wired, You're Hired: The Canadian Guide to Job Hunting Online.* Scarborough, ON: Prentice-Hall Canada Inc.

Tapscott, Don. (1997) *Growing up Digital: The Rise of the Net Generation.* Toronto: McGraw-Hill.

Tapscott, Don. (1995) *The Digital Economy : Promise and Peril in the Age of Networked Intelligence.* Toronto: McGraw-Hill.

Tobias, Michael. (1994) *World War III : Population and the Biosphere at the End of the Millennium.* Bear & Company.

Tremblay, Miville. (1996) *A Country Held Hostage: How the World Finances Canada's Debt.* Toronto: Stoddart Publishing Co. Limited.

Twombly, Dianne. (1997) *Getting Back to Work: The Ultimate Jobseeker's Guide for Canadians over 45.* Toronto: Macmillan Canada.

Vance, Jonathan F. (1997) *Death So Noble : Memory, Meaning, and the First World War.* Vancouver: University of British Columbia Press.

Wattenberg, Ben. (1987) *The Birth Dearth.* New York: Pharos Books.

Weele, Maribeth Vander. (1994). *Reclaiming Our Schools: The Struggle for Chicago School Reform.* Chicago: Loyola Press.

Westlake, Donald E. (1997) *The Ax.* New York: Warner Books, Inc.

Wilson, William Julius. (1997) *When Work Disappears: The World of the New Urban Poor.* New York: Alfred A. Knopf, Inc.

Winslow, Philip C. (1997) *Sowing the Dragon's Teeth: Land Mines and the Global Legacy of War.* Boston: Beacon Press.

Worzel, Richard. (1998) *The Next Twenty Years of Your Life: A Personal Guide into the Year 2017.* Toronto: Stoddart.

Zuboff, Shoshana. (1988) *In the Age of the Smart Machine: The Future of Work and Power.* New York: Basic Books, Inc.

Image Credits

Photographs

Cover Flag-skewered beaver by Uku Casements.

Cover Corporate Careers Expo. 1997 The Washington Post Writers Group. Reprinted with permission.

Cover Dr. J. William Pfeiffer by Stephen McNeill.

Glossary Image of people by permission of CN Railway.

iii Requiem to the Great Depression: June, 1935. Canadian Press.

v "The Shot Heard Around the World" Reproduced from an original watercolour by Walter Burden.

v ACME pollsters cartoon by Graham Harrop.

vii Broom Hilda © Tribune Media Services, Inc. All Rights Reserved. Reprinted with permission.

viii Gertrude L. Thebaud Schooner. Painting by J. Franklin Wright, commissioned by SOE Inc.

viii Lions Gate Bridge by permission of Lions Gate Project Office.

001 Beaver with dunce cap by Uku Casements.

004 Reality Check reprinted by permission of United Feature Syndicate, Inc.

006 Dilbert reprinted by permission of United Feature Syndicate.

007 Cortez: Hospital de Jesus, Mexico, D.F.

008 Ford Taurus by permission of Ford Motor of Canada, Limited.

009 Auckland Harbour permisssion of New Zealand Tourist Board.

010 Caesar's Ghost: UTNE Reader.

011 Confederation Bridge. Barrett & MacKay.

012 Victoria's Crest. The House of Lords.

012 British soldiers in India. National Army Museum.

013 Fathers of Confederation painting by Robert Harris. Rogers Cantel Inc.

014 Hudson's Bay Company Coat of Arms. HBCA 1987/363-C-43/41 (N72-75). Hudson's Bay Company Archives, Provincial Archives of Manitoba.

014 General Wolfe dying on the Plains of Abraham, 1759. Benjamin West.

014 Hammer down: last spike. Canadian Pacific Archives Image No. NS 1960.

014 Copy of J.D. Kelly 1938 painting of Cabot. Rogers Cantel.

015 Pierre Trudeau by Jean Demers.

019 Roberta Bondar. Canadian Press.

022 Igloo cartoon by permission of Graham Harrop.

022 Nungak/Inuit. Canadian Press.

023 Anthropomorphic Theatre. 1987 The Washington Post Writers Group. Reprinted with permission.

024 Potlatch. Museum of Civilzation and Culture.

025 Artist's Wife and Daughter, 1931. Norval Morriseau. McMichael Canadian Art Collection.

026 Traditional headwear. Gable. Reprinted with permission from The Globe and Mail.

026 Phil Fontaine and Jane Stewart. Canadian Press.

029 Louis Riel being hanged. National Archives of Canada, Neg. no. C11789.

029 Louis Riel. National Archives of Canada, Neg. no. C52177.

031 Fort "Prince of Wales", 1734. HBC's 1922 calendar illustration. Artist: A.H. Hider (from an engraving by Samuel Hearne). HBCA P-386 (N87-47). Hudson's Bay Company Archives, Provincial Archives, Manitoba.

032 "Harvester" by Fitzgerald. Permission Fitzgerald Copyright.

033 Government compensation cartoon permission Theo Moudakis.

036 Wizard of ID. Permission Johnny Hart and Creators Syndicate.

048 "Long Distance Call" Rex Woods, 1971. Rogers Cantel Inc.

048 "Klondike" J. D. Kelly and Thomas Wilderforce Mitchell, 1954. Rogers Cantel Inc.

055 Adam. © 1997 Universal Press Syndicate.

057 "Luddite Riots" 1811. Mansell/Time Inc.

058 Take Back the Nation 2 cover. By permission of Maude Barlow.

058 The Wealthy Banker's Wife cover. © 1993 by Linda McQuaig. Cover by permission of Penguin Books Canada Limited.

059 Between Friends. Reprinted permission of King Features.

060 Dave. © Tribune Media Services, Inc. All Rights Reserved. Reprinted with permission.

061 Dave. © Tribune Media Services, Inc. All Rights Reserved. Reprinted with permission.

062 Strike cartoon. Reprinted with permission – S. Dewar, Ottawa Sun.

063 Strikers. Canadian Press.

064 UPS cartoon. © Tribune Media Services, Inc. All Rights Reserved. Reprinted with permission.

066 Mad as a Hatter. Illustration by Tenniel.

068 Eaton's cartoon. Reprinted permission of Adrian Raeside.

074 Fishers cartoon. Reprinted with permission of John Carter.

078 I Need Help by Vic Lee. Reprinted with special permission of King Features Syndicate.

081 Hunger's Face. Reuters / Archive Photos.

082 "Non-violence" sculpture. UN Photo 182966 / M. Tzovaras. DOC 1031L.

083 B.C. By permission of Johnny Hart and Creators Syndicate.

084 Hell's Angels. Canadian Press.

085 Brazil Jail. Canadian Press.

088 Ross Rebagliati. Canadian Press.

090 Amendments cartoon. By permission of Malcolm Mayes.

093 Bound and Gagged. © Tribune Media Services, Inc. All Rights Reserved. Reprinted with permission.

094 Skulls. Canadian Press.

094 General Romeo Dallaire. Canadian Press.

095 The End of the Nation State cover. Reprinted with permission – University of Minnesota Press.

095 & 239 Reprinted with permission from the publisher. From When Corporations Rule the World. © by David Korten, Berrett-Koehler Publishers, Inc. San Francisco, CA. All rights reserved.

099 Dhaka beggers. Reuters/Rafiqur Rahman/Archive Photos.

100 Ivaan Kotulsky.

101 Ivaan Kotulsky.

103 Video Lottery Terminal. Canadian Press.

108 Lord Beaverbrook. University of New Brunswick, Harriet Irving Library, Archives and Special Collections

111 Debt and Deficit cartoon. Permission – John Carter.

112 Dilbert reprinted by permission of United Feature Syndicate.

115 Charlie by Rodriguez. © Tribune Media Services, Inc. All Rights Reserved. Reprinted with permission.

116 Debt/Deficit marquee by permission of Peter Pickersgill.

117 MacDonald and MacKay bridges. Halifax-Dartmouth Bridge Commission, photos by Sun Dancer Air Shows Ltd., HDBC AG-WIN.

118 Loon roasting cartoon. BADO, Le Droit, Ottawa.

118 IMF cartoon. Bruce Mackinnon. Halifax Chronicle Herald.

119 Canada's gold coin. Royal Canadian Mint.

120 Amalgamated Bank cartoon by Gable. Reprinted with permission from TheGlobe and Mail.

121 Who Killed Confederation Life cover. McClelland and Stewart.

125 Nest Egg cartoon by permission of Dale Cummings, 1997, Winnipeg Free Press.

126 Ponzi. Courtesy of the Boston Public Library, Print Department.

126 CPP cartoon by Jenkins. Reprinted with permission from The Globe and Mail.

127 Year 2020 cartoon. Reprinted with permission of Adrian Raeside.

131 Sheila Copps by Peter Bregg.

131 By permission of Brian Tobin's office.

131 By permission of Jean Charest's office.

131 By permission of John Nunziata.

132 Charlie by Rodriguez. © Tribune Media Services, Inc. All Rights Reserved. Reprinted with permission.

132 John Glenn by permission of National Aeronautics and Space Administration.

134 Pinochet. Canadian Press.

135 Empty your pockets cartoon by permission of Graham Harrop.

145 ENIAC. UPI photo.

146 © 1998 Iridium Canada.

152 Gin cartoon by permission of Graham Harrop.

152 Mr. Jefferson. Reuters/HO/Archive Photos.

152 Dolly. Reuters/Jeff Mitchell/Archive Photos.

152 George and Charlie. Reuters/HO/Archive Photos.

153 PPL Therapeutics.

154 Hands off my DNA! Canadian Press.

154 Male order cartoon. Copyright 1997, The Toronto Sun, a division of Sun Media Corporation.

155 Grocery store cartoon. 1997 The Washington Post Writers Group Reprinted with permission.

160 © Air Canada 1997, A319.

160 Canada Post logos by permission of Canada Post.

160 Electronic Age Meteor cartoon. Reprinted with permission – Toronto Star Syndicate.

161 Reprinted with permission – Canadian Airlines.

161 Hong Kong Tourist Association.

162 Homer Hydro cartoon reprinted with permission of Adrian Raeside.

170 Chretien and the Great Wall of China. Canadian Press.

172 Barbie is a trademark owned by Mattel, Inc. C 1998 Mattel, Inc. All Rights Reserved. Used with permission.

178 US Arms. Los Angeles Times Syndicate.

179 CF5 reprinted with permission – Department of National Defence (DND).

179 Nukes cartoon. Reprinted with permission – Jim Margulies.

180 Shohei Nozawa resigning. AP/Wide World Photos.

180 Suh Sang-rok, former chairman of Sammi Group, training as a waiter. Reuters/Yun Suk-bong/Archive Photos.

181 Hagar. Reprinted with permission of King Features Syndicate.

182 Boer War soldiers. National Archives of Canada C7981.

183 Unknown Canadian Soldier, 1942. Sam Morse Brown.

183 Andre Dunoyer de Segonzac: Seriously Wounded Man, Somme, 1916

183 Vimy Ridge Memorial. Government of Canada Veterans Affairs.

184 Rusting Russian sub. AP/Wide World Photos.

185 F/A-18 Hornet. US Navy photo by Cmdr. Anthony Kiggins (950315-N-0000K-001).

187 Saddam Hussein. Canadian Press.

189 NATO cartoon. Alan King. Reprinted with permission – The Toronto Star Syndicate.

190 Princess Diana with land mine victims. Canadian Press.

190 Tag Along cartoon by permission of Alan King.

191 Mine guzzler. Bofors Weapons Systems.

191 Land mines. Reprinted with permission of Colin King.

193 General Rot cartoon. Reprinted by permission of Roy Peterson.

194 DND logo. Reprinted by permission of the Department of National Defence (DND).

195 CF18s. Reprinted by permission of the Department of National Defence (DND).

195 Removing hydro towers near St. Cesair, PQ. Journal La Press; Robert Nadon, 19-1-98.

196 Navy tub cartoon. Reality Check by permission of United Feature Syndicate, Inc.

197 British sub cartoon. Reprinted with permission of Adrian Raeside.

199 Graduation day. 1997 The Washington Post Writers Group. Reprinted with permission.

207 Petrified Campus cover. Random House Canada.

207 Beaver in medieval garb. Uku Casements.

211 & 238 From Emotional Intelligence. (Jacket Cover) by Daniel Goleman. Copyright – Used by permission of Bantam Books, a division of Bantam Doubleday Dell Publishing Group, Inc.

213 The Better Half by Glasbergen. Reprinted with permission – King Features.

217 Dilbert reprinted by permission of United Feature Syndicate.

Annotated Bibliography

From Sex in the Snow by Michael Adams. Copyright © 1997 by Michael Adams. Cover reprinted by permission of Penguin Books Canada Limited.

Women's Work cover by permission of W.W. Norton & Company

1967: The Last Good Year. Doubleday Canada Limited.

Surviving the Information Age. Prentice Hall Canada, Inc.

Reprinted by permission of Jeremy P.Tarcher, Inc., a division of the Putnam Publishing Group from Age Wave by Ken Dychtwald and Joe Flower. Copyright © 1989 by Ken Dychtwald and Joe Flower.

Naming Rumpelstiltskin. Key Porter Books.

Fixing Broken Windows. Free Press.

Preparing for the Twenty-First Century. Harper Collins Publishers.

The Wealth and Poverty of Nations. W.W. Norton & Co. Inc.

Shakedown: How the new Economy is Changing our Lives. Doubleday Canada Limited.

Reprinted by permission of Jeremy P.Tarcher, Inc., a division of the Putnam Publishing Group from The End Of Work by Jeremy Rifkin. Copyright © 1995 by Jeremy Rifkin.

K. Sale, Rebels Against the Future © 1995 Kirkpatrick Sale Reprinted by permission of Addision Wesley Longman.

The Art of the Long View. Currency Doubleday.

Growing up Digital. McGraw-Hill Companies.

A Country Held Hostage: How the World Finances Canada's Debt. Stoddart Publishing Co. Limited.

Citations [•]

1 Curtis, Ken. Quoted by Newman, Peter in *"The Man Who Would Move Markets,"* MacLean's August 26, 1996.

2 Lipsey, Dr. Richard G. (Professor of Economics, Simon Fraser University) Canadian Institute for Advanced Research and Economics.

3 Loewen, James W. (1995) *Lies my Teacher Told Me: Everything Your American History Textbook Got Wrong.* New York: The New York Press.

4 KK. *Report on Business.* May, 1997.

5 Cage, John.

6 Finley, Michael. *Get Real: The Unsugarcoated Philosophy of Morris Shechtman.* The Masters Forum 1996. www.mastersforum.com/shecht.htm

7 This quote may be falsely attributed as the accuracy cannot be verified.

8 Anonymous. This version has been wordsmithed by John Seidel, EDP Consulting Incorporated, Oakland, CA.

9 His Excellency John Wood, Ambassador of New Zealand to the United States. *New Zealand: A Blueprint for Economic Reform.* (June 16, 1995).

10 Utne Reader, July-Aug., 1997, p.32, originally printed in *Kyoto Journal.*

11 Sears, Stephen W. (1973) *The Horizon History of the British Empire.* US American Heritage Publishing Co., Inc.

12 Francis, Daniel. (1997) *National Dreams: Myth, Memory and Canadian History.* Vancouver: Arsenal Pulp Press.

13 McKenna, Frank. (Former premier of New Brunswick). *The Globe & Mail.* June 20, 1996.

14 *Odds & Ends* A Newsletter of Eagles Byte Historical Research. May, 1997, No. 20.

15 http://www.dnd.ca

16 *Report on Business.* January, 1998.

17 Statistics Canada, U.S. Bureau of Statistics

18 Privy Council. Report: *Key Issues Facing Canada to the Year 2005.*

19 Statistics Canada.

20 Levine, Robert. *A Geography of Time.*

21 Hughes, Campbell. (1971)

22 The source of this wisdom is lost, the author acknowledges Dr. Michael Fullan, of OISE/University of Toronto for bringing a slightly different form of it to his attention.

23 Statistics Canada.

24 Statistics Canada.

25 Kidd, Kenneth. *Grain Storm. Report on Business Magazine.* June, 1997. pp. 32 - 40.

26 Monsebraaten, Laurie. *The End of Welfare. The Toronto Star.* May 2, 1998.

27 McGeary, Johanna and Michaels, Marguerite. *Africa Rising. Time* March 30, 1998.

28 Simpson, Jeffrey. *The Globe and Mail.*

29 United Nations. (1997)

30 The Voluntary Human Extinction Movement (VHEMT). www.vhemt.org/

31 Statistics Canada. Report on Demographic Situations in Canada 1997.

32 Foot, David K. and Stoffman, Daniel. (1997) *Boom, Bust and Echo: How to Profit from the Coming Demographic Shift.* Toronto: MacFarlane Walter Ross. This section relies heavily on Foot & Stoffman.

33 *The Globe and Mail* August, 1998.

34 Citizenship & Immigration Canada.

35 Commission for Environmental Co-operation (1997) *Taking Stock.*

36 David Suzuki Foundation. *"Why Stabilization Won't Work." Finding Solutions newsletter.* December, 1997.

37 Statistics Canada. Catalogue No. 82-221-XDE.

38 *Atlantic Progress* (Jan/Feb., 1998)

39 Citizenship and Immigration.

40 Barber, Elizabeth Wayland. (1994) *Women's Work: The First 20,000 Years: Women, Cloth and Society in Early Times.* New York: W.W. Norton & Company. This section relies heavily on Barber.

41 Statistics Canada 1996 Census data published in *The Globe and Mail.*

42 Statistics Canada 1996 Census data published in *The Globe and Mail.* May 13, 1998.

43 Statistics Canada 1996 Census data cited by Philp, Margaret. *The Globe and Mail*

44 The Heritage Foundation/Wall Street Journal. *1998 Index of Economic Freedom.*

45 Runzheimer Canada.

46 OECD / *The Economist.*

47 Gutmann, Manfried and Kalt, Daniel. *Prices and Earnings Around the Globe 1997.* Economic Research Department of the Union Bank of Switzerland.

48 Faculty of Nursing of Laval University / Quebec City Public Health Unit.

49 Dychtwald, Ken and Flower, Joe. (1989) *Age Wave: The Challenges and Opportunities of an Aging America.* Los Angeles: Jeremy P. Tarcher, Inc.

50 Black, Conrad. *"Taking Canada Seriously," Saturday Night,* February, 1998.

51 Barber, John. *The Globe & Mail.* May 19, 1998.

52 Stark, Judy. (Financial Planner/Educator).

53 Statistics Canada.

54 Finlayson, Ann. (1996) *Naming Rumpelstiltskin: Who Will Profit and Who Will Lose in the Workplace of the 21st Century.* Toronto: Key Porter Books.

55 OECD.

56 Chaykowski, Richard. (November 1, 1997) *"Not Going Quietly"* in *POST 2000* and Gordon, John. *Work Around the Clock.*

57 Dagg, Alex. Advisory Committee for Ladies' Dress and Sportswear.

58 Bains, Anne. *"Thirty-eight cents a shirt." Toronto Life.* February, 1998.

59 Stinson, Marian. *"Generics win on Prozac Look-Alike." The Globe and Mail.* April 29, 1997.

60 Crymes, Jacquie. PR Department, Manpower Milwaukee Headquarters and www.manpower.com

61 Bellemare, Diane and Poulin-Simon, Lise. (1994) *What is the Real Cost of Unemployment in Canada* Ottawa: Canadian Centre for Policy Alternatives.

62 Harriman, H.I. (President of the US National Chamber of Commerce).

63 Picot, Garnett and Lin, Zhengxi. *Research Paper 96: Are Canadians More Likely to Lose their Jobs in the 1990's?* Ottawa: Statistics Canada.

64 *"Statistics Canada Labour Force Survey." The Daily,* Oct. 24, 1997. Cat. No. 11-001E.

65 Nesbitt Burns Economics Department.

66 OECD. *Standardised Employment Rates* (February, 1997) www.oecd.org

67 Post TAGS Review Team. (1998) *The Atlantic Groundfish Strategy: Post TAGS Review Report.* Ottawa: HRDC.

68 Angell, Ian O.

69 Statistics Canada data published by Fennell, Tom. *A Mountain of Debt. MacLean's* Feb. 2, 1998.

70 Statistics Canada data published in *The Globe and Mail.*

71 Fellegi, Ivan P. (1996-97) *On Poverty and Low Income.* Statistics Canada.

72 The National Council on Welfare *Poverty Profile 1996.*

73 Campaign 2000 Report. (1997)

74 Doherty, Gillian (child psychologist and early childhood educator/consultant). Cited by Lewington, Jennifer. *"Attitudes Lay Foundation for Student Performance," The Globe and Mail.* April 19, 1997.

75 Safe Motherhood Initiative.

76 Hall, Barbara. (Former Toronto mayor and head of a 1998 federal initiative on crime prevention).

77 Statistics Canada data cited by Dr. Bob Horner, M.P Chairman. *Excerpt from the Twelfth Report of the Standing Committee on Justice and the Solicitor General.*

78 Reid, Angus. (1996) *Shakedown: How the New Economy is Changing Our Lives.* Toronto: Doubleday Canada Ltd.

79 Statistics Canada.

80 Nemeth, Mary and Cardwell, Mark. *"Circle of Justice"* Vol. 107, *MacLean's,* 09-19-1994, p. 52.

81 Camp, Dalton. *"Farewell to the Idea of a Nation-state." The Toronto Star.*

82 Worldwide Institute. *Vital Signs 1997.*

83 Veith, Dr. Gene. (Sept./Oct., 1995) *Modern Reformation* Annaheim, CA: CURE.

84 Guehenno, Jean-Marie. (1995) *The End of the Nation-State.* Minneapolis, MN: University of Minnesota Press.

85 Rifkin, Jeremy. (1995) *The End of Work: The Decline of the Labor Force and the Dawn of the Post-Market Era.* New York: G.P. Putnam's Sons.

86 Barnet, Richard J. and Cavanagh, John. (1994) *Global Dreams: Imperial Corporations in the New World Order.* Toronto: Simon & Schuster.

87 *The Economist* "The Nation-state is Dead. Long live the Nation-state." Vol. 337, 12-23-95.

88 Tocqueville, referring to America. Cited by Guehenno, Jean-Marie. (Translated by Victoria Elliot). (1995) *The End of the Nation-State.* Minneapolis, MN: University of Minnesota Press.

89 Finlay, Richard. (Chairman of Toronto-based Centre for Public and Corporate Governance).

90 Ramphal, Sir Shridath. (1997) *15th Annual Attlee Lecture.*

91 Centre for the Study of Living Standards

92 *Tramp on the Street:* traditional southern gospel song.

93 Emson, H.E. (Professor of Pathology and Medical Bioethicist).

94 Picard, Andre. *A Call to Alms: The Voluntary Sector in the Age of Cutbacks. The Globe and Mail.* Atkinson Foundation.

95 Picard, Andre. *"Top Court Asked to be Charitable." The Globe and Mail.* Feb. 24, 1998.

96 Ketch, Jack. "The Man who invented Christmas," Vol. 8, *World & I,* 12-01-1993, pp. 321. News World Communications.

97 Pinney, Chris. *Imagine:* Canadian Centre for Philanthropy.

98 Imagine: Canadian Centre for Philanthropy.

99 Murphy, Sandra. (Executive Director, Volunteer Centre, St. John's).

100 Royal Bank of Canada

101 OECD Economic Outlook, June, 1997.

102 Canada West Foundation. (1998) *Red Ink IV: Back from the Brink?* Charts derived from Budgets, Public Accounts, DBRS, CBRS, and Investment Dealer's Association.

103 *The Globe and Mail.* / Angus Reid Survey. (November, 1997).

104 Halifax-Dartmouth Bridge Commission. Document 902-483-2466.

105 OECD. Using OECD 1996 data, the difference was 29% with the purchasing power parity methodology (a better method) or 43% using the exchange rate methodology.

106 Bank of Canada, International Monetary Fund

107 McQueen, Rod. (1996) *Who Killed Confederation Life: The Inside Story.* Toronto: McLelland & Stewart Inc.

108 Healy, C. Ross and Sgromo, Enrico. (1995) *Phoenix Rising (the 2% Solution) A Plan to Eliminate Canada's Deficit and Debt Crisis.* Toronto: Strategic Analysis Corporation.

109 McQuaig, Linda. *"Making sure the rich stay rich." The Toronto Star.* March 22, 1998.

110 ACPM Report: *A Retirement Income Strategy for Canada,* Toronto: The Association of Canadian Pension Management.

111 Investors Group, July, 1997.

112 McCarthy, Shawn. *"No Promises Given on Limits for CPP Premiums," The Globe and Mail.* November 7, 1997.

113 Certified General Accountants' Association of Canada. (May, 1996) Submission to the Federal/Provincial/Territorial consultation panel reviewing the Canada Pension Plan.

114 Foot, David K. *"To relieve pension headaches," The Globe and Mail.*

115 The Reform Party of Canada, Sarnia Lambton Constituency Association. *What a Friend they Have in Taxes!* www.sarnia.com/reform#waste

116 Canadian Institute of Actuaries. (January, 1995) *Troubled Tomorrows – The Report of the Canadian Institute of Actuaries' Task Force on Retirement Savings.*

117 Organization for Economic Co-operation and Development. Nov., 1997.

118 *The Economist.* The Intelligence Unit.

119 Deloitte & Touche.

120 Micklethwait, Brian. *The Top Rate of Income Tax Should be Cut to Zero.* Economic Notes No. 68. Libertarian Alliance.

121 KPMG. (Dec., 1997) *Final Project Report: Strategic Analysis of Underground Employment in the Construction Industry.* Ottawa.

122 Citizens for an Alternative Tax System. *Creating a National Retail Sales Tax. This section relies heavily on the CATS article.*

123 Price Waterhouse.

124 Statistics Canada.

125 Jorgenson, Dr. Dale. (Chairman, Economics Department, Harvard University).

Citations, *continued*

126 Qualls, Dr. (Economist)

127 Nesbitt Burns and StatsCan.

128 Iridium Canada www.iridium.ca

129 Crossette, Barbara. *The New York Times* as quoted by Gee, Marcus in *The Globe and Mail* (May 13, 1998).

130 Gee, Marcus. *The Globe and Mail.* (May 13, 1998).

131 IDC, US high technology research company.

132 Software Human Resource council estimates '92-99 and census figures 1971 - 91.

133 Gray, Kenneth C. and Herr, Edwin L. (1995) "High Skill/High Wage Jobs for the Non-Degreed" in *Other Ways to Win: Creating Alternatives for High School Graduates.* California: Corwin Press, Sage Publications.

134 McCarthy, Shawn. "Report charts Internet tax path" in *The Globe and Mail.* May 1, 1998.

135 Wilmut, Dr. Ian. (Co-ordinator of the work at the Roslin Institute near Edinburgh). As told to a news conference.

136 Davidmann, Manfred. (1996) *Creating, Patenting and Marketing New Forms of Life.*

137 Feynman, Richard P. "An Invitation to Enter a New Field of Physics." American Physical Society at the California Institute of Technology *Engineering and Science.* Feb., 1960.

138 KPMG. August, 1997.

139 Richie, Gordon. (A former civil servant who has studied Canada Post).

140 Statistics Canada data cited by Bruce Little, *The Globe and Mail* May 15, 1998.

141 Kenney, Jason. Alberta Association of Taxpayers.

142 World Trade Organization, March 23, 1998

143 Coopers & Lybrand. The Autofacts division.

144 Canadian Association of Japanese Automobile dealers.

145 Drobis, David R. (Nov. 12, 1996). Address Delivered to the Public Relations Society of America National Conference. City News Publishing Co.

146 Kolko, Dr. Gabriel. (Professor Emeritus: York University) *Vietnam: Anatomy of a Peace.*

147 Gee, Marcus. "Japan Inc., Korea Inc., red ink" *The Globe and Mail.* Jan., 1998.

148 Reisen, Helmut. OECD.

149 Little, Bruce. "Exports top Internal Trade" in *The Globe and Mail.*

150 Crane, David. "Where do Barbies come from?" in *The Toronto Star.* Oct. 13, 1996.

151 Transparency International (see Appendix E)."TI Corruption Index" in *The World Competitiveness Yearbook.* DRI/McGraw Hill.

152 Asia-Pacific Economic Cooperation (APEC). *Key Indicators of Member Economies.* www.apecsec.org.sg/member/ind.html

153 International Monetary Fund.

154 Hopkins, J. Castell.

155 International Institute for Strategic Studies. *The Military Balance 1996 - 1997.* Figures involving nuclear weapons from the US Natural Resources Defence Council.

156 U.S. Defense Department

157 White House; Senator Patrick Leahy; Vietnam Veterans of America Foundation; Human Rights Watch; US Department of Defence.

158 Department of National Defence.

159 Department of National Defence. (December, 1997) *Canada's Defense Team in Action.* Ottawa.

160 Canadian Coast Guard College internal review. October, 1997.

161 Carty, Arthur. President: National Research Council. Convocation speech delivered on June 14, 1997 on being given an honorary doctorate by Carleton University.

162 Golden, Anne. President: The United Way of Metropolitan Toronto. Cited by Andre Picard in *A Call to Alms.* (Citation #94).

163 Bell, Terrel. (1983) *A Nation at Risk: The Imperative for Education Reform.* Note: in the original "unfriendly power" quote, Bell refers to the American education system.

164 Shenk, Joshua Wolf. "Saving Education: The Public Schools' Last Hurrah?" in *The Washington Monthly* March, 1996.

165 Card, David and Krueger, Alan. (Princeton economists).

166 Third International Mathematics and Science Study.

167 Statistics Canada. (1994)

168 SchoolNet workshop. (1996) *Vision of Learners in the 21st Century.* Toronto.

169 Logan, Robert K. (1995) *The Fifth Language: Learning a Living in the Computer Age.* Toronto: Stoddart Publishing Co.

170 Human Resources Development Canada / National Literacy Secretariat. (1997) *Literacy Skills for the Knowledge Society.*

171 International Conference on Technology and Education.

172 Chang, Ifay. *Cyber Assisted Responsive Education (CARE): Paradigm Shifts in Education Stimulated by Information Technology and Future Education Situations.* Hawthorne, NY: Polytechnic Research Institute for Develoment Enterprise. *This section relies heavily on Chang's article.*

173 Bercuson, D., Bothwell, R. and Granatstein, J.L. (1997) *Petrified Campus: The Crisis in Canada's Universities.* Toronto: Random House of Canada.

174 Tuathail, Gearoid O. *Thinking Critically About Geopolitics*

175 Stager, David. (Professor of Economics: The University of Toronto).

176 Graham, Bill. (Professor of Philosophy: The University of Toronto).

177 Southam's Directory of Canadian Schools, 1993-96.

178 Statistics Canada, CANSIM matrix 8008, Catalogue no. 81-229.

179 Statistics Canada. *University Enrolment by Field of Study, 1994-5.*

180 Henry George, (1884) *Progress and Poverty.*

181 Global Information Network, Some factual data from Reuters Ltd. Wire Service.

182 Ehrenreich, Barbara, (1997) *Blood Rites: Origins and History of the Passions of War.* New York: Henry Holt & Company.

183 Winslow, Philip C.(1997) *Sowing the Dragon's Teeth: Land Mines and the Global Legacy of War.* Boston: Beacon Press.

184 Professor McLaren, Simon Fraser University.

185 Tom Grey, National Coalition Against Gambling Expansion.

186 Caledon Institute.

Index

Website

Understanding how Canada works in the rapidly-changing world of the post-modern, soon-to-be-post-nation, information age is an ongoing challenge. We are plagued by economic ignorance, apathy, congenital self-interest and a tidal wave of content-free journalism that almost always chooses sizzle over substance.

However, there is an abundance of valuable resources that are sometimes just difficult for the concerned citizen to find among the stories on the scandal of the week: Clinton's sex life, new Lady Di revelation, Chrétien's succession of foot-in-the-mouth comments, and the most recent disaster–plan crash, tidal wave, fire, or earthquake.

The *RoadKill* web site is intended to focus on key issues that concern:
• The salient issues that impact the future of work.
• Ways to get government out of the business of competing with the private sector.
• The widening gulf between the Haves and Have-Nots on both a national and international level.
• Real answers for halting the alarming growth in the number of Canada's poor children — our most shameful national disaster.

Some material on the site will be original observations, some summaries from obscure or complex sources.

The site will feature many hot keys that will take you to source documents on key issues that will help keep you and the ones you love from being *RoadKill On The Information Highway*.

roadkill-drjobs.com